AF764970

Anti-corruption Laws and Regulations

A Global Guide

Consulting Editor **Roberto Hernández-García**

Consulting editor
Roberto Hernández-García

Managing director
Sian O'Neill

Anti-corruption Law and Regulation, A Global Guide
is published by

Globe Law and Business Ltd
3 Mylor Close
Horsell
Woking
Surrey GU21 4DD
United Kingdom
Tel: +44 20 3745 4770
www.globelawandbusiness.com

Printed and bound by CPI Group (UK) Ltd, Croydon CR0 4YY

Anti-corruption Law and Regulation, A Global Guide

ISBN 9781787421172
EPUB ISBN 9781787421189
Adobe PDF ISBN 9781787421196
Mobi ISBN 9781787421202

© 2018 Globe Law and Business Ltd except where otherwise indicated.

All rights reserved. No part of this publication may be reproduced in any material form (including photocopying, storing in any medium by electronic means or transmitting) without the written permission of the copyright owner, except in accordance with the provisions of the Copyright, Designs and Patents Act 1988 or under terms of a licence issued by the Copyright Licensing Agency Ltd, 6–10 Kirby Street, London EC1N 8TS, United Kingdom (www.cla.co.uk, email: licence@cla.co.uk). Applications for the copyright owner's written permission to reproduce any part of this publication should be addressed to the publisher.

DISCLAIMER
This publication is intended as a general guide only. The information and opinions which it contains are not intended to be a comprehensive study, or to provide legal advice, and should not be treated as a substitute for legal advice concerning particular situations. Legal advice should always be sought before taking any action based on the information provided. The publishers bear no responsibility for any errors or omissions contained herein.

FSC www.fsc.org
MIX
Paper from responsible sources
FSC® C013604

Table of contents

Introduction

Roberto Hernández-García
COMAD, SC

1. Corruption: a difficult to eliminate international enemy

In recent years, a map of the world with red, orange and yellow colours assigned to different countries has been published every year, making nations tremble and question their situation with regarding to the existence and effects of corruption on them.

Of course, we are speaking about the *Corruption Perceptions Index* (the Index) prepared and published annually by the non-governmental organisation (NGO) Transparency International. According to this highly respected organisation:

> *The index, which ranks 180 countries and territories by their perceived levels of public sector corruption according to experts and businesspeople, uses a scale of 0 to 100, where 0 is highly corrupt and 100 is very clean.*[1]

In the 2017 edition of the Index, a worrying statement frames the study: "CORRUPTION PERCEPTIONS INDEX 2017 SHOWS HIGH CORRUPTION BURDEN IN MORE THAN TWO-THIRDS OF COUNTRIES". The authors go on to explain that:

> *Analysis of results from Transparency International finds crackdowns on NGOs and media are associated with higher levels of corruption.*[2]

The most significant aspect of the background to this story is, however, that international and national anti-corruption instruments are, more than ever before, working efficiently toward the end of international corruption. A number of international anti-corruption treaties, such as those of the United Nations (UN) and the Organisation for Economic Co-operation and Development (OECD) have been signed and have come into force. National legal frameworks against corruption have also been designed and implemented in many countries.

Furthermore, there has been unprecedented growth in the number of NGOs that are focused especially on anti-corruption and which work continuously to help governments to draft, implement and modify legislation and to be effective in the fight against corruption.

Current technology allows the identification, investigation and efficient prosecution of criminal masterminds, while cases like *Lava Jato* (Operation Car Wash) and *Odebrecht* in Brazil demonstrate that international corruption can be tackled and identified through cooperation between and the unstinting political will of governments.

1 www.transparency.org/news/feature/corruption_perceptions_index_2017.
2 www.transparency.org/news/pressrelease/corruption_perceptions_index_2017_shows_high_corruption_burden_in_more_than.

2. What is necessary for anti-corruption initiatives to succeed?

Notwithstanding all of the initiatives discussed at 1 above, however, it seems that we are far from winning the war. It is therefore necessary for all who are involved in anti-corruption to think about the situation and consider the following questions.

1. Should we expect such results at present?
2. Are the wrong strategies being adopted?
3. Are governments and societies really trying to eliminate corruption?
4. What is the way forward if we are to succeed?

A number of thoughts on these questions are set out below.

2.1 Should we expect such results at present?

Some politicians have said – without scientific evidence – that when a corruption scandal emerges, and even if it has been prosecuted successfully, the perception of corruption of that country increases. Conversely, other politicians have said that, by making cases public, people become aware of corruption scandals and therefore feel that corruption is growing even if the government is doing its work, so that if the position of a country in the Index falls, it is because corruption is being fought.

I have heard this argument put by public officers mainly to justify a lower ranking in a country's place in the Index. In any case, speaking about my own country (Mexico) and with colleagues from other countries, this argument is not enough to justify a lower ranking and society's perceptions about corruption. This is because, given all the anti-corruption initiatives discussed at 1 above, ideally we should not be in situation whereby two-thirds of the countries worldwide remain immersed in corruption.

The idea of minimising corruption by making it analogous to little more than a bribe given to a police officer after passing a red light is ridiculous. Corruption has pervasive effects on all citizens worldwide. By giving misleading pretexts to their positions in the annual Index and to all the efforts made by organisations and individuals, countries are failing to consider what terrible effects corruption has in all our lives. This is explained in an OECD paper,[3] which briefly summarises the corrosive effects of corruption by saying that:

- it increases the cost of doing business;
- it leads to waste or the inefficient use of public resources;
- it excludes poor people from public services and perpetuates poverty; and
- it corrodes public trust, undermines the rule of law and ultimately delegitimises the State.

So, the answer is simple: we should not be going backwards when speaking about the fight against corruption, since we have the necessary elements to evolve rapidly in this battle rather than diminishing our presence in it.

2.2 Are the wrong strategies being adopted?

Finding an answer to this question is more difficult, since at least two factors have to be taken into account: the legal framework and political will. If a country has a

---

3 The rationale for fighting corruption (OECD CleanGov.Biz initiative, 2014), available at www.oecd.org/cleangovbiz/49693613.pdf.

sophisticated legal framework but at the same time there is a lack of political will and intention to implement it, where will its government's anti-corruption strategy go?

This is an important question to answer with regard to the overall topic of this book, since in its content experts from different parts of the world discuss the legal efforts in their own jurisdictions to tackle corruption. The authors of many of the chapters speak optimistically about the situation in their countries, the way in which their laws are being implemented efficiently and real results have been achieved, while others (even from countries that are well positioned, according to Transparency International) have doubts regarding the reality of their countries' situation and the way forward. In a very few cases, authors have been really proud and willing to share views and evidence that their countries have succeeded in the fight against corruption. Most of the authors, however, feel that there is still a long way to go. In any case, what is very positive is that all authors enthusiastic about improving their countries' anti-corruption efforts.

In any case, strategies vary from jurisdiction to jurisdiction, and we can say with certainty that they are not limited to the legal framework. Thus, a general formula has not yet been found and we need to keep seeking it in every case and envisioning international strategies. The task is to keep on thinking, trying and sharing success stories.

2.3 Are governments and societies really trying to eliminate corruption?

While it is clear that the answer to this question should be an absolute 'yes', there are still a growing number of individuals and companies in both the public and the private sectors who, directly or indirectly, benefit from corruption and illegal activities and operate outside of the law. This creates a non-linear answer to the question: while many individuals and companies want to end corruption, others do not, since it is their way of living. The former will find the way to make the corrupt individuals and companies pay for their actions, commencing with 'baby steps', such as not buying their products or allowing those bad elements to grow in the market.

In some way, the answer is simple: there are 'good guys' and there are 'bad guys', and the former will unify and be intelligent enough to succeed against the latter.

2.4 What is the way forward if we are to succeed?

First, every individual and/or company on the 'good side' must not diminish their efforts in fighting corruption. Strategies for this include, of course, not only compliance programmes but also other actions, such as recruiting, retaining and promoting people with high ethical standards. Such efforts can, however, also mean the 'good guys' losing business or not growing as fast and to the extent expected. This can be a painful way forward in a complex world.

Secondly, while in many sectors and markets, working without bribery may seem impossible, clean individuals and companies are finding ways to work effectively by evolving in their processes and standards of conduct. This does not mean that it is easy, but by starting there is a chance to begin advancing.

Finally, and in connection with the overall purpose of this book, individuals and companies are obliged to be familiar with their applicable legal frameworks and to demand their application without hesitation. The only way to win the anti-corruption battle in a world that cries out for the rule of law is to apply the rule of law. Creating a clean new environment means understanding applicable international treaties and national laws and standards, demanding their effective application and enforcing them by prosecuting and convicting, in particular, the ruling criminal minds.

3. Conclusion

For sure, the task of fighting corruption is not an easy one. A large number of people around the world, from among both top tier companies and individuals, lead corruption, which pervades all the way down to the poorest neighbourhoods in a remote country. The fight still has a long way to go and it is therefore necessary not to quit in seeking a better world for our future generations.

It is sincerely hoped that this book will be received as an honest seed from leading authors around the world, and as a contribution to efforts to defend the honour of countries that is so craved by their citizens.

The International Chamber of Commerce: the business pioneer in the fight against corruption

Viviane Schiavi
International Chamber of Commerce
Denis Simonneau
L'Oréal
François Vincke
Member of the Brussels Bar

1. An advocate for open trade as a vehicle for inclusive growth and prosperity

The International Chamber of Commerce (ICC) was founded in 1919 in the aftermath of the First World War when no world system of rules governed trade, investment, finance or commercial relations. Without waiting for governments to fill the gap, its founders acted on their conviction that the private sector was best qualified to set global standards for business.[1] They called themselves "the merchants of peace".

ICC works to promote international trade and responsible business conduct by combining its global influence in trade advocacy with its unique expertise in dispute resolution, standard-setting activities and global services. It sets its sights on the future of globalisation, working to promote inclusive and sustainable growth for the benefit of all.

ICC (motto: 'The World Business Organization') has long upheld the critical role of compliance by enterprises with self-imposed rules while at the same time recognising the basic responsibility of governments in the fight against corruption and in promoting responsible business conduct.

Nationalism and protectionism are currently presenting new and genuine threats to open societies and economies, while new technologies are rapidly changing the way we work. ICC acknowledges the perspective of those who have lost out and those who fear they could lose out tomorrow to trade or to technological change.

1 ICC's first Chairman, Étienne Clémentel, who had been the French Minister of Commerce, Industry, Posts and Telegraphs during the First World War, had witnessed the benefits of cooperation between Allied nations (the Allies) in international trade during the war. After the war, he proposed that the Allies pursue such collaboration further, on the basis of 'organised liberalism'. When the Allies did not concur with his ideas in 1919, he turned toward the business world, which agreed to create ICC. One of the members of Clémentel's staff during the war was Jean Monnet, who would devote his life to international economic cooperation.

The ICC recognises that business needs to play its role in making open economies and the rule of law work for the benefit of countries and all members of society, and to create equitable opportunity for all to participate in growth.

2. Self-regulatory rules to facilitate trade

2.1 A pioneering role

ICC emphasises the critical role of corporate compliance and responsibility through self-regulation while recognising the basic role of international organisations and national governments in the fight against corrupt practices and in favour of corporate responsibility.

Self-regulation and best practice standards may be deemed to be 'soft law', ie, they are adopted, within the framework of a trade or professional association, on a voluntary basis and their enforcement will not be pursued through the courts of any jurisdiction (even if a number of courts refer to ICC provisions in their rulings). They are not compulsory, but enjoy a status bordering on customary law as they are often used by professionals and trades people in all spheres. Over the years, ICC documents have gradually transformed into a form of *lex mercatoria*, becoming another source of law in the international business environment. Of course, private rules, accepted on a voluntary basis, cannot replace international conventions and national statutes but can usefully supplement them.

Setting rules for the international business community has been defined as the "making of the rules that govern the conduct of business across borders".[2] As a result, ICC is a leader in the area of business best practices. In the banking world, the ICC Uniform Customs and Practice for Documentary Credits (UCP)[3] are in use everywhere. Across the world, all those who are involved in international trade use its International Commercial Terms or INCOTERMS®.[4]

The various texts are based on best international practice and drafted by ICC's policy commissions. They are processed through a lengthy, involved and critical procedure of internal approval, involving ICC National Committees, individual experts who serve as members of the relevant policy commissions, and the top governance bodies of the organisation.

2.2 ICC self-regulatory tools for business integrity

ICC has spearheaded the drive for greater integrity in business transactions as it believes that only a corruption-free system will enable all participants to compete on a level-playing field. ICC has also been a pioneer in asserting the business community's commitment to act responsibly by taking into account human rights, social requirements and environmental considerations when conducting business.

---

2 ICC, *About The International Chamber of Commerce*, available at www.icchkcbc.org/aboutus.html.

3 The UCP were issued for the first time in 1933 and their sixth and latest revision (under the name 'UCP 600') dates from 1 July 2007.

4 The INCOTERMS were first issued in 1936 and their latest revision (under the name 'INCOTERMS ® 2010') dates from 1 January 2011: see www.iccwbo.org/products-and-services/trade-facilitation/incoterms-2010/.

Fighting corruption consists of prohibiting and condemning all corruptive practices but also, and perhaps even more essentially, implementing all reasonably available measures to avoid or prevent these practices. Public authorities play a role in matters of prevention, but both the private sector and civil society must also take a proactive part in this. Indeed, the private sector has understood for a long time that corruption not only undermines the foundations of democracy through the breach of the trust vested in public officials but also that it undercuts the very basis of sound corporate governance, fair competition and ultimately the liberal economy.[5]

2.3 The key international anti-corruption conventions and frameworks

As early as 1975, ICC created a Committee on Extortion and Bribery. This committee, called the Shawcross Committee after its Chairman,[6] issued a report in 1977[7] setting out ICC's Rules of Conduct on Extortion and Bribery, which were influenced mainly by the United States Foreign Corrupt Practices Act 1976 (FCPA). The report was welcomed as a breakthrough and, by issuing these rules, ICC became the first non-governmental organisation to produce rules of conduct on matters as sensitive as extortion and bribery.[8]

The ICC Rules on Combating Corruption have since been updated in 1996, 1999, 2005 and 2011 to reflect the adoption of key laws and international legal instruments, such as the OECD Convention on Combating Bribery of Foreign Public Officials in International Business Transactions 1998 (OECD Convention) and the United Nations (UN) Convention Against Corruption 2003 (UNCAC). These conventions are recognised as major milestones in the fight against corruption and their adoption, implementation and enforcement have garnered the strong support of the business community at large.[9]

2.4 Codifying good commercial practice

ICC's aim in issuing the Rules on Combating Corruption was to provide business with precise and practical guidelines on how to put into place, on a voluntary basis, effective processes and mechanisms for concrete action against corruption and

---

5 François Vincke, 'The business community's attitude towards corruption, special focus on private-to-private corruption', in A Benoit-Moury *et al*, *Liber Amicorum: Commission Droit et Vie des Affaires* (1998, Brussels: Bruylant), pp192 *et seq.*

6 Hartley William Shawcross (1902–2003), British barrister and politician. Lord Shawcross served as a Member of Parliament from 1945 to 1958 and held the position of Attorney-General from 1945 to 1951. He was the much respected lead British Prosecutor at the Nuremberg War Crimes Tribunal.

7 ICC, *Extortion and Bribery in Business Transactions: Report Adopted by the 131st Session of the Council of the ICC, 29 November 1977* (1977, Paris: The Chamber) (the Shawcross Committee Report).

8 Professor Antonio Argandona, The 1996 ICC Report on Extortion and Bribery in International Business Transactions (1997) 6(3) Business Ethics: A European Review 134–146 and Fritz F Heimann, 'Combating International Corruption: The role of the Business community', in Kimberley Ann Elliott (Ed), *Corruption in the Global Economy* (1997, Washington DC, Institute for International Economics (now Peterson Institute for International Economics)), pp150–152.

9 The Shawcross Committee had a mandate limited in time. After the outbreak of a number of corruption scandals at the start of the 1990s, a new Ad Hoc Committee on Extortion and Bribery was created with the mission of updating ICC's position on integrity in business in light of the most recent international legal developments. The new committee enjoyed the enthusiastic cooperation of many ICC National Committees and leading corporate experts. In turn, it established useful and fruitful cooperation with a number of international organisations, such as the OECD and the UN Office on Drugs and Crime (UNODC).

extortion. Bribery and corruption in all forms had not only to be condemned in rigorous terms but enterprises were also to be encouraged to put in place effective corporate ethics and compliance programmes with the aim of avoiding any corruptive acts being committed in the conduct of their business. These flagship ICC rules make up what is considered good commercial practice but are without prescriptive legal effect.

3. ICC anti-corruption guidance and rules

3.1 Introduction

ICC's international business experts and practitioners from all sectors of industry, commerce and finance have developed a suite of robust best practice guidance and regulatory tools for business integrity over the past decade to supplement the ICC Rules on Combating Corruption. These tools provide guidance to companies of all sizes, ranging from multinationals to small- and medium-sized enterprises (SMEs).

3.2 RESIST: a success story

The RESIST project (which stands for *Resisting Extortion and Solicitation in International Transactions*) was developed jointly by ICC, Global Compact, the Partnership Against Corruption Initiative (PACI) and Transparency International. Based on 21 real-life scenarios, RESIST was designed in 2010 as a training tool to provide practical guidance for company employees on how to prevent and/or respond to an inappropriate demand by a client, business partner or public official in the most efficient and ethical way. RESIST, which has been translated into French, Spanish, German, Chinese and Arabic, is used worldwide and offers a practical, easy and user-friendly tool for training and teaching co-workers on how to oppose illicit demands.

3.3 The ICC Anti-corruption Clause

Not all ICC integrity initiatives have their origin in policy commissions seated at ICC's Paris headquarters. Indeed, it was ICC's Mexican National Committee that came forward with the idea that ICC should propose a new instrument for use by companies of all sizes, but particularly by smaller ones, in their contracts: the ICC Anti-corruption Clause (the ICC Clause). The Mexican initiative was welcomed by the Paris headquarters and it was decided that two policy commissions would cooperate to forge an instrument that would be legally strong and practically efficient: the Anti-corruption Commission and the Commission on Commercial Law and Practice. In tandem with the fruitful cooperation of a number of ICC National Committees, the document was launched in 2012. The ICC Clause is intended to be a practical instrument for use in private contracts, to proscribe corruption at all phases of the negotiation and implementation of contractual relationships.

The basic reasoning underlying this initiative is very straightforward and may be illustrated by a hypothetical common scenario. A business person commences negotiations with a potential customer, supplier or any other business partner. Everything proceeds smoothly, but when that business person comes close to concluding the deal, his or her advisers will induce him or her to broach one of the most sensitive subjects – an anti-corruption provision. He or she will not be enthusiastic about this idea: it is delicate – but unavoidable – to start talking about such a subject. Nobody likes to see his or her reputation being put into question and nobody wishes to be interrogated on such matters. Furthermore, smaller companies will feel dwarfed by larger ones, while bigger companies will fear that the resistance of a small company against their model anti-corruption clause may hide some desire to continue illicit practices. ICC therefore wished to create a clause that was usable by any kind of company in all circumstances.

The other idea underlying the new instrument was that, by hitting corruptors and/or corruptees in their wallets, terminating or suspending their contracts under strict and fair conditions was a sure way of meting out a strong, appropriate and dissuasive sanctions.

To avoid the difficult dialogue outlined above in the hypothetical scenario, parties can prefer to opt for the ICC Clause as a neutral solution. This instrument is built upon the most common practices in business and allows both parties to move from corporate compliance to contractual compliance. A party to a contract containing the ICC Clause will not only comply with its anti-corruption provisions, as summarised in Part I of the ICC Rules on Combating Corruption (2011) (the 2011 Rules), but can also expect the counterparty to do the same, failing which the former may either suspend or terminate the contract. Alternatively, both contractual parties may commit to each of them having put in place (or being about to do so) a corporate anti-corruption compliance programme, as described in article 10 of the 2011 Rules.

Many leading companies have expressed interest in using the ICC Clause. The hope is that the ICC Clause will be so frequently and universally used that it will become part and parcel of customary international law. In this way, the ICC will contribute in a significant way to impeding breaches of anti-corruption provisions.

3.4 The ICC Guidelines on Gifts and Hospitality

The ICC Guidelines on Gifts and Hospitality (2013) provide guidance to companies on how to establish and maintain a policy relating to gifts and hospitality, based on the most recent international, regional and national rules and regulations, and on commercial best practice. ICC recommends that enterprises establish clear procedures covering the offer or receipt of gifts and hospitality in order to ensure that such arrangements:

- comply with national law and applicable international instruments;
- are limited to reasonable and *bona fide* expenditures;
- do not improperly affect, or may be perceived as improperly affecting, the recipient's independence of judgment toward the giver;
- are not contrary to known provisions of the recipient's code of conduct; and
- are neither offered nor received too frequently nor at an inappropriate time.

3.5 ICC Anti-corruption Third Party Due Diligence: A Guide for SMEs

The ICC Guidelines on Agents, Intermediaries and Other Third Parties were released in 2011. This document highlights the fact that third parties, if not carefully selected and supervised, could expose enterprises to considerable risk and damage. Thus, enterprises need to ensure that their agents expressly commit to not paying bribes. First of all, however, it is incumbent on enterprises to choose an appropriate due diligence method for evaluating the agents they may select.

Furthermore, ICC issued its seminal *ICC Anti-corruption Third Party Due Diligence: A Guide for SMEs* (the 2015 Guide) in 2015. It developed this guidance particularly for SMEs out of the recognition that while smaller companies are drivers of economic growth in many economies, they often need capacity-building assistance to enable them to do their part in developing responsible supply chains and sustainable growth. Small- and medium-sized enterprises are often on the receiving end of burdensome due diligence processes implemented by larger multinational companies. These requirements can be overwhelming and SMEs may find that they have insufficient resources to comply with them.

The 2015 Guide encourages SMEs to engage in due diligence by creating achievable and manageable due diligence goals. It provides practical advice on how SMEs can cost-effectively conduct due diligence on third parties they engage to perform services on their behalf. It focuses on the corruption risks associated with engaging third party suppliers, contractors and consultants in both an international and a domestic setting and gives advice on how those risks can be managed.

3.6 The ICC Business Integrity Compendium

This ICC publication, which was issued in 2017,[10] brings together for the first time all of the ICC guidance and rules for anti-corruption and corporate responsibility (including those discussed at 3.2–3.5 above) in one document.

3.7 ICC Guidelines on Conflicts of Interest in Enterprises

Work on integrity in business will always be a work in progress. The ICC Commission has, in the light of this reality, taken up the difficult but necessary task of drafting Guidelines on Conflicts of Interest in Enterprises. Such effort requires contributions from many parts of business life and, at the time of writing, is about to be finalised.

3.8 ICC training programmes for ethics and compliance

It has gradually become clear over the past decade that every company has a duty to implement an efficient corporate anti-corruption programme. Such a programme should be adapted to the particular circumstances of an enterprise and be set up with the aim of preventing and detecting corruption and of promoting a culture of integrity. Pioneers in legally requiring the putting in place of effective corporate compliance programmes include the laws of the United States, Italy and the United Kingdom.

To promote business integrity further, ICC has published four editions of its *ICC Ethics and Compliance Training Handbook* (the *ICC Handbook*)[11] (the latest in 2013), a

10 Available at https://cdn.iccwbo.org/content/uploads/sites/3/2017/12/icc-business-integrity-compendium 2017-web.pdf.

11 ICC Product No 741E (2013, Paris: ICC Publications).

publication designed by business for business, which sets forth specific guidance on ethics and compliance and the problems confronting them. Further, in keeping with the concrete and practical, training approach of the *ICC Handbook*, ICC released its ICC Ethics and Compliance Training for Anti-corruption to its National Committees in March 2017 for them to use in their face-to-face training activities in different national contexts.

3.9 Conclusion

In summary, ICC's anti-corruption guidelines, rules, *Handbook* and training programmes have been published, read, implemented and referred to by policy-makers and business leaders across the world as leading standards for best practice by companies. All were originally written in English and, to enhance their outreach further, many of them have been translated into several languages and are available at the ICC website (www.iccwbo.com).

4. Self-regulation: working with the law

4.1 Introduction

As is widely acknowledged, corruption distorts markets, disincentivises investment, diminishes potential growth, deprives companies of their legitimate gains, distorts competition and reduces job opportunities. It is therefore evident that ICC, whose mission is to promote free trade and competition, has long been concerned with this form of illicit action, which is, disturbingly, still too common in a global economy.

Some may question the relevance of ICC's action in the prevention of corruption. They may contend that those who support self-regulation seek to attribute to themselves state-like functions by giving themselves the roles of legislator and judge all at once. Further, some may contend that, by engaging in best practices, companies may seek to give themselves an aura of ethical conduct, while in reality they are only concerned with maximising their profits.

4.2 The real reach of ICC action

In responding to these possible contentions, one needs to focus on ICC's underlying mission. The aim of ICC's standard-setting work in the fight against corruption is to bolster the positive actions of governments by putting in place adequate and appropriate measures to support and assist enterprises. In summary, ICC's self-regulatory guidance supports mandatory law rather than seeking to replace or contravene it.

The OECD echoed this perspective in 2010, when it issued its *Good Practice Guidance on Internal Controls, Ethics, and Compliance* (the OECD Guidance) (see, in particular, Annex II). The OECD Guidance is an integral part of the Recommendation of the OECD Council for Further Combating Bribery of Foreign Public Officials in International Business Transactions of 26 November 2009. In the Guidance, the OECD asserts that:

Business organizations and professional associations may play an essential role in assisting companies, in particular SMEs, in the development of effective internal control, ethics, and compliance programmes or measures for the purpose of preventing and detecting foreign bribery.

Best practices by enterprises, coupled with legal standards by governments and/or inter-governmental organisations, can therefore help to achieve what the European Commission has described as "co-regulation", which couples mandatory legislative or regulatory measures with measures taken by those actors most incentivised to put their practical experience into practice – the enterprises themselves.[12]

The measures implemented by a particular company to combat corruption may, it is true, present a corollary 'communications advantage' by giving itself a favourable image and underscoring its commitment to ethics. This public relations dimension, while real, cannot however, override a good faith policy of prevention undertaken by an enterprise.

It is also difficult to conceive that an enterprise would accept extensive expense in implementing an integrity programme that only has the objective of projecting a flattering image, whether deserved or not. One needs to take into account in this context not only the monetary costs involved but also the potential damage to the company's reputation. Indeed, for a company to put in place an integrity program as mere 'window dressing' while at the same time continuing to engage in unlawful practices is particularly risky, for the company could be very poorly perceived by shareholders, analysts, clients and the business community. It could also result in a serious breach of trust and reputational damage.

5. A forum for public-private partnership: the B20

In the wake of the G20 Summit in Seoul in 2010, the G20 leaders asked experts of the business world, who were gathered in the Business 20 (B20) meeting, to give them help and advice on a number of issues, including the fight against corruption. B20 anti-corruption processes have consistently focused since then on areas in which business leaders perceived that urgent action was required. These have included responsible business conduct in infrastructure projects and public procurement, the need for recognition by governments of companies' compliance efforts (through training and capacity building), voluntary self-disclosure ('self-reporting'), beneficial ownership transparency and transparency for state-owned enterprises.

ICC has consistently championed two main initiatives in this context:

- anti-corruption training and capacity building, and
- the development of tools, especially for SMEs.

ICC has been particularly well positioned in the B20 context as a pioneer in building the capacity of businesses to fight corruption and has been honoured by regular invitations to chair or co-chair B20 expert groups in this process.

---

12 See European Commission and the Economic and Social Committee. *European Self- and Co-Regulation,* which defines this term at p11; available at www.eesc.europa.eu/resources/docs/auto_coregulation_en—2.pdf and also https://ec.europa.eu/digital-single-market/en/news/principles-better-self-and-co-regulation-and-establishment-community-practice.

6. ICC's lead on anti-corruption: its impact now and in the future

Fighting corruption and building an even stronger sense of corporate responsibility and good corporate governance is an ongoing process and requires sustained efforts from all parties to work together – whether they are public officials or business people, and at all levels of the corporate world.

The fight against corruption and anti-competitive practices is ingrained in ICC's DNA. However, the mere condemnation of corruption is not enough. ICC has expanded its mission over the years to help companies generate a culture of integrity. This has been done through the development of ICC corporate codes of conduct, its guidance on business integrity, its ethics and compliance programmes and its anti-corruption training. This is clearly a way to contribute effectively to the 'social responsibility' of business and is the reason why the ICC Commission is now developing its work on corporate social responsibility. Companies are increasingly in need of down-to-earth integrity and responsibility tools provided by experienced practitioners. ICC is committed to continuing to contribute to this daunting task.

Anti-corruption and the legal profession

Ashleigh Buckett
Lawyer
Rocío Paniagua
International Bar Association

1. Introduction

1.1 The International Bar Association

The International Bar Association (IBA) is the global voice of the legal profession. It is a professional association, the members of which are bar associations, law societies, law firms, corporations and individual legal practitioners from around the world.[1] Its structure includes a number of committees that focus on particular areas of law. For example, there are committees on anti-trust, corporate and mergers and acquisitions law, litigation and technology law.

Relevant to the focus of this chapter is the IBA's Anti-Corruption Committee. The Anti-Corruption Committee provides an international forum for private and public sector practitioners to meet and discuss anti-corruption laws, compliance practices, enforcement trends and asset recovery issues. It facilitates the sharing of best practice and the regular communication of information on legal and other developments, including new legislation, case law, prosecution guidance and government policy, as well as developments in civil society, the private sector and international organisations. It has a number of sub-committees that focus on asset recovery, double jeopardy, drivers of corruption and structured criminal settlements.[2] IBA members who wish to contribute to the work of the Anti-Corruption Committee are free to join it.

1.2 Anti-corruption and the IBA

The role of the legal profession in anti-corruption is critical. The IBA, principally its Anti-Corruption Committee and its Legal Policy & Research Unit (LPRU, formerly the Legal Projects Team[3]), based in London, recognised early on the key role the legal profession has to play in anti-corruption in the international context. In particular, the IBA recognised that ignorance of the laws that prohibit the bribery of foreign public officials meant that many lawyers potentially could be at risk of contravening those laws. In that context, the IBA developed the Anti-Corruption Strategy for the

1 More information about the IBA can be found at www.ibanet.org/Default.aspx.
2 More information on the IBA Anti-Corruption Committee can be found at www.ibanet.org/LPD/Criminal_Law_Section/AntiCorruption_Committee/Default.aspx.
3 More information about the IBA LPRU can be found at www.ibanet.org/Legal_Policy_Research_Unit.aspx.

Legal Profession. This was done by the IBA LPRU in tandem with the IBA's Anti-Corruption Committee and with the cooperation of the Organization for Economic Co-operation and Development (OECD) and the United Nations Office on Drugs and Crime (UNODC).

The IBA LPRU has built on this work and has expanded its project portfolio to include anti-corruption related projects, such as judicial integrity, whistleblower protection and 'sextortion'.

2. Where it all began

In developing the IBA/OECD/UNODC Anti-Corruption Strategy,[4] the IBA identified growing trends in anti-corruption compliance and the need for the legal profession to integrate these anti-corruption processes in law firms. The IBA, OECD and UNODC agreed that the best way to raise awareness of the role of legal professionals in international corruption, anti-corruption and the application of international instruments and extra-territorial legislation to legal practice was through in-country workshops. The three partners conducted 35 workshops in as many countries over a five-year period to 2015.

The findings set out in two reports informed the approach and content of these workshops. The first report – *Global Anti-Corruption Report for the Legal Profession*, published in 2010, was based on the responses of more than 700 lawyers in almost 100 jurisdictions to a survey on:

- their perception of the impact of corruption on their profession at home and abroad;
- the risks associated with international corruption for the legal profession;
- their levels of awareness of the international anti-corruption regulatory framework that exists to address these risks and;
- the role which local bar associations, law societies and law firms play in addressing the challenge of corruption in the legal profession.

The second report – *Anti-Corruption Compliance and the Legal Profession: The Client Perspective*, published in 2013, was based on the views of senior in-house legal and compliance counsel of leading companies from 20 countries. The purpose of this report was to understand how businesses were managing the corruption risks posed by engaging external legal counsel.

The IBA also developed a set of anti-corruption guidelines and tools for bar associations, law firms and compliance officers as part of its Anti-Corruption Strategy for the Legal Profession. A major benchmark of this project was the adoption of the Anti-Corruption Guidance for Bar Associations, a compact document drafted by the IBA's LPRU, which sets out several key ways in which bar associations can support anti-corruption initiatives in their jurisdictions. For example, bar associations can

---

4 For more information on the IBA/OECD/UNODC Anti-Corruption Strategy, see www.ibanet.org/LPRU/Anti-corruption.aspx.

5 See www.ibanet.org/Publications/publications_IBA_guides_and_free_materials.aspx. Details of the JII and its results can be found at www.ibanet.org/Legal_Projects_Team/ judicialinte grityinitiative.aspx. The JII was launched by David W Rivkin, the then President of the IBA (2015–2016).

educate lawyers, provide information resources, offer technical assistance and apply/reform ethical codes). The IBA Council approved the Guidance in May 2013.[5]

The IBA LPRU intends to continue its work on anti-corruption. In particular, it hopes to continue to educate legal professionals and to equip them with the requisite skills to identify and act against corruption. In the next few years, the IBA LRPU proposes to develop an online toolkit for lawyers. This toolkit will contain information and reference materials relevant to anti-corruption, anti-money laundering, asset recovery and illicit enrichment. Participants in the IBA/OECD/ UNODC workshops identified all these topics as being of interest to them.

The IBA's work on anti-corruption has highlighted other areas in which it considers further work is required. This includes the importance of having integrity in judicial systems.

3. Out of the frying pan and into the fire

Corruption in judicial systems can be especially damaging to society. If a country's judicial system is corrupt, it follows that anti-corruption initiatives in the legal profession, the executive and the legislature are unlikely to be effective. The judiciary is, by nature of its function, the legal and institutional mechanism through which to curb corruption.

Awareness of corruption in various judicial systems has influenced the IBA, through the LPRU, to initiate the Judicial Integrity Initiative (JII),[6] a research project which focuses on the types of corruption affecting judicial systems and the roles that professionals in judicial systems have in facilitating it.

The LPRU used a combination of quantitative and qualitative research methods for the first part of its project.[7] The work revealed information about the complex nature of corruption and presented a number of key findings.[8]

- Firstly, bribery and undue influence were the most widespread forms of corruption observed, the degrees of which depended on the strength of the rule of law within a country. Bribery occurs more often in countries where the rule of law is weak. Undue influence occurs more widely. However, neither of these forms of corruption occurs in a uniform way within judicial and governmental structures.
- Secondly, public perception is an influential factor. For example, in countries where political corruption is high, the public also perceives the judicial system as highly corrupt even where this is not the case.

---

6 Details of the JII and its results can be found at www.ibanet.org/Legal_Projects_Team/judicial integrityinitiative.aspx. The JII was launched by David W Rivkin, the then President of the IBA (2015–2016).

7 The research project was carried out in collaboration with the Basel Institute of Governance and comprised three elements. First, the LPRU conducted a comprehensive analysis of the legal instruments and literature already in existence on the topic. A survey was then issued at the global level and garnered 1,577 responses from 120 countries, which proved significant in providing the biggest variety of data in terms of geography and judicial structures. Finally, in-depth consultations were undertaken with judicial professionals from two different countries – Mexico and the Philippines.

8 The outcome of the research was a report published in May 2016, entitled *The International Bar Association Judicial Integrity Initiative: Judicial Systems and Corruption*, published by the International Bar Association Press Office on 27 May 2016.

The findings of the survey highlight that judges who engage in corrupt conduct do so more frequently with other judges or lawyers, which suggests that they have a focus on internal interactions. Those most involved in corrupt practices tend to be the judicial professionals part of the system itself, including judges, lawyers and court personnel. On the other hand, lawyers reportedly serve as intermediaries with third parties and can influence cases more frequently because of their interaction with a broader range of parties. Prosecutors too are at risk of third party influence. Conversely, the findings suggest that court personnel do not actively seek bribes themselves but are subject to such requests from external actors.

These findings place significant stress on states to find an appropriate balance between independence and accountability in their judicial systems. This concept underpins the second phase of the JII, which is now under way.

The IBA LPRU, working with the National Centre for State Courts (NCSC) and the Research Institute on Judicial Systems (IRSIG), is focusing on the various constraints experienced within the judicial systems of four countries as case studies. Through these case studies, the partners seek to determine the methods of investigation and punishment following alleged corruption of members of the judiciary. This may be through internal disciplinary mechanisms or criminal proceedings.

The objectives of this project are several.

- Firstly, to ascertain the various obstacles faced by criminal courts and disciplinary systems in investigating members of the judiciary.
- Secondly, to compare the standards for findings of corruption in criminal and disciplinary proceedings.
- Thirdly, to examine the legal frameworks and policies governing the investigation and prosecution of corruption and the culture surrounding this.
- Finally, to examine the interconnectedness of and/or overlap between processes in terms of responsibility, investigatory collaboration and findings in criminal and disciplinary proceedings, and the extent to which, if any, one influences the other.

The IBA LPRU, NCSC and IRSIG prepared a detailed set of questions, which address the criminal and disciplinary processes of a number of jurisdictions. These questions reflect the aims and objectives outlined above; analyse the regulations and procedures in place for both criminal and internal hearings, and cross-reference them. The research partners have conducted a series of interviews and gathered a range of data, in collaboration with members of international associations of judges, jurists and prosecutors. The research partners have completed draft analyses of four different countries – Costa Rica, France, Ghana and the Philippines. This information will be presented in a report, the preliminary findings of which the partners have been presented at the Conference for the Launch of the UNODC Global Judicial Integrity Network in April 2018.

4. What about those who reveal misconduct?

The protection of those who bring the misconduct of others to light is well recognised. As always, they usually have the most to lose by doing so. The protection of whistleblowers is multi-faceted and is not specific to anti-corruption. However, it is clear that international discourse with regard to whistleblower protection is driven primarily by the anti-corruption agenda.

In 2016, the IBA LPRU and officers of a number of IBA committees formed a working group to undertake a project on whistleblower protection. The project was intended to identify key elements essential to effective whistleblower programmes and frameworks across all sectors, not only anti-corruption. Given the relevance of whistleblower protection to anti-corruption, however, it is included here for completeness.

The project's focus was multi-faceted and drew on excellent work done by:

- various international organisations, such as the OECD and UNODC;
- academics, such as those involved in the International Whistleblower Research Network;
- non-governmental organisations, such as Public Concern at Work, Transparency International and the Government Accountability Project; and
- the private sector, such as Vodafone, Axa and the ING Group.

The IBA recognises that different countries are at different stages of experience in and exposure to whistleblowing laws and practice. For example, the US and its legal systems have significantly more history and experience on whistleblowing than most other jurisdictions. The IBA also recognises that people in many countries, particularly those with histories of repression, regard whistleblowing or reporting, however so called, with a great deal of suspicion. These issues are recognised and addressed in the report. Finally, the IBA is aware that many countries have excellent whistleblower protection laws in place, but that their implementation and practice are wanting. The IBA has sought to identify possible options that users may wish to consider to overcome these problems. The project culminated in the publication of *Whistleblower Protections: A Guide* in April 2018.

In 2017, the LPRU participated by invitation in an expert's workshop on whistleblower protection hosted by the European Commission. This follows the roundtable on *Protecting Whistleblowers: A legal framework*, which the LPRU co-hosted with the European Economic and Social Committee in 2016, at which Ms Beate Gminder, Secretary-General of the European Ombudsman's Office, provided the keynote address.

The roundtable:

- provided an opportunity to learn about initiatives that stakeholders are currently undertaking (principally in Europe) to improve whistleblower protection;
- established, through case studies, elements of successful whistleblower protection frameworks; and
- explored how to resolve issues of contention that commonly arise in relation to whistleblower protection.

It also provided an opportunity for the IBA LPRU to identify how the legal profession can best contribute to and potentially work with stakeholders to improve whistleblower protection. Following the publication of *Whistleblower Protections: A Guide*, the IBA LPRU co-hosted an event with MEP Virginie Rozière at the European Parliament to discuss the European Commission's recent proposal for European Union-wide whistleblower protections. Future events are planned.

5. What happens when sex, not money, is the benefit demanded?

When people think of corruption, particularly bribery, they tend to think of a person or business handing over or transferring money to another party to secure some benefit or approval illegally. For example, a developer may pay some money to a local councillor to secure approval for a particular project that does not meet regulatory requirements. Conversely, it may be that someone in authority demands money from another to process paperwork or to accept a job application; for example, a migration official may demand cash from an individual in order to process his/her paperwork.

A corruptly obtained benefit, however, is not restricted to money. Individuals in authority can also demand sex from a person in exchange for something that person seeks or requires. A classic example is a male producer demanding sex from a female actor before he is prepared to cast her in a movie (the 'casting couch'). Other disturbing examples include demands for sex in exchange for aid and basic necessities or due process in legal proceedings.

In 2008, the International Association of Women Judges (IAWJ) coined the term 'sextortion' to describe:

> *[A] form of sexual exploitation and corruption that occurs when people in positions of authority[,] whether government officials, judges, educators, law enforcement personnel, or employers[,] seek to extort sexual favours in exchange for something within their power to grant or withhold. In effect, sextortion is a form of corruption in which sex, rather than money, is the currency of the bribe.*

While there is growing international recognition of sextortion, significant legal reform is required to address the full scope of such conduct. Sextortion may fall under existing anti-corruption frameworks if the definition of 'benefit' (in relation to a corrupt transaction) is sufficiently broad. However, further research is required to establish whether this is the most effective avenue through which to pursue sextortion claims. This topic is of particular relevance to the legal profession, given that sextortion frequently occurs within legal settings and reform in this area rests on lawyers, particularly prosecutors and members of the judiciary, being cognisant of the issue. It is also relevant to in-house counsel faced with internal claims of sextortion.

The IBA LPRU is currently undertaking a project on sextortion. This project aims to:

- establish whether definitions of 'benefit' under anti-corruption frameworks are broad enough to encompass sextortion, and the extent to which sextortion claims are successfully brought under this framework;
- identify barriers to addressing sextortion through existing legal frameworks;
- develop recommendations on how to address the full scope of sextortion through legal frameworks; and
- promote awareness of sextortion and the legal issues relevant to it.

Through this project, the IBA LPRU hopes to further awareness of sextortion and the legal issues relevant to it.

6. Conclusion

Through its work on anti-corruption since 2010, the IBA LPRU has identified myriad other areas to which it can contribute. It remains convinced that the role of the legal profession is critical to addressing corruption and seeking redress for those who have suffered from it.

The United Nations Convention Against Corruption (Merida Convention) and its effect in local law

Lorena de la Barrera
Carlos Hernández
UNODC LPO Mexico

1. Introduction: the importance of the Merida Convention in the international community

It was the last month of 2003, the winter season of a city that has never known snow, cold or any weather hazards related to this time of the year. This was Merida, the capital of the Mexican state of Yucatán as well as the largest city of the Yucatán Peninsula. It is located in the northwest part of the state, about 35 kilometres from the Gulf of Mexico coast. Merida, specifically, has the highest percentage of indigenous people of any city in Mexico, with approximately 60% of all inhabitants being of Mayan ethnicity.

It was in this culture-rich city, on 9 December 2003, that the United Nations Convention Against Corruption (UNCAC) – the latest international convention on the subject – was opened for signature. It was not a coincidence that the opening of the convention for signature took place in this location. There had been strong lobbying from the Mexican delegation along with the full support of the country. The relevance of this convention relies on its universal legally binding nature (it was signed by 183 states parties) and its comprehensive and inclusive nature.

Mr Kofi Annan, the then Secretary-General of the United Nations (UN), recognised the fragmented efforts that had been made by the international community against corruption and celebrated them during his speech, in which he acknowledged the UNCAC as an "important victory" in the global fight against corruption. At last, this new convention, together with the United Nations Convention Against Transnational Crime of 2000, offered to the international community "useful mechanisms to attack transnational crime and corruption at [*sic*] a global scale". Ninety-Six states parties signed the UNCAC, which would, from then on, be informally known as the Merida Convention.

More than a decade later, the balance between the political commitments that came from Merida have been crystallised in sets of mechanisms, projects, initiatives and compromises put into effect through the UNCAC, which have had a very positive overall effect. An example of this is the successful UNCAC Implementation Review Mechanism (IRM) (see 9 below), which is a mutual and voluntary peer review process aimed at encouraging and showing continuous advances in normative and operational instruments, thus assisting states parties to implement the convention effectively. As a result, the IRM promises the implementation of a national legal framework and the sharing of best practices to implement actions operationally to prevent and counter corruption.

Even though the UNCAC is directed mainly toward states, focusing primarily on the strengthening of their institutions, the convention also clearly promotes the active participation of all sectors of society – the public and private sectors, academia and civil society. For each and every one of these key actors, shared responsibility is the main goal.

The term 'shared responsibility', can be understood – and has been strongly emphasised by all of the UNODC's work since 2003 – as a mutual responsibility by virtue of which every citizen in every country should respond to and uphold the country's duty and obligations in the daily fight towards integrity. This is because it is precisely at that first level of responsibility – the citizenry – that all democratic values, followed by legal and practical tools and, finally, the more complex institutions, are shaped. This series of steps, from the individual to the institutional levels, is part of the sense of what shared responsibility stands for. Further, shared responsibility is the term that differentiates the UNCAC from all its predecessors and sets up a challenge to all societies in the 21st century.

By now, the question for consideration must be something among the lines of: how precisely can a convention establish such an ambitious and comprehensive approach? In the discussion that follows, more detail is offered on the history of the UNCAC, its challenges, its effects and, – more importantly – ongoing activities, in order to provide a snapshot of the impact of the UNCAC on people's daily lives.

2. A brief history of the UNCAC

Corruption evolves faster than controls, policies and regulations. It does not respect the economic, financial or administrative systems of any country in the world. This phenomenon has endemically affected all aspects of human civilisation and the 21st century world has not been the exception. It probably remains more notorious than ever in modern societies, thanks to the digitalisation and globalisation of economies, is one of the biggest obstacles to development and democracy and represents a strong enemy of democratic political systems.

The reason why the UNCAC has become such an efficient legal tool resides in its capacity to involve every sector of society, that is to say, by facilitating:

- the definition and development of normative frameworks and national regulations;
- the design and implementation of prevention campaigns and outreach efforts; and
- the measurement and reporting of illicit acts related to corruption.

The road toward signature of the UNCAC started on 4 December 2000, when UN

General Assembly Resolution 55/61 recognised the need to give the international community a universal legal instrument against corruption. Under this resolution, an *ad hoc* committee was created to facilitate the negotiation of a new instrument. For this task, the then Centre for the Prevention of International Crime of the Office on Drug and Crime Prevention (now the United Nations Office on Drugs and Crime, or UNODC), was asked to serve as the secretariat for the negotiation process.

Two years and seven negotiation sessions later, the UN General Assembly approved Resolution 58/4 on 31 October 2003, allowing the UNCAC to see the light of day. Having been opened for signature on 9 December 2003, the Merida Convention came into force on 14 December 2005 with its 20th instrument of ratification.

3. What is the UNCAC?

The aims of the UNCAC are:

- to promote and strengthen measures to prevent and combat corruption more efficiently and effectively;
- to facilitate and support international cooperation and technical assistance;
- to promote integrity, accountability and the proper management of public affairs and public property; and
- to provide all sectors of society with a clear mandate to counter corruption and to seek to decrease its incidence toward the year 2030.

To achieve these goals, the convention covers five main subject areas:

- preventive measures (Chapter II);
- criminalisation and law enforcement (Chapter III);
- international cooperation (Chapter IV);
- asset recovery (Chapter V); and
- technical assistance and information exchange (Chapter VI).

In general, the UNCAC manifests an international commitment to support the creation of strong and just societies in which the management of the *res publica* is conducted with transparency, impartiality and with due respect for the rule of law. The following discussion describes the actions that UNCAC requests state parties to take in the different areas on which it focuses.

4. Shared responsibility for preventing corruption

Two sides co-exist in any act of corruption: the corruptor and the corrupted. Both sides come together to violate the law and generate benefits for the perpetrators of the crime. The price of this criminal pact is paid by society as a whole. Corruption therefore:

- undermines the credibility of governing institutions and their resources;
- distracts those institutions from the proper exercise of their functions;
- diverts public resources;
- drives costs as well as burdens; and

- reduces investment, distorting free market rules and reducing the quality of products and services.

The Merida Convention recognises this criminal pact between corruptors and the corrupted as a central element. It therefore postulates the need to prevent or overcome this pact with a new and more vigorous co-responsibility pact between institutions and civil society, the sector that is most vulnerable to the costs of corruption. The goal of this new pact is good governance, meaning more efficient, fair and effective government in which public management is subordinated to the criteria of transparency and accountability.

Given this dynamic, and in addition to the instruments and mechanisms that the UNCAC imposes on its signatory states, the convention makes an important call for state parties to involve civil society, academia and the private sector actively in the design and implementation of prevention of corruption policies.

5. The broad sweep of the UNCAC

Article 5, paragraph 1 of the UNCAC requires state parties to formulate and implement "effective, coordinated anti-corruption policies that promote the participation of society". In implementing this article, countries are requested to promote the principles of the rule of law, proper management of public affairs and public property, integrity, transparency and accountability. This approach underlies Chapter II of the convention, 'Preventive measures'.

Article 7 is addressed exclusively to the public sector. It promotes the adoption, maintenance and strengthening of systems for the recruitment, hiring, retention, promotion and retirement of civil servants and, where appropriate, other non-elected public officials. Such a recruitment system would be based on principles of efficiency, transparency and the application of objective criteria, such as merit, equity and aptitude, as well as adequate procedures for the selection and training of individuals for public positions, especially for those who are vulnerable to corruption.

In this regard, article 8 states the need for institutions to adopt codes of ethics for public officials. Through the implementation of such tools, states parties are required actively to promote personal standards (integrity, honesty and responsibility) and professional responsibilities (correct, impartial, honourable and proper performance of public functions) among all public officials.

Article 12 covers what is expected from the private sector with regard to the prevention of corruption. The convention:

- directly calls on its signatories to strengthen the control and audit mechanisms of companies;
- indirectly calls on the private sector to:
  - exercise initiative in the development and implementation of mechanisms aimed at promoting transparency along with ethics;
  - prevent conflicts of interest;
  - design and consolidate good practices; and
  - cooperate actively with authorities in the fight against corruption.

The standard of shared responsibility through the participation of civil society is developed by article 13, whereby signatory states are requested to take the necessary measures to ensure the "active participation of individuals and groups outside the public sector, such as civil society, non-governmental organizations and community-based organizations, in the prevention of and the fight against corruption and to raise public awareness regarding the existence, causes and gravity of and the threat posed by corruption".

To ensure the compliance of civil society participation with anti-corruption efforts, the convention suggests four possible strategies:

- fostering transparency and citizen participation in the decision-making processes of the institutions;
- ensuring public access to information;
- developing information and educational campaigns on corruption, with particular attention to school and university education; and
- protecting and promoting the right to report corruption.

Chapter II of the UNCAC contains a number of other articles which deal with public procurement and transparency.

In summary, then, the term 'shared responsibility' reflects a strategy to create an effective prevention of corruption policy. Prevention must therefore be the public policy that countries consider as the best tool to counter corruption. Citizens must trust their authorities, and vice versa, which can only be achieved by living in an environment of democratic governance.

6. The features of corruption and its criminalisation: summary of salient provisions of the UNCAC

Nowhere in the UNCAC is a definition of 'corruption' offered. The various illicit acts that constitute this crime are, however, identified and explained, and authorities in all jurisdictions are encouraged to typify, investigate, prosecute and punish them.

A disclaimer has to be made at this point in the discussion, since it is clear that although the list that follows is not exhaustive of the different typologies of illicit act related to corruption, these definitions have achieved the almost unachievable: to define the global parameters of corruptive acts according to the perspective of criminal codes, thus facilitating their prosecution and promoting their prevention.

In this regard, Chapter III of the UNCAC, "Criminalization and law enforcement", sets out provisions relating to the criminalisation of the different facets of corruption, generating an obligation for signatory states to pursue these types of crime within their criminal legal frameworks. Thus, Chapter III clearly identifies the main corruptive offences as follows:

- bribery of national and foreign public officials (articles 15 and 16 respectively);
- bribery in the private sector (article 21);
- embezzlement, misappropriation or other diversion of property by a public official (article 17);
- trading in influence (influence peddling) (article 18);

- abuse of functions (article 19);
- illicit enrichment (article 20);
- embezzlement of property in the private sector (article 22);
- laundering of proceeds of crime (article 23);
- concealment (article 24);
- obstruction of justice (article 25);
- liability of legal persons (article 26);
- participation and attempt (article 27); and
- knowledge, intent and purpose as elements of an offence (article 28).

An important new feature of the UNCAC is the broadening of the typology of corruption-related offences. In addition to traditional categories of crime, the convention calls on its signatories to consider prosecuting new criminal offences that reflect the evolution of corruption and apply to corrupt acts that relate to the commission of and participation in crimes, regardless of their outcome.[1]

An important element of the classification of crimes under the UNCAC is extension of the concept of a 'benefit' that is derived from an act of corruption. According to the convention, the benefit would be understood not only as the transfer of tangible and/or pecuniary goods but also as the promise of such a transfer, including everything that seeks an undue reward, even if this reward is given to third parties and/or persons (ie, organisations, companies or political parties).[2]

In this sense, the UNCAC consolidates and universalises the tendency to hold juridical persons accountable for financial crimes and corruption as stated by the Organisation for Economic Co-operation and Development (OECD),[3] the Organization of American States (OAS),[4] the Commission of the European Communities[5] and the Financial Action Task Force (FATF).[6] At the same time, the convention seeks to develop a set of measures and mechanisms to facilitate the prosecution of corrupt acts by requesting states to establish time limits for prosecution along with mechanisms that allow time limits to be interrupted where alleged perpetrators raise obstacles to investigations (article 29).

In light of the economic nature of corruption offences, article 30 of the UNCAC calls on signatory states to adopt the necessary measures to arrest and detain alleged offenders for the duration of investigations and prosecutions and to confiscate ill-gotten assets after judgment. In the latter instance, the convention provides that states may recover the value of proceeds of crime along with other property of the

---

1 Article 27, paragraph 1 requests states to pursue "any form of participation, whether as an accomplice, collaborator, or instigator" and suggests that states should criminalise "any attempt to commit an offence established in accordance with this Convention" (paragraph 2), along with "preparation for an offence established in accordance with this Convention" (paragraph 3).

2 Articles 15, 16, 18, 19 and 21.

3 OECD Convention on Combating Bribery of Foreign Public Officials in International Business Transactions 1997, article 2.

4 OAS, Model Regulations on Laundering Offenses Relating to Illicit Drug Trafficking and Other Serious Offenses 2005, article 15.

5 *Green Paper on the criminal-law protection of the Community's financial interests*, COM (2001) 715, section 5.4, available at http://eur-lex.europa.eu/LexUriServ/site/es/com/2001/com2001_0715es01.pdf.

6 FATF's Forty Recommendations against money laundering 2003, recommendation 2, paragraph b.

offender. Furthermore, it enables national legislation to assert the principle of *onus probandi*, which requires the offender to prove the legal origin of alleged proceeds of crime or confiscated property.

Articles 32, 33 and 37 of the UNCAC address the key roles of witnesses, victims, experts and whistleblowers in investigating and prosecuting crimes, and call upon signatory states to establish mechanisms and processes that provide these actors, together with their families, with not only physical but also legal protection, in order to motivate and facilitate their collaboration with justice.

States parties to the UNCAC are also obliged to assign responsibility for prosecuting corruption offences to one or more specialised bodies or persons. Steps must be taken to ensure that these actors have the necessary functional and operational independence to carry out their functions "effectively and without any undue influence" (article 36).

Recognising the complexity of investigations for corruption offences and with a view to facilitating their investigation and prosecution by specialised bodies, the UNCAC invites states to promote cooperation between their public bodies (article 38). This necessary cooperation extends also to the private sector and in particular to financial institutions (article 39), under the principle of shared responsibility. Lastly, article 40 seeks to remove legal obstacles to bank secrecy that may make it difficult to investigate crimes under the convention.

Chapter III of the UNCAC shows the importance of having strong law enforcement agencies. Once the law has been broken, state authorities need to understand which crime(s) should be prosecuted and ensure that they have the technical capacities to punish them. By contrast with many other crimes, corruption is difficult to understand and even more difficult to document. There is usually confusion between investigations from the criminal and administrative standpoints. For this reason, Chapter III represents the most important technical tool for state parties in countering corruption.

7. Closing spaces for transnational corruption: international cooperation

An indispensable part of the fight against corruption is undoubtedly international cooperation, which is dealt with by Chapter IV, 'International cooperation'. Such cooperation (or its omission) can determine the success or failure of national strategies, reducing or consolidating the impact of measures taken in the prevention, investigation and prosecution of offences and the seizure and restitution of illicit assets. From this perspective, the UNCAC builds upon the progress made in judicial matters by the UN Convention against Transnational Organized Crime 2000, adopting and strengthening such instruments as extradition (article 44) and mutual legal assistance during the phases of investigation, prosecution, trial and post-judgment proceedings (articles 46, 47 and 48).

With regard to the problem of double criminality,[7] which frequently undermines

7 The principle of double criminality provides that a state party to an international convention on criminal matters is not obliged to extradite a person wanted for acts allegedly committed abroad if the same acts are not criminalised in its own territory.

the scope of international cooperation in criminal matters, article 43, paragraph 2 of the UNCAC urges signatory states to consider this requirement fulfilled where the conduct constituting the offence for which cooperation is invoked "shall be deemed fulfilled irrespective of whether the laws of the requested State Party place the offence within the same category of offence or denominate the offence by the same terminology as the requesting State Party, if the conduct underlying the offence for which assistance is sought is a criminal offence under the laws of both States parties."

Finally, the erosion of the principle of double criminality in the prosecution of corruption offences is further reflected in extradition, whereby the UNCAC recognises the possibility that national legislation may allow the extradition of a person for a crime of corruption even if this offence is not punishable under the domestic law of the requested state (article 44, paragraph 2).

In order to combat corruption more effectively, the UNCAC encourages states to develop bilateral and multilateral agreements to carry out joint investigations (article 49), as well as to make use of special investigative techniques such as electronic surveillance, covert operations and supervised deliveries (article 50).

At the local level, and through the IRM (see 1 above and 9 below), a number of recommendations, the sharing of practices and closer collaboration have been successfully reported in the last decade.

Corruption is not only a local crime but also represents a global threat. For this reason, the UNCAC highlights the need to promote significant levels of working partnership between states parties and all other global actors (eg, non-governmental organisations (NGOs) such as Transparency International), that should lead to more effective, responsive and prompt international cooperation to combat corruption.

In order to combat corruption effectively at the international level, appropriate legal frameworks are required to support the implementation by states parties of their treaty obligations; thus, sufficient resources, experienced personnel and institutional capacity are also required to foster this cooperation. The UNCAC provides this framework of collaboration once it has been signed and ratified by countries.

8. Crime does not pay: the challenge of asset recovery

Another unique element in the UNCAC is Chapter V, "Asset recovery" which deals with the recovery of assets derived from crimes related to corruption. The convention clearly indicates that corruption victimises both citizens and institutions and that the benefits related to corruption become unacceptable economic, social and political burdens and costs for every society. It is therefore natural that the convention should try to reverse this dynamic, allowing the party who has been robbed to recover assets diverted by an act of corruption.

To this end, article 51 of the UNCAC emphasises that asset recovery is "a fundamental principle" of the convention, since it fulfils three important functions:

- it operates as a preventive measure, reducing the possibility that offenders can enjoy the proceeds of crime or use them to ensure their impunity;
- it contributes toward consolidating the rule of law; and
- it operates as an instrument to repair the damage caused, clearly reaffirming the collective victimisation brought about by all acts of corruption.

The convention therefore seeks to close opportunities for impunity in the corruption of VIPs and PIPs,[8] who generally manage to hide abroad the proceeds of their crimes, thanks to their political influence.

Lastly, article 56 of the convention invites states parties to promote international cooperation in the area of asset recovery with special cooperation initiatives, such as information transfer without request from the receiving State and the conclusion of bilateral and multilateral agreements in the areas of investigation and prosecution.

In this regard, and thanks to the support of the international community, in 2007 the UNODC and the World Bank launched the Stolen Asset Recovery Initiative (StAR). The StAR initiative, in addition to generating and transmitting information and data on mechanisms to prevent and prosecute asset diversion for corruption offences, provides technical assistance to many states for the recovery of assets held abroad.

Although this is an issue in relation to which a number of states parties have shown reluctance, several new compromises and sets of good practices were implemented throughout the globe as a result of the Seventh session of the Conference of the States Parties to the UNCAC held on 6–10 November 2017 (the 2017 Conference).[9] These included, in particular, actions by civil society in the states to foster the agenda of the asset recovery, such as the StAR initiative (see above), in relation to which the discussions included the role that civil society could play in overcoming challenges in the asset recovery process.

In particular, ways in which civil society organisations (CSOs) from both developing and developed countries can collaborate to uncover the money trail of stolen wealth include taking part in or initiating investigations into where stolen wealth has been hidden, such as properties in developed countries and banks in developed countries or offshore jurisdictions. Other ways in which CSOs can play a role in highlighting the impact of corruption and the harm done by corrupt acts is to ensure that courts and prosecutors take this into account in setting high standards for and levels of compensation for victims. Finally, there are other mechanisms in which CSOs can help monitor returned assets to ensure that they are used in a transparent and accountable way that benefits the victims of corruption. The 2017 Conference shared experiences of both government and civil society in this regard. It is also useful to look at examples of best practices for each of the areas discussed above in which civil society can and does contribute to enhancing the asset recovery process.[10]

9. The birth and nature of the peer-to-peer Implementation Review Mechanism

The UNCAC adopted a mechanism to keep its processes alive and make them work efficiently: the Implementation Review Mechanism (IRM), a mutual and voluntary peer evaluation mechanism to encourage and show the continuous advances in

8 VIP: Very Important Person; PIP: Political Important Person.

9 www.unodc.org/unodc/en/corruption/COSP/session7-resolutions.html.

10 For further information, see https://css.unodc.org/unodc/en/corruption/COSP/session7-specialevents.html and http://star.worldbank.org/corruption-cases/assetrecovery/?amp%3Bf%5B3%5D=dm_field_pup_scheme_began%3A%5B2012-01-01T00%3A00%3A00Z%20TO%202013-01-01T00%3A00%3A00Z%5D&f%5B0%5D=bundle%3Aarw&f%5B1%5D=sm_field_arw_jurisdiction_recove%3AUnited%20Kingdom.

normative and operational instruments under the convention. Under the IRM, each state party is voluntarily reviewed by two peers – one of which comes from the same regional group – which are selected by drawing lots at the beginning of each year of the review cycle. The functioning and performance of the IRM is guided and overseen by the Implementation Review Group, an open-ended intergovernmental group of states parties that is a subsidiary body of the Conference of the States Parties to the UNCAC (CoSP) and was created together with the IRM by UN General Assembly Resolution 3/1.

The purpose of the IRM is to harmonise national regulatory frameworks to facilitate the implementation of the UNCAC at a universal level and to reduce the incidence of impunity arising from corruption.

The guiding principles of the IRM include:

- a transparent, efficient, non-intrusive, inclusive and impartial approach;
- a non-adversarial and non-punitive approach, without any form of ranking;
- opportunities to share good practices and challenges;
- technical guidance, promoting constructive collaboration; and
- serving as a way to complement existing international and regional review mechanisms.

The IRM provides to each signatory state the opportunity to be assessed by governmental experts from two other states parties. The evaluation, which is always limited to a couple of pre-determined chapters of the convention, usually involves a first phase of desk work, comprising study of a self-assessment submitted by the state under review and of supplementary information provided by that state. This is followed by an on-site visit in which experts from governmental organisations can develop a direct dialogue with the institutions of the country under review.

At its Third session held in Doha on 9–13 November 2009, the CoSP decided that each thematic review cycle should be conducted in two phases, each lasting five years. The first cycle, which included chapters III (Criminalization and enforcement) and IV (International cooperation), began in 2010 and ended in 2015. By November 2016, 170 states parties had submitted their responses to the verification list for self-assessment; 161 direct dialogues were held and 144 abstracts were finalised. The second review cycle was launched in November 2015 and covers chapters II (Preventive measures) and V (Recovery of assets). All reports produced by the Implementation Review Group are published and are available on the UNODC website.[11]

10. The 2030 Sustainable Development Agenda and the anti-corruption indicators of the UN Sustainable Development Goals (SDGs)

In September 2015, all UN member states committed themselves to the 2030 Sustainable Development Agenda to measure their progress in development as well as their progress in reducing corruption. This was achieved through the adoption of Sustainable Development Goal (SDG) 16, which aims to promote peaceful and

11 www.unodc.org/unodc/en/treaties/CAC/country-profile/index.html.

inclusive societies for sustainable development, provide access to justice for all and build effective, accountable and inclusive institutions at all levels.

Moreover, all states parties are committed to reaching and evaluating the improvements discussed below, such as target 16.5: "Substantially reduces corruption and bribery in all its forms." Proposed indicators for this target include presenting revenues, expenditures and financing of all central government entities on a gross basis in public budget documentation authorised by the legislature. A first survey to measure bribery under Target 16.5 is being developed by the UNODC and its task force, to standardise this measurement and shed more light on the measurement of the impacts of all corruption-related crimes.

Measurement of the perception of public sector corruption is the subject of Target 16.6: "Develop effective, accountable and transparent institutions at all levels." Proposed indicators for this target include one in identical terms to that discussed for Target 16.5 above.

Another important target to accomplish under the SDGs for the year 2030 is Target 16.7: "Ensure responsive, inclusive, participatory and representative decision-making at all levels." Key indicators include the percentage of seats held by women and minorities in national parliaments and/or sub-national elected offices in accordance with their respective share of the population (the modified Millennium Development Goals (MDG) Indicator).

11. Conclusion

As shown in the previous discussion, the UNCAC is both ambitious and universal in its reach. The UNODC works to implement it through all available mechanisms: policies, recommendations and inter-sectoral actions that are crystallised every year through the UNODC's annual campaign as part of International Anti-Corruption Day. The latest campaign, 'Together Against Corruption', was launched on 9 December 2017, reflecting that nowadays it is clear that the degree of responsibility of every citizen, business, government, NGO and CSO is crucial in preventing and countering corruption.

The UNCAC has influenced and had an impact on the development of a number of important tools and initiatives to take its reach from global to local realities. Ultimately, it is only in the hands of every global citizen, every community and every sector's willingness to act with integrity that the UNCAC will continue to be a useful tool and to guide our daily lives.

Argentina

Roberto P Bauzá
Santiago Oliva Pinto
Rattagan Macchiavello Arocena

1. Overview: corruption in Argentina

1.1 Preliminary remarks

Corruption has been a long-standing problem in Argentina. Some of its deepest roots can be traced back to Spanish colonial times and it has been present in practically all governments throughout the country's history.

Under President Mauricio Macri's administration, however, Argentina has entered an era of promised transparency and concerted efforts to battle corruption, which is now acknowledged as a widespread, endemic evil and a major obstacle to sustainable development.

In addition to other contributing measures,[1] during 2016 the executive branch sent to Congress three main pieces of projected legislation that constitute the backbone of its anti-corruption efforts, namely:

- a mechanism allowing for reduced sentences for corruption crimes – among other offences – benefiting indicted individuals who collaborate with investigations;
- a bill establishing corporate criminal liability for acts of corruption; and
- a bill proposing the forfeiture of title over assets that are the product of, or are otherwise connected with, criminal activity (including acts of corruption).

Cambiemos,[2] the political alliance that placed Mr Macri in the presidential seat, does not have a majority in either of the legislative chambers.[3] This situation calls for permanent negotiation with opposition forces and poses additional challenges to the progress of the anti-corruption legislation. However, by building legislative consensus, the government has managed so far to pass into law two of the three bills mentioned above.

Further, and even if all projected legislation is adopted, there are still several question marks and hurdles in the way towards reducing corruption effectively. Some of these obstacles are:

- an historically low level of anti-corruption enforcement;,
- a judiciary still perceived as inefficient and corrupt;

1 Such as greater publicity of acts of administration, electronic government and a self-proclaimed non-interference with the judiciary.
2 Spanish for "Let us Change".
3 The Chamber of Deputies and the Senate.

- the lack of a corporate compliance culture; and
- substantial cultural, legislative and economic differences among the federal and provincial jurisdictions that would ultimately be in charge of applying the laws.

1.2 The political background to corruption in Argentina

Following Argentina's latest return to democracy in 1983, and prominently among the successive administrations, allegations of big time corruption plagued the two presidential terms of Carlos Menem (1989–1999), although very few were investigated and even fewer resulted in convictions. After a very protracted investigation, Mr Menem – who is now 87 years old – has himself been convicted by the highest Argentine criminal court on counts of illegal sales of weapons to Ecuador. This conviction – which is subject to review – has not, however, been an obstacle to Mr Menem's election and tenure as a senator for several terms since stepping down as President.

Most recently, however, Argentina showed a particularly poor record in the fight against corruption during the presidencies of Nestor Kirchner (2003–2007) and his wife Cristina Fernández (2007–2015). During those years, the word 'corruption' was squarely absent from presidential speeches and acts of government. Quite the contrary, a series of official and unofficial acts or omissions had the effect of tolerating – if not openly boosting – the rampant corruption swelling in all levels of the administration.

Among other actions, the Kirchners dismantled or rendered ineffective most internal control agencies, exercised heavy interference and pressure over the judiciary, showed a lack of transparency in governmental proceedings, doctored public statistics, attempted to pass laws to control the media and manipulated the body in charge of appointing and removing federal judges. Against this backdrop, a small group of the Kirchners' associates and close family members allegedly made fortunes dealing with federal or provincial administrations, under the appearance of legitimately awarded bidding processes or direct contracts. Even more seriously, there appears to be substantial evidence supporting allegations that the presidential family itself was directly involved in a scheme for illicit enrichment and money laundering.

Most of these actions are presently under criminal investigation, which have resulted in Ms Fernández, her children, her Vice President, several cabinet ministers and a number of other politicians and businessmen facing indictments for corruption-related crimes.[4]

1.3 Public cases involving corruption

In fact, Ms Fernández has been involved in several investigations since she stepped down from her two terms as President (2007–2015), which have not, however, prevented her from being elected as a senator in the congressional elections of October 2017. These include the following.

- Ms Fernández has been indicted on the basis of testimony by Leonardo Fariña, an imprisoned former associate of businessman and alleged Ms

4 Nestor Kirchner died on 27 October 2010 while his wife was in office.

Fernández 'frontman' Lázaro Báez. In a plea bargain, Mr Fariña implicated Ms Fernández and her late husband in a case related to money laundering and embezzlement of funds earmarked for public works. According to press reports, Mr Fariña testified to the movement out of Argentina of tens and possibly hundreds of millions of US dollars, through offshore companies in Panama, Belize and the Seychelles to a Swiss bank. In Argentina, this investigation is referred to as *'The Route of the K-Money'*.[5]

- Ms Fernández has also been indicted – along with her son and daughter – in a case involving a family real estate company. According to federal judge Claudio Bonadio, there was enough evidence to indict them for conspiracy over allegations of renting properties from the Kirchners' real estate company (Los Sauces), in exchange for public works contracts and other favours. Judge Bonadio also ordered the freezing of assets of about $8.5 million each for Ms Fernández and her son, and $6.5 million for her daughter (found in cash in a safety deposit box). Lázaro Báez, a construction businessman in Patagonia (who was detained in the money laundering case referred to above) and a casino magnate, Cristóbal López, were also indicted in this case along with 16 other persons. They are all forbidden from leaving the country. According to the judge, the two businessmen and their associates set up a system to 'illegally reimburse' the presidential family for public works projects awarded to them.[6]
- Allegations of steering public contracts to the mentioned businessmen also led to charges of fraudulent administration being laid against Ms Fernández by Judge Julian Ercolini, who also ordered the freezing of $633 million of Ms Fernández's assets. She said the case is politically motivated and accused current President Macri of plotting against her: "Illicit association is a legal concept that has been used by all dictatorships to persecute their political opponents", she tweeted. She presented national budget documents as part of her evidence, highlighting that the accounts had been approved by parliamentary bodies and the country's Auditor General. Judge Ercolini also approved corruption charges against two of Ms Fernández's close aides: former Planning Minister Julio de Vido and former Public Works Secretary José Lopez.[7] In June 2016, Mr Lopez was caught throwing bags filled with almost $9 million in cash over the walls of a monastery and was arrested on suspicion of money laundering.[8] Mr de Vido was also arrested on 25 October 2017 on charges of fraud against the public administration.

---

5 In Spanish, '*La ruta del dinero K*' ('K' stands for 'Kirchnerism'). This political scandal began with reports on the *Periodismo Para Todos* television programme on the results of an investigation, led by journalist Jorge Lanata. Embezzlement and an associated money trail involved Argentine presidents Néstor and Cristina de Kirchner and their employee, businessman Lázaro Báez. The investigation concluded that Báez diverted money intended for public infrastructure to tax havens. For more information, see www.theguardian.com/world/2016/apr/09/argentina-cristina-fernandez-de-kirchner-money-laundering-investigation?CMP=share_btn_link.

6 www.nytimes.com/2017/04/04/world/americas/argentina-cristina-fernandez-de-kirchner-corruption-indictment.html.

7 www.bbc.com/news/world-latin-america-39499004.

8 www.reuters.com/article/us-argentina-corruption/former-argentine-official-arrested-after-throwing-cash-over-monastery-walls-idUSKCN0Z02KM.

Most of these investigations were started by the media. In fact, during the last decade, journalists have played a key role in uncovering many of the public corruption scandals in Argentina. This renewed role of the media has in a certain manner been 'blessed' by Argentina's Supreme Court of Justice, which in more than one ruling stated that:

> *[I]n these times in which the phenomenon of corruption does not only affect peripheral countries but also embraces the central countries [sic], the press has a key responsibility to fulfill, which should be encouraged and facilitated by the State and especially by the Judicial Branch.*[9]

1.4 Perceptions of society regarding corruption and changes under Macri administration

As at the end of 2016, Argentina had a score of only 36 (out of a maximum grade of 100) in the Corruption Perception Index published by Transparency International, thus ranking 95th out of the 176 countries surveyed.[10]

The violent and still unsolved death of Special Prosecutor Alberto Nisman on 18 January 2015, immediately after accusing President Cristina Fernández and Argentina's Foreign Affairs Minister Alberto Timerman of covering up Iran's responsibility for a terrorist attack that had occurred in 1994, marked a sad rock-bottom and acted as a powerful symbol of the corrupt atmosphere of the times.

Things were, however, about to change. Immediately after taking office in December 2015, following a presidential election that marked the end of 12 years of Kirchner rule, President Macri assumed a public engagement with transparency and the fight against all forms of corruption.

One of the first steps taken in this direction was revitalising key areas of the administration that bore heavily on corruption matters, such as the Anti-Corruption Office and the Financial Information Unit (the agency in charge of fighting and preventing money laundering). In parallel, the administration reached out to the private sector, engaging in dialogue and cooperation with recognised Argentine and foreign experts in anti-corruption and compliance, in order to bring laws, regulations and procedures up to the highest international standards.

It is no coincidence that Argentina requested admission as a full member of the Organisation for Economic Co-operation and Development (OECD) member in 2016, and that several OECD missions had visited the country ever since to review progress in areas such as trade, statistics, financial regulation and anti-corruption.

Regarding anti-corruption specifically, the new administration has concentrated its legislative efforts on the three bills referred to at 1.1 above. To date, the individual plea-bargaining mechanism and the corporate criminal responsibility bill have made it into a law. Further progress is expected to be achieved in the coming months.

---

9 Corte Suprema de Justicia de la Nación. See for example,the decisión in *Fallos*, 321:2848.

10 Available at www.transparency.org/news/feature/corruption_perceptions_index_2016.

2. International anti-corruption treaties signed by Argentina and their effects on the fight against corruption

2.1 Introduction

As the OECD has noted,[11] international anti-corruption conventions play a key role in the global fight for integrity by:

- bringing the fight against corruption to the political forefront;
- setting legally binding standards and principles by which signatory States can be held to account; and
- fostering both the domestic action and international cooperation needed to tackle the many facets of corruption.

Pursuant to the Argentine Constitution,[12] international treaties signed by Argentina, upon ratification by Congress, take precedence over federal and provincial laws. In addition, Supreme Court precedents have held that international treaties cannot be repealed by subsequent domestic legislation. Thus, international treaties signed by Argentina are a privileged part of the country's legislation.

Argentina is a party to several international treaties concerning anti-corruption measures. The importance of compliance with those treaties has been specially stressed by Argentine's Supreme Court of Justice, which ruled that:

> *[W]henever there is a case involving the management of public funds and property, the decision to be adopted must be determined with a greater rigour in assessing the facts, bearing in mind the international commitments made by Argentina in signing treaties with other countries, such as the Inter-American Convention against Corruption and the United Nations Convention against Corruption, approved by laws 24,759 and 26,097, non-compliance with which could generate international responsibility and which, therefore, also require consideration by judges of all instances.*[13]

2.2 International treaties on anti-corruption signed by Argentina

(a) The United Nations Convention against Corruption (UNCAC)

This convention, which was approved in 2003 by the UN General Assembly, became the first international anti-corruption legal instrument to establish binding rules for the signatory countries. The signatories commit to prevent and criminalise corruption, to cooperate openly with one another in cases of cross-border corruption activities, and to return stolen assets to their countries of origin. Under the UNCAC review mechanism, compliance is reviewed through a process involving country self-assessments, a country visit and the drafting of a report submitted to the country under review for approval.

Argentina ratified the UNCAC on 28 August 2006, following its approval on 10 May 2006 by Law No 26.097,[14] and filed a self-assessment report on its implementation.[15]

---

11 www.oecd.org/cleangovbiz/internationalconventions.htm.
12 Sections 31 and 75, § 22.
13 Corte Suprema de Justicia de la Nación, *Fallos* 339:1628, 11/22/2016.

In 2011, Transparency International provided support to the *Asociación Civil por la Igualdad y la Justicia* (ACIJ), a non-governmental organisation (NGO) specialising in anti-corruption, to monitor and contribute to the official UNCAC review of Argentina's implementation of selected articles of the UNCAC.[16]

With regard to the report's conclusions,[17] specifically those concerning the criminalisation of conduct highlighted in the UNCAC, Argentina has generally satisfied its obligations by criminalising offences such as bribery of national and foreign officials, illicit enrichment and money laundering. Thus, from a legal point of view, Argentina meets the legislative requirements of the UNCAC by criminalising some behaviour related to corruption. The NGO has, however, found serious shortcomings in Argentina's implementation of UNCAC provisions concerning anti-money laundering, corporate liability, asset freezing, seizure and confiscation, protection of witnesses and whistleblowers, and bank secrecy.[18]

Further, an official report on Argentina's implementation of the UNCAC was recently issued[19] within the framework of the Follow-Up Mechanism for the Implementation of the Inter-American Convention against Corruption (MESICIC[20]). The report concludes that Argentina:

- has successfully adopted measures aimed at establishing objective and transparent criteria for determining the remuneration of public officials; and
- should establish, within the powers of the national executive, a centralised data registry to keep records of amounts collected by each official and the purposes of payments.

(b) The Convention on Combating Bribery of Foreign Public Officials in International Business Transactions

Argentina is a signatory to the OECD Convention Against Bribery of Foreign Public Officials (Anti-Bribery Convention) and as such it is subject to periodic reviews implemented by this organisation.[21]

The Anti-Bribery Convention is the first and only international anti-corruption

14 The country played also an important role, since it hosted the informal preparatory meeting of the Ad Hoc Committee for the Negotiation of the Convention.

15 www.unodc.org/documents/treaties/UNCAC/WorkingGroups/ImplementationReviewGroup/ExecutiveSummaries/V1388719Ae.pdf.

16 The UNCAC provisions that received particular attention in the report are those concerning bribery (article 15), foreign bribery (article 16), embezzlement (article 17), illicit enrichment (article 20), money laundering (article 23), corporate liabilities (article 26), statute of limitations (article 29), freezing, seizure and confiscation (article 31), witness protection (article 32), whistleblower protection (article 33), compensation for damage (article 35), bank secrecy (article 40), jurisdiction (article 42) and mutual legal assistance (article 46).

17 Full version available at https://acij.org.ar/wp-content/uploads/2012/02/civil-society-review-argentina-2011.pdf.

18 Articles 23, 26, 32, 33 and 40 of the UNCAC.

19 www.fiscales.gob.ar/wp-content/uploads/2017/03/Mesicic-informe-final-Argentina.pdf.

20 The MESICIC is a process of reciprocal evaluation between the States that are parties to it, within the framework of successive 'rounds' that review how the States are implementing the UNCAC provisions selected for each round. For these purposes, country reports are adopted which formulate concrete recommendations for each State, in order for them to close legal gaps that have been detected, correct inadequacies that have been found, and put indicators in place that allow an objective determination of the results that have been achieved in relation to the implementation of those provisions.

21 The Convention was signed by Argentina in 1997 and entered into force on 9 April 2001, following ratification by the Argentine Congress through Law No 25.319.

instrument focused on the 'supply side' of bribery transactions. It establishes legally binding standards to criminalise bribery of foreign public officials in international business transactions and provides for related measures, such as rigorous country monitoring and extensive follow-up mechanisms, to ensure effective implementation. The convention was signed by OECD member states, with the addition of Brazil, Argentina, Bulgaria, Chile and Slovakia, on 17 December 1997. It entered into force in 1999.

The OECD has strongly urged Argentina to comply fully with the Anti-Bribery Convention. In a report published on its website,[22] the OECD remarked (among other things) that:

- 16 years after joining this convention, Argentina remains in serious non-compliance;
- Argentina still cannot hold companies liable for foreign bribery or prosecute its citizens who commit this crime abroad; and
- Argentina must take urgent steps to address concerns about judicial and prosecutorial independence.

In its *Phase 3bis Report*[23] on Argentina's implementation of the Anti-Bribery Convention and related instruments, the OECD Working Group on Bribery made further recommendations to improve Argentina's fight against foreign bribery. These include:

- significantly reducing delay in complex economic crime investigations and prosecutions;
- proactively investigating and prosecuting all foreign bribery cases, as appropriate;
- reducing the very high number of judicial vacancies and the use of surrogate judges; and
- ensure investigative judges and prosecutors are adequately resourced.

This report has been especially critical regarding Argentina's non-compliance with key articles of the convention:

The Working Group acknowledges that efforts to implement the Phase 3 recommendations began in earnest only after the current government took office in December 2015. A Corporate Liability Bill meant to address some of these issues was introduced into Congress in October 2016 but has yet to be adopted. As a result, Argentina still cannot hold legal persons liable for foreign bribery, or exercise jurisdiction to prosecute its citizens who commit this crime abroad.

As discussed below, this last observation has been recently overcome by the passage of the Law of Corporate Criminal Responsibility for Acts of Corruption.

The report also notes a number of positive developments, including that:

- a corporate liability bill is high on the agenda of the current government (since passed into law in March 2018: see 3(c) below);

22 www.oecd.org/daf/anti-bribery/argentina-must-urgently-enact-corporate-liability-bill-to-rectify-serious-non-compliance-with-anti-bribery-convention.htm.

23 '*Phase 3bis report on implementing the OECD Anti-bribery Convention in Argentina*', available at www.oecd.org/corruption/anti-bribery/Argentina-Phase-3bis-Report-ENG.pdf.

- an express prohibition of the tax deduction of bribes to foreign officials has been enacted;
- Argentine authorities have made substantial efforts to engage the private sector and promote corporate compliance programmes;
- efforts to raise awareness of foreign bribery within the Argentine public administration have been made;
- judicial investigations have been opened in several foreign bribery cases, though some of them should be pursued more proactively;
- Argentina has taken steps to extend the application of International Financial Reporting Standards;
- the regime to debar companies from obtaining public procurement contracts has been expanded; and
- there has been an increase in the forwarding of financial information to law enforcement authorities.

The report lists all of the recommendations of the Working Group to Argentina at pages 63–68 and includes an overview of recent enforcement actions and specific legal, policy and the institutional features of Argentina's framework to fight foreign bribery.

Argentina will report to the Working Group in March 2018 on progress made in implementing certain key recommendations. It will then report by March 2019 on its implementation of all of the recommendations. These reports will be made publicly available.

The Working Group may take additional measures, depending on Argentina's progress in implementing the Phase 3bis recommendations.

(c) The United Nations Convention against Transnational Organized Crime

The UN Convention against Transnational Organized Crime recognises combating corruption, among other issues, as an integral part in the fight against transnational organised crime. It requires signatory countries to take measures to prevent and criminalise corruption as well as to curb money-laundering. It further provides for a broad framework to reinforce international cooperation on these matters.

Argentina signed this convention in December 2000 and ratified it in November 2002.

(d) The Inter-American Convention against Corruption

Sponsored by the Organization of American States (OAS), the Inter-American Convention against Corruption was signed on 29 March 1996, in Caracas, Venezuela.

Under article II, the convention has two goals:

- to promote and strengthen the development by each of the States parties of the mechanisms needed to prevent, detect, punish and eradicate corruption; and
- to promote, facilitate and regulate cooperation among the States parties to ensure the effectiveness of measures and actions to prevent, detect, punish

and eradicate corruption in the performance of public functions and acts of corruption specifically related to such performance.

Argentina signed and Congress ratified the Convention in 1997.

Under the Convention, Argentina voluntarily agreed in May 2002 to be examined in the first round of evaluation of the Committee of Experts of the Follow-up Mechanism (Committee of Experts) for implementation. Conclusions of the first report include the following:

- the agreements signed and mutual technical cooperation activities undertaken by Argentina are relevant for promotion of the purposes of the Convention;
- Argentina has considered and adopted measures to establish, maintain and strengthen standards of conduct intended to prevent conflicts of interest and enforcement mechanisms, among them Law No 25.188 (the Public Ethics Law) and its regulations within the framework of national public administration, including the establishment of the Anticorruption Office; and
- the Committee of Experts suggested developing procedures for assessing the effectiveness of the appropriate systems and mechanisms.

In turn, in the opinion of the Argentine Supreme Court of Justice, Argentina is fully compliant with this Convention:

The internal rules that arise from Article 13 of Law 25.233 and its reference to Articles 26, 45 and 50 of Law 24,946 and National Decree 102/99, are strictly in accordance with the purposes and objectives of the Inter-American Convention against Corruption (Preamble and Articles 2, 3, 2, 8, 9 and 7), as approved by law 24,759.[24]

3. The concept of 'corruption': corruption-related offences within the Argentine legal framework

3.1 The Argentine Criminal Code

Although 'corruption' is not defined as a specific criminal offence within Argentina's legal framework, anti-corruption provisions are largely contained in the Criminal Code (the Code), which prohibits (among other things) the active and passive bribery of public officials and foreign public officials. The Code does not provide an exception for facilitation payments, and gifts are prohibited, but enforcement of anti-corruption provisions is lacking. Perceptions are that companies consider irregular payments and bribes to be a standard way of conducting business in many sectors.[25]

Apart from the provisions contained in the international conventions on corruption that Argentina has signed and which are also part of the Argentine legal system (see 2.2 above), the Code also contains provisions sanctioning corrupt behaviour, including:

---

24 Corte Suprema de Justicia de la Nación, *Fallos*, 329:1984.
25 GAN Business Anticorruption Portal, at www.business-anti-corruption.com/country-profiles/argentina.

- bribery and trading in influence;
- money laundering;
- embezzlement;
- abuse of functions; and
- illicit enrichment.

It also contains general provisions that have direct implication in corruption offences, such as obstruction of justice and participation and attempt.

In line with the above, Argentina has also introduced anti-bribery provisions in non-criminal legislation. Thus, for example, it has recently enacted legislation[26] that prohibiting the deduction of bribes from the taxable base of income tax.

3.2 The 'Repentant' law (individual plea bargaining)

Law No 27.304, of 19 October 2016 (the 'Repentant Law') modified section 41 of the Argentine Criminal Code by introducing the figure of the 'repentant' for several criminal offences. The basic feature of the law is to allow a sentence reduction negotiated by the prosecutor with a 'repentant' indicted individual in exchange for relevant information. That information may, for example, help the progress of the investigation, avoid further occurrences of the crime, contribute to identifying or indicting accomplices or revealing sources of financing for criminal enterprises.

Even though the 'repentant' figure already existed in some isolated statutes for several specific crimes, the Repentant Law has made it a part of the Criminal Code and specifically extended it to corruption-related offences, such as bribery. In this connection, the Argentine government has undoubtedly looked for precedent to Brazil, where plea-bargaining has achieved astounding success in bringing down large-scale corruption conspiracies and indicting highly placed politicians and businessmen in the so-called *Lava Jato* ('Car Wash') investigation.

Relevant aspects of the Repentant Law include the following:

- convictions may be reduced by between one third and one half of the applicable prison time. Life sentences may be reduced to up to 15 years in prison;
- an individual may only provide information about facts for which he/she is criminally responsible;
- information concerning other persons must refer to individuals whose criminal responsibility is equal to or of a higher level than that of the 'repentant';
- politicians subject to constitutional impeachment may not benefit from the plea-bargaining mechanism;
- plea-bargaining agreements must be implemented in writing, with assistance from legal counsel, and must be approved by the court in a special hearing;
- individuals making use of this mechanism are entitled to claim the benefits of a witness protection programme; and
- the information provided by the 'repentant' individual in the context of the plea-bargaining agreement may not be the sole ground for a conviction. This

---

26 Decree No 1246/2016, December 2016.

information must be confirmed and complemented by other evidentiary elements on the record.

Since its entry into force is relatively recent, the value of the 2016 Law as an effective mechanism for combating corruption and bringing down 'big fish' has yet to be proved. A number of characteristics of Argentine culture and its criminal justice system may limit the intended effect of this tool, as further discussed below. Most significantly, while a number of businessmen and mid-level public officials from the Kirchner era have been indicted and even imprisoned in ongoing corruption investigations, no significant plea-bargaining agreements have been announced signalling responsibility up the political chain.

3.3 Law of Corporate Criminal Responsibility for Acts of Corruption

In response to long-standing requirements and recommendations by the UN and the OECD, in honouring certain commitments assumed by Argentina in meetings of the G-20 and following the latest international trends in anti-corruption prevention and enforcement, the Argentine government sent to Congress in October 2016 a bill intended to establish the criminal responsibility of corporations for acts of corruption (bribery and other related crimes). The bill was the subject of much political debate and underwent a number of amendments at successive stages in the Chamber of Deputies and the Senate. It was eventually approved and became law on 8 November 2017 (Law No 27.401 of Criminal Responsibility of Legal Entities) which officially entered in force on 1 March 2018.

As mentioned previously, until recently only individuals were criminally responsible for corruption-related crimes, while criminal corporate responsibility was limited to several other crimes.[27]

Influenced by theories of economic analysis of the law, the explicit purpose of the Law of Corporate Criminal Responsibility for Acts of Corruption (Law No 27.401 of Corporate Criminal Responsibility) is to create strong and effective incentives for compliance in the private sector. Faced with the prospect of receiving heavy penalties themselves, corporations and other legal entities should cooperate in discouraging, preventing, detecting and sanctioning corrupt behaviour by their employees, agents and other related third parties.

The law follows in many aspects the Brazilian Clean Companies Act No 12.846 which, together with the Chilean Corporate Criminal Liability Law 2009, the UK Bribery Act 2010 and the US Foreign Corrupt Practices Act 1977, are expressly recognised as relevant precedents in the statement of purpose of the legislation.

The main features of the law are as follows:

(a) *Scope*

- The law imposes liability on private Argentine- or foreign-owned legal entities (even if they are partially owned by the State) for the following crimes:

---

27 Such as money laundering, financing of terrorism and some violations of the customs, foreign exchange and competition regimes.

  - bribery and influence peddling (national or transnational);
  - negotiations incompatible with the exercise of public functions (ie, where there is a conflict of interest on the part of a public official);
  - extortion;
  - illicit enrichment of public officials; and
  - false financial statements and reports, where used to conceal bribery.
- Companies are responsible for criminal activity committed directly or indirectly on their behalf, for their benefit or in their interest. A company will be exempt from liability only if the persons who committed the crime acted for their exclusive benefit and without generating any benefit to the company.
- In cases of transformation, merger, spin-off or any other corporate modification, the liability of the company passes on to the continuing or surviving entity.

(b) Extinction of a criminal action

A criminal action against the company may only be extinguished by means of an amnesty or the expiry of the statute of limitations. Termination of actions involving individuals (ie, authors or participants in the criminal act), will not affect the validity of the action against the company.

(c) Penalties

- In all cases, a fine shall be applied, ranging from 2 to 5 times the undue benefit obtained by the company as a result of the criminal activity.[28]
- Additionally, penalties may include (upon judicial assessment):
  - suspension of the company's activities for up to 10 years;
  - loss or suspension of any subsidies or other government-granted benefits;
  - exclusion from public contracts and calls for bids for up to 10 years;
  - termination of legal existence, but only in cases where the commission of crimes is the principal activity of the legal entity; and
  - publication of the judgment.
- Loss of title over goods and disgorgement of profits obtained from the illicit activity are also contemplated, in accordance with applicable provisions of the Argentine Criminal Code.

(d) Exemption from responsibility

Companies may be exempted altogether from criminal responsibility and penalties, provided that three elements are present:

- the company has voluntarily reported the criminal activity to the authorities;
- an adequate compliance programme was in place before the crime was committed; and
- the company has returned any undue benefit obtained.

---

28 Pursuant to the law, judges will determine the specific penalty in accordance with certain parameters established therein, such as the amount of damage, involvement of high management, size and economic capacity of the company, violation of internal rules, self-denunciation by the company, collaboration with the authorities and recidivism.

(e) ***Collaboration agreements***

The entity being indicted may enter into a collaboration agreement with the prosecutor and obtain a reduced penalty in exchange for relevant information and collaboration in the investigation. Terms of the agreement must, as a minimum, include payment of a reduced fine, disgorgement of profits and loss of title over assets obtained from illicit activities. Other terms may include performance of community service, disciplinary measures against involved individuals, payment of damages and implementation of compliance programmes (see below) or improvement of existing ones.

(f) ***Compliance programmes***

- The law establishes general criteria and some specific content that compliance programmes must fulfil to qualify for penalty mitigation or exemption.
- An adequate compliance programme will also be a requirement for entering into public concession agreements and other contacts with the federal administration.
- Mandatory elements include a code of ethics or conduct, specific rules for interaction with the public sector and periodic training sessions. In turn, there are a number of optional components, which include periodical risk-analysis, internal communication channels to report irregularities, whistleblower protection mechanisms, internal investigation systems, proper due diligence of third parties and during corporate reorganisations, constant monitoring and assessment and an internal compliance officer or responsible person.

(g) ***Recidivists registry***

- The law mandates registration of sanctions at the National Recidivism Registry, which is a part of the National Ministry of Justice and Human Rights.
- A company shall be considered a repeated offender if it commits a new crime within three years from the issuance of a previous judgment.

(h) ***Extra-territorial effects of bribery of foreign public officials***

The law modifies section 1 of the Argentine Criminal Code, by extending the jurisdiction of Argentine courts over the crime of bribery of foreign public officials[29] committed abroad by Argentine citizens or legal entities domiciled in Argentina. This amendment had been a specific recommendation by the OECD and is relevant because, prior to its implementation, this crime could only be prosecuted to the extent that it was committed within or had effects in Argentine territory.

(i) ***Fines for certain corruption-related crimes***

The law further modifies the Penal Code by including substantial fines (in addition

29 Section 258 bis of the Argentine Criminal Code.

to prison sentences) for several corruption-related crimes involving public officers or interposed persons.

(j) ***Statute of limitations***

The law sets the statute of limitations at six years for corruption crimes attributable to companies.

3.4 Bill on Forfeiture of Title Over Assets Related to Crime

On 23 June 2016, the Argentine Chamber of Deputies approved a bill sent by the Executive Branch that establishes a procedure for forfeiture of title (*extinción de dominio*) in favour of the Argentine state over assets that are the product of illicit activities or are otherwise connected with crime.

This bill is currently awaiting consideration by the Senate in order to become law. The discussion below is based on the text as approved by the Chamber of Deputies which is subject to potential further amendment by the Senate.

The bill provides a list of situations in which a judicial action may be started with the purpose of extinguishing legal title over relevant assets, including assets directly resulting from criminal activity, assets used to commit crimes and unjustified patrimonial increases related to illicit activities.

Legal proceedings pursuing forfeiture must be commenced by a state attorney before a court of law having civil and commercial jurisdiction. Those proceedings are independent of any criminal proceedings existing against the persons who have title over, or are in the possession of, the assets. However, it is a condition for the admission of the forfeiture petition that the affected person had been indicted in a criminal investigation. Any persons affected by the forfeiture proceedings shall have all legal and constitutional guarantees to appear before the court and exercise their rights of defence.

The bill authorises the Attorney General Office, with the support of the executive branch, to form special units dedicated to investigating relevant cases and, if necessary, commencing and pursuing forfeiture proceedings.

State attorneys are empowered to perform preliminary investigations, request information and cooperation from governmental agencies, private individuals and entities, and may request court orders where they may be necessary for obtaining that information.

Private legal entities or individuals who voluntarily provide evidence leading to asset forfeiture may become entitled to a reward of up to 5% of the value of the forfeited assets. Cooperating individuals may provide testimony without disclosing their identity and/or request inclusion in a witness protection programme.

State attorneys may request from the court injunctions or preliminary measures necessary for the freezing or seizure of the assets while proceedings are under way or even before they are formally commenced.

The bill establishes an expedited procedure for forfeiture actions, with oral arguments before the court and strict procedural deadlines. The forfeiture decision shall declare extinction of title over the assets and their transfer to a special governmental agency created for that purpose. Grounds of appeal are very restricted and appeals shall also be dispatched expeditiously.

Forfeited assets may be applied to a number of public uses detailed in the bill, such as education, public housing, drug rehabilitation programmes, the justice system and law enforcement.

3.5 Ethical standards for public officials: the Public Ethics Law

Law No 25.188 (the Public Ethics Law) stipulates duties, prohibitions and conflicts of interest for all persons acting as public officials at all levels and hierarchies of state. The law applies to public officials who are elected to their positions and also to officials who are hired in a direct way for temporary or permanent positions. Judicial employees are also included within the scope of this law.

The main duties of public officials established by the Public Ethics Law are the following:

- to comply with the Federal Constitution, the laws and applicable decrees and to protect the republican and democratic form of government;
- to comply with the standards of ethics established by this law: honesty, probity, rectitude, good faith and republican austerity;
- to satisfy in all acts the general goodwill and uphold the general interest over particular interest;
- to avoid receiving any inappropriate benefit related to their job as public officials;
- to show transparency in all acts and decisions;
- to protect the property of the state and use that property only for authorised purposes.
- to avoid using for their own benefit information obtained through their jobs;
- to avoid using the property or services of the state for their own benefit or that of their families;
- to follow the legal procedures for any contract with the state in accordance with the principles of publicity, equality and reasonableness; and
- to refrain from acting in cases where there is a conflict of interest.

The law also establishes:

- a detailed system of patrimonial disclosure in the form of sworn statements for public officials. As a general rule, all upper ranking public officials up to the category of director are obliged to file an affidavit of all property of their own, of their spouse or other person living with them and property of their children under the age of eighteen;
- a mechanism for any individual to obtain a copy of the aforementioned affidavits. Moreover, a number of jurisdictions, such as the City of Buenos Aires, have published the affidavits of a number of of their public officials online;[30]
- guidelines relating to conflicts of interest, which establish general prohibitions for public officers from:
    - acting as administrators, officers, advisers, representatives or in any other manner render services to a supplier of the government, when the public

30 www.buenosaires.gob.ar/declaracionesjuradas.

    - officer has direct responsibilities for hiring, managing or overseeing that supplier, or
    - being a supplier (directly or indirectly) of goods or services to the governmental office in which they render services;
- that public officers cannot receive gifts, subject to two exceptions:
    - that the gifts are given as courtesy,[31] or
    - that they are offered as a matter of diplomatic practice.[32]

In such cases, these gifts must be included in the Register of Gifts granted to Public Officers.

Pursuant to the provisions of this legislation, public officers may accept the payment of travel or hotel expenses by third parties only if certain requirements are met.[33] Public officers who receive these benefits must register them at the Register of Trips Financed by Third Parties.

4. Authorities responsible for regulating, enforcing and punishing corruption

The investigation of offences begins with a charge made either by a public organ or a private individual. The Public Prosecutor must initiate an action, as the holder of the public right of action in respect of the offence; without such a request from the Public Prosecutor, it is not possible for a judge to begin proceedings for corruption offences.

Criminal proceedings may also be initiated by means of preventive actions on the part of the security forces, but this is not usual in corruption crimes. The federal procedural system requires an examining judge to direct the proceedings, and it is this judge who may take any measures deemed pertinent to the discovery of the truth (including raids and seizures, telephone tapping and requests for information). The judge may, at his or her discretion, delegate to prosecutors the investigation of these crimes and may resume the investigation whenever he or she deems convenient.

The procedural system allows an individual affected by an alleged offence to become a plaintiff in the proceedings and to suggest measures or appeal any decision that is not favourable to him or her. This role may be assumed either by the public entity affected by the particular case of corruption or by the Anti-Corruption Office.

Judges and prosecutors for federal criminal and correctional matters are competent to enforce the law in corruption cases. The Office of Coordination for Crimes against the Public Administration (OCDAP), which was created with the goal

---

31 That is, because such gifts, donations, benefits or gratuities may be deemed to be demonstrations or acts indicating recognition of, respect for or affection towards another person on the occasion of certain events in which it is usual to award them.

32 That is, because as a matter of protocol, recognition or gestures received from governments, international organisations or non-profit entities are permissible in accordance with conditions under which law or usual official custom admit those benefits.

33 That is, (i) they are allocated for the organisation of conferences, courses or academic or cultural activities, or for participation in them; (ii) they do not originate from governments, entities, individuals or agencies who are forbidden from giving gifts to public officers; and (iii) their acceptance is neither incompatible with a public officer's functions nor forbidden by any special rules.

of cooperating with prosecutors working on corruption cases, has been replaced by the Office of the Prosecutor for Economic Crime and Money-laundering (PROCELAC),[34] of the office of the Attorney General. This new organisational structure comprises a team of specialised prosecutors and officials who coordinate various areas of operation.

Argentina also has a Prosecutor's Office for Administrative Investigations, a body specialised in the investigation of acts of corruption and administrative irregularities committed by agents of the national administration, as well as an Anti-Corruption Office,[35] which is an agency under the Ministry of Justice and Human Rights and which aims to develop and coordinate programs to combat corruption.

Other relevant institutions in relation to corruption cases are the office of the Controller General of the Nation[36] and the Auditor General's Office.

Under the Code of Criminal Procedure, public officials and public employees are obliged to report offences that are prosecutable *ex officio* of which they gain knowledge during the exercise of their functions. Such public officials and employees fulfil their legal duty by informing the Anti-Corruption Office of the facts and/or evidence in support of the presumption of the commission of an offence that is prosecutable *ex officio* committed within the national public administration or any public or private entity with state participation.[37] Presumed offences that are not investigated by the Anti-Corruption Office are to be reported to a judge, a prosecutor or the police by such officials and employees.

5. Conclusion

As acknowledged by the OECD's *Phase 3bis Report*, there are positive developments in some areas regarding corruption in Argentina, although efforts to implement the report's recommendations began in earnest only after the current government took office in December 2015.

(a) The Law of Corporate Criminal Responsibility for Acts of Corruption represents a fundamental improvement in the Argentine anti-corruption system. However, it presents, in the authors' view, several practical concerns. Since it establishes a purely criminal responsibility system (with no prior administrative stage), it will necessarily rely on the existing structure of the Argentine criminal judiciary to be enforced. Some limitations of this approach are:

- the absence of a central, specialised body or agency in charge of investigating and prosecuting, in accordance with unified criteria, corruption cases against legal entities;
- uncertainties concerning the determination of monetary sanctions and the implementation of collaboration agreements;
- different procedural laws and systems for criminal enforcement at federal level, in each of the Argentine provinces and the City of Buenos Aires;

34 Created by resolution No 914/12 of 20 December 2012.
35 Created by Law No 25.233 of 10 December 1999.
36 SIGEN.
37 In accordance with article 1 of Decree-Law No 1162/00.

- criminal judges and prosecutors with little experience or education in corporate matters and compliance programmes; and
- excessive formalism and protracted average duration of criminal proceedings.

These factors, absent coordinated efforts to create uniform enforcement culture and practices, may result in diverging judgments, lack of predictability about expected corporate behaviour and slow-moving enforcement proceedings, and eventually work against the incentives that the bill aimed at creating in the private sector.

(b) Since the individual plea-bargaining ('repentant') law entered into effect, no substantial developments have occurred of public record concerning plea-bargaining in anti-corruption investigations. In the authors' view, there may be two reasons for this.

- Firstly, in accordance with judicial criteria followed by most criminal courts in Argentina, very few individuals are actually jailed in anti-corruption investigations and so the effectiveness of the mechanism is somehow reduced. By comparison, most plea-bargaining deals[38] in Brazil have been struck by negotiating with people already behind bars.
- Secondly, the law does not permit complete immunity to be granted to the 'repentant' individual. Considering, in addition, the overwhelmingly low rate of convictions for corruption crimes in Argentina and protracted litigation, the potential reduction of a jail sentence is probably not that much of an incentive for individuals to self-incriminate or reveal the involvement of others further up the criminal hierarchy.

In short, this measure (which is by itself positive) may be rendered almost moot if not accompanied by a change in the behaviour of prosecutors and judges, a modernisation of criminal procedure and a general perception of tougher and more effective anti-corruption enforcement.

(c) A law on forfeiture of title over assets related to crime has been signalled for a long time as a necessary tool to fight corruption most effectively. However, the current bill has been stuck in Congress for over a year and it is still the subject of much political and legal discussion, as it has been criticised for not observing constitutional guarantees regarding due process of law.

(d) Finally, some other important steps are being taken, such as:

- increased judicial activity in cases involving corruption, including indictment of high-level public officers;
- the enactment of legislation that expressly prohibits the tax deductibility of bribes;
- Argentina's efforts to adopt the OECD's Common Reporting Standard regarding automatic exchange of financial information;

---

38 *Delações premiadas.*

- greater enforcement of money laundering controls; and
- the encouragement and promotion of corporate compliance programmes.

The effectiveness of the tools aimed at combating and reducing corruption will, however, depend on greater cultural change that must include the cooperation of all political forces, and active involvement and commitment by the judiciary and the corporate sector. Only then will Argentina be able to show that it has started to turn the page on its corruption-ridden past, always bearing in mind that, as Theodore Roosevelt accurately stressed more than a century ago:

> *[O]ther offenses violate one law while corruption strikes at the foundation of all law... The exposure and punishment of public corruption is an honor to a nation, not a disgrace. The shame lies in toleration, not in correction.*[39]

39 Third Annual Message, 7 December 1903.

Australia

Jocasta Giles
King & Wood Mallesons
Robert Wyld
Johnson Winter & Slattery

1. Introduction and overview

1.1 Perceptions of corruption in Australia

Australia has a reputation as a corruption-free country, a reputation that has perhaps been achieved more by accident than design. Australia was ranked 13th (of 176 countries) in Transparency International's Corruption Perception Index 2017, although that represents a slide in the rankings since 2012.[1] More locally, Transparency International interviewed more than 20,000 people in 16 countries, regions and territories across the Asia-Pacific region between 2015 and 2017 about their perceptions and experiences of corruption, and reported that:[2]

- people in Australia were the most positive, of those surveyed, about levels of corruption in their country;
- while the survey results suggest overall that the police are an institution widely suspected of corruption across the Asia-Pacific region, only 5% of people in Australia surveyed said the police were highly corrupt;
- fewer than 5% of the people surveyed in Australia said they had paid a bribe when accessing public services; and
- a majority of the people surveyed in Australia (80%) said they felt empowered to fight against corruption.

The report shows Australia had the best results from the survey overall. Nonetheless, the survey results suggest that people in Australia think their government's efforts to fight corruption are mediocre. This view is undoubtedly influenced by media coverage of ongoing corruption and financial scandals.

Momentum is building, however, for changes to strengthen Australia's approach to bribery and corruption, including amendments to the Criminal Code Act 1995 (Cth) (Criminal Code), the proposed introduction of a scheme for Commonwealth deferred prosecution agreements and improvements to whistleblower protections (see 6 below).

1 Transparency International, *Corruption Perceptions Index 2017*, available at www.transparency.org/news/feature/corruption_perceptions_index_2017.

2 Coralie Pring, *People and Corruption: Asia Pacific* (February 2017) Transparency International, available at www.transparency.org/whatwedo/publication/people_and_corruption_asia_pacific_global_corruption_barometer.

1.2 Government responses to corruption

In 2016, in its first Open Government National Action Plan, the government of the Commonwealth of Australia (Commonwealth Government) made 15 commitments split across five key areas.[3] Of particular relevance to anti-corruption and anti-bribery are the following commitments:

- from the 'transparency and accountability and business' key area:
  - improving whistleblower protections in the tax and corporate sectors;
  - combating corporate crime;
- from the 'integrity in the public sector' key area:
  - a national integrity framework.

In September 2017, the Commonwealth Government published its Midterm Self-Assessment Report for Australia's First Open Government National Action Plan 2016–2017 (Midterm Report).[4] Each of the 'transparency and accountability and business' commitments identified above have been self-assessed as being "on track",[5] noting the following achievements to date:

- referral by the Senate of an inquiry into whistleblower protections in the corporate, public and not-for-profit sectors to the Parliamentary Joint Committee on Corporations and Financial Services in November 2016 (Parliamentary Joint Committee) (the report was released in September 2017);[6]
- public consultation on draft legislation for whistleblower protection;[7]
- release by the Minister for Justice of public discussion papers on a proposed Commonwealth deferred prosecution agreement (DPA) scheme and on possible reform of the laws applicable to bribery of foreign public officials in March and April 2017 respectively.

At the time the *Midterm Report* was published, the Commonwealth Government was considering the proposed law reforms, which incorporate views expressed in the submissions and through the public consultation sessions which are discussed in more detail at 6 below.[8]

Progress on the national integrity framework has been self-assessed as being "delayed".[9] The *Midterm Report* states that the Attorney-General's Department is

---

3 Commonwealth of Australia, Department of the Prime Minister and Cabinet, *Australia's First Open Government National Action Plan 2016–18,* available at https://ogpau.pmc.gov.au/sites/default/files/posts/2017/07/first-open-government-national-action-plan-final.pdf.

4 Commonwealth of Australia, Department of the Prime Minister and Cabinet, *Midterm Self-Assessment Report for Australia's First Open Government National Action Plan 2016–18,* available at https://ogpau.pmc.gov.au/sites/default/files/posts/2017/09/midterm_self-assessment_report_for_australias_first_open_government_national_action_plan_2016-18.pdf.

5 *Ibid,* p8.

6 *Ibid,* p10; Parliamentary Joint Committee on Corporations and Financial Services, Parliament of Australia, *Whistleblower Protections* (September 2017).

7 Midterm Report (note 5 above), p10.

8 *Ibid,* p16.

9 *Ibid,* p9.

10 *Ibid,* p45. For the text of the report, see www.aph.gov.au/Parliamentary_Business/Committees/Joint/Australian_Commission_for_Law_Enforcement_Integrity/Jurisdiction_of_ACLEI/Report.

continuing consultations with affected agencies to develop a government response to the report of the Parliamentary Joint Committee Inquiry into the jurisdiction of the Australian Commission for Law Enforcement Integrity (ACLEI).[10]

1.3 History of legislative reform

Australia's anti-corruption laws were enacted in the Criminal Code in 1999 as a result of Australia complying with its international obligations (see 2 below). There have been some minor reforms since 1999, but nothing of substance until more significant reforms were proposed in 2017.

Some of the recent legislative reforms have been noted above. It is hoped that the Commonwealth Government will adopt these reforms and enact them to update Australia's overall capability to target financial crime and corruption.

2. International anti-corruption treaties to which Australia is a party

Australia became a signatory to the Organisation for Economic Co-operation and Development (OECD) Convention on Combating Bribery of Foreign Officials in International Business Transactions 1997 (the OECD Convention) in 1997 and ratified it in October 1999.[11] Australia's implementing legislation for the convention became effective in December 1999 and is contained in section 70 of the Criminal Code, which is discussed at 3 below.

Australia is also a signatory to the following international anti-corruption treaties:

- United Nations Convention against Transnational Organized Crime 2000 – ratified by Australia in 2004;[12]
- United Nations Convention against Corruption 2004 – ratified by Australia in December 2005;[13] and
- Agreement for the Establishment of the Anti-Corruption Academy as an International Organization 2010 – ratified by Australia in June 2012.[14]

In addition to signing and ratifying international treaties, Australia is active in other ways in the international community in the fight against corruption and bribery. For example it was a founding member of the Financial Action Task Force.[15] Australia is also an active member of:

---

11 Department of Foreign Affairs and Trade, Government of the Commonwealth of Australia, Convention on Combating Bribery of Foreign Officials in International Business Transactions, available at www.info.dfat.gov.au/Info/Treaties/treaties.nsf/AllDocIDs/8521B7F9B2E2282ACA256B20000EE392.

12 Department of Foreign Affairs and Trade, Government of the Commonwealth of Australia, United Nations Convention Against Transnational Organized Crime, available at www.info.dfat.gov.au/Info/Treaties/treaties.nsf/AllDocIDs/52DAAC7EB03FA201CA256B3E000E05F4.

13 Department of Foreign Affairs and Trade, Government of the Commonwealth of Australia, United Nations Convention against Corruption, available at www.info.dfat.gov.au/Info/Treaties/treaties.nsf/AllDocIDs/D928C58E62238FDECA256DF900837FEE.

14 Department of Foreign Affairs and Trade, Government of the Commonwealth of Australia, Agreement for the Establishment of the Anti-Corruption Academy as an International Organization, available at www.info.dfat.gov.au/Info/Treaties/treaties.nsf/AllDocIDs/206C10EE6DCF0267CA25781D00147DC2.

15 Attorney-General's Department, Government of the Commonwealth of Australia, *Australia's engagement with the Financial Action Task Force*, available at www.ag.gov.au/CrimeAndCorruption/AntiLaunderingCounterTerrorismFinancing/Pages/FATF.aspx.

- the OECD Working Group on Bribery in International Business Transactions;[16]
- the G20 Anti-Corruption Working Group;[17] and
- the Asia-Pacific Economic Cooperation (APEC) Anti-Corruption and Transparency Working Group.[18]

Australia has significant involvement in anti-bribery and anti-corruption efforts in the Asia-Pacific region. For example:

- Australia has been actively involved since 2003 in the Asia Development Bank-OECD Anti-Corruption Initiative;[19]
- in 2004 Australia endorsed the APEC Santiago Commitment to Fight Corruption and Ensure Transparency and the APEC Course of Action on Fighting Corruption and Ensuring Transparency;[20] and
- Australia had a leading role in developing the APEC Code of Conduct for Business.[21]

3. Bribery and corruption laws in Australia

The Criminal Code is the primary source of liability in Australia for offences both of bribery of a foreign public official[22] and bribery of public officials of the Commonwealth of Australia.[23]

The Criminal Code applies to bodies corporate in the same way as it applies to individuals (with such modifications as are set out and/or necessary by the fact that criminal liability is being imposed on bodies corporate rather than individuals).[24] Sections 12.1–12.6 of the Criminal Code deal with corporate criminal responsibility. While a corporation may be found guilty of any offence under the Criminal Code (including one only otherwise punishable by imprisonment), no company has been prosecuted for bribery under these provisions since their introduction in 2001.[25]

While the Criminal Code is the primary source of liability, sources of secondary liability for bribery both of a foreign public official and public officials of the Commonwealth of Australia, include the Crimes Act 1914 (Cth) and the Proceeds of

---

16 OECD Working Group on Bribery in International Business Transactions available at www.oecd.org/corruption/anti-bribery/anti-briberyconvention/oecdworkinggrouponbriberyininternationalbusinesstransactions.htm. The OECD Working Group is made up of representatives from the States parties to the OECD Anti-Bribery Convention.

17 Attorney-General's Department, Government of the Commonwealth of Australia, Anti-corruption, available at www.ag.gov.au/CrimeAndCorruption/AntiCorruption/Pages/default.aspx.

18 *Ibid.*

19 Anti-Corruption Division, Directorate for Financial and Enterprise Affairs, Organisation for Economic Co-operation and Development, *Steps Taken by State Parties to Implement and Enforce the Convention on Combating Bribery of Foreign Public Officials in International Business Transactions* (2011), available at www.oecd.org/investment/anti-bribery/anti-briberyconvention/46881297.pdf.

20 *Ibid.*

21 *Ibid.*

22 The term "foreign public official" is defined broadly in section 70.1 of the Criminal Code.

23 The term "public official" is defined in the Dictionary at the end of the Criminal Code to include a range of persons in or holding official positions.

24 Criminal Code, section 12.1.

25 The Reserve Bank of Australia subsidiaries, Securency Pty Ltd and Note Printing Australia Pty Ltd, were prosecuted for foreign bribery offences in 2011 but the status of those proceedings is subject to Australia-wide non-publication orders made by the Supreme Court of Victoria: see 5 below.

Crime Act 2002 (Cth) to target the proceeds of crime,[26] and State criminal laws which particularly focus on commercial fraud, financial deception, corruption and secret commissions.

There are also Commonwealth and State criminal laws for domestic criminal offences (which include commercial corruption). Bribery involving state or local public officials is also criminalised by legislation in each of Australia's States and Territories.

3.1 Domestic bribery and corruption laws

(a) Offences involving Commonwealth public officials

Sections 141 and 142 of the Criminal Code deal with bribery offences involving Commonwealth public officials, including:

- giving a bribe;[27]
- receiving a bribe;[28]
- giving a corrupting benefit;[29]
- receiving a corrupting benefit;[30] and
- abuse of public office.[31]

The penalties for the offences of giving or receiving a bribe are:

- for an individual: imprisonment for not more than 10 years, a fine of not more than 10,000 penalty units[32] (A$2,100,000), or both;[33] and
- for a body corporate: a fine of not more than the greatest of 100,000 penalty units (A$21,000,000), three times the value of the benefit obtained (if the court can determine the value) or, if the court cannot determine the value of the benefit obtained, 10% of the annual turnover of the body corporate during the period of 12 months ending at the end of the month in which the offending conduct occurred.[34]

The penalty for the offences of giving or receiving a corrupting benefit is imprisonment for five years.[35]

For offences of giving a bribe or a corrupting benefit, it is not necessary to prove that the defendant knew the public official was a Commonwealth public official or that the duties were duties as a Commonwealth public official.[36]

For offences of giving or receiving a corrupting benefit, it is immaterial whether the benefit is in the nature of a reward.[37]

---

26 Offences include dealing with the proceeds or instruments of crime and obstruction of justice.
27 Criminal Code, section 141.1(1).
28 *Ibid*, section 141.1(3).
29 *Ibid*, section 142.1(1).
30 *Ibid*, section 142.1 (3).
31 *Ibid*, section 142.2.
32 One Penalty Unit is defined in section 4AA of the Crimes Act 1914 (Cth) to mean the amount of A$210, subject to indexation on 1 July 2020 and each third 1 July following that day.
33 Criminal Code, section 141.1(5).
34 *Ibid*, section 141.1(6).
35 *Ibid*, section 142.1(1), (3).
36 *Ibid*, sections 141.1(2), 142.1(2).
37 *Ibid*, section 142.1(4).

The Criminal Code also deals with other offences involving fraudulent conduct, including dishonestly obtaining a gain from,[38] or causing a loss to,[39] a Commonwealth entity, or doing anything with the intention of dishonestly influencing a Commonwealth public official in the exercise of that person's duties as a public official.[40] Each of these offences carries a penalty of imprisonment for five years.

The Criminal Code deals only with conduct involving Commonwealth public officials or foreign public officials; it does not expressly deal with bribery in private commercial practices. There are, however, criminal and civil laws in various Australian State and Territory jurisdictions that may impose liability on individuals and companies involved in such conduct. An example is the Crimes Act 1900 (NSW) (NSW Crimes Act), the provisions of which cover conduct involving the corrupt receipt or giving of commissions and other corrupt practices.[41]

(b) Offences involving state or local public officials

Taking New South Wales as an example, the primary source of liability for offences of bribery is the NSW Crimes Act. This act includes offences against both payers and payees of bribes, with such offences carrying a sentence of up to seven years' imprisonment.[42]

Under the Local Government Act 1993 (NSW), local government officials may face dismissal if a finding of 'serious corrupt conduct' is made by the NSW Independent Commission Against Corruption (NSW ICAC),[43] which may refer such conduct to the NSW Director of Public Prosecutions (DPP) for criminal prosecution.

3.2 Laws governing foreign bribery

(a) Applicable provisions

The Criminal Code is the primary source of liability in Australia for bribery of foreign public officials. In substance, it is an offence under section 70.2 of the code to offer, promise or provide, or cause to be provided, a benefit to another person, directly or indirectly, where that benefit is not legitimately due, and with the intention of influencing a foreign public official in the exercise of that person's duties as a foreign public official in order to obtain or retain business or a business advantage that is not legitimately due.[44]

The term "benefit" is defined broadly by the Criminal Code to include any advantage and is not limited to property.[45]

The term "foreign public official" is also defined broadly by the Criminal Code and includes employees or officials of a foreign government body, as well as:

---

38 *Ibid*, section 135.1(1).
39 *Ibid*, section 135.1(5).
40 *Ibid*, section 135.1(7).
41 Sections 249A–249J.
42 *Ibid*, section 249B.
43 Section 440B.
44 Criminal Code, section 70.2(1).
45 *Ibid*, section 70.1.

- individuals who perform work under a contract for a foreign government body or a public international organisation;
- individuals who hold or perform duties of an appointment, office or position, either under the law of a foreign country, or created by a custom or convention of a foreign country;
- individuals who are otherwise in the service of a foreign government body or public international organisation;
- individuals who are members of either the executive, judiciary or magistracy of a foreign country, or members or officers of the legislature of a foreign country;
- individuals who hold or perform duties of an office or position in a public international organisation; or
- individuals who are authorised intermediaries, or hold themselves out to be authorised intermediaries, of foreign public officials as defined by the Criminal Code.[46]

In the above list, references to 'foreign country' include part of a foreign country.

For the purposes of an offence under section 70.2 of the Criminal Code (bribing a foreign public official), it is not necessary for the person providing the bribe to intend to influence a particular foreign public official, and a business or business advantage does not need to be actually obtained or retained.[47]

The offence of bribing a foreign public official will not have been committed unless the conduct occurs wholly or partly in Australia (or wholly or partly on board an Australian aircraft or ship).[48] If the conduct occurs wholly outside of Australia, an offence still may have been committed if, at the time of the alleged offence, the offender was an Australian citizen or resident of Australia, or a body corporate incorporated by or under Australian law.

The penalties for the offence of bribing a foreign public official are:

- for an individual: imprisonment for not more than 10 years, a fine not more than 10,000 penalty units (A$2,100,000), or both;[49] and
- for a body corporate: a fine of not more than the greatest of 100,000 penalty units (A$21,000,000), three times the value of the benefit obtained (if the court can determine the value) or, if the court cannot determine the value of the benefit obtained, 10% of the annual turnover of the body corporate during the period of 12 months ending at the end of the month in which the offending conduct occurred.[50]

If the primary offence of foreign bribery is not open to the prosecutor, the secondary offence of conspiracy may be available.[51]

---

46 *Ibid*.
47 *Ibid*, section 70.2(1A).
48 *Ibid*, section 70.5(1).
49 *Ibid*, section 70.2(4).
50 *Ibid*, section 70.2(5).
51 *Ibid*, section 11.5. See also other 'aiding and abetting' offences: Criminal Code, sections 11.1–11.6. See also *R v Jousif; R v I Elomar; R v M Elomar* [2017] NSWSC 1299.

(b) Defences

Limited defences are available under the Criminal Code to a prosecution under section 70.2 for bribery of a foreign public official. Essentially, these defences apply where:

- the conduct occurs wholly in a foreign jurisdiction, it is lawful in that jurisdiction and is permitted by a written law of that country;[52]
- the payment is a facilitation payment;[53] or
- for corporations, where there is proof that a corporation exercised adequate due diligence to prevent the conduct.[54]

In order to rely on the 'facilitation payment' defence, the value of the benefit provided must have been of a minor nature.[55] A successful 'facilitation payment' defence under the Criminal Code also requires that the paying person's conduct was engaged in for the sole or dominant purpose of expediting or securing the performance of a routine government action of a minor nature.[56] The type of government action that is routine and of a minor nature is set out in the Criminal Code.[57] In addition, as soon as practicable after the relevant conduct, the paying person must have made a record of it with that person's identity clearly disclosed, or he or she must have signed the record,[58] and either:

- that person retained the record;[59]
- the record was lost or destroyed by a person or event outside the control of the paying person and the paying person could not reasonably be expected to guard against such conduct or event;[60] or
- a prosecution for the offence is instituted more than seven years after the conduct occurred.[61]

The 'facilitation payment' defence remains law in Australia (and only under the laws of the United States, New Zealand and South Korea), despite the international community seeming to move in the opposite direction. Facilitation payments are often, in substance, small bribes and paying a facilitation fee, once or more than once, can lead unintentionally to significant reputational and legal risks. While the Australian Senate References Committee Report on Foreign Bribery published in March 2018 recommended the abolition of the facilitation payment defence, describing a facilitation payment as "not materially different from a small bribe",[62] it remains to be seen if the Australian government will act on the recommendation.

---

52 Criminal Code, section 70.3.
53 *Ibid*, section 70.4.
54 *Ibid*, section 12.3(3).
55 *Ibid*, section 70.4(1)(a).
56 *Ibid*, section 70.4(1)(b).
57 *Ibid*, section 70.4(2).
58 *Ibid*, sections 70.4(1)(c), 70.4(3).
59 *Ibid*, section 70.4(1)(d)(i).
60 *Ibid*, section 70.4(1)(d)(ii).
61 *Ibid*, section 70.4(1)(d)(iii).
62 Senate References Committee, *Foreign Bribery Report* (March 2018) at paragraph 7.101, available atwww.aph.gov.au/Parliamentary_Business/Committees/Senate/Economics/Foreignbribery45th/Report.

4. Investigative and prosecuting authorities

Set out below is a description of the anti-corruption investigative and prosecuting authorities in Australia. At the time of writing, there is no Commonwealth anti-corruption commission.

4.1 The Australian Federal Police (AFP)

The AFP investigates criminal offences against Commonwealth laws. One of the areas of operational emphasis of the AFP is "investigating complex, transnational, serious and organised crime".[63] The AFP is responsible for investigating crimes which may then, subject to certain threshold requirements, be prosecuted by the Commonwealth Director of Public Prosecutions (CDPP). A significant operational arm of the AFP is the Serious Financial Crime Task Force.

4.2 The Commonwealth Director of Public Prosecutions (CDPP)

The CDPP is the independent statutory prosecutor who is responsible for prosecuting criminal offences against the Commonwealth.[64] There are two key threshold issues about which the CDPP must be satisfied before pursuing a prosecution for foreign bribery:

- that there is sufficient evidence to prosecute and that there are reasonable prospects of securing a conviction; and
- that it is evident from the facts of the case that a prosecution would be in the public interest.[65]

In addition to the threshold issues set out above, the Prosecution Policy of the Commonwealth also provides guidance for prosecutions for the bribery of foreign public officials under the Criminal Code, including a direction that the prosecutor deciding whether to prosecute must not be influenced by considerations of national economic interest, the potential effect upon relations with another State, or the identity of the natural or legal persons involved.[66] This direction is consistent with article 5 of the OECD Convention.

During 2014, the Commonwealth Government (through the Department of Foreign Affairs and Trade, (DFAT)), obtained a suppression order in relation to the Securency prosecution (discussed further at 5 below) with a view to protecting the identity of various political figures in Asia who had been named in evidence but not charged with any offence, thereby allegedly protecting Australia's international relations.[67] However, the Victorian Supreme Court discharged the initial suppression orders in June 2015, stating that the DFAT had failed to establish that the strong public interest consideration in the public knowing about the Securency case was, on balance, outweighed by the public interest of "protecting the administration of

---

63 Australian Federal Police, *Our Organisation*, available at www.afp.gov.au/about-us/our-organisation.

64 Director of Public Prosecutions Act 1983 (Cth).

65 Commonwealth Director of Public Prosecutions, *Prosecution Policy of the Commonwealth: Guidelines for the making of decisions in the prosecution process* (August 2014), available at www.cdpp.gov.au/sites/g/files/net2061/f/Prosecution-Policy-of-the-Commonwealth_0.pdf.

66 *Ibid*, p19 (Annexure A).

67 The individuals concerned did not seek to apply for any suppression orders from the court.

justice and Australia's national security".[68] In addition, the fact that the identity of the political figures was well known outside Australia and had been published by WikiLeaks made the continuation of the court's non-publication orders moot.[69]

4.3 The Australian Criminal Intelligence Commission (ACIC)

The ACIC is a Commonwealth statutory authority with coercive powers to compel the production of documents and information that might assist in the investigation of serious and organised crime.[70] For example, the ACIC can compel persons to give evidence in private examinations, or to produce documents or things relevant to a special operation or investigation.[71] Persons who are the subject of the ACIC's coercive powers are required to give testimony or produce documents even where such testimony incriminates them as witnesses.[72] A witness is, however, protected in relation to any evidence given under compulsion to the ACIC, in that such evidence is inadmissible in subsequent criminal or civil proceedings against that person, save in proceedings for perjury.[73] Care must be taken in how the ACIC disseminates information it obtains pursuant to its powers, so that a person's right to a fair trial is not prejudiced.[74]

4.4 The national Fraud and Anti-Corruption Centre (FAC)

The FAC is a multi-agency initiative, hosted by the AFP with involvement from the Australian Taxation Office (ATO), the ACIC, the Department of Human Services, the Australian Border Force, the Australian Securities and Investments Commission (ASIC), the DFAT, the Department of Defence, the Australian Transaction Reports and Analysis Centre (AUSTRAC), the Attorney-General's Department and the CDPP. The FAC has several objectives, including "strengthening law enforcement capability to respond to serious and complex fraud, foreign bribery, corruption by Commonwealth Government employees and complex identity crime".[75]

4.5 The Australian Commission for Law Enforcement Integrity (ACLEI)

The ACLEI assists the Commonwealth Integrity Commissioner in investigating, assessing, reporting on and preventing corruption in a number of prescribed Commonwealth Government law enforcement agencies, namely:

- the ACIC;
- the AFP;
- AUSTRAC;
- prescribed functions of the Department of Agriculture and Water Resources;

---

68 Commonwealth *DPP v Barry Thomas Brady* [2015] VSC 246.

69 WikiLeaks, *Australia bans reporting of multi-nation corruption case involving Malaysia, Indonesia and Vietnam* (29 July 2014), available at wikileaks.org/aus-suppression-order/.

70 Australian Crime Commission Act 2002 (Cth).

71 *Ibid*, sections 21A, 28.

72 *Ibid*, sections21A(5)(note 2), 21E, 30(2), 30(4).

73 *Ibid*, section 21E, 30(4)–(5).

74 *Ibid*, section 25A(9A). See also *X7 v Australian Crime Commission* [2013] HCA 29; *Lee v The Queen* [2014] HCA 20.

75 Australian Federal Police, *Fraud and Anti-Corruption Centre*, available at www.afp.gov.au/sites/default/files/PDF/fac-centre-fact-sheet.pdf.

- the Department of Immigration and Border Protection (including the Australian Border Force);
- the former National Crime Authority; and
- any other Commonwealth Government agency that is prescribed by regulation under the Law Enforcement Integrity Commissioner Act 2006 (Cth).[76]

4.6 Other central government agencies

There are a number of other Government agencies that may assist or be involved in the investigation and/or prosecution of bribery and/or commercial crime offences, including:

- ASIC (where directors' duties and other offences arise under the Corporations Act 2001 (Cth));
- the ATO (where taxation-related offences arise under Commonwealth tax laws);
- the Australian Competition and Consumer Commission (ACCC) (where offences involve consumer protection, anti-competitive and cartel conduct); and
- AUSTRAC (which is the statutory regulator ensuring compliance with Australia's anti-money laundering and counter-terrorism financing laws).[77]

4.7 State commissions

Each Australian state has an anti-corruption commission. Taking New South Wales as an example, the NSW ICAC (Independent Commission Against Corruption) was established in 1988.[78] Its remit is to investigate corruption as it concerns government officials (local or state), public assets or money relevant to New South Wales. The NSW ICAC's jurisdiction includes all public sector agencies in the state other than the NSW Police. It has powers to investigate and make findings but cannot prosecute. The power to prosecute for breaches of domestic bribery laws lies with the NSW DPP.

The NSW ICAC's findings are based on evidence it obtains pursuant to compulsive powers and such evidence is inadmissible against the witness who gave the evidence in any subsequent criminal proceedings against that witness. Accordingly, in order to exercise its prosecutorial powers, the NSW DPP has to establish a case independently of the evidence obtained by the NSW ICAC pursuant to its compulsive powers, using admissible evidence that can be used in criminal proceedings. This can often lead to the result that NSW ICAC findings of corruption do not result in criminal prosecutions as the NSW DPP cannot be satisfied that it is

---

76 Australian Commission for Law Enforcement Integrity, Government of the Commonwealth of Australia, *ACLEI's role*, available at www.aclei.gov.au/acleis-role.

77 In 2017, AUSTRAC commenced two prosecutions for breaches of Australia's anti-money laundering laws. The first, brought in early 2017 against Tabcorp, secured an agreed settlement of A$49 million. The second prosecution, civil penalty proceedings brought against the Commonwealth Bank of Australia (CBA) in August 2017, is continuing before the Federal Court of Australia. The Australian media has reported that the CBA allegedly breached anti-money laundering laws by not reporting suspicious transactions involving its smart automated teller machines. The CBA also faces investigation by a number of foreign agencies.

78 Independent Commission against Corruption Act 1988 (NSW).

appropriate, based on admissible evidence, to commence or to continue a case against a particular person.

The scope of the NSW ICAC's investigative powers was challenged in 2015. Following an ultimately unsuccessful investigation into the conduct of a senior Crown Prosecutor (and subsequent rulings by the High Court of Australia about the circumstances in which the NSW ICAC could not investigate),[79] the NSW Government amended the Independent Commission against Corruption Act 1988 (NSW) to:

- limit the power of the NSW ICAC to make findings of corrupt conduct only in relation to cases where there is serious corrupt conduct;
- clarify the definition of 'corrupt conduct' to include particular conduct that impairs (or could impair) public confidence in public administration;
- enhance the NSW ICAC's functions of advice, education and prevention; and
- expand the NSW ICAC's functions to include investigating certain conduct referred to it by the Electoral Commission.[80]

5. Relevant bribery and corruption cases

5.1 Foreign bribery

(a) Introduction

There have been two criminal prosecutions for foreign bribery in Australia since 1999, when the Criminal Code was amended to prohibit bribery of a foreign public official. One of the most high profile, and ongoing, prosecutions is that of two subsidiaries of the Reserve Bank of Australia (RBA), Securency International Pty Ltd (Securency) and Note Printing Australia Pty Ltd (NPA).[81] The second was against Lifese Pty Ltd and its officers.

(b) The Securency and NPA case

In the first case, in July 2011, the AFP charged Securency and NPA, as well as several individuals, with foreign bribery offences. The AFP alleged that Securency, NPA, and several senior executives paid (or conspired to pay) bribes to foreign public officials in several jurisdictions in order to secure contracts for the printing of polymer banknotes. Pursuant to non-publication orders, details about these prosecutions have been supressed. The prosecutions are ongoing and are yet to be listed for trial. However, in 2012, David John Ellery, the former CFO of Securency, was sentenced to imprisonment for a term of six months (wholly suspended for two years) on one count of false accounting[82] to which Mr Ellery pleaded guilty.[83]

---

79 *Independent Commission against Corruption v Cunneen* [2015] HCA 14; *Duncan v Independent Commission against Corruption* [2015] HCA 32 (upholding the constitutional validity of the laws).

80 Independent Commission Against Corruption Amendment Act 2015 (NSW) (commentary by the NSW ICAC is available at www.icac.nsw.gov.au/about-the-icac/legislation/history-of-act).

81 NPA is wholly owned by the RBA. Securency was a joint venture between the RBA and a UK-based company, Innovia Films. However, the RBA is no longer a shareholder in Securency, having sold its interest to Innovia. (Reserve Bank of Australia, *Sale of Securency* (Media Release 2013-02, 12 February 2013), available at www.rba.gov.au/media-releases/2013/mr-13-02.html).

82 In contravention of section 83(1)(a) of the Crimes Act 1958 (VIC).

83 *The Queen v David John Ellery* [2012] VSC 349.

(c) ***The Lifese case***

In the second case, in 2015, three men faced allegations of conspiracy to bribe a foreign official for the purposes of winning contracts for their company, Lifese, in Iraq. In July 2017, the defendants, Mamdouh Elomar, Ibrahim Elomar and John Jousif, each pleaded guilty to conduct constituting a conspiracy to engage in foreign bribery. On 27 September 2017, the Supreme Court of New South Wales sentenced each of them to imprisonment for a period of four years, with a non-parole period of two years. The court also imposed a fine of A$250,000 each on two of the three accused.[84]

(d) ***Other extant prosecutions***

Following a long-running investigation into the conduct of Leighton Holdings and its construction contracts in the Middle East, two former executives of the company, Peter Gregg and Russell John Waugh, have been charged by the ASIC with engaging in conduct that resulted in the falsification of the company's books in contravention of the Corporations Act 2001 (Cth). At the time of writing, the prosecutions are continuing, with the matter having been listed for trial to commence on a date in October 2018.[85]

5.2 Domestic corruption

In 2017, the New South Wales Court of Criminal Appeal[86] upheld the 2016 decision of the Supreme Court of New South Wales to sentence a former New South Wales politician to imprisonment for five years (with a non-parole period of three years) for the common law offence of wilful misconduct in public office.[87] This prosecution and conviction emerged after lengthy investigations by the NSW ICAC and findings of corruption against the former politician.

Other examples of successful prosecution for wilful misconduct in public office include the sentencing of Mr Ian Macdonald (a former NSW Government minister) to 10 years' imprisonment (with a non-parole period of seven years)[88] and Mr John Maitland (a business colleague of Mr Macdonald) to six years' imprisonment (with a non-parole period of four years).

6. Future reform

6.1 Domestic bribery and corruption reform

For a number of years, the penalties for 'white collar crime' have been regarded in Australia as too low. On 23 October 2017, the ASIC Enforcement Review Taskforce published a consultation paper calling for substantial increases in penalties against individuals and companies for contraventions of the Corporations Act and other Commonwealth laws. Substantial penalties are proposed, including terms of

---

84 *R v Jousif; R v I Elomar; R v M Elomar* [2017] NSWSC 1299.

85 Australian Securities and Investments Commission, *Former Leighton executive charged* (Media Release 17-004MR, 10 January 2017); Australian Securities and Investments Commission, *Former Leighton employees charged* (Media Release 17-020MR, 31 January 2017).

86 *Obeid v R* [2017] NSWCCA 221.

87 *R v Obeid* (No 12) [2016] NSWSC 1815.

88 *R v Macdonald; R v Maitland* [2017] NSWSC 337; *R v Macdonald; R v Maitland* [2017] NSWSC 638.

imprisonment of up to 10 years and fines of up to A$525,000 for individuals and, for companies, A$2.65 million or three times the benefit or 10% of turnover. Together with civil disgorgement powers and a standardised penalty regime, this will add considerably to ASIC's powers in prosecuting individuals and companies for domestic offences. Any new laws are likely to be considered in 2018.

In terms of criminal reforms, the Commonwealth and State criminal laws, provisions on proceeds of crime and domestic tax laws are regularly updated to address the ongoing challenge of keeping up with financial crime.

6.2 Foreign bribery and corruption reform

(a) Introduction

The OECD's Working Group on Bribery published its Phase 4 evaluation of Australia in December 2017.[89] The OECD recognised the substantial steps taken by the Australian government to improve its framework for detecting and investigating foreign bribery (with 19 ongoing investigations and 13 referrals under evaluation), that enforcement had increased markedly since the 2012 Phase 3 Report and that a number of legislative and institutional reforms have strengthened or are in the process of strengthening the focus on targeting foreign bribery.

The Phase 4 Report makes the following substantive recommendations for the future:

- to address the risks that the proceeds of foreign bribery could be laundered through the Australian real estate sector;
- to enhance private sector whistleblower protections;
- to resource the AFP and CDPP adequately;
- to pursue criminal charges against companies for foreign bribery and related offences (false accounting, money laundering and tax evasion); and
- to continue to encourage companies, particularly SMEs, to develop and adopt adequate internal controls, ethics and compliance programmes to prevent and detect foreign bribery.

The OECD Phase 4 Review of Australia's performance under the OECD Convention is, arguably, a significant motivation for the proposed legislative reforms to Australia's approach to bribery and corruption.

In addition, the Australian Senate concluded its long-running review of Australia's foreign bribery laws in September 2017 and published its report in March 2018 (see 3.2 above). The report made 22 recommendations designed to enhance Australia's approach to foreign bribery and to make its laws and practices consistent with 'best practices' being used overseas. A number of the recommendations concern reforms that are already the subject of draft Bills before the Australian Parliament (see the topics discussed below).

---

89 Working Group on Bribery in International Business Transactions, OECD, *Monitoring Schedule December 2016-June 2024*, available at www.oecd.org/daf/anti-bribery/Phase-4-Evaluation-Calendar-2016-2024.pdf.

(b) ***Statutory amendments to offences***

As discussed at 2 above, Australia has given effect to its obligations under the OECD Convention primarily through provisions of the Criminal Code. Australia is currently exploring ways of improving the effectiveness of anti-bribery and anti-corruption measures, one example of which is amendments to the Criminal Code that would:

- extend the definition of 'foreign public official' to include candidates for office;
- remove the requirement that the benefit or business advantage must be "not legitimately due" (in the section 70.2 foreign bribery offence) and replace it with the concept of 'improperly influencing' a foreign public official;
- extend the foreign bribery offence to cover bribery to obtain a personal advantage;
- create a new strict liability corporate offence of failing to prevent foreign bribery (discussed further at 6.2(b) below);
- remove the requirement of influencing a foreign public official in the exercise of his or her official capacity; and
- clarify that the offence does not require the accused to have a specific business or advantage in mind, and that business or an advantage can be obtained for someone else.[90]

These reforms have yet to be enacted (as at the date of publication). They do, however, have widespread support.[91]

(c) ***New corporate offence of failing to prevent foreign bribery***

A draft bill was published in December 2017 proposing a new offence for a corporation failing to prevent foreign bribery.[92] The proposed new offence would impose strict liability and a company would be guilty of the offence if:

- an 'associate' of the company engages in conduct that constitutes an offence against the new proposed section 70.2 Criminal Code offence of intentional bribery of a foreign public official;
- if an 'associate' engages in such conduct outside of Australia, and that conduct (if it had occurred in Australia) would constitute an offence against (the proposed new) section 70.2 of the Criminal Code; and
- the 'associate' acts for the profit or gain of the company.[93]

---

90 Attorney-General's Department, Government of the Commonwealth of Australia, *Combatting bribery of foreign public officials: Proposed amendments to the foreign bribery offence in the Criminal Code Act 1995*, Public Consultation Paper (April 2017), available at www.ag.gov.au/Consultations/Documents/Foreign-bribery-offence/public-consultation-paper-amendments-to-the-foreign-bribery-offence.pdf.

91 The reforms set out in the Crimes Legislation Amendment (Combatting Corporate Crime) Bill 2017 were reviewed and accepted by a report published in April 2018 by the Australian Senate Legal and Constitutional Affairs Legislation Committee, available at www.aph.gov.au/Parliamentary_Business/Committees/Senate/Legal_and_Constitutional_Affairs/CombattingCrime/Report

92 Crimes Legislation Amendment (Combatting Corporate Crime) Bill 2017

93 Exposure Draft, 'Crimes Legislation Amendment Bill 2017', available at www.ag.gov.au/Consultations/Documents/Foreign-bribery-offence/Exposure-draft-provisions-amendments-to-the-foreign-bribery-offence.pdf.

The proposed new offence would impose absolute liability unless the company could prove that it had in place 'adequate procedures' to prevent such conduct occurring. Under the proposed laws, the Commonwealth Government would be obliged to publish guidance on what companies must do to satisfy the 'adequate procedures' defence. No such guidance has yet been published. It is likely to be similar to guidance published by the UK Ministry of Justice under the Bribery Act 2010.

The term 'associate' is defined broadly in the proposed amendments to the Criminal Code and would include employees, agents, contractors and subsidiaries of companies, as well as a person or entity controlled by a company, or who otherwise performs services for or on behalf of the company.

The proposed new offence is one of the ways in which Australia is trying to overcome the difficulty in prosecuting companies for instances of bribery or other corrupt conduct. One such difficulty that often arises is that the conduct occurs outside Australia (through subsidiaries or third party intermediaries). This offence, if enacted, would have the potential under Australian law to pierce the corporate veil and to impose strict criminal liability on a company for any conduct by an associate, whether in Australia or overseas, that amounts to the offence under Australian law of reckless or intentional bribery of a foreign public official. The Australian Senate's report considered that the introduction of such an offence was "overdue" and that it was "appropriate to require corporations to prove the existence of an adequate compliance regime".[94] This would make it critical for Australian businesses to know, understand and supervise the entire supply chain and all intermediaries, agents or third parties acting on their behalf. If a business cannot demonstrate that it had adequate procedures in place to prevent such conduct from occurring, it would face severe criminal liability and all that flows from it.

6.3 Commonwealth Deferred Prosecution Agreements

There has been widespread support for the introduction of a Commonwealth DPA Scheme.[95] In December 2017, the Australian government published a model DPA scheme covering identified serious offences contained in the Corporations Act 2001 (Cth), the Criminal Code, the Autonomous Sanctions Act 2011 (Cth), the Charter of the United Nations Act 1945 (Cth) and the Anti-Money Laundering and Counter-Terrorism Financing Act 2006 (Cth).[96] The proposed DPA scheme only applies to these Commonwealth offences and not to any State or Territory offences. The key features of the proposed DPA scheme include the following:[97]

94 See the Senate report (note 62 above), paragraphs 4.96-4.98.

95 In 2016, the Minister for Justice released a public consultation paper seeking comment on the introduction of a DPA scheme in Australia and all but two of the 17 submissions received either endorsed or conditionally endorsed the proposal. See: Attorney-General's Department, Government of the Commonwealth of Australia, *Improving enforcement options for serious corporate crime: A proposed model for a Deferred Prosecution Agreement scheme in Australia*, Public Consultation Paper (March 2017), available at www.ag.gov.au/Consultations/Documents/Deferred-prosecution-agreement-scheme/A-proposed-model-for-a-deferred-prosecution-agreement-scheme-in-australia.pdf.

96 Attorney-General's Department, Government of the Commonwealth of Australia, *Improving enforcement options for serious corporate crime: A proposed model for a Deferred Prosecution Agreement scheme in Australia*, Public Consultation Paper (March 2017), available at www.ag.gov.au/Consultations/Documents/Deferred-prosecution-agreement-scheme/A-proposed-model-for-a-deferred-prosecution-agreement-scheme-in-australia.pdf.

97 *Ibid.*

- the DPA would be available for companies, not individuals, and only for certain nominated Commonwealth 'serious corporate crime' offences;
- the decision whether to enter into a DPA would be at the discretion of the prosecutor (the CDPP) and the Commonwealth government would be required to publish guidance on the factors the prosecutor may consider in exercising this discretion, under a proposed DPA Code of Practice;[98]
- the terms of the DPA would be determined by the parties and may include the payment of financial penalties (including fines, disgorgement of profits and compensation), agreed statements of facts and the appointment of an independent monitor to ensure compliance with the terms of the DPA; and
- the approval of a DPA would be determined by a retired judge (or panel of retired judges) and, if approved, the DPA would be published. If a DPA is not approved, the parties may continue to negotiate or abandon negotiations.

6.4 A possible new investigative and prosecuting agency – the Australian SFO

For a number of years, there has been criticism of the fractured and diffuse manner in which Australia and its regulatory agencies tackle corruption. Leaving aside State corruption commissions, at the Commonwealth level there is no corruption commission. Rather, the Commonwealth prefers to have an Integrity Commission oversee nominated agencies and otherwise leaves it up to the AFP to investigate serious financial crime whenever it receives a referral of suspicious conduct. Over many years, the Commonwealth Government (whatever the political persuasion) has cut resources to regulators while increasing the numerous policing and investigative obligations on them. Now, however, with a focus on national security, terrorism and money laundering, the focus has changed and more money is starting to be spent, but again in a fragmented manner.

Over the past few years, the Commonwealth Government has established the FAC (see 4.4 above) and sought to coordinate serious financial crime matters (from investigation to prosecution) through one coordinating centre (although the CPDD is, by definition, the independent statutory prosecutor). While the creation of the FAC is a good starting point, its overall success is hard to measure independently. The Commonwealth Government seems resistant to the notion of one dedicated financial crime agency, properly resourced and funded, to tackle financial crime and corruption. Serious fraud offices (SFOs) exist in both the UK and New Zealand. While the UK SFO has experienced its ups and downs in the past, it is now a considerable force to be reckoned with. Australia would benefit greatly from creating an Australian SFO that could independently investigate and prosecute serious financial crime whether in Australia (domestic financial crime) or offshore where Australian companies, citizens or Australian residents engage in such conduct.

---

98 On 20 December 2017, the CDPP published its *Best Practice Guideline: Self-reporting of foreign bribery and related offending by corporations* (the Guideline). The Guideline outlines how the CDPP and the AFP will respond to a voluntary report of foreign bribery (or other serious offences) by a corporation and the manner by which the CDPP will assess the corporation's conduct in determining whether or not to prosecute the corporation consistent with the Commonwealth's *Prosecution Policy*.

6.5 Whistleblower protection

The improvement of whistleblower protection forms one of the commitments made by the Commonwealth Government as part of the first Open Government National Action Plan.

A Parliamentary Joint Committee report, released in September 2017,[99] contained a number of important recommendations for reform relating to whistleblower protections applicable to the disclosure of misconduct in the private sector (which would include domestic and/or foreign bribery), including:

- that Commonwealth private sector whistleblowing legislation be brought together in a single act;
- that the Commonwealth, States and Territories should harmonise whistleblowing legislation across Australia;
- a broader definition of 'whistleblower' that would include both current and former staff (whether public officials or in the private sector), contractors (to both the Australian Public Service and in the private sector), and volunteers (in the private sector);
- removal of the 'good faith' test as a requirement for protection (although a person would be required to have a reasonable belief of the existence of disclosable conduct to receive protection);
- provision for anonymous disclosures by private sector whistleblowers, consistent with public sector legislation;
- protection for disclosure, in limited circumstances, to the media and politicians;
- enhanced provisions for compensation and rewards available to whistleblowers; and
- the establishment of a 'one-stop shop' whistleblower protection authority to cover both the public and private sectors.

Implementation of these recommendations would assist agencies in Australia charged with investigating and prosecuting acts of bribery and corruption, in particular by providing a greater pool of potential witnesses to the AFP for its investigations against corporations (and therefore a source of more readily admissible evidence to the CDPP).

In December 2017, the Australian government introduced the Treasury Laws Amendment (Enhancing Whistleblower Protections) Bill 2017 (the Whistleblower Bill) to Parliament. The Whistleblower Bill was reviewed and accepted by the Senate's Economics Legislation Committee in a report published in March 2018.[100] While the Whistleblower Bill proposed a number of important changes, particularly with regard to enhancing the anonymity of whistleblowers and their statutory protections and requiring listed corporations and large proprietary corporations to have in place whistleblower policies consistent with the new laws by 1 January 2019, it failed to

---

99 The report is available at www.aph.gov.au/Parliamentary_Business/Committees/Joint/Corporations_and_Financial_Services/WhistleblowerProtections/Report.

100 The report is available at www.aph.gov.au/Parliamentary_Business/Committees/Senate/Economics/WhistleblowerBill2017/Report.

address certain key weaknesses in Australia's private sector whistleblower protection laws, which were the subject of the Parliamentary Joint Committee's report. This means that:

- whistleblowers must make their own claims for compensation in court proceedings, although costs orders cannot be made against them unless a court is satisfied that a claim was vexatious or made without reasonable cause;
- there is no independent authority to represent the interests of whistleblowers or to act in their name;
- while the proposed compensation provisions are improved, there are no rewards (or US-style bounties).

The Whistleblower Bill represents a significant improvement on existing whistleblower protection laws for the private sector in Australia. However, there is likely to be a way to go before whistleblowers will feel able to come forward on their own to report corporate misconduct without any independent agency to protect their interests.

7. Conclusions

Domestic bribery and corruption are and remain an ongoing focus for the State-based anti-corruption commissions. The independent regulation of domestic corruption at a Commonwealth (or national) level is still patchy, uneven and only recently has the Australian government (and indeed the opposition political parties), moved closer to accepting the need for a Commonwealth anti-corruption commission. It is hoped that some real concrete action will emerge for the establishment of a national and independent anti-corruption commission.

In relation to foreign bribery, over the last 20 years, anti-corruption initiatives in Australia have been at best occasional, at worst, reactive and piecemeal. Australia was quick to accede to the OECD Convention in 1999, update its laws, criminalise foreign bribery, create corporate criminal liability and espouse compliance through its international obligations.

However, subsequent foreign-related bribery investigations and enforcement in particular have told a different story. There appeared to be an inability to cut through complex cross-border cases and to prosecute Australian companies and individuals engaged in illegal conduct outside Australia. While the AFP had numerous foreign bribery investigations under way between 1999 and 2011, there was only one prosecution. A second prosecution commenced in 2016. The difficulties involved in bringing foreign bribery cases to court have rarely been publicly discussed by the Australian authorities except to say they are complex, expensive, time-consuming and take many years to progress. It is likely that the complexity of Australia's existing foreign bribery laws and the difficulties of proving complex commercial crime cases with hard to secure offshore evidence may partly explain the paucity of prosecutions.

It is refreshing to be able to say that over the last three to four years, this rather pessimistic outlook has changed markedly and for the better. The Commonwealth Government has initiated more proactive reforms to tackle foreign bribery. The call for one unified financial crime agency remains and resources and the continuity of experience remain a challenge for investigators and prosecutors. However, a far better level of coordination and work are being undertaken by the AFP and the CDPP through the FAC and the Serious Financial Crime Task Force. Australia secured its first foreign bribery convictions in September 2017, while the foreign bribery prosecution in the much-publicised Securency banknote printing case is yet to be listed for trial after many years of legal arguments before the courts shrouded in secrecy and non-publication orders. Significant legislative reforms are well in progress, from amendments to the foreign bribery offence to a new corporate offence of failing to prevent foreign bribery, a Commonwealth DPA scheme and much improved whistleblower protection laws for the private sector.

While these legislative reforms will take time, they bode well for a much more proactive approach by the Commonwealth Government. The AFP and the CDPP are likely to be armed with more flexible options to pursue companies and individuals for illegal conduct, and those who blow the whistle in the private sector should feel and it is hoped, will be better protected. The outlook for the next few years is likely very much to reflect the focus of the OECD's Phase 4 Report on Australia – solid work with the focus now being on targeted enforcement. Australian business understands the importance of a culture of ethical behaviour. The laws are increasingly directed towards achieving that end, an achievement that will be to the benefit of Australian business, consumers and, more broadly, society at large.

Bolivia

Estefania Paz
Lindsay Sykes
Ferrere

1. Overview

1.1 Introduction

Anti-corruption reforms have gained momentum in the Plurinational State of Bolivia over the past 30 years. Following a period of several dictatorships, leaders elected democratically began to put transparency and anti-corruption on the political agenda in the late 1990s and early 2000s.[1] During his 1997–2001 term, President Hugo Banzer Suarez created the Technical Unit for the Fight against Corruption (the Unit), which was part of the Office of the Vice President. From 2002 to 2003, during President Gonzalo Sanchez de Lozada's second presidential term, the Unit was renamed the Secretariat for the Fight against Corruption and Special Policies (the Secretariat). During the term of President Carlos Mesa (2003–2005), the Secretariat was replaced by the Presidential Delegation, an institution of the Ministry of the Presidency authorised to fight corruption.[2]

Most recently, President Evo Morales' political party, *Movimiento Al Socialismo* (MAS) advocated a zero-tolerance policy against corruption during his campaign for the presidential election in 2005. In line with this, the Morales administration oversaw the implementation of a new Political Constitution (CPE) in 2009, which includes a duty of all citizens to report acts of corruption. That same year, Morales established a Ministry for Institutional Transparency and the Fight against Corruption,[3] and, in 2010, the Legislative Assembly promulgated the country's first anti-corruption law.

Despite these reforms, the public generally still perceives corruption as pervasive and a significant obstacle to doing business and the administration of justice in the country. Although the state has prosecuted corruption cases, such cases have generally lacked transparency and many consider them to reflect political influence.

---

1 Between 1980 and 1981, under the dictatorship of Luis García Meza Tejada, several thousand civil servants were prosecuted for embezzlement; in 1986, García Meza was charged with treason and sedition, among other crimes, along with 55 of his associates.

2 Karina Ingrid Medinaceli Diaz, *Transparencia y acceso a la información en Bolivia*, (last accessed 17 October 2017), available at www.revistasbolivianas.org.bo/scielo.php?pid=S1997-44852013000100005&script=sci_arttext.

3 The Ministry of Institutional Transparency and the Fight against Corruption was created by Supreme Decree No 29894 of 7 February 2009 (see 2.3(b) below).

1.2 Legislative reforms under the Morales administration

Since his election in 2006, current President Evo Morales and his political party MAS have vowed to fight corruption. As Bolivia's first president to self-identify as indigenous, part of Morales' political platform included a promise to overhaul what he claimed was the previous status quo of self-interested elites allowing foreign powers to pillage the country's natural resources while profiting personally. As part of the pledge to establish a transparent and corruption-free government, Morales created in 2009 what is today the Ministry of Justice and Institutional Transparency (previously the Ministry of Institutional Transparency and Fight Against Corruption) (Ministry of Transparency).[4] His administration also oversaw the implementation of the Political Constitution referred to at 1.1 above.

Following this, in 2010, the MAS-controlled Legislative Assembly promulgated Law No 004 of 31 March 2010, Law on the Fight Against Corruption, Illicit Enrichment and Investigation of Wealth *'Marcelo Quiroga Santa Cruz'* (the Anticorruption Law), the country's first anti-corruption law, which broadly criminalises bribery and unjust enrichment of public officials, as well as contracts harmful to the state.

1.3 Judicial reforms

As part of its overhaul of government, the Political Constitution provided, among other things, for the popular election of judges for the Plurinational Constitutional Court (the highest constitutional authority), the Agro-Environmental Court (a specialised court for agrarian and environmental matters), the Supreme Court (the highest judicial authority), and the Judicial Council (the body in charge of supervision, control and disciplinary regime of the judicial organ of the state).[5] This change has been widely criticised, including by the current administration, as having worsened corruption in the judiciary.

Indeed, polling reflects that the public perceives the judiciary as one of the most corrupt public sector organisations,[6] with case backlogs, lack of staff and resources, and problems with corruption being the most frequently cited complaints.[7] Miller & Chevalier's *2016 Latin American Corruption Survey*[8] reported that 81% of Bolivian respondents ranked judicial corruption as the highest among public institutions, along with police corruption.

---

4 The Ministry of Institutional Transparency and Fight against Corruption merged with the Ministry of Justice in 2017 to form a new combined ministry: see 2.3(b) below.

5 Other lower court judges are elected by the Supreme Court or designated by higher judicial authorities.

6 76% of respondents in Bolivia felt that judiciary was corrupt/extremely corrupt.
Transparency International, *Global Corruption Barometer, Bolivia* (last accessed 14 October 2017), available at www.transparency.org/gcb2013/country/?country=bolivia.

7 Bureau of Economic and Business Affairs, *Investment Climate Statements for 2017 – Bolivia* (last accessed 14 October 2017), available at www.state.gov/e/eb/rls/othr/ics/investmentclimatestatements/index.htm?year=2017&dlid=270048.

8 Miller & Chevallier, *2016 Latin American Corruption Survey* (last accessed October 2017), available at www.millerchevalier.com/sites/default/files/resources/2016-Latin-America-Corruption-Survey-Full-Report.pdf.

1.4 Public perceptions of corruption

These reforms, however, have not resulted in corresponding changes in public opinion regarding corruption. For example, according to a national poll conducted in 2017, seven out of ten Bolivians believe that the level of corruption in the country is the same or more than in previous governments.[9] Miller & Chevalier's 2016 *Latin American Corruption Survey* similarly found that almost 60% of Bolivian respondents reported corruption to be a significant obstacle to doing business in Bolivia. Indeed, during his public address on the tenth anniversary of his election in January 2016, President Morales recognised that justice and the fight against corruption remain significant problems in Bolivia.[10]

External observers mirror these perceptions. For example, Transparency International's *2016 Corruption Perception Index* ranks Bolivia as 113 out of 176 (with 176 being the most corrupt). The ranking measures the perceived levels of public sector corruption and qualifies Bolivia with a score of 33 out of 100 (0 being highly corrupt and 100 being very clean).[11] Furthermore, in September 2016, the World Economic Forum released a ranking for global competitiveness which contained an *Ethics and Corruption Index* that placed Bolivia as the second most corrupt out of 138 countries surveyed. The World Economic Forum ranking identified corruption as the most problematic factor for doing business in the country.[12] Similarly, the World Bank's *Worldwide Governance Indicators* (WGI) place Bolivia in the lowest half of the percentile ranks in the Control of Corruption dimension, with a score of 26.92 for 2016, on a scale from 0 to 100 (with 0 indicating higher levels of corruption).[13]

2. The anti-corruption legal framework

2.1 International anti-corruption treaties

Bolivia is a signatory to both the United Nations Convention against Corruption (2003 ratified in 2005) and the Inter-American Convention against Corruption (1996, ratified in 1997).[14]

---

9 Página Siete, *La Corrupción en la mente de la gente* (last accessed 24 October 2017), available at www.paginasiete.bo/opinion/editorial/2017/6/8/corrupcion-mente-gente-140378.html.

10 El Comercio, *Morales dio discurso de casi 6 horas por 10 años en el poder* (last accessed 14 October 2017), available at https://elcomercio.pe/mundo/latinoamerica/morales-dio-discurso-6-horas-10-anos-265456; El Agencia EFE, *Morales se explaya en logros y admite fallos en salud, justicia y corrupción* (last accessed 14 October 2017), available at www.efe.com/efe/america/politica/morales-se-explaya-en-logros-y-admite-fallos-salud-justicia-corrupcion/20000035-2818216.

11 Transparency International, *Corruption by Country: Bolivia* (last accessed 13 October 2017), available at www.transparency.org/news/feature/corruption_perceptions_index_2016#table.

12 World Economic Forum, *Competitiveness Rankings 2016–2017 – Ethics and Corruption* (last accessed 11 October 2017), available at http://reports.weforum.org/pdf/gci-2016-2017-scorecard/WEF_GCI_2016_2017_Scorecard_GCI.A.01.01.02.pdf; World Economic Forum, *Competitiveness Rankings 2016–2017* (last accessed 11 October 2017), available at www3.weforum.org/docs/GCR2016-2017/05FullReport/TheGlobalCompetitivenessReport2016-2017_FINAL.pdf. The new version of the ranking for 2017–2018 no longer considers Bolivia among the countries ranked. World Economic Forum, *Competitiveness Rankings 2016–2017* (last accessed 11 October 2017), available at http://reports.weforum.org/global-competitiveness-index-2017-2018.

13 Worldwide Governance Indicators project, Full Data set (last accessed 23 October 2017), available at http://info.worldbank.org/governance/wgi/#home.

14 The United Nations Convention against Corruption was ratified through Law 3068 of 1 June 2005. The Inter-American Convention Against Corruption was ratified through Law 1743 of 15 January 1997.

Bolivia has been subject of reports on the implementation of both conventions through the Follow-Up Mechanisms (FUMs) for the Implementation of the Inter-American Convention against Corruption (MESICIC) and for the United Nations Office on Drugs and Crime (UNODC) Implementation Review Mechanism respectively. The most recent MESICIC and UNODC reports[15] found that Bolivia had addressed some of the FUMs' recommendations, principally through its promulgation of the Anticorruption Law and the creation of the Ministry of Transparency.

These conventions have served as the backdrop to and motivation for Bolivia's domestic anti-corruption legislation.

2.2 National legislation

(a) *The Anti-corruption Law (2010)*

In 2010, the Legislative Assembly enacted the Anticorruption Law. This law provides a judicial framework to:

- prevent corruption and investigate allegations of corruption;
- sanction individuals involved in acts of corruption; and
- recover the proceeds of corruption.

The Anticorruption Law resulted in part from efforts to comply with the international conventions on corruption, including the UN and Inter-American conventions.[16]

Prohibited conduct: The Anticorruption Law broadly defines 'corruption' as the solicitation or acceptance by a person of either a direct or indirect offering of any article of financial value or other benefit (ie, a gift, favour, promise, political, social or economic advantage for himself or herself or another person or entity) in exchange for any act or omission to act that affects state interests.

The Anticorruption Law criminalises the following acts:

- passive and active bribery;
- extortion;
- illicit enrichment;
- misuse, stealing and/or misappropriation of public funds, and/or goods and services;
- abuse of office or undue use of influence;
- business incompatible with public office;
- issues of justice, including (a) obstruction of justice, (b) delayed or denied justice, and (c) breach of duty by judges; and

---

15 Organization of American States, MESICIC, Bolivia (last accessed 24 October 2017), available at www.oas.org/juridico/english/blv.htm; United Nations Office on Drugs and Crime, *Corruption Country Profiles, Bolivia* (last accessed 24 October 2017), available at www.unodc.org/unodc/treaties/CAC/country-profile/CountryProfile.html?code=BOL.

16 EABolivia, *Cámara de Diputados aprueba ley anticorrupción Marcelo Quiroga Santa Cruz* (19 March 2010), available at www.eabolivia.com/politica/3515-camara-de-diputados-aprueba-ley-anticorrupcion-marcelo-quiroga-santa-cruz.html.

- economic crimes, including (a) false declaration of goods and income or failure to declare goods and income; (b) contracts harmful to the state; (c) economic disloyalty; and (d) breach of contract harming state interests.

Scope of application: The Anticorruption Law applies to the following individuals and entities:

- current and former Bolivian public servants;
- Bolivian state-run entities, including the Public Ministry, the Central Bank and universities;
- the Bolivian police and armed forces;
- entities and organisations in which the Bolivian government has an ownership interest; and
- individuals or entities who commit acts of corruption that cause economic damage to the state or who unduly benefit from their resources.

Penalties: Penalties for individuals include:

- imprisonment (from one to 10 years per crime, with a maximum sentence of 30 years);
- monetary fines;[17] and
- other sanctions, including (a) the seizure of goods illegally acquired, and (b) disqualification from public office.

Bolivian law generally provides for criminal responsibility exclusively for natural (ie, individual) persons and legal entities are generally not subject to criminal liability. Rather, the entity's legal representative or other employees involved in misconduct would be the target of criminal prosecution. The Anticorruption Law provides, however, that companies may also be subject to criminal sanctions, including:

- restitution of all state assets affected by illicit conduct;
- seizure of all goods illegally obtained; and
- a fine equivalent to 25% of total corporate assets.

Under the Anticorruption Law, an individual or entity can receive credit for their cooperation in resolving corruption cases, which can reduce the penalty imposed by up to two-thirds.

(b) The National Council Against Corruption

The Anticorruption Law establishes a National Council for the Fight against Corruption, Illicit Enrichment, and Money Laundering (CNLCC). The CNLCC comprises:

---

17 The judge can elect to impose a fine of 0 to 500 'days'. The amount of each 'day' depends on the individual's economic capacity and income. The daily rate cannot exceed the individual's maximum daily salary and the total amount of the fine cannot surpass monthly 25 days of the national minimum salary (in 2017, the national monthly minimum salary was 2,000 Bol (approximately $287)). The resolution will state the exact number of days as well as the daily fee amount and payment period (Bolivian Criminal Code, articles 29 and 30).

- the Ministry of Institutional Transparency and the Fight against Corruption (now the Ministry of Justice and Institutional Transparency: see 2.3(b) below);
- the Ministry of Government;
- the Public Prosecutor;
- the Comptroller General;
- the Financial Intelligence Unit;
- the State Attorney General; and
- representatives of civil society organisations.

The CNLCC has regular meetings and is required to report yearly to the President, the Legislative Assembly and civil society on its plan for combating corruption, as well as the status of its efforts. The CNLCC is not authorised to investigate, prosecute or sanction violations of the Anticorruption Law.

(c) ***Anti-corruption tribunals***

The Anticorruption Law creates new anti-corruption tribunals and courts to adjudicate on charges of corruption. It also requires the Public Prosecutor's Office (*Ministerio Publico*) to dedicate prosecutors exclusively to the investigation and prosecution of corruption-related crimes. These specialised prosecutors are currently working with designated police investigators from newly-created anti-corruption divisions in the police departments.

(d) ***The Integrated System for Anticorruption Information and Recovery of State Property (SIIARBE)***

The Anticorruption Law has created an Integrated System For Anti-Corruption Information And Recovery Of State Property (SIIARBE), which has the objective of centralising and exchanging information between public entities involved in the fight against corruption. Under SIIARBE, the System For The Compilation Of Information From Financial Entities (SIRIEFI) transmits online information requests to financial entities and reviews the sworn statements of assets and income from state employees directly, all through a web application. The system aims not only to accelerate the processes of investigation but also to eliminate the risk of violations of the confidentiality of the information exchanged.

SIIARBE's implementation was coordinated through conventions with the State General Comptrollership and the Financial System's Authority of Supervision (ASFI). Financial entities required to participate include banks and similar financial institutions, brokerage firms, investment fund managers and the Bolivian Central Bank.

Information requests: Through the web application, Bolivian financial entities must respond to any information request within a 48-hour period to determine whether they have the required information, regardless of whether the person investigated is a customer of the institution. In any case, the institution must provide the information within 15 business days by compiling and uploading it to the electronic system to make it available to the Ministry of Transparency's officials.

Sworn declarations: The General Comptrollership uploads public officials' required sworn declarations of assets to the system to make them available for their review.

Evidentiary value: Data collected via the SIRIEFI web application constitutes admissible evidence in judicial proceedings involving corruption and related crimes. Regulations provide that electronic data is valid evidence and that the normal banking secrecy protections do not apply in cases involving corruption.

(e) Transparency Units

Transparency Units ('TUs') were created in 2009 through Supreme Decree No 29894 for the Organization of the Executive, which required each ministry under the Organization of the Executive in the Country to create a Transparency Unit to operate access to information, promotion of ethics, social control and accountability systems. Law 974 for Transparency Units (4 September 2017) extended the jurisdiction of TUs to operate not only within Executive Ministries but also within all public institutions at the central level of the state, public companies, public-private partnerships and financial institutions. This law requires that such TUs be autonomous and permanent, responsible for handling corruption reports and investigating possible corruption crimes and related misconduct. They have authority to request supporting documents regarding the entities' public contracting processes for investigative purposes, as a corruption-prevention measure.

2.3 Anti-corruption authorities

The Anticorruption Law designates the Transparency Ministry, the Attorney-General's Office, the Bolivian Police and the Financial Investigation Unit as the entities involved in the fight against corruption.

(a) The Ministry for Institutional Transparency and the Fight against Corruption

The Ministry for Institutional Transparency and the Fight against Corruption was established in 2009 by Supreme Decree No 29894 of 7 February 2009. On 22 January 2017, this ministry was merged with the Ministry of Justice to create the present Ministry of Justice and Institutional Transparency, which now performs the functions of both ministries.

Within the Ministry of Justice and Institutional Transparency, a new regulation[18] created a Vice Ministry of Institutional Transparency and the Fight Against Corruption, which supervises two directorates: the General Directorate of Prevention, Promotion Of Ethics And Transparency, and the General Directorate Of The Fight Against Corruption.[19] Its mandate is to:

- present and execute policies and programmes on ethics, transparency, prevention and the fight against corruption, as well as on institutional coordination;
- propose the regulation on corruption;

---

18 Supreme Decree 3058 of 22 January 2017.
19 Supreme Decree 3058 of 22 January 2017.

- supervise the lawful fulfilment requirements for public office;
- file reports on corruption;
- participate as a civil party in corruption cases and coordinate related investigations; and
- work to fulfil obligations under international conventions against corruption.

(b) ***The Financial Investigations Unit***

The Financial Investigation Unit (FIU) (*Unidad de Investigaciones Financieras*, or UIF) is part of the Ministry of Economy and Public Finance. It is an autonomous unit charged with the fight against money-laundering, corruption and related offences through financial intelligence activities, policy development and the monitoring of compliance.

The FIU's activities include:

- receiving and requesting reports on suspicious transactions;
- collecting information from public entities in connection with investigations into suspicious activities; and
- providing public authorities with information obtained from its investigations in connection with criminal prosecutions.

(c) ***The Public Prosecutor's Office***

The Public Prosecutor's Office (*Ministerio Publico*) represents the public in criminal cases. It has an operative technical unit specialising in corruption. This unit is authorised to oversee the investigation and prosecution of corruption crimes and coordinate institutional policies for criminal prosecution and the prevention of corruption. As per the Anticorruption Law, the Public Prosecutor's Office designates special corruption prosecutors for every department in the country.

3. Corruption cases

3.1 The Ministry of Transparency

In its *Annual Report* for 2016, the Ministry of Transparency stated that its Unit For The Investigation Of Corruption In Public Entities had processed 599 reports of corruption, out of which 263 (44%) were conclusive. Twenty-one administrative and four criminal processes were initiated as a result of such reports. Fifty-five technical reports were issued, out of which 15 found misconduct by public servants.[20]

3.2 Noteworthy public cases

Publicly available information about corruption-related cases is limited. However, the following cases were publicly and successfully prosecuted.

- Santos Ramirez Valverde, President of state-owned oil and gas company of

---

20 *Ministerio de Transparencia y lucha contra la corrupción, Informe-Gestion 2016* (last accessed 24 October 2017), available at www.justicia.gob.bo/index.php/normas/doc... Ascenso y caída de un hombre fuerte c/361-informe-de-gestion-2016-mtilcc.

Bolivia YPFB (*Yacimientos Petroliferos Fiscales Bolivianos*) (2008–2009), was sentenced in January 2012 to 12 years' imprisonment. Mr Ramirez was found guilty of influence peddling, economic damage to the state and bribery, among other crimes. The case involved the award of a contract to Catler-Uniservice for the construction of a gas extraction plant. Jorge O'Connor, an executive of Catler-Uniservice, was murdered in a thwarted robbery attempt. Investigation later revealed that, at the time of the murder, Mr O'Connor was carrying $450,000, which was intended as a bribe for Mr Ramirez.[21]

- Gabriela Zapata was convicted of crimes of corruption and sentenced to ten years' imprisonment. Ms Zapata is currently appealing the sentence. Specifically, she was accused of the crimes of money laundering, criminal association, use of false documents and misuse of public goods, among others. Ms Zapata acted as an executive of the company CAMC, an affiliate of a Chinese entity, which had been awarded state contracts valued at over $600 million.[22]

4. Conclusion

Bolivia has implemented significant legislative and institutional reforms over the past 30 years aimed at fighting corruption. Most recently, President Morales' administration has brought new energy and focus to anti-corruption efforts. Public perceptions of corruption nonetheless remain high, indicating that corruption remains a significant challenge to conducting business and accessing justice and other public services in Bolivia.

Future criminal law reform efforts will likely aim to develop further the anti-corruption framework, specifically with regard to the introduction of corporate criminal liability. Such a reform was included in the new Criminal Code, which was enacted on 15 December 2017. The new Code was, however, quickly repealed in its entirety on 25 January 2018,[23] following popular rejection of certain reforms, such as penalties for medical malpractice and the decriminalisation of abortion.[24]

The Criminal Code contemplated corporate criminal liability for certain crimes, including illicit enrichment, tax fraud and financial crimes. Sanctions included monetary fines, suspension of business activities and corporate dissolution. When combined with other factors, a company's internal compliance programme and procedures could fully exculpate it from liability. Given that this particular change was not the subject of widespread protests, it is likely that it will resurface in a new reform effort in the future.

---

21 Eju TV, Santos Ramirez, *Ascenso y caída de un hombre fuerte cercano a evo* (last accessed 24 October 2017), available at http://eju.tv/2012/01/santos-ramrez-ascenso-y-cada-de-un-hombre-fuerte-cercano-a-evo.

22 CNN, *Condenan a 10 años de cárcel a Gabriela Zapata, expareja de Evo Morales*, last accessed 24 October 2017, available at: http://cnnespanol.cnn.com/2017/05/23/condenan-a-10-anos-de-carcel-a-gabriela-zapata-expareja-de-evo-morales/.

23 Law 1005 for the new Criminal Code, dated 15 December 2017 and Law 1025 of 25 January 2018, which repeals Law 1005.

24 La Razón, *Presidente promulga ley que abroga el Código del Sistema Penal* (last accessed 27 February 2018), available at www.la-razon.com/nacional/Codigo_Penal-Evo_Morales-abrogacion-ley_0_286351 3668.html.

Brazil

Mariana Duprat Ruggeri
Camargo Corrêa Infra
Leopoldo Pagotto
Freitas Leite Advogados

1. Overview of the country *vis-à-vis* corruption

This chapter considers the increasing level of anti-corruption enforcement in Brazil from a number of perspectives, including the context of corruption, the challenges it poses to the country and the consequent pressure for effective law reform.

Comparatively, Brazil has been ranking better than all the other three largest emerging countries since the Corruption Perception Index (CPI) was created by Transparency International.

Figure 1: Corruption perception index

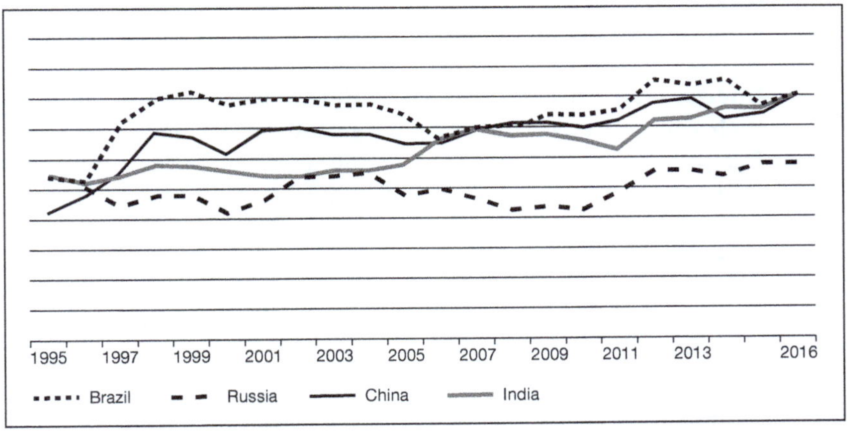

Source: Transparency International, www.transparencyinternational.org

Although corruption in Brazil is not as serious as in China, Russia or India, German NGO Transparency International often brands Brazil as a corrupt country. In 2016, the country scored 40 out of 100, which means that it holds the rank of 79 out of the 175 countries surveyed by the NGO, which is the same as that obtained by China and India. For compliance officers, this is a red flag to watch out for and, some would say, it is a significant obstacle to the private sector's development in the country.

What differentiates Brazil from the other BRICS countries is the current level of enforcement. A combination of factors have played a role in increasing enforcement, leading to what several experts have labellied the 'Anti-Corruption Revolution'. It is hard to pinpoint the specific factors, but the legal landscape has been changing, legal entities included. On 29 January 2014, Law No 12,846/2013, the Clean Company Act (the 2014 Act) came into force and boosted enforcement against companies involved in the bribery of public agents. The 2014 Act established a strict liability regime for companies involved in violations of the statute. Before this, companies could be held liable for corrupt practices under Law No 8,492/92, the Improbity Law, but since the focus of this statute was the liability of public agents, enforcement against companies had historically been secondary.

The strict liability regime established by the 2014 Act means that legal entities may be held liable for acts of corruption committed by any of their employees or by third parties without the need to evidence intent or to show that the company's management had actual knowledge of or had approved the specific improper acts. The authorities need only show that the illegal acts were committed for the benefit or interest of the legal entity.

Since the enactment of the 2014 Act, companies have increasingly become involved in implementing anti-corruption compliance programmes in order to avoid incurring liability for violations of the statute. This concern is also reflected in the public sector. On 1 July 2016, Law No 13.303, the State-Owned Companies Law, came into force, laying down a number of compliance obligations on state-owned companies. Likewise, Decree No 9.203 came into force on 23 November 2017, laying down similar obligations in respect of direct and indirect federal administration.

2. International anti-corruption treaties applicable to the country and their concrete effect in the fight against corruption.

Essentially, three anti-corruption conventions apply in Brazil:

- the Inter-American Convention Against Corruption (1996) (the 1996 Convention);
- the OECD Convention on Combating Bribery of Foreign Public Officials in International Business Transactions (1997) (the 1997 Convention); and
- the United Nations Convention against Corruption (2003) (the 2003 Convention).

2.1 The 1996 Convention

Negotiated in Caracas, the 1996 Convention was the first international instrument to address both preventive and coercive measures against corruption. It was adopted in Brazil in June 2002 and promulgated in October 2002. Ratified without restriction by Brazil, the 1996 Convention listed twelve preventive measures basically aimed at

- hindering the concealment of payment of and receipt of bribes; and
- encouraging the control and reporting of corrupt practices.

2.2 The 1997 Convention

The 1997 Convention was approved by the Brazilian National Congress in June 2000 and ratified in August 2000, taking effect in October 2000. Although not binding *per se* and having a generic content, the incorporation of the convention into the Brazilian legal system was the first step toward the country's commitment to the international fight against corruption. Under the terms of the compromise, Brazil committed itself to criminalising corruption involving foreign public authorities, prohibiting tax deductions attributable to the costs of bribery of foreign authorities and adopting concrete and effective measures to combat international bribery. It should be noted that the text of the Convention has been ratified without reservations and is now fully in force in Brazil.

As part of the commitments assumed in the context of the 1997 Convention, Law No 10.467 was passed in June 2002, amending Chapter II-A (articles 337-B to 337-D) of the Criminal Code, creating a new category of 'Crimes Practised by a Private Person against the Foreign Public Administration'. This inclusion expanded the scope of the enforcement against corruption, creating types of crime having extraterritorial effects, such as active corruption in international transactions (article 337-B) and influence trafficking in commercial transactions (article 337-C).

Despite the delay in approving the 1997 Convention and promulgating legislation, Brazil received a good evaluation during the first phase review of the convention in August 2004. The OECD Working Group has so far evaluated Brazil on four occasions: Phase 1 (September 2004),[1] Phase 2 (December 2007),[2] Phase 2 Monitoring Report (June 2010)[3] and Phase 3 (October 2014).[4] In June 2010, Brazil had implemented eight out of the 16 Phase 2 recommendations. The recommendations highlighted in the last report (Phase 3) covered topics such as lack of accountability of legal entities, sanctions, asset confiscation, public awareness and benefits. According to the latest review report, dated October 2014, although the Working Group welcomed Brazil's approval of the 2014 Act, there was still concern with several aspects of the legislation because they were unclear and could impair its adequate application.

2.3 The 2005 Convention

The 2005 Convention, which was ratified in May 2005 and took effect in January 2006, is the international anti-corruption treaty of the widest scope with regard to foreign officials. It regulates asset recovery and deals with the criminalisation of corruption, international cooperation and preventive measures.

Even before the entry into force of this Convention, however, Brazil had already taken steps to improve its anti-corruption mechanisms, particularly with regard to money laundering. Law No 9.613/98 defines the crime of 'money laundering' and implements preventive and coercive measures to combat it. This law also created the Department for Combating Exchange and Financial Violations (DECIC) at the

---

1 See *Brazil Phase 1: Review of Implementation of the Convention and 1997 Recommendation*. available at: www.oecd.org/daf/anti-bribery/anti-briberyconvention/33742137.pdf.

2 See *Brazil: Phase 2 – Report on the application of the Convention on Combating Bribery of Foreign Public Officials in International Business transactions and the Recommendation on Combating Bribery in International Business Transactions*, available at www.oecd.org/daf/anti-bribery/anti-briberyconvention/39801089.pdf.

3 See *Brazil: Phase 2 – Follow-up Report on the Implementation of the Phase 2 Recommendations*, available at www.oecd.org/daf/anti-bribery/anti-briberyconvention/45518279.pdf.

4 See (1) *Brazil: Phase 3 – Report on Implementing the OECD Anti-bribery Convention in Brazil, October 2014*, available at www.oecd.org/daf/anti-bribery/Brazil-Phase-3-Report-EN.pdf.
(2) *Brazil: Follow-up to the Phase 3 Report & Recommendations, February 2017*, available at www.oecd.org/corruption/anti-bribery/Brazil-Phase-3-Written-Follow-Up-Report-ENG.pdf.

Central Bank and the Financial Activities Control Council (COAF), which is subordinate to the Ministry of Finance and which is the Brazilian financial intelligence unit responsible for receiving, examining and forwarding reports on suspected money-laundering practices. Under Law No 9.613/98, the COAF is in charge of disciplining and applying administrative penalties, as well as coordinating and proposing mechanisms for cooperation and exchange of information to enable swift action to combat concealment of assets, rights and values. The COAF has been an essential focus in coordinating the efforts of the tax authorities and the financial system with the objective of tracking suspicious transactions involving money. As a result of tracking conducted by COAF, there have been numerous investigations that have led to the detection of corrupt activities.

Chapter IV of the 2005 Convention makes provision for mutual assistance in the exchange of information about and prosecution of individuals in the fight against corruption. During its first years, international cooperation was not that effective in Brazil, due both to the still low rate of anti-corruption enforcement and the 'inertial red tape', ie, that whenever new rules were promulgated, they tended to be interpreted in a manner similar to the preceding rules.

However, for a variety of reasons, national authorities have started exchanging information at the international level at a growing pace. Requests are being handled in a less formal manner compared to one decade ago. This has happened as the result of the development of stronger institutional and personal ties between prosecutors from different jurisdictions, who now meet regularly, narrowing down geographic distance. Of course, technology will also have played a role: it is said in some quarters that details are even exchanged between prosecutors through WhatsApp groups.

Such a swift pace in the exchange of information has made international cooperation certain. Some ten years ago, a certain investigation was halted because nobody knew how to reach the United States Department of Justice. No one should expect that the corruption investigations will move as slowly now as they did 20 years ago in the Maluf cases.

This new scenario has forced practitioners and prosecutors to work at a faster pace. Cases once took a long time to decide in Brazil, and this is still true in most situations. By contrast, the process of commencing anti-corruption cases in Brazil is astonishingly brisk. There was a time when attorneys would only worry about investigations and their repercussions caused by US Department of Justice involvement. Currently, there are even cases that have reached a swift conclusion in Brazil by comparison with other jurisdictions. For this reason, more than ever, it is vital to coordinate strategies, both in criminal litigation and in settlement.

3. The concept of 'corruption' in Brazilian legislation

The Brazilian Criminal Code, which applies to individuals, creates the crime of 'active corruption', which is defined as offering or promising an undue advantage to a public agent in order to influence him or her to perform, hide or delay a public act within the scope of his or her duties. In turn, the crime of 'passive corruption' is defined by the Criminal Code as asking, receiving or accepting a promise of any undue advantage, including for the benefit of third parties, directly or indirectly, and whether prior to or after accepting a public position. The Criminal Code also defines as crimes the offences of active and passive corruption perpetrated against foreign officials, as discussed in section 2 above.

With regard to corporate liability, the 2014 Act lays down a broader concept of 'corruption' that includes a number of conducts considered harmful to the public administration, either national or foreign. The following conducts are prohibited by that law:

- to promise, offer or give, directly or indirectly, an undue advantage to a public agent, or to a third party related to him/her;
- to finance, defray, sponsor or in any way subsidise, in a proven way, any wrongful acts provided for in the law;
- to make use of an individual or legal entity interposed to conceal or conceal a public agent's real interests or the identity of the beneficiaries of the acts performed, in a proven way;
- with regard to public tenders and contracts:
    - to thwart or defraud, through an adjustment, arrangement or any other means, the competitive character of a public tender process;
    - to prevent, disturb or defraud the performance of any act of a public tender process;
    - to remove or try to remove a tenderer by fraudulent means or by the offering of any type of advantage;
    - to defraud a public tender process or a contract arising therefrom;
    - to create, in a fraudulent or irregular manner, a legal entity to participate in a public tender or enter into an administrative contract;
    - to gain an undue advantage or benefit, in a fraudulent way, from modifications of or extensions to contracts entered into with the public administration, without authorisation provided by law or in the public tender invitation or the respective contractual instruments;
    - to manipulate or defraud the economic and financial balance of contracts entered into with the public administration; or
    - to hinder the investigation or auditing activities by public agencies, entities or agents, or to interfere with their work, including that falling within the scope of the regulatory agencies and supervisory bodies of the national financial system.

Furthermore, the 2014 Act also creates jurisdiction for the Brazilian authorities over acts of corruption committed abroad by entities based in Brazil or which have subsidiaries or affiliates in Brazil.

4. Administrative and criminal regulations and the competent authorities responsible for regulating, enforcing and punishing corruption

There is no criminal liability for legal entities under the 2014 Act. The available sanctions under that act in such cases are therefore limited to administrative and judicial sanctions and responsibility for enforcing them is divided accordingly. While criminal judicial enforcement is undertaken by independent prosecutors and judges, administrative sanctions may be imposed by different authorities under specific procedures. The nature and effectiveness of judicial sanctions also depend on the courts in which they are imposed.

4.1 Judicial sanctions

Judicial sanctions include:

- loss of assets, rights or valuables representing, directly or indirectly, the advantage or benefit gained from the infringement;
- partial suspension or interdiction of the legal entity's activities;
- compulsory dissolution of the legal entity; and
- prohibition from receiving incentives, subsidies, grants, donations or loans from public agencies or entities and from public financial institutions or institutions controlled by the government, for between one and five years.

Judicial sanctions follow the same procedure as that applicable to the Brazilian class action (*Ação Civil Pública*) set out in Law No 7.347/1985 and may be imposed by federal or state courts.

4.2 Administrative sanctions

The highest authority of the relevant agency or entity of the executive, legislative and judiciary has standing to investigate and impose administrative sanctions under the 2014 Act. At the federal executive branch level, the Office of the Federal Comptroller General (CGU) has jurisdiction to prosecute companies and audit investigations conducted by other authorities. The CGU also has authority to impose sanctions for corruption involving foreign authorities.

There are two kinds of administrative sanction pursuant to the 2014 Act:

- a fine ranging from 0.1% to 20% of the gross revenue of the legal entity in the fiscal year prior to the initiation of the administrative proceedings, excluding taxes, which shall never be lower than the advantage obtained, where it is possible to estimate it; and
- publication of the condemnatory decision.

If it is not possible to use the criterion of the value of the gross revenue of the legal entity, the fine will range from R$ 6,000 to R$ 60 million.

The 2014 Act sets out (among others) the following criteria for determining fines:

- the seriousness of the offence;
- the advantage gained or sought;
- whether the offence was fully or partially completed;
- the degree of damage; and
- the negative effects produced by the offence.

In turn, Decree No 8.420/2015 sets out objective criteria, based on those factors, to determine the percentage of the gross revenue that will be used to calculate fines. If the legal entity demonstrates that it had an effective compliance programme in place when the illegal act was committed, the sanctions to be imposed on the company could be significantly reduced.

The criteria set out by Decree No 8.420/2015 still leave too much room for interpretation, however; compared with US sentencing guidelines, too much discretion is conferred in imposing fines. Since its enactment, there have been a number of examples of how fines should be calculated under the 2014 Act, though access to the information is limited. The chart below summarises how the fine should be calculated under Decree No 8.420/2015:

The calculation of the fine begins with the sum of the amounts corresponding to the following percentages of the gross earnings of the latest fiscal year of the legal entity prior to the initiation of administrative proceedings, excluding taxes:	**From the sum of the amounts in the left hand column, the amounts corresponding to the following percentages of the gross earnings of the latest fiscal year of the legal entity prior to the initiation of the administrative proceeding, excluding taxes, will be deducted:**
(i) 1% to 2.5% if the violations continued over time	(i) 1% where the infraction was not completed
(ii) 1% to 2.5% if members of the board of directors or management of the legal entity tolerated or were aware of the violations	(ii) 1.5% where there is evidence that damage caused by the legal entity can be compensated in damages
(iii) 1% to 4% in the case of interruption of provision of public service or interruption of public construction	(iii) 1% to 1.5% depending on cooperation with the investigation or with the ascertainment of the violation regardless of a leniency agreement;
(iv) 1% for the economic condition of the violator based on the presentation of General Solvency (GS) and General Liquidity (GL) indexes superior to one and of net profit in the fiscal year prior to the violation	(iv) 2% in the event of voluntary self-disclosure by the legal entity before the initiation of the administrative proceeding relating to the violation
(v) 5% in the event of recidivism, defined as the occurrence of a new violation less than five years from the publication of the decision on the previous violation	(v) 1% to 4% where there is evidence of the existence and enforcement of a compliance programme (integrity programme) pursuant to the criteria set out in Decree No 8.420
(vi) In the case of contracts executed or intended to be executed with the affected public entity, the following percentages will be considered: (a) 1% on contracts of an amount higher than R$1.5 million (b) 2% on contracts of an amount higher than R$10 million (c) 3% on contracts of an amount higher than R$50 million (d) 4% on contracts of an amount higher than R$250 million (e) 5% on contracts of an amount higher than R$1,000 million	

Moreover, Decree No 8.420/2015 provides guidance on what needs to be covered in an entity's compliance programme for that programme to be considered effective. The compliance programme must be individualised and structured pursuant to the characteristics of each legal entity and by reference to its particular activities, ie, there are no 'off-the-shelf' compliance programmes.

The 2014 Act provides that, in the case of merger or incorporation, the liability of the successor entity will be limited to the payment of the fine and reimbursement for the damage (except where there is evidence of concealment or fraud), limited to the total value of the assets transferred.

It is possible to enter into a leniency agreement under 2014 Act. The legal entity must cooperate with the investigation and help the authorities identify other entities or individuals involved in the wrongdoing. The legal entity must also be the first to come forward to the authorities, and a 'guilty' plea is mandatory. Leniency agreements under the 2014 Act only protect the company, and the employees involved cannot be included. Such a mismatch in the legislation has been tested and it has recently become common practice to negotiate the leniency agreement together with its equivalent in the criminal sphere (*Colaboração Premiada*, which is equivalent to the notion of state's evidence or plea agreements).

5. Relevant public cases and how have they been handled and resolved.

There have been a number of corruption scandals in Brazil, most of which related to facts arising prior to the enactment of the 2014 Act. In those cases, the focus of the authorities was the criminal liability of the individuals involved in the schemes and many of those scandals resulted in the arrest of politicians and public servants. As some of the facts continued to arise even after the 2014 Act was passed, leniency agreements were therefore entered into. Prosecutors accept the use of leniency agreements even in cases of violations of the Improbity Law.

The largest case was *Operation Car Wash*, which started as a money laundering investigation targeting a black market dollar operator who laundered money from gas stations and car washes. As the investigation continued, it was discovered that the initial target, the *doleiro* (black market money dealer) Alberto Youssef, had bought a Land Rover vehicle for Paulo Roberto Costa, a director of Brazilian oil company Petrobras. Further evidence revealed improper payments to Youssef from companies that won Abreu & Lima (Petrobras) refinery contracts. Costa and Youssef both struck a plea bargain with prosecutors in exchange for information on a kickback scheme in which several top Petrobras public agents colluded with a cartel of Brazilian construction companies to overcharge the oil company for construction and service work. Following these two plea deals, the operation mushroomed, revealing the largest corruption scheme under investigation in the world. The cartel would decide which construction company should win a contract bid to, for example, service an oil rig or build part of a refinery. This fake competition was overseen by Petrobras directors and agents, who were rewarded with bribes. They kept some of the money but shared much of it with politicians. Petrobras, while publicly traded, is 51% government-owned. Many Petrobras executives owe their jobs to elected public officials.

After three years of investigations, *Operation Car Wash* has become the largest anti-corruption case in the world, leading to the arrest of tycoons (two out of the 10 richest men in Brazil were jailed), senior politicians and civil servants. For many Brazilians, the last two years seemed to be a 'real' version of TV drama *House of Cards*: Arrests and convictions of politicians, including active ministers, and high level company executives, such as the CEO of Odebrecht (a Brazilian construction company). There were also investigations of alleged money laundering, fraud, corruption and obstruction of justice involving former President Inácio Lula da Silva ('Lula'), resulting in his detention, a raid on his house, and an unsuccessful attempt to make Lula's Chief of Staff protect him from such investigations by the then President Dilma Rousseff. Lula was found guilty of corruption in July 2017, while this chapter was being written. An appeal against conviction failed and Lula is in jail and this is the end of his political career unless the conviction is quashed by the Brazilian Supreme Court. Rousseff is also alleged to have been involved in the Petrobras scheme and is under investigation, but has not yet been charged. She was impeached by Congress in August 2016 for fiscal crimes, *viz* fraudulent adjustments of government accounts by taking loans from state banks and the opening of supplementary credits without congressional approval. Her impeachment was broadcast live on television and closely watched. Furthermore, the Speaker of the lower house, Eduardo Cunha, was subsequently removed from office for, among other allegations, receiving $5 million in kickback payments from the Petrobras scheme. He was jailed for 15 years for these offences in March 2017. He remains in prison, having lost all appeals.

Since March 2015, the Federal Prosecutor's Office and the Federal Police have been investigating a major corruption scheme in the Federal Administrative Tax Court (CARF, *Conselho Administrativo de Recursos Federais*). Essentially, companies pursuing causes of substantial value (the Federal Police estimates the losses at R$19 billion) allegedly paid bribes to judges who were linked to law firms and lobbyists. The bribes were paid mostly to law firms and then transferred to the judges.

Perhaps one of the most striking developments involves Marcondes Machado. According to media sources, he was arrested for helping to secure incentive regulations for the automobile industry. He is said to have paid the consulting company of one of the sons of former President Lula. Media sources claimed that Marcondes Machado had told three different associations that he had "political influence in Brasília" to secure legislative and government measures conferring tax incentives on industries. According to one police officer, "Marcondes asked BRL 500,000.00 just to start working. If all went well, he would still have won a success fee between 3% and 5% of the total benefit given to the industry". These allegations would be connected to a similar scheme within the Development and Trade Ministry to obtain favourable measures. The Federal Police claims that Mr Marcondes Machado's main contact was Gilberto Carvalho, former head of the private office of former President Lula.

Corruption cases under the 2014 Act are mostly ongoing and companies are increasingly considering settlements with authorities, in order to avoid severe sanctions such as the prohibition on contracting with the government or receiving public funding. To date, the CGU has successfully completed two sets of leniency negotiations, one with Brazilian construction company UTC and the other with Austria-based company Bilfinger.

UTC's leniency agreement involved conducts investigated by *Operation Car Wash* and included the payment of R$574 million by way of a fine, restitution and damages. The leniency agreement also included an obligation to implement a compliance programme, which will be monitored by the CGU.

On the other hand, Bilfinger's leniency agreement did not involve conduct falling within the scope of *Operation Car Wash*. Bilfinger committed to pay R$9.8 million by way of a fine, restitution and damages, and also to improve its compliance programme with regard to Brazil.

Federal and state prosecutors have entered into several leniency agreements with *Operation Car Wash*-implicated companies. However, the validity of those agreements is being challenged in the courts for a number of reasons, including discussions over the jurisdiction of prosecutors to enter into leniency agreements.

The officers of Odebrecht (see above) finally entered into plea agreements and Odebrecht itself entered into a leniency agreement with the Federal Prosecutor's Office. Its impact on jurisdiction in other cases remains unclear, however.

6. Next steps

As with every process involving the maturing of institutions, the fight against corruption entails advances and setbacks. There is considerable fear that the current high level of anti-corruption enforcement will be dissipated as the political players have a dominant and clearly defined strategy, ie, to fight with all the tools available against the anti-corruption enforcers. Even so, there are a number of nascent measures that represent possible future developments.

The dimensions and speed of *Operation Car Wash* have spurred legislative proposals that seek either to harden or to restrain criminal enforcement.

In relation to anti-corruption regulation, several civil society entities are placing much hope in Bill No 4.850, which embodies the proposals of a public campaign called '10 Measures Against Corruption', which has the support of more than two million subscribers. Drafted by the Federal Prosecutor's Office, the objective of the bill is to enhance the tools for tackling corruption by addressing a number of loopholes in existing legislation. Bill No 4.850 has been subjected to harsh criticism, since a number of interest groups have deemed it to be draconian. While some of the criticism may be reasonable, it is strange to see people under investigation for corruption attacking the bill for allegedly violating human rights. In any event, nobody expects the bill to be passed easily; it is unlikely that it will be passed until 2018, when the mandates of the current representatives expire.

Among the '10 Measures Against Corruption' proposed by the Federal Prosecutor's Office are a number of changes to the criminal law and criminal procedure. These include the following:

- higher penalties for corrupt practices, faster enforcement of final convictions, limitation of appeals, the authorised use of unlawful evidence if obtained in good faith, and reform of criminal statute of limitation rules;

- the accountability of political parties and the criminalisation of political slush funds. A political party would be liable for crimes committed for its benefit. A new criminal offence would be introduced, whereby individuals directly involved in the handling and use of political slush funds would face imprisonment of between four and five years; and
- legalising sting operations and introducing civil asset forfeiture. The latter would allow law enforcement authorities to seize private property of unlawful origin. Legitimate owners, who were eventually subject to wrong allegations of illegitimate origin of the assets and who are seeking the return of seized assets, would have to prove that those assets were not involved in criminal activity.

In this context, it is worth mentioning that existing whistleblowing provisions do not create appropriate incentives for individuals and corporations to cooperate with criminal investigations. Incentives to disclose and cooperate are still weaker in Brazil than in the United States. Brazil only has a provision enabling prosecutors to enter into plea bargain agreements with criminal defendants who provide information that leads to the discovery of other wrongdoers and the recovery of ill-gotten gains. Plea bargain agreements are playing a key role in conducting investigations. The protection of whistleblowers and the facilitation of voluntary reporting have occupied a significant place in the implementation of the OECD 2005 Convention as a strategy for promoting a standard and an organisational culture of integrity and responsibility. In spite of the recommendations of the OECD anti-bribery Working Group, Brazil still has no legal provisions regulating a whistleblower programme. In order to fill this gap, the National Strategy to Combat Corruption and Money Laundering (ENCCLA) has drafted a law providing financial rewards and protections to whistleblowers pursuant to a 'Programme of Protection and Incentive to Report Information of Public Interest'.

Currently under consideration in Congress is a Whistleblower's Reward Bill. Individuals who, on their own initiative, give relevant information to authorities on an act constituting either a crime or administrative improbity, thus successfully triggering an investigation, would be entitled to a share of up to 10% of the assets forfeited by the government, as well as compensation for damage caused to them. The whistleblower's identity would be protected with appropriate measures. The bill is still at a preliminary stage and could face many changes before it is possibly enacted.

Although the above-mentioned proposals have been rejected in the House of Representatives, the possibility of approval still remains because a justice of the Federal Supreme Court of Justice, Luiz Fux, has ruled that the project should be submitted to a vote again, this time in the terms originally proposed as a project of popular initiative, which had the support of more than two million voters. As a result, the regulations drawn up by ENCCLA may also be subject to reconsideration.

The sabotaging of these bills is just one of the attempts to render anti-corruption enforcement more difficult. Another relates to the Abuse of Authority Bill, which was proposed by Senator Renan Calheiros in 2016. This bill is seen as an attempt to constrain enforcement agents (police, prosecutors and even judges) currently engaged in *Operation Car Wash*, especially those involved in plea bargain negotiations, which have become a key element in anti-corruption investigations in Brazil. The bill would only allow plea agreements for individuals who are not under arrest and would veto the acceptance of criminal complaints based solely on plea agreements. Senator Calheiros's criticism also appears to be based on personal grounds, since he has been mentioned in several plea bargain agreements arising out of *Operation Car Wash*.

Bulgaria

Kamen Chanov
Vanya Evtimova
Dessislava Fessenko
Kinstellar

1. Perceptions about corruption in Bulgaria: an overview

Among the Member States of the European Union (EU), Bulgaria consistently ranks at the bottom of international surveys as the country with the highest perceived level of corruption. Deficiencies in the judiciary, coupled with ineffective and inefficient prosecution of high-profile corruption cases, have been regarded as contributing factors to the country's poor image. This perception is also due to the ostensible lack of consensus among the political establishment as to the adoption of comprehensive anti-corruption legislation and the creation of an effective and independent institutional infrastructure to enforce it.

Bulgaria slipped from 69th place in Transparency International's *Global Corruption Perceptions Index* for 2015 to 75th place in 2016.[1] With regard to the public sector, this is largely due to the limited pace of long-contemplated judicial reform and the introduction of efficient anti-corruption legislation.

Bulgaria also scored worse in the benchmark for absence of corruption of the World Justice Project's *Rule of Law Index Report*, falling in the ranks from 71st place in 2015 to 79th place in 2016.[2] This benchmark takes into account three forms of corruption: bribery, improper influence by public or private interests, and misappropriation of public funds or other resources.

According to the World Economic Forum Global Competitiveness Report 2016–2017, corruption represents the single most important barrier to doing business in Bulgaria.[3] It has been estimated that the cost of corruption to the Bulgarian economy ranges from 14.57% to 22.01% of the country's gross domestic product.[4]

While 2016 saw the introduction of a number of changes to the institutional framework, they did not fully match the expectations set by the wider public and the European Commission's recommendations under the Co-operation and Verification Mechanism. The impression of ineffectiveness or even of bias on the part of local prosecutors has persisted as a result of revelations of the possible involvement of

1 Both reports are available respectively at www.transparency.org/cpi2015 and www.transparency.org/news/feature/corruption_perceptions_index_2016.

2 Both reports are available respectively at https://worldjusticeproject.org/sites/default/files/roli_2015_0.pdf and https://worldjusticeproject.org/sites/default/files/documents/RoLI_Final-Digital_0.pdf.

3 The report is available at hwww3.weforum.org/docs/GCR2016-2017/05FullReport/TheGlobalCompetitivenessReport2016-2017_FINAL.pdf.

4 European Parliament, *Organised Crime and Corruption: Cost of Non-Europe Report*, Annex II – RAND Europe, Research paper on the Cost of non-Europe in the Area of Corruption (2016), available at www.europarl.europa.eu/RegData/etudes/IDAN/2016/558779/EPRS_IDA(2016)558779(ANN2)_EN.pdf.

politicians and high-ranking judges in power brokerage and possible misuse of power that the Prosecution Office had decided not to probe.

Proposed anti-corruption legislation has not received sufficient support from the major political stakeholders, leaving the impression of a political class unwilling to target and cope with bribery within the higher ranks of the state. Although several new draft laws are currently in the pipeline, they are still at the early stages in Parliament and far from becoming effective, let alone yielding significant results. Further light is shed on those initiatives and on the current legal framework in sections 2 and 3 below.

Considerable shortcomings in the level of enforcement of existing legislation on corruption-related offences leave much room for improvement. The case law largely comprises convictions for small-time crimes, such as police officers accepting bribes for not issuing fines to speeding motorists. Section 4 provides a summary of several of the most well-known cases that have proceeded to court.

The international community plays an important role as a driver for reform in Bulgaria. Section 5 describes international legal instruments against corruption to which Bulgaria is a party and their effect on the country's legal framework.

Section 6 discusses the steps ahead and proposes a number of issues that will need to be addressed in the years to come.

2. The concept of corruption in Bulgaria

Current Bulgarian anti-corruption legislation is fragmented and does not contain a specific, clear-cut definition of 'corruption'. Several pieces of legislation mention this term, most notably the Act on Defence and Armed Forces of the Republic of Bulgaria,[5] the Administration Act,[6] the Act on the Ministry of Interior and the Rules on the Implementation of the Act on the Ministry of Interior.[7]

A new Act on Counteraction to Corruption and Forfeiture of Illegally Acquired Property, was adopted at the beginning of 2018.[8] It provides that corruption in the public sector occurs when:

> *as a result of a senior public position, the person abuses power, violates or fails to fulfil official duties for the purpose of obtaining, directly or indirectly, undue tangible or intangible benefit for himself or others.*

This appears to be a somewhat modified version of the definition of 'corruption' already contained in article 2 of the Council of Europe's Civil Law Convention on Corruption (1999), which was ratified by Bulgaria on 3 August 2006. This provision stipulates that 'corruption' means "requesting, offering, giving or accepting, directly or indirectly, a bribe or any other undue advantage or prospect thereof, which

---

5 Promulgated in *State Gazette* No 35/12.05.2009, effective as of 12 May 2009, last amendment promulgated in *State Gazette* No 85/24.10.2017.

6 Promulgated in *State Gazette* No 130/5.11.1998, effective as of 6 December 1998, last amendment promulgated in *State Gazette* No 58/18.07.2017.

7 Adopted with Decree No 168 of 16 August 1999 of the Council of Ministers promulgated in *State Gazette* No 75/24.08.1999, last amendment promulgated in *State Gazette* No 89/17.11.2015, effective as of 1 January 2016.

8 Promulgated in *State Gazette* No 7/9.01.2018, effective as of 23 January 2018, last amendment promulgated in *State Gazette* No 21/09.03.2018

distorts the proper performance of any duty or behaviour required of the recipient of the bribe, the undue advantage or the prospect thereof".

Although corruption in the private sector is not explicitly regulated by the new act, corruption-related crimes in the private sector are currently regulated by the Bulgarian Criminal Code. It is also expected that the legal framework of corruption in the private sector will be further developed so that the effective prosecution of these crimes is better guaranteed.

3. The national legal framework on anti-corruption in Bulgaria

3.1 Overview of national legislation

At the national level, the primary legislation encompassing different corruption-related offences is the Bulgarian Criminal Code.[9] The Criminal Code applies to most offences related to corruption, such as bribery, embezzlement, extortion, power brokerage and abuse of office. Proposed amendments to the code have recently been published for consultation[10] and are expected to be adopted in 2018. Their main objective is to harmonise the regime for corruption-related crimes by permitting the criminal law to be applied symmetrically both for public officials and for officials in the private sector.

Whistleblowing and procurement have traditionally been regulated by a number of different pieces of legislation (including, among others, the Administrative Procedure Code,[11] the Civil Servants Act,[12] the Public Procurement Act[13] and the Judiciary System Act[14]). The fact that whistleblowing regulation is so fragmented has been considered a significant disadvantage.

The new Act on Counteraction to Corruption and Forfeiture of Illegally Acquired Property is a step in the right direction towards codifying the rules concerning whistleblowers. In particular, it outlines a procedure for reporting the involvement of senior officials in acts of corruption or conflicts of interest. Another novelty is the power of the Chairman of the Commission for Counteraction to Corruption and Forfeiture of Illegally Acquired Property to request the assistance of authorities within the Ministry of the Interior in providing additional protection to whistleblowers. With the exception of the above, the new act does not go far beyond what was already prescribed by the now repealed Conflict of Interest Prevention and Ascertainment Act[15] and the Act on Forfeiture of Illegally Acquired Property.[16] Officials processing reports by whistleblowers are still subject to the same confidentiality obligations as under the old regime. Furthermore, anonymous alerts

---

9 Promulgated in *State Gazette* No 26/2.04.1968, effective as of 1 May 1968, as amended.

10 A draft Law on amendment of and supplements to the Criminal Code was published for consultation on 17 October 2017.

11 Promulgated in *State Gazette* No 30/11.04.2006, effective as of 12 July 2006, as amended.

12 Promulgated in *State Gazette* No 67/27.07.1999, effective as of 28 August 1999, as amended.

13 Promulgated in *State Gazette* No 13/16.02.2016, effective as of 15 April 2016, as amended.

14 Promulgated in *State Gazette* No 64/07.08.2007, as amended.

15 Promulgated in *State Gazette* No 94/31.10.2008, effective as of 1 January 2009, as amended, repealed by the Act on Counteraction to Corruption and Forfeiture of Illegally Acquired Property.

16 Promulgated in *State Gazette* No 38/18.05.2012, effective as of 19.11.2012, as amended, repealed by the Act on Counteraction to Corruption and Forfeiture of Illegally Acquired Property.

are still not subject to review. Bulgaria offers no other legal protection specifically to whistleblowers, apart from leniency processes in competition cases, civil law compensation for unjustly dismissed, harassed or prosecuted employees, and the ability to file administrative complaints. There are no public records on whistleblowing cases.

Key enforcement priorities may also be found in the Integrated Strategy for Prevention and Counteraction of Corruption and Organised Crimes adopted by the Ministry of the Interior and the Action Plan for Prevention and Counteraction of Corruption, which used to be updated on a yearly basis by the Commission for Prevention and Counteraction of Corruption. These instruments are of particular importance because they contain firm policy steps that are considered to be a priority in the fight against corruption for the following year.

3.2 Competent authorities

Prior to the adoption of the Act on Counteraction to Corruption and Forfeiture of Illegally Acquired Property, a number of authorities were responsible for combating different aspects of corruption-related offences.

- *Council for Anti-Corruption Policies to the Council of Ministers:* chaired by the Minister of the Interior, this body coordinates and monitors the preparation and implementation of anti-corruption strategic documents.
- *Centre for Prevention and Countering Corruption and Organised Crime:* also supervised by the Council of Ministers, this body was established in 2010 with the particular aim of conducting the so-called BORKOR project. A risk assessment tool, BORKOR is a complex cyber model for planning and exploiting anti-corruption measures, in particular those relating to the prevention of corruption in public procurement. It is said that this is a unique tool that is used only in Bulgaria.
- *Commission for Prevention and Ascertainment of Conflict of Interests:* this body became operational in 2011. It has not succeeded in acting systematically to prevent or uncover risks of political corruption.
- *Commission Against Corruption, Conflict of Interests and Parliamentary Ethics to the National Assembly:* this is one of the permanent commissions to the National Assembly. Its main duties relate to the supervision of ethical behaviour of members of parliament. Citizens may also file an alert alleging corruption or embezzlement by an MP. It is, however, important that the commission should not take anonymous alerts into consideration.
- *Supreme Judicial Council:* this body probes cases of alleged corruption within the judiciary. Both individuals and organisations may lodge alerts or information regarding alleged graft within the judiciary with the Inspectorate at the Supreme Judicial Council, which will then conduct an investigation.
- *Inspectorates within different ministries:* special inspectorates for fighting corruption exist in almost all ministries within the Bulgarian government. Their particular purpose is to monitor and prevent corruption within the respective ministries.
- *State Agency for National Security (SANS):* this body was established in 2008

with significant resources to fight high-profile corruption and serious organised crime. Its early existence was, however, marked by controversy. Only two years after SANS's establishment, a new government revised its mission and decreased its staff and budget, transforming it into a security agency dealing mostly with counter-intelligence matters.

The activities of investigatory authorities as they currently stand are fragmented and lack independence and external oversight. Institutions tasked with investigating conflicts of interest and the forfeiture of illegal assets lack autonomy and resources.

The new Act on Counteraction to Corruption and Forfeiture of Illegally Acquired Property aims to bridge these gaps. It provides for the creation of a new and unified anti-corruption body, ie, the Commission on Counteraction to Corruption and Forfeiture of Illegally Acquired Property (the Commission), which should improve interaction between the institutions in dealing with acts of corruption. The Commission brings together under the same umbrella the former Commission for Prevention and Ascertainment of Conflict of Interests, the Centre for Prevention and Countering Corruption and Organised Crime and the relevant SANS directorate tasked with counteracting corruption by senior public officials.

4. Enforcement

4.1 Introduction

The lack of a solid track record in high-profile cases of alleged corruption has been a recurring theme in eastern European countries. Unfortunately, Bulgaria is more often the norm rather than the exception. While public pressure and encouragement from the EU have undoubtedly resulted in moderate political impetus to break this trend, the judicial attitudes and practice speak for themselves.

Before delving more deeply into detail, a preliminary note on a jurisdictional issue is in order. Until recently, corruption offences, such as bribery and abuse of power committed by magistrates, members of the executive branch, persons with immunity and other public figures at the highest levels of the state apparatus, fell within the domain of the Sofia City Court as a court of first instance. An amendment to the Criminal Procedure Code which entered into force on 5 November 2017 has placed such cases within the competence of the Specialised Criminal Court instead.

There is notable scepticism among the judiciary about the positive impact of this change. In a report of December 2016 of the work done by the Specialised Criminal Court and the Appellate Specialised Criminal Court (collectively, the specialised courts) during the period 2012–2015,[17] the Supreme Court of Cassation concluded that settlements and lighter sanctions, such as probation and conditional sentencing for serious crimes, dominated the decisional practice of those courts.

Seeking to reinforce this scepticism, on 25 October 2017 the Sofia City Court

17 Supreme Court of Cassation of the Republic of Bulgaria, *Report on the Work Done by the Specialised Criminal Court and the Appellate Specialised Criminal Court Since Their Inception in 2012 Until the End of 2015* (December 2016), available at www.vks.bg/Docs/analiz_spec_sud_2012-2015.pdf.

published statistics on all corruption-related indictments filed by the Prosecution Office for the past three years.[18] This document shows that the number of indictments amounted to 26, casting further doubt on the suitability of the specialised courts to steer enforcement of the criminal legislation in the desired direction. For the sake of completeness, however, it is worth mentioning that in its annual report for 2016,[19] the Prosecution Office alone reported having filed 491 indictments for corruption-related acts, of which 141 concerned genuine corruption crimes in that year alone.

With a view to providing a glimpse of how prosecutors and the courts handle corruption-related offences, three noteworthy recent cases that attracted public attention are summarised below.

4.2 The case of Prosecutor Rumen Penev

Rumen Penev, a regional prosecutor, was arrested in 2011 on allegations of having requested a bribe amounting to Lev 21,000 (€10,737) from a businessman in order to exert influence over a fellow prosecutor not to indict that person.

The case spent some time going back and forth from one higher instance court to another. Sofia City Court had sentenced Penev to three and a half years' imprisonment in an open penitentiary. However, the Sofia Court of Appeal disagreed with the punishment, reduced the sentence to three years' imprisonment and suspended its enforcement for five years – the longest allowed under the Criminal Code currently in force.[20] The Supreme Court of Cassation sharply criticised the Court of Appeal's view that Penev's relatively young age (39) amounted to mitigating circumstances rendering him incapable of reacting properly to bribe-related situations. The Supreme Court of Cassation partially set aside the Court of Appeal's judgment and referred the case back to the second instance for a new review and verdict.

This situation was repeated on two further occasions until the Supreme Court of Cassation itself finally decided the case on its merits as it was no longer possible to refer it back to the Court of Appeal. The court set aside the Court of Appeal's conditional sentence and simply sentenced Rumen Penev to three years' imprisonment.

4.3 The case of Philip Zlatanov

In mid-2011, Philip Zlatanov was appointed and acted as the Chair of the Bulgarian Commission on Prevention and Ascertainment of Conflict of Interest (the Commission or CPACI). Following suspension from service two years later after having been indicted for abusing his powers as a public official, he officially resigned in September 2013.

---

18 The statistics published by the Sofia City Court are available at http://scc.bg/?p=6969.

19 Prosecution Office of the Republic of Bulgaria, *Report on the Application of the Law and the Activity of the Prosecution Office and the Investigating Authorities in 2016*, available at www.prb.bg/media/filer_public/a6/4e/a64eace3-f2d0-4c85-9781-64e82cad9e68/godishen_ doklad_na_prb_2016.pdf.

20 It should be noted that, under article 66 of the Criminal Code, conditional sentencing is permissible in Bulgaria only where the punishment imposed by the court is imprisonment for up to three years and provided that the perpetrator has never been sentenced for a crime of a general nature.

The first of two more serious accusations also involved the then acting President of the Republic of Bulgaria, against whom proceedings aimed at ascertaining conflicts of interest were initiated. Intending to preserve the acting President's reputation in the eyes of the public, Zlatanov had ordered the system administrator to abstain from uploading to the CPACI website the decision by which the Commission terminated the proceedings without pronouncing on the merits of the case. Sofia City Court held that this was an infringement of the Chair's duties to publish all decisions and reports related to the CPACI's activities. More importantly, the court considered this violation as having potentially serious repercussions for the Commission as it could erode the public's esteem for its work as an independent institution tasked with preventing and ascertaining conflicts of interest by persons holding public office.

The second accusation related to a former Deputy Chair of the Financial Supervision Commission (FSC) in charge of the Investments Supervision Department. Following an alert filed by the then Chair of the FSC, the Commission examined a potential conflict of interest against the former Deputy Chair and found her to be in violation of the Prevention and Ascertainment of Conflict of Interest Act. Once again, Zlatanov had ordered the system administrator not to upload the CPACI's decision to its website. In the Sofia City Court's view, this had stripped the former Deputy Chair of her right of defence and had once more put the Commission in a position where its reputation in the eyes of the public was at stake.

As a result, the Sofia City Court sentenced Zlatanov to three and a half years' imprisonment in an open hearing and deprived him of his right to take up any managerial or elected position in the country's administration for a period of five years. This case reached the Supreme Court of Cassation in 2015. The court ultimately reduced Zlatanov's sentence to three years' imprisonment and suspended its enforcement for five years. In the Supreme Court of Cassation's view, the initial punishment was disproportionate to the individual weight of the crime committed when assessed against its true content and specific features. Moreover, the infringements at issue were not as significant as other powers falling within the discretion of the CPACI's Chair and his behaviour had had no real serious repercussions.

Two of Zlatanov's personal notebooks served as evidence in his conviction. Their contents revealed that, in the exercise of his duties as Chair of the CPACI, he had coordinated his actions with and received instructions from other persons outside the Commission's structure, allegedly at the highest levels of the state hierarchy. However, only the initials of those persons were available and their full names remained unknown. Before the prosecution could establish their real identities in the course of the intermediate appellate review proceedings, the notebooks were stolen from the car of the investigating officer in charge of their safekeeping. In its judgment, however, the Sofia Court of Appeal listed exhaustively all the names and initials written in the notebooks. Among them were those of senior public officials, such as the then director of the National Health Insurance Fund, the interim Prime Minister and several city mayors.

4.4 The case of Christo Biserov

In November 2013, the Deputy Chair of Parliament, Christo Biserov, submitted his resignation for personal reasons. Several days later, the prosecutor announced that Biserov and his stepson, Ivaylo Glavnikov, had been the subjects of pre-trial proceedings.

There were several allegations against Biserov: for money laundering, tax evasion and document-related crimes. The prosecution decided not to pursue a conviction on the counts of money laundering at the pre-trial stage and instead indicted Biserov for:

- failure to pay income taxes as a natural person in the amount of Lev 18,965.49 (€9,696.90);
- failure to declare currency transactions amounting to Lev 700,960.63 (€358,395.56); and
- failure to declare to the Bulgarian National Audit Office, contrary to the Act on Public Disclosure of the Assets of Persons Holding Senior Government and Other Positions, that he held large sums in foreign currencies amounting to Lev 417,752.64 (€213,593.58).

Both the Sofia City Court and the Sofia Court of Appeal found Biserov not guilty on all counts because the prosecution had failed to prove the offences objectively. Only the tax evasion indictment reached the Supreme Court of Cassation but this was also struck down and Biserov was fully acquitted by an effective judgment. The outcome in the case was largely due to the lack of evidence, which the Prosecution Office could not collect via mutual legal assistance processes.

5. International legal instruments applicable to anti-corruption in Bulgaria and their effects

Political turmoil and unsatisfactory levels of enforcement aside, Bulgaria does not shy away from participating in international legal instruments in the fight against corruption. It has ratified all available instruments of the United Nations (UN), the Council of Europe, the EU and the Organisation for Economic Co-operation and Development (OECD)

Ever since the establishment of the Group of States against Corruption (GRECO) in 1999, the Council of Europe has been regarded as the most active international institution in the fight against corruption. As a member state both of GRECO and the Council of Europe, Bulgaria is bound by:

- the Criminal Law Convention on Corruption (1999) and its corresponding Additional Protocol (2003);
- the Civil Law Convention on Corruption (1999);
- Resolution (97) 24 on the Twenty Guiding Principles for the Fight against Corruption;
- Recommendation No R (2000) 10 on Codes of Conduct for Public Officials; and
- Recommendation No R (2003) 4 on Common Rules against Corruption in the Funding of Political Parties and Electoral Campaigns.

With regard to the UN, Bulgaria has ratified the Convention against Transnational Organized Crime (2000) with its corresponding Protocols and the Convention Against Corruption (2003). It is also a signatory to the OECD's Convention on Combating Bribery of Foreign Public Officials in International Business Transactions (1997).[21]

As a Member State of the EU, Bulgaria is bound by the *acquis communautaire,* which includes legal acts in the fields of justice and home affairs. The most relevant EU instruments in the fight against corruption are Council Framework Decision 2003/568/JHA of 22 July 2003 on combating corruption in the private sector and Commission Decision of 6 June 2011 Establishing an EU Anti-corruption reporting mechanism for periodic assessment.

Bulgaria's accession to international anti-corruption initiatives and legislation usually translates into amendments of existing domestic criminal legislation in order to align it with international obligations. It is worth noting that the Criminal Law Convention on Corruption contains provisions on corporate criminal liability. This convention was not incorporated into Bulgarian criminal legislation but was introduced instead in the Administrative Violations and Sanctions Act.[22] Legal entities that have enriched themselves as a result of a crime, such as bribery and power brokerage, face the imposition of a pecuniary sanction of up to Lev 1,000,000 (€511,292).

For example, with a view to ratifying the Criminal Law Convention on Corruption, Bulgaria introduced a number of changes to the Criminal Code in the section on bribery in 2000. In particular, offering a bribe to a local or a foreign public official was criminalised, as was the requesting of a bribe by such persons.

The ratification of the OECD Convention on Combating Bribery of Foreign Public Officials in International Business Transactions led to an amendment to the Criminal Code on the definition of a 'foreign public official' and the criminalisation of bribery in international business transactions.

6. The way ahead

Bulgaria persists in its efforts to reform its judiciary and to install sufficient safeguards against high-ranking corruption. One driver behind those efforts is ongoing annual monitoring by the European Commission of Bulgaria's progress with regard to judicial reform and the fight against corruption as part of the EU Co-operation and Verification Mechanism. Another factor is mounting social pressure on the political establishment to introduce the necessary checks and balances in order for graft and power brokerage to be curbed.

These external and internal factors will likely prevail and lead to the enactment of effective anti-corruption legislation. The only two questions remaining are how waterproof those legislative mechanisms would be and how effectively they would be enforced. Measures or practical solutions to that effect may include:

---

21 Bulgaria was in fact the first non-OECD contracting State to ratify this convention.

22 Article 83a of the Administrative Violations and Sanctions Act, promulgated in *State Gazette* No 92/28.11.1969, last amendment promulgated in *State Gazette* No 63/408.2017, effective as of 5 November 2017.

- sufficient legislative safeguards to depoliticise the state administration and the judicial system and prevent conflicts of interests by public officials;
- a legal framework containing provisions aimed at ensuring the transparency of funding for political parties as well as provisions pertaining to disclosure of the assets of public officials;
- mechanisms for facilitating whistleblowing (eg, bespoke whistleblower protection) and cooperation with authorities by offenders (ie, effective remorse) in the course of establishing and investigating corruption;
- specialisation of investigation teams in corruption and economic crimes in order to ensure better understanding of the genesis of crimes and their perpetrators' *modus operandi* and more efficient evidence-gathering;
- greater effectiveness in cross-border cooperation in criminal matters, including with respect to evidence-gathering.

Canada

Wendy Berman
Lara Jackson
Stephanie Voudouris
Cassels Brock & Blackwell LLP

---

1. Overview of the country *vis à vis* corruption matters

The Canadian government has a stated commitment to combat domestic and foreign corrupt practices as a key aspect of its efforts to engender confidence in the integrity of Canadian businesses. The country has implemented a range of tools to detect, deter and prosecute corruption. The Corruption of Foreign Public Officials Act 1998 (the 1998 Act)[1] is the principal Canadian statute designed to combat corruption and bribery of foreign public officials in international business transactions. In addition to the implementation of a domestic legal regime, Canada has ratified various international treaties designed to address corruption. Moreover, Canada's courts recognise the importance of national and international cooperation in prosecuting corruption[2] and interpret domestic legislation to ensure that Canada's authorities are not constrained in their enforcement of the country's international obligations.[3]

2. International anti-corruption treaties applicable to Canada and their concrete effect in the fight against corruption.

Canada has ratified two primary treaties designed to address corruption:[4] the United Nations (UN) Convention Against Corruption 2003 (the UN Convention)[5] and the Organisation for Economic Co-operation and Development (OECD) Convention on Combating Bribery of Foreign Public Officials in International Business Transactions (the OECD Convention).[6]

The UN Convention covers five main areas:

- preventive measures;
- criminalisation and law enforcement;

---

1 SC 1998, c 34.

2 *World Bank Group v Wallace*, 2016 SCC 15. In this case, the Supreme Court of Canada upheld the immunity applying to certain documents and information held by the World Bank and rejected the applicants' request for a wiretap and search and seizure to obtain access to such information. The court specifically noted that waiving such immunity could have a chilling effect on collaboration with domestic law enforcement, which would be particularly harmful since organisations like the World Bank are well-placed to investigate corruption and "serve at the frontlines of international anti-corruption efforts".

3 See for example, *R v Karigar*, 2017 ONCA 576, (*Karigar*), [40]-[44].

4 Canada has also ratified the UN Convention Against Transnational Organized Crime and the Inter-American Convention Against Corruption.

5 UN Convention Against Corruption, 21 May 2004, General Assembly resolution 58/4.

6 OECD Convention on Combating Bribery of Foreign Public Officials in International Business Transactions, 17 December 1998.

- international cooperation;
- asset recovery; and
- technical assistance and information exchange.

Furthermore, the convention introduces standards and rules that member countries can apply to strengthen their domestic and regulatory anti-corruption regimes.[7]

The OECD Convention requires member states to introduce legislation making the payment of bribes to foreign officials illegal, in order to create a level playing field in international business.[8]

In addition to the 1998 Act, Canada has a number of other legislative regimes to fight economic crimes. These include the Criminal Code 1985,[9] the Extractive Sector Transparency Measures Act 2014,[10] the Proceeds of Crime (Money Laundering) and Terrorist Financing Act 2000,[11] the Mutual Legal Assistance in Criminal Matters Act 1985,[12] the Extradition Act 1999,[13] the Freezing Assets of Corrupt Foreign Officials Act[14] and the Witness Protection Program Act 2011.[15] Canada has enacted or enhanced such legislation to align with the mandates of and obligations under the UN and OECD conventions and continues to work with international and domestic organisations to ensure that it remains compliant with these conventions and consistently improves the prevention, detection and prosecution of corruption.

3. The concept of 'corruption' in Canada

3.1 Introduction

Canada has demonstrated a strong commitment to combating corruption through its implementation and enforcement of the above legal framework.

The concept of 'corruption' in Canada can be measured by reviewing the country's commitment to and performance under the conventions it has ratified, as well as the enforcement of its own regulatory framework in combating corruption. Most recently, Transparency International – a non-government organisation[16] – released its *Corruption Perceptions Index 2016*, which measures the perceived levels of

---

7 UN Convention, piii, available at www.unodc.org/documents/brussels/UN_Convention_Against_Corruption.pdf. In particular, the UN Convention introduced first-of-its-kind provisions requiring member states to return assets obtained through corruption to the country from which they were stolen.

8 The OECD Convention is supplemented by a number of additional instruments including: (1) the OECD Recommendation for Further Combating Bribery of Foreign Public Officials, which aims to strengthen the means for prevention, detection and investigation of foreign bribery; and (2) the OECD Guidelines for Multination Enterprises, which contains guidance on corporate social responsibility for companies investing abroad. See further Global Affairs Canada, *Canada's Fight Against Foreign Bribery, Eighteenth Annual Report to Parliament* (6 October 2017), available at www.international.gc.ca/trade-agreements-accords-commerciaux/topics-domaines/other-autre/corr-18.aspx?lang=eng (*Eighteenth Annual Report to Parliament*).

9 RSC 1985, c C-46.

10 SC 2014, c 39, section 376.

11 SC 2000, c 17.

12 RSC 1985, c 40 (4th Supp).

13 SC 1999, c 18.

14 SC 2011, c 10.

15 SC 1996, c 15.

16 Transparency International, 'Our Organisation', available at www.transparency.org/whoweare/organisation.

public sector corruption worldwide. Canada scored 82 in an index of 0 (highly corrupt) to 100 (very clean) and had the highest-ranking score of all of the countries in North and South America.[17]

In May 2013, the OECD issued a report focused on monitoring Canada's implementation of the Anti-Corruption Convention.[18] By that time, Canada had introduced Bill S-14: An Act to Amend the Corruption of Foreign Public Officials Act (Bill S-14),[19] which aimed at strengthening Canada's ability to detect, investigate and prosecute corruption-related offences. The report stated that it welcomed the significant steps taken by Canada to improve the 1998 Act through Bill S-14.

Also in 2013, Transparency International published an annual report entitled *Global Corruption Barometer 2013: Report*, which surveyed more than 1,000 people from each of 107 countries to assess the perception of corruption within each country.[20] Highlights of the Canadian survey results include the following:

- Canadians ranked political parties as the institution with the highest level of perceived corruption (the other institutions being the police, judiciary, public officials/civil servants, the legislature, medical and health services, media, religious bodies, business and the private sector);[21]
- 61–80% of Canadian respondents said they believed in ordinary people's ability to make a difference in response to corruption;[22] and
- more than 90% of Canadian respondents said that they would be willing to report an incident of corruption.[23]

The report found that the majority of respondents across the globe view political parties as the institution with the most corruption.[24] It set out a variety of recommendations, including increasing transparency within government and enhancing integrity in the public procurement process.[25] The percentages listed above suggest that Canada has been successful in creating an environment in which its citizens feel comfortable reporting incidents of corruption as well as in educating its citizens about the consequences of participating in corruption-related offences.

---

17 Transparency International, *Corruption Perceptions Index 2016*, available at www.transparency.org/news/feature/corruption_perceptions_index_2016.

18 This report is part of the mandatory peer monitoring process, which has so far been carried out in three phases. See OECD, *Canada – OECD Anti-Bribery Convention*, available at www.oecd.org/daf/anti-bribery/canada-oecdanti-briberyconvention.htm.

19 Parliament of Canada, *Legislative Summary of Bill S-14: An Act to amend the Corruption of Foreign Public Officials Act* (28 May 2013), available at https://lop.parl.ca/About/Parliament/LegislativeSummaries/bills_ls.asp?ls=s14&Parl=41&Ses=1

20 Transparency International, *Global Corruption Barometer 2013*: Report, available at www.transparency.org/gcb2013/report (*Global Corruption Barometer 2013*). This is the most recent such report published by Transparency International. Drawing on the results of a Transparency International survey of more than 114,000 respondents in 107 countries, it addresses people's direct experiences with bribery and details their views on corruption in their countries' main institutions. Transparency International has announced that over the course of 2015–2017 it will release a *Global Corruption Barometer* accompanied by five regional surveys which will track people's experience of corruption in their countries. Transparency International's website states that the survey for the Americas is forthcoming: see www.transparency.org/research/gcb/gcb_2015_16/0.

21 *Global Corruption Barometer 2013*, p17.

22 *Ibid*, p21.

23 *Ibid*, p22.

24 *Ibid*, p3.

25 *Ibid*, p4.

Canada was also reviewed under the UN's Implementation Review Mechanism (IRM), a peer-review process designed to monitor and ensure the effective implementation of the UN Convention. An executive review[26] of Canada's implementation of certain chapters of the Convention, including criminalisation and law enforcement and international cooperation, was published in 2014.[27] The review highlighted several "successes and good practices", including:

- the 2013 amendments to the 1998 Act to expand jurisdiction and increase penalties (discussed further at 4.2 below);
- the strategic restructuring of the Royal Canadian Mounted Police (RCMP) to increase the efficiency and effectiveness of corruption investigations;
- extending the scope and breadth of provisions of the Criminal Code addressing conspiracy, aiding and abetting, and other participation in offences of corruption;
- the acceptance of a wide variety of legal bases for the extradition of individuals in relation to corruption offences, including bilateral and multilateral treaties, the domestic Extradition Act and the UN Convention itself;
- the adoption of a multilateral memorandum of understanding that allows for more effective exchange of information and provides mutual legal assistance to participating countries; and
- the adoption of a flexible approach to the establishment of joint investigations with law enforcement bodies from other countries.

The review also identified several areas for improvement including:

- engagement with civil society organisations to improve public awareness;
- the detection and reporting of corruption cases;
- the creation of more protective measures for those who report corruption; and
- encouraging cooperation between government and the private sector to facilitate proactive reporting of instances of corruption.

The IRM Executive Summary also encouraged Canada to eliminate the exemption of facilitation payments (also known as 'grease payments'). As discussed further at 4.2 below, Canada implemented this suggestion in October 2017.

---

26 United Nations, *Conference of the States Parties to the United Nations Convention Against Corruption* (13 February 2014), Implementation Review Group, Executive Summary: Canada, available at www.unodc.org/documents/treaties/UNCAC/WorkingGroups/ImplementationReviewGroup/ExecutiveSummaries/V1400913e.pdf (UN *Executive Summary*).

27 Each country goes through the IRM review process during a given cycle. The timing for when each country goes through its review, or acts as a reviewing State, is determined by lottery. The review is carried out by government experts who have been nominated by their respective States to carry out the review process. The first cycle of the review mechanism started in 2010 and covers the chapters of the UN Convention on criminalisation and law enforcement and on International cooperation. Canada was evaluated in 2013, year 3 of the first review cycle. The second cycle, which was launched in November 2015, covers the chapters on preventive measures and asset recovery. Canada was scheduled to be evaluated during 2016, the second year of the cycle. See further www.unodc.org/unodc/en/corruption/implementation-review-mechanism.html.

3.2 The domestic framework for enforcement of Canada's anti-corruption regime

Canada has adopted a two-pronged approach to the fight against foreign corruption, focusing on both prevention and enforcement. This approach relies on a number of federal departments, agencies and Crown corporations to play significant roles in combating foreign bribery.[28]

The federal police agency, the RCMP, has exclusive authority to investigate and lay charges for foreign corruption and bribery offences. The RCMP currently has special investigation units in two major cities dedicated to the investigation of corruption offences. The RCMP manages the International Anti-Corruption Program through its Federal Coordination Centre. It also provides expertise nationally and internationally on corruption-related matters and works with the Department of Justice to prioritise international requests for assistance in corruption-related investigations.[29]

RCMP investigators are tasked with a number of responsibilities including:

- investigating allegations that a Canadian person or business has bribed, offered or agreed to bribe a foreign public official;
- investigating allegations that a foreign person has bribed a Canadian public official;
- investigating allegations that a foreign public official has secreted or laundered money in or through Canada;
- providing assistance on international assistance requests; and
- developing and delivering outreach activities to various target groups.

In April 2017, the RCMP established a tip-off line in partnership with the Competition Bureau whereby the RCMP may receive information regarding allegations of bid-rigging, bribery, price fixing, conflict of interest, false invoicing and product switching. While the Competition Bureau is responsible for triaging the information that is presented to the RCMP, the RCMP retains the ultimate responsibility for investigating allegations. This partnership also coincides with the development of the Competition Bureau's Federal Contracting Fraud Tip Line, which allows Canadians anonymously to report fraud, collusion or corruption in federal government contracts and real property agreements. Canadians can provide tips either online or by telephone and the information collected may be relied on to gather further intelligence and introduce greater due diligence measures.[30]

The RCMP also works with the Public Prosecution Service of Canada (PPSC), which prosecutes criminal offences under the 1998 Act and the Criminal Code, as well as under other federal statutes. The PPSC consults with the RCMP and other government agencies involved in the investigation and enforcement under the 1998 Act.[31]

Global Affairs Canada (GAC) is tasked with representing Canada at international anti-corruption conventions like the OECD Working Group and is responsible for

---

28 *Eighteenth Annual Report to Parliament* (note 8 above).
29 *Ibid*, pp5–6.
30 *Ibid*, p10.
31 *Ibid*, p6.

coordinating Canada's approach to meeting its obligations under the international conventions. GAC works closely with Canadian companies operating abroad to promote awareness of and compliance with the 1998 Act.[32] GAC has also been involved in the review and revision of the OECD Methodology for Assessment of Procurement Systems (MAPS), featuring enhanced accountability, integrity and transparency assessment criteria.[33]

Other government agencies and departments, such as Export Development Canada, the Canada Revenue Agency, the Department of Justice Canada, and Public Services and Procurement Canada are all tasked with the responsibility of educating, preventing and detecting instances of corruption.[34]

4. Regulation and the authorities that are responsible for regulating, enforcing and punishing corruption

4.1 Introduction

Canada's primary legislation for combating foreign corruption is the 1998 Act. However, a variety of domestic statutes work in tandem to prevent, detect, investigate and prosecute corruption, including the Criminal Code and the Extractive Sector Transparency Measures Act 2015. Each of these three pieces of legislation is discussed in turn below.

4.2 Overview of the 1998 Act

The basic offence of bribery of a foreign public official is set out in section 3(1) of the 1998 Act, which provides:

> *3(1) Every person commits an offence who, in order to obtain or retain an advantage in the course of business, directly or indirectly gives, offers or agrees to give or offer a loan, reward, advantage or benefit of any kind to a foreign public official or to any person for the benefit of a foreign public official*
>
> *(a) as consideration for an act or omission by the official in connection with the performance of the official's duties or functions; or*
>
> *(b) to induce the official to use his or her position to influence any acts or decisions of the foreign state or public international organization for which the official performs duties or functions.*

In 2013, Canada enacted a number of amendments to strengthen the 1998 Act and enhance Canada's ability to prevent, detect, investigate and prosecute corruption-related offences. In particular:

- the definition of 'business' under the 1998 Act was broadened to remove the previous reference to "for profit" under the definition, thereby ensuring that a company or individual could not escape liability on the basis that a bribe was not paid for a 'or profit' enterprise or that the business was not profitable;

---

32 *Ibid*, pp6–8.
33 *Ibid*, p7.
34 *Eighteenth Annual Report to Parliament* (note 8 above).

- a new books and records offence was created by section 4 to criminalise the making, falsifying or concealing of records and payments related to the bribery of a foreign public official. Payments for bribes are often facilitated as a result of weak internal controls over financial reporting as such payments are typically inaccurately recorded in the books and records of a company. The creation of a books and records offence creates potential criminal exposure for a company and its directors and senior officers in cases where there have been inadequate internal controls and compliance programmes or the false or inaccurate recording of payments of bribes in the company's financial records;
- stricter penalties for breaches of the 1998 Act. Individuals found guilty of bribing a foreign public official under section 3, or of breaching the books and records provision under section 4, are guilty of an indictable offence and face a maximum term of imprisonment of 14 years. The 1998 Act does not specify a maximum fine for corporations; however, section 735(1) of the Criminal Code provides that in lieu of a prison sentence, corporations convicted of an indictable offence, such as a breach of the 1998 Act, are subject to a fine at the court's discretion;[35]
- granting the RCMP exclusive authority to lay charges under the 1998 Act. This eliminates the potential for jurisdictional conflicts between federal and provincial law enforcement agencies;
- extending the jurisdictional reach of the 1998 Act. Previously, this act only applied to actions that were committed in or connected to Canada – in other words, the actions had to have a 'real and substantial connection' to Canada to fall within the purview of the 1998 Act. The 2013 amendments broadened Canada's jurisdiction beyond the territorial link requirement of a 'real and substantial connection' by deeming any act in contravention of the 1998 Act committed abroad by a Canadian company, citizen or permanent resident to have been committed in Canada.[36] The mere fact of nationality is therefore sufficient to attract liability under the 1998 Act. More specifically, companies may be liable under the 1998 Act if a Canadian director, or a Canadian employee with a sufficiently important role, has knowledge of, condones, permits, fails in an oversight role, is wilfully blind to or fails to prevent the bribery of a foreign public official. A company or a person would not have to

35 In assessing the financial penalty to impose on a corporation for breaches of the 1998 Act, courts will consider a number of factors, such as the advantage realised as a result of the offence. Courts will also consider mitigating factors, such as whether the corporation has taken steps to reduce the likelihood of a subsequent offence. In the context of a breach of the 1998 Act, this could include the implementation of a rigorous compliance and training programme.

36 Section 5 of the 1998 Act. To date, only one case has interpreted the application of this section. In *Chowdury v Canada*, 2014 ONSC 2635, the court had to determine whether the 1998 Act extended Canada's jurisdiction to a foreign national for the purpose of charging him with an offence under the act. In this case, the foreign national was acting as an agent for SNC Lavalin Group Inc and was charged with offering bribes to foreign public officials in Bangladesh. The foreign national was not a citizen of Canada, nor had he ever been in Canada. The court applied the principle of sovereign equality: ie, that countries will generally not adjudicate matters that occurred within the borders of another country or exercise jurisdiction over foreign nationals unless those foreign nationals commit an offence within the country's borders. The court concluded that section 5 does not extend Canada's jurisdictional reach over a foreign national who commits an act in a foreign country, unless and until that foreign national physically attends Canada or the foreign country offers to surrender him to Canada.

be in Canada and the act would not have to occur in Canada or be connected to Canada for such person to be tried and convicted under the 1998 Act; and

- perhaps most notable is the elimination of the facilitation payment exemption from the offence of bribery under the 1998 Act. Facilitation payments, often referred to as 'grease payments', are payments made to facilitate or expedite routine government actions such as processing permits or visas or other paperwork. The Canadian government eliminated the exception allowing for facilitation payments under Canada's anti-corruption regime with effect from 31 October 2017.[37] The elimination of the facilitation payments exception aligns the Canadian regime with other countries, including the United Kingdom, but importantly differentiates the Canadian regime from the United States and Australian regimes, which maintain a facilitation payment exception.[38]

4.3 The Criminal Code

The Criminal Code governs corruption within Canada in relation to both the bribery of government officials, judicial officers, police officers, municipalities and obstructing justice. 'Unconventional' corruption offences, such as breach of trust and misconduct of officers, as well as private corruption (that which is applicable to private sector organisations), are also criminalised by the Criminal Code.[39]

Two recent cases decided under the Criminal Code involved government officials. In 2016, the Ontario Court of Justice dealt with 31 charges that had been laid against a Senator in relation to certain Senate expense claims.[40] The court dismissed the charges, finding that the expenses related to honest mistakes or in any event fell short of criminal conduct. In 2017, the Ontario Court of Appeal overturned the acquittal of a senior adviser in the Office of the Prime Minister from 2006 to 2008 and 2009.[41] The adviser had a history of involvement with water treatment and waste disposal issues in First Nations communities. In 2010, he negotiated a contract with

---

37 The repeal of the facilitation payment exception in 2013 had been held in abeyance to allow Canadian companies adequate time to adjust their operations to comply with it.

38 This divergence between regimes continues to present ongoing challenges to Canadian companies that are dual-listed or operate in countries that still maintain a facilitation payment exception. Moreover, Canadian companies that are dual-listed or operate in such jurisdictions will need to abide by the stricter Canadian legislation, since the 1998 Act extends its reach to any act in contravention of it committed abroad by a Canadian company, citizen or permanent resident. Canadian companies, especially those operating in high risk countries, should continue to review the effectiveness of their compliance regimes for the detection and prevention of any facilitation payments. In particular, Canadian companies should ensure robust, ongoing training with regard to the new Canadian prohibition on facilitation payments and take appropriate steps to ensure compliance with this requirement by any third party consultants, contractors or agents working with the company. See further Wendy Berman, "*Proposed Amendments to the Corruption of Foreign Public Officials Will Have Significant Impact on Canadian Companies Doing Business Abroad*" (22 February 2013), available at www.casselsbrock.com/CBNewsletter/Proposed_Amendments_to_the_Corruption_of_Foreign_Public_Officials_Act_Will_Have_a_Significant_Impact_on_Canadian_Companies_Doing_Business_Abroad; Arthur Hamilton & Wendy Berman, Canada's Corruption of Foreign Public Officials Act: Mitigating Old and New Risks, available at www.casselsbrock.com/files/file/docs/CanadaCorruptionofForeignPublicOfficialsAct.pdf.

39 Public Safety Canada, *Corruption in Canada: Definitions and Enforcement* (May 2014), available at http://publications.gc.ca/collections/collection_2015/sp-ps/PS18-10-2014-eng.pdf (Corruption in Canada).

40 *R v Duffy*, 2016 ONCJ 220 (Duffy). For other cases involving bribery and fraud involving police and public officials, see *R v Kozitsyn*, 2009 ONCJ 540; *R v O'Brien*, 249 CCC(3d) 237, 2009 CarswellOnt 7803.

41 *R v Carson*, 2017 ONCA 142 (*Carson*).

a company which contained a provision for commissions to be paid to his then girlfriend on all sales of water treatment systems to First Nations. The Court of Appeal held that the adviser had presented himself as someone with influence over the government to extract a benefit for his then girlfriend. As such, the court set aside the acquittal and entered a conviction.

A number of cases have interpreted and applied the Criminal Code to instances of domestic corruption. However, the predominant focus in recent years has been on strengthening Canada's foreign anti-corruption regime under the 1998 Act.[42]

4.4 The Extractive Sector Transparency Measures Act 2015

The Extractive Sector Transparency Measures Act[43] (ESTMA) came into force on 1 June 2015.[44] Parliament enacted the legislation in response to a commitment that Canada had made at the 2013 G8 Leaders' Summit, where "leaders agreed to raise global standards of transparency in the extractive sector, reduce the potential for corruption and ensure that citizens benefit fully from the extraction of natural resources."[45] Natural Resources Canada (NRCan) describes the purpose of the ESTMA as follows:[46]

> *The Act requires businesses to publicly report certain payments they make to all levels of government in Canada and abroad in relation to the commercial development of oil, gas and minerals. The purpose of the ESTMA is to deter corruption in the global extractive sector by making government revenues from natural resources transparent to the public. The reports will be made available on publicly accessible websites by reporting businesses, and a link to every report submitted will be available on the ESTMA website.*

Reports made by business pursuant to the ESTMA are made publicly available on the NRCan website and must remain publicly available online for a minimum of five years.[47] The ESTMA applies to 'entities', as defined. To qualify as an 'entity', a business must be engaged in the commercial development of oil, gas or minerals in Canada or elsewhere, or control (directly or indirectly) a business engaged in the commercial development of oil, gas or minerals in Canada or elsewhere. A business must report if it qualifies as an entity. Pursuant to two exclusive tests under the ESTMA, an entity must report:

- either if it or its securities are listed on a stock exchange in Canada; or
- if it:
    - has a place of business in Canada, does business in Canada or has assets in Canada; and
    - meets two of the following minimum thresholds in one of its two most recent financial years:

42 *Corruption in Canada* (note 41 above).

43 SC 2014, c 39, section 376.

44 On 31 March 2016, Natural Resources Canada (NRCan) finalised implementation tools that had previously been released to the public for comment. For example, the 'Guidance' is a substantive supplement to the Act, published to assist extractive resource entities in interpreting and understanding the reporting requirements under the ESTMA: available at www.nrcan.gc.ca/sites/www.nrcan.gc.ca/files/mining-materials/PDF/ESTMA–Guidance.pdf.

45 NRCan, *Extractive Sector Transparency Measures Act* (ESTMA) FAQs, available at www.nrcan.gc.ca/node/18802/#A1.

46 *Ibid.*

47 NRCan, *Links to ESTMA Reports*, available at www.nrcan.gc.ca/mining-materials/estma/18198?.

- it has at least C$20 million in assets;
- it has generated at least C$40 million in revenue;
- it employs an average of at least 250 employees.

To date, no cases have been decided under the ESTMA.

5. Relevant public cases and how have they been handled and resolved

There have only been four prosecutions under the 1998 Act (three companies and one individual) and approximately 35 active investigations to date. The four convictions are as follows:

- on 10 January 2005, Hydro-Kleen Group Inc entered a guilty plea to one count of bribery and was fined C$25,000. The company had bribed a US immigration official to process visa applications for its employees favourably;
- on 24 June 2011, Niko Resources Ltd entered a guilty plea for one count of bribery and was fined C$9.5 million and subject to probation and monitoring for three years. The company was charged under the 1998 Act for providing gifts to a foreign public official worth approximately C$200,000. Niko cooperated with the police investigation but did not self-report;
- on 22 January 2013, Griffiths Energy International Inc pleaded guilty to a charge related to securing an oil and gas contract in Chad and was fined. C$10.35 million.[48] The company commenced an independent internal investigation, self-reported and shared the results of its internal investigation with the police and the PPSC and implemented a robust anti-corruption compliance programme; and
- in May 2014, the Ontario Superior Court convicted the first individual, Nazir Karigar, under the 1998 Act. This was also the first prosecution that proceeded to trial. Mr Karigar was an employee or agent of Cryptometrics Canada. He was charged and convicted of conspiracy to bribe Indian officials to secure a multi-million dollar contract with Air India. Mr Karigar was in charge of handling the strategy to win the contract, including the proposed offering of bribes. Two US-based executives were responsible for making the ultimate strategic decisions. Despite Mr Karigar's jurisdictional challenge, the trial court determined that Canada had jurisdiction because:
  - he was a Canadian businessman who had approached a Canadian company in Ottawa and acted as its employee or agent in his efforts to secure the Air India contract;
  - the benefit to be obtained was for the contracting Canadian company, with a great deal of the work to be done by its employees in Ottawa;
  - nearly all of the real evidence — documents and emails — was seized in Canada, and all the witnesses who testified were from Canada.[49]

---

48 (2013) AJ No 412.

49 The offence was committed prior to the enactment of Bill S-14. The trial judge considered this new provision but concluded that the new section 5 did not have retroactive effect and instead applied the 'real and substantial connection' test.

Mr Karigar did not lead any evidence at trial. He appealed the conviction, which was upheld by the Ontario Court of Appeal.[50]

As at April 2018, the following investigations by the RCMP were ongoing:[51]

- on 19 February 2015, Groupe SNC Lavalin Inc and two of its subsidiaries were charged with bribery and fraud for payments made in connection with a construction project in Libya. The company and its subsidiaries are also charged with defrauding various organisations in the amount of C$129,832,830;[52]
- on 31 January 2014, Sami Bebawi, Constantine Kyres and Stéphane Roy were charged in relation to payments made to foreign officials in Libya. Messrs Bebawi and Roy were executives of SNC Lavalin and were charged with fraud, bribery, possession of stolen property and possession of proceeds of crime. Mr Kyres was Mr Bebawi's lawyer and was charged with obstruction of justice and extortion; and
- on 4 June 2014, Robert Barra, Dario Berini and Shailesh Govindia, all US nationals and executives or agents for Cryptometrics Canada, were charged with agreeing to pay bribes to Indian officials in violation of the 1998 Act. These charges flow from the same circumstances that led to the conviction of Nazir Karigar, as described above.

6. Next steps: comments on what needs to be modified, strengthened or addressed

Canada does not have a formal self-reporting or leniency regime through which companies or individuals can voluntarily disclose most economic crimes, including violations of the 1998 Act or other domestic legislation designed to combat corruption. While many Canadian regulatory and law enforcement agencies state that voluntary disclosure will result in a more lenient resolution, few provide any specific guidance or guidelines. With little or no assurance as to the likely benefit from self-reporting, corporations are faced with uncertainty and must weigh unknown and uncertain benefits against the risks of voluntary disclosure, including

---

50 Mr Karigar appealed the conviction on three main grounds: (1) that the court did not have territorial jurisdiction over what had occurred because there was no sufficient connection to Canada; (2) that proof of conspiracy was not enough – instead, the Crown had to prove an agreement between the accused and a foreign public official; and (3) that the trial judge incorrectly applied the co-conspirators exception to the hearsay rule and misapprehended some of the evidence. The Court of Appeal dismissed each ground and upheld the conviction.

51 *Eighteenth Annual Report to Parliament* (note 8 above). Since the inception of the 1998 Act, the RCMP has been involved in over 45 active investigations. From September 2014 to August 2015, it pursued 12 active investigations. From September 2015 to August 2016, it pursued 10 active investigations. See: Global Affairs Canada, *Canada's Fight Against Foreign Bribery, Sixteenth Annual Report to Parliament*, available at www.international.gc.ca/trade-agreements-accords-commerciaux/topics-domaines/other-autre/corr-16.aspx?lang=eng; Global Affairs Canada, *Canada's Fight Against Foreign Bribery, Seventeenth Annual Report to Parliament* (20 October 2016), available at www.international.gc.ca/trade-agreements-accords-commerciaux/topics-domaines/other-autre/corr-17.aspx?lang=eng.

52 Certain employees of SNC Lavalin have also been charged with corruption-related offences for their involvement with the planned construction of the Padma Bridge in Bangladesh (*R v Wallace*, 2017 ONSC 132). The dispute has not proceeded to trial and the decision referred to focused on the applicants' challenge to the interception of their private communications through wiretapping. The court found that the wiretapping authorisations should not have been granted and ordered that all communications obtained thereunder be excluded from evidence at trial.

reputational damage. Companies must also consider the consequences of any admissions on other potential or existing civil proceedings, such as class actions, or other cross-border investigations or proceedings.

Many countries, including the United States and the United Kingdom, offer a range of alternatives to prosecution that encourage self-reporting by companies, including deferred prosecution and non-prosecution agreements. For companies operating in multiple countries, the lack of non-prosecution agreements or deferred prosecution agreements, for example, creates an additional challenge where a company will need to consider whether to disclose in the jurisdiction that does offer non-prosecution agreements or deferred prosecution agreements.

Current corporate best practice in Canada requires the establishment of an effective compliance programme to detect and mitigate the risk of foreign corruption. An effective compliance programme is one that "promotes an organizational culture that encourages ethical conduct and a commitment to compliance with the law."[53] The existence of a compliance programme not only increases the likelihood that a company will be able to detect and prevent breaches of the 1998 Act but also influences how charges will be resolved if the company is unable to prevent a breach.

Some key elements of an effective compliance policy include:[54]

- a clear, concise, and accessible code of conduct and anti-corruption policy that contain a commitment from senior management to detect and mitigate risk of corruption;
- a compliance officer assigned the responsibility for implementing and overseeing the company's compliance programme;
- a charitable donation policy;
- a system for pre-approval of payments to public entities and officials;
- a system for third party due diligence and risk assessment;
- a system for confidential reporting.

---

53 *Resource Guide* (note 56 below).

54 *Risky Business, A Primer on Canada's Foreign Anti-Corruption Enforcement Regime,* Cassels Brock & Blackwell LLP; US Department of Justice and US Securities and Exchange Commission, *A Resource Guide to the US Foreign Corrupt Practices Act,* available at www.sec.gov/spotlight/fcpa/fcpa-resource-guide.pdf (Resource Guide); DLA Piper, *Charitable Contributions and the FCPA – 6 simple steps to help ensure your company is giving responsibly* available at www.dlapiper.com/en/us/insights/publications/2014/09/ the-global-anticorruption-perspective-q3-2014/charitable-contributions-and-the-fcpa/?; Arnold & Porter LLP, *Anti-Corruption Compliance: Special Considerations for Charitable Contributions* by Company Giving Programs and Foundations, available at https://files.apks.com/advisory%20anti-corruption_compliance_special_considerations_for_charitable_contributions_co_giving_programs_foundations.pdf; FCPA Compliance & Ethics, Anheuser-Busch Inbev and Lessons in Joint Venture FCPA Compliance, available at http://fcpacompliancereport.com/2016/09/10710/ ; OECD, *Good Practice Guidance on Internal Controls, Ethics, and Compliance* (OECD Good Practice), available at www.oecd.org/daf/anti-bribery/44884389.pdf; International Chamber of Commerce, *ICC Guidelines on Agents, Intermediaries and Other Third Parties,* available at https://cdn.iccwbo.org/content/uploads/ sites/3/2017/02/ICC-Guidelines-on-Agents-and-Third-paries-ENGLISH-2010.pdf; Transparency International UK, *Anti-Bribery Due Diligence for Transactions,* available at www.transparency.org.uk/publications/anti-bribery-due-diligence-for-transactions; Association of Corporate Counsel, *The Foreign Corrupt Practices Act and Global Anti-Corruption Law,* available at www.acc.com/ethicsxchange/bundle.cfm?ctpid=352; World Economic Forum, *Good Practice Guidelines on Conducting Third Party Due Diligence,* available at www3.weforum.org/docs/WEF_PACI_Conducting ThirdPartyDueDiligence_Guidelines_2013.pdf.

- a system to complete periodic internal audits to ensure compliance with the programme;[55]
- periodically reminding employees about anti-corruption policies and providing training regarding compliance with anti-corruption policies to new and current employees; and
- creating a committee or assigning personnel who can provide confidential guidance and advise on complying with the policy, including in situations where urgent advice is needed.[56]

The implementation of effective compliance programmes also recognises that the private sector is an integral part of Canada's ability to prevent, detect, investigate and prosecute corruption. Going forward, collaboration between the private, public and government sectors ought to be encouraged to ensure a robust approach to combating corruption.

55 OECD, *Good Practice* (note 54 above).
56 *Ibid*.

Chile

Juan Eduardo Figueroa
FIHS Abogados; Former judge of the Supreme Court of Chile
Sergio Huidobro Martínez
FIHS Abogados

1. Country overview with regard to corruption

The historic perception of Chile with regard to the phenomenon of corruption has generally been positive. That is to say, in a country with a low index of 'corruption', this perception is confirmed by rankings published annually by international organisations such as the non-governmental organisation (NGO) Transparency International (TI) and others. For example, according to TI's *Corruption Perceptions Index 2016*, Chile now ranks 24th out of 76 countries in terms of the perception of corruption.

There was an historic 17-year period, between 1973 and 1990, during which Chile lived under military rule. As is characteristic of such governmental regimes, there was no documented information about corruption until democracy was restored in 1990, after which certain actions and activities became widely known.

At the beginning of the 1990s, the democratic government used a policy of transparency to promote citizen interest in corruption. Beginning in 1994, the people of Chile became increasingly concerned with 'a fungus that grows in the dark' which was evident in a series of in-house irregular operations involving future sales of copper contracts through Codelco (Copper Corporation). This situation had a national resonance, as the company significantly influenced the national budget and, subsequently, government public policies.

A direct result of the Codelco corruption case was the organisation of a commission comprising outstanding political and academic representatives. This integrated commission issued a report with multiple recommendations including draft laws, administrative reforms, self-regulatory codes for ethics and seminars.

Later, in 2003, a number of incidents of corruption occurred that related to the wages of public servants and which once again captured the public interest as well as the attention of social media. These incidents were a direct outcome of a private-public sector partnership for the construction of public facilities, particularly roads, prison facilities and airports under the modality of 'public works concessions'.

During 2014 and 2015, a number of other examples of corruption were revealed in both the public and private sectors. These incidents related to political funding as well as other issues. Once again, these allegations strongly impacted on citizens, leading to the creation of another commission, the Engel Commission, whose report contained multiple proposals for action and recommendations.

Scholars on the subject of corruption have formulated a useful summary classification of the phenomenon against which to understand the Chilean situation: accidental, systemic and systematic. In other words, these categories describe, respectively, whether corruption is an isolated instance, periodic or frequent.

Historically, Chile has had low levels of corruption. Globalisation and existing transparency in the public, private, national and international arenas have driven the country to systematic corruption. That is to say, sectors of society such as finance, politics and police institutions are affected by the phenomenon of corruption, unlike other countries in which the entire state apparatus is infected by systemic corruption.

The volume of foreign investment in Chile has, to date, been relatively unaffected by the issue of corruption.

The current situation in Chile reveals the need to review standards and regulations with regard to integrity, good practices and the financing of political activity. In addition, the delineation of exclusive areas and reciprocal relations between the public and private sector are recommended. Chilean society is becoming accustomed to transparency and accountability as essential bases for the necessary trust in the operation of public institutions.

Similarly, in private enterprise or entrepreneurial ventures, Chileans expect that those involved, such as entrepreneurs, owners and principals, should be bound by juridical rules and ethical codes. In addition, when these principles are violated, there should be mechanisms and agencies for enforcement as well as effective sanctions.

With regard to political activity, the public expects that politicians, both individually and as members of parties, should serve in accordance with their ideals, let their actions be guided by and for the wellbeing of society in general, be prepared to fulfil their duties, act with honesty and independence and not let their personal interests overshadow their consciences.

2. The concept of 'corruption' in Chile

The term 'corruption' has a very unclear definition, both nationally and internationally. It is difficult to encapsulate all of its intended meaning. This results in a misuse of the term and its interchangeability with many other words that may, or may not, truly convey the same overall idea or emphasis. Thus, for not only theoretical but also practical reasons, there is justification for defining the term 'corruption' as it manifests itself in the community.

Two main concepts are generally accepted as being part of corrupt behaviour:

- power and its use (or misuse); together with
- damage to the common good and general wellbeing.

Abuse of power (whether public or private) perpetrated by a third party is extremely prevalent. A popular and very accurate phrase, to quote the 19th century British politician Lord Acton, is that "absolute power corrupts absolutely". The approach to damage to the common good or general wellbeing is revealed in the definition of 'administrative integrity' in article 54 of Law 18.575 of 5 December 1986 on the General Rules of the State Administration:

to observe impeccable official conduct and honest and loyal performance as a function or position with prevalence of the general interest over the particular.

The objective is to have people understand the idea of the common good as opposed to their own individualised personal interests. Indeed, working for the general wellbeing in fact ultimately turns out to be in the interest of individuals. This is one of the most challenging antidotes to corruption in which states seek to reduce their rankings in national corruption indices.

The breadth of the concept of 'corruption' in Chile comprises both the public and private sectors and encompasses a wide range of situations, viz "profiting from influential positions with public or private decision making power for one's own benefit" (Law 19.645 of 11 December 1999 on Modifications to the Criminal Code Sanctioning Crimes of Corruption).

In the authors' opinion, Chilean corruption is not only identified with bribery (ie the giving of gifts to public servants in order to act in an illegal sense), but in a broader perspective, it is also seen as 'public corruption'. This means that those who (whether by representation or designation) exercise rights or perform public functions in such a manner that they primarily fulfil the particular interests of an individual, organisation, group or party instead of the general interest on which every public action must focus, are involved in 'public corruption'. In this situation, there is a violation or a postponement of the public interest to favour the private interest. 'Corruption' is, therefore the use of public facilities for private interests where these differ from the general interest which every public action should fulfil.

Corruption is also manifested in the contravention of ethical principles. The ethical-social context of a country and the moral environment or universe of society normally determine the corruption index ranking of a country. It therefore influences the country's moral environment with regard both to so-called 'minor' as well as 'major' corruption, whether public, municipal and private, national and international. Minor acts of corruption are reflected in daily activities and act as the starting point from which major corruption often evolves. Both minor/private and major/public acts of corruption have disloyalty as a common denominator.

All of the above explains the idiosyncrasies of the complex definition of 'corruption' in both international and domestic law. The reality is that Chilean legislation broadly includes the complexities of this definition in its administrative, penal and commercial laws

3. The regulatory framework and the authorities responsible for anti-corruption enforcement and sanctions

In Chile, the majority of the regulations to fight corruption stem from laws enacted by Parliament.

The authorities responsible for enforcement and the imposition of sanctions in corruption cases are as follows.

3.1 The judicial branch

This is one of the three branches of the state and is in charge of hearing and resolving all civil and criminal lawsuits and executing their outcomes. With regard to criminal matters, the Judiciary Branch performs its functions through the Examining Court and the Oral Criminal Court, which decide whether or not a crime has been committed in addition to deciding on the application of pertinent sanctions (ie, penalties). The decisions of these courts are subject to review by the appellate courts and the Supreme Court.

3.2 The Public Prosecution Office

This body leads the investigation of crimes in collaboration with the *Carabineros de Chile* (uniformed police) and the *Policía de Investigaciones* (PDI, civil police). The Public Prosecution Office may bring criminal actions in respect of the majority of crimes involving corruption without the need for a complaint to be filed by a citizen or organisation. It has a specialised anti-corruption unit that acts in a coordinated and strategic manner with the State Defence Council (see 3.6 below) and with the General Comptroller Office of the Republic (see 3.4 below).

3.3 The *Carabineros de Chile* and the *Policía de Investigaciones*

Both of these organisations, which are referred to at 3.2 above, are auxiliary entities of the Public Prosecution Office with regard to carrying out investigations. They perform (among other things) raids, interception of communications and seizures of documents and computers. This is the best way to obtaining proof or evidence leading to convictions for crimes of corruption.

3.4 The *Contraloría General de la República* (CGR – General Comptroller Office of the Republic)

The State Treasury supervises and examines the flow of investment funds to the Treasury from the municipalities and other organisations. It also examines the accounts of those who are responsible for the assets of those entities.

Every public servant, citizen or entity receiving or having custody of, managing or paying state funds must report and be accountable to the *Contraloria* (General Comptroller Office). If an investigation conducted by the *Contraloría* reveals that public funds have been misused or used for bribery or other corruption-related crimes, the *Contraloria* must submit this information to the Public Prosecution Office and may act in any subsequent criminal proceedings.

Some 44% of enforcement activities by the *Contraloria* during the last year were generated from the complaints made by citizens on its website.[1]

The most recent *National Survey on the Perception of Corruption* published by *Libertad y Desarrollo* (Liberty and Freedom Institute), has enhanced the reputation of the *Contraloría* as the best qualified public institution in anti-corruption matters.[2]

---

1 Manuel Aris, (Deputy Director of Incidencia, Director of Proyecto Chile Check), *Corrupción y participación. La ciudadanía tiene un rol central en la prevención y control de la corrupción (Participation and corruption. The citizenry has a central role in prevention control of corruption)*, available at espaciopublico.cl/corrupción-y-participacion/.

2 *El Mercurio*, Editorial, 13 August 2017.

3.5 The Financial Analysis Unit (*Unidad de Análisis Financiero* – UAF)

The UAF is responsible for preventing and impeding the use of the financial system and of other economic sector activity for the commission of asset laundering and the financing of terrorism. There have previously been allegations of corruption based on evidence of suspicious operations in particular business sectors. For this reason, the backgrounds of all people involved in a number of sectors (including banks, financial institutions, money exchange houses, stock exchange agencies, insurance companies and notaries public) are scrutinised and examined thoroughly.

The UAF has a broad remit to investigate accusations of asset laundering. In relation to drugs, terrorism, weapons, securities markets, banks, customs officials, intellectual property, the ax code, public servants, the use of illicit or privileged information and the trafficking of women and children. Many of these issues develop into more serious corruption.

Having detected irregularities, the UAF can impose an administrative sanction (a fine) and submit its information to the Public Prosecution Office.

3.6 The *Consejo de Defensa del Estado* (CDE, State Defence Council)

The main objective of the CDE is the legal defence of state interests. It takes penal action against crimes that can damage the State Treasury economically as well as in crimes committed by public servants, particularly bribery and negotiating against the interests of the state.

The CDE website (www.cde.cl) reports that 103 criminal cases were completed in 2016, with 86.4% of decisions rendered in favour of the state with regard to crimes committed by public servants.

3.7 *Servicio de Impuestos Internos* (SII – Internal Revenue Service)

The SII applies and enforces all internal taxes of the country. The Director decides whether or not to pursue punitive action for infringements, for which the penalities are fines and imprisonment. The SII acts as complainant in criminal cases relating both to taxes and to crimes of corruption.

The power of the Director to decide whether or not to file criminal complaints has been criticised by both the Public Prosecution Office and the General Comptroller Office of the Republic, who believe that it lacks objectivity and therefore take on the task themselves of deciding what action to take.

3.8 *Tribunal de Defensa de la Libre Competencia* (TDLC – Chilean Competition Tribunal) and the *Fiscalía Nacional Económica* (FNA – National Economic Prosecution Office)

Both of these entities are regulated by the Decree-Law 211, the objective of which is to promote and defend free market competition.

Decree-Law 211 penalises as a crime any collusion that contemplates incidents of corruption between citizens (such as entering into agreements to fix sale prices, to acquire goods and services in one or more markets, or to limit the production or provision of goods and services).

Criminal investigations for crimes involving collusion can only commence pursuant to claims filed by the FNA. The result of an investigation is then ruled upon by the TDLC, resulting in a final and executory judgment establishing the existence of a criminal agreement.

3.9 *Consejo para la Transparencia* (Council for Transparency)

This entity was created in 2008 by Law 20,285, Access to Public Information. Its aim is to promote transparency, enforcing compliance with norms on transparency and the publication of information in keeping with the guarantee of the right of access to information from the state administration. This law and the work of the Council are seen as one of the final efforts by Chile to ensure the proper application to the International Convention on Corruption.[3]

3.10 *Chile Transparente* (Chile Transparent)

This body is the Chilean chapter of the Transparency International NGO. Its mission is to make a substantial contribution to the fight against corruption and bad practices in Chile and to promote the creation of a culture based on probity and transparency. Its overall aim is to position Chile among the 20 countries with the lowest level of corruption in the *Corruption Perception Index of Transparency International.*

4. International anti-corruption treaties applicable to Chile and their concrete effects in fighting corruption

Chile has ratified the following international anti-corruption instruments:

- the Inter-American Convention Against Corruption (1996);
- the Organisation for Economic Co-Operation and Development (OECD) Convention on Combating Bribery of Foreign Public Officials in Foreign Business Transactions (1998) (the OECD Convention);[4] and
- the United Nations Convention against Corruption (2004) (the UN Convention).

The provisions and principles of these conventions have been direct sources of applicable Chilean legislation but have varied in their practical application. Such variance has occurred in relation to (among other things):

- statutes governing crimes of bribery;
- the law on penal responsibility of legal persons;
- the disposition of goods that are the subject of corruption;
- investigatory and adjudicatory norms;
- prescription periods;
- asset laundering;
- mutual legal assistance; and
- extradition.

---

3 Leslie Montoya Rivera, *Análisis de los instrumentos internacionales contra la corrupción (Analysis of international instruments against corruption).*

4 The OECD Convention (1960) became effective in Chile in August, 2010.

As an example, with regard to bribery, the Penal Code was amended in October 2002 and April 2009 to comply with the obligations of the OECD Convention, allowing for the first time the prosecution of offences of bribery involving foreign public servants (the current articles 251 bis and 251 ter of the Penal Code).

Then, in December 2009, in order to comply further with the OECD Convention, but even though it was unnecessary, Law 20.393 was enacted to declare the legal responsibility of citizens and companies. This law imposed penal responsibility on companies for asset laundering, financing terrorism, bribery and offences relating to the receipt of stolen money or assets. As a result, many companies (both public and private) have adopted measures to avoid involvement in such crimes, since applicable penalties range from the dissolution of a company to fines of 936 million Chilean pesos.[5] Many companies have created 'Models of Crime Prevention', accompanied by external certification. They have also designated Prevention Officers, who must create Crime Prevention Models[6] and who must coordinate their activities with organisations such as the UAF (see 3.5 above) and the Public Prosecution Office (see 3.2 above), as well as with the boards of their companies. In reaction to criticism made in 2015 by Transparency International, the law was amended in July 2016 to ensure that all companies respond to allegations of bribery offences against foreign public officials.

In Chile, however, there is still a need to clarify what will be the real consequence for companies that have adopted Crime Prevention Models in criminal investigations to which they are exposed. This is, because it remains unclear whether the models will act to exempt from or extenuate criminal responsibility, even with certificates, or if they will have no effect on prosecutors and judges. For the moment, it has been indicated by criminal judges and prosecutors that the models will not be enough *per se* but that it will be necessary to demonstrate that they are really 'living' and truly functioning documents, not just 'good' documents that 'sleep' in the drawers of company employees and executives.

In Chile today, the issuance of public information and transparency apply pursuant to the norms of article 10 of the UN Convention. This provision essentially proposes the application of procedures that allow the public to obtain information on the organisation, operation and adoption processes applicable to public administrative decisions. Article 10, which was motivated by *Chile Transparente* (see 3.10 above), has allowed both private persons and different groups to request and (where successful) receive information from public organisations and state administration authorities. Furthermore, Law 20.285 of August 2008 on Access to Public Information allows public and private enterprises to make much of their relevant information available on the internet and obliges them to deliver information requested by the authorities or by citizens.[7]

In preventing corruption through improving accounting and auditing standards,

---

5 $1,509,677 as at October 2017.

6 That is, not merely paper documents but model documents used daily in companies.

7 Where information is not provided by an entity of the state administration, on grounds of secrecy or otherwise, the applicant can appeal to the Council for Transparency (see 3/9 above) also created by this law. In spite of its strengths, however, this entity also has weaknesses, eg, as to the processes for the appointment and removal of its members.

and thus avoiding penalties, the UN Convention has encouraged more companies to improve their corporate structures and compliance.

In terms of the civic participation envisaged by article 13 of the UN Convention, organisations such as the *Contraloria* (see 3.4 above), which organise seminars and conferences for the private sector, invite the review of subjects such as the prevention of corruption as well as specific topics such as the raising of false invoices or receipts for fees in order to secure the lowering of tax calculation.[8] This is as much a means of fighting corruption as more direct methods, as the existence of corruption has severe consequences and poses a threat to society and the economy.

5. Pertinent public cases and how they have been managed and resolved

5.1 The *Inverlink* case:

In 2003, the President of the Central Bank detected an anomaly in the bank's computer. It was discovered that his secretary had been leaking confidential information to the stock brokerage Inverlink in exchange for payment.

One month after the investigation, which also disclosed that the Head of Treasury in the State Production Development Corporation (CORFO) had been removing security documents that represented money and had endorsed them to Inverlink in such a manner that Inverlink could submit them as guarantees to the bank and, in this manner, obtain liquidity. He would then return the guarantees before CORFO carried out its monthly balance reconciliations. Inverlink therefore operated in the market utilising privileged information and obtained more than sufficient liquidity, unwittingly thanks to CORFO.

News of the information leak from the Central Bank generated alarm among investors in Inverlink who, in turn, withdrew their funds, significantly affecting the liquidity of their holdings. Inverlink reacted by withdrawing more than Ps 80,000,000,000 ($125.618.277,460) in instruments from CORFO, which funds were never returned.

All of the above nearly resulted in a financial collapse. These actions generated uncertainty in the mutual fund market, which in turn lost 35% of the value of hedge funds in five days.[9]

Thirteen public servants and private persons were arrested for such crimes as as misuse of public funds, fraud and infringement of the General Law of Banks. In addition, a number of civil lawsuits were initiated both by private persons and CORFO, which was unable to recover its losses entirely.

5.2 The *MOP-Gate* case

The corporation GATE SA was founded by a former officer of the Ministry of Transportation to provide consultancy services in engineering, environmental and hydro projects, among others.

---

8 This practice constitutes a tax crime in Chile, under article 97 No 4 of the Tax Code.

9 Antonio Recabarren, *'Caso CORFO-Inverlink, el impacto de la confianza en los mercados[('The CORFO/Inverlink Case, the impact on market trust')*; in *Entrepreneurial Ethics, Approaches from Senior Management* (2005, Business School, Universidad de Los Andes, Santiago), p68.

As a result of the investigation of the *Coimas* case (the '*Kickback* case'), in which eight people were subsequently convicted of bribery, it was revealed that the Ministry of Public Works (MOP) and GATE had concluded contracts for non-existent, repeat or overvalued services in order to obtain payments and had then distributed those funds among MOP officials. The then Minister of Public Works, Carlos Cruz, publicly acknowledged that he had received every month an envelope containing cash, which he understood was part of his salary.

This meant that the State Treasury had been the victim of a fraud to the amount of Ps 1,250 million ($1,962,785,590), for which another 13 people were convicted (among them Mr Cruz) and received prison sentences ranging from 60 days to 5 years. In addition, the State received a civil court damages award of Ps 799,142,217 ($1.254.835,860).

5.3 The *Penta* case

This case began with the so-called 'FUT Fraud'[10] in which an officer of the Internal Revenue Service (SII – see 3.7 above), Ivan Alvarez, took advantage of a system failure to increase tax returns from a number of companies in exchange for money, defrauding the Treasury of almost Ps 3,000 million ($4,710,685,400) In the middle of 2012, the SII detected the irregularities and started an internal investigation, passing its findings later to the Public Prosecution Office.

The case involved relatives and close associates of a number of Chilean politicians who were issued fee receipts (a tax instrument used to provide services without a labour contract) or invoices (a tax instrument for sales and services) by Penta for work and services that were never in fact performed. Penta therefore financed political campaigns in an irregular way. The recipients appeared to have paid fees pursuant to false invoices or receipts, while lowering the calculation of their taxes.[11]

The only involved politician convicted to date is Jovino Novoa, a former Senator, who in December 2015, and after admitting that he had received from Penta the sum of Ps 30,000,000 ($47,106,850) through the mechanisms discussed above, was sentenced to three years' imprisonment. For his part, Iván Alvarez was sentenced to five years' probation.

5.4 The *Ceresita* case

This was one of the first cases involving a legal entity found guilty of the crime of bribery under Law 20.393.

At the end of 2011, a number of entrepreneurs alleged that the Director of Works for the Municipality of Recoleta, Carlos Reyes, had requested money to authorise extensions to commercial premises. The Public Prosecution Office began an investigation and discovered that Ceresita, a leading paint manufacturer, had

10 According to the Internal Revenue Service, the FUT or Taxable Profit Fund is a "control book that must be filled by the taxpayer who declares effective incomes in first category, demonstrated by means of a complete accounting system and a consolidated balance, in which the history of taxable and nontaxable profits generated by the Company and perceived from companies that have participation" (sic).

11 This practice constitutes a tax crime in Chile according to Art 97 No 4 of the Tax Code.

obtained a permit for a production plant in an area of the municipality in which industrial activities were not allowed. Reyes would have received Ps 20,000,000 ($31,404,570) for the authorisation through the company Carpediem, which was allegedly hired by Ceresita to expedite the permit process.

Ceresita reached an agreement with the Public Prosecution Office for a conditional suspension of the prosecution. Among the conditions imposed on the company were a donation of land located in Recoleta for the construction of a park, the provision of health services and respiratory disease equipment to the commune and the conduct of a soil study. For his part, Mr Reyes (who had been accused of receiving bribes of approximately Ps 114,000,000, ($179,006,050)) was convicted of bribery and falsification of a public instrument in 2013.

6. The next steps: comments on what should be modified, strengthened or addressed

6.1 Introduction

One of the central suggestions in a report of March 2015 of the Presidential Advisory Council against conflicts of Interest, Influence Trafficking and Corruption (known as the '*Engel Report*') was the creation of a new financing system for political parties, predicated upon a profound change in current practices with regard to transparency, accountability and internal democracy. A second suggestion was the creation of effective regulations for financing politics and for market operations, with effective penalties for the most severe transgressions.

In the authors' view, there are, in particular, five specific areas in which existing laws in Chile should be improved, each of which is discussed below:

- the prevention of corruption;
- the regulation of conflicts of interest;
- political system financing policy, in order to strengthen democracy;
- generating greater confidence in the operation of markets; and
- strengthening ethics and citizens' rights though civic education.

6.2 Prevention of corruption

Improvements should be made to the regulatory framework, particularly in the following areas:

- *integrity and the strengthening of municipalities* – so that decisions are taken at the local level with maximum transparency, which would mean increasing levels of citizen participation and limit the exercise of sole discretion by authorities, eg, in the generation and processing of territorial planning instruments that determine (among other things) land use, zoning, equipment, density and the use of public and private space;
- *reform of high-level public sector management system* – this must be consolidated as a professional and merit system on the understanding that there are positions of confidence in each new government. There is a question of the existence of an appropriate mechanism for seeking and selecting people for the highest positions in public institutions, starting with the headquarters,

and working down to the next hierarchical level. In all cases, this system should appoint professionals who meet suitability requirements, who demonstrate an eminently professional trajectory and who value public service;

- *reform of the public procurement system* – because this is a key aspect within the state administration and represents a determining factor in the quality of the services delivered and in the infrastructure that it provides. Good performance of this system promotes the general interest and it is of vital importance that the mechanism and process ensure transparency and efficiency, promoting competition and minimising the risk of corruption;
- *the prosecution of corruption* – among the problems identified are the relatively low penalties for crimes against probity, in comparison both with other countries and with other crimes in Chile. There remain legal gaps in the typology of a number of crimes that are known to other countries and under the UN Convention, eg, abuse of functions, corruption between private and public sectors and influence trafficking. Further, prescription periods are too short for crimes that take a long time to identify, investigate and prosecute;
- *transparency and access to public information* – Law 20.285, Transparency of the Public Function and Access to Information of the State Administration, has meant important progress in matters of transparency for Chile: it has generated incentives so that the exercise of public functions is framed by the principle of probity, facilitating the social control of state power and working as a preventive measure against bad practices and corruption. However, in spite of the progress achieved owing to good performance and to the work of the Council for Transparency, there still remain a number of aspects that can be strengthened and the governing rules improved, in line with international standards and the proposals made by the Presidential Advisory Council;
- *penal responsibility of legal persons* – the model adopted by the law to attach criminal responsibility to legal persons has been internationally criticised. This is because, firstly, the natural person who commits the base crime must have a power of decision or be under the supervision or direction of somebody who has that power; secondly, the crime is of direct benefit to the legal person, and thirdly that the commission of the crime is attributable to non-compliance by the legal person with directors' duties and its non-supervision. In Chile, a number of companies have published a Crime Prevention Model in their websites (where they have them), but it is not known with certainty how many of these are adequate and efficient. To be able to gauge this, it is necessary that the legal system should establish a mandatory system of integrity assurance that incorporates crime prevention models and ethical components and that this is backed up by a verification process;
- *the creation of an evaluation process service for public policies* – under the Budget Law of 2015, the national budget amounts to Ps 33,356 billion ($52,390,675,842,900). The way in which the budget is submitted, in spite of the effort to improve the information on which it is based, makes it difficult

to control and generates asymmetries of information that translate to a lack of an effective system of analysis and global monitoring.

There are a broad body of laws and measures that actually prevent the best use of public expenditure. However, there are other areas in which an estimate pertinent to increased transparency, in addition to an increase in the capacity for efficacy and efficiency of programmes, could be resourced through and monitored by an independent agency. At the same time, results necessary to facilitate access to information on the various programmes is necessary, so that experts become part of the efforts to evaluate the use of public resources.

6.3 Regulation of conflicts of interest

Progress has been achieved in Chile on establishing mechanisms to inhibit interference by the private interests of authorities and public servants with their duties. It is possible to identify gaps and deficiencies that still impede a strict separation between public functions and personal interests. When comparing domestic institutional norms and Chilean legislation with international standards such as those utilised by the OECD, these particular gaps become apparent.

Within the ambit of the aim indicated above, it should be possible to review the causes of incompatibilities or inabilities between public and private sector positions and activities in Chile. Equally, work should be undertaken to:

- strengthen the obligations of the national authorities in terms of a declaration of equity and interest;
- establish a system of blind trust for authorities, such that they do not participate in management of their equity when performing high-level public management functions; and
- improve the regulation of lobbying and the management of private interests in dealing with authorities.

6.4 Political system financing policy

With regard to financing the political system, adequate mechanisms to strengthen democracy must be sought out. In Chile, a number of institutional incentives that influence the performance of politics have contributed to weakening political parties as organisations. These include, among others, the binomial electoral system, whereby two positions are elected by districts, Law No 18.603 of 23 March 1987, The Organic Constitutional Law of Political the Parties, lack of public funding and weak rule enforcement.

For political parties to function well, they must strengthen their role in representing interests – that is, mediating between society and the state. This is vital to the global functioning of a democratic regime.

The efficacy of enforcing rules determines the soundness and depth of democratic government. The weakness of the current control system, low penalty level and the inability to impose them, have generated risks for probity, capturing a collective agenda for particular interests, distorting equity in electoral competence and weakening the overall system and collective character of the political parties.

Moreover, they have contributed to denting the confidence of citizens with regard to politics and its institutions.

6.5 Generating greater confidence in market operations

With regard to the need to strengthen public confidence in the markets as an instrument in the fight against corruption, several bills are currently under discussion in Parliament on market competition and consumer protection. In general, efforts are afoot to discover institutional weaknesses in searching for a better system. However, one of the major issues is to contribute to the recovery of public confidence in the markets and to prevent the occurrence of practices that work against probity. Threefold efforts are being made in this regard:

- firstly, to provide a higher degree of efficacy to regulators and supervisors in controlling improper conduct by the private sector;
- secondly, to strengthen corporate governance of the regulators themselves; and
- thirdly, to promote a higher level of commitment by government in the realm of self-regulation, through a process of internal audit and, externally, by preventing the occurrence of illicit conduct.

6.6 Strengthening of ethics and the rights of citizens through civic education

Lastly, in terms of a comprehensive or holistic approach, the strengthening of ethics and the rights of citizens as tools to combat corruption and to prevent and decrease the incidence of corrupt acts and a lack of probity, an educational system is required which instils civic values of respect, co-existence and the promotion of common wellbeing. Education on the challenges that the country faces must set civic education at the forefront, allowing the preparation of children and young people to face ethical dilemmas in their lives.

7. Conclusion

Progressing a culture of prevention of corruption requires an effort on the part of all institutions and sectors of society to strengthen systems of integrity: viz, all the branches of the state and its respective institutions; parties and political movements; NGOs and civil society; guilds, unions and professional associations; the media; the educational system, and families and citizens. Establishing codes of conduct, regulations and procedures that effectively define and promote anti-corruption principles and values is the most significant national challenge that Chile faces.

This chapter was prepared with the collaboration of lawyers Mr Luis Bates Hidalgo and Ms Isidora Espinosa Aravena. Ms Espinosa collaborated in particular with regard to section 5.

China

Zhaopeng Yang
Haixiao Helen Zhang
Zhong Lun Law Firm

---

1. Overview of anti-corruption in China

1.1 Introduction

Chinese citizens have long voiced concerns about corruption, dating back even as far as the Xia dynasty (2146 BC/BCE-1675 BC/BCE).[1] The struggle between corruption and anti-corruption is woven through the long history of China. Even since the founding of the People's Republic of China (PRC) in 1949, corruption has continued to be one of the primary root causes of social unrest. Over the past 30 years, Chinese Communist Party leaders and government leaders have issued numerous laws, regulations and policies to combat corruption. Particularly in the last couple of years, President Xi Jinping has launched a more effective anti-corruption campaign focusing on reducing very visible extravagant spending and official bribery. Businesses that once served officials, such as extravagant restaurants and nightclubs, now face difficulties surviving. These developments have been welcomed by Chinese citizens.

1.2 A new stance

President Xi's crackdown is unprecedented as it not only targets officials accepting bribes (the demand side) but also concurrently targets businesses offering bribes (the supply side). The bribe payer is often a state-owned enterprise (SOE) or multinational company (MNC) which pays an official or private citizen to gain certain business advantages. As a prime example of President Xi's efforts, the Chinese subsidiary of Glaxo Smith Kline (GSK) was famously fined a record Rmb 492 million for bribing hospitals and doctors to prescribe GSK's medications to their patients (see 5 below). Five of GSK's top executives in China, including Mark Reilly, a United Kingdom national, were convicted of corruption-related crimes and received suspended sentences. This demonstrates the Chinese government's new stance and will to curb corruption on the supply side, even if it means imposing significant penalties on big name MNCs.

To strengthen the implementation of its anti-corruption efforts, the Chinese government created the National Bureau of Corruption Prevention (NBPP) in 2007. The NBPP is subject to the direct supervision of the State Council of the PRC. It is responsible for coordinating national corruption prevention measures, formulating

---

1 http://fanfu.people.com.cn/n/2014/0812/c64371-25453180-2.html.

comprehensive policies, rules and regulations and plans for fighting corruption and supervising and inspecting anti-corruption efforts. In two years, the NCPB established 18 provincial level anti-corruption institutions across 31 provinces and municipalities.

2. Anti-corruption laws and regulations in China

2.1 Introduction

China has two overarching laws that deal with corruption:

- the Criminal Law of the PRC (the Criminal Law of 1997) which, as its name suggests, is a general criminal measure; and
- the Anti-Unfair Competition Law of the PRC (the AUCL of 1993), which is an economic (ie, commercial) law measure.

The Criminal Law concerns bribery payments made to officials, while the AUCL concerns bribery payments in the context of commercial transactions.

Further, a number of rules and regulations are frequently applied in support of these laws. These include:

- the Interim Provisions on Prohibition of Commercial Bribery, effective as of November 1996 (the Interim Provisions);
- the 2007 opinion of the Supreme People's Court (SPC) and Supreme People's Procuratorate (the SPP) on certain issues concerning application of law in handling criminal cases of bribe acceptance (the 2007 Opinion);
- the 2008 opinion of the SPC and the SPP on several issues concerning application of laws for handling criminal cases of commercial bribery (the 2008 Opinion); and
- the 2016 interpretation of the SPC and the SPP on certain issues concerning application of law in handling criminal cases involving embezzlement and bribery (the 2016 Interpretation).

These rules and regulations govern the controversial matter of judicial definition of new types of bribery crime, including commercial bribery.

2.2 The Criminal Law and its interpretation

The Criminal Law criminalises offering bribes by way of "money and property".[2] Based on an authoritative judicial interpretation, "money and property" include cash, cash equivalents, material objects and "property-like benefits", which include material benefits with monetary value, such as renovations, debt forgiveness and other intangible benefits that may be paid, such as memberships, services and travel.[3]

The Criminal Law further categorises bribery and corruption into two groups: accepting bribes and offering bribes.

---

2 Article 389 of the PRC Criminal Law.
3 Article 12 of the 2016 Interpretations.

(a) *Accepting bribes*

It is a criminal offence for a state functionary, an SOE, a state organ or a people's organisation (being a non-party organisation established for a specific purpose, eg, the China Association for Science and Technology), or a 'close relative' of or a person 'closely related' to any of the foregoing parties, to demand or accept bribes and for individuals in commercial dealings to 'take advantage' of his or her position in a company to demand or accept bribes.[4]

Although the Criminal Law does not expressly define the terms 'close relative' or 'closely related', judicial interpretation of the law provides a highly persuasive definition, encompassing spouses, parents, children, siblings, grandparents, grandchildren and other dependents within the scope of these terms.[5]

(b) *Offering bribes*

It is a criminal offence for an individual or an entity to:

- offer bribes to any state functionary, SOE, people's organisation or a 'close relative' of or someone 'closely related to' any of the foregoing parties; or
- serve as an intermediary in the offering of bribes to any of the foregoing parties (ie, the indirect offering of bribes).

(c) *Improper interests and improper commercial interests*

The Criminal Law further stipulates that it is an offence to offer bribes to:

- a legal entity to seek 'improper benefits'; or
- a foreign public official or international public organisation official to seek "improper commercial benefits".[6]

The SPC and the SPP define "improper commercial benefits" as the pursuit of an interest that breaches, or requires any state official to provide any form of assistance or conditions to facilitate the breaching, of any law, regulation, national policy or any regulations promulgated by the State Council.[7]

(d) *Timing of a bribe*

There was previously ambiguity as to whether a bribe offered and/or accepted after the fact, ie, one that was only offered and/or accepted following the receipt of a benefit, constituted an offence. This was because it was unclear whether the recipient of the bribe had been induced by the bribe to deliver certain unlawful benefits. This is now no longer the case. The loophole has been closed as to whether a bribe may be offered or accepted before or after the delivery of illicit benefits.[8] This makes bribery punishable retroactively, and together with a statute of limitation period that ranges between five to 20 years, the closing of this loophole provides law enforcement authorities with much greater power to fight corruption.

---

4 Article 163 of the Criminal Law.
5 Article 11 of the SPC Interpretation on Certain Issues of the Enforcement of the Administrative Procedure Law.
6 Article 164 of the Criminal Law.
7 Article 9 of the 2008 Opinion.
8 Article 13(3) of the 2016 Interpretation.

2.3 The AUCL and its interpretation

The AUCL penalises the act of offering bribes to an individual who is neither a state official nor performs public duties, and the acceptance of bribes by that person. The AUCL deals with bribes relating to commercial activities.

As a matter of the law applicable to commercial bribery, it is an offence for a commercial operator to offer bribes in the form of money or material, or by any other means, to make a purchase or sale. Any 'under the table' arrangement, such as a kickback or rebate not recorded in the books[9] constitutes an offer to bribe, and any acceptance thereof constitutes an acceptance of a bribe.

Consistent with one of the general principles of corporate law, an employer will be held accountable for an act of bribery committed by its employees as if that employer committed the bribery itself, unless the employer can prove otherwise.

(a) The AUCL and adapting to business reality

The AUCL was amended in November 2017 (effective as of January 2018) (the 2017 amendment) to adapt to the dynamic realities of business. Prior to the 2017 amendment, the threshold standard for commercial bribery focused on bribery having been committed for the purpose making a purchase or sale. The 2017 amendment expands the standard beyond simple purchases or sales, penalising illicit acts committed for the purpose of obtaining "transaction opportunities" and "competitive advantage". The PRC judiciary interprets the term "transaction opportunities" literally where any transaction or opportunity will fall within the scope of this definition. The term "competitive advantage" encompasses an even broader meaning. A party who provides any form of benefit to another party in order to gain a certain advantage, whether that advantage is direct or indirect, will fall within the scope of a "competitive advantage".

The 2017 changes capture a much broader array of actions that may constitute commercial bribery, so that schemes designed to offer or accept a bribe but which deliberately circumvent the actual making of a purchase or sale may be punishable as an offence. In fact, this increases the autonomy of the PRC's law enforcement authorities and judiciary, who may, under the AUCL as amended, exercise greater discretion in determining what constitutes "transaction opportunities" and "competitive advantage". Historically practised activities that have been at the core of corruption in China in maintaining relationships and providing gestures of good will, such as feasts, gifts and favours (eg, helping a child to gain admission to a prestigious college) are now expected to be examined closely to determine whether bribery may be involved. This is a significant advance in the PRC's efforts to fight corruption.

As previously explained, 'under the table' arrangements, such as a kickback or a rebate not recorded in the books, constitutes bribery. The 2017 amendment to the AUCL removed this negative connotation and instead expressly recognises the reality of business that giving discounts to a counterparty or paying commissions to

---

9 As explained at 2.3(a) below, the AUCL was amended in November 2017 so that discounts and commissions are lawful if they are properly recorded in the books.

a middleman is a necessity in completing business deals. So long as these perks are truthfully recorded in the books, they are acceptable business practices and so do not constitute bribery.

3. International anti-corruption treaties applicable in China

In addition to its domestic laws and regulations, China relies on international treaty commitments to combat corruption, both domestically and internationally.

At the international level, China became a signatory to the United Nations (UN) Convention Against Corruption of 2004 (UNCAC) in October 2005, and the UN Convention Against Transnational Organized Crime of 2000 (UNCATOC) in December 2000.

At the regional level, the members of the Asia-Pacific Economic Cooperation (APEC), at China's initiative, issued the Beijing Declaration on Fighting Corruption (BDFC) and established the APEC Network of Anti-Corruption Authorities and Law Enforcement Agencies (both in 2014).

Furthermore, at both a global and a regional level, China has entered into extradition and judicial assistance treaties with over 70 countries.[10]

3.1 The UNCAC

(a) Implementation

Recognising that corruption is not only a regional issue but also a transnational epidemic afflicting all societies and economies, the UNCAC devises five policy mechanisms in an attempt to stem this tide:

- prevention of corruption;
- criminalisation and law enforcement;
- international judicial and law enforcement cooperation;
- asset retrieval; and
- performance supervision.

The aim of UNCAC is to promote and strengthen diverse various measures and resources in order to:

- prevent and combat corruption more effectively and forcefully;
- facilitate and support relevant international cooperation and technical assistance; and
- promote incorruptible accountability mechanisms for public affairs and property administration.

In October 2005, the 18th meeting of the 10th Standing Committee (Standing Committee) of the National People's Congress of China (NPC) unanimously voted for and approved China joining the UNCAC.

Shortly after its entry, China established a ministerial coordinating body to handle affairs pertaining to the UNCAC. Member units of this body include the SPC,

10 www.fmprc.gov.cn/web/ziliao_674904/tytj_674911/wgdwdjdsfhzty_674917/t1215630.shtml.

the SPP and other high-ranking departments of the central government. The Criminal Law and the Criminal Procedure Law of 1996 were amended in June 2006 and the Standing Committee adopted the Law of the People's Republic of China on Anti-Money Laundering (the Anti-Money Laundering Law) in October 2006. The intention of both sets of provisions was to adapt Chinese law to the terms and the spirit of the UNCAC. The Sixth Amendment of June 2006 to the Criminal Law expanded the category of serious crimes to include the crime of money laundering, which encompasses bribery, crimes of destroying the financial order and financial fraud.[11] The Criminal Procedure Law as amended incorporates a special confiscation procedure[12] for illegal gains that are in line with relevant provisions of the UNCAC.[13] Following the approach of the UNCAC, the Anti-Money Laundering Law targets not only financial but also non-financial institutions.

(b) *The International Association of Anti-Corruption Authorities*

As part of a further effort to fight corruption at the international level, the International Association of Anti-Corruption Authorities (IAACA) was established by the UN in Vienna in October 2006 and has its headquarters in Beijing. The IAACA is an independent, non-governmental and non-political organisation that aims to promote the implementation of the UNCAC, provide international assistance to signatory nations' anti-corruption authorities and promote international cooperation to facilitate evidence collection, investigation, detention, the pursuit of fugitives and the confiscation of assets.

China is a founding member of and major participant in the IAACA, which has served for China as a platform for sharing anti-corruption experience, enhancing the possibility and practicability of criminal cooperation that may help China in extraditing corrupt criminals back to the country to face justice and retrieving unlawful gains. Being an initiator of the IAACA reflects the determination of the Chinese government to take an active part in the global anti-corruption cause and demonstrates its willingness to make a concrete contribution to this endeavour.

3.2 The UNCATOC

The UNCATOC initially targeted such issues as the trafficking of women and children and the illicit manufacture and sale of firearms. Over time, the scope of the UNCATOC was expanded to combat crimes relating to terrorist activities, money laundering and corruption. With regard to corruption, efforts under the UNCATOC are concentrated on the criminalisation of public corruption and derivative corporate liability and the development of measures to prevent, investigate and punish the perpetrators of public corruption.

In August 2003, the Standing Committee of the NPC approved accession to the UNCATOC, by virtue of which China's efforts could be facilitated in conducting bilateral, regional and international cooperation to prevent and crack down on

---

11 Article 16 of the Sixth Amendment to the Criminal Law.
12 Article 280 of the Criminal Procedure Law.
13 Article 54(1) of the UNACC.

organised crime as well as corruption. Under this legal framework, China could join with other member countries in combating crimes of money laundering and bribery, and strengthen bonds with those countries in implementing comprehensive prevention measures against a multiplicity of organised crimes.

3.3 The Beijing Declaration on Fighting Corruption

The BDFC, the first international anti-corruption declaration drafted by China, was approved at an unofficial meeting of leaders of APEC in November 2014. The adoption of the BDFC clearly demonstrates China's initiative and aspirations to strengthen regional cooperation and its willingness to join forces with APEC member countries in jointly fighting corruption.

The BDFC has formalised the framework of cooperation between APEC member countries, greatly supplementing international treaties to which those countries are signatories. In practice, the BDFC mandates APEC member countries not only to cooperate (with regard to which international treaties are often ineffective, resulting in uncoordinated and perhaps even half-hearted efforts) but also to follow a set of procedures aimed at managing corruption issues spanning the region.

More specifically, the BDFC prescribes three sets of policy frameworks:

- information sharing;
- judicial cooperation; and
- a law enforcement network.

With regardect to information sharing, member countries should jointly establish a secretariat to maintain daily operations and provide a vehicle for member countries to share information and experience. With regard to judicial cooperation, each member country should respect and enforce each other's judgments or decisions of other member countries or decisions in its own pursuit of fugitives and the retrieval of illicit gains. With regard to the law enforcement network, member countries should develop and promote anti-corruption manuals and other new types of anti-corruption tool for each jurisdiction. These frameworks are expected to streamline the transnational pursuit of fugitives in a less bureaucratic and less costly manner.

3.4 Bilateral treaties combating corruption

On 4 May 1987, China signed a Civil and Commercial Judicial Assistance Treaty with France, China's first such agreement concluded with a foreign country.[14] By January 2017, China had signed judicial assistance treaties, asset retrieval and sharing treaties, extradition treaties and treaties to combat 'three forces' with 70 countries. As part of these anti-corruption endeavours, China has strenuously negotiated and cooperated with the United States, Canada and Australia in particular, because corrupt officials and relevant personnel tend to treat these countries as 'asylum paradise' jurisdictions.

14 www.fmprc.gov.cn/web/ziliao_674904/tytj_674911/wgdwdjdsfhzty_674917/t1215630.shtml (in Chinese).

(a) Cooperation between China and the US

At the time of writing, China and the US had made preliminary arrangements for judicial cooperation and the establishment of joint processes for combating corruption and pursuing transnational fugitives.

In May 1998, the two countries established a Joint Liaison Group on Law Enforcement Cooperation (JLG). The scope of its work encompasses economic crimes, anti-money laundering, illegal immigration, anti-terrorism and drug prohibition. In practice, the JLG has formed a Repatriation and Fugitive Working Group and an Anti-Corruption Working Group, along with other special working groups.

The working mechanism of the JLG is regular meetings and negotiations pursuant to which bilateral cooperation on anti-corruption endeavours can be achieved. On 19 June 2000, the two countries signed the Agreement between the United States of America and the Government of the People's Republic of China Mutual Legal Assistance in Criminal Matters, which took effect on 8 March 2001. Pursuant to this agreement, the countries have conducted effective and solid cooperation on criminal judicial assistance, investigation assistance, evidence provision, intelligence sharing, retrieval of illegal assets and the supervision and pursuit of criminals. On 29 July 2006, they issued the Joint Statement by the Ministry of Public Security of the PRC and the Department of Justice of the United States of America on Further Strengthening Law Enforcement Cooperation, which emphasises that they should deepen their bilateral law enforcement cooperation.

In one of the most significant recent Sino-US anti-corruption developments, China concluded an agreement with the US in June 2014, pursuant to the latter's Foreign Account Tax Compliance Act 2010 (the FATCA). Under this agreement, China may request the US to provide it with financial information on Chinese nationals possessed by US-based institutions. This has effectively provided China with a means of tracing and tracking the movement of assets from China to the US arising out of corrupt behaviour. At least in theory, therefore, China has succeeded in reducing the ability of corrupt officials to exploit the US as a 'safe haven' by corrupt officials. The development of China's efforts in this regard in the next few years will be critical to the effectiveness of the FATCA.

(b) Cooperation between China and Canada

In April 1996, China and Canada signed a landmark memorandum of understanding that detailed cooperation mechanisms and procedures to fight jointly crimes relating to money-laundering, terrorism, cross-border criminal activities and trafficking. This is the practice framework under which the two countries have fought the relevant crimes to date.

In December 2009, after many years of diplomacy and negotiation, and after China had attempted but failed for many years to extradite high-profile fugitives from Canada, the two countries finally issued a joint declaration to reinforce their mutual cooperation on the extradition of fugitives and the retrieval of illicit assets. This joint declaration finally established a previously long-absent foundation for extraditing high-profile officials from Canada to China to face trial. In June 2010, a memorandum of understanding was signed between the Ministry of Public Security of China and the Royal Canadian Mounted Police to give this joint declaration 'teeth', putting its spirit into actual practice by Canada's police forces. This memorandum provided China with a channel to negotiate with Canadian institutions the recovery of potentially illicit assets located in Canada and owned by corrupt Chinese officials. If China successfully recovers any such assets, the relevant corrupt officials who own them will be unable to use them at will. Thus, Canada is no longer a 'safe haven' jurisdiction in this regard. This is a major milestone and a breakthrough for China in its fight against corruption.

(c) Cooperation between China and Australia

By comparison with the US and Canada, the history of judicial cooperation with Australia is much shorter and its scope and depth are also weaker than in those jurisdictions.

On 3 April 2006, the two countries concluded the Agreement on Mutual Legal Assistance in Criminal Matters between the Commonwealth of Australia and the People's Republic of China, which took effect on 28 March 2007.

It has been more than 10 years since two countries signed the Treaty on Extradition Between Australia and the People's Reopublic of China on 6 September 2007. At the time of writing, this treaty has not come into effect because it has failed to pass through Australia's parliamentary ratification process. In the light of this, repatriation, persuasion to return or recourse to other places is the main platform for cooperation between the two countries.

4. Competent authorities regulating crimes of corruption

As discussed previously, corruption in China can be classified into two types, namely commercial bribery in the business field and corruption and bribery in the political field, which can be determined by the status of and posts held by corrupt officials, the severity of the alleged corruption and other traits of the people who commit corruption. Further, these two types of corruption can be regulated and punished by different authorities.

4.1 The State Administration of Industry and Commerce (SAIC)

The SAIC and its corresponding local administrations have the power and authority to investigate, enforce and prosecute commercial bribery cases that are not of the highest level of criminal severity in administrative proceedings.

These authorities have the right to make enquiries of relevant persons of a company and third party witnesses, demand the disclosure of relevant documents, carry out onsite inspections, and seal or seize material evidence. The SAIC can decide to impose an administrative penalty; if, however, the company fails to pay the penalty, the SAIC will need to apply to the people's court to enforce the penalty.

If a company offers bribes for the purpose of selling or purchasing goods or services but has not triggered any criminal liability, the SAIC has power to confiscate the illegal income from the bribery and impose a government fine of between Rmb 100,000 and Rmb 3,000,000, which is much more severe than the previous level of fine (Rmb 10,000-200,000) stipulated in the original AUCL in 1993.

4.2 The Public Security Bureau (PSB)

Where commercial bribery constitutes a crime and is committed by people who are neither public officials nor officials of SOEs, the SAIC will transfer the case to the PSB for further criminal investigation.

In reality, some cases are complicated because they involve, on the one hand, public officials and/or officials of SOEs and, on the other, people who are neither public officials nor officials of SOEs. In these circumstances, the principal crime will be dealt with by the PSB pursuant to the Criminal Procedure Law and its corresponding regulations, and the PSB will have the principal jurisdiction to investigate the case and the local People's Procuratorate will provide assistance. If, however, the principal crime is to be dealt with by the People's Procuratorate, the PSB will provide the necessary assistance.

4.3 The Supreme People's Procuratorate (SPP)

In accordance with the Constitution of the PRC (the PRC Constitution) and the Criminal Procedure Law, the SPP and its local procuratorates are the legal supervision authorities. Anti-corruption or anti-graft is the main task of the SPP and its local entities.

Although many authorities enjoy the power to regulate and punish corruption, the SPP and its local entities are the most fundamental and effective in combating it. The PRC Constitution bestows powers on the SPP and its local entities to supervise other governmental agencies and public officials. In another words, the procuratorate authorities represent the nation and its people in implementing compulsory legal powers of supervision. Bringing corrupt officials to justice is by its nature, the most powerful form of impeachment-type supervision against those who abuse their powers in such a way as to give rise to opportunities to commit crimes.

The Criminal Procedure Law stipulates that corruption and graft crimes shall be handled by procuratorate authorities. This is because, on the one hand, they implement superior-subordinate leadership between the judicial and law enforcement authorities and, on the other, they are independent from any other governmental agency, thus excluding or reducing possibilities of interference from other institutions.

4.4 The Central Commission for Discipline Inspection and the Ministry of Supervision

The Central Commission for Discipline Inspection of the Communist Party of China (CCDI) is the inspection and supervision authority for the Communist Party (CPC or the Party).

The main tasks dealt by the CCDI are:

- to maintain the Constitution of the CPC (CPC Constitution) and other rules;
- to reinforce Party infrastructure;
- to inspect the Party's policies and their enforcement processes;
- to educate Party members in matters of discipline;
- to make decisions upholding Party discipline; and
- to inspect and handle major and complex cases where it has been alleged that a Party unit or member has breached the CPC Constitution, or other Party rules.

In March 1993, in accordance with decisions made by the Central Communist Party and the State Council, the CCDI and the Ministry of Supervision (MOS) were merged into one working office and classified as a direct institution of the Central Government. The MOS is also an administrative supervision department led by the State Council. Following the merger, the MOS's local supervision authorities continue to conduct supervision work under the joint leadership of their local governments and superior supervision authorities.

5. Review of anti-corruption cases

The GlaxoSmithKline commercial bribery case is the most significant anti-corruption case in China in recent years.

On 28 June 2013, the police in Changsha in Hunan Province announced investigations into alleged economic crimes committed by GlaxoSmithKline (GSK) subsidiary GlaxoSmithKline (China) (GSK China). On 11 July 2013, the Ministry of Public Security (MPS) confirmed that it had ordered police departments in a number of cities to investigate GSK China executives for serious economic crimes, including commercial bribery and embezzlement. Shortly afterwards, GSK pledged to cooperate fully with the Chinese authorities and confirmed that the general manager of GSK China, a British citizen, would return to China to cooperate with the investigations. On 14 May 2014, the official Xinhua News Agency reported that the bribery investigation of GSK China had been completed and that the case had been transferred to prosecutors for official charges to be laid.

On 19 September 2014, the Intermediate People's Court of Changsha tried GSK China and its managers. The court convicted GSK China on that day of offering money or property to non-government personnel in order to obtain improper commercial gains. There was solid evidence that company had paid hundreds of millions of pounds sterling in bribes, via travel agencies, to doctors, healthcare officials and hospitals to use its products. The court sentenced GSK China to pay a fine of Rmb 3 billion, while the individual executives who had been convicted were sentenced to between two and three years' imprisonment, suspended by between two and four years.

The GSK case had a profound effect on big business. It not only shocked the pharmaceutical industry but also shook all multinational companies operating in China into overhauling their anti-corruption compliance programmes. The Chinese government struck with an iron fist to show its ambition and toughness in combating corruption and graft in the business world.

6. Next steps for anti-corruption in China

Eradicating corruption is not a linear effort. It needs cooperation and coordination from start to finish. It is essential to form an anti-corruption 'ecosystem' in which supervision, prevention, control and punishment mechanisms can operate smoothly.

Having a supervision mechanism means forming a supervisory infrastructure under which the public may have a direct channel to report corruption to the authorities, while the institution that receives and investigates complaints of corruption must be independent and highly authoritative.

Having a prevention mechanism means forming a basic anti-corruption system under which asset reporting and other corruption prevention procedures will be adopted and implemented, both for public officials and for companies. Records of the offer and acceptance of payments must be regularly submitted to the authorities, guaranteeing them free access to monitor acts of offer and acceptance involving companies.

Having a control mechanism means forming a swift and effective law enforcement team by which evidence can be collected and analysed in a short time and any suspect can be detained before fleeing to other countries.

Having a punishment mechanism means regulating procedures pursuant to which penalties are handed down, whether by administrative authorities or the courts, and strengthening cooperation between the various enforcement authorities. Each authority must have a clear jurisdiction, work according to clear procedures and exercise powers of punishment within their jurisdiction. Further, penalties must be made public, and swiftly, for the purposes of both deterrence and education.

With specific regard to commercial bribery, it is necessary to enact an anti-commercial bribery law in which the acts of both persons offering bribes and those accepting them will be expressly, clearly and consistently regulated by law. Moreover, the law should also expand the its scope to regulate those who offer and accept bribes to all participants in the business world, not merely business operators, in order to keep pace with an ever-changing business world and patterns of commerce.

From the administrative perspective, administrative authorities must, when enforcing laws, not only abide by the applicable laws and regulations but also further improve their law enforcement measures so as to perform their duties better in cracking down on commercial bribery. This may be done in four ways.

- First, the authorities should establish a supervision mechanism specifically targeting those fields in which bribery regularly occurs, such as the construction, medical and hygiene industries. For such fields of endeavour, the authorities should establish corresponding approval and admission thresholds, and formulate strict industry regulations against commercial bribery.
- Secondly, the authorities should establish a coordinating platform through which commercial bribery cases could be handled smoothly by a major agency, thus avoiding inter-agency conflict or cross-management by different agencies, which can lead to inefficiency and a situation in which no one agency steps in to crack down on commercial bribery.
- Thirdly, the authorities should establish a system of incentives in support of public supervision. Owing to the common interests shared by the demand and supply sides of bribery, both sides may present a common front in order to avoid discovery by the authorities. Thus, the authorities could give rewards to those who report facts showing commercial bribery, thus enhancing the effective deployment of powers of public supervision.
- Fourthly, the authorities should construct a 'social credit' database. Commercial bribery, by its nature, is a dishonest act aimed at inducing the pursuit of improper interests. A social credit database should be constructed

to record the credit status of companies and associated individuals. Once a company or individual is caught with evidence showing the commission of an act of commercial bribery, the database would record the relevant information and make it available to the public. This would directly exert a bad image of the parties involved and make it difficult or impossible for them to do business later on.

Czech Republic

Jitka Logesová
General Prosecutor's Office (Czech Republic)
Kristýna Del Maschio
Filip Široký
Kinstellar

1. The history of corruption and the perception of society in the Czech Republic

If you don't rob from the state, you rob your family.

This axiom to a great extent expressed the attitude of many citizens of the former Czechoslovakia during more than 40 years of the communist regime. Corruption was a characteristic of the communist system in the Soviet Union prior to its fall in 1989 and, as a satellite State, Czechoslovakia was no exception.

The main reason for corruption was quite straightforward back then – shortages in almost every aspect of life created an environment in which people had to look for unofficial ways to satisfy their needs. Thanks to the centrally planned economy, the distribution of goods and services was in hands of a few bureaucrats, who could easily cut one off from resources. Moreover, the general public perceived any part of the administrative apparatus as an oppressive body. The state was considered an enemy of its citizens and, as such, small-scale misuse and theft of public property became part of passive opposition to communism.[1] Altogether, this situation created a perfect storm for corruption – mainly in the form of bribery – as people considered paying a 'little extra' to behave normally in order to get at least some, or better, goods or services; such behaviour was therefore generally accepted during the communist era.

After the fall of the Czechoslovak communist regime in 1989, corruption continued to prevail. People did not change overnight, and the general enthusiasm triggered by the Velvet Revolution did little to affect the corrupt practices that were so rooted in society. Instead, the transition to a free market economy caused corruption to shift from its primary sphere of small- to mid-scale corruption in general sales and services to mid- to large-scale corruption in the area of state administrative services.[2] The process of post-communist transformation to a market economy in the later Czech Republic was accompanied by a series of harsh legal, economic and institutional measures that – with more than 25 years of hindsight – certainly opened another door for corruption in the republic. One example of such harsh measures was the privatisation of enterprises through the distribution of vouchers to Czech citizens, who could subsequently exchange them for shares in

1 Lubomír Lizal & Evžen Kočenda, *State of Corruption in Transition: The Case of the Czech Republic* (2001) 2(2) Emerging Markets Review 138–160.

2 Lubomír Lizal & Evžen Kočenda, *The Paradox of Czech Crusaders: Will They Ever Learn the Corruption Lesson?* CERGE-EI Working Paper No 171 (2001, CERGE-EI, Praguee/W Davidson Institute, University of Michigan Business School/CEPR, London).

companies. Although the voucher bidding process was meant to eliminate corruption and give individuals an equal chance at acquiring Czech state assets, voucher privatisation was instead a window of opportunity for corrupt practices. Along with the non-transparent funding of newly-established political parties and associated corruption scandals that emerged from time to time and, in some cases, brought down governments, one could guess why the expression term 'wild '90s' is used when talking about this period.

These days are not as wild as the 1990s, but this does not mean that corruption has been extinguished. It is more subtle and more sophisticated but still very widespread among the Czech population. While in the past the level of corruption in the Czech Republic could be attributed mainly to the communist legacy and the loosening of the economic system in the 1990s, today's corruption risks rest mainly in the entanglement of corruption with business and politics as well as in the increasing oligarchisation of politics and the media. On the other hand, a clear shift can be seen nowadays in how society as a whole approaches corruption. Corruption has become a political theme that is discussed among the general public and perceived by that public as amoral behaviour rather than as the status quo. Furthermore, various social networks play an important role in this process.

The shift is also reflected in the growth of anti-corruption legislation. One recent example is Act No 340/2015, on the Register of Contracts, as amended, which came into force in July 2016. This establishes a register for contracts (an online electronic information database) in which contracts involving public entities, resources and property are published. The aim of the Contract Register is to ensure that details concerning publicly-related contracts are in the public domain to ensure openness and reduce the risk of corruption in their awarding and performance. Another recent example is an amendment to Act No 253/2008, on Selected Measures against Legitimisation of Proceeds of Crime and Financing of Terrorism (the AML Act) adopted in 2016, under which Czech legal entities are required to disclose information about their ultimate owners or persons having significant control over them in a beneficial ownership registry. However, the most significant change relating to anti-corruption laws remains Act No 418/2011 Coll. on the Criminal Liability of Corporations and Proceedings against Them, which took effect on 1 January 2012 and both establishes broad criminal liability of corporations and covers corruption-related criminal offences.

Looking at the statistics, the Czech Republic was ranked as the 47th least corrupt country out of 176 countries in Transparency International's *Corruption Perceptions Index 2016*, which serves as one of the benchmarks of the level of perceived corruption in the countries surveyed, with scores ranging from 0 (very corrupt) to 100 (very clean). The Czech Republic's corruption ranking averaged 45.86 from 1996 until 2016, reaching a high of 57 in 2011 and a record low of 25 in 1996.

Anti-corruption enforcement seems to be on the rise, with several high-profile investigations emerging during the last few years. Nevertheless, the country still lacks large-scale corruption-related criminal convictions and there are numerous instances of bribery or domestic corruption by officials that are not dealt with effectively by prosecutors or the courts. However, there are several large-scale criminal matters in relation to corruption-related crimes, such as violations of public tender rules or the misuse of European Union (EU) and domestic grants that are currently being investigated.

2. International treaties to which the Czech Republic is a party

The Czech Republic is a signatory to several international anti-corruption conventions, most significantly:

- the United Nations Convention against Corruption (2004, in force in the Czech Republic since 29 November 2013), which is the only legally binding universal anti-corruption instrument;
- the United Nations Convention against Transnational Organised Crime (2000, in force in the Czech Republic since 24 September 2013);
- the Organisation for Economic Co-operation and Development (OECD) Convention on Combating Bribery of Foreign Public Officials in International Business Transactions (1998, in force in the Czech Republic since 21 March 2000) (the OECD Convention);
- the Criminal Law Convention on Corruption of the Council of Europe (1999, in force in the Czech Republic since 1 July 2002); and the Civil Law Convention on Corruption of the Council of Europe (1999, in force in the Czech Republic since 1 January 2004).

A number of EU legal instruments also bind the Czech Republic. These include, for example the Convention against Corruption Involving Officials of the European Communities or Officials of Member States of the European Union of 25 June 1997 and Council Framework Decision 2003/568/JHA on combating corruption in the private sector, which was ratified by the Czech Republic on 31 July 2003.

Unfortunately, there are not many statistics available that would provide relevant data on the implementation and actual enforcement of the international anti-corruption treaties adopted by the Czech Republic. In general, international anti-corruption treaties are transposed into specific provisions of existing laws, and as such become part of the national laws. For example, in line with the OECD Convention, which requires each signatory to criminalise the bribery of foreign public officials, an amendment to the Criminal Code was adopted in 2008 which extended the definition of 'public official' in relation to bribery offences.

The OECD regularly issues reports the main goal of which is to evaluate particular challenges to and achievements of countries pertaining to corruption of foreign public officials; these reports also provide general insights and comments on the status of corruption in the respective countries. The latest report, *Implementing the OECD Anti-Bribery Convention, Phase 4 Report: Czech Republic*, was issued in June 2017. With regard to the positives evaluated in the report, the OECD considers the use of mutual legal assistance requests from foreign jurisdictions to detect foreign bribery cases as a potentially good practice. The OECD also highlights initiatives to establish a beneficial ownership register and contract register mentioned at 1 above. On the other hand, the OECD expresses concerns about the dearth of prosecution of foreign bribery cases in the Czech Republic. In fact, 17 years after ratification of the

OECD Convention, not a single case of foreign bribery has been prosecuted. This is a cause for concern for the OECD, owing to the export-oriented nature of the Czech economy and the fact that Czech exports include high-risk sectors for bribery, such as machinery and defence *matériel*, where many of the Czech Republic's export destinations for arms are at high risk of corruption. The OECD also comments on the Czech legal system's lack of whistleblower protection.[3] According to Transparency International reports, the Czech Republic still ranks among countries with little or no enforcement of the OECD Convention.[4] This is definitely not a very positive ranking for the Czech Republic, and although indisputable progress in the adoption of various anti-corruption laws and implementation of international treaties can be seen, there is still a long road ahead.

3. The concept of 'corruption' in the Czech Republic

Czech anti-corruption legislation is mainly embodied in criminal law regulations, in particular the Criminal Code. In addition, a number of other statutes contain obligations in connection with anti-corruption, such as the anti-money laundering and public procurement laws.

The Criminal Code recognises several crimes of corruption, including not only bribery but also other related crimes of corruption, such as abuse of office by a public official, violation of the obligation of trust and various public procurement crimes. With regard to bribery, the Criminal Code defines a 'bribe' in a manner similar to that by which the Civil Law Convention on Corruption defines the term 'corruption',[5] ie, as an unjust benefit consisting of direct material enrichment or other advantage provided to the bribed person or to another person with the bribed person's consent to which they are otherwise not entitled. There are no minimum thresholds for considering such benefit to be a bribe, which means that facilitation payments are not allowed at all. The Criminal Code recognises bribery in both the public and private sectors – the Criminal Code's terminology uses the phrases "in the public interest" and "in connection with business". The only difference between public and private bribery is that more stringent sanctions apply in relation to public sector bribery, as this form of corruption constitutes an aggravated crime.

Czech law recognises both active bribery (giving a bribe) and passive bribery (accepting one). The Criminal Code also recognises another offence: that of accepting a bribe in order to influence a public official, which is a form of indirect bribery. As mentioned previously, bribery of foreign public officials is punishable in the same manner as bribery of domestic public officials under the Criminal Code, although there is no specific criminal offence for it. Instead, in order to conform to the OECD Convention, lawmakers decided to extend the definition of 'public official' in relation to bribery offences so that it now also covers persons who:

---

3 Available at www.oecd.org/daf/anti-bribery/Czech-Republic-Phase-4-Report-ENG.pdf.

4 Available at www.transparency.org/exporting_corruption/Czech%20Repub.

5 Article 2 of the convention defines 'corruption' as requesting, offering, giving or accepting, directly or indirectly, a bribe or any other undue advantage or prospect thereof, which distorts the proper performance of any duty or behaviour required of the recipient of the bribe, the undue advantage or the prospect thereof.

- have a position in a legislative, judicial or other public authority of a foreign country;
- act or are employed in an international judicial authority or in an international or supranational organisation; and act in the capacity of a legal person in which the Czech Republic or a foreign country has a decisive influence, such as a state-run company.

The risk of corruption is always most prevalent where public funds are involved. Where a company is owned by an individual, that person wants to ensure that the company's funds are used effectively, but this is not necessarily the case with public funds. A politician entrusted by the people with managing public property will not see any additional personal enrichment if he or she manages it effectively, apart from receiving a monthly salary, unless that politician finds illegal ways of profiting from the management and distribution of public funds. This is why state aid – including, of course, EU subsidies and public procurement – is the most prone to corruption.

Under Czech law, a person, who intentionally conceals or distorts information or provides false information when seeking a subsidy or subvention, commits the crime of subsidy fraud. Ever since the Czech Republic acceded to the European Union in 2004, a substantial number of high profile cases have involved potential misuse of EU funds. However, in the majority of these cases, a final decision is still pending or prosecution was terminated before any decisions could be delivered.

To ensure that not only subsidy fraud but all various types of criminal conduct related to embezzling public funds are punishable, the Czech legal framework also includes the general crime of breach of trust.

Furthermore, another corruption-related issue that is worth mentioning – and which is currently a hot topic of discussion in the Czech Republic – is the giving of expert opinions. Whenever a factual question arises in proceedings that cannot be determined without an expert opinion, an expert in the relevant field is chosen from a list to provide a report. In some cases this report may be the most critical piece of evidence and at times could turn a case around. Because of this the temptation exists to offer an expert a bribe in exchange for a report that favours the briber's side. This system often leads to the public prosecutor and defendant serving new expert opinions on each other until the court calls for a truly 'independent' expert. This is exactly what happened in the case of Roman Janoušek, the infamous Czech businessman and lobbyist who intentionally hit a woman while driving, claiming afterwards he did not see her. The expert reports produced by the lobbyist's attorney and the public prosecutor offered completely different opinions – Janoušek's expert, unsurprisingly, opined that he could not have seen the victim. Both sides then procured new experts, who again proffered opposing opinions, prompting the court to call in its own expert, who finally stated in his report that Janoušek had to have seen the victim, leading to Janoušek's conviction and imprisonment.

4. Regulations and relevant authorities

4.1 Regulations

Unlike many Western countries, the Czech Republic does not have any specialised statute dealing with corruption or bribery. Instead, Czech lawmakers have chosen a different approach: all criminal conduct is covered by the Criminal Code, including all corruption-related crimes. While in past, countless amendments made it almost impossible to navigate through the previous Criminal Code, the present Criminal Code, which has been in place since 2009, is more transparent.

The second most important piece of criminal legislation has, unfortunately, not yet been modernised. The Code of Criminal Procedure currently in effect dates from 1964 (ie, from the communist era). The Ministry of Justice, together with academics and practitioners, are currently working on its recodification. It is unclear, however, when a new version is likely to be enacted.

In order to meet the objectives of applicable international treaties, the Czech Republic recently adopted a new piece of legislation,, Act 418/2011 Coll., on Corporate Criminal Liability (the 2011 Act), which imposes criminal liability on corporate entities.

Under the 2011 Act, corporations (or any other legal entities) can be criminally liable for all crimes covered by the Criminal Code, unless specifically excluded. The crimes that are excluded are mostly those that only an individual can commit due to their nature (eg, assault or bigamy). The criminal liability of legal entities does not pose an obstacle to the liability of individuals; both a company and an individual may be convicted of the same criminal conduct. A widely discussed issue is the possibility of corporate entities discharging themselves from criminal liability by employing a compliance defence. The 2011 Act states that:

a corporate entity can discharge itself from criminal liability if it has implemented all necessary measures that could be reasonably required in order to prevent the crime.

This especially gives rise to the question of what the phrase "necessary measures that could be reasonably required" really means. However, the courts have so far provided only a hint, ruling that a corporation's compliance programme must not be merely on paper; rather, it is the company's culture that really counts.

Even though criminal liability has been widely discussed among academics, attorneys, compliance officers and CEOs since the 2011 Act was adopted, its impact has not been very significant, especially due to the ridiculously low fines that the courts have imposed on companies so far. Thus, the Czech Republic still awaits the exemplary conviction of a company.

4.2 Relevant authorities

The investigation of offences of corruption is entrusted to police authorities under the supervision of state prosecutors. Unlike France or the United Kingdom, the Czech Republic does not have any specialised anti-corruption branch of the public prosecutor's office or any special office of this kind at all.

Where the police are concerned, in addition to the special anti-corruption and financial crime departments that can be found in the police administration, there is also a special body that has been established in order to fight corruption and other organised crime: the National Centre against Organised Crime (the Centre). This new body was created in 2016 by merging two special police forces – the Anti-corruption Office and the Office for Combatting Organised Crime. The creation of this new body has been plagued by serious doubts, as it was part of a wider reorganisation of the police in general that was criticised by many state officials. Nevertheless, the new Centre is currently up and running, with four crime units under its competence: organised crime, cybercrime, corruption and terrorism.

Final conviction and sentencing are solely in the hands of the courts. In the Czech Republic, three court branches are generally recognised: general, administrative and constitutional. The administrative branch consists of the Regional Administrative Courts and the Supreme Administrative Court, while the Constitutional Court is the only one covering the whole country.

The general branch consists of the District and Regional Courts, two High Courts and one Supreme Court. Each first instance court is internally divided into departments, one of these being a criminal department; criminal cases are therefore judged by special judges with a certain expertise in the field. Basically, an alleged crime is tried by the District Court, subject to possible appeal to the relevant Regional Court, but if the crime is more serious the Regional Court becomes the court of first instance, while a possible appeal lies to one of the High Courts. Following an unsuccessful appeal to either of these courts, there remains, in certain circumstances, the possibility of an extraordinary appeal to the Supreme Court.

5. The role of NGOs in the fight against corruption

A very substantial amount of work in preventing corruption is carried out by a number of non-governmental organisations (NGOs). The most recognised NGOs in the Czech Republic are Transparency International and Reconstruction of the State (*Rekonstrukce státu* in Czech). Reconstruction of the State was founded as a result of the highly corrupt environment in the totalitarian era and the perception of corruption after the 1989 Velvet Revolution and the room for improvement that was recognised in relation to laws aimed at fighting and preventing corruption, money laundering and the financing of terrorism.

Reconstruction of the State devised nine essential goals from these areas and pressured representatives across the political spectrum before the 2013 parliamentary elections to pledge support for future statutes aimed at meeting those nine objectives. Since then, five of those goals have already been achieved: statutes omitting irrelevant amendments, asset declarations by politicians, a public register of the state's business agreements, transparency in political party financing and, finally, the abolition of anonymous shareholdings. Nevertheless, four objectives remain to be met: a broadening of the competency of the Czech Supreme Control Authority (ie, Supreme Audit Office), depoliticisation of the state administration, independent investigations of corruption (especially by the establishment of a special anti-corruption public prosecution branch) and an end to providing lucrative positions in various state companies' boards in return for political concessions.

6. Relevant cases[6]

In many cases, corruption remains a hidden crime as it is very difficult to prove. However, even if police authorities are often not able to prove bribery, offenders are at least prosecuted for related crimes, such as abuse of office by a public official or public procurement crimes. Nevertheless, even where this happens, it very often takes a long time before cases are finally concluded and the offenders punished.

6.1 The *Pandur* case

One of the most high-profile cases concerns Marek Dalík, a Czech lobbyist who was closely linked to former Prime Minister Mirek Topolánek. Back in 2006, the Czech government decided to purchase 200 Pandur armoured personnel carriers (APCs), choosing through a tender the Austrian company Steyr as the supplier. The estimated price of the vehicles was Kr24 billion (approx. €1 billion). However, before the actual purchase took place, the APCs (according to press reports) failed certain military tests, which resulted in the Czech government backing out of the deal. This was when Dalík saw an opportunity and asked Steyr's representatives for a bribe of close to Kr460 million (approx. €20 million), in return for which he would persuade the government not to withdraw from the agreement. When the case finally got to court almost 10 years after the actual event, Dalík was charged with bribery. Nevertheless, the appellate court found that he did not in fact have sufficient influence over the government to prevent it from killing the deal. Instead the court classed Dalík's conduct as fraud. The lobbyist was sent to prison for four years. After several months, however, the Supreme Court decided that the appellate court should reconsider its decision in the case, as there were errors concerning the application of the old and new versions of the Criminal Code. Eventually, Dalík was sentenced to five years' imprisonment and a fine of Kr4 million (approx €160 000); he is currently serving his sentence.

6.2 The *David Rath* case

Another interesting case of a senior political representative involved former Minister of Health David Rath and a wine crate which was filled with Kr7 million (approx. €300,000). In May 2012, the police arrested Rath – who at the time was a member of the Chamber of Deputies (the lower house of Parliament) – while he was carrying the

---

6 The following case studies are collected from a variety of local news articles appearing in the press. These include: *The Big Marek Dalík Game* (Respekt, 15 January 2016); *One year later, Dalík's Pandur trial continues. Former US ambassador giving remote testimony in court* (iHNed.cz – Local News, 15 January 2016); *The Pandur Case: Former US Ambassador has not confirmed Dalík's corruption. Yet, the prosecutor is satisfied* (Newton Media – Daily News – Industry, 15 January 2016); *Former US Ambassador stood up for lobbyist Dalík in the Pandur case* (lidovky.cz, 16 January 2016); *Commentary of Peter Kremsky: Big step for Slovakia – the ministers will go to jail* (aktuality.sk, 6 April 2017); *Decision of the Supreme Court: wiretapping in the Rath's case was legal and the courts should take it into account* (irozhlas.cz, 8 August 2017); *Through the Rath case labyrinth: 1165 days that destroyed the ex-deputy's career* (lidovky.cz, 23 July 2012); *The court decided, that Rath should remain in custody, but maybe only for another week* (zpravy.idnes.cz, 8 August 2012); *Tatra case: the secret services have not found any corruption* (novinky.cz, 10 July 2012); *The court finally liberated ex-minister Barták in the Tatra army vehicles case* (ihned.cz, 4 December 2014); *Barták and Smrž will get 180,000 CZK compensation for the prosecution in the Tatra case* (zpravy.idnes.cz, 14 May 2016); *The court deals with ROP Northwest subsidy case. The prosecutor wants a new trial* (zpravy.idnes.cz, 18 April 2017); and *First custody proposal in the ROP Northwest case, but Vaňhová still remains free* (lidovky.cz, 14 December 2016).

wine crate, and charged him with receiving a bribe and embezzlement of EU structural funds. In the Czech Republic, deputies have immunity from prosecution for criminal conduct unless Parliament decides to allow them be prosecuted. However, the Czech Constitution permits the arrest of a deputy if it immediately follows the alleged commission of a crime.

According to police, this was exactly the case with Rath and, to ensure compliance with the law, the chairman of the Chamber of Deputies, Miroslava Němcová, officially agreed to the process. Rath was also stripped of his immunity a month later. There were several other arrests in addition to Rath: Kateřina Pancová (the head of the regional hospital and a member of the Social Democratic Party (ČSSD), of which Rath was also a member); her partner (a former member of the Chamber of Deputies and a close colleague of Rath), and five others, all executive directors or owners of companies that were part of the alleged scheme. Everyone arrested was charged with damaging the financial interests of the EU, passive and active bribery, and creating an advantage from a public procurement. The public prosecutors and police officers claimed that these crimes happened in relation to the renovation of a castle in the Central Bohemia region. Prosecutors argued that since there was a strong likelihood of Rath absconding or influencing witnesses, it was essential that he remain in custody. The case was enormously complicated and the process took some time; as a result Rath was held in custody for almost two years, prompting him to file a complaint with the Constitutional Court. The Constitutional Court ruled in his favour and the former minister received financial compensation for his distress. However, justice is omnipresent and Rath was eventually sentenced to eight and a half years' imprisonment for accepting bribes on multiple occasions. Adding to the already complicated case, Rath's attorneys questioned the legality of wiretapping that had been the most important evidence in the case. The issue wound up before the Supreme Court, which ultimately ruled that the wiretapping of Rath was entirely legal.

6.3 The *Tatra* case

An ideal example of the low rate of enforcement in bribery cases in the Czech Republic is the *Tatra* case. Its key players were former Minister of Defence Martin Barták and an arms dealer, Michal Smrž. The public prosecutors claimed that Barták and Smrž had asked Tatra representatives for a bribe in order to ensure that Tatra would win future public tenders organised by the ministry. The prosecution argued that Barták had asked for a bribe of Kr80 million (approx. €3.2 million) during a trip he made to the United States in 2008, when he was deputy defence minister. He was refused by Tatra's then-supervisory board chairman, William Cabaniss, who also filed a criminal complaint. The other person accused in the affair, Barták's friend Smrž, allegedly tried to persuade Tatra representatives that he had influence with the Czech government and particularly within the Ministry of Defence. The trial of both men began in 2010 and lasted until the court finally found them not guilty in 2014, triggering a strong critical response in the media.

6.4 The *ROP Northwest* case

One of the most infamous cases related to the misuse of EU subsidies is the *ROP Northwest* case. In order to improve the development of the poorest regions in the country (the Ústí nad Labem and Karlovy Vary regions) the Regional Operational Programme Northwest (ROP Northwest) was created to draw from EU subsidies and invest the money into these regions. The redistributions of those subsidies – multiple instances amounting to Kr20 billion (approx. €800 million) – has long been criticised, but so far the courts have handed down only one final judgment. This related to the planned reconstruction of a football pitch and two local hotels. However, according to press reports, an audit performed by the Ministry of Finance (in cooperation with Deloitte Advisory) disclosed that the Subsidy Office of ROP Northwest made mistakes in all 35 redistribution cases in question. Apart from the one final court decision, the European Commission is of the opinion that the two regions should be liable for the misuse of EU funds. The Commission therefore decided that the Ústí nad Labem and Karlovy Vary regions would have to repay Kr2.5 billion (approx. €100 million) to the ROP Northwest fund. However, the governor of the Ústecký Region, Oldřich Bubeníček, strongly disagreed with the decision, claiming that the regions would pay no more than half of the amount sought by the Commission, leaving the rest to be repaid by the Ministry of Finance, which Bubeníček claimed was partly to blame for the scandal.

7. The way forward

While the fight against corruption in the Czech Republic certainly seems to be advancing – through the adoption and enforcement of various pieces of anti-corruption legislation – there is still a long road ahead. One of the areas that still remains under discussion without any specific outcome is whistleblower protection. Currently, the issue of whistleblowers and how to protect them is receiving considerable international attention. Nevertheless, the Czech Republic still lacks comprehensive legal regulation on whistleblowing and, as such, the protection of whistleblowers remains fragmented under a variety of statutes. In the authors' view, this should be the main issue for legislators in the near future, as encouraging people to report unlawful or unethical behaviour and ensuring that subsequent legal protection be provided to them when they do so is vital to effectively fighting corruption.

Motivating individuals as well as companies to self-report to authorities should be another area of focus in anti-corruption efforts. In the Czech Republic, the obligation to report crimes relates to certain listed crimes, which include bribery, but not other related crimes, such as public procurement manipulation or abuse of office. Despite the reporting obligation, individuals as well as companies are often reluctant to report alleged crimes to authorities, and as a result many corruption offences remain undiscovered. This unwillingness results from a lack of incentives that law enforcement authorities could offer in exchange for reporting a criminal offence, eg the possibility of an effective settlement that does not result in a criminal prosecution, as is the case in the United Kingdom and the United States.

France

Stéphane de Navacelle
Sandrine dos Santos
Julie Zorrilla
Navacelle

1. A wide array of major corruption scandals and an inefficient system have led to improvements to anti-corruption legislation

1.1 Introduction

France's exposure to corruption has received considerable attention since 2010. A succession of major political scandals, foreign decisions against French multinationals and highly critical reports by international organisations have led to significant changes in anti-corruption laws and their enforcement. These legislative amendments and their application aim at aligning France with international standards and demonstrate an intention to put an end to the general sense of impunity in the fight against corruption.

In 2011, a former French President was handed a two-year suspended sentence after being found guilty of embezzling public funds to illegally finance the conservative party of which he was the leader during his time as Mayor of Paris.[1] The number of political figures involved in corruption-related scandals has since increased, resulting in significant repercussions. These include the resignation of the Budget Minister in 2013 over allegations of tax fraud and corruption[2] and the disruption of the 2017 presidential election due to similar allegations against the frontrunner.[3]

Between 2010 and 2016, French companies Technip,[4] Alcatel,[5] Total[6] and Alstom[7] were forced to pay millions of dollars to the United States authorities for alleged violations of the Foreign Corrupt Practices Act 1976 (FCPA). Three of them were also forced to allow monitors reporting to US authorities to have access to their operations, pursuant to deferred prosecution agreements (DPAs).

Furthermore, French efforts to tackle corruption have generally been deemed insufficient by international experts and non-governmental organisations (NGOs) alike.[8]

1 *Jacques Chirac condamné à deux ans de prison avec sursis*, Le Monde, 15 December 2011.
2 *Jérôme Cahuzac démissionne du gouvernement en réaffirmant son '"innocence"*, Le Monde, 19 March 2013.
3 *De quoi est soupçonné François Fillon*, Le Monde, 7 February 2017.
4 *Technip SA Resolves Foreign Corrupt Practices Act Investigation and Agrees to Pay $240 Million Criminal Penalty*, US Department of Justice press release, 28 June, 2010.
5 *Alcatel-Lucent SA and Three Subsidiaries Agree to Pay $92 Million to Resolve Foreign Corrupt Practices Act Investigation*, US Department of Justice press release, 27 December 2010.
6 *French Oil and Gas Company, Total, SA, Charged in the United States and France in Connection with an International Bribery Scheme*, US Department of Justice press release, 29 May 2013.
7 *Alstom Sentenced to Pay $772 Million Criminal Fine to Resolve Foreign Bribery Charges*, US Department of Justice press release, 13 November 2015.
8 *Pour l'OCDE, la lutte contre la corruption manque de vigueur*, Les Echos, 16 March 2016.

As a consequence of the recurrent scandals and in order for France to regain credibility on the issue, politicians (through legislative intervention) and enforcement authorities have placed an emphasis on the fight against tax evasion and corruption.

1.2 Anti-corruption laws and treaties

(a) *The Sapin I Law (1993) and developments to 2014*

In 1993, the Sapin I Law[9] created the Central Corruption Prevention Department (SCPC), a department within the Ministry of Justice headed by a judge. The SCPC's core missions were to:

- centralise and exploit information on the prevention and detection of corruption;
- guide and assist administrative and judicial authorities in the prevention and detection of corruption; and
- increase awareness of and provide training in the prevention of corruption and in international action.

The SCPC's mandate was also to ensure that documents passed on to foreign authorities in the context of monitoring missions imposed under DPAs did not infringe the terms of the so-called 'Blocking Statute',[10] in that it prohibits the communication of certain information to foreign public authorities and carries a fine and a prison term for violations, or were not otherwise prohibited by law from being sent abroad.[11] The powers assigned to the SCPC were, however, considered insufficient as the institution did not have the same investigatory authority as its counterparts in the fields of antitrust and financial markets regulation.[12]

The Organisation for Economic Co-operation and Development (OECD) Convention on Combating Bribery of Foreign Public Officials in International Business Transactions (the OECD Convention) was adopted in 1997 and France's tax laws were amended to prohibit the deductibility of domestic or foreign bribes. The OECD Convention brought about notable progress in France's anti-corruption framework, namely through the OECD Working Group on Bribery's monitoring of implementation and enforcement, which is regarded by Transparency International as the "gold standard" of monitoring.[13]

---

9 Law No 93-122 of 29 January 1993 on the prevention of corruption and the transparency of economic life and public procurement.

10 Law No 68-678 of 26 July 1968 on the communication to individuals and legal entities of documents and information on economic, commercial, industrial, financial and technical matters (otherwise known as the 'Blocking Statute'), article 1 of which provides:

> *Subject to international treaties or agreements, it is prohibited for any individual of French nationality or with usual residence in France or any manager, agent or representative of a legal entity with its headquarters or established in France, to communicate documents or information of an economic, commercial, industrial, financial or technical nature – of which the disclosure is liable to infringe upon French sovereignty, security, economic interests or public order – in any form and place whatsoever to foreign public authorities.*

11 SCPC, *Report for year 2014 to the Prime Minister and the Minister of Justice.*

12 SCPC, *Report for year 2001 to the Prime Minister and the Minister of Justice.*

13 OECD, *Better Policies for Development 2014: Policy Coherence and Illicit Financial Flows* (OECD Publishing, 28 April 2014).

In 2005, France ratified the United Nations Convention against Corruption of 2003 (the UN Convention), aiming at reducing cross-border corruption and providing legally binding mechanisms for international asset recovery.

On 13 November 2007, the law on the fight against corruption,[14] which was largely inspired by reports of the OECD and the Group of States against Corruption (GRECO) working groups on bribery:

- created a new offence of influence peddling for state officials;[15]
- introduced legal entity criminal liability for economic offences committed on their behalf;
- granted protection to whistleblowers in the private sector for the first time; and
- made further provision as to sentences for the offences of corruption and influence peddling.

On 25 April 2007, the Council of Europe's Criminal Law Convention on Corruption of 1998 came into force in France. The country nevertheless reserved the rights not to criminalise 'influence peddling' (as defined in article 12 of the convention) and to establish its jurisdiction on the basis of reciprocity, whereby if the offender is a French national, the relevant offence must be punishable under the legislation of the country in which it was committed.

In October 2012, the OECD Working Group on Bribery reported on the application in France of the OECD Convention as part of Phase 3 of its monitoring process (Phase 3 Report).[16] The OECD condemned the very low number of convictions for bribery of foreign public officials handed down in France – merely four final convictions and one conviction under appeal since the offence came into being – considering the size of the economy and the exposure of companies to the risk of transnational bribery. While welcoming the progress made and the newly implemented measures – with regard to the independence of the prosecutors in particular – the OECD recommended:

- that France abolish the reciprocity requirement;
- that France ensure that companies and their subsidiaries/consultants could not avoid criminal liability;
- that prosecutors be awarded more independence in the instigation and conduct of criminal proceedings, regardless of political power and other considerations, such as national economic interests;

---

14 Law No 2007-1598 of 13 November 2007 on the fight against corruption.

15 Article 433-2 of the Criminal Code, which provides:

Any person who requests or agrees, at any time, directly or indirectly, offers, promises, gifts, presents or any advantages, for himself or for others, in order to misuse his real or supposed influence in order to obtain distinctions, jobs, contracts or any other favorable decision from an authority or public administration is punished by five years' imprisonment and a fine of 75 000 euros. To accept the requests provided for in the first paragraph or to suggest offers, promises, gifts, presents or any advantages to any person, for herself or for others, at any time, directly or indirectly and without having the right to, in order to abuse his real or supposed influence in order to obtain distinctions, jobs, contracts or any other favorable decision from an authority or public administration is sanctioned in the same way.

16 OECD Working Group on Bribery, *Phase 3 Report on Implementing the OECD Anti-bribery Convention in France*, October 2012.

- the implementation of a less burdensome mechanism with regard to classified information; and
- that self-reporting to prosecutors by public officers should be encouraged.

The OECD also criticised the fact that France neglected to modify its Blocking Statute,[17] which restricts the cross-border gathering of information, that France had not implemented the offence of influence peddling on foreign public officers and had not modified the statute of limitation.

Following the Phase 3 Report and the revelations about corrupt schemes involving prominent politicians, Law No 2013-1117 of 6 December 2013 on action against tax fraud and serious economic and financial crime was enacted. It reinforced the French anti-corruption framework by establishing the National Financial Prosecutor office (PNF, a financial prosecutor with national jurisdiction), enabled anti-corruption groups to bring civil party claims in criminal proceedings for probity offences (including corruption and influence peddling), increased penalties for bribery of foreign public officials to 10 years' imprisonment and to a €1 million fine or a fine of up to twice the proceeds of the offence, and extended whistleblower protection to the public sector. The law encouraged self-reporting, whereby an individual who stops acting in a criminal manner and reports such acts will not be sanctioned or will receive a lesser sentence, thus extending the notion of self-reporting to corruption, influence peddling and money laundering.

Since its inception, the office of the PNF has been intent on fighting tax evasion, financial offences and corruption. This special prosecutor currently has more than 100 open corruption cases, of which over 20 involve international corruption. On 24 April 2018, the CEO of a major investment group was arrested and interviewed over allegations of corruption in Africa relating to one of the company's subsidiaries. The PNF is investigating how the company obtained contracts to operate ports in West Africa and potentially indirectly influenced election outcomes for the governments involved.[18]

The PNF includes 22 magistrates and 10 specialised investigating magistrates, with a dedicated office in charge of the fight against corruption and financial offences comprising 92 police officers.[19] It has nationwide jurisdiction over stock market offences, corruption of public officials and complex proceedings.[20]

Law No 2013-1117 of 6 December 2013 also provides investigative powers to fight corruption, including infiltration, the interception of correspondence, the use of wiretaps in public or private places and the interception of data. This law abolished the power of the Ministry of Justice to give individual instructions to the NPC in order to increase the latter's' independence *vis-à-vis* the exercise of political power. A specialised chamber with specialised magistrates was created within the

---

17 Law No 68-678 of 26 July 1968 on the communication to individuals and legal entities of documents and information on economic, commercial, industrial, financial and technical matters.

18 *French Billionaire Vincent Bollore Arrested For Alleged Corruption In Africa*, Forbes, 24 April 2018; *Vincent Bolloré déféré devant les juges*, Les Echos, 24 April 2018.

19 *Le Parquet national financier, jeune pousse judiciaire*, Libération, 15 February 2017.

20 Administrative circular of criminal policy of 31 January 2014 on the Financial National Prosecutor, *Supplementary Official Gazette*, 14 February 2014 – JUSD1402887C.

Paris *Tribunal de Grande Instance* to prioritise cases from the PNF office, allowing for faster scheduling of corruption-related hearings.

In October 2014, France presented the OECD Working Group on Bribery with its written follow-up report[21] on the recommendations of the Phase 3 Report, pointing to the increased volume of ongoing proceedings. On 23 October 2014 however, the Working Group on Bribery published a formal declaration stating that France had still failed to meet the standard set by the OECD Convention and the 2012 Recommendation and requesting expeditious implementation of the convention.[22]

(b) *The Sapin II Law (2016) and subsequent developments*

Further to Law No 2013-1117, a number of other major advances were made under François Hollande's presidency with the adoption, in 2016, of the Sapin II Law and decrees made pursuant to it,[23] which was widely regarded as bringing France into line with the highest international standards in the areas of transparency. It aims at supplementing and strengthening the existing anti-corruption framework.

The Sapin II Law was intended to further the effects of the Sapin I Law by rendering public life more transparent and addressing shortcomings in the existing anti-corruption framework. The law therefore also serves a defensive purpose against the extra-territorial application of foreign legislation (such as the US FCPA and the UK Bribery Act 2010). Indeed, the Sapin II Law extends the extra-territorial application of the provisions of the Criminal Code on corruption by providing that French law is applicable in 'all circumstances' to offences of corruption committed abroad by French persons, persons ordinarily residing in France or exercising all or part of their economic activity on French territory.

The Sapin II Law aims at countering corruption more effectively – and particularly in international business – through preventive and punitive measures. This prevents the sanctioning of French companies by foreign judicial and regulatory authorities and strengthens French judicial sovereignty. It also seeks to avoid the leaking of strategic information and economic espionage where a foreign monitor is appointed within French companies.[24]

As a result of the Sapin II Law, and as of 1 June 2017, large French companies and foreign subsidiaries of French groups (those with over 500 employees and an average annual turnover of over €100 million) are required to implement mandatory compliance programmes to prevent and detect corruption (including codes of conduct, internal reporting procedures and risk mapping).[25]

The French Anticorruption Agency (AFA), the national detection and prevention agency placed under the joint authority of the Ministry of Justice and the Ministry

---

21 OECD, *France: Follow-Up to The Phase 3 Report & Recommendations*, December 2014.

22 OECD press release, 23 October 2014, *Statement of the OECD Working Group on Bribery on France's implementation of the Anti-Bribery Convention.*

23 Law No 2016-1691 of 9 December 2016 on transparency, the fight against corruption and modernisation of the economy; Decree No 2017-329 of 14 March 2017 on the Anti-Corruption Agency; Decree No 2017-564 of 19 April 2017 on the procedures for the collection of reports issued by whistleblowers in public or private law corporations or state administrations.

24 *Ibid*, article 3, 5°.

25 *Ibid*, article 17.

of the Budget,[26] monitors companies' compliance with these provisions. The AFA has replaced the SCPC established under the Sapin I Law.[27] It participates in administrative coordination by preparing a multi-annual plan against corruption-related offences and assisting the competent French authorities with regard to cooperation with international organisations in order to define and implement the positions they have adopted on corruption and related offences.

The AFA engages in training, awareness-raising and assistance activities for the prevention and detection of risks of corruption and related offences.[28] In this capacity, it issued its first recommendations on 22 December 2017 (after a public consultation of all parties concerned), which are aimed at assisting legal entities to prevent and detect facts of corruption. The recommendations address:

- the role of management;
- codes of conduct;,
- internal alert mechanisms;
- risk-mapping;
- third-party evaluation;
- accounting controls;
- anti-corruption training; and
- internal evaluation mechanisms.[29]

These recommendations apply throughout French territory to ensure compliance with international anti-corruption treaties. They target every organisation, including private companies and public entities, regardless of their size, corporate form, area of business, annual revenue or number of employees. The AFA also contributes to the pursuit of France's international commitments through its cooperation, support and technical assistance functions.

When it succeeded the SCPC, the AFA received additional resources and powers, such as an enlarged workforce and budget. It is headed by a judge with relative autonomy, M Charles Duchaine,[30] who is appointed by the President of the French Republic for a non-renewable six-year term. It exercises administrative powers to control the quality of anti-corruption compliance mechanisms implemented by companies, administrative entities of the state and public bodies by conducting on-site investigations,[31] and has power to issue warnings and/or impose injunctions and fines of up to €200,000 for individuals and €1 million for legal entities.[32] While the first audits launched on 10 October 2017 only concern private companies, the AFA has announced that it will determine a schedule for auditing public entities at the

---

26 *Ibid*, article 1.

27 *Ibid*, article 5.

28 *Ibid*, article 3.

29 *Recommendations from the French Anticorruption Agency aimed at assisting public and private entities to prevent facts of corruption, influence peddling, bribery, illegal taking of interest, embezzlement of public funds and favouritism*, JORF no 0298 of 22 December 2017.

30 Decree of 17 March 2017 on the appointment of the Director of the French Anti-corruption Agency, M Duchaine (Charles).

31 Law No 2016-1691 of 9 December 2016 (note 18 above), article 4.

32 *Ibid*, article 17.

beginning of 2018.[33] The AFA will request documentation on a voluntary basis and will then conduct on-site visits to acquire more information under existing mechanisms.[34] At the end of the audit, the AFA will send a warning letter or refer cases of serious violations to its Sanctions Committee.

On 28 March 2018, the AFA signed a cooperation agreement with the PNF, aimed at strengthening the effectiveness of the provisions of the Sapin II Law and better articulating the different mechanisms of prevention, detention and punishment of probity offences. This agreement seeks to improve coordination and communication between the AFA and the PNF in the context of offences of corruption and follow-up on the implementation of recommendations by international bodies and legislative developments. It also lays down specific steps to be taken once a *convention judiciaire d'intérêt public* (CJIP, a public interest agreement – the French equivalent of a US DPA) proposed by the PNF is approved by a judge.[35]

Alongside the establishment of the AFA and the whistleblowing mechanism, monitorship, an additional compliance-related penalty, may now be imposed upon legal entities convicted of offences of corruption or influence peddling under the Sapin II law.[36]

Where medium- and small-sized companies do not yet fall within the scope of this compliance obligation, they are already subject to the implementation of internal reporting procedures. Companies with over 50 employees must provide for whistleblower protection (which is broadly defined by the law) and implement escalating internal reporting procedures under penalty of incurring civil or criminal liability.[37] Companies must guarantee the anonymity both of whistleblowers and of persons identified by them, as well as the confidentiality of information reported.

The Sapin II Law also introduces into French law the possibility of signing a CJIP. A CJIP may be proposed by the prosecutor (which includes PNF prosecutors) for select probity offences before the initiation of criminal proceedings or by the investigating magistrate (*juge d'instruction*) where an inquiry (*instruction*) is ongoing.[38]

These agreements allow a company that is being prosecuted for probity offences to negotiate a fine without going to trial. The charges are dropped against the incriminated company, which is thereby spared the reputational risk of a court case.

The introduction of the CJIP mechanism illustrates the legislature's intent to address some of the OECD's criticisms, particularly as to the absence of effective sanctions and respond to the harsh fines imposed upon French businesses in the United States. A CJIP may be put forward to a legal entity questioned by the public prosecutor over a breach of probity (viz, corruption, influence peddling, money laundering, laundering of tax fraud proceeds and other related offences):

- at the inquiry stage, so long as no investigating magistrate is involved; or

---

33 *Le Directeur de l'AFA lance les premiers contrôles sur les entreprises*, Ministry of Justice, French Anti-corruption Agency press release, 10 October 2017.

34 *L'Agence française anticorruption mise sur la prévention*, Le Point, 7 November 2017.

35 *L'AFA signe un protocole de coopération avec le PNF*, French Anti-Corruption Agency press release, 28 March 2018.

36 Article 131-39-2 of the Criminal Code.

37 Law No 2016-1691 of 9 December 2016 (note 23 above), article 8.

38 *Ibid*, article 22.

- after the transmission of the file by the investigating magistrate once the legal entity being examined acknowledges the facts and accepts the potential legal definition of the facts.[39]

A CJIP requires the validation of a judge at different stages of the procedure and must allow for the compensation of potential victims.[40] Once it has been validated, the prosecutor will issue a press release, the validation order and the amount of the fine imposed and the CJIP will be published on the AFA website.[41] A CJIP does not issue an opinion on the defendant's guilt and is not of the same nature and status as a court conviction. It is therefore not registered on the criminal record of the legal entity concerned.[42]

The first CJIP was concluded on 30 October 2017 between HSBC Private Bank (Suisse) SA and the National Financial Prosecutor following a four-year investigation into alleged laundering of tax fraud and unlawful cross-border banking solicitation. HSBC agreed to pay a €300 million fine, inclusive of both a 'public interest fine' (disgorgement of profits and an additional financial penalty) and damages for the victim.[43] Two more CJIPs with the Nanterre Prosecutor were signed in early 2018. On 14 February 2018, Set Environnement agreed to pay an €800,000 fine on account of commissions paid to obtain its contract with a corrupt EDF employee.[44] On 15 February 2018, SAS Kaefer Wanner agreed to pay a €2,710,000 fine on account of similar payments made by some of its employees to an EDF employee.[45] Both companies also agreed to subject themselves to a compliance programme under the AFA's control, for a two-year period for the former and an 18-month period for the latter.

Finally, the Sapin II Law provides a framework for lobbyists with the creation of a digital register of "interest representatives" (ie, lobbyists) to the High Authority for transparency in public life (HATVP).[46] Established in 2014, this independent administrative authority aims to promote the integrity of public life by requiring the highest-ranking public officials to disclose their assets and interests when taking up their official duties and preventing conflicts of interests in general. Moreover, it manages a public register of lobbyists in order to inform citizens on the rapports interest representatives share with public officials.

(c) Extension of the limitation period in corruption cases

Addressing the OECD Working Group's concerns over the French statute of limitations, the Law of 27 February 2017[47] doubled the statutory limitation periods

---

39 Article 41-1-2 of the Criminal Code.
40 *Ibid.*
41 *Ibid.*
42 *Ibid.*
43 *Convention judiciaire d'intérêt public* (CJIP) between the National Financial Prosecutor of the Paris first instance court and HSBC Private Bank (Suisse) SA, 30 October 2017.
44 *Convention judiciaire d'intérêt public* (CJIP) between the Nanterre Prosecutor and Set Environment, 14 February 2018.
45 *Convention judiciaire d'intérêt public* (CJIP) between Nanterre Prosecutor and SAS Kaefer Wanner, 15 February 2018.
46 Created under Chapter 3bis of Law No 2013-907 of 11 October 2013 on transparency in public life.
47 Law No 2017-242 of 27 February 2017 amending the statute of limitations period for criminal matters.

for the prosecution of criminal offences, extending them to 20 years for *crimes* (felonies) and six years for *délits* (misdemeanours). With regard to 'clandestine' offences (breach of trust, misappropriation of corporate assets, tax fraud and other financial and economic offences), the law introduced a deadline of 30 years for felonies and 12 years for misdemeanours, after which the prosecution of offences, even if not discovered until later, is time-barred. The limitation periods start running from the date on which an offence was committed.[48]

(d) A new obligation to identify risks of corruption for parent and contracting companies

The new compliance obligations imposed on companies by the Sapin II Law are part of a wider trend of transparency and corporate accountability, as outlined by the enactment of the Law of 27 March 2017,[49] which requires large companies to implement a monitoring programme allowing the identification of risks and the prevention of serious violations of human rights and fundamental freedoms, damage to the health and security of individuals or to the environment where the same result from the activities of:

- a company;
- the companies it controls; and
- sub-contractors and suppliers with which these companies have an established commercial relationship.[50]

2. Overview of the concept of 'corruption' in France

2.1 Active and passive corruption of national public officials

'Corruption' may be defined as the action by which a person with a specific function, public or private, requests or accepts a donation, gift or promise in order to accomplish, delay or refrain from accomplishing an act falling directly or indirectly within his or her functions. It therefore implies the violation of the duties related to the functions of the accused by the accused. French criminal law distinguishes between active corruption and passive corruption. These two offences are distinct and autonomous. They can be prosecuted and tried separately.

'Active corruption of national public officials' is defined by article 433-1 of the Criminal Code as unlawfully offering:

> *at any time, directly or indirectly, benefits, promises, donations, gifts or any other advantages to persons exercising public authority, performing public duties or holding elective public office, for themselves or others, to induce them to perform or refrain from performing actions in accordance with or facilitated by their duties, functions or office; or to abuse their real or supposed influence to obtain from a public authority or department distinctions, employment, contracts or any form of favourable decision.*

The definition "persons exercising public authority, performing public duties or

---

48 *Ibid.*
49 Law No 2017-399 of 27 March 2017 on the duty of care of parent companies.
50 *Ibid.*

holding elective public office" encompasses all national public officials. Offering "benefits, promises, donations, gifts or any other advantages" encompasses the notions of "promising, offering or giving" under the Council of Europe Criminal Law Convention on Corruption[51] (see 1.2 above).

The penalties that may be imposed on individuals for active corruption in the public sector is 10 years' imprisonment and a fine of €1 million or twice the proceeds of the offence. Perpetrators may also incur supplementary sentences, including:

- exclusion from business activities;
- loss of civic, civil or family rights for up to five years;
- disqualification from public office or duties or the occupational or social activity in, or in connection with, the exercise of which the offence was committed (either temporary, for up to five years, or permanent);
- confiscation of the object used in or intended for use in committing the offence;
- confiscation of the direct or indirect proceeds of the offence and assets of which the offender is unable to justify the origin;
- publication and dissemination of the decision; and exclusion from French territory for foreign nationals found guilty of active bribery of judicial personnel.[52]

Legal entities may incur a fine of €5 million or ten times the proceeds of the offences as well as supplementary sentences, including:

- up to five years' disqualification from performing the activity in connection with which the offence was directly or indirectly committed;
- judicial supervision;
- closure of establishments, or one of them, in which the offence was committed;
- exclusion from public procurement;
- ineligibility for public funding;
- a ban on issuing cheques or using payment cards;
- confiscation of the object used in or intended for use in the commission of the offence;
- confiscation of the direct or indirect proceeds of the offence and assets of which the perpetrator is unable to justify the origin; and
- publication or dissemination of the decision.[53]

'Passive corruption of national public officials' is defined, by article 432-11 of the Criminal Code, as unlawfully requesting or agreeing to:

at any time, directly or indirectly, offers, promises, donations, gifts or any other advantages, for themselves or others, in exchange for: performing or refraining from performing actions in accordance with or facilitated by their duties, functions or office

---

51 Article 2 of the Criminal Law Convention on Corruption, Council of Europe, Strasbourg, 27 January 1999.

52 Article 433-1 of the Criminal Code.

53 *Ibid*, article 131-38.

or abusing their real or supposed influence to obtain from a public authority or department distinctions, employment, contracts or any form of favourable decision.

The same penalties apply to both active and passive bribery in the public sector.[54]

2.2 Active and passive corruption in the private sector

'Active bribery in the private sector' is defined by article 445-1 of the Criminal Code as unlawfully offering:

at any time, directly or indirectly, benefits, promises, donations, gifts or other advantages, for themselves or others, to persons who do not exercise public authority, perform public duties or hold elective public office but who hold a managerial position or undertake other work, in an occupational or social capacity, for an individual or legal person or for any other body, in exchange for performing or refraining from performing actions in accordance with or facilitated by their activities or duties, in breach of their legal, contractual or professional obligations.

The sanctions incurred by individuals for active corruption in the private sectors are five years' imprisonment and a fine of €500,000 or twice the proceeds of the offence. Perpetrators may also incur supplementary sentences.[55] Legal persons may incur a fine of €2.5 million or ten times the proceeds of the offences as well as supplementary sentences.[56]

'Passive corruption in the private sector' is defined by article 445-2 of the Criminal Code. It does not concern persons who exercise public authority, perform public duties or hold elective public office but those who hold a managerial position or undertake work for an individual or a legal entity and who unlawfully request or agree to:

at any time, directly or indirectly, for themselves or others, benefits, promises, donations, gifts or any other advantages in exchange for performing or refraining from performing actions in accordance with or facilitated by their activities or duties, in breach of their legal, contractual or professional obligations.

The same penalties apply to both active and passive corruption in the private sector.[57]

A specific regime applies to active and passive corruption of judiciary personnel, which includes magistrates, clerks, mediators, conciliators and arbitrators.[58] The same applies to the corruption of foreign judicial personnel and of foreign public officials.

2.3 Related offences

Influence peddling by persons holding public office is covered by article 432-11 of the Criminal Code on the passive bribery of public officials and by article 433-1 of the Criminal Code on the active bribery of national public officials – both of which are discussed at 2.1 above. The offence is thereby punishable by the same penalties as corruption of a public official.

---

54 *Ibid*, article 432-11.
55 *Ibid*, article 445-1.
56 *Ibid*, article 131-38.
57 *Ibid*, article 445-2.
58 *Ibid*, articles 434-9 and 434-9-1.

'Influence peddling between individuals aimed at national authorities' is defined by article 433-2 of the Criminal Code, which penalises persons who request or agree to, at any time, directly or indirectly, benefits, promises, donations, gifts or other advantages, for themselves or others, to abuse their influence, real or supposed, to obtain from a public authority or department distinctions, employment, contracts or any other favourable decision, with five years' imprisonment and a €500,000 fine. This provision also states that the same penalties shall apply to persons who respond to requests specified in the first paragraph or who, at any time, directly or indirectly, unlawfully offer other persons benefits, promises, donations, gifts or other advantages for themselves or others to abuse their influence, real or supposed, to obtain from a public authority or department distinctions, employment, contracts or any other favourable decision.

Other offences related to corruption include illegal taking of interest, misappropriation of public funds and favouritism. Under article 432-14 of the Criminal Code, the offence of favouritism:

- applies to any person holding public authority or discharging a public service mission or holding a public electoral mandate or acting as a representative, administrator or agent of the state, territorial bodies, public corporations, mixed economy companies of national interest discharging a public service mission and local mixed economy companies, or any person acting on behalf of any of the aforementioned bodies;
- in respect of obtaining or attempting to obtain for others an unjustified advantage by an act breaching statutory or regulatory provisions designed to ensure freedom of access and equality for candidates in respect of tenders for public service and delegated public services; and
- is penalised by two years' imprisonment and a €200,000 fine or twice the proceeds of the offence.[59]

3. Practical enforcement of anti-corruption laws

3.1 Criminal liability of individuals and legal persons

The criminal liability of employees depends on whether they have sufficient autonomy in the decision-making process. Executives may be held liable as accomplices if they have provided specific instructions.

The criminal liability of a legal entity as a perpetrator depends on whether it has acted through an "organ" or "representative" who committed an offence on its behalf.[60] The legal entity may be held liable even though the organ or representative was not prosecuted.

Judges must examine the company's hierarchy to determine whether an executive was aware of the employees' misconducts. A *de facto* manager of a company may be considered a representative of the company, for example.[61]

59 *Ibid*, article 432-14.
60 *Ibid*, article 121-2.
61 Cass crim, 11 December 2012, No 11-88.643, 7548.

Moreover, the *Cour de Cassation* (French Supreme Court) held in 2006 that "it was not essential to identify the individual when the offence could only be attributable to the legal entity or be the result of the company's business policy",[62] thus creating a presumption that the offence is committed by an organ or representative. Legal entities may also be held liable as accomplices by providing "aid or assistance" or "instructions".[63]

3.2 Criminal procedure

"Criminal procedure" is defined by law as fair and adversarial in order to preserve a balance between the rights of the parties.[64] Article 1 of the Criminal Procedure Code provides for separation between authorities responsible for prosecuting offences and those responsible for ruling on them. A public prosecution leading to the imposition of penalties is initiated by prosecutors or civil servants entrusted by law and adjudicated by judges.

The prosecution may also be initiated by the injured party, including anti-corruption organisations under the conditions set forth in the Criminal Procedure Code.[65] The investigating judge is in charge of investigations after having been seized of the case by a submission made by the district prosecutor or by a complaint containing a petition to become a civil party.[66]

The investigating judge is autonomous and independent and is conferred with powers of investigation. Investigations, particularly in international corruption matters, can last for more than a decade due to their complexity, the lack of direct evidence available and the lack of resources allocated to investigation teams.

3.3 Examples of leading French corruption cases

(a) ***The* 'Biens mal acquis' *case***

The *Bien mal acquis* (which can be translated as 'improperly acquired assets') case is indicative of the challenges raised by the fight against international corruption. It originated in a report by a French NGO in 2007 aimed at assessing the value of accumulated assets of several foreign leaders held in western countries. In March 2007, several NGOs filed a criminal complaint against foreign presidents and their relatives alleging that they held significant real estate assets in French territory, the purchase of which, according to the complainants, was unjustifiable.

A police investigation was initiated but the charges were then dropped by the Public Prosecutor in November 2007 as the evidence was considered insufficient.

On 2 December 2008, the NGOs filed a petition to join the case as civil parties. After a three-year procedural battle, the issue finally reached the Criminal Chamber of the Supreme Court. On 9 November 2010, it ruled that Transparency International had standing to institute corruption proceedings and permitted the appointment of

62 Cass crim, 20 June 2006, No 05-85.255, Bull crim no 188.
63 Article 121-7 of the Criminal Code.
64 Preliminary article of the Criminal Procedure Code.
65 *Ibid*, article 2 to 2-24.
66 *Ibid*, article 49.

an investigating judge and the opening of a judicial investigation.[67] A decade after the first criminal complaint however, only one of the accused has been tried at first instance.[68]

(b) Allegations of fraud following a €400 million arbitral award

Following years of judicial proceedings between the subsidiary of a large French bank and a former French Minister of City Affairs, the parties entered into an arbitration agreement. The former minister was awarded approximately €400 million following proceedings pursuant to the arbitration agreement. However, doubt was cast over the independence and impartiality of the arbitral tribunal. On 17 February 2015, the Paris Court of Appeal held that the award was tainted by fraud.[69] Following a criminal investigation, five individuals, including the former minister, one of his attorneys and one of the arbitrators will (at the time of writing) stand trial for embezzlement of public funds and fraud, either as authors or accomplices.[70]

(c) Double jeopardy: **ne bis in idem** *protection*

One of the difficulties encountered by French authorities in enforcing French anti-corruption laws is the *ne bis in idem* protection shielding individuals and corporations from double jeopardy. Indeed, under article 113-9 of the Criminal Code, which applies to offences committed outside of French territory, no prosecution may be initiated against a person who establishes that he or she was subject to a final decision abroad for the same offence and, in the event of conviction, that the sentence has been served or extinguished by limitation. Article 14(7) of the International Covenant on Civil and Political Rights (ICCPR) also provides for protection against double jeopardy by providing that:

> *[n]o one shall be liable to be tried or punished again for an offence for which he has already been finally convicted or acquitted in accordance with the law and penal procedure of each country.*

This rule has led to acquittals by first instance courts in a number of jurisdictions in several high-profile cases, district courts taking into account the settlements concluded with foreign authorities to determine whether the accused could stand trial on the same facts.

On 26 February 2016, the Paris Court of Appeal refused to apply the double jeopardy provision of the Code of Criminal Procedure to a DPA,[71] giving a cross-border application to article 14.7 of the ICCPR, on the ground that a separate provision of the Code of Criminal Procedure did not distinguish between national and foreign jurisdictions in enforcing double jeopardy. On 14 March 2018, in reviewing the decision, the *Cour de Cassation* held that article 14.7 – an obstacle to double jeopardy for unique facts within the same jurisdiction – is not applicable in

67 Cass crim, 9 November 2010, No 09-88.272.

68 *Teodorin Obiang, premier condamné dans l'affaire dite des 'biens mal acquis'*, Le Monde, 27 October 2017.

69 Paris Court of Appeal, 17 February 2015, No 13/13278.

70 *Arbitrage du Crédit Lyonnais : la justice ordonne un procès pénal pour Tapie*, Le Point, 20 December 2017.

71 *Pétrole contre nourriture : précisions en matière de corruption d'agents publics étrangers et d'abus de bien sociaux*, Dalloz actualité, 4 April 2018.

the case of a prior conviction in foreign jurisdictions. This had the effect of curtailing the scope of international double jeopardy protection.

In light of the appearance of CJIPs, international double-jeopardy protection is to be expected. There is a risk nevertheless that CJIPs will be perceived as too lax, in that they do not include the confiscation or disgorgement of gains brought to companies by their misconduct.[72] UK and US authorities in particular – which follow a more strenuous approach – may therefore wish to pursue parallel settlements, thus threatening the *ne bis in idem* principle.

3.4 Internal investigations

In light of the new compliance and anti-corruption framework, companies are, for a number of reasons, increasingly willing to conduct internal investigations following allegations of corruption. These include the ability to inform their boards about the background and circumstances surrounding an issue, enabling the companies to state that they have investigated the matter and taken relevant action, while complying with regulatory obligations, addressing employee misconducts and/or discouraging regulators or prosecutors from initiating official investigations.

This new level of activity has led the Paris Bar Council to issue recommendations addressing privilege, document retention and other issues. Indeed, in a legal culture in which negotiating a deal with a prosecutor or an investigating magistrate is uncommon and in-house counsel have no legal privilege, attorney–client privilege should be an important concern in internal investigations.[73]

4. Conclusion

Over the past 20 years, French justice has acquired considerable expertise in dealing with financial crimes. The anti-corruption framework has gained comprehensiveness and precision and the magistrates' technical knowledge in financial matters has vastly improved. The case law in these matters has increased accordingly, Transparency France counting (in 2016) 660 corruption-related cases that led to convictions by French courts, 440 of them having been adjudicated since 2014.[74]

By refusing to give effect to an agreement obtained through corruption in an *exequatur* case on 13 September 2017, the French Supreme Court showed that the fight against international corruption is a matter of public policy that should extend beyond pure criminal justice.[75]

The fight against corruption has long been enshrined in the international political system, and important progress has been made over the past decades in cooperation between national judicial systems, including joint investigations and mutual legal assistance in criminal matters.

Following the important progress that has been made, the success of the fight will ultimately depend on political continuity and the level of general involvement.

---

72 Article 131-21 of the Criminal Code.

73 *Nouvelle annexe XXIV : Vademecum de l'avocat chargé d'une enquête interne,* Paris Bar Council, 13 September 2016.

74 *Une carte collaborative de la corruption en France,* Le Monde, 12 February 2017.

75 Cass crim, No 16-25657, 13 September 2017.

In this regard, compliance, monitoring and open data exchange are tools to be reckoned with in guaranteeing the transmission of information and achieving a better enforcement of anti-corruption laws.

Germany

Volker D Popp
Compliance and AML Officer

1. Introduction

Participating in international anti-corruption conferences is always an interesting experience. Apart from communicating with colleagues who work on the prevention of corruption and money laundering, the author learns a lot about how Germany is perceived by other countries. People regularly say that bribery payments in Germany used to be tax-deductible until 1999. This causes, with few exceptions, intensive head-shaking and incomprehension on the part of participants. It is interesting, though, that perceptions change when it comes to German citizens. Germans are mostly described as 'straight, honest, deliberate, serious and rule-consistent'. Corruption in the country is barely perceived, both by Germans themselves and by visitors. In the annual Transparency International (TI) publication *Corruption Perceptions Index* (CPI), Germany is ranked tenth as one of the countries with the least perception of corruption.[1] TI is one of the most well-known non-governmental organisations (NGOs) in the global fight against corruption.

It surprises the author that, in his experience, the German criminal law is barely an issue, both in panel discussions and in informal conversations with international experts working against corruption. Instead, there are lively discussions about developments concerning the Foreign Corrupt Practices Act 1976 (FCPA) of the United States and the Bribery Act 2010 of the United Kingdom. This is a puzzling fact, since Germany, owing to its foreign investments, is the biggest economy in Europe and currently the fourth-largest economy globally,[2] and thus plays an important role at an international level. In 2014, only two countries in the world made more foreign investments than Germany: the United States and Japan.[3] This demonstrates the considerable volume of worldwide trade and business relations that Germany is maintaining.

This chapter aims to provide basic information about corruption in Germany. Moreover, it will outline relevant provisions of the criminal law and discuss the main features of relevant past and current legislative provisions. The chapter will conclude with a brief survey of current trends in the fight against corruption in Germany.

1 Cf, Transparency International (2017), *TI-Corruption-Index 2016*, available at www.transparency.org/news/feature/corruption_perceptions_index_2016 (accessed 10 January 2018).
2 Cf, International Monetary Fund (2017), available at www.imf.org/external/pubs/ft/weo/2017/01/weodata/index.aspx (accessed 10 January 2018).
3 Cf, OECD, *OECD Fact book 2015–2016: Economic, Environmental and Social Statistics* (2016, OECD Publishing, Paris), available at http://dx.doi.org/10.1787/factbook-2015-en (accessed 8 January 2018).

Another priority of this chapter is to provide the reader with realistic guidelines. It is not, however, possible to offer a deep analysis, particularly with regard to existing standards in the criminal law and in corresponding legislation. In specific cases, it may be advisable to consult a specialist attorney.

2. History and perceptions of corruption

Perceptions of corruption in Germany are not confined to the 21st century. Following the definition of 'corruption' formulated by TI in 2017 ("the abuse of entrusted power for private gain"[4]), it is interesting to see that discussions about potential corruptive actions can be frequently found in German history.

The foundation of the German Second Empire (1871–1918) was apparently possible only due to bribery payments made by the former Chancellor of the North German Confederation and later Reich Chancellor Otto von Bismarck. It is said that Bismarck used confiscated private assets to buy the approval and support of King Ludwig II of Bavaria for the nomination of the German Kaiser Wilhelm I by paying him an annual amount of 300,000 Goldmarks (the currency then used in the German Empire). King Ludwig II apparently used the money to pay for his excessive lifestyle and his weakness for expensive buildings.[5]

Corruption scandals were also numerous in the Weimar Republic (1919–1933). Examples included that of a former minister who was accused of taking bribes from representatives in exchange for private, economic or political benefits. Apparently, he received 187 bottles of wine for only 7% of their actual market price in return for assigning extra supplies of sugar to a wine growers' association.[6]

During the Nazi era (1933–1945), probably the darkest chapter in German history, corruption seems to have been more common than was publicly known.[7] Apparently, legal proceedings were often suspended in exchange for bribery payments.[8] Historical research has also revealed the common misappropriation of public funds, as well as the payment of excessive fees for doubtful services.[9]

Bribery scandals have also been known in the Federal Republic of Germany (1949–the present). Instances include alleged bribery payments during the establishment of the post-World War II German capital in Bonn,[10] alleged

---

4 Cf, Transparency International (2017), available at www.transparency.org/what-is-corruption#define (accessed 10 January 2018).

5 Cf, Heinz Höhne, (1984), *Das Große Schmieren*, in *Der Spiegel*, available at www.spiegel.de/spiegel/print/d-13512339.html (accessed 10 January 2018); Detlef Jena (2011), *Korruption dank Bismarcks 'Reptilienfonds'*, in *Thüringische Landeszeitung*, available at www.tlz.de/web/zgt/kultur/detail/-/specific/Korruption-dank-Bismarcks-Reptilienfonds-120195142 (accessed 10 January 2018).

6 Cf, Annika Klein (2014), *Korruption und Korruptionsskandale in der Weimarer Republik*, pp 159 *et seq*.

7 Cf, Tillmann Bendikowski (2001), *Korruption in der NS-Zeit – Die schwarzen Kassen der 'Volksgemeinschaft'*, in *Der Spiegel*, available at www.spiegel.de/kultur/gesellschaft/korruption-in-der-ns-zeit-die-schwarzen-kassen-der-volksgemeinschaft-a-121421.html (accessed 12 January 2018).

8 Cf, Erik Lindner (2007), *Die Reemtsmas. Geschichte einer deutschen Unternehmerfamilie*, in *Cicero*, available at www.cicero.de/wirtschaft/zwölf-millionen-für-göring/38290 (Accessed 3 January 2018).

9 Cf, for example, Ingo Bach (2001), *Korruption in der NS-Zeit: Die Gier der Goldfasane*, in *Der Tagesspiegel*, available at www.tagesspiegel.de/weltspiegel/gesundheit/korruption-in-der-ns-zeit-die-gier-der-goldfasane/249726.html (accessed 2 January 2018).

10 Cf, Deutscher Bundestag (German Federal Parliament) (1949), *Drucksache 2274*, available at http://dipbt.bundestag.de/doc/btd/01/022/0102274.pdf (accessed 8 January 2018).

manipulation of votes during the World Cup draw of 2006,[11] and bribery payments for big construction projects like the new Berlin Airport.[12]

It remains uncertain, however, how to categorise the corresponding criminal offences. The Federal Criminal Police Office (*Bundeskriminalamt*, or BKA), "the national central police agency",[13] distinguishes between situational and structural corruption.

- 'Situational corruption' is understood to be a spontaneous act that occurs without concrete planning or preparation and as a direct reaction to an official act.[14] A typical example is the offering of a bribe to a traffic police officer in order to avoid a fine for violating road traffic regulations (*Straßenverkehrsordnung*, or *StVO*).
- By contrast, 'structural corruption' describes planned situations that require a long-term relationship between bribe giver and taker and does not include spontaneous actions.[15] A possible example of this arises where a long-time supplier bribes a public official during a public tender process.

This distinction is important in construing the distinction between real and perceived corruption. According to the *Corruption Perceptions Index* and with regard to the corruption scandals discussed above, it seems paradoxical that the perception of corruption in Germany is considered to be very low.[16] This discrepancy was studied by the research project Crime & Culture with the University of Konstanz as lead contractor.[17] A possible explanation may lie in the fact that situational corruption is understood within the classical understanding of corruption, which in Germany is considered to be morally unacceptable. According to the *Crime and Culture* study, situational corruption basically does not exist in German everyday life[18] and may therefore explain the non-existent or limited perception of corruption.[19] By contrast, structural corruption would be perceived and rationalised only as an individual offence.[20] However, public discourse can influence the perception of structural corruption. It therefore remains to be seen how the *Corruption Perceptions Index* for Germany will change in the future as a result of ongoing public discourse.

11 Cf, Deutscher Bundestag (2017), *Drucksache 18/10869*, available at http://dip21.bundestag.de/dip21/btd/18/108/1810869.pdf (accessed 12 January 2018).

12 Cf, *Süddeutsche Zeitung* (2016), *Ehemaliger BER-Manager muss ins Gefängnis*, available at www.sueddeutsche.de/wirtschaft/korruption-ehemaliger-ber-manager-muss-wegen-korruption-ins-gefaengnis-1.3202879 (accessed 12 January 2018).

13 Cf, Bundeskriminalamt (Federal Criminal Police Office) (2018), *The BKA*, available at www.bka.de/DE/UnsereAufgaben/unsereaufgaben_node.html;jsessionid=1B8738AD016914048FE56D85B89CE905.live2302 (accessed 18 February 2018).

14 Cf, Bundeskriminalamt (2018), *Korruption*, available at www.bka.de/DE/UnsereAufgaben/Deliktsbereiche/Korruption/korruption_node.html (accessed 12 January 2018).

15 *Ibid.*

16 Cf, Transparency International (1995–2017), *Corruption Perceptions Index*, available at www.transparency.org/research/cpi/overview (accessed 12 January 2018).

17 Cf, University of Konstanz/European Commission Specific Targeted Research Project (STREP), *Crime & Culture: Final Report* (undated), available at www.uni-konstanz.de/crimeandculture/docs/STREP_Crime_and_Culture_Final_Project_Report.pdf (accessed 12 January 2018).

18 *Ibid*, p 113.

19 Cf, Angelos Giannakopoulos & Joerg Tänzler (2009),'Deutsche Ansichten zur Korruption', in *Aus Politik und Zeitgeschichte*, Edition 3-4/2009, p 16.

20 *Crime & Culture* (note 17 above).

3. International anti-corruption agreements and their impacts on German law

3.1 Introduction

Acceding to a number of international anti-corruption agreements has played a crucial role in the further development of German criminal law. The key agreements, the standards they apply and the term 'public official' as defined both in section 11, paragraph 1 No 2 of the StGB (*Strafgesetzbuch*, or the German Criminal Code) and in section 11, paragraph 1, No 2a of the StGB are discussed below in outline only. In cases of doubt, readers should obtain independent legal advice and analysis.

3.2 The EU Anti-Corruption Act 1998[21]

The EU Anti-Corruption Act of 10 September 1998 (*EU-Bestechungsgesetz*, or *EUBestG*) (the 1998 Act)[22] made it possible to transpose two EU instruments into national law, thus illustrating the importance of EU conventions to the development of German anti-corruption law:

- the EU Protocol of 27 September 1996 to the Convention on the Protection of the European Communities' Financial Interests (1995);[23] and
- the EU Convention of 26 May 1997 on the fight against corruption involving officials of the European Communities or officials of member states of the European Union.[24]

The objective of the 1998 Act is:

die verstärkte Bekämpfung der Bestechung und Bestechlichkeit, an der Gemeinschaftsbeamte oder Amtsträger der Mitgliedstaaten der Europäischen Union beteiligt sind,[25]

which translates as the "intensified fight against bribery and corruption involving civil servants of the Community or public officials of the Member States of the European Union".[26] It should be emphasised that section 1 of the EUBestG extends the scope of offences governed by the following provisions of the German Criminal Code:

- "taking bribes intended as an incentive to violate one's official duties" (section 332 of the StGB);

---

21 Cf, Bundesgesetzblatt (Federal Law Gazette) , Year 1998, Part II, No 37 of 21 September 1998 pp 2340 *et seq*, available at www.bgbl.de/xaver/bgbl/start.xav?startbk=Bundesanzeiger_BGBl&jumpTo=bgbl298s2340.pdf (accessed 13 January 2018).

22 The full name of the law is 'Law on the EU Protocol of 27 September 1996 to the Convention on the Protection of the European Communities' Financial Interests' (EU-Bestechungsgesetz - EUBestG) of 10 September 1998.

23 Cf, Official Journal of the European Communities (1996), C313, Volume 39, dated 23 October 1996, pp 1 *et seq*, available at https://eur-lex.europa.eu/legal-content/EN/TXT/PDF/?uri=OJ:C:1996:313:FULL&from=EN (accessed 11 May 2018).

24 Cf, Official Journal of the European Communities (1997), C195, Volume 40, dated 25 June 1997, pp 1 *et seq*, available at https://eur-lex.europa.eu/legal-content/EN/TXT/PDF/?uri=OJ:C:1997:195:FULL&from=EN (accessed 11 May 2018).

25 Cf, Deutscher Bundestag, *Drucksache 13/10424 vom 20.04.1998*, available at http://dip21.bundestag.de/dip21/btd/13/104/1310424.asc (accessed 13 January 2018).

26 Author's free translation.

- "giving bribes as an incentive to violation of the recipient's official duties" (*ibid*, section 334);
- particularly serious cases of taking and giving bribes (*ibid*, section 335);
- "omission of an official act" (*ibid*, section 336); and
- "confiscatory expropriation order and extended confiscation" (*ibid*, section 338).

Prior to the implementation of the 1998 Act, corresponding provisions applied only to domestic public officials. Under the 1998 Act, however acts of bribery concerning a future action or service of a European judge, a member of the European Commission or the European Court of Auditors and a civil servant of the EU, as well as a judge or any other public official of an EU member state, are made punishable offences. Furthermore, article 2, paragraph 2 of the EUBestG extends territorial applicability, regardless of the place (*Recht des Tatorts*) where a conviction for an alleged offence committed by a German national in a foreign state is recorded. Moreover, this also applies to the the recording of convictions of foreigners regarded as 'public officials', as defined in section 11, paragraph 1(2) of the StGB.[27] Under article 2, section 2(2) of the EUBestG, an offence committed abroad can be prosecuted under German law if the person involved is a German judge, a German public official or, under article 2, section 1(1) of the EUBestG, a person who is treated as such, if that person is German.

3.3 The Act on Combating International Bribery 1998[28]

The Act on Combating International Bribery of 10 September 1998 (*Gesetz zur Bekãmpfung internationaler Bestechung*, or *IntBestG*) implements the OECD Convention on Combating Bribery of Foreign Public Officials in International Business Transactions of 17 December 1997[29] (the OECD Convention). The objective of this convention is to protect open competitive markets from the negative impacts of corruption.[30] Among other things, under article 2(1) of the IntBestG, similar to the 1998 Act, bribing foreign public officials shall be treated equally to bribing national public officials if it refers to a future action or service and is performed in the course of international trade in order to provide oneself or a third party with an order or an unfair advantage. Article 2, section 2 of the IntBestG governs the bribery of foreign members of parliament in the context of the course of international trade. Furthermore, article 1(3) of the 1998 Act has extended territorial application. Likewise, sections 334–336 of the StGB apply regardless of the law of the place of commission of the alleged offence where these provisions have been violated by a German person. The OECD Convention therefore plays a key role in the fight against bribery outside of the EU.

---

27 The definition in article 2(1b)(bb) of the IntBestG is expressly waived.

28 Cf, Bundesgesetzblatt, Year 1998, Part II, No 37 of 21 September 1998, pp 2327 *et seq*, available at www.bgbl.de/xaver/bgbl/start.xav?startbk=Bundesanzeiger_BGBl&jumpTo=bgbl298s2327.pdf (accessed 13 January 2018).

29 Available at www.oecd.org/daf/anti-bribery/ConvCombatBribery_ENG.pdf (accessed 13 January 2018).

30 Cf, Deutscher Bundestag, *Bundesdrucksache 13/10428 vom 20.04.1998*, available at http://dip21.bundestag.de/dip21/btd/13/104/1310428.pdf (accessed 13 January 2018).

3.4 Extension of section 299 of the German Criminal Code to include foreign competition[31]

Relevant to the extension of German criminal law was the now repealed joint action of 22 December 1998 adopted by the Council on the basis of article K.3 of the Treaty on European Union, on corruption in the private sector (98/742/JHA).[32] Up to that point, private sector corruption theory was based on the fact that the former version of section 299 of the German Criminal Code ('Taking and giving bribes in commercial practice') mainly concerned domestic competition, ie, bribery payments made abroad were prosecutable in the course of trade only if the interests of German competitors were affected. Implementing the 1998 joint action through the extension of section 299 was intended to result in the prosecution of all competition-related acts of bribery, regardless of the location of the market and the identity of the competitors.[33]

3.5 Extension of the criminal offence of bribing delegates to legislatures[34]

Together with the 48th Criminal Law Amendment Act (*48. Strafrechtsänderungsgesetz*) of 23 April 2014, Germany has implemented the Council of Europe's Criminal Law Convention on Corruption of 27 January 1999,[35] its Additional Protocol to the Criminal Law Convention on Corruption of 15 May 2003[36] and the United Nations Convention Against Corruption of 31 October 2003 (the UN Convention).[37] Germany was, however, criticised internationally for taking 11 years to ratify the UN Convention.[38]

The previous version of section 108e of the StGB on bribing delegates did not correspond to the international agreements signed by Germany. Until the commencement of the 48th Criminal Law Amendment Act, only the buying and selling of votes and ballots during elections was a punishable offence,[39] whereas

---

31 Cf, Bundesgesetzblatt, Year 2002, Part I, No 61 of 29 August 2002, pp 3387 *et seq*, available at www.bgbl.de/xaver/bgbl/start.xav?startbk=Bundesanzeiger_BGBl&jumpTo=bgbl102s3387.pdf (accessed 13 January 2018).

32 Cf, Official Journal of the European Communities, L358/2, dated 31 December 1998, pp 1 *et seq*, available at http://eur-lex.europa.eu/legal-content/EN/TXT/PDF/?uri=CELEX:31998F0742&rid=12 (accessed 11 May 2018).

33 Cf, Deutscher Bundestag, *Bundesdrucksache 14/8998 vom 13.05.2002*, p 9, available at http://dip21.bundestag.de/dip21/btd/14/089/1408998.pdf (accessed 13 January 2018).

34 Cf, Bundesgesetzblatt, Year 2014, Part I, No 17 of 29 April 2014, pp 410 *et seq*, available at www.bgbl.de/xaver/bgbl/start.xav?startbk=Bundesanzeiger_BGBl&jumpTo=bgbl114s0410.pdf (accessed 13 January 2018).

35 Cf, Council of Europe, *Sammlung Europäischer Verträge*, Nr 173 vom 27.01.1999, pp 1 *et seq*, available at https://rm.coe.int/168007f589 (accessed 13 January 2018).

36 Cf, Council of Europe, *Sammlung Europäischer Verträge*, Nr 191 vom 15.05.2003, pp 1 *et seq*, available at https://rm.coe.int/1680083735 (accessed 13 January 2018). *Note:* The Additional Protocol was actually implemented in 2017: cf, Bundesgesetzblatt, Year 2017, Part II, No 15 of 28 June 2017, pp 696 *et seq*, available at www.bgbl.de/xaver/bgbl/start.xav?startbk=Bundesanzeiger_BGBl&jumpTo=bgbl217s0696.pdf (accessed 13 January 2018).

37 Cf, UN Office on Drugs and Crime (UNODC), *United Nations Convention Against Corruption*, available at www.unodc.org/pdf/crime/convention_corruption/signing/Convention-e.pdf (accessed 12 January 2018).

38 Cf, *Deutsche Welle* (2014), *Belatedly, Germany ratifies UN anti-corruption convention*, available at www.dw.com/en/belatedly-germany-ratifies-un-anti-corruption-convention/a-18066424 (accessed 13 January 2018).

39 Cf, Deutscher Bundestag, *Bundesdrucksache 18/476 vom 11.02.2014*, pp 1 *et seq*, available at http://dip21.bundestag.de/dip21/btd/18/004/1800476.pdf (accessed 13 January 2018).

exercising influence over members of parliament or delegates in the course of lobbying was not. Furthermore, prior to the 48th Criminal Law Amendment Act, offering, promising or granting benefits to a foreign member of parliament for an action or omission to act related to his or her mandate was a punishable offence (the former article 2, section 2 of the IntBestG), whereas the same situation in relation to a national member of parliament was not subject to prosecution.

Pursuant to the amendment of section 108e of the German Criminal Code on bribing delegates:[40]

- a person who acts as a member of the federal or a regional parliament and who requests or accepts a promise or accepts unjustifiable benefits for himself or herself or a third party in return for an action or omission to act, and who fulfils such a promise in respect of a matter related to his or her mandate, is liable to up to five years' imprisonment or a fine; and
- likewise, it is an offence to offer, promise, or grant an unjustifiable benefit to a member of the federal or regional parliaments to his or her advantage or the advantage of a third party in exchange for an action or omission to act related to the bribee's mandate.

3.6 The Anti-Corruption Act 2015[41]

Together with the substantial revision of the criminal law on corruption (as discussed below and at 3.5 above), and implementation of the Council of Europe standards (see 3.5 above), Germany has also implemented EU Council Framework Decision 2003/568/JHA on combating corruption in the private sector of 22 July 2003.[42] This Framework Decision goes back to an initiative of the Kingdom of Denmark,[43] which remarked that several member states had not yet ratified the EU convention of 26 May 1997 (see 3.2 above) and the transposition of the joint measure 98/742/JHA (see 3.4 above) was not yet available. Finally, 2003/568/JHA repealed the joint measure 98/742/JHA.

The key amendments made by the Anti-Corruption Act of 20 November 2015 (*Gesetz zur Bekämpfung der Korruption*) are as follows.

- As a result of the amendment of section 299 of the StGB ('Taking and giving bribes in commercial practice'), the condition that the contribution of an advantage intended to disadvantage national or foreign competition ceased to apply. Instead, as provided in section 299, paragraph 1(2) of the StGB, the acceptance of a contribution by a donee violates his or her duties to his or her principal (the so-called '*Geschäftsherrenmodell*'). These amendments have

---

40 The scope of application does not merely apply to the parliaments of the *Bund* and the *Länder*: cf, section 108e, article 3 of the StGB.

41 Cf, Bundesgesetzblatt, Year 2015, Part I, No 46 of 25 November 2015, pp 2025 *et seq*, available at www.bgbl.de/xaver/bgbl/start.xav?startbk=Bundesanzeiger_BGBl&jumpTo=bgbl115s2025.pdf (accessed 13 January 2018). This law is also called the *Korruptionsbekämpfungsgesetz*.

42 Cf, Official Journal of the European Communities, *L* 192/54, Volume 46, dated 31 July 2003, pp 1 *et seq*, available at https://eur-lex.europa.eu/legal-content/EN/TXT/PDF/?uri=CELEX:32003F0568&from=en (accessed 11 May 2018).

43 Cf, Official Journal of the European Communities, C184, Volume 45 dated 2 August 2002 (2002/C 184/04), pp 1 *et seq*, available at: http://eur-lex.europa.eu/legal-content/EN/TXT/PDF/?uri=CELEX:52002IG0802(02)&from=nl (accessed 11 May 2018).

far-reaching consequences for compliance practice, since the provisions of internal company regulations can confer ability on a company to influence behaviours that could give rise to criminal liability.[44]

- There is now full equality between European and national public officials under the criminal law on corruption. Under the amendments to sections 331 and 333 of the StGB, granting an undue advantage to a European public official and its acceptance is now considered a criminal offence. Thus, facilitation payments to European public officials as well as business courtesies (the so-called '*Klimapflege*') are no longer permissible.
- The criminal offence of bribing foreign public officials has been amended, pursuant to section 335a of the StGB. Now, not only active but also passive bribery (section 334 of the StGB) is a criminal offence. It is, however, remarkable that every act of bribery of a foreign public official is now considered a criminal offence so long as a German person is involved. Furthermore, a foreign public official can now be prosecuted under German criminal law.

4. Corruption under the German criminal law

4.1 Introduction

The term 'corruption' does not exist in the German Criminal Code (StGB). Moreover, it is not defined by the German legislature and so does not represent a normative term. The following discussion is intended to be an overview of key provisions of the Criminal Code. Due to the complexity of the criminal law on corruption[45] and for reasons of space, it is not possible to provide detailed explanations of the individual norms. The objective is, rather, to provide an international readership with an inside view on relevant norms of the German criminal law on corruption. Specialist legal advice should be sought with regard to specific cases.

4.2 "Offences committed in public office" (sections 331–336 of the StGB)

"Taking bribes" (section 331 of the StGB) and "taking bribes meant as an incentive to violating one's official duties" (section 332) can only be committed by the following categories of beneficiary:

- public officials;
- European public officials;
- persons entrusted with special public service functions (*Verpflichtete*);
- judges; and
- members of a court belonging to the EU or arbitrators.

The difference between these provisions of the StGB lies in whether the acceptance of a benefit occurs in the "discharge of an official duty" (section 331) or

---

44 Joerg Bielefeld & Lenard Wengenroth, (2015), *Compliance-Berater*, 10/2015, pp 367 *et seq*.

45 Cf, for example (as to the application of section 299 of the StGB), Anja Nöckel (2013), *Grundprobleme zu § 299 StGB*, in *ZJS 1/2013*, pp 50 *et seq*, available at http://zjs-online.com/dat/artikel/2013_1_665.pdf (accessed 14 January 2018).

by violating a beneficiary's official duty (section 332). Taking bribes[46] as a public official or as an entrusted person can lead to up to three years' imprisonment or a fine (section 331). "Taking bribes meant as an incentive to violating one's official duties" (section 332) can lead to between six months' and five years' imprisonment for non-minor offences. Attempted bribery is also punishable under section 332 of the StGB.

It is worth mentioning that the offence does not necessarily need to be complete. The mere willingness of a public official or entrusted person to violate his or her duties through his or her actions or by acting for his or her own benefit while taking a discretionary decision is sufficient.

"Giving bribes" (section 333 of the StGB) and "Giving bribes as an incentive to the recipient to violate his official duties" (section 334) are the converse of the offences to which sections 331 and 332 of the StGB apply. In these cases, the benefactor is the offender, who can be anybody. Under sections 333 and 334, the offender is not necessarily a public official or entrusted person.

Particularly serious cases of the offences to which sections 332 and 334 of the StGB apply are governed by section 335. Under that provision, a particularly serious case arises if "the offence relates to a major benefit", the offender continuously accepts benefits violating his or her official duties or "the offender acts on a commercial basis or as a member of a gang whose purpose is the continued commission of such offences".[47] An offence under section 335, paragraph 1(1) of the StGB is punishable by between one and 10 years' imprisonment.

Section 335a of the StGB governs the application of sections 331–335 to foreign and international public servants. This provision does not stipulate a criminal offence as such but, rather, applies a standard of equality. By so doing, the legislature ensures that the criminal offences stipulated in sections 332 and 334 of the StGB apply to their full extent to foreign and international public servants, so long as they are considered equal within the meaning of section 335a, paragraph 1 and the offence relates to a future judicial act or official duty. The same applies to the giving and taking of bribes.

Under section 336 of the StGB, "the omission to act shall be equivalent to the performance of an official act or a judicial act within the meaning of sections 331 to 335".

4.3 "Taking and giving bribes in commercial practice" (sections 299 and 300 of the StGB)[48]

The criminal offence of taking bribes in commercial practice, the so-called 'passive bribery', is governed by section 299, paragraph 1 of the StGB. Under this provision, the offender must be:

an employee or agent of a business who demands, allows himself to be promised or accepts a benefit for himself or a third party in a business transaction as consideration

46 The situation for judges, members of any court within the EU and arbitrators is considered in outline only.

47 See section 335, paragraph 2 Nos 1–3 of the StGB.

48 Section 337 of the German Criminal Code (*Schiedsrichtervergütung*) is not analysed herein.

for according an unfair preference to third party in the competitive purchase of goods or commercial services.

This provision also applies to acts affecting competition abroad. Furthermore, bribery governed by this provision is punishable if an employee or agent of a business demands, allows himself or herself to be promised or accepts a benefit for himself or herself or for a third party in exchange for an action or omission to act without the approval of his or her company while purchasing goods or commercial services and, in doing so, violates his duties to his principal.

Section 299, paragraph 2 of the StGB applies to the benefactor in the situation to which section 299, paragraph 1 applies. Thus, offering, promising or granting a benefit in this situation is equally punishable. Active or passive bribery in commercial practice is liable to up to three years' imprisonment or a fine.

Particularly serious cases of taking and giving bribes in commercial practice (section 300 of the StGB) are liable to between three months' and five years' imprisonment. The definition of a particularly serious case for the purposes of section 300 corresponds to that in sections 335, paragraph 2(1) and 335, paragraph 2(3).

4.4 "Taking and giving bribes in the healthcare sector" (sections 299a, 299b and 300 of the StGB)

The Act on Fighting Corruption in the Healthcare Sector (*Gesetz zur Bekämpfung der Korruption im Gesundheitswesen*) of 14 April 2016 (the 2016 Act) came into effect on 4 June, 2016.[49] This legislation was passed in response to a decision by the Great Senate of the Federal Court of Justice in a case in which a resident doctor with a concession to provide panel doctor services was held to have acted neither as a public official nor as a statutory health insurance representative for the purposes of section 299 of the StGB, thus creating a lacuna in that provision.[50] The result was that section 299 applied neither to the malpractices alleged nor to the normative rules regarding the taking and giving of bribes in commercial practice. Since the application of section 229 of the StGB was not applicable to resident doctors, pharmacists or other self-employed medical professionals, key risks of corruption could not be covered by the legislation.[51] The 2016 Act was passed to remedy this unsatisfactory legal situation.

Following the implementation of the 2016 Act by section 299a, paragraph 1 of the StGB, corruption in the healthcare sector is now punishable if a member of a medical profession, whose work or job title requires regulated education, demands, allows himself or herself to be promised or accepts a benefit that illegally favours a national or foreign competitor. Furthermore, obtaining the benefit of purchasing pharmaceutical or other medical products is now punishable if they are used directly

---

49 Cf, Bundesgesetzblatt, Year 2016, Part I, No 25 of 3 June 2016, pp 1254 *et seq*, available at www.bgbl.de/xaver/bgbl/start.xav?startbk=Bundesanzeiger_BGBl&jumpTo=bgbl116s1254.pdf (accessed 13 January 2018).

50 Bundesgerichtshof, *Beschluss GSSt 2/11 vom 29.03.2012*, available at http://juris.bundesgerichtshof.de/cgi-bin/rechtsprechung/document.py?Gericht=bgh&Art=pm&Datum=2012&Sort=3&nr=60679&linked=bes&Blank=1&file=dokument.pdf (accessed [14 January 2018).

51 Bundesrat, *Bundesdrucksache 360/15 vom 14.08.2015*, p 7, available at http://dipbt.bundestag.de/dip21/brd/2015/0360-15.pdf (accessed 13 January 2018).

by the member of the medical profession or his or her assistant (section 299a(2) of the StGB) or if demanding, accepting a promise or accepting the benefit was done with a view to transferring patients or materials (section 299a(3)).

Offences under section 299a are liable to up to three years' imprisonment or a fine. Active corruption is governed by section 299b of the StGB, while particularly serious cases are punishable pursuant to section 300.

4.5 "Bribing voters" and "bribing delegates" (sections 108b and 108e of the StGB)

Under section 108b of the StGB, both active and passive bribery are defined punishable offences. A person who offers, promises or grants gifts or other benefits in order to influence a decision by someone else on whom to vote for is liable to up to five years' imprisonment or a fine. Likewise, it it is a punishable offence for a person to demand, allow himself or herself to be promised or to accept gifts or other benefits in exchange for voting or not voting in a certain manner.

Section 108e of the StGB is discussed at 3.5 above.

4.6 Offences related to corruption

Offences directly related to corruption offences, the so-called *Begleitdelikte* (associated crimes) include, for example:

- assistance in avoiding prosecution or punishment in an official capacity (section 258a of the StGB);
- money laundering (section 261);
- "Fraud" (section 263);
- "Embezzlement and abuse of trust" (section 266); and
- "Forgery" (of documents) (section 267).

The following discussion refers exclusively to tax evasion, as defined in section 370 of the Fiscal Code of Germany (*Abgabenordnung*, or AO), as an associated crime. Following the German Annual Tax Law of 11 October 1995,[52] the deduction of business expenses for bribes and bribery payments was restricted for the first time, with effect from the 1996 assessment period. The purpose of this was to deny the possibility of making deductions for bribery where a benefactor or donee is finally convicted or criminal proceedings are terminated (under sections 153 *et seq* of the German Code of Criminal Procedure (*Strafprozessordnung*, or StPO)).[53] Corresponding to section 4, paragraph 5(10), first sentence of the German Income Tax Act (*Einkommenssteuergesetz*, or EStG), bribery payments ceased to be tax deductible (*Abzugsverbot*, or restriction on tax deductions) once the annual tax law of 1996 came into effect. However, if a benefactor intends to claim tax deductions by declaring a bribery payment as a business expense, he or she would be guilty of tax evasion under section 370 of the AO. The same applies if a donee does not declare a bribery payment in his or her income tax return in addition to other income (*sonstige*

---

52 Cf, Bundesgesetzblatt, Year 1995, Part I of 20 October 1995, pp1250 *et seq*. Available at www.bgbl.de/xaver/bgbl/start.xav?startbk=Bundesanzeiger_BGBl&jumpTo=bgbl195s1250.pdf (accessed 5 January 2018).

53 Cf, *Deutsches Steuerrecht* (German Tax Law Journal) (2002), p1990.

Einkünfte) (section 22(3) of the EStG).[54] Tax evasion is liable to up to five years' imprisonment or a fine (section 370, paragraph 1 of the AO).

5. Legislative, judicial and prosecutorial powers

5.1 Introduction

As in other democracies, state authority in Germany is shared between several branches of government. Under article 20, paragraph 2(2) of the Basic Law (*Grundgesetz*, or GG) of the Federal Republic of Germany (FRG, or BRD), these are the legislative, executive and judicial branches.

5.2 Legislative powers

The FRG consists of 16 *Länder* (federal states) and one national state, ie, the Federation, which is called the *Bund*. It should be noted that the *Länder* as well as the *Bund* can enact laws in accordance with powers to legislate conferred by the Basic Law.[55] In the case of the German Criminal Code,[56] the *Bund* and the *Länder* have concurrent powers to legislate. The *Bund* has the principal responsibility to legislate. The *Länder* may only legislate under concurrent powers if the *Bund* does not do so.[57] As the *Bund* regularly complies with its responsibilities, it is responsible.

The *Bundestag* in Berlin is the German Federal Parliament and, at the same time, the most important legislative body in the country. Comprising delegates and parliamentary groups and with the participation of the *Bundesrat* (federal council), "it decides on all laws that fall within its sphere of competence of the German Federation in a legislative process that also requires the participation of the *Bundesrat*".[58] For example, the Anti-Corruption Act of 20 November 2015 was passed by the *Bundestag*. The *Bundestag* is also entitled to introduce bills, which are "debated, deliberated and voted on".[59]

As soon as the *Bundestag* and the *Bundesrat* have approved a federal bill, it is submitted to the Chancellor and to the relevant ministers for signature. The minister responsible for the criminal law is also the Minister of justice and Consumer Protection. Once signed, the Federal President examines the constitutionality of the law. If no objections are raised, the law is published in the *Bundesgesetzblatt* and so comes into effect.[60] Involving the Chancellor and the Minister of Justice and

---

54 Bundesgerichtshof (German Federal High Court), *Urteil vom 02.12.2005*, 5 StR 119/05, available at http://juris.bundesgerichtshof.de/cgi-bin/rechtsprechung/document.py?Gericht=bgh&Art=en&sid=5fe92aa16795c5d5273598d40358d5f5&nr=34961&pos=1&anz=2&Blank=1.pdf (accessed 14 January 2018).

55 Cf, for example, articles 30, 70 and 71 of the *Grundgesetz* (*GG* , the Basic Law of the Federal Republic of Germany).

56 *Ibid*, article 74.

57 Cf, Deutscher Bundestag, available at www.bundestag.de/parlament/aufgaben/gesetzgebung_neu/gesetzgebung/bundesstaatsprinzip/255460 (accessed 13 January 2018).

58 Cf, German Bundestag, available at www.bundestag.de/en/parliament/function/legislation/legislation/197614 (accessed 11 May 2018).

59 Cf, Deutscher Bundestag, available at www.bundestag.de/parlament/aufgaben/gesetzgebung_neu/gesetzgebung (accessed 13 January. 2018).

60 Deutscher Bundestag, available at www.bundestag.de/parlament/aufgaben/gesetzgebung_neu/gesetzgebung/weg/255468 (accessed 13 January 2018).

Consumer Protection in this review process ensures that the Federal Government, ie, the executive branch, takes part in the legislative process.[61] The Federal Government, as the central level of the executive branch, the *Bundesrat* and parliamentary groups all have the right to introduce federal bills in the *Bundestag*.

5.3 Judicial powers

Under article 92 of the GG, the judicial power is entrusted to the judiciary. It is exercised by the Federal Constitutional Court, by the federal courts and by the courts of the *Länder*. The judges are independent and exclusively subject only to the law.[62] The court having subject-matter jurisdiction, such as in cases of corruption, depends on whether the case concerns a felony (section 12, paragraph 1 of the StGB) or a misdemeanour (section 12, paragraph 2 of the StGB). Felonies are liable to a minimum sentence of one year's imprisonment. "Misdemeanours are unlawful acts punishable by a lesser minimum term of imprisonment or by fine."[63]

The jurisdiction of the respective courts is defined in the Courts Constitution Act (*Gerichtsverfassungsgesetz*, or GVG) in the version published on 9 May 1975,[64] last amended by article 10, paragraph 6 of the Law of 30 October 2017.[65]

- If a penalty more severe than a two-year sentence of imprisonment is not to be expected, jurisdiction lies with a local court (section 25(2) of the GVG).
- If the likely term of imprisonment is between two and four years, jurisdiction lies with the *Schöffengericht* (court of first instance for criminal matters, comprising one judge and two lay judges) within the local court (sections 24 and 28 of the GVG).
- The district court has jurisdiction where a term of imprisonment is likely to exceed four years. It also has jurisdiction over an appeal filed against a first instance decision made by a local court (section 74, paragraph 2, second sentence of the GVG).
- The Higher Regional Courts (*Oberlandesgerichte*) are responsible for an appeal against decisions of the aforementioned courts (section 121 of the GVG). Furthermore, they have jurisdiction for hearing and deciding cases at first instance involving crimes against the security of the state (section 120 of the GVG).

The Federal Court of Justice (*Bundesgerichtshof*) located in Karlsruhe is the final instance court for criminal matters and has jurisdiction to hear and rule on the legal remedy of appeal on points of law only (Revision) against judgments of the Higher Regional Courts at first instance and against judgments of the Regional Courts at first instance (section 135 of the GVG), if the Higher Regional Court is not responsible.

61 Cf, article 62 of the GG.
62 *Ibid*, articles 97, paragraph 1 and 20, paragraph 3.
63 *Bundesministerium der Justiz und Verbraucherschutz*, available at: www.gesetze-im-internet.de/englisch_stgb/englisch_stgb.html (accessed 11 May 2018).
64 Federal Law Gazette, Part I, p1077.
65 Federal Law Gazette, Part I, p2618.

5.4 Prosecutorial powers

In Germany, criminal prosecution is the responsibility of the *Staatsanwaltschaft* (Public Prosecutor's Office), the police and the tax investigation authorities (*Steuerfahndung*).

The Public Prosecutor's Office is the investigative authority; its powers are exercised by investigating officials (section 152 of the GVG). By contrast with judges, public prosecutors are not independent but are bound by superior orders as they are not judicial officers. Thus, the Attorney General is assigned to and bound by instructions of the minister of justice of the relevant *Land*. At the federal level, the Federal Attorney General is bound by instructions given by the Minister of Justice and Consumer Protection. The Public Prosecutor, by contrast, is assigned to and bound by instructions given by the department of justice of the relevant *Land*. Its duties include initiating and entrusting the police with investigations. This is often called '*Herrin des Ermittlungsverfahrens*', which means the leading role of the Public Prosecutor in investigations.[66] The Public Prosecutor also decides whether charges are to be pressed, an order for punishment given or proceedings closed. At the same time, it acts as the investigating, accusatory and executory authority.

Corruption can be investigated by the local police or, in particularly serious cases, by the State Office of Criminal Investigation (*Landeskriminalämter*, or LKA).[67] The Criminal Police Office (*Bundeskriminalamt*, or BKA) supports the federal state authorities within its role as the central office.[68]

The duties of the tax investigation authorities are defined by the Fiscal Code of Germany. Under section 208 of the AO, it is in charge of "investigating tax crimes and tax-related administrative offences as well as detecting and investigating unknown tax cases". Furthermore, the tax investigation authorities are responsible for external audits in the context of tax investigation and other tasks by order of the revenue authorities. In the case of detecting bribery payments, the tax investigation authorities are legally bound by section 4, paragraph 5(10), third sentence of the EStG to inform the Public Prosecutor's Office or the relevant administrative authority. Thus, on a legal basis, it is apparent that there is an intensive exchange of information between the Public Prosecutor's Office and the tax investigation authorities.

6. Statistics of corruption offences for 2016

Before addressing the statistics for 2016, it is worth mentioning the estimated number of unreported cases, which is probably quite significant. Former public prosecutor and compliance expert Wolfgang Schaupensteiner has stated that, based on estimates, at best, 5% of corruption offences in Germany are detected.[69] This

66 Cf, for example, Volker Krey (2006), *Deutsches Strafverfahrensrecht* (*Criminal Procedure Law*), pp 166 *et seq.*

67 Cf, for example, *Abteilung 3 des LKA* (State Office of Criminal Investigation) in Berlin, available at www.berlin.de/polizei/dienststellen/landeskriminalamt/lka-3/ (accessed 13 January 2018).

68 Cf, section 1, paragraph 2 of the *Gesetz zur Neustrukturierung des Bundeskriminalamtgesetzes* (Law to restructure the Law on the *Bundeskriminalamt*) of 1 June 2017.

69 Wolfgang Schaupensteiner, commenting in a television documentary, *Wie korrupt ist Deutschland?* (ZDF, 14 September 2017), available at www.zdf.de/dokumentation/zdfzeit/korruption-100.html (accessed 13 December 2017).

implies a non-detection rate of 95% or more. The discussion below seeks to amplify these comments.

The following information is taken from the *Bundeslagebild Korruption 2016*, a report on corruption offences published annually by the Criminal Police Office (*Bundeskriminalamt*, or *BKA*). Due to the implementation of the Anti-Corruption Act 2015 and the subsequent extension of criminal liability for corruption offences, a comparison of 2016 with previous years is possible only to a limited extent.[70] The author therefore focuses exclusively on 2016.

In 2016, a total of 6,502 corruption offences were registered by the police. The five most recorded categories were:

- active bribery ("Giving bribes as an incentive to the recipient's violating his official duties", section 334 of the StGB), with 1,844 offences;
- "taking bribes meant as an incentive to violating one's official duties" (section 332), with 1,209 offences;
- taking bribes (section 331), with 952 offences;
- particularly serious cases of taking and giving bribes in commercial practice (section 300), with 866 offences; and
- "taking and giving bribes in commercial practice" (section 299), with 701 offences.[71]

It was possible to determine financial damage in only 18% of cases, amounting to almost €124 million.[72] Given the low detection rate and the estimated number of unreported cases, it is most likely that financial damage could amount to several billion Euros.

The areas most affected were:

- general public administration, with 49% of cases;
- economic authorities (30%);
- legal and prosecution authorities (18%); and
- politicians (only 3%).[73]

In 66% of cases, the donee was a public official.[74]

Reasons for giving bribes ranged from obtaining an official authorisation (37.9%), improperly obtaining an order (33%) and securing a competitive advantage (8.8%).[75] Consideration took the form of either money in cash (35.3%), non-monetary benefits (31.09%) or entertainment (15%). It is striking that the usage of cash has decreased while non-monetary benefits and entertainment has increased.[76]

According to the statistics of the industry affiliations of benefactors, the sectors

---

70 Cf, BKA (2017), *Bundeslagebild Korruption 2016 vom 17.10.2017*, available at www.bka.de/DE/AktuelleInformationen/StatistikenLagebilder/Lagebilder/Korruption/korruption_node.html (accessed 20 December 2017).

71 *Ibid*, pp 3 *et seq*.

72 *Ibid*, p 9.

73 *Ibid*, p 8.

74 *Ibid*, p 10.

75 *Ibid*, p 13.

76 *Ibid*, p 11.

of logistics (16.3%), construction (14%) and services (21.4%) turned out to be particularly prone to corruption. The fact that the biggest group of benefactors consisted of private persons (47.9%) illustrates that corruption is not only a problem with industries but, rather, is related to society as a whole.[77]

In more than half of the cases, a different preliminary proceeding (eg, for drug trafficking) led to criminal proceedings for corruption. Other corruption offences were detected owing to informants and anonymous reports (22.5%) and information coming from other authorities (13.9%). Comparing the percentages regarding informants and anonymous reports in Germany with a study on how work-related cases of fraud were detected in Western Europe (47.4%, as a result of reports received),[78] it is striking that the number for Germany is comparatively low.

7. Conclusion

It is clear that Germany has made considerable legislative efforts in the fight against corruption. The transposition of international agreements into national law has played a key role. However, even after ratification of the respective agreements, the fight against corruption in Germany is still a matter for discussion and development. The following discussion seeks to give a brief insight.

With regard to white collar crime, the importance of professionalism by authorities in criminal prosecutions is stressed. This seems logical: given the ongoing specialisation of investigators, the risk of detection rises for offenders who commit economic crimes, which in turn may have a deterrent effect. In the past, some *Länder* in Germany have set up so-called *Schwerpunktstaatsanwaltschaften* (Public Prosecutors' Offices with specialised tasks) for white-collar crime.[79] They have managed to prosecute highly complex corruption offences by using specially trained staff. This may well lead to further *Schwerpunktstaatsanwaltschaften* working on white collar crime. Challenges for all criminal prosecution authorities include obtaining appropriately qualified and skilled staff, equipment and resources, issues that are often discussed in public.[80] It remains to be seen how this area of conflict will be resolved in the future.

A decision of 9 May 2017[81] by the Federal Court of Justice has received special attention from compliance and legal experts. In an *obiter dictum*,[82] the Federal Court of Justice stated that the existence of an efficient compliance management system can be a mitigating factor for companies. This decision is also interesting in light of discussions about establishing a criminal law for corporations in Germany. It is

---

77 *Ibid*, p 12.

78 Cf, Association of Certified Fraud Examiners (ACFE) (2016), *Report to the Nations*, available at www.acfe.com/rttn2016/detection.aspx (accessed 14 January 2018).

79 For example, the *Schwerpunktstaatsanwaltschaften* (Specialised State Prosecutor's Offices) in Munich, Stuttgart, Bochum, Mannheim and Frankfurt.

80 Cf, for example, Ralph Knispel (2017), *Staatsanwaltschaft Berlin fehlt Personal*, available at www.rbb24.de/politik/beitrag/2017/10/staatsanwaltschaft-fehlen-mitarbeiter-berlin-knispel.html (accessed 14 January 2018) and Dr Peter Schneiderhan, commenting in the ZDF documentary, *Wie korrupt ist Deutschland?* (note 69 above).

81 Cf, Bundesgerichtshof, *Urteil des 1 Strafsenats vom 09.05.*2017, 1 StR 265/16, p 46, available at http://juris.bundesgerichtshof.de/cgi-bin/rechtsprechung/document.py?Gericht=bgh&Art=en&nr=78723&pos=0&anz=1 (accessed 10 January 2018).

82 Cf, Dr Moritz Jenne & Dr Jan Henning Martens (Eds) (2017), *Corporate Compliance Zeitschrift*, p285.

worth mentioning that, even though it has not yet been possible to enact such a law, under the so-called *Kölner Entwurf eines Verbandssanktionengesetzes*[83] (draft of a criminal law on associations developed by a research group of the University of Cologne, together with external experts), proposed financial penalties imposed on a legal entity could eventually amount to 15% of an entity's income.[84] It remains to be seen, however, whether and how these developments will have an actual impact on the prevention of corruption.

During the coalition negotiations in the aftermath of the 2017 elections to the German Bundestag, discussion arose with regard to the protection of whistleblowers in Germany. It was pointed out by some that whistleblowers are not sufficiently protected and that they have to fear legal consequences for their actions under German labour and criminal laws.[85] Others have argued instead that whistleblowers are already sufficiently protected and that there is no need for amendments to the legal framework.[86] However, since the protection of whistleblowers is a key factor for anti-corruption and the detection of economic crimes generally, it is quite conceivable that the ongoing discussion will lead to legal amendments in the future.

At the political level, a further intensification of transparency regulation is very possible. In 2011, the European Parliament and the European Commission introduced a Transparency Registry at the EU level. This registry lists organisations that wish to influence legislation enacted by and the policymaking of European institutions.[87]

In this context and with particular regard to Germany, Transparency International is currently promoting the implementation of a lobbyist registry, mandatory disclosure of conflicts of interest within executive branch authorities and the Federal government, and improved transparency for donations to political parties in Germany.[88]

83 Cf, Universität zu Köln (2017), *Kölner Entwurf eines Verbandssanktionengesetz*, available at www.verbandsstrafrecht.jura.uni-koeln.de/sites/fg_verbandsstrafrecht/user_upload/Koelner_Entwurf_eines_Verbandssanktionengesetzes__2017.pdf (accessed 14 January 2018).

84 Cf, Simone Kämpfer & Christoph Knauer (2017), *Kommt das Unternehmensstrafrecht?*, in *Legal Tribune Online*, available at www.lto.de/recht/hintergruende/h/unternehmensstrafrecht-koelner-entwurf-verbandssanktionengesetz-haftung-leitung/2/ (accessed 14 January 2018).

85 Dietmar Neurer (2017), *Paradise Papers rücken Informanten in den Fokus*, in *Handelsblatt*, available at www.handelsblatt.com/politik/deutschland/whistleblower-schutz-paradise-papers-ruecken-informanten-in-den-fokus/20552028.html (accessed 8 January 2018).

86 Cf, Deutscher Bundestag (2015), *Hinweisgeber-Schutz kontrovers diskutiert*, available at www.bundestag.de/dokumente/textarchiv/2015/kw12_pa_arbeit_soziales/360644 (accessed 5 February 2018).

87 Cf, Europäische Kommission (European Commission), *Transparenz-Register*, available at: https://ec.europa.eu/info/about-european-commission/service-standards-and-principles/transparency/transparency-register_de (accessed 5 February 2018).

88 Cf, Transparency International, available at www.transparency.de/themen/politik/?L=0 (Accessed 23 December 2017).

Ghana

David Ofosu-Dorte
AB & David

1. Overview of the country *vis-à-vis* corruption

Ghana is often cited as a good example of democracy and good governance in Africa. However, corruption still remains a matter of concern and a topic that keeps coming up in regular mainstream and social media debates. The debate appeared to have reached a climax in 2015, when several judges were caught on video participating in a scandal that was reported widely in local and international media. This was the result of the work of an investigative journalist and resulted in a massive shake-up of the judiciary.

Unfortunately, this was soon followed by the case of *Lolan Ekow Sagoe-Moses & 6 Others v Minister of Justice & Attorney General*,[1] popularly known as the 'Bus Branding case'. In this case, the government awarded a contract worth $818,182 (equivalent to 3,600,000 Ghanaian Cedis (GHS)[2]) to a company called Smarttys. Under the contract, the company was required to brand 116 intra-city buses acquired for the municipal authorities. Investigations conducted into the bus branding in 2015 revealed that, Smarttys overpriced the branding to the tune of $431,818.20 (about GHS1,900,000. This led to huge public outcry and, even though it became apparent that the decision to award the contract was taken without the involvement of Ghana's Ministry of Transport, the scandal led to the resignation of the then Minister of Transport. The government subsequently concluded an agreement with Smarttys for the return of $351,956.37 (GHS1,548,608.04) to the treasury coffers.

These are a couple of examples of matters that appear to shape recent perceptions of corruption in Ghana. On paper, however, Ghana has been placed higher than many African countries in the Transparency International *Corruption Perceptions Index*. Nevertheless, there appears to be a perception in Ghana that government-related corruption is far from having been eradicated. Worldwide, the *Corruption Perceptions Index 2016* ranked Ghana 70th most corrupt country out of 176 countries that were evaluated.

2. The concept of 'corruption' in Ghana

Traditionally, Ghanaians have long had a culture of expressing appreciation in the form of token gifts. Thus, the giving and receiving of token gifts in Ghana is considered to be cultural. However, the Ghanaian culture of gifts may be said to have three key features, whereby a gift is:

1 High Court of Justice (Suit No HR/0027/2015), 13 April 2016.
2 At the prevailing exchange rate of $4.4 to a Cedi as at 7 November 2017.

- a token, eg, in the form of a bottle of whisky;
- given on special occasions only, eg, at Christmas; and
- outside of special occasions, given voluntarily after the performance of a service, in similar fashion to a 'thank you' note.

In other words, gift-giving has become a general custom. However, this cultural approach to gifts appears to have been used as an excuse by some people to perpetrate acts of bribery. For example, the giving of expensive gifts, the acceptance of gifts ahead of the performance of a duty or a demand for a gift in exchange for the performance of a duty have never been part of Ghanaian culture. Thus, any attempt to equate such 'gifts' as cultural is misplaced.

There have been a number of instances in which public officials have even exploited the bureaucratic systems of public institutions in some sectors in order to induce indirectly persons seeking permits or licences to part with money.

3. The legal framework

3.1 Introduction

In Ghana, there is no single composite law that governs corruption. Anti-corruption provisions are therefore scattered across several pieces of legislation. Most of the laws focus on corruption and economic crime in the public sector.

3.2 Key components of the legal framework

(a) The Constitution

Chapter 24 of Ghana's Constitution (the Republican Constitution of 1992) obliges the state to take steps to eradicate corrupt practices and the abuse of power by public officials. All other laws of Ghana are required to be consistent with the Constitution.

(b) The Criminal Offences Act 1960 (Act 29)

This act sets out the offences of active and passive bribery of public officers. It provides that a public officer should not be influenced by a gift, promise or prospect of any valuable consideration in the conduct of duties.

Several amendments were made to the act in 1993 and one of them in particular has since attracted a lot of public debate. The rather notorious section 179A of the act, which makes provision for 'Special Offences', added the criminal offence of wilfully causing financial loss to the state. The charge of causing financial loss is founded on the premise that any person through whose wilful, malicious or fraudulent act or omission the state incurs a financial loss commits an offence. Although, this is not directly a corruption-related offence, it is worthy of note as charges under it have often been combined with charges of corruption. There have been several prosecutions founded on allegations of economic malfeasance under this law in recent years. The amendment has since led to outcries, particularly from politicians who take turns (when in opposition) to accuse their opponents (when in power) of using it as a means of punishing political opponents.

Perhaps the most well-known prosecution based on section 179A occurred in *Republic v Ibrahim Adam & 4 Others*.[3] This case arose out of an agreement signed in 1995 between the government of Ghana and the Export Import Bank of the United States of America (Exim Bank) in respect of the financing of an irrigation and rice production project at Aveyime in the Volta Region of Ghana. In 1996, the Parliament of Ghana approved the credit facility in favour of the rice producer, Quality Grain Company (Ghana) Limited (Quality Grain), a company which had been presented as a party to a joint venture between Mrs Renee Cotton (then Woodard), a US citizen, and the government of Ghana. It turned out that Quality Grain did not in fact exist. Following prosecutions, two government officials[4] were charged with wilfully causing financial losses totalling over $13,274,305.00 without parliamentary approval, in violation of the Constitution of Ghana and the Loans Act 1970 (Act 335).

(c) ***The Economic and Organised Crime Act 2010 (Act 804)***

This act established the Economic and Organised Crime Office (EOCO) as a specialised government agency mandated to monitor, investigate and, where authorised by the Attorney General, prosecute any offence involving serious financial or economic loss to the state.

(d) ***The Anti-Money Laundering Act 2008 (Act 749)***

It is believed that the proceeds of corruption, like those of drugs, are often laundered. Accordingly, Ghana has followed the international trend of passing anti-money laundering legislation. Pursuant to the Anti-Money Laundering Act and its Regulations (LI 1987), the Financial Intelligence Centre (FIC) was set up for the purpose of monitoring and detecting suspicious financial transactions relevant to money laundering activities from financial and non-financial institutions. The law is also intended to assist government organisations in maintaining a comprehensive financial intelligence database for information collection and exchange with counterpart financial intelligence and law enforcement agencies around the world. It is believed that the FIC also assists in tracing money gained from corruption.

(e) ***The Public Procurement Act 2003 (Act 663, as amended by Act 914)***

This act provides administrative and institutional structuring for public procurement procedures. 'Corruption' under the act is defined by reference to the Criminal Offences Act 1960 (see 3.2(b) above). Under the act, it is an offence for any person to exert influence in order to obtain an unfair advantage in a procurement award. It is also an offence to give or agree to give directly or indirectly to any current or former public official, a gratuity in any form, employment, a thing of service or value as an inducement with respect to anything connected with a procurement entity or procurement proceedings. The act enjoins public officials not to put themselves in a

3 Fast Track High Court, Accra, 28 April 2003.

4 The then Minister of Finance and the Director of Legal Sector, Private and Financial Institutions of the Ministry of Finance.

position in which personal interest conflicts or is likely to conflict with the performance of their functions. The Public Procurement Authority publishes a monthly bulletin containing information notices of proposed procurement, notices of invitation to tender and contract award information.

(f) ***The Whistleblower Act 2006 (Act 720)***

To further enhance the fight against corruption, this act was passed to empower individuals, in the public interest, to disclose information that relates to unlawful or other illegal conduct or corrupt practices of others. The disclosure of impropriety may be made where a person has reason to believe that:

- an economic crime has been committed or is about to be committed;
- another person has not complied with a law or is in the process of breaking a law which imposes an obligation on that person; and
- there has been misappropriation or mismanagement of public resources in a public institution.

The act allows a whistleblower to disclose the information to his or her employer, a police officer, the Attorney-General or members of Parliament. A whistleblower is not liable to civil or criminal proceedings in respect of a disclosure unless it is proved that the disclosure was made with malicious intent. A whistleblower has protection against victimisation by his or her employer or fellow employees or by other persons. Where a whistleblower raises an issue against an employer, he or she is deemed to have been subjected to victimisation if, as a result of making the disclosure, the whistleblower is threatened with dismissal, suspended, declared redundant, denied promotion, transferred against his or her will or intimidated in any form.

(g) ***The Public Financial Management Act 2016 (Act 921)***

To ensure adherence to ethics in public finance, this act was passed to regulate financial management of the public sector. It prescribes the responsibilities of persons entrusted with financial management of public funds. The Minister of Finance has oversight of the use of public funds. The relevant provision on corruption states that any person connected with the management of public funds or assets who demands, accepts or receives money or valuable consideration for the performance of official duties or as an inducement to influence any decision commits an offence and is liable to a fine or to imprisonment for a term not exceeding 10 years, or both.

(h) ***The Audit Service Act 2000 (Act 584)***

This act governs the periodic audit of public offices, public corporations and institutions established by an Act of Parliament. Any member of the Audit Service who demands or takes any bribe for the neglect or non-performance of his or her duty commits an offence and is liable on conviction to a fine or to imprisonment for a term not exceeding two years, or both.

(i) ***The Internal Audit Agency Act 2003 (Act 658)***

This act established the Internal Audit Agency (the Agency) to coordinate and supervise the provision of quality assurance for internal audit activities and so ensure the efficient use of state resources. It applies to internal audits within ministries, departments and agencies of state and the metropolitan, municipal and district assemblies. Any member of staff or employee of the Agency who demands or takes a bribe, gratuity, recompense or reward for the neglect, omission, commission or performance of duty under this act is liable to a fine or to imprisonment for a term not exceeding five years, or both.

(j) ***The Income Tax Act 2015 (Act 896, as amended)***

Anti-corruption provisions are also found in the Income Tax Act. This provides that an officer or employee of the state who directly or indirectly asks for or receives, in connection with his or her duties, a payment or promise or security for that payment or reward is liable on summary conviction to imprisonment for a term of not less than one year and not more than three (3) years, or a fine, or both.

(k) ***Comment***

It has been advocated that offences of corruption should be treated as more 'serious' crimes, ie, that punishment should be made appropriately painful by also providing civil remedies to recover ill-gotten gains. It has also been proposed that Ghana should consider enacting a consolidated Bribery and Corruption Act.

3.3 'Soft law'

It has generally been recognised that the culture of gifts has been abused. In an attempt to arrest the situation, the government published the Code of Ethics for Ministers and Political Appointees (the Code) on 8 July 2013. Under the Code, gifts exchanged during an official visit are to be deemed as gifts to the office and not to the official occupying the office. Gifts may only be retained by an official if their value is not more than GHS200 ($60) and any gift exceeding GHS500 ($151) must be relinquished when leaving office.

4. Institutions established to enforce the law and punish corruption

For the purposes of enforcement, the most relevant institutions assigned the responsibility for the fight against corruption include the following.

4.1 The Commission on Human Rights and Administrative Justice (CHRAJ)

The Constitution mandates the CHRAJ to investigate complaints of corruption and abuse of power by public officers and the misappropriation by them of public moneys. The CHRAJ is also mandated under the Constitution to take appropriate steps, including reporting to the Attorney General and the Auditor General of the results of such investigations. The CHRAJ, as part of its mandate, has investigated a number of high level cases that have been successfully prosecuted in the courts. The CHRAJ was created by the Commission on Human Rights and Administrative Justice Act 1993 (Act 456).

4.2 The Criminal Investigation Department (CID) of the Ghana Police Service

The CID has a mandate to carry out investigations based on complaints or allegations made by the public which are forwarded to the office of the Attorney General for prosecution.

4.3 The EOCO

As part of its mandate under the Economic and Organised Crime Act 2010 (see 3.2(c) above), the EOCO also has power to carry out investigations and recommend the prosecution of offences relating to serious financial and economic loss to the state.

4.4 The Financial Intelligence Centre (FIC) of the Bank of Ghana

The Bank of Ghana has set up the Financial Intelligence Centre (FIC) (see 3.2(d) above), the main role of which is to monitor and detect suspicious financial transactions and the identity of persons behind these transactions. It allows the tracking of illegal money transactions in banks and other financial institutions and is mandated to (among other things); process, analyse and interpret reports of suspicious financial transactions, including those used to fund illegal activities. The FIC is also required to cooperate with investigating authorities and their foreign counterparts where necessary.

4.5 The Office of Accountability

This unit was established by the President in 2003 as a watchdog agency for the close monitoring of ministers and other government executives.

4.6 The Financial and Economic Crimes Court (FECC)

This is a specialised division of the High Court created by the Chief Justice to handle high profile corruption and other related cases involving public office holders. The court has jurisdiction in all matters, both civil and criminal, including offences created under legislation discussed at 3.2 above, including the Criminal Offences Act 1960, the Public Financial Management Act 2016, the Public Procurement Act 2003 and the Internal Audit Agency Act 2003. The court also has jurisdiction under the Anti Money Laundering Act 2008 and the Economic and Organised Crime Act 2010, in addition to jurisdiction conferred on it by any other enactment.

With the exception of the CHRAJ, these institutions do not have direct prosecution powers and may only carry out prosecutions if expressly authorised by the Attorney-General.

5. Ghana's international anti-corruption commitments and their effects on the fight against corruption

5.1 Introduction

Ghana is a signatory to a number of international anti-corruption treaties. Currently, it has signed and ratified the following international agreements:

- the United Nations Convention Against Corruption (2003) (UNCAC);
- the African Union Convention on Preventing and Combating Corruption (2003) (AUC); and

- the Economic Community of West African States (ECOWAS) Protocol on the Fight Against Corruption (2001).

5.2 Codification by Ghana of international obligations

Ghana's legal and institutional framework is generally compliant with the UNCAC. Obligations under the UNCAC have been codified in Ghanaian law in the following respects.

(a) Article 7(3) of the UNCAC: political parties

Article 7(3) of the UNCAC is codified by the Political Parties Act 2000 (Act 574). This act provides that only citizens may contribute in cash or kind to the funds of a political party. Provision of funds to political parties by non-citizens (directly or indirectly) is therefore outlawed.

(b) Article 9 of the UNCAC

Article 9 (public procurement and management of public finances) has been codified in the following laws.

- The Public Procurement Act 2003: see 3.2(e) above.
- The Public Financial Management Act 2016: see 3.2(g) above.
- The Internal Audit Agency Act 2003: see 3.2(h) above.

(c) Article 10 of the UNCAC and article 9 of the AUC: the right to information

Both article 10 of the UNCAC and article 9 of the AUC seek to enhance transparency in public administration through access to information. Further, article 13 of UNCAC makes provision for effective access to information and the right to receive information. Although the Constitution of Ghana provides for a right to information and for the legislation to implement it, the Right to Information Bill has been pending before Parliament for about 20 years.

(d) Other steps

- National Anti-Corruption Action Plan (NACAP): The recommendation of a report of the United Nations Office on Drugs and Crime[5] for countries to adopt national anti-corruption plans has been implemented in Ghana by the NACAP. The Plan integrates anti-corruption measures into the programmes of state agencies and allows for sustained coordination between agencies and other stakeholders. There is, however, a need for capacity building for financial investigations, the establishment of an asset declaration system and better developed extradition laws to foster international cooperation.
- The US Foreign Corrupt Practices Act 1976 and the UK Bribery Act 2010.

It has been observed that, as a result of the extra-territorial application of the US

---

5 United Nations Office on Drugs and Crime (UNDOC), *The United Nations Convention against Corruption, National Anti-Corruption Strategies – A Practical Guide for Development and Implementation* (September 2015), available at www.unodc.org/documents/corruption/Publications/2015/National_Anti-Corruption_Strategies_-_A_Practical_Guide_for_Development _and_Implementation_E.pdf.

Foreign Corrupt Practices Act 1976 and the UK Bribery Act 2010, most American and UK entities and their intermediaries operating in Ghana are increasingly taking steps to ensure that their businesses are compliant with both of these acts.

6. Recent inquiries and cases

6.1 General observations

(a) *Number of cases*

It appears that, notwithstanding the numerous laws passed and institutions set up to prevent and fight corruption, very few corruption cases have been prosecuted. This observation is based upon the numerous allegations versus the number of prosecutions. Additionally, it appears that prosecution of public officials who are alleged to have been involved in corrupt acts often occurs only where the political party under whose regime the offence occurred is out of power. Allegations made against persons in public office are at times met with a response asking those making the allegation to 'produce the evidence'.

In *Republic v High Court, Accra, ex parte CHRAJ (Richard Anane, Interested Party)*,[6] the CHRAJ sent a letter inviting Dr Anane (the then Minister of Roads and Transport) to comment on an investigation that it was conducting. In his reply, he requested that the evidence be submitted to the CHRAJ by the complainant. The CHRAJ responded that there was no complainant and that it was undertaking the investigations of its own volition without a formal complaint, on the basis of its understanding of its mandate under the Constitution and also the provisions contained in the CHRAJ Act.

The Supreme Court held that for the CHRAJ to act on the alleged corrupt practices of Dr Anane or any government official, a written or oral complaint must first be made against such person to the CHRAJ. The Supreme Court ruled further that the complaint must be made by an identifiable individual or corporate body.

A number of commentators have taken the view that anti-corruption agencies, such as the CHRAJ and the EOCO, have not been ineffective in combating the menace of corruption. Many of them have explained this away with the excuse of 'lack of resources'. For example, it is said that the CHRAJ has been unable to attract a high calibre of lawyers and other professional staff owing to relatively low salary levels. There are also commentators who blame the apparent ineffectiveness on 'lack of real autonomy' and 'lack of political will' to fight corruption.

(b) *Relevant inquiries and cases*

Notwithstanding the criticisms, there have been a number of prosecutions which have led to the conviction of public officials for corrupt practices. There have also been a number of investigations into corrupt practices. The following are some examples.

---

6 [2007–2008] SCGLR 213.

Investigation into allegations of conflict of interest against the President of the Republic of Ghana:[7] On 15 June 2016, media reports alleged that the President had (when he was Vice President) engaged in corrupt practices in relation to the grant of two contracts to a contractor from Burkina Faso, Djibril Kanazoe. The reports indicated that the President had received a Ford Expedition vehicle sometime in 2012 and receipt of this gift was in conflict with his duty to award such contracts using the appropriate procurement methods.

A petition was submitted to the CHRAJ by three complainants on the basis that the President, in accepting the vehicle as a gift from the contractor, had placed himself in a conflict of interest situation. On 28 September 2016, the CHRAJ decided that the President had breached the 'gift policy' section in its Code of Conduct for Public officers of Ghana and Conflict of Interest Guidelines (2006) when he accepted the gift. However, the CHRAJ also concluded that the President was not culpable of bribery or conflict of interest.

The concluding part of the decision stated:

At the end of the preliminary investigation the Commission has come to the conclusion, based on the extensive evidence assembled, that the allegations that the Respondent has contravened Article 284 of the 1992 Constitution by putting himself in situations of conflict of interest has not been substantiated. Consequently, the Commission holds that full or further investigations into the allegations are not warranted. The allegations therefore, are hereby dismissed.

Bribery scandal involving judges: As discussed at 1 above, Ghana was plunged into a state of shock in 2015 by the biggest corruption scandal ever to hit the judiciary. News broke of revelations by an investigative journalist, Anas Aremeyaw Anas, of corruption on the part of 34 judges from the High Court, the circuit courts and the magistrates' courts. Mr Anas produced video recordings of judges allegedly collecting bribes at various times that were intended to influence their judgments. The persons allegedly caught on camera attempted to prevent the screening of the recording.[8] The premier showing of the video recording subsequently revealed that some of the judges implicated were the same judges who had either sat in cases relating to the alleged payment of bribes or had actually ruled in favour of persons on whose behalf the various bribes were paid.

A disciplinary committee set up by the then Chief Justice commenced investigations into the bribery allegations and indicated that swift and decisive sanctions would be applicable to judges found to be culpable of corruption. Some of the judges involved lost their jobs and the Judicial Service has initiated measures to salvage the integrity of the judiciary.

The GYEEDA scandal: In 2010, the media reported on a scandal relating to the Ghana Youth Employment and Entrepreneurial Development Agency (GYEEDA) in

---

7 See http://citifmonline.com/2016/09/29/full-text-chrajs-report-on-mahamas-ford-gift-saga.

8 *His Lordship Justice Paul Uuter Dery v Tiger Eye PI and others* (J1/29/2015), [2016] GHASC 10 (4 February 2016).

which it was alleged that the Director of GYEEDA had entered into a memorandum of understanding (MOU) with a company without following due process. There were further allegations that a number of payments of about $931,818.20 (about GHS4.1 million) had been made to the company for various services that were never performed.

As a result of the scandal, the State instituted an action against the former National Coordinator of GYEEDA, Mr Abuga Pele, for wilfully causing financial loss to the state, abetment of crime and intentionally misapplying public property; and the Chief Executive Officer of Goodwill International Group, Mr Philip Assibit, for defrauding by false pretences and dishonestly causing loss to public property.[9] The High Court found them guilty and sentenced them to six and 12 years' imprisonment respectively on 23 February 2018. The High Court further ordered the state to recover all assets and money belonging to it from them.

The Mabey & Johnson case: In another case that had international dimensions and related to the construction sector, United Kingdom company Mabey & Johnson Ltd was accused by the UK Serious Fraud Office (SFO) of having been involved in corrupt activities in Ghana. As a result, the SFO was reported to have made available to the government of Ghana documentary evidence of corruption involving public officers and ministers of state in Ghana, specifically that Mabey & Johnson had paid bribes to those persons for construction projects in Ghana sometime in 2009. Former President John Evans Atta Mills (the then President of Ghana) invited the CHRAJ to investigate the allegations involving the Ghanaian officials. CHRAJ commenced its investigations in 2010.

However, the Ghanaian officials allegedly involved in the bribery scandal instituted an action in the Human Rights Court to restrain the CHRAJ from investigating the matter. They claimed that some prejudicial comments attributed to the then Commissioner of the CHRAJ had been made to and published by a television station.[10] The High Court ruled in favour of the applicant and ordered the CHRAJ to cease investigations into the matter. The ruling was subsequently overturned by the Court of Appeal but a further appeal was made to the Supreme Court. At the time of writing, public records indicate that the CHRAJ has since put the investigations on hold pending the result of the final appeal, which was still pending as at 30 April 2018.

The basis of the Mabey & Johnson case was an application of the UK's Bribery Act 2010 in Ghana and an example of the application of the UK's cross-border enforcement action and global settlement agreements in the investigation and prosecution of corporate global bribery and corruption violations.

---

9 *Republic v Abuga Pele & Philip Assibit* (FTRM 122/14).

10 *Republic v Commission on Human Rights and Administrative Justice, ex parte Kwame Reprah and 5 others* (unreported ruling of the Human Rights Division of the High Court, Accra (Suit No HRCM 46/10), 11 June 2010, UP Dery J).

Alfred Agbesi Woyome v Attorney General of the Republic of Ghana & Another:[11] In July 2004, Ghana won the right to host the 2008 African Cup of Nations football tournament, popularly known as CAN 2008. As a result of this, there was a need to rehabilitate football stadia and other sporting facilities in Ghana and the contract was awarded to Vamed Engineering Gmbh & Co KG. Vamed later assigned all its rights and obligations under the contract to Waterville Holdings.

The government of Ghana signed two separate but similar agreements with Waterville for the rehabilitation of a number of stadia in Ghana (relating to, respectively, the Ohene Djan and El Wak stadia in Accra and the Baba Yara stadium in Kumasi). Even though the agreements did not take effect, Waterville commenced some works on the stadia sites. In 2006, the government terminated the agreements with Waterville on the ground that the contracts had not received approval from Ghana's Cabinet in accordance with clause 17 of the contracts, so that they never became effective.

Waterville sued, claiming fees and pre-financing costs for the initial construction works from the government and not their sub-contractors, Vamed, as agreed. The court gave judgment in favour of Waterville.

Waterville had engaged a number of persons, including Alfred Agbesi Woyome, a Ghanaian businessman, to provide services to the company. In 2012, Woyome[12] was charged with corruption as a beneficiary of an $11,590,909.10 (GHS51 million) judgment debt pursuant to a suit against the state, which sum was paid to him as compensation for illegal termination of a financial engineering contract by the previous government. A former Attorney General, Martin Amidu, instituted an action in the Supreme Court against the then Attorney General, Woyome and Waterville Holdings (BVG) Ltd for a declaration that the contract between the government of Ghana and Waterville, which formed the basis for the claim by Woyome was void. According to the claim, Waterville's contract had been properly abrogated and the subsequent decision awarding it compensation for breach of contract was null and void.

The Supreme Court in the first instance declared the Waterville contract to have been properly abrogated. No order for a refund of damages received by Woyome was made, however. Mr Amidu then brought an application for review against Woyome and the Attorney General for an order for the refund of the monies paid to Woyome. On 29 July 2014, the Supreme Court, after hearing the review application, ordered Woyome to refund the sum of $11,636,363.64 (GHS51.2 million) paid to him by the state.

In 2015, however, the High Court, acquitted Woyome of any criminal liability for corruption as a beneficiary of $11,590,909.10 in the matter.

Martin Amidu v Attorney General, Isofoton and Anane Agyei-Forson:[13] In this case, a Spanish company called Isofoton entered into two international business agreements with the government of Ghana in 2006 without parliamentary approval

11 Suit No RPC/152/10, High Court (Commercial Division), Accra.
12 *Martin Amidu v Attorney-General & 2 others* (J1/23/2012).
13 [2013–2014] SCGLR 167.

for agricultural irrigation and rural electrification projects in Ghana based on solar technologies. Under article 181(5) of the Constitution of Ghana, the government requires parliamentary approval before executing contracts involving international business or economic transactions. Press reports indicated that the government of Ghana re-awarded the contract to another Spanish company, Elecnor. Isofoton therefore sued the government for wrongful termination of the contract, seeking more than $1.3 million (about GHS5,850,000)[14] in damages.

Isofoton obtained judgment in default of appearance by the government. Settlement negotiations then took place between the parties which led to the setting aside of the default judgment and the entry of a consent judgment by the court in favour of Isofoton, pursuant to which the government paid $325,472 (about GHS1,464,624)[15] of the claim.

Martin Amidu (the former Attorney General referred to in the Woyome case discussed above), a gentleman often referred to in social media in Ghana as a champion of citizen vigilantism, brought an application before the court stating (among other things) that Isofoton had no basis to make the claims because it had no contract with the government of Ghana that could result in payment of damages for breach. The Supreme Court held (among other things) that the contract between Isofoton and government, which had not been laid before Parliament, was void and of no effect. The Supreme Court further ordered Isofoton to refund the Cedi equivalent of $325,472.00 that had been paid to it.

CHRAJ and PV Obeng & Others: In 1996, a much earlier case on corruption involving four very high ranking officials made major headlines. Following the publication of allegations in the press, the CHRAJ was requested by the then President to investigate allegations of corruption, illegal acquisition of wealth and abuse of office against four individuals.[16] At the end of the investigations, adverse findings were made against three of them, while one (the Presidential Adviser on Government Affairs, Mr PV Obeng) was exonerated.

7. Conclusions and recommendations

The following conclusions may be reached and recommendations made from the above analysis.

- Notwithstanding the numerous allegations of corruption made in the media, the actual number of prosecutions and convictions do not reflect the frequency of allegations.
- The fight against corruption in Ghana may be given a boost if:
  - the boards of both public and private institutions provide adequate training on anti-corruption to their staff and institute measures that act as a deterrent;

14 At the prevailing exchange rate of $4.5 to a Cedi as at 27 April 2018.

15 At the prevailing exchange rate of $4.5 to a Cedi as at 27 April 2018.

16 See Dr Sam K Asibuo, *The Role of The Commission on Human Rights and Administrative Justice (CHRAJ) in Promoting Public Service Accountability Under Ghana's Fourth Republic*, available at http://unpan1.un.org/intradoc/groups/public/documents/CAFRAD/UNPAN017693.pdf.

- civil society were to increase its demands for accountability. Further, civil society may mobilise its own resources or collaborate with other parties to conduct preliminary investigations into corruption allegations, where necessary or appropriate. This would enable them to gather preliminary evidence, which might then make it difficult for government officials to forestall further investigations.

- Amendments to the applicable laws should be made to enable anti-corruption agencies such as the CHRAJ to carry out direct prosecution of offences without having to await the approval of the Attorney General. This is necessary because the Attorney General and the Minister of Justice are the same person and it often appears that the political will to prosecute such offences is lacking.
- Attempts should be made to give full effect to article 21(1)(f) of the Constitution of Ghana by enacting the long overdue Right to Information Bill (see 5.2(c) above).

Hong Kong

Ada SW Chan
Sophia SY Lam
Felix KH Ng
Haldanes

1. Overview: history and perception of corruption in Hong Kong

1.1 History of corruption

Anti-corruption laws have had a long history in Hong Kong since the colonial era. As early as 1898, bribery had been a criminal offence in Hong Kong with the enactment of the Misdemeanours Punishment Ordinance. This was subsequently replaced by the Prevention of Corruption Ordinance 1948, which was enforced by the Anti-Corruption Office of the Hong Kong Police Force.

In the 1960s and 1970s, there was rapid social and economic development in Hong Kong. The insatiable needs of the swelling population, coupled with scarcity of resources, made Hong Kong a hotbed of corruption; to earn a living and to secure a higher priority in obtaining goods and services, many people resorted to the 'backdoor route' by taking and offering bribes. Corruption was particularly rampant within the Police Force; corrupt police officers would offer protection to vice, gambling, drug and triad activities in return for illicit remuneration.

The government at the time was powerless to deal with the widespread syndicated corruption, as a result of which the community gradually lost patience. The situation reached a tipping point in the early 1970s, when Chief Police Superintendent Peter Godber, who had been under investigation for controlling disproportionate assets of over HK$4.3 million, fled Hong Kong undetected by abusing his senior position in the Police Force. Students took to the streets to protest and condemned the government for failing to tackle corruption in the territory. Protestors carrying placards with slogans like "Fight Corruption, Arrest Godber" could be seen everywhere, demanding that he be extradited to stand trial.

In response to the public outcry, a Commission of Inquiry into Godber's escape was formed under the chairmanship of Mr Justice Alastair Blair-Kerr. He pointed out that:

> *responsible bodies generally feel that the public will never be convinced that Government really intends to fight corruption unless the Anti-Corruption Office is separated from the Police …*

Thereafter, Governor Sir Murray Maclehose delivered a speech to the legislature in which he advocated the establishment of an independent agency solely dedicated to eradicating corruption.

1.2 Establishment of the Independent Commission Against Corruption

Such initiatives were instrumental to the inception of the Independent Commission

Against Corruption (ICAC) in 1974 with the enactment of the Independent Commission Against Corruption Ordinance (Cap 204) (ICACO). The ICAC is independent of the civil service and the police. It was only answerable directly to the Governor of Hong Kong before 1 July 1997. It remains so to the post-1997 equivalent officer, the Chief Executive of the Hong Kong Special Administrative Region (HKSAR). The ICAC adopts a three-pronged approach to the fight against corruption: law enforcement, prevention and education, which are undertaken by its Operations Department, Corruption Prevention Department and Community Relations Department respectively.

The cornerstone of the ICAC's anti-corruption framework is the Prevention of Bribery Ordinance (Cap 201) (POBO). The ICAC's strenuous efforts over the last four decades have successfully transformed Hong Kong from a city plagued with syndicated corruption into a highly regulated business environment with a level playing field.

1.3 Recent developments

Up to the present, Hong Kong has continued to enjoy a stellar reputation as an Asian business and financial hub, thanks to its rigorous and effective anti-corruption regime. This is evidenced by the following commentaries.

- In the 2017 Index of Economic Freedom published by the Heritage Foundation,[1] Hong Kong continues to be the world's freest economy for the 23rd consecutive year, with the commendation that:

  > *there is little tolerance for corruption and government integrity is buttressed by a high degree of transparency.*

  With regard to the rule of law, the report further acclaims Hong Kong for having "an excellent track record in combating corruption".
- According to the *Corruption Perceptions Index*, published by Transparency International, Hong Kong has consistently been identified as among the top 20 economies with very low levels of corruption since its launch in 1995. Hong Kong's latest ranking in the *Corruption Perceptions Index 2016*[2] is 15th out of 176 countries and territories surveyed and fourth in the Asia-Pacific region, immediately behind New Zealand, Singapore and Australia.

2. The concept of 'corruption' in Hong Kong

The ICAC's most common forms of ammunition against corruption are the statutory offences created under the POBO and the originally English common law offence of misconduct in public office, which has existed since the 18th century.

Under the POBO, the most important element of corruption and bribery is 'advantage', which is the bedrock of the territory's anti-corruption regime. Generally speaking, offering, soliciting or accepting an advantage as a reward or inducement for doing (or forbearing to do) an act or showing favour (or disfavour) constitutes an

---

1 Heritage Foundation, 2017 *Index of Economic Freedom*, available at www.heritage.org/index/country/hongkong.

2 Transparency International, *Corruption Perceptions Index 2016*, available at www.transparency.org/news/feature/corruption_perceptions_index_2016.

offence under the POBO. Both the offeror and the recipient of an advantage would be criminally liable.

2.1 Meaning of "advantage" under the POBO

Under section 2 of the POBO, the definition of "advantage" encompasses a broad spectrum of benefits, including:

- property (including a gift, loan, fee, reward or commission consisting of money or of any valuable security or other property or interest in property);
- discharge of a debt;
- employment;
- any other service or favour other than entertainment;
- forbearance from or exercise of any right, power or duty; and
- any promise or offer of any of the aforesaid benefits.

2.2 Application of the POBO to the public and private sectors

The provisions of the POBO apply to both the public and private sectors.

The public sector encompasses government departments, public bodies, prescribed officers and public servants. In general terms, under section 2 "prescribed officers" means all government and judicial officers, while "public servants" is a broader concept that includes prescribed officers and employees of any public bodies (eg, a bus company or a power company).

With regard to the private sector, offences under the POBO apply to anyone who is in a 'principal' and 'agent' relationship. In a business context, this usually applies to an employer and employee relationship.

Three main types of *actus reus* apply under the POBO in both the public and private sectors: offer, solicitation or acceptance of advantages. The application of these concepts is discussed at 3 below.

2.3 The "entertainment" exemption

While the term "advantage" appears to be a catch-all concept in business and governmental dealings, the POBO has specifically carved out entertainment as a permissible exception. That said, "entertainment" is very narrowly defined as:

> *the provision of food or drink, for consumption on the occasion when it is provided, and of any other entertainment connected with, or provided at the same time.*

In other words, the provision of drinks and meals and other forms of entertainment (eg, attendance at a musical performance before or after a meal) for consumption on a particular occasion will not be deemed an "advantage" for the purposes of the POBO.

It is, however, noteworthy that according to the guidelines on conduct and discipline of civil servants issued by the government of the HKSAR,[3] officials should not accept any –

> *lavish or unreasonably generous or frequent entertainment, or indeed any entertainment that is likely to give rise to any potential or real conflict of interest, put the officers in*

---

3 Administration of the Civil Service, *Summary of the Regulatory Regime on Acceptance of Advantages and Entertainment by Civil Servants*, available at www.csb.gov.hk/english/admin/conduct/ files/aae_e.pdf.

an obligatory position in the discharge of their duties, compromise their impartiality or judgment, or bring them or the public service into disrepute bearing in mind public perception …

While government officials who receive entertainment may be able to take advantage of the statutory exemption under the POBO, they may still be subject to the government's disciplinary actions or the common law offence of misconduct in public office.

2.4 No *de minimis* exemption

No *de minimis* exemption is prescribed under the POBO, which means that the value of an advantage offered or obtained is completely irrelevant to criminal liability, so that even a minor amount of advantage would suffice.

For example, in *HKSAR v Cheung Shiu Chor*,[4] the Court of First Instance upheld the decision of the magistrates' court in which the defendant was convicted for providing red packets containing cash which ranged in amount from HK$100 to HK$800 (approximately US$13–$103) to supermarket managers in return for their disclosure of information on milk powder sales and purchases. The defendant was found guilty under the POBO and sentenced to 6 months' imprisonment.

2.5 *Quid pro quo* is not an essential element

Quid pro quo is not an essential element of bribery and corruption under the POBO. Section 11 specifically provides that it is no defence that the conduct for which an advantage was offered or received did not materialise. For example, if a person receives an advantage from a third party without his or her employer's authorisation, it is irrelevant whether he or she had actual intention or power to carry out the required conduct, or whether the actual required conduct was in fact carried out.

3. Anti-corruption laws and regulations in Hong Kong

There are two main statutes in Hong Kong which govern corruption and bribery and the fairness of the electoral process. In addition, a common law offence specifically targets the abuse of power by government officials. These are discussed below.

3.1 The POBO

As previously stated, the cornerstone of the ICAC's mechanism of enforcement against public and private sector corruption and bribery is the POBO, which not only defines a number of types of criminal offences but also provides the investigative powers of the ICAC.

(a) Public sector corruption: sections 3–8 and 10

Public sector corruption offences under the POBO apply to government officials ranging from the Chief Executive, prescribed officers (mainly government and judicial officers) and public servants (a broader concept covering prescribed officers and employees of public bodies): see 2.2 above.

---

4 [2014] HKCFI 1690, 18 September 2014 (judgment in Chinese).

The most common offence prosecuted by the ICAC is that under section 4, which prohibits public servants and the Chief Executive from unlawfully soliciting or accepting advantages in return for performing or abstaining from performing their official duties. Both the recipient and the offeror of advantage would be liable and the offence covers a broad spectrum of corrupt transactions.

Sections 5, 6 and 7 of POBO cover offences concerning advantages in connection with public sector contracts, tenders and auctions respectively.

Section 3 makes it an offence for prescribed officers to accept or solicit an advantage without the general or special permission of the Chief Executive. Section 8 prohibits offering of an advantage to prescribed officers and public servants while having dealings with government departments and public bodies. It is noteworthy that sections 3 and 8 do not require the advantage to be paid for a corrupt purpose. In other words, the mere act of offering, soliciting and accepting advantages would be sufficient to constitute an offence, which is in stark contrast with the offences under sections 4–7 discussed above. Furthermore, sections 3 and 8 do not apply to the Chief Executive, which is a controversial lacuna in the law that is currently under active debate in Hong Kong.

In addition to bribery, the ICAC has another powerful weapon in investigating corrupt government officers, one that is particularly useful where the officer concerned conceals his or her illicit fortune without leaving any trace of its origin. Under section 10 of the POBO, a prescribed officer or the Chief Executive who possesses assets disproportionate to, or maintains a standard of living not commensurate with his or her official emoluments, shall be guilty of an offence unless he or she can give a satisfactory explanation in relation to how the assets are legitimately acquired or how such a lavish lifestyle could be maintained.

(b) Private sector corruption: section 9

Private sector corruption is frequently prosecuted by the ICAC under sections 9(1) and (2) of the POBO, which target corrupt transactions with agents. The offences under these provisions comprise three elements:

- the offer, solicitation or acceptance of an advantage;
- as a reward for certain conduct; and
- such conduct is related to the principal's affairs or business.

Similar to the public sector corruption offence, both the offeror and the recipient of the advantage will be liable. The most typical scenario is where an employee receives an 'under the table' commission from a supplier or customer without his or her employer's approval, in return for special favours provided by the employee.

Further, section 9(3) penalises agents who use falsified receipts, accounts or other documents for the purpose of misleading their principals. This is a useful tool for the ICAC in cases where false instruments are used while substantive evidence of bribery is absent.

(c) The defences of lawful authority and/or reasonable excuse

With the exception of offences under sections 3, 9(3) and 10 of the POBO, an affirmative defence is generally available for public and private bribery offences in cases where a public servant and/or agent has acted with 'lawful authority' or 'reasonable excuse'. While the POBO does not define these terms, the Hong Kong courts have provided useful guidance on their meanings in previous judgments.

In *HKSAR v Chan Chi Cheung*,[5] the court defined the defence of "lawful authority" as "a statutory provision that empowered the defendant to conduct himself in a way that would otherwise be an offence". A similar definition can be found in *HKSAR v Yan Pak Cheung*,[6] which defined "lawful authority" in the context of the POBO as a defence that is "sourced in a positive rule of law that expressly or impliedly empowers, countenances or authorizes the defendant to conduct himself in a way that would otherwise be a defence".

In relation to what constitutes a "reasonable excuse" under the POBO, the Court of Appeal held in *HKSAR v Chan Chi Wan Stephen*[7] that the scope of this defence was wider than that of the defence of lawful authority. In the Court of Final Appeal's judgment in the same case,[8] the court further elaborated that the absence of prejudice to the principal or the fact that the defendant's act was beneficial to the principal would not constitute a reasonable excuse. However, a reasonable excuse could include an honest belief by the defendant that his or her principal would not raise any objections to the advantage being accepted.

Under section 24 of the POBO, the burden of proving a defence of lawful authority or reasonable excuse rests with the accused.

Specifically in relation to offences under section 3 of the POBO, a statutory defence of general or special permission from the Chief Executive is available.

(d) Penalties

The Hong Kong courts have made it clear that deterrent sentences will be imposed for corruption offences in both the public and private sectors. As such, immediate imprisonment is the customary sentence for such offences.

The statutory penalties are set out in section 12 of the POBO. Under section 3, bribery is the only summary offence that carries a maximum prison sentence of one year, while other offences under the POBO are indictable offences, which are more serious in nature. On indictment, offences under sections 5, 6 and 10 carry a maximum prison term of 10 years, while other offences can lead to imprisonment of up to seven years.

In addition, section 3 carries a maximum fine of HK$100,000 (US$13,000), while other offences carry maximum fines ranging from HK$500,000 to HK$1 million (US$64,000–$128,000) on indictment.

The courts can also make orders under the POBO to disgorge any illicit advantage and confiscate the assets of persons convicted under it.

---

5 [2016] 1 HKLRD 1448.
6 [2009] 2 HKLRD 82.
7 [2016] 3 HKLRD 186.
8 *Secretary for Justice v Chan Chi Wan Stephen* (2017) 20 HKCFAR 98.

3.2 **The Elections (Corrupt and Illegal Conduct) Ordinance**

The Elections (Corrupt and Illegal Conduct) Ordinance (Cap 554) (ECICO) seeks to ensure that the public electoral process is conducted in an open and fair manner and is free from corruption. It is enforced by the ICAC and sets out a number of corruption offences related to elections of (among others) the Chief Executive, the Legislative Council, District Councils and rural committees in Hong Kong. For example, the ECICO prohibits the offer, solicitation and acceptance of advantages to influence a person to stand or not stand as a candidate in elections,[9] and of advantages to influence votes.[10]

3.3 **The common law offence of misconduct in public office**

Corruption in the public sector is no longer confined to the traditional 'bribe for favour' type of offence. The common law offence of misconduct in public office, despite its long history since the 18th century, continues to exist and effectively complements the POBO offences. It is wider in scope and encompasses any serious misuse of power or position by public officials, even if the conduct in question falls short of the evidentiary requirements under the POBO. This offence remains a powerful weapon of the ICAC, particularly in the prosecution of high-ranking government officials in recent years; a number of cases are discussed at 6 below.

In laying down a test for this common law offence, the Court of Final Appeal (CFA) stated in the landmark case of *Sin Kam Wah v HKSAR*[11] that it contains five elements:

- a public official;
- in the course of or in relation to his public office;
- wilfully misconducts himself, by act or omission, for example, by wilfully neglecting or failing to perform his duty;
- without reasonable excuse or justification; and
- where such conduct is serious, not trivial, having regard to the responsibilities of the office and the office-holder, the importance of the public objects which they serve and the nature and extent of the departure from those responsibilities.

With regard to the third of the above points, the CFA held that the misconduct must be deliberate rather than accidental, in the sense that the official either knew that his or her conduct was unlawful or wilfully disregarded the risk that his or her conduct was unlawful.

In *Sin Kam Wah v HKSAR*, the defendant, a Senior Superintendent in the Hong Kong Police Force was held to have wilfully and intentionally misconducted himself by accepting sexual services from women over whom another defendant had exercised control, while he was aware of the fact that the other defendant had interests in four nightclubs in Hong Kong. The CFA found that the police were

9 Section 7 of the ECICO.
10 *Ibid*, section 11.
11 *Sin Kam Wah v HKSAR* (2005) 8 HKCFAR 192.

conducting continuous checks on the clubs and that these favours had been provided to the defendant as sweeteners to him.

Another example of what constitutes 'misconduct' can be found in *HKSAR v Yu Sum Fat Troson Zab*.[12] In that case, misconduct was established when an ambulanceman switched off the device showing the location of his ambulance during journeys conveying patients to hospitals. He had also deliberately inputted wrong locations that were far away from any hospitals so that he would not need to answer ambulance calls requiring immediate responses from ambulances in the vicinity.

To constitute the offence of misconduct in public office, wilful misconduct that has a relevant relationship with the defendant's public office would suffice. Misconduct otherwise than in the performance of the defendant's public duties may have such a relationship with his public office as to bring that office into disrepute, in circumstances where the misconduct is both culpable and serious and not trivial.

Under section 101I of the Criminal Procedure Ordinance (Cap 221), a public official convicted of this common law offence is liable to imprisonment for seven years and a fine. The Hong Kong courts generally adopt a deterrent sentencing policy in such cases.

4. The powers of the ICAC

As an anti-corruption body operating independently of other government departments and law enforcement bodies, the ICAC has extensive investigative powers to do the following under the ICACO and the POBO:

- arrest without a warrant if the officers reasonably suspect a person to be guilty of an offence under the POBO, ECICO or ICACO;[13]
- detain suspects for inquiries;[14]
- grant bail following the arrest of an accused;[15]
- search premises and seize evidence;[16]
- inspect and take copies of accounts, books or documents for investigation purposes;[17]
- make an *ex parte* application to the Court of First Instance (CFI) to compel a suspect or any other relevant persons to furnish information on his or her assets, expenditure and liabilities, etc;[18]
- make an *ex parte* application to the CFI to impose a restraining order on the relevant property held by a suspect or a third party;[19] and
- make an *ex parte* application to a magistrate for the surrender of suspects' travel documents.[20] It is noteworthy that this power can be exercised upon a suspect before he or she is charged with any criminal offence.

---

12 [2016] HKEC 1148.
13 Section 10 of the ICACO.
14 *Ibid*, section 10A.
15 *Ibid*, section 10AA.
16 *Ibid*, sections 10B and 10C; section 17 of the POBO.
17 *Ibid*, section 13.
18 *Ibid*, section 14.
19 *Ibid*, section 14C.
20 *Ibid*, section 17A.

In practice, the ICAC normally conducts the questioning of suspects by way of video recorded interviews, while taking statements from witnesses in written form. For interviews with suspects, ICAC officers must caution an interviewee by stating the nature and particulars of the alleged offence and saying words to the effect that "you are not obliged to say anything unless you wish to do so, but whatever you say will be put into writing and maybe given in evidence", otherwise the admissibility of such evidence could be subject to challenge in the criminal courts. A suspect has a right to remain silent and may therefore choose whether or not to answer any questions posed by the ICAC officers. He or she also has a right to legal representation throughout the interview process.

It is also noteworthy that the ICAC only commences an investigation pursuant to corruption-related complaints. However, if other forms of criminal conduct are uncovered during its investigations (which typically include (among others) conspiracy to defraud, theft and false accounting), the ICAC can always switch its focus of investigation and lay the appropriate criminal charges.

5. International anti-corruption treaties and other arrangements applicable to Hong Kong

The primary basis of criminal jurisdiction in Hong Kong is territorial, following the English position that the function of the English criminal courts is to maintain the Queen's peace within her realm. As such, absent any statutory exceptions, the courts are not concerned with any criminal conduct committed abroad. In contrast with recent legislative developments in the United States and the United Kingdom, there is only very limited extra-territorial jurisdiction under anti-corruption legislation in Hong Kong: this is discussed at 7 below.

That said, the ICAC may cooperate with overseas regulators in combating corruption via international treaties, bilateral agreements for mutual legal assistance and 'soft laws', such as memoranda of understanding and anti-corruption initiatives.

International anti-corruption treaties applicable to Hong Kong include the United Nations (UN) Convention against Corruption (2003) (UNCAC) and the UN Convention Against Transnational Organized Crime (2000) (UNCATOC), which have been implemented in Hong Kong through several pieces of local legislation.[21] These treaties provide mechanisms whereby the signatories thereto can jointly combat international and cross-border corruption via mutual legal assistance in investigations, prosecutions and judicial proceedings.

Furthermore, Hong Kong is part of the Anti-corruption Initiative for Asia-Pacific and the related Action Plan jointly launched by the Asia Development Bank (ADB) and the Organisation for Economic Co-operation and Development (OECD), which further set out goals and standards for sustainable safeguards against corruption in the region's economic, political and social spheres.

---

21 For example, the Fugitive Offenders (Corruption) Order (Cap 503AB) and the Mutual Legal Assistance in Criminal Matters (Corruption) Order (Cap 525W) implement the UNCAC, while the Mutual Legal Assistance in Criminal Matters (Transnational Organized Crime) Order (Cap 525X) and the Fugitive Offenders (Transnational Organized Crime) Order (Cap 503AE) implement the UNCATOC.

6. Recent case law

6.1 *Secretary for Justice v Stephen Chan Chi Wan* (FACC 11 and 18/2016, 14 March 2017): section 9 of the POBO

This is a high-profile bribery case involving the former general manager of the largest television broadcasting company in Hong Kong. The case lasted for more than 7 years, with two trials, two appeals and one final appeal. It clarifies the offence of bribery of agents and the scope of sections 9(1) and (2) of the POBO by setting out the CFA's interpretation of the element "in relation to the principal's affairs or business", which has significant implications on Hong Kong's anti-bribery regime, particularly in the private sector.

(a) Background

The defendant, Mr Stephen Chan was the former General Manager (Broadcasting) of Television Broadcasts Limited (TVB). Apart from being an executive of TVB, he also hosted a popular television talk show, 'Be My Guest', for TVB with no remuneration for his services. His co-defendant, a Mr Tseng, ran an advertising and production company and acted as the defendant's agent for outside commercial engagements.

Against this background, TVB produced and broadcasted a countdown event for a Hong Kong shopping mall on New Year's Eve 2009. The shopping mall entered into a separate agreement with Mr Tseng's production company for Mr Chan to host a special episode of his 'Be My Guest' programme at the countdown event. The shopping mall paid HK$160,000 to Mr Tseng's production company, of which Mr Chan received HK$112,000 for hosting the show. Mr Chan neither sought nor obtained permission from TVB to appear on or to be paid for hosting his show, notwithstanding the contractual obligation under his employment contract to seek approval for outside work.

The defendants were subsequently charged with conspiracy for an agent to accept an advantage, contrary to section 9(1)(a) of the POBO and, alternatively, with the substantive offences of an agent accepting an advantage (in Mr Chan's case) and offering an advantage to an agent (in Mr Tseng's case).

(b) The trial, retrial and appeals

Both defendants were acquitted at the District Court in their first trial in 2011. The trial judge held that Mr Chan's conduct did not fall within the "in relation to his principal's affairs or business" element of the alleged offence. The Department of Justice (DOJ) appealed against the decision to the Court of Appeal in 2012. The Court of Appeal allowed the appeal and directed a retrial. It also directed the District Court to consider whether Mr Chan could rely on the defence of 'reasonable excuse'.

The retrial took place in 2013 and the District Court acquitted the defendants on the basis of the defence of 'reasonable excuse'. Subsequently, the DOJ lodged an appeal, which was heard by the Court of Appeal in 2014. The Court of Appeal held that there was insufficient primary evidence to establish that the defendants had a reasonable excuse. It then directed the District Court to convict them for breaching section 9 of the POBO.

In the ultimate appeal, the CFA unanimously quashed the convictions of both defendants.

(c) ***The CFA's interpretation of "in relation to the principal's affairs or business"***

The majority of CFA judges held that Mr Chan was not acting "in relation to his principal's affairs or business" when he accepted HK$112,000 as an inducement or reward for appearing in the special episode of 'Be My Guest'. In particular, the CFA held that, upon a true construction of section 9, the agent's act or forbearance must be:

> *aimed at and intended to influence or affect the principal's affairs or business in a manner that undermines that integrity of the agency relationship by injuring the bond of trust and loyalty between principal and agent. ... [It] ... does not need to involve immediate or tangible economic loss to the principal or benefit to the agent at the principal's expense.*

In addition, the CFA ruled that it was not the legislature's intent to stigmatise as criminal the conduct of an agent that was beneficial to and congruent with the interests of the principal. Since Mr Chan's hosting of the show helped boost TVB's audience ratings, his conduct was beneficial to TVB and he had therefore not violated section 9 of the POBO.

(d) ***The defence of "reasonable excuse"***

The defence of "reasonable excuse" was also canvassed by the dissenting judge in the CFA, who took the view that, even if Mr Chan's conduct fell within the meaning of section 9, he had a reasonable excuse to accept the advantage as the facts showed that, by having Mr Chan participate in the countdown show, TVB must have impliedly consented to him performing in the programme and be paid for his appearance.

(e) ***The impact of the CFA judgment***

In essence, this landmark CFA judgment adopts a more liberal and commercial approach to the construction of the scope and intent of section 9 of the POBO. It distinguishes between corruption, which causes detriment to the principal's affairs or business, and 'moonlighting' which will generally not be caught by the statute.

6.2 *HKSAR v Kwok Ping-kwong Thomas, Hui Rafael Junior and others* (FACC 12-15/2016, 14 June 2017): misconduct in public office

This is another high-profile corruption case. It involved two property tycoons, Mr Thomas Kwok Ping Kwong (Thomas Kwok) and Mr Raymond Kwok Ping Luen (Raymond Kwok), together with Mr Rafael Hui Si Yan (Rafael Hui), a former Chief Secretary of Hong Kong (the second highest position in the HKSAR government).

This case, which was recently heard in the CFA, is internationally noteworthy not only because of the large scale of evidence and transactions (involving more than 120 witnesses, 230 local and overseas bank accounts and thousands of transactions spanning over a decade), but also because it involved two tycoons at the top of the Hong Kong social pyramid and the highest civil servant, all of whom were put behind bars. In this landmark CFA judgment, the court clarified the scope of the common law offence of misconduct in public office and gave insights on the interpretation of its various elements.

(a) *Background*

Rafael Hui was appointed the Chief Secretary of the HKSAR government on 30 June 2005. He then became an Official Member of the Executive Council. Thomas Kwok was a Co-Chairman and Managing Director of Sun Hung Kai Properties Limited (SHKP), a major property developer and publicly listed company in Hong Kong.

In late June 2005, immediately before Rafael Hui took office as Chief Secretary, a total sum of HK$8.5 million was transferred into his bank account at the direction of Thomas Kwok and Raymond Kwok with the aid of their assistants.

During Rafael Hui's term of office as Chief Secretary, there were substantial commercial negotiations between SHKP and the HKSAR government, including with regard to the Ma Wan Park Project and the West Kowloon Cultural District Project, in both of which SHKP had significant and substantial interests.

The prosecution alleged that the payments of HK$8.5 million were advantages to secure an improper inclination and in exchange, Rafael Hui had agreed to be or remain favourably disposed to SHKP, its subsidiaries or associated companies in his capacity as Chief Secretary. The prosecution further alleged that the payments were consideration for a verbal agreement which supplemented a consulting contract between Rafael Hui and SHKP in 2003.

The High Court jury trial lasted 130 days. Raymond Kwok having been acquitted, the remaining defendants were convicted and sentenced to imprisonment for terms of between five and seven and a half years.

(b) *'General sweetener payments'*

Rafael Hui and Thomas Kwok eventually appealed to the CFA against conviction. This final appeal centered on one of the charges, specifically a joint count of conspiracy to commit misconduct in public office.

The appellants argued that 'general sweetener payments' made to a prospective public officer before his appointment, absent any agreed or intended act in his capacity as a civil servant, were insufficient to constitute the offence of misconduct in public office. It was contended that there was no relevant act of misconduct and that the prosecution's allegation of intended misconduct was merely a state of mind. The appellants argued that the common law did not recognise mere 'inclination' or 'motive' to be "sufficient for the commission of a criminal offence".

The appeal was heard and determined by the CFA in June 2017. The five presiding judges were asked to decide whether favourable disposition was a sufficient criminal element for the offence. The court unanimously dismissed the appeal.

The court considered the background and the history of the law on misconduct in public office and corruption in Hong Kong. Since the first Hong Kong legislation on corruption in 1898, the core element of a corrupt advantage has been its tendency to obtain improper effect or secure a disloyal inclination. Subsequent legislative developments in Hong Kong have broadened the anti-corruption interpretation while maintaining this centrepiece concept.

The court held that a broad range of acts and omissions can constitute misconduct in public office, while the essence of the offence is the abuse of public trust by the accused officer. The misconduct must be serious and not trivial in view of the responsibilities of the public servant and the office held.

Given the seniority of Rafael Hui's office in the HKSAR government and his membership of the Executive Council, he not only possessed confidential information concerning the Ma Wan Project and the West Kowloon Cultural District Project, but he also had an essential role in the decision-making process under the relevant government policy and contracts as a "sentinel of the public welfare". Since the relevant agreement with SHKP resulted in Rafael Hui being paid HK$8.5 million in return for his favourable disposition in his capacity as Chief Secretary, the CFA accepted that the advantage was clearly corrupt.

As such, therefore, the CFA ruled that despite the lack of any specific act, by accepting the payment of HK$8.5 million, Rafael Hui had committed serious misconduct by placing his independence in the 'golden fetters' and a 'hopelessly compromised' position constituted by the payments during his entire tenure.

(c) ***Implications of the CFA judgment***

It is apparent from this judgment that the CFA has broadened the interpretation of the common law offence of misconduct in public office to include a compromised public position caused by corrupt payments, which is in sharp contrast with the requirement of specific acts under the POBO. Furthermore, this is also the first case in Hong Kong in which a court has convicted a public officer for advantages accepted prior to taking office and held that pre-office acceptance would amount to an abuse of public trust and constitute an offence. The CFA has effectively reiterated the message to the general public that Hong Kong has zero tolerance toward corrupt conduct by civil servants and public officials.

7. Possible reforms

7.1 Extra-territorial jurisdiction and bribery of foreign officials

Unlike the Foreign Corrupt Practices Act 1976 in the United States and the Bribery Act 2010 in the United Kingdom, one of the major loopholes in the Hong Kong anti-corruption regime is the failure effectively to criminalise foreign bribery. Section 4 is the only provision of the POBO that carries extraterritorial jurisdiction (as it encompasses bribery by Hong Kong public servants "whether in Hong Kong or elsewhere"); nevertheless, its practical effect is relatively limited.

Further, recent court cases have confirmed that all other bribery offences under the POBO require that the relevant conduct (offer, solicitation or acceptance of advantages) take place in Hong Kong. Failing this, such conduct would not amount to an offence. As such, the anti-corruption regime in Hong Kong principally focuses on domestic rather than foreign bribery.

With regard to the bribery of foreign public officials, while the concept of "agent" under section 9 of the POBO is broad enough to cover a foreign government official, the conduct of offering, soliciting and accepting an advantage has to occur in Hong Kong in order to constitute an offence, given the lack of extraterritorial jurisdiction. This restrictive provision renders the POBO rather toothless in tackling the bribery of foreign officials.

The OECD Convention on Combating Bribery of Foreign Public Officials in International Business Transactions (1997) was adopted on 15 February 1999. Under the OECD Convention, the signatory nations shall adopt national legislation making it a crime to bribe foreign public officials, with a broad definition of 'bribery' and commitments to providing mutual legal assistance. Given the restrictions discussed above, however, Hong Kong is currently lagging behind the OECD nations in combating offshore bribery and this is a major area for potential reform.

7.2 Corporate criminal liability

Although companies (including foreign companies) can technically be liable for corruption offences under the POBO, the ICAC's operations mainly target individuals and prosecutions against corporations are very rare. However, in the United States and the United Kingdom, corporations may be held criminally liable for the acts of their employees in certain circumstances and for failing to prevent corrupt activities, and the authorities there are very robust in commencing such prosecutions. Further, the prosecution may enter into non-prosecution agreements or deferred prosecution agreements with corporations to encourage their self-reporting and full cooperation with investigations.

In light of recent reforms in other major jurisdictions, Hong Kong's anti-corruption laws may be extended by specifically providing for corporate criminal liability for corruption offences with a view to fostering a culture of proactive prevention and detection of corrupt activities. Leniency programmes and non-prosecution/deferred prosecution agreements may be explored in an attempt to cultivate a responsible corporate culture in preventing corruption.

India

Ramesh K Vaidyanathan
Advaya Legal

1. Introduction

I used to look down on the world for being corrupt, but now I adore it for the utter magnificence of that corruption.

This quote by Canadian humour columnist Richard J Needham (1912–1996) aptly sums up the state of play of corruption in India. Corruption is present both in the public and private sectors in Indian society. To a large extent, low level or petty corruption has gained social acceptance in India as it is often seen as a convenient though expensive way of getting things done where public services or benefits are involved. This is especially true in cases involving liaison with authorities for business licences or approvals and the payment of 'fees' to the corrupt officials to facilitate or expedite matters is a routine occurrence. This has even led to many globally reputed international companies being penalised under the anti-corruption laws of their own countries for such acts where committed by their Indian subsidiaries. One of the companies that recently suffered this fate was Mondelez Inc, the international snack-food manufacturer. Mondelez was sanctioned by the United States' Securities Exchange Commission because its Indian subsidiary Cadbury India made 'facilitation payments' in violation of the US Foreign Corrupt Practices Act 1976 (FCPA) to obtain approvals for its unit in India. The matter was closed when Mondelez agreed to pay $13 million in settlement, without admitting to the charges.

Large scale bureaucratic corruption in the public sector resulting in the squandering and diversion of resources meant for the public good is a menace that is condemned by most Indians, particularly the younger generation. As a result, every other political movement today has 'anti-corruption' as its agenda and the government has over the years taken a number of steps to tackle the menace. Regardless, the menace still subsists.

This chapter seeks to chart the course of corruption through the Indian history and to examine the steps taken by governments over the years to curb it. It concludes by examining the various measures anti-corruption measures that are being rolled out and what this entails for the future.

2. Corruption in India: historical evolution

There are several references to the prevalence of official corruption in ancient India.[1] However, the text that provides the most elaborate description of corruption in

1 Available at http://cbi.nic.in/coffeetable/1.pdf, accessed 24 September 2017.

India during that period is the *Arthashastra*, an ancient Indian treatise on statecraft, economic policy and military strategy.[2] It was written by Kautilya, a minister in the Kingdom of Chandragupta Maurya during the period 317–293 BC/BCE. Arthashastra cited cases of embezzlement of funds by officials and also acknowledged the prevalence of corruption in judicial administration in ancient India.

Corruption reached new heights during the Mughal reign and not much changed during British rule. The brief period of rule by the East India Company (the Company) saw rampant corruption in India, with the merchants of the Company, who were also the administrators, embezzling money from the British Crown to amass personal wealth. When the Company was disestablished following the Indian Mutiny of 1857, the British government took direct control of India and introduced measures to prevent the increasing prevalence of corruption in the country. Laws were made to curb corruption in public offices, but bribery and regular theft of resources together continued to be common practice. Commissions to officials became an unwritten rule, not only to secure special favours but also to make them perform their official duties. By the time of the Second World War, such corruption had become a significant problem. A Special Police Establishment (SPE) was set up by the British administration to deal with offences relating to bribery and corruption within the government. Initially, the SPE's responsibility was limited to investigating cases of bribery within the government that arose during the war. However, in 1943, the SPE's power was extended to cases related to the Indian Railways, initially through an ordinance[3] that was later re-enacted as the Delhi Special Police Establishment Act, 1946.

Independence failed to bring about any change in the societal mindset or practices where corruption was concerned. In fact, the 'socialist economic policy' followed by the first government of independent India involving a licensing regime for all industrial activities led to the institutionalisation of corruption. Practically all commercial activities in the country were regulated and required a prior licence, while manufacturing quantity was strictly controlled and competition was stifled as only a few private entities were given entry to a limited number of sectors. Most sectors were reserved for public bodies and the economy was closed to foreign players. Any violation of the draconian licensing rules resulted in serious repercussions. The only way to cut through the labyrinth of red tape and governmental suppression was through bribery and other unscrupulous means, leading to an exponential increase in corruption.

In 1991, the Indian economy was liberalised and many of the sectors exclusively set aside for public sector entities were de-reserved for the private sector and even for some foreign entrants, ending the infamous licensing regime. Although this move resulted in a boom in the Indian economy, it failed to mitigate corruption. On the contrary, with the increase in stakes brought about by the liberalisation, the scale of corruption also increased. Several public office and government scams surfaced every year in India, covering the entire spectrum from coal allocation to telecommunications. India was ranked 79th out of 176 countries surveyed in the

2 Roger Boesche, *The First Great Political Realist: Kautilya and His Arthashastra* (2002, Lexington Books), p 7.
3 Criminal Law (Amendment) Ordinance (No XXIX of 1943).

Corruption Perception Index 2016 released by the Berlin-based corruption watchdog Transparency International. India's bad reputation on this score has severely tarnished its image globally and is at odds with various government initiatives to make India one of the most investor-friendly destinations in the world.

3. Laws against corruption

3.1 Introduction

The Prevention of Corruption Act 1988 (PCA) and the Indian Penal Code 1860 (IPC) are the primary legislations that deal with the offence of corruption in public office in India. Other anti-corruption-related laws include the Whistle Blowers' Protection Act 2011 (WBPA), the Lokpal and Lokayuktas Act 2013 (LLA) and the Prevention of Money Laundering Act 2002 (PMLA).

The scope of almost all anti-corruption laws in India is restricted to corruption in the public sector, with little or no emphasis on the private sector. Further, these laws only seek to prosecute public officials who accept bribes and not the persons offering them, who may at most be convicted of the offence of abetment. The current legislative framework is discussed briefly below.

3.2 The IPC

The IPC originally covered a range of corruption and related offences. These included any form of 'gratification' received by public servants over and above legal remuneration to influence a public servant unduly. An amendment to the IPC was introduced in 1952 in order to make abetment of bribery also an offence under that statute. The IPC also has provisions to prosecute public servants for criminal breach of trust, which is punishable by up to 10 years' imprisonment. A number of offences of corruption under the IPC were repealed upon the enactment of the PCA.

3.3 The PCA

Enacted in 1988, the PCA is India's principal anti-corruption legislation. It consolidates all laws relating to offences of corruption by public servants that primarily involve accepting illegal gratification or payment (other than official remuneration) and also stipulates the penalties for the same. A number of significant aspects of the PCA are discussed below.

The PCA has also enlarged the scope of the term 'public servant' to encompass a large number of public sector employees within its ambit.

The scope of this term has been further expanded by judicial interpretations over the years. While bribe-taking activities by public servants have been criminalised under the PCA, bribe-giving falls within the scope of the offence of abetment of bribe-taking offences by public servants. It may also be noted that although the scope of the PCA is limited to public servants, courts have over the years expanded the interpretation of the term 'public servant'. In *Central Bureau of Investigation, Bank Securities & Fraud Cell v Ramesh Gelli & Ors,*[4] the scope of the term 'public servant'

---

4 Crl App 1077–1081 of 2013.

under the PCA was further expanded by the Supreme Court of India to include the chairman and directors of a private bank.

(a) *The concepts of 'public servant' and 'public duty'*

The most important issue under the PCA has been the interpretation of the terms 'public servant' and 'public duty' as the act criminalises activities such as the receipt of 'gratification', ie an unlawful inducement (section 7 of the PCA) and the acceptance of gifts by public servants in the course of performing their public duties. 'Public duty' is defined by the PCA as "a duty in the discharge of which the State, the public or the community at large has an interest".[5] This definition is an inclusive one, whereby persons who are remunerated by government for public duties and those who perform public duties are both 'public servants' under the PCA.

The definition of the term 'public servant' under the PCA has been interpreted broadly. The expression is not restricted to the instances set out in the interpretation section and the courts have taken the view that further categories of person may be included within its ambit.[6] The definitions of 'public duty' and 'public servant' were considered further in *PV Narasimha Rao v State of Andra Pradesh*.[7] While this case dealt with the corrupt practices of a member of Parliament, it is relevant as the Supreme Court interpreted the definition of 'public servant' in an expansive manner. Applying the same elucidation in the *Ramesh Gelli* case, the Supreme Court concluded that even though the concerned individuals were neither employees of the state nor of its instrumentalities, the public duty element and the nature of the work performed by bank managers meant that, for the purposes of the PCA, such officers would qualify as public servants.

(b) *Presumption of taint*

Another significant principle under the PCA regime is the presumption of taint. In respect of any valuable thing or any form of gratification that is found in the possession of a person under investigation, there is a presumption that such valuable thing is for the purposes of gratification as laid down by the PCA. This is a rebuttable presumption and the burden of proof is on the person under investigation to demonstrate that the valuable thing or gratification was not received in connection with an offence under the PCA.[8] Thus, where evidence is not led to rebut the presumption, a person under investigation would be convicted. The PCA also provides immunity to a bribe giver, such that a statement given by that person shall not subject him or her to prosecution. The immunity accorded to bribe givers has, however, been considered to be both a major flaw in the PCA and inconsistent with international standards.

(c) *Offences and penalties*

The scope of the offences created under the PCA is very wide. The act addresses,

---

5 Section 2(b) of the PCA.
6 Note 4 above.
7 (1998) 4 SCC 626.
8 (2001) 1 SCC 691.

among other things, gratification received through intermediaries, gifts and other non-pecuniary gratification, and certain conduct described as 'criminal misconduct' by public servants (including the possession of assets disproportionate to their income). Sections 7–11 of the PCA make provision as to the instances that qualify as taking gratification, influencing public servants or accepting gifts. While it is intended to amend the PCA in the near future, in line with India's obligations under the United Nations Convention against Corruption (2003), the provisions as they currently exist are discussed below.

The taking of gratification other than legal remuneration by a public official in respect of an official act is a punishable offence under the PCA. An explanatory note in section 7 states that 'gratification' "is not restricted to pecuniary gratifications or gratifications estimable in money".[9] However, it is an equally important ingredient of the offence that a demand for such sum should have been made by a public servant. Further, the mere fact that the individual has a valuable thing may not, in the absence of proof of such demand, lead to a conviction under the PCA.[10]

The PCA also prohibits public servants from taking gratification by corrupt or illegal means to exercise their influence. The term 'corrupt' has not been defined, leaving scope for ambiguity. The Supreme Court has attempted to clarify the same in the *Parkash Singh Badal* case, in which it was held that if a public servant accepts gratification as an inducement to do or to forbear from doing any official act, he or she would fall within the purview of an offence under the PCA.[11] In considering examining the nature of the gratification obtained in the same case, the Supreme Court held that the gratification could be of any kind, so that the PCA was of wide application to it.

Section 11 of the PCA also provides that it is an offence for a public servant to obtain a 'valuable thing' from a person who is concerned with any business or transaction relating to that public servant. The Supreme Court has interpreted this provision to imply that a public servant must obtain a valuable thing while acting in his or her official capacity.[12] The court has held further that in order to convict a person under this provision, there must be evidence on record that the person under investigation 'obtained' for himself or herself or for any other person any valuable thing or pecuniary advantage by either corrupt or illegal means or by abusing his or her position as a public servant or that he obtained for any person any valuable thing or pecuniary advantage without any public interest.[13] However, in the absence of any proof of a demand for illegal gratification, the use of corrupt or illegal means or abuse of position as a public servant to obtain any valuable thing or pecuniary advantage cannot be held to have been proved.[14] As a result of this ambiguity in the law and the complexity involved in marshalling definitive proof in bribery cases, more often than not public servants are acquitted and so escape the grasp of the law.

---

9 *Parkash Singh Badal v State of Punjab* (2007)1 SCC 1.

10 *P Satyanarayana Murthy v The District Inspector of Police* (2015) 10 SCC 152.

11 Note 10 above.

12 *Ibid.*

13 *Subash Parbat Sonvane v State of Gujarat* (2002) 5 SCC 86.

14 *P Satyanarayana Murthy v The District Inspector of Police* (2015) 10 SCC 152.

Persons found guilty of offences under the PCA are liable to terms of imprisonment that may range from six months to seven years, in addition to payment of a fine.

It is pertinent to note that certain proposed amendments to the PCA by way of a bill entitled the Prevention of Corruption (Amendment) Bill, 2013 (PCA Amendment Bill) was introduced in Parliament soon after India ratified the UNCAC, to align the provisions of the PCA with the UNCAC. However, the amendments still await consideration by Parliament.

The PCA Amendment Bill seeks to amend the PCA in order to safeguard former public servants from vexatious litigation by stipulating that proceedings against them require prior sanction by certain named authorities. This bill also requires that any property proved to have been acquired by public servants through corrupt means must be forfeited to the government, and prescribes a procedure for attaching such property before a court passes judgment. In the context of penalties, the bill proposes to relate the quantum of fines to the pecuniary resources of the accused or the value of property for which the accused is unable to account satisfactorily. Most significantly, however, the PCA Amendment Bill introduces specific provisions criminalising the giving or offering of a bribe to a public servant.

A number of other changes proposed by the PCA Amendment Bill include the following:

- specific provisions relating to the bribery of public officials by commercial organisations and the liability of officials of such organisations for such acts;
- a defence to prosecution where a commercial organisation can demonstrate that an offence was committed without its knowledge, consent or neglect and that it had exercised all due diligence to prevent the offence; and
- abolition of immunity for persons abetting offences under the PCA.

3.4. The WBPA

The WBPA was enacted in May 2014. Its basic objective is to protect whistleblowers against corruption in the public sector. The preamble to the WPA provides for the establishment of a mechanism to receive complaints relating to the disclosure of allegations of corruption, to enquire into such disclosure and to provide adequate safeguards against victimisation of persons making such complaints.

Disclosures may relate to an incidence of corruption or the wilful misuse of power. The WBPA further provides as to (among other things) the entities eligible or entitled to make such disclosures, the subject-matter that may be covered by the disclosures, the competent authority for various public sector bodies to whom disclosures or complaints are to be made, inquiry into disclosures, powers of competent authorities, the protection of persons making disclosures, offences and the penalties therefor.

The WBPA makes it mandatory for the identity of the complainant to be disclosed to the relevant competent authority. However, the act also requires the competent authority to conceal the identity of the complainant except when such disclosure is necessary for the inquiry. Even where this is so, however, the complainant's written consent to this is mandatory and the head of the relevant department shall be directed not to disclose the complainant's identity.[15] The WBPA also makes it mandatory for the disclosure to be accompanied by full particulars and supporting documents.[16]

Upon receipt of a complaint, the competent authority established under the WBPA is required to decide if the matter is one that needs investigation. If the authority determines that this is the case, it shall conduct a discreet inquiry to ascertain whether there is a basis to proceed. If the authority finds such a basis, it will seek an explanation or a report from the head of the department concerned, who will then recommend measures including the initiation of proceedings or corrective measures against the public servant.[17] The public authority will then take a decision within three months of receiving the recommendation on whether a given course of action should be pursued. If it decides not to proceed further, it will record its reasons for electing not to take action.

To safeguard the inquiry process, the WBPA prescribes a whole raft of penalties:

- making *mala fide* or false disclosures can lead to imprisonment of up to two years and a fine of $460 (approx).[18]
- if reports are not furnished to the competent authority during an inquiry, the person in default may face a fine of around $4 per day, up to a sum of $770 (approx);[19]
- the penalty for revealing the identity of a complainant is imprisonment for up to three years, accompanied by a fine of $770 (approx);[20] and
- knowingly providing false or incomplete information to a competent authority attracts a penalty of $770 (approx).

3.5 The LLA

The LLA provides for the establishment of a Lokpal for the Union and of Lokayukta for States (collectively, Lokpal) to inquire into allegations of corruption against certain public functionaries and for related matters. The basic tenet of Lokpal in India is borrowed from the concept of an ombudsman. The ombudsman acts as a watchdog of the government in power and investigates complaints by citizens against acts of corruption by government officials. In modern times, the office of ombudsman comes within the framework of the government but with a certain degree of independence.

The LLA allows the setting up of an anti-corruption ombudsman called Lokpal at the centre and Lokayukta at the state level. The Lokpal covers all categories of public servant, including the Prime Minister. The armed forces do not, however, fall within its ambit. The LLA also incorporates provisions for the attachment and confiscation of property acquired by corrupt means, even while a prosecution is pending. The biggest advantage under the LLA regime is its independence from the legislature and executive and its ability to dispose of cases in a brisk manner.

---

15 Section 5(4) of the WBPA,
16 *Ibid*, section 4(4).
17 *Ibid*, section 3(h).
18 *Ibid*, section 17.
19 *Ibid*, section 15(a).
20 *Ibid*, section 16.

3.6 The PMLA

The PMLA forms the core of the legal framework put in place by India to combat money laundering. It came into force in 2005.

The PMLA defines the offence of money laundering and provides for the freezing, seizure and confiscation of proceeds of crime. Some salient features of this act are as follows:

- the banking, financial and insurance business regulators, namely the Reserve Bank of India (RBI), the Securities Exchange Board of India and the Insurance Regulatory and Development Authority, have been brought under the purview of the PMLA. The provisions of the act therefore apply to all financial institutions, banks, mutual funds, insurance companies, and their financial intermediaries;
- the agency monitoring anti-money laundering activities in India is the Financial Intelligence Unit (FIU-IND). This agency is responsible for receiving, processing, analysing and disseminating information relating to suspect financial transactions. FIU-IND is also responsible for coordinating and strengthening the efforts of national and international intelligence, investigation and enforcement agencies in pursuing global efforts against money laundering and related crimes. FIU-IND is an independent body reporting directly to the Economic Intelligence Council (EIC) headed by the Finance Minister. Significantly, the RBI has also laid down certain 'know your customer' (KYC) norms that banks and financial institutions must follow with regard to the opening of accounts and monitoring transactions of a suspicious nature for the purpose of reporting the same to an appropriate authority, such as FIU–IND and the RBI; and
- with regard to penalties for money laundering, an offender is liable to between three and seven years' imprisonment, together with a fine of up to \$7,705 (approx). However, the upper limit of \$7,705 (approx) was removed by an amendment of 2012. In the case of offences under the Narcotic Drugs and Psychotropic Substances Act 1985, the penalty is imprisonment for up to 10 years.

4. India's international obligations against corruption

India signed the United Nations Convention against Corruption of 2003 (UNCAC) on 9 December 2005. India ratified both the UNCAC and the United Nations Convention on Transnational Organised Crime of 2000 (UNCTOC). While the central government has competence under Indian law to enter into treaty obligations, a legislative enactment is required to the extent that such treaty obligations will affect any justiciable rights of Indian nationals. The UNCAC recognises the far-reaching impact of corruption and economic crimes that undermine the value of democracy, sustainable development and the rule of law. The UNCTOC requires signatory states to adopt a series of measures to prevent and control transnational organised crime, including:

- criminalising participation in an organised criminal group, money laundering, related corruption and the obstruction of justice; and

- the adoption of frameworks for extradition, mutual legal assistance and international cooperation.

In June 2010, India also became a member of the Paris-based Financial Action Task Force (FATF), an intergovernmental body established in 1989 by the G7 that aims to develop national and international policies to prevent money laundering and terrorism financing arising out of bribery.[21]

5. Investigative authorities

Three main agencies are involved in enquiring into, investigating and prosecuting corruption charges against both central and state government departments, government companies, local government bodies and public servants: the Central Vigilance Commission (CVC), the Central Bureau of Investigation (CBI) and the state Anti-Corruption Bureau (ACB).

The CBI and the state ACBs are responsible for investigating corruption cases under the PCA and the IPC. The CBI's jurisdiction encompasses the central government and Union Territories, while the ACBs of each state investigate cases within their states. The states can, nevertheless, also refer cases to the CBI.

The CVC is a statutory body that supervises corruption cases in government departments. The CBI works under the supervision of the CVC, which can refer cases either to the Central Vigilance Officer (CVO) in each department or to the CBI. The CVC or the CVO may recommend the action to be taken against a public servant, but the decision to take any disciplinary action against a civil servant rests on the authority of the respective government department.[22] An investigating agency can initiate a prosecution once it has the prior sanction of the central or a state government to do so. Government-appointed prosecutors undertake prosecution proceedings in the courts. All cases brought under the PCA are tried by special judges who are appointed by the central or a state government.

The Serious Fraud Investigation Office, which is the investigating arm of the Ministry of Corporate Affairs, probes incidents of fraud in the case of private companies.

6. Relevant case law

6.1 *Association of Unified Tele Services Providers and Others v Union of India*[23]

In this case, the Supreme Court held that the Comptroller and Auditor General of India (CAG) had powers to conduct revenue audits of the accounts of private telecom service providers. The CAG is a constitutional body responsible for auditing the accounts of central and state governments as well as all departments and public sector entities and organisations under their control. The court ruled that the statutory powers of the CAG extended to the right to audit the accounts of private entities having revenue sharing arrangements with government bodies and

---

21 See www.fatf-gafi.org/media/fatf/documents/reports/2009%202010%20ENG.pdf.

22 See www.prsindia.org/administrator/uploads/general/1302844978_PRS%20Note%20on%20corruption%20laws.pdf.

23 Civil Appeal No 4591 of 2014.

contributing to the government exchequer. With this ruling, the Supreme Court paved the way for all private entities engaged in business under the public-private partnership (PPP) model to be brought within the purview of CAG audits.

6.2 *Manzoor Ali Khan v Union of India and Others*[24]

This case upheld the validity of the requirement to obtaining prior sanction from the competent authority for the prosecution of public officials under the PCA. 'Competent authority' essentially refers to the authority empowered to remove such an official from public office. Firstly, the Supreme Court held that the mere possibility of abuse of this requirement did not make it unconstitutional and emphasised the importance of both punishing the corrupt and protecting the innocent from *mala fide* prosecution. Secondly, the court also required that decisions regarding the issue of a sanction must be taken expeditiously and also laid down the guidelines applicable to the grant of such a sanction.

6.3 *MR Purushotham v State of Karnataka*[25]

In this case, the Supreme Court held that a requirement for obtaining the conviction of a public official under the PCA for criminal misconduct on account of obtaining any valuable thing or pecuniary advantage by corrupt means or by abusing his or her office was that it had to be proved that the accused official made a demand for such valuable thing or pecuniary advantage. The court further observed that mere possession of and recovery of currency notes from the accused did not by default amount to proof of having obtained the same by corrupt means or by abusing his or her office. This judgment once again highlights the fact that although the PCA seeks to punish corrupt officials, the judiciary is committed to preventing any abuse of its provisions that may lead to victimisation of innocent public servants discharging their duty in good faith.

6.4 *Rakesh Kapoor v State of Himachal Pradesh*[26]

In this case, the Supreme Court ruled that, in the absence of any material or evidence as to a demand for a bribe, a conviction for corruption under the PCA was not sustainable. In this case, the prime prosecution witness claimed that the demand was made over a mobile phone, but call history details were not adduced in evidence. When another prosecution witness was examined by the investigating officer, however, he had claimed that the demand was made over a land line, so that call details could not be obtained. Thus, the only evidence for the charge that the accused had demanded a bribe was contradictory oral testimony of two prosecution witnesses. Accordingly, the accused was acquitted of charges of demanding a bribe or gratification for performing his duties under the PCA. Another legal issue settled in this case was that, in the absence of proof of demand and acceptance, the accused was entitled to the benefit of the doubt.

---

24 (2015) 2 SCC 33.
25 (2015) 3 SCC 247.
26 (2012) 13 SCC 552.

6.5 The Hawala scam (*LK Advani v Central Bureau of Investigation*)[27]

Hawala refers to an unofficial system of money transfer around the world. The *Hawala* scam was an Indian political scandal involving illicit payments allegedly sent by top politicians through *hawala* brokers. This scandal saw some of the country's leading politicians implicated in a $18 million bribery scam, leading to a huge public outcry. However, with little or no *prima facie* evidence against the accused politicians that could form the basis of probative legal evidence, the case fell apart and the accused were acquitted by the Delhi High Court.

6.6 The 2G scam

The second generation (2G) telecom spectrum loss was a scam involving politicians and government officials under the erstwhile central government. In this case, the Minister of State for Communications and other officials illegally undercharged mobile telephone companies for frequency allocation licences used to create 2G subscriptions for mobile phones. The shortfall between the money collected and the money that the law required to be collected was Rs 1.76 trillion or approximately $27 billion, as estimated by the CAG. The then minister, along with several other politicians and bureaucrats, were alleged to have awarded 2G mobile phone services licences arbitrarily to nine telecom companies at much discounted prices on a first-come-first-served basis rather than through a competitive auction, resulting in a huge loss to the government. In his defence, the accused minister maintained that it was a deliberate move to keep customer tariffs low and denied any losses. However, it was soon established that there had been a massive scam, with the CAG revealing that a huge amount had been lost by the government due to the arbitrary allocation of 2G telecom licences.

In early 2012, the Supreme Court delivered a judgment in public interest litigation directly related to the 2G scam. Declaring the allotment of the spectrum as "unconstitutional and arbitrary", the court quashed all 122 telecom licences issued in 2008 by the accused minister. Thus, even telecom operators not involved in the scam had to bear the brunt of the cancellation of licences and lost their initial investment.

It is safe to conclude, however, that while there have been several cases in which the law has managed to catch up with perpetrators of corruption, it has failed to do so on most occasions, due to inability of the authorities to assemble foolproof evidence.

7. The way forward

The principal focus of the anti-corruption legislative framework in India is on the government and public sector. It only seeks to prosecute public officials accepting bribes and not the persons offering them. The bribe giver may be convicted, on rare occasions, at best for abetment. The PCA is proposed to be amended through the PCA Amendment Bill, which is currently pending in Parliament. Although the PCA Amendment Bill seeks to encompass private entities and related bribe givers within

27 1997 IIIAD Delhi 53

its penal coverage, the bill does not set out a comprehensive anti-corruption legal regime.

While the inclusion of private entities within the scope of PCA is a progressive step, it may not be sufficient to combat effectively the colossal problem of corruption in India. What is needed is the introduction of a number of additional provisions under the PCA Amendment Bill, including corporate governance standards, criminalisation of bribe giving activities, identification of extraterritorial offences of corruption and the introduction of penalties in line with the US FCPA, the UK Bribery Act and other international best practices.

The author would like to thank Laxmi Joshi and Probal Bose at Advaya Legal for their contributions to this chapter.

Italy

Marco Dalla Vedova
Luca Pietrantuono
Dalla Vedova Associazione Professionale

1. The phenomenon of corruption in Italy: a brief introduction and historical notes

The task of identifying the broad range of detrimental consequences, both economic and political, that result from the modern phenomenon of corruption is not a straightforward endeavour in any society. A review of the situation in Italy reveals the difficulty of fulfilling this task.

Indeed, a close relationship between corrupt behaviours among public institutions and private stakeholders, together with the resulting loss of competitiveness of the country's economic and financial fabric, did arise with dramatic intensity over the last few decades. The situation has been worsening, to the extent that public opinion is compelled to face such a social emergency on a daily basis whenever an arrest occurs, an investigation is opened or a disputed ruling is issued by a judicial authority.

As the current President of Italy's National Anti-Bribery Authority recently stated,[1] the disease of corruption seriously risks undermining the foundations upon which democratic institutions have rested in the 70 years or so since the Constitution of the republic was adopted – and, accordingly, their reliability.

A line of continuity can be traced between the present and a scandal that erupted in the early 1990s, as an investigation conducted by the Milan Prosecutor's Office and dubbed 'Clean Hands' (*Mani Pulite*) revealed a tightly-knit network of illicit collusion and systemic bribery between the political and business environments at all levels.

It did not take long to figure out the endemic proportions of the problem Italy was facing, to the extent that, within a couple of years (1992–1993), an investigation that originated in the areas of public tendering would cause first the fall of the government, followed shortly after by that of the entire political establishment, and therefore the end of the so-called 'First Republic' (*Prima Repubblica*).

It was during such an age of change that the expression 'systemic bribery' (*corruzione ambientale*) was coined to indicate the common and undisputed practice, jointly adopted by politicians and business people, to subject the award of tenders pursuant to public procurement processes to interested companies on the promise or receipt of money or other undue advantages.[2] The amounts of money collected were

1 Speech by Raffaele Cantone, (President of the National Anti-Bribery Authority and a former magistrate), to the opening of the academic year 2017/2018 ceremony of the School of Politics, University of Perugia.

2 This expression was used first by Antonio Di Pietro, a member of the pool of magistrates that were leading the *Mani Pulite* investigations.

then distributed among representatives across political party lines, according to their respective political strength, following a well-tested pattern that had been supporting Italian politics for decades alongside legitimate public funding.

The current situation looks far from having changed since the years of *Tangentopoli* (literally, 'City of Bribes'), as the system described above was dubbed. Not much later, in 2013, the outbreak of another scandal – *Mafia Capitale* ('Capital City of the Mafia') – which involved the management of public affairs within the city of Rome, led to the resignation of the Mayor in 2015 and to the appointment of a special commissioner to oversee city governance until new elections were held in 2016.

Once again, public anger and discontent was turned towards all public administrations, which were blamed for sharp increases in public expenditure in the face of excessively high taxation and the inadequacy of public services. In turn, this fuelled anti-political feelings and favoured the rise of populist movements.

Meanwhile, the urge to combat the phenomenon of corruption on a massive scale led the Italian legislature to establish an *ad hoc* independent authority in 2012, ie, the National Anti-Bribery Authority. This authority was provided with specific skills and a full array of powers was conferred on it in order to achieve set targets and will be more fully discussed at 4 below.

The new course of the fight against corruption, in light of the failure both of European regulation and international conventions adopted in the late 1990s and early 2000s, saw the enactment of a series of laws aimed at strengthening the stability of public administrations. Efforts to make the public tendering system bribery-proof reached their apex in 2016, with the introduction of even more restrictive measures concerning transparency and publicity.

In the wake of the push to restore the rule of law within both the private and public sectors, a set of new legislative provisions aimed at protecting those who reported crimes of which they have become aware as a result of the offices they hold or the professions they practise were enacted in November 2017. Through such an acknowledgment, therefore, whistleblowing has come to play a key role in detecting and rooting out instances of corruption in economic and financial circles.

In light of the above, and as will be discussed below, a new concept of 'administrative corruption' appears to be developing separately in Italy. This demonstrates that criminal prosecution is no longer capable of being the only tool in fighting bribery, and proves that it is absolutely necessary that the criminal justice system should be accompanied by preventive and regulatory action.

2. The modern concept of corruption and the definitions commonly used by international institutions and supranational legislation

2.1 The meaning of the term 'corruption' according to the World Bank and the International Monetary Fund

Before assessing the impact of corruption on the social and economic system, the underlying concept must be unambiguously identified. This is necessary in order to dispel any doubts about which conduct is truly deplored by the community and so deserves to be criminally prosecuted as well as prevented by the competent authorities.

It must be stressed that a number of definitions have been provided for over the years by a variety of sources, within both public opinion and national legislation, with each one of them mirroring a different approach to tackling the issues arising.

For example, the most common formulation, shared by the majority of experts in the field of economics who have dealt with bribery matters and often used in relevant studies and papers, must be taken into account. According to this definition, corruption means "the abuse of a public office for a private gain".[3]

Although such a definition may still be considered valid to explain the most ancient and typical forms assumed by the phenomenon, ie, those related to a distortion in the management of a function or service respectively performed or provided in the interest of the community, it is unable to embrace the entire range of misconducts in which bribery may nowadays manifest itself.

Indeed, as discussed further below, the need to combat corrupt practices, as they have evolved and been finessed, has progressively gone beyond public affairs to include those illicit behaviours that take place within private business.

Nevertheless, within the scope of application of the aforementioned definition, and despite the constraints referred to above, at least six types of corruption can be identified and described, in the view of the World Bank.

- First of all, *grand corruption* has been defined as one that may involve heads of state, ministers or other senior government officials and which serves the interests of a narrow group of business people and politicians, or criminal elements.
- *Political corruption*, which is likely the most typical case, appears to be quite different and means the conduct of "lawmakers, such as monarchs, dictators, and legislators, acting in their role as creators of the rules and standards by which a polity operates", who seek "bribes or other rewards for their own political or personal benefit and in return provide political favors to their supporters at the expense of the public interest".[4]
- *Corporate corruption* occurs within relationships between private business corporations and their suppliers or clients, as well as within corporations themselves: for example, where an employee, a member of a board of directors or other professional at any level of the company's organisation uses its resources for private gain, at the expense of the shareholders.
- *Administrative corruption* is the use of "favoritism to allow certain individuals or businesses to lower their taxes, escape regulations, or win low-level procurement contracts".[5]
- So-called *petty corruption* deserves separate analysis, as it concerns "payment

3 World Bank, *Helping Countries Combat Corruption: The Role of the World Bank* (1997, Washington DC: World Bank Group), p8. See further the October 2005 paper by a former Director of the World Bank's International Affairs Department, Dr Vinay Bhargava, to the Global Issues Seminar series: VK Bhargava, 'Curing the Cancer of Corruption', in VK Bhargava (Ed), *Global Issues for Global Citizens: An Introduction to Key Development Issues* (2006, Washington DC, World Bank Publications), chapter 18.

4 Bhargava, *op cit* (note 3), p1.

5 *Ibid.*

of comparatively small amounts of money to 'facilitate' routine official transactions, such as customs clearance or the issuing of building permits".[6]

- Finally, *systemic corruption* refers to the phenomenon that has spread throughout all levels of society, ie, precisely the situation Italy faced during the years of *Tangentopoli*, as discussed above.[7]

Regardless of their level of accuracy and exhaustiveness, the wordings adopted by the World Bank in these classifications are the result of an in-depth analysis of the nature of corruption, its causes, its genesis and its development, as well as its consequences on society.

In this regard, the lack of clear and strict rules on the management of the public sector has been strongly asserted[8] to be the first suspect in creating dangerous loopholes for individuals or companies struggling to gain benefits to which they might not otherwise be entitled. This also demonstrates that legislation, although unambiguous and stringent, nevertheless allows officials an excessively wide discretion in the pursuit of the public interest.

Such a dynamic creates a breeding ground for abuses committed by those on whom public powers are conferred. They may impose unfair costs, in terms of monetary demands or other undue performance on companies or individuals subject to their regulatory, taxation or law enforcement powers and take advantage of a 'wide mesh' legal system.

Finally, poverty, lack of social development and the weakness of media cannot be ignored as factors which negatively affect the corruption rate of any country in any era, since they inevitably lead to the decline of the rule of law, thus making the demarcation between public and private property less clear.

The definitions so far discussed, as well as the arguments upon which they are based, have been criticised for being incapable of fully understanding the other side of the issue, represented by so-called corporate corruption. According to a more general perspective, the relevant major literature seems to have neglected or failed to understand those instances of corruption that occur within private business relationships. In fact, this topic has been the subject of a short treatment[9] that has appeared as a result of an as yet non-comprehensive consideration by the World Bank and which is indicative of that institution's tendency to label bribery primarily as a matter of public affairs.

In 1998 Vito Tanzi, in his capacity both as the *pro tempore* Director of the International Monetary Fund's Fiscal Affairs Department and as an economist, stressed the weakness of the concepts traditionally used to make the public aware of the harmful effects of corruption on the market economy in the face of the growth of international trade and finance. In particular, Tanzi emphasised the misunderstanding that would have occurred if corruption had been considered as in no way affecting private sector activities. On the contrary, he showed that it "clearly

---

6 *Ibid*, p2.
7 See 1 above for further discussion.
8 Bhargava, *op cit* (note 3).
9 *Ibid*.

does exist",[10] – for example, within the hiring procedures of a large private enterprise, where candidates offer or are required by recruiters to do, give or promise something for which there should be no compulsion.

The same reasoning may apply to private services, the fees of which are regulated by competent authorities rather than by free interplay between supply and demand. An Italian example of this, is medical assistance rendered according to the *intra moenia* mode (ie, a private service legally acknowledged and provided by physicians outside of working hours, using facilities and equipment of the hospital in which they work), in relation to which a price higher than that subject to regulation may be charged to patients.

It is also important – as Tanzi points out – to make a distinction between a standard bribe and what may in fact be a simple gift: although it may sometimes be very difficult to distinguish between them, basically the former usually implies some form of reciprocity, whereas the latter does not.

Likewise, not all corrupt behaviours result in the payment of a bribe, as they may involve some form of generic abuse by public officials of their position for a personal benefit. Such circumstances have led the Italian legislature to introduce several types of offence in addition to 'pure' bribery, as discussed in more detail below.

Thus, depending on a number of variables, a lot of different categories may currently be used to classify possible misconducts. Apart from the adjectives 'bureaucratic' and 'political' – which are referred to by Tanzi as synonymous with, respectively, the adjectives 'petty' and 'grand' already used by the World Bank – corruption may be:

- cost-reducing (for the briber) or benefit-enhancing (with regard to the bribe);
- briber-initiated as well as bribee-initiated;
- coercive or collusive;
- centralised or decentralised;
- predictable or arbitrary; and, of course,
- committed by means of cash payments or otherwise.

Each of these attributes may be used to refer to same notion, identified as "the intentional non-compliance with [an] arm's length relationship aimed at deriving some advantage from this behaviour for oneself or for related individuals".[11]

Beyond the formal framework attributed to the problem of corruption, which has been analysed more from an economic than a legal perspective, Tanzi's approach has the merit of focusing on which factors must be considered as directly contributing to the spread of corruption in modern society.

Paradoxically, it should be noted that, at least at a certain stage of development, the more an economic and financial system grows, the more favourable conditions there are for an increase in the levels of corruption.

Indeed, there is no doubt that most private activities require a large number of

---

10 See Vito Tanzi, *Corruption Around the World – Causes, Consequences, Scope, and Cures*, IMF Staff Papers, Vol 45, No 4 (December 1998) 559–594 at 564.

11 *Ibid*, p564, note 11.

licences, permits and authorisations of various kinds to be obtained and compliance with relevant regulations. This inevitably causes an exponential growth in the need for contact between citizens and bureaucrats, as well as pressure on public institutions by lobbyists on behalf of large corporations, thus giving rise to occasions to put in place conducts somehow bound with bribery.

Among administrations that are at a high risk of being affected by bribery, tax and customs offices certainly play a key role. This is due to several factors, including but not limited to the following:

- the complexity and/or obscurity of the legal framework, compared to other sectors;
- the lack of transparency and the weak monitoring of the relevant administrative procedures; and, above all,
- too wide a discretion granted to responsible officials.

Finally, Tanzi recalls Gary Becker's 1968 theory on the importance of the enforcement of penalties as a deterrent against criminal conduct[12] in asserting the existence of a close relationship between the probability of acts of bribery taking place and the fact that in most cases penalties, far from being effectively imposed under the relevant legislation and regulations, "tend to be more lenient than the statutory ones".[13]

Likewise, the weakness of institutional controls plays a central role in the spread of corruption, thus leading several countries, including Italy (as discussed at 4 below) – to establish special commissions or ethics offices charged with the task of fighting bribery.

Insiders have complained about such authorities' lack of accountability as they are often subject to a requirement to report their activities solely to governments rather than to legislative bodies and thus fall outside the scope of any proper monitoring. The former Director of the IMF's Fiscal Affairs Department has, however, wished for an improvement in their level of independence from political establishments as well as in the associated integrity of their personnel, and argued that direct powers to enforce penalties should be conferred on the administrations concerned.[14]

2.2 The meaning of 'corruption' under the current international and supranational legal framework

By comparison with the definitions discussed thus far, which have been drawn up pursuant to a socio-economic approach, the concept of corruption as enshrined within the relevant international and European legal frameworks, derive from the need to narrow down the parameters of corrupt conducts that deserve particularly serious law enforcement action.

As a result, the governments, as well as parliaments, administrations and judicial

12 See more thoroughly GS Becker, *Crime and punishment: an economic approach*, Journal of Political Economy 76, No. 2 (March-April, 1968).

13 *Ibid*, p574.

14 *Ibid*, p575.

bodies of a number of countries have been granted essential tools aimed at strengthening their cooperation and identifying a series of broad categories of corruption in relation to which each individual jurisdiction may tailor its own preferred strategy in tackling bribery.

For example, the United Nations Convention against Corruption 2004 (the UN Convention) – which was adopted in New York pursuant to UN General Assembly Resolution 58/4 dated 13 October 2003 and ratified by Italy via Act no 116/2009 – provides a general definition of 'corruption', seeking to facilitate the passage by contracting states of provisions most suitable to them, in accordance with the specific features prevailing in each jurisdiction.

The UN Convention is therefore limited to binding the contracting states to implement all necessary measures for preventing, investigating and prosecuting the corruption offences listed therein. These measures include:

- the establishment of anti-corruption bodies;
- making provision for policies aimed at improving the management of public finance and tightening discipline in public procurement; and
- the promotion of transparency and accountability, both in public and private business relationships.

Among the obligations that contracting states are required to fulfil is that provided for by article 15 of the UN Convention, concerning 'Bribery of national public officials'. Pursuant to this provision, every conduct resulting in the promise, offering or giving of undue advantage to a public official in order to procure him or her acting or refraining from acting within his or her duties, where intentionally committed, is a criminal offence, together with the solicitation or acceptance of the same by a public official himself or herself.[15]

The same reasoning may apply with respect to article 16 of the UN Convention, which concerns 'Bribery of foreign public officials and officials of public international organizations', which substantially reflects the wording of article 15, save that it extends the parameters of the behaviours to be prosecuted and punished to those committed by foreign public officials or public officials of an international organisation.[16]

---

15 See article 15 of the United Nations Convention against Corruption (2004), which refers to "(a) [t]he promise, offering or giving, to a public official, directly or indirectly, of an undue advantage, for the official himself or herself or another person or entity, in order that the official act or refrain from acting in the exercise of his or her official duties; (b) [t]he solicitation or acceptance by a public official, directly or indirectly, of an undue advantage, for the official himself or herself or another person or entity, in order that the official act or refrain from acting in the exercise of his or her official duties."

16 *Ibid*, article 16, pursuant to which: "1. Each State Party shall adopt such legislative and other measures as may be necessary to establish as a criminal offence, when committed intentionally, the promise, offering or giving to a foreign public official or an official of a public international organization, directly or indirectly, of an undue advantage, for the official himself or herself or another person or entity, in order that the official act or refrain from acting in the exercise of his or her official duties, in order to obtain or retain business or other undue advantage in relation to the conduct of international business. 2. Each State Party shall consider adopting such legislative and other measures as may be necessary to establish as a criminal offence, when committed intentionally, the solicitation or acceptance by a foreign public official or an official of a public international organization, directly or indirectly, of an undue advantage, for the official himself or herself or another person or entity, in order that the official act or refrain from acting in the exercise of his or her official duties."

In addition to the offences provided for by articles 15 and 16, which encompass the core notion of corruption encapsulated in much of the relevant international legislation, the UN Convention also lists a number of forms of ancillary misconduct that domestic legislation of the majority of jurisdictions, including Italy, deem to have negative effects. Among these, several forms of infringement are just as important as those previously mentioned. They include:

- the embezzlement, misappropriation or other diversion of any public or private property obtained by a public official by virtue of his or her position, in order to gain a personal benefit (article 17),[17] as well as the same misconduct committed by any professionals in the course of economic, financial or commercial activities (article 22);[18]
- the promise, offering or giving to a public official or any other person of an undue advantage, as well as its solicitation or acceptance, pursuant to his or her actual or supposed influence over public institutions, in order to obtain undue benefits for the instigator (article 18);[19]
- the abuse by a public official of functions or positions in violations of laws for the purpose of obtaining an undue advantage for himself or herself or another person or entity (article 19);[20]
- illicit enrichment, ie, an unjustified increase in the assets of a public official relative to his or her lawful income (article 20);[21] and
- bribery in the private sector stemming from the same forms of misconduct as those dealt with by article 15 of the UN Convention, where they are carried out within private business relationships (article 21).[22]

---

17 *Ibid*, article 17, pursuant to which: "Each State Party shall adopt such legislative and other measures as may be necessary to establish as criminal offences, when committed intentionally, the embezzlement, misappropriation or other diversion by a public official for his or her benefit or for the benefit of another person or entity, of any property, public or private funds or securities or any other thing of value entrusted to the public official by virtue of his or her position."

18 *Ibid*, article 22, pursuant to which: "Each State Party shall consider adopting such legislative and other measures as may be necessary to establish as a criminal offence, when committed intentionally in the course of economic, financial or commercial activities, embezzlement by a person who directs or works, in any capacity, in a private sector entity of any property, private funds or securities or any other thing of value entrusted to him or her by virtue of his or her position."

19 *Ibid*, article 18, pursuant to which: "Each State Party shall consider adopting such legislative and other measures as may be necessary to establish as criminal offences, when committed intentionally: (a) [t]he promise, offering or giving to a public official or any other person, directly or indirectly, of an undue advantage in order that the public official or the person abuse his or her real or supposed influence with a view to obtaining from an administration or public authority of the State Party an undue advantage for the original instigator of the act or for any other person; (b) [t]he solicitation or acceptance by a public official or any other person, directly or indirectly, of an undue advantage for himself or herself or for another person in order that the public official or the person abuse his or her real or supposed influence with a view to obtaining from an administration or public authority of the State Party an undue advantage."

20 *Ibid*, article 19, pursuant to which: "Each State Party shall consider adopting such legislative and other measures as may be necessary to establish as a criminal offence, when committed intentionally, the abuse of functions or position, that is, the performance of or failure to perform an act, in violation of laws, by a public official in the discharge of his or her functions, for the purpose of obtaining an undue advantage for himself or herself or for another person or entity."

21 *Ibid*, article 20, pursuant to which: "Subject to its constitution and the fundamental principles of its legal system, each State Party shall consider adopting such legislative and other measures as may be necessary to establish as a criminal offence, when committed intentionally, illicit enrichment, that is, a significant increase in the assets of a public official that he or she cannot reasonably explain in relation to his or her lawful income."

There is no doubt that this international legal framework has given a fundamental impetus to the fight against corruption worldwide, so far as it imposes a specific duty on contracting states to implement as much legislation as deemed necessary to achieve the required objectives.

The Organisation for Economic Co-operation and Development (OECD) Convention on Combating Bribery of Foreign Public Officials in International Business Transactions (OECD Convention)[23] binds contracting states to implement all necessary measures to prosecute as criminal offences in their jurisdictions the same kinds of conduct those dealt with under the UN Convention. The main differences between the OECD Convention and the UN Convention are the use of the adjective 'pecuniary' with regard to undue advantages obtained by corrupt officials and the application of criminal liability in the context of international business.[24]

Attention is also drawn to a provision of the OECD Convention concerning a number of further illicit behaviours aimed at preparing, causing and supporting the commission of an act of bribery. These behaviours merit separate grounds for criminal prosecution, whether they are committed by foreign public officials or those of an OECD contracting state.[25]

No less important is the contribution made by European Union (EU) conventions – among other instruments[26] – ratified by Italy through Act No 300/2000. Pursuant to this act, a number of amendments have been made to the Criminal Code and other related laws aimed at fighting bribery, as described more fully below.

Starting with the European Union Convention on the fight against corruption involving officials of the European Communities or officials of member states of the European Union 1997 (the EU Convention),[27] it should be noted that such provisions

---

22 *Ibid*, article 21, pursuant to which: "Each State Party shall consider adopting such legislative and other measures as may be necessary to establish as criminal offences, when committed intentionally in the course of economic, financial or commercial activities: (a) [t]he promise, offering or giving, directly or indirectly, of an undue advantage to any person who directs or works, in any capacity, for a private sector entity, for the person himself or herself or for another person, in order that he or she, in breach of his or her duties, act or refrain from acting; (b) [t]he solicitation or acceptance, directly or indirectly, of an undue advantage by any person who directs or works, in any capacity, for a private sector entity, for the person himself or herself or for another person, in order that he or she, in breach of his or her duties, act or refrain from acting."

23 This convention was adopted in Paris on 21 November 1997.

24 *See* article 1, paragraph 1 of the OECD Convention, pursuant to which: "Each Party shall take such measures as may be necessary to establish that it is a criminal offence under its law for any person intentionally to offer, promise or give any undue pecuniary or other advantage, whether directly or through intermediaries, to a foreign public official, for that official or for a third party, in order that the official act or refrain from acting in relation to the performance of official duties, in order to obtain or retain business or other improper advantage in the conduct of international business."

25 *Ibid*, article 1, paragraph 2, pursuant to which: "Each Party shall take any measures necessary to establish that complicity in, including incitement, aiding and abetting, or authorisation of an act of bribery of a foreign public official shall be a criminal offence. Attempt and conspiracy to bribe a foreign public official shall be criminal offences to the same extent as attempt and conspiracy to bribe a public official of that Party."

26 Including the European Union Convention on the protection of the European Communities' financial interests, signed in Brussels on 26 July 1995, its First Protocol, signed in Brussels the same day, and its Second Protocol, signed in Dublin on 27 September 1996.

27 This convention was drawn up pursuant to article K.3(2)(c) of the Treaty on European Union and signed in Brussels on 27 May 1997.

set out a notion of 'corruption' very similar to those provided for by the UN Convention several years later, in particular by mirroring the same two-fold approach to active and passive bribery.

Thus, in order to avoid any possible shortcomings in the regulatory framework, EUs member states, as contracting parties under EU conventions, are required to establish as a criminal offence the promise or giving of any advantages whatsoever by whomsoever to a public official,[28] as well as the request or receipt of same by such public official,[29] in order for the latter to act or refrain from acting in accordance with his or her duties or in breach of them, depending on the requirements of the briber.

The express definition of 'public official', as one of the figures liable for such crimes as well as the briber, must be considered one of the most remarkable achievements of the EU Convention, since it allows domestic legislative and judicial bodies to adopt as many precise notions as possible of who benefits from a bribe, thus improving their ability to enforce against such offences.

In this regard, no distinction is made between national officials of each of the member states and those entrusted with the management of public functions within the EU, as well as their employed personnel, with regard to the prohibitions listed in the EU Convention.[30]

Finally, the role played by EU Council Framework Decision 2003/568/JHA of 22 July 2003 on combating corruption in the private sector (the Council Framework Decision) should not be ignored, as it anticipates a more sophisticated approach to bribery as a result of pressure exerted by the most informed commentators with the

28 See article 3 of the European Union Convention, pursuant to which: "1. For the purposes of this Convention, the deliberate action of whosoever promises or gives, directly or through an intermediary, an advantage of any kind whatsoever to an official for himself or for a third party for him to act or refrain from acting in accordance with his duty or in the exercise of his functions in breach of his official duties shall constitute active corruption. 2. Each Member State shall take the necessary measures to ensure that conduct of the type referred to in paragraph 1 is made a criminal offence."

29 *Ibid*, article 2, pursuant to which: "1. For the purposes of this Convention, the deliberate action of an official, who, directly or through an intermediary, requests or receives advantages of any kind whatsoever, for himself or for a third party, or accepts a promise of such an advantage, to act or refrain from acting in accordance with his duty or in the exercise of his functions in breach of his official duties shall constitute passive corruption. 2. Each Member State shall take the necessary measures to ensure that conduct of the type referred to in paragraph 1 is made a criminal offence."

30 *Ibid*, article 1, pursuant to which: "For the purposes of this Convention:
(a) 'official' shall mean any Community or national official, including any national official of another Member State;
(b) 'Community official' shall mean:
– any person who is an official or other contracted employee within the meaning of the Staff Regulations of officials of the European Communities or the Conditions of Employment of other servants of the European Communities,
– any person seconded to the European Communities by the Member States or by any public or private body, who carries out functions equivalent to those performed by European Community officials or other servants.
Members of bodies set up in accordance with the Treaties establishing the European Communities and the staff of such bodies shall be treated as Community officials, inasmuch as the Staff Regulations of officials of the European Communities or the Conditions of Employment of other servants of the European Communities do not apply to them;
(c) 'national official' shall be understood by reference to the definition of 'official' or 'public officer' in the national law of the Member State in which the person in question performs that function for the purposes of application of the criminal law of that Member State.
Nevertheless, in the case of proceedings involving a Member State's official initiated by another Member State, the latter shall not be bound to apply the definition of 'national official' except insofar as that definition is compatible with its national law."

support of public opinion. Under this approach, the fight against corruption within private business relationships must be considered equally important to the struggle in the field of public affairs in restoring and upholding the rule of law.

The Council Framework Decision – which has been recently implemented in Italy by virtue of Legislative Decree No 38/2017, despite new criminal provisions having already been introduced into the Civil Code by virtue of Act no 190/2012 – imposes a duty on EU member states to make criminal offences several instances of bribery that once took place between private individuals in the course of business.

The Council Framework Decision refers to the promise, offer or giving of any undue advantage to any individual in his or her capacity as a director and/or employee of a private sector entity, as well as a request for or the receipt of such undue advantage by such director and/or employee, in order for him or her to act or refrain from acting in breach of his or her duties.[31]

3. The Italian legal framework with regard to the provisions aimed at fighting corruption

3.1 Criminal legislation

Criminal legislation in Italy is the result of a merger between domestic experience, gained over time, in the fight against corruption and the ever-growing number of guidelines and recommendations emanating from relevant EU bodies and aimed at building a common framework of legal tools and so harmonising a shared system of law enforcement by EU member states.

Accordingly, as discussed previously, a number of provisions set out in the Italian Penal Code and other related laws have been amended over the past few decades in order to comply with the international and supranational instruments referred to at 2 above and to keep updating them to match the evolution of methods of bribery.

This is exactly the case with article 317 of the Penal Code – which has most recently been amended by Act No 69/2015, which contains 'Provisions regarding offences against public administration, mafia organizations and false accounting' – pursuant to which those behaviours constituting generic abuse of a public position are made criminal offences.

Put more precisely, where a public official or a person in charge of a public service abuses his or her powers by requiring another to give or promise, to him or her or to a third party, money or other undue benefits, he or she will be sentenced to six to 12 years' imprisonment.[32] Ancillary penalties may also be imposed, such as permanent

31 See more pertinently article 2 of Council Framework Decision 2003/568/JHA, pursuant to which: "1. Member States shall take the necessary measures to ensure that the following intentional conduct constitutes a criminal offence, when it is carried out in the course of business activities: (a) promising, offering or giving, directly or through an intermediary, to a person who in any capacity directs or works for a private-sector entity an undue advantage of any kind, for that person or for a third party, in order that that person should perform or refrain from performing any act, in breach of that person's duties; (b) directly or through an intermediary, requesting or receiving an undue advantage of any kind, or accepting the promise of such an advantage, for oneself or for a third party, while in any capacity directing or working for a private-sector entity, in order to perform or refrain from performing any act, in breach of one's duties. 2. Paragraph 1 applies to business activities within profit and non-profit entities."

32 See article 317 of the Italian Penal Code 1930 as amended (2009 version).

disqualification from holding a public office, though this may be made temporary if mitigating circumstances can be shown.[33]

With regard to passive bribery, the Italian Supreme Court of Cassation has recently stated that coercion, which is integral to the subjective element of the crime, may also consist of an implicit threat, provided that it is capable of coercing the will of the private individual. The existence of coercion will be evaluated on a case-by-case basis by reference to the broad discretion under which a public official exercises his or her powers.[34]

The Supreme Court of Cassation has also held, in a separate ruling, that an attempted passive bribery may take place, for example, in relation to any request and/or illicit pressure by a public official following the submission of a complaint to the competent authorities by the victim of a crime.[35]

The offence under discussion must be distinguished from that introduced by Act No 190/2012 (the so-called 'Severino Act'), pursuant to which the conducts covered by article 317 of the Penal code are punishable with between six and ten-and-a-half years' imprisonment (for the bribed public official) and up to three years' imprisonment (for the briber) where they are deemed to have a lower negative value. Such a distinction rests upon the manner in which the public official requires a passive bribe to be made. Thus, behaviour resulting in a conviction for an offence under article 317 features some form of psychological threat or violence capable of limiting the victim's freedom of choice, whereas an offence under article 319-*quater*, only implies a form of pressure or a deceptive inducement that the victim may refuse or resist.[36]

Article 318 of the Penal Code, as amended by Act No 190/2012, makes criminal offences of several forms of conduct that may be considered close to those referred to as "passive bribery" by article 2 of the EU Convention above. Article 318 provides that a public official who, in the exercise of his or her functions or powers, unduly receives, for himself or herself or for a third party, money or other benefits or accepts the promise of such money or benefits, shall be punishable by between one and six years' imprisonment.

In this regard, the Supreme Court of Cassation has specified that the article 318 offence, as formulated following amendments made by Act No 190/2012, shall be deemed to have been committed even if an agreement between a public official or a person charged with a public service and a briber in relation to the performance or otherwise of a public function or a public service in exchange for a promise or the giving of undue benefits is not followed by an actual distortion of such public function or service.[37] The reason for such an interpretation is that, according to the 2012 amendments, the core of the crime is to be found in the 'monetisation' of a public office, as expressed by the agreement between the briber and the bribed; such agreement deserves to be criminally prosecuted regardless of its effective execution.

---

33 *Ibid*, article 317-*bis*.
34 See Court of Cassation, ruling No 47602/2017.
35 See Court of Cassation, ruling No 25677/2016.
36 See Court of Cassation, ruling No 35/2017.
37 See Court of Cassation, ruling No 36769/2017.

Article 319 of the Penal Code punishes with terms of six to 10 years' imprisonment any public official who either fails or delays or has failed or delayed the performance of an act within his or her official duties, or who performs or has performed an act contrary to his or her official duties, receives money or other benefits or accepts the promise of such money or benefits,[38] for himself or herself or for a third party.

Such penalties, which are harsher than those laid down by article 318 of the Penal Code, are intended to increase, pursuant to article 319-*bis*, in the event that the article 319 offence relates to the award of state employments, salaries or pensions, or contracts in which the public administration employing the bribed public official is interested, as well as to the payment or reimbursement of taxes.[39]

With regard to an offence arising under article 319, the Supreme Court of Cassation has recently stressed that the offence shall also be deemed to have been committed in the case of acts that, although formally legitimate (except those strictly determined by the law as to the *an*, to the *quod* and to the *quomodo*[40]), are committed in the context of the pursuit by a public official of purposes other than public or institutional ones.[41]

Particular attention must be paid to corruption affecting judicial proceedings such as to upset their smooth course. Accordingly, article 319-*ter* of the Penal Code makes specific provision where any of the behaviours governed by articles 318 or 319 are committed to the favour or the detriment of a party to any judicial proceedings, whether civil, criminal or administrative. Indeed, in such cases the penalty of imprisonment increases from six to 12 years. If one of the abovementioned offences results in the unfair conviction of any person to imprisonment not exceeding five years, article 319-*ter* increases the penalty to between six and 14 years. If the wrongful imprisonment is for longer than five years or a life sentence, the same provision increases the penalty to between eight and 20 years.

According to case law, one of the most typical forms that the offence of bribery within judicial proceedings may take is the promise or giving of money by anyone to a witness, and accepted by him or her, resulting in the false testimony of that witness favouring a party to a trial.[42]

Moreover, article 320 of the Penal Code is concerned with extending the punishment for the crimes governed by articles 318 and 319 to persons in charge of a public service.

The discussion above concerns the criminal legal framework with regard to the most ancient form of corruption, ie, that which affects the management of public affairs. A number of other provisions introduced into the domestic legal system by international and EU instruments require a separate analysis, as they deal with bribery that may take place within private business relationships.

The applicable provision in Italy is article 2635 of the Italian Civil Code, as last

38 See article 319 of the Italian Penal Code.

39 *Ibid*, article 319-*bis*.

40 These Latin expressions mean, respectively, (1) the need for prosecution of the concerned behavior, and (2) the degree of gravity to be reached by the offence to trigger a criminal prosecution and the extent of the relevant penalties.

41 See Court of Cassation, ruling No 3606/2016.

42 See Court of Cassation, ruling No 40759/2016.

amended by Legislative Decree No 38/2017. Directors, managers, executives responsible for preparing corporate accounting documents, statutory auditors, liquidators and other related professionals of companies or private entities who, even through a third party, solicit, receive or accept a promise, for themselves or others, of money or other undue benefits, in order to perform or refrain from performing an act in violation of their duties or fidelity obligations, are punishable with between one and three years' imprisonment.

The same penalties may be imposed on bribers, even those acting through a third party, but they will be doubled in the event that the offence is committed within companies with securities listed on regulated Italian or other EU stock markets or widely traded publicly.[43]

However, pursuant to article 2635-*bis* of the Civil Code, penalties for bribees and bribers may be reduced by one-third in cases where an offer, the promise or the solicitation of money or other undue benefits is not accepted (so-called 'inducement to bribery').[44]

The prosecution of bribery between private individuals can only be initiated following a report made by the victim, unless the offence has caused a distortion in competition for the purchase of goods and services. Where seizure of the product, of the profit or the means used to commit the offence is ordered (whether a judicial authority or not), its value must be at least equal to the amount of any given or promised bribes.[45]

According to the Supreme Court of Cassation, a vote or even a simple opinion expressed for the purpose of formulating or influencing a resolution of the collective ruling body of a company may be an example of bribery under article 2635 of the Civil Code.[46]

In any event, those who are found guilty of the forms of conduct discussed above are subject to an ancillary penalty of temporary disqualification from holding an executive office within private companies or other private legal entities.[47]

3.2 Administrative corporate liability arising out of criminal offences

Following the ratification by Italy, pursuant to Act No 300/2000, of the EU and OECD instruments of the late 1990s aimed at strengthening cooperation between EU member states in tackling bribery, Legislative Decree No 231/2001 was enacted to implement article 6 of the EU Convention[48] and article 2 of the OECD Convention,[49] both of which impose on member states and contracting States respectively a duty

---

43 See article 2635, paragraph 4 of the Italian Civil Code 1942 as amended.

44 See article 2635-*bis* of the Italian civil code, added by Legislative Decree No 38/2017.

45 *Ibid*, article 2635, paragraphs 5 and 6.

46 See Court of Cassation, ruling No 5848/2012.

47 See article 2635-*ter* of the Italian Civil Code, added Legislative Decree No 38/2017.

48 See article 6 of the EU Convention, pursuant to which: "Each Member State shall take the necessary measures to allow heads of businesses or any persons having power to take decisions or exercise control within a business to be declared criminally liable in accordance with the principles defined by its national law in cases of corruption, as referred to in Article 3, by a person under their authority acting on behalf of the business."

49 See article 2 of the OECD Convention, pursuant to which: "Each Party shall take such measures as may be necessary, in accordance with its legal principles, to establish the liability of legal persons for the bribery of a foreign public official."

to take such measures as may be necessary, in accordance with their legal principles, to establish the liability of legal persons and their highest executives for acts of bribery. The enactment of this decree marks a turning point in the long-standing debate on the opportunity, if not the need, to establish a form of administrative liability arising out of criminal offences committed within private legal entities. This is in order to increase the deterrent capability of penalties, taking into account the fact that in most cases fines are too high to be borne effectively by the physical persons who are have actually committed corporate crimes.

According to the Roman law *maxim societas delinquere non potest* (legal persons cannot commit crimes), the Italian legal system traditionally barred any kind of criminal liability on the part of companies and other private legal entities, due to their lack of consciousness, on the assumption that no-one can be punished for an offence that cannot be ascertained to have been psychologically pursued.

Such a framework has now been reversed on the basis that, legal persons actually do commit crimes (*societas delinquere potest*). This is because it appears extremely difficult to imagine a real distinction between the very will of a company and the conduct of its top management, bearing in mind that the former turns out to be nothing but the result of a strategy adopted by the latter, who have been entrusted with the power to take decisions within a collective business organisation.

As a result, article 5 of Legislative Decree No 231/2001 envisages that a legal person may be held liable for crimes committed in its interest or for its benefit by the following categories of professional, provided that they did not act solely in their own personal interest or for their own benefit:

- persons holding representative, administrative or executive offices within an entity or a financially-independent organisational unit of that entity, as well as persons who exercise, even if only as a matter of fact (*de facto*), the management and control of the entity itself; and
- persons subject to an executive or supervisory power of the persons mentioned in the previous category.

As to the first category above, companies and other legal entities may be exempted from liability where it can be shown that they have adopted and effectively implemented so-called 'compliance programmes', a concept borrowed from North American legal systems. This exemption will only apply provided that the following conditions are met:

- that an independent body within the collective organisation has been entrusted with supervisory and updating tasks under a compliance programme; and
- an alleged offence has been committed as a result of a deceitful bypassing of such a programme and its monitoring by the independent body, provided that it has properly carried out its functions.[50]

As to the second category above, the exemption of legal entities from liability

50 See more pertinently article 6 of Legislative Decree No 231/2001.

stems directly from compliance by top management with the executive and supervisory duties by which it is bound toward employed personnel. The exemption will apply provided that a compliance programme has been adopted and effectively implemented prior to the commission of an offence of the type that has in fact occurred and top management would have otherwise have been able to prevent the commission of the same offence.[51]

In any case, it must be stressed that, in order to strengthen the effectiveness of penalties, legal persons will be found liable even if the author of the crime has not been identified or cannot be charged with it, as well as if the offence is extinguished due to a cause other than amnesty, such as a statute of limitation or the death of the author of that offence.[52]

With regard to the penalties envisaged by Legislative Decree No 231/2001, a distinction is made by article 9 between the following:

- pecuniary sentences;
- interdictory measures;
- seizure; and
- publication of the conviction and sentence.

Pecuniary sentences are imposed in accordance with the seriousness of the offence committed, the degree of responsibility of the legal person, its financial and economic position, and measures undertaken to eliminate or mitigate the consequences of the offence and prevent or deter the commission of further ones.[53]

There is no doubt, however, that greater attention should be paid to interdictory measures. They are the fundamental tools for ensuring compliance with regulations by legal entities, given the ability of those measures to freeze temporarily – or, at worst, to end – the course of business run by companies on which such measures are imposed.[54]

Finally, Legislative Decree No 231/2001 provides a list of offences – updated from time to time – the commission of which trigger a charge of administrative liability on companies and other private legal entities in the interest of or for the benefit of which such offences have been committed. Among those crimes, the most significant for present purposes are those set out in article 25, pursuant to which active and passive bribery, as well as an inducement to give or promise money or other gains are all capable of triggering liability of a legal person within the organisation of which they have been committed.

Such a mechanism was intended to strengthen law enforcement action against those corrupt forms of behaviour that are nowadays widespread throughout private

---

51 *Ibid*, article 7.

52 See, more pertinently, article 8 of Legislative Decree No 231/2001.

53 See, more pertinently, article 11 of Legislative Decree No 231/2001.

54 *Ibid*, article 9, paragraph 2, pursuant to which: "The interdictory measures are: a) disqualification from pursuing a business activity; b) suspension or revocation of permits, licences or concessions functional to the commission of the occurred offence; c) prohibition from contracting with public administration, except for obtaining the performance of a public service; d) exclusion from benefits, loans, grants or subsidies and the possible revocation of those already granted; e) prohibition from advertising goods or services."

business relationships and with respect to which the lack of strict legal constraints could have led to a quicker than expected deterioration of the social and economic fabric. As a matter of fact, however, this objective has not yet been achieved, for reasons due to the reasons that are detailed below.

3.3 Administrative legislation

As stated at 1 above, one of the most important achievements in the fight against corruption is the awareness that this phenomenon is not merely a matter of criminal law, it being necessary to broaden approaches to it by reference to different perspectives, both preventive and regulatory.

In this regard, the key role played by Act No 190/2012 mentioned above (the so-called 'Severino Act'), which contains "Provisions aimed at preventing and combating corruption and unlawfulness within public administration", cannot be ignored in addressing bribery issues. This is because of several remarkable amendments made by this act to existing legislation, in addition to the establishment of the independent National Anti-Bribery Authority, which is discussed in greater detail at 4 below.

With regard to the fundamental need for transparency, the Severino Act, as implemented by regulations adopted under it,[55] imposes a general duty on all public entities to disclose the most significant data regarding their organisations and activities by publishing them on their institutional websites. In other words, the entire flow of data regarding, for example, composition of bodies, expenditure caps, salaries of employees of any public administration, the financial situation of public officials and their relatives and documents pertaining to any administrative procedure whatsoever has now been made fully available to citizens.

Furthermore, in order to allow them a true monitoring of the administrations and of their compliance with constitutional principles such as equality, impartiality, good performance, responsibility, effectiveness and efficiency of public action, a new general right to access public documents has been established.

With regard to preventive measures undertaken, the Severino Act identifies the most sensitive areas of public affairs at risk of being affected by corruption, such as those dealing with the grant of economic gains to private stakeholders or with the award of public goods and procurements, in relation to which an internal anti-bribery plan must be adopted in compliance with guidelines issued every three years by the National Anti-Bribery Authority and known as the National Anti-Bribery Plan, discussed at 4 below.

Moreover, pursuant to article 1, paragraph 44 of the Severino Act, a genuine ethical code has been implemented by virtue of Decree of the President of the Republic No 62/2013, which lays down a minimum core of duties with which public servants must comply with regard to diligence, loyalty, impartiality and good behaviour. Failure to comply with the code, in addition to triggering disciplinary liability, is punishable under criminal, civil, administrative and accounting legislation.

---

55 See Legislative Decrees Nos 235/2012, 33/2013 and 39/2013, together with Decree of the President of the Republic No 62/2013.

The engagement of a professional figure to be specifically appointed by every individual administration so as to prevent corrupt forms of behaviour,[56] subject to the supervisory power of the National Anti-Bribery Authority, is another major innovation under the new system. Such appointees are charged with (among other tasks) a duty to oversee the smooth conferral of executive positions, both in-house and external, to persons who can demonstrate that they meet a number of requirements.

Under Legislative Decree No 39/2013, adopted pursuant to Act No 190/2012, supervisory appointees to administrations may deal, for example, with a previous conviction in relation to offences committed against the public administration, or, alternatively, with an existing or potential conflict of interest on the part of candidates. Such cases of incompatibility must be challenged by the responsible appointee, whether they have arisen prior to or following a person's appointment as a public officer, so that relevant violations of the law are notified to the National Anti-Bribery Authority.[57]

More recently, administration appointees responsible for the prevention of corruption, together with the National Anti-Bribery Authority and judicial authorities, have been entrusted by Act No 179/2017 with the responsibility of receiving reports by public employees who have become aware of illicit behaviour by an office of which they are part and to maintain the strict confidentiality of such reports in order to encourage whistleblowing as an essential tool in fighting bribery and illegality in the management of public affairs. Accordingly, the authors of such reports must be protected from any possible consequences of their choice to cooperate with justice, ie, disciplinary actions, demotion, dismissal and transfer, as well as any other organisational measure having negative effects, whether direct or indirect, on their working conditions.

Legislative Decree No 97/2016 (the so-called Madia Decree), adopted pursuant to Act No 124/2015 (the so-called Madia Act), is another important step towards rooting out corruption. This decree is committed to the following major targets:

- to broaden the scope of application of the duties imposed on public administrations with regard to the prevention of bribery;
- to adopt organisational measures for publishing documentation pertaining public activities; and
- to identify the authorities conferred with powers to impose penalties in relation to detected violations of transparency requirements.

For this purpose, the Madia Decree has increased the number of public entities on which a general duty of transparency has been imposed, so as to include the following categories:

- non-economic entities;
- companies subject to public control, except for those listed on a stock exchange;

56 See article 1, paragraph 7 of Act No 190/2012.
57 See article 15 of Legislative Decree No 39/2013.

- corporations with a major public shareholding;
- associations, foundations and other private entities, including those without a legal personality, that are financed mainly by a public administration holding a right to appoint their entire management and where their financial statements are above the threshold of €500,000.

From another perspective, the Madia Decree, in order to protect the rights of citizens by facilitating their efforts to monitor administrative procedures, confers on to them a general right to access public documents regardless of any demonstration by applicants that they possess a legitimate interest in relation to those procedures. Furthermore, the procedure for allowing access must result in a reasoned decision, to be notified to applicants and other concerned parties within 30 days from the filing of the relevant application. In the event that access is totally or partially denied, applicants can request the responsible supervisory appointee of the relevant administration for the prevention of corruption to review the application. An appeal against his or her decision may be filed with the Regional Administrative Court (TAR).

Finally, the Madia Decree envisages a number of violations of matters to which it applies that may trigger a specific liability on the part of responsible executives with regard to their duties to allow citizens access to public documents and to make available the most significant data regarding the management of public affairs. The power to impose appropriate penalties for such liability is exercisable by the National Anti-Bribery Authority.

4. National authorities responsible for regulating and enforcing provisions aimed at fighting corruption

The entire national juridical machinery aimed at tackling corruption matters has rested, at least since the enactment of Act No 190/2012, upon dialectical cooperation between three main actors. Each of them has been conferred with different powers within the framework of the struggle against such an ever-growing phenomenon.

Firstly, as discussed at 3.3 above, public administration must currently be considered as the first guarantor of transparency and compliance with legislative provisions, particularly with regard to discipline in public procurement and the smooth administration of public tenders.

Secondly, the law enforcement actions exercised by judicial authorities, by means of investigating, prosecuting and ruling upon the most typical forms of corruption-related misconduct, as described above, is fundamental.

Finally, the National Anti-Bribery Authority (*Autorità Nazionale Anti-Corruzione*, or ANAC) has been charged with, on the one hand, regulating specific issues that are already subject to primary legislation of both a domestic and a European pedigree and, on the other, enforcing these enactments by means of conducting supervisory activity and investigations into alleged violations of the law, as well as punishing the authors of those violations. As such, it is likely that the ANAC will exercise a leading role in the fight against corruption in the next few years, following the same path as that taken by the National Commission for Corporations and the Stock Exchange

(*Commissione Nazionale per le Società e la Borsa*, or CONSOB), the national supervisory body for the financial markets, over the past few decades.

Established by the Severino Act in 2012, pursuant to article 6 of the UN Convention, the ANAC evolved from the Independent Commission for the Assessment, Integrity and Transparency of Public Administrations (*Commissione Indipendente per la Valutazione, l'Integrità e la Trasparenza delle pubbliche amministrazioni*, or CIVIT). It is required to control, prevent and counteract corruption acts and illegality within the public administration.[58] For this purpose, the ANAC is committed to fulfilling a number of tasks, including but not limited to:

- collaborating with foreign counterpart bodies and competent regional and international organisations;
- approving the National Anti-Corruption Plan prepared by the Public Function Department;
- analysing the causes of corruption and identifying which forms of intervention can help to prevent and fight it; and
- advising public administrations with regard to the compliance of acts of and behaviour by public officials with laws, codes of conduct and contracts, both collective and individual, regulating the public employment relationship.[59]

The ANAC shall report to Parliament every year in respect of these duties. Furthermore, as already discussed, the ANAC is charged with supervising the activities of the appointees of each public administration who are specifically responsible for the prevention of corruption in their organisations. In this capacity, the ANAC receives reports made by those appointees concerning any violation of laws detected in relation to procedures for the appointment of any public officers within the administrations for which those appointees are responsible.

The National Anti-Corruption Plan must meet the following requirements:[60]

- to identify activities in which the risk of corruption is highest;
- to make provision for mechanisms for training, implementation and monitoring of decisions aimed at preventing such risk;
- to monitor compliance with terms laid down by law or by regulations for completing procedures; and
- to monitor relationships between administrations and private contractual counterparts or stakeholders concerned with regard to procedures for authorising, granting or providing benefits of any kind, including checking any relationship between owners, directors, members and employees of those private entities and public executives and employees.

Furthermore, it must be stressed that the ANAC has absorbed the national Public Works, Services and Supplies Contracts Supervisory Authority (*Autorità per la vigilanza sui contratti pubblici di lavori, servizi e furniture*, or AVCP) by virtue of Law

58 See article 1, paragraph 1 of Act No 190/2012.
59 *Ibid*, article 1, paragraph 2.
60 *Ibid*, article 1, paragraph 9.

Decree No 90/2014, as implemented by Act No 114/2014. By absorbing the AVCP's functions and personnel, the ANAC has also become the reference institution with regard to acts of bribery affecting the sectors formerly covered by the AVCP.

As a result, in order to combine an improvement in the quality of public procurements with a reduction in their costs, procuring entities have benefited from a wider margin of discretion in choosing private companies to which public tenders are to be awarded, provided they have met a number of requirements. Among these requirements is an obligation to undertake all measures that may be necessary to highlight and prevent any conflicts of interest that may arise within procedures aimed at awarding procurements, and to provide rules aimed at ensuring the accountability of private companies. Accordingly, private enterprises that appear to be at a high risk of being affected by corruption are automatically barred from any tender, so as to prevent them from entering into any agreements with public administrations.

That said, the effectiveness of the system of anti-corruption bodies described above has been confirmed by the most recent review of the relevant legal framework under the Madia Decree. The provisions of that decree containing the 'Review and simplification of the provisions concerning prevention of corruption, publicity and transparency' state that (among other things) the ANAC's anti-corruption duties and corresponding powers have significantly increased. This regulator has therefore been entrusted with a number of additional tasks compared to those originally assigned to it when it was established in 2012. These include but are not limited to:

- identifying data, information and documents that are subject to compulsory publication, but with regard to which full publication has been replaced by publication in summarised form;
- providing for simplified ways in which municipalities with fewer than 15,000 inhabitants may be enabled to fulfil their anti-corruption obligations; and
- adopting standards, forms and schemes aimed at ensuring the smooth implementation of transparency obligations.

Moreover, the adoption of the National Anti-Corruption Plan, which was previously the responsibility of the Public Function Department, subject to the ANAC's approval, is now entirely the responsibility of the ANAC and must be prepared on a yearly basis. This plan is an official guideline both for public administrations (as to the drafting of their relevant internal plans), and private enterprises (as to the implementation of anti-corruption measures additional to those provided for by Legislative Decree No 231/2001).

5. An assessment of progress in the fight against corruption

The above analysis gives an overall picture of the progress made by Italy in fighting corruption up to the present day. The relevant legal framework and, accordingly, the related case law, as well as social perceptions of the phenomenon, have been subject to many frequent changes in line with political will and changes in public policy.

One preliminary feature must be stressed in this regard: despite the anti-corruption system initially having rested on preventive actions and risk assessment processes, combined with the key role played by the responsible appointees to public authorities, a new approach seems to be emerging that is based on different solutions with regard to discipline and the supervision of public contracts.

Likewise, the concept of 'anti-corruption' is evolving and being finessed as the various regulatory and enforcing authorities experience constant enhancement in the array of powers conferred on them to restore the rule of law within the management of public affairs.

As a result, the prosecution of the major bribery-related offences has not been an exhaustive process. Not only have judicial authorities been bound to establish the criminal liability of individuals, but now they must also, following the enactment of Legislative Decree No 231/2001, pursue private legal entities charged with such offences.

Furthermore, as has already been highlighted, ancillary penalties are not necessarily effective penalties; their failure in this regard renders criminal proceedings at risk of being a huge waste of time and effort.

In real terms, serious law enforcement action requires reinforcement in terms of prevention. This may be gained by ensuring compliance by the stakeholders concerned with a set of organisational standards and guarantees aimed at reducing the risk of corrupt behaviour to a level that may be deemed as acceptable or tolerable in a democratic society.

Thus, as the President of the ANAC has recently stated,[61] objections raised against the authority having recently been entrusted with additional responsibilities to exercise control over public procurement and award of contracts entered into by any public administration – which in some quarters was deemed an inadequate solution – seem to be groundless.

Certain juridical tools – some of which have been transposed from the international framework, while others are the results of domestic efforts to face corruption – can be said to have reached the goals set for them. Unfortunately, this cannot be said of many others, owing mainly to a 'cultural heritage' that is difficult to eradicate.

Since corruption is a disease that affects both the body politic and the entire administrative, social and economic systems, causing serious prejudice to the opportunities that would otherwise be available to the community overall, a shared commitment by society is required to tackle and defeat it.

Accordingly, the authors of this chapter extend an invitation to the body politic and public opinion to undertake an educational campaign aimed at raising awareness by insiders and outsiders alike with regard to bribery issues.

61 See note 1 above.

Japan

Naoki Iguchi
Nagashima Ohno & Tsunematsu

1. Overview

Japan has been one of the leading states in United Nations (UN) and Organisation for Economic Co-operation and Development (OECD) projects for anti-corruption conventions and treaties (see 2 below). Historically, the crime of bribery (*wairo-zai*) set out in the Japanese Criminal Code (Act No 45 of 1907[1]) (the 1907 Criminal Code) only had a limited extra-territorial reach; in other words, it did not extend to acts of bribery committed outside the territory of Japan, except with regard to the acts of 'public officials' to whom bribes were given or promised to be given outside of Japan (article 4). There was no penalty for the act of offering or promising to offer bribes to public officials of foreign governments. By acceding to, in particular, the UN's anti-corruption instruments and by adding a new set of provisions to the Unfair Competition Act 1993 (Act No 47 of 1993) (the 1993 UCA), Japan accepted UN convention principles and extended its jurisdictional outreach to corrupt conduct committed overseas (paragraphs 19–23).

As an increasing number of Japanese businesses become more active in overseas markets in Asia and elsewhere, they are eager to study the extraterritorial anti-corruption legislation and regulations of other jurisdictions, including but not limited to the United States Foreign Corrupt Practices Act 1976 (FCPA) and the United Kingdom Anti-Bribery Act 2010, both of which may apply to them. The Ministry of Economy, Trade and Industry (METI) recently published *Guidelines for Preventing Bribery of Foreign Public Officials* (the Guidelines) (which were originally published in 2014 and revised in 2017). The Guidelines address the needs of Japanese businesses and cover not only Japanese legislation but also that of foreign jurisdictions. With regard to domestic legislation and regulations, articles 197 and 198 of the 1907 Criminal Code have taken the leading role in preventing and punishing acts of bribery. Many state-owned businesses were privatised during the 'privatisation' age in the early 1990s. In connection with this, the scope of application of anti-bribery penalties was extended by special legislation to businesses transitioning from state-owned to privately-owned status (see 3.4 below).

Furthermore, after a series of corruption scandals in the 1990s involving high-ranking public officials damaged people's trust in the integrity of government

1 Note: Almost all of the codes and statutes referred to have subsequently been amended. In this chapter, codes and statutes are referred to by their original titles unless those titles have expressly been changed or the entire structure of those instruments has been substantially changed or substituted.

officials, the Diet enacted the National Public Service Ethics Act (Act No 129 of 1999) (the 1999 Act). Furthermore, the National Public Service Ethics Code (Cabinet Order No 101 of 2000) (the 2000 Code), which is subordinate regulation of the 1999 Act, sets out concrete and detailed restrictions on minor and potential 'payoffs' to officials (see 3.6 below).

In the field of public procurement (see 3.7 and 3.8 below), competitive bidding processes are required under the Public Accounting Act (Act No 35 of 1947) (the 1947 PAA) and the Local Autonomy Act (Act No 67 of 1947) (the 1947 LAA) and their subordinate rules and regulations. Any "fraudulent means or force used to commit an act which impairs the fairness of a public auction or bid" and any "person who colludes for the purpose of preventing a fair determination of price or acquiring a wrongful gain" is punishable by imprisonment or a fine under the 1907 Criminal Code (article 96-3 of the 1947 PPA, 'Crime of Obstruction of Auctions and Public Bidding' (*keibai-nado-bogai*)). In addition, after the end of World War II, the Act on Prohibition of Private Monopolization and Maintenance of Fair Trade Act (Act No 54 of 1947) (the 1947 Antitrust Act) became another source of law against 'bid-rigging' by prohibiting "unreasonable trade restraint" (*fusei-na-torihiki-seigen*). Furthermore, in the past two decades, the legislature has become quite active in enacting rigorous regulations applicable to the public by enacting statutes such as the Act on Elimination and Prevention of Involvement in Bid-Rigging, etc and Punishments for Acts by Employees that Harm Fairness of Bidding, etc (Act No 101 of 2002) (the 2002 Fair Bidding Act).

2. International anti-corruption treaties

2.1 Introduction

Japan became a signatory to the Convention on Combating Bribery of Foreign Public Officials in International Business Transactions (1997) (the OECD Convention) in October 1999, immediately after adding corresponding new provisions to the 1993 UCA in September 1999 (the 1999 UCA Amendment).

Furthermore, Japan gave effect to the United Nations Convention Against Corruption (2003) (the UN Convention) after adding new corresponding provisions for 'anti-terror conspiracy' to the Act on Punishment of Organized Crimes and Control of Crime Proceeds (Act No 136 of 1999) (the 1999 Organized Crimes Act).

As shown in the preceding paragraphs, all international conventions are finally given effect after the enactment of domestic legislation. This is because Japan has taken the position that, unless otherwise expressly stated in the text, conventions need to be codified in domestic statutes in order to be enforced.

2.2 The OECD Convention and the 1999 UCA Amendment

Historically, Japan did not punish the act of bribing foreign public officials, whereas any act of bribery involving Japanese public officials, regardless of the venue of such action or promise, was punishable (article 4 of the 1907 Criminal Code). By accepting the OECD Convention and enacting the 1999 UCA Amendment, Japan extended its extra-territorial jurisdiction to Japanese nationals and businesses that commit acts of bribery. Corresponding to article 1 of the OECD Convention, article 18(1) of the 1993 UCA, which was added by the 1999 UCA Amendment, provides:

No person shall give, or offer or promise to give, any money or other benefit to a Foreign Public Official, etc for the purpose of having such Foreign Public Official act or refrain from acting in a particular way in relation to the performance of such official's duties, or for the purpose of having a Foreign Public Official, etc use his/her position to influence another Foreign Public Official, etc to act or refrain from acting in a particular way in relation to the performance of such other official's duties, in order to obtain illicit gains in business relating to international commercial transactions.

The term 'Foreign Public Official' may include officials of local government, state-owned enterprises and international organisations (articles 18(2)–18(5) of the 1993 UCA). Mirroring article 2 of the OECD Convention, a 'judicial person' is also subject to punishment (articles 21(2)[7] and 22(1)[3] of the 1993 UCA (per the 1999 UCA Amendment)).

Provisions on 'Anti-money-laundering prevention' (article 7 of the OECD Convention) are also set out in articles 2-2 and 10 of the 1999 Organized Crimes Act.

Provisions of the OECD Convention on 'Mutual Legal Assistance' (article 9 OECD Convention) and 'Extradition' (article 10) have been affirmed by, respectively, amendments to the Act on International Assistance in Investigations and Other Related Matters 1980 (Act No 69 of 1980) and the Act of Extradition 1953 (Act No 68 of 1953). However, the Japanese government has taken the position that bilateral or multilateral treaties on extradition are necessary to enforce an extradition order and, as of 2017, such treaties have been concluded only with the United States and South Korea, owing to differences of position regarding the death penalty between other OECD signatory states and Japan.

It is well known that Commentary 9 to the OECD Convention provides that "small 'facilitation' payments"[2] do not constitute payments made "to obtain or retain business or other improper advantage" within the meaning of article 1, paragraph 1 of the OECD Convention. Japanese laws do not have such a concept, either in the 1907 Criminal Code or in the 1993 UCA. Similar problems have been discussed in the interpretation of the term "Bribe(s)" in the 1907 Criminal Code (see paragraphs 16–18).

---

2 According to the OECD Commentaries adopted and published by the Negotiating Conference on 21 November 1997:

8. Small 'facilitation' payments do not constitute payments made 'to obtain or retain business or other improper advantage' within the meaning of paragraph 1 and, accordingly, are also not an offence. Such payments which, in some countries are made to induce public officials to perform their functions, such as issuing licenses or permits, are generally illegal in the foreign country concerned. Other countries can and should address this corrosive phenomenon by such means as support for programs of good governance. However, criminalisation by other countries does not seem a practical or effective complementary action.

However, in 2008, the OECD Council published its 'Recommendation of the Council for Further Combating Bribery of Foreign Public Officials in International Business Transactions', which clearly –

URGES all countries to raise awareness of their public officials on their domestic bribery and solicitation laws with a view to stopping the solicitation and acceptance of small facilitation payments.

Since the Japanese legal system has never accepted the concept of 'facilitation payment', its position has not changed.

3. The definition of 'bribe(s)' or 'corruption' and the basic framework of anti-corruption laws

3.1 Introduction

The legal term 'corruption' (*oshoku*) is expressly used in only two statutes: the 1907 Criminal Code and the Attorney Act 1949 (Act No 205 of 1949).[3] Under Japanese laws, the term 'corruption' seems to be too vague and broad to be enforced. Chapter 25 of the 1907 Criminal Code is titled 'Crime of Corruption' but defines several types of crime of corruption without using the term 'corruption' itself. These are entitled as follows:

- Abuse of Authority by Public Officials (*komuin-shokken-ranyo*) (article 193);
- Abuse of Authority by Special Public Officials (*tokubetsu-komuin-shokken-ranyo*) (article 194);
- Assault and Brutality by Special Public officials (*tokubetsu-komuin-boko-ryogyaku*) (article 195);
- Abuse of Authority Causing Death or Injury by Special Public Officials (*tokubetsu-komuin-boko-ryogyaku-to-chishisho*) (article 196);
- Acceptance of Bribes (*shuwai*) (article 197);
- Acceptance of Bribes with Request (*jutaku-shuwai*) (article 197);
- Acceptance of Bribes before Taking Office (*jizen-shuwai*) (article 197);
- Passing of Bribes to a Third Party (*dai-sansha-kyowai*) (article 197–2);
- Aggravated Acceptance of Bribes (*kaju-shuwai*) (article 197–3);
- Acceptance of Bribes after Resignation of Office (*jigo-shuwai*) (article 197–3);
- Acceptance of Bribes for Exertion of Influence (*assen-shuwai*) (article 197–4);
- Confiscation and Collection of a Sum of Equivalent Value (*bosshu-oyobi-tsuicho*) (article 197–5); and
- Giving or Offer of Bribes (*zowai*) (article 198).

As is apparent from the short titles of each type of crime, the legal concept of 'corruption' is not necessarily equivalent to 'bribery-corruption' and also includes 'police abuse' and 'police brutality' against citizens, and cases where no economic incentives are received from citizens. These points should be noted when interpreting the statutes.

Accordingly, in order to understand Japanese 'anti-corruption' laws and practices in the context of the UN anti-corruption project, focus should be placed on the term 'bribe' rather than 'corruption'.

3.2 "Bribes (*wairo*)": the 1907 Criminal Code

The 1907 Criminal Code by itself does not provide a detailed definition of 'Bribe' (*wairo*) and leaves the matter to interpretation by the courts. The Japanese Supreme Court has provided a general interpretation of the term 'bribe' in several cases: any illegal and unlawful rewards paid to a public official in connection with such officer's

---

3 The Attorney Act prohibits attorneys from accepting any economic incentives from a counter-party to a case for which the same attorney is representing or advising his or her client.

duties (judgment of the former Supreme Court of Judicature (*Dai-Shin'in*),[4] 19 December 1910). Bribes include, but are not limited to:

- money payment;
- goods;
- properties;,
- assumption of debts;
- financial interest;
- invitation to dining or entertainment; and
- assistance for job placement.

The courts have interpreted 'bribe' very broadly. For example, giving shares in a joint stock company before its listing on a stock exchange may fall within the scope of a bribe, so long as such shares are expected to gain in price when listed (judgment of the Supreme Court of Japan, 18 July 1988).

The courts have never recognised the concept of the 'facilitation payment' as a means of decriminalising the conduct of an accused person.

It has been argued that 'social gifts' (*shako-girei*) should not constitute bribes. In reality, there is certainly a tradition of social gifts which a person or company gives to another person or company as a token of long-term friendship or seasonal greetings. Even in business communities, it is still common for companies to exchange such gifts on special occasions or at seasonal events, ie, mid-year, year-end and new year. If such gifts are given or offered to a public official purely on the basis of a personal relationship and without any connection to the public official's duties, they may be accepted. It should be noted, however, that the Supreme Court of Japan has never accepted 'social gifts' as a safe harbour. Furthermore, as explained in detail at 3.6 below, Japan codified the ethics applicable to public officials by enacting the 1999 NPS Ethics Act and the 2000 NPS Ethics Code. These instruments impose detailed prohibitions and restrictions with regard to even minor social gifts exchanged by public officials and other persons or companies. Accordingly, it is recommended that no party should attempt to give money, goods or incentives of any kind to public officials, except for ceremonial gifts and payments that are unquestionably of a personal nature.

3.3 The 1999 UCA Amendment

Article 18(1) of the 1993 UCA, which was introduced by the 1999 UCA Amendment, first introduced express provisions prohibiting bribes given or offered to foreign public officials:

No person may give, or offer or promise to give, any money or other benefit to a Foreign Public Official, etc. in order to have them act or refrain from acting in relation to the performance of official duties, or in order to have the Foreign Public Officials, etc., use their position to influence another Foreign Public Official, etc. to act or refrain from

4 The Supreme Court of Judicature (*Dai-Shin'in*), which was abolished in 1947, was the highest judicial body in the Empire of Japan, and its rulings are still treated as part of Japanese case law to the extent that the relevant body of law has not been changed by the Diet.

acting in relation to the performance of official duties, in order to make any wrongful gain in business with regard to international commercial transactions.

Technically, the 1999 UCA Amendment does not use the term 'bribe'; rather, this instrument adopts the descriptive term "any money or other benefit". Furthermore, it sets out a single provision that covers various types of bribery crime.

Article 2 of the 1993 UCA, which was introduced by the 1999 UCA Amendment, also provides a definition of 'Foreign Public Official':

(i) any person who engages in public service for national or local foreign governments; (ii) any person who engages in the business affairs of an entity established under foreign special laws to carry out specific business affairs in the public interest; (iii) any person who engages in the business affairs of an enterprise in which one or more of the national or local governments of foreign states directly owns a number of voting shares or an amount of capital subscription that exceeds 50 percent of that enterprise's total issued voting shares or total amount of capital subscription, or in which the majority of the Officers (meaning directors, auditors, council members, inspectors, liquidators, and other persons engaged in management of the business) are appointed or designated by one or more of the national or local foreign governments, and to which special rights and interests are granted by the national or local government of the foreign states for performance of its business, or a person specified by Cabinet Order as an equivalent person; (iv) any person who engages in public services for an international organization (meaning an international organization which is formed by governments or intergovernmental international organizations); or (v) any person who engages in the business affairs under the authority of the national or local government of a foreign state or an international organization and is delegated by them.

Violations of the provisions of the 1993 UCA as amended are punishable by "imprisonment with labour for not more than five years, a fine of not more than five million yen, or both" (article 21(2)(iiv) of the 1993 UCA as amended).

The amendments made to the 1993 UCA by the 1999 UCA Amendment also adopted the 'extraterritorial application' principle for acts of Japanese nationals (including Japanese companies) (article 21(6) of the 1993 UCA as amended) in a manner similar to crimes of bribery in the 1907 Criminal Code (article 8 (Extraterritorial Application) of the 1907 Criminal Code). Furthermore, since the 1993 UCA as amended applies to "any person" who commits the acts stipulated in the statutes, the 1999 UCA Amendment applies it to foreign nationals and foreign companies to the extent that any part of alleged acts of the accused are made in the territory of Japan or any outcome of the acts occurred there.

3.4 Special bribery-corruption crime (1): directors, officers and employees of designated corporations

As explained previously, the crime of bribery in the 1907 Criminal Code only applies to bribes given or offered to public officials. In Japan, any payments or economic incentives given to the officers of private companies do not constitute bribes.

On the other hand, in common with other jurisdictions, the Japanese government has established a number of special financial institutions in order either to provide financing and guarantees to small- and medium-sized enterprises (SMEs) or to provide long-term financing for large projects. From the mid-1980s, the government started to privatise its businesses in other areas, starting with the telegraph and telecommunications, tobacco businesses, railways, postal services and, finally, the airport operation business, which was privatised in late 2010. In addition, together with funds from the private sector, the government has provided funds to newly established organisations for the purpose of facilitating the revitalisation of companies that require rehabilitation. Some of these companies are expected to continue over a limited period, while others are in transition before their shares are completely transferred to the private sector. In either case, the operation of these special-status corporations and funds, in whole or in part, closely relates to pubic services; each statute that gives a legal basis to these corporations and funds has a set of provisions similar to those applicable to the crime of bribery. They are applicable to the directors, executive officers, auditors and employees of such corporations and funds. The statutes set out in the following (non-exhaustive list) contain such provisions.

- Regional Economy Vitalization Corporation Act 2009 (Act No 63 of 2009), articles 68–70;
- Industrial Revitalization Corporation Act 2003 (Act No 27 of 2003), articles 60–62–2;
- Industrial Competitiveness Enhancement Act 2013 (Act No 98 of 2013), articles 144–146;
- Shoko Chukin Bank Limited Act 2007 (Act No 74 of 2007), articles 67–69;
- Small and Medium-Sized Business Investment and Consultation Corporation Act 1963 1963 (Act No 101 of 1963), articles 13 to 14–2;
- Development Bank of Japan Act 2007 (Act No 85 of 2007), articles 30–32;
- Act on Advance Payment Guarantee for Public Works 1952 (Act No 184 of 1952), 1952), article 29;
- Japan Tobacco Act 1984 (Act No 69 of 1984), articles 14 to 15–2;
- Japan Post Holdings Corporation Act 2005 (Act No 98 of 2005), articles 18–20;
- Japan Post Corporation Act 2005 (Act No 100 of 2005), articles 19–21;
- Nippon Telegraph and Telecommunication Corporation Act 1984 (Act No 85 of 1984), articles 19 and 20;
- Nippon Expressway Company Act 2004 (Act No 99 of 2004), articles 18–20;
- Japan Environmental Storage and Safety Corporation Act 2003 (Act No 44 of 2003), articles 16–18;
- Narita International Airport Corporation Act 2004 (Act No 124 of 2004), articles 18–20;
- Act on Construction and Management of Chubu Centrair International Airport, Nagoya 2008 (Act No 36 of 2008), articles 24 to 25–2;
- Act on Integrated and Efficient Construction and Management of Kansai International Airport and Osaka International Airport 2011 (Act No 54 of 2011), articles 25 to 26–2;
- Japan Railway Corporation Act 1986 (Act No 88 of 1986), articles 16–18;
- Tokyo Metro Corporation Act 2002 (Act No 188 of 2002), articles 12–14.

Some of the companies concerned are expected to be listed on the stock exchange in the near future. Once all of the shares are sold to the private sector, they will become private companies and the special provisions will no longer apply.

3.5 Special bribery-corruption crime (2): Diet members and secretaries

Traditionally, the crime of 'Acceptance of Bribes for Exertion of Influence' (article 197–4 of the 1907 Criminal Code) only applied if an influenced public official performed his or her duties in an illegal and unlawful manner. In the 1990s, however, the government and the Diet were confronted with harsh criticism of undue influence, technically not illegal, that was exercised by members of the Diet on subordinate public officials in the executive branch. Given that such influence was hardly appropriate to the fairness and transparency of public services, lawmakers enacted the Act on Prevention of Undue Influence on Public Officials by Diet Members and Their Staff 2000 (Act No 130 of 2000).

3.6 The 1999 NPS Ethics Act and the 2000 NPS Ethics Code

A series of scandals involving public officials was revealed in the 1990s, as a result of which the government faced severe criticism. Among other things while the amount or size of bribes given to public officials working in several regulatory bodies was not huge, its continuous and unfathomably cosy relationship with financial institutions came under closer scrutiny. A number of public officials and company officers were accused of the crime of bribery under the 1907 Criminal Code.

In order to enforce strict official discipline for the future, the 1999 NPS Ethics Act was enacted and the 2000 NPS Ethics Code was subsequently promulgated as delegated legislation under the former, by means of Cabinet Orders.

With regard to what the 1999 NPS Ethics Act and the 2000 NPS Ethics Code provide, these instruments did not in fact change any principles of the 1907 Criminal Code. Instead, they have provided more concrete additional rules, some of which have been refined by the courts. They provide that public officials should obtain an Ethics Supervisor's approval for some social activities with private individuals and impose 'reporting/disclosure obligations' on public officials for other minor activities. Thus, for example, public officials:

- may not receive any services *gratis*;
- may not accept any cost-free goods or rent-free properties;
- may not be entertained with meals and drinks;
- may not play golf or travel with interested parties; and
- shall, if they go out for meals with private individuals, report and disclose the details thereof to an Ethics Supervisor if their cost exceeds ¥10,000.

Even though the 1999 NPS Ethics Act and the 2000 NPS Ethics Code regulate minor acts of public officials, the government views these rules and regulations as important and have enforced them effectively up to now.

3.7 Public procurement (1): framework

A general legal framework for public procurement processes is provided by:

- the 1947 PAA;
- the Cabinet Order on Budgets, the Settlement of Accounts and Accounting (Imperial Ordinance No 165 of 1947) (the 1947 Budget Order); and
- the Contract Administration Rules (Order of the Ministry of Finance, Order No 52 of 1962).

Article 29 of the 1947 PAA adopts the principle of "public competitive bidding" (*kokai-kyoso-nyusatsu*) for public procurements, with limited exceptions for "designated competitive bidding" (*shimei-kyoso-nyusatsu*) and "negotiated contracts" (*zuii-keiyaku*).

Following a series of scandals involving public officials in connection with public procurement projects, the Diet enacted the Act on Improvement of Open Tendering and Contracting of Public Construction Works 2000 (Act No 127 of 2000) (the 2000 Public Procurement Improvement Act), which provides for:

- disclosure of information;
- punishment of illegal conduct;
- appropriate management of performance of construction contracts; and
- guidelines for improvement.

The 2000 Public Procurement Improvement Act was followed by the promulgation of the Guidelines for Improvement of Public Tendering and Contracting of Public Construction Works (Cabinet Decision of 2006) (the 2006 Guidelines) (collectively, the 2000 and 2006 instruments).

The 2000 and 2006 instruments, which have been revised several times since their promulgation, apply to all public procurement projects. The most recent (2014) revisions to the 2006 Guidelines emphasise the following points:

- reinforcement of anti-dumping measures;
- the making illegal of inadequate pressure by a project owner for a price discount;
- making 'variation' procedures more transparent; and
- reinforcement of measures against 'bid-rigging'.

Furthermore, with regard to the technical aspects of public procurement, the Diet enacted the Act for Promoting Quality Assurance in Public Works 2005 (Act No 18 of 2005). This act places emphasis on the fair evaluation of technical aspects of bids or proposals provided by bidders. In actual practice, governments have developed a method of 'comprehensive evaluation' (*sogo-hyoka-hoshiki*), by which a project owner takes into account both the economic perspective (ie, price) and the technical aspects of bids or proposals when it determines a winning bidder. A method of comprehensive evaluation has been widely accepted by most central and local government project owners.

3.8 Public procurement (2): prohibition of 'bid-rigging'

Three statutes strictly prohibit 'bid-rigging' in public procurement:

- the 1907 Criminal Code;

- the 1947 Antitrust Act; and
- the 2002 Fair Bidding Act.

Article 96-3 of the 1907 Criminal Code provides for the crime of 'Obstruction of Auctions and Public Bidding' (*keibai-nado-bougai*) as follows:

- a person who, by the use of fraudulent means or force, commits an act which impairs the fairness of a public auction or tender, shall be punished by imprisonment with labour for not more than two years or a fine of not more than ¥2,500,000; and
- the same shall apply to a person who colludes for the purpose of preventing a fair determination of price or acquiring a wrongful gain.

Article 6 of the 1947 Antitrust Act strictly prohibits 'cartels' as follows:

An enterprise must not enter into an international agreement or an international contract which contains such matters which fall under unreasonable restraint of trade or unfair trade practices.

The term 'unreasonable restraint of trade' is defined by article 2(6) of the 1947 Antitrust Act as:

such business activities, by which any enterprise, by contract, agreement or any other means irrespective of its name, in concert with other enterprises, mutually restrict or conduct their business activities in such a manner as to fix, maintain or increase prices, or to limit production, technology, products, facilities or counterparties, thereby causing, contrary to the public interest, a substantial restraint of competition in any particular field of trade.

Last but not least, the Diet enacted the 2002 Fair Bidding Act. This act focuses on public officials, prohibiting them from being involved in bid-rigging acts. This is because, even though no bribes may have been given to public officials, some public officials, particularly those in local governments, may have been involved in the local business community and sometimes leaked important information regarding ongoing or upcoming public procurement processes to the local business community. In some of the worst cases, public officials even indicated the preferred price and preferred allocation of the works to individual bidders. The 2002 Fair Bidding Act was the Diet's response to harsh public criticism.

Any prohibited acts by public officials in violation of the 2002 Fair Bidding Act shall be punished, even if such officials do not accept any bribe from potential bidders. Prohibited acts are:

- giving instructions to bidders for the performance of a bid-rigging conduct;
- indicating a project owner's preference on which bidder should take work or what price should be tendered;
- disclosing confidential information regarding public procurement; and
- abetting particular bid-rigging conduct by potential bidders.

3.9 The 1999 Organized Crimes Act

Another area of the law contributing to anti-corruption is the 1999 Organized Crimes Act, which prohibits illegal money-laundering.

4. Responsible authorities

Police and public prosecutors offices are authorised to commence a criminal investigation for any crime. If the police initiate an investigation, the case will be reported. When the police have completed their investigation, and if a determination is made that the suspected conduct constitutes a crime, evidence collected will be forwarded to the Public Prosecutor's Office, which has exclusive power of indictment for all crimes.

The Japan Fair Trade Commission (JFTC), the administrative body that is authorised to enforce the 1947 Antitrust Act and other relevant laws, also enforces the 2002 Fair Bidding Act. The JFTC conducts administrative investigations of the public procurement practices of central and local governments and gives advice and instructions to such entities if it finds any inadequate practices. The JFTC also publishes guidelines.

The METI (see 1 above) is also active in interpreting the 1993 UCA Amendment and the OECD Convention. It has published and regularly revised guidelines for Japanese companies with regard to how the 1993 UCA Amendment is applied. However, it is the police and the public prosecutor's offices that have authority to commence criminal investigations.

Furthermore, under the 1999 NPS Ethics Act and the 2000 NPS Ethics Code, the National Public Service Ethics Board (the NPS Ethics Board) was established within the National Personnel Authority. Ministries that receive disclosure reports from individual public officials regarding regulated conduct must forward a copy of such disclosure reports to the NPS Ethics Board for public disclosure. Furthermore, even though each ministry reserves the power to take disciplinary measures against subordinate public officials, it must first seek the approval of the NPS Ethics Board before taking enforcement measures. The NPS Ethics Board also works as an educational centre for national public service ethics.

5. Relevant public cases

There have been numerous court cases reflecting a standard categorisation of bribery corruption. As explained at 3.2 above, the definition and interpretation of 'bribe' have been established by case law.

There have recently been an increasing number of cases in which public officials have been indicted for violation of the 2002 Fair Bidding Act. Searching a popular case law database using the 2002 Fair Bidding Act as the search keywords, 30 cases may be found, including three appeal cases (two appeals to the High Court and one to the Supreme Court of Japan). Accordingly, a net total of 27 cases have been decided by the courts. In all cases, the defendants were found guilty and all appeals against conviction were dismissed.

In fact, in most 2002 Fair Bidding Act violation cases, the accused were concurrently indicted under the 1907 Criminal Code (by consolidated punishment, per article 45 of the 1907 Criminal Code) for crimes of bribery, and were typically found guilty of acceptance of bribes (*shuwai*), acceptance of bribes with request (*jutaku-shuwai*) or aggravated acceptance of bribes (*kaju-shuwai*). There is only one case in which the accused was found guilty solely of violating the 2002 Fair Bidding

Act. In that case, the defendant was a medical doctor who was the chief of a radiotherapy department in a public hospital funded by a local community. He was indicted because, the hospital having arranged a designated competitive bidding procedure for a radiation therapy machine, he informed one potential bidder of a standard price informally determined by the mayor, while informing the other bidders of different price information. He was convicted of violating the 2002 Fair Bidding Act, although he was not found to have accepted any bribe from that potential bidder.[5]

Two cases of violation of the 1993 UCA (as amended by the 1999 UCA Amendment) have also been reported. The first is the *Pacific Consultants International* case.[6] In this case, employees of an engineering consulting company gave bribes of approximately $2,200,000 to a public official of Vietnam in return for the favour of being awarded a consultancy contract. The court found the employees and the company guilty of violating the 1993 UCA as amended. Another 1993 case under the same provisions is the *Japan Transportation Consultants* case.[7] In this case, a director and employees (together with an accounting department chief) were indicted by reason of the fact that the director and employees had given bribes totalling approximately ¥55 million to officials in Vietnam, Indonesia and Uzbekistan, while the accounting department chief, at the request of the other defendants, had managed the raising of money for the bribes. All of the defendants and their company were found guilty of violating the 1993 UCA as amended.

6. Outlook and conclusions

At the time of writing, a number of mega-sized general contractors are being prosecuted on charges of violating the 1947 Antitrust Act by organising a cartel for the purpose of obtaining contracts to build several sections of the Maglev line between Tokyo and Nagoya. This shocked the business community because all of the top construction companies were accused of involvement. Furthermore, since two of the companies strenuously deny their involvement, the criminal process is expected to continue for more than a year. It is difficult to predict the final outcome of the process and necessary to keep developments under review.

5 For the cases discussed in this paragraph, see the judgments of the Asahikawa District Court, 29 June 2016; the Sapporo High Court, 4 October 2016; and the Supreme Court of Japan, 9 February 2017.

6 Judgment of the Tokyo District Court, 29 January 2009.

7 Judgment of the Tokyo District Court, 4 February 2015.

Mexico

Roberto Hernández-García
Cynthia Irene Osio Sanchez
COMAD, SC

1. Overview

Corruption does not depend on a country's level of development; it is, however, more prevalent in weak institutional and legal systems that encourage opacity and impunity and focus on protecting public servants and corrupt private interests over society's interests.

Mexican citizens are well aware that the national legal framework and institutional structure are better than in the past with the implementation of the National Anticorruption System (NAS) that entered into force on July 2016. Regrettably, however, society has not seen the necessary political interest and will in implementing and/or strengthening this complex system correctly. Thus, at the time of writing, there is not only a perception but also the reality that corruption is not being attacked head on in Mexico.

As a consequence of this situation, corruption is a matter of discussion in almost every meeting or gathering and its social, economic and political consequences are becoming more and more palpable every day.

Unlike other countries, where it is often limited to politics and the upper class, corruption in Mexico has filtered through all levels of society. According to the National Corruption and Good Governance Index, an average of 14% of a family's income goes in bribes,[1] but this percentage goes up to 33% in the case of the poorest members of society.[2]

A recent study on Latin America and the Caribbean by the Transparency International *Global Corruption Barometer* indicates that, regionally, Mexico has one of the most alarming corruption rates in the delivery of public services to citizens, particularly in education and health services and in obtaining official personal documents. An astounding 51% of the survey respondents admit having paid a bribe to access basic utility services.[3]

Mexico's place in international comparative surveys is especially unsettling. Mexico ranked 135 out of 180 countries in the Transparency International *Corruption Perceptions Index* 2017,[4] while the *National Survey of Quality and Governmental Impact*

1 Transparency Mexico, *2010 National Corruption and Good Governance Index*, executive report available at www.tm.org.mx/wp-content/uploads/2013/05/01-INCBG-2010-Informe-Ejecutivo1.pdf.

2 www.elfinanciero.com.mx/economia/el-costo-de-la-corrupcion-en-mexico-en-graficas.html.

3 Transparenchy International, *People and Corruption: Latin America and the Caribbean*, (9 October 2017), available at www.transparency.org/whatwedo/publication/las_personas_y_la_corrupcion_america_latina_y_el_caribe.

4 www.tm.org.mx/ipc2017/.

delivered an incidence of corruption of 12,590 for every 100,000 inhabitants in their encounters with safety, judicial and administrative authorities.[5]

According to US Foreign Corrupt Practices Act (FCPA) statistics, Mexico has appeared among the countries where bribes were offered or paid in every FCPA Group listed in the Stanford University Foreign Corrupt Practices Clearing House *Heat Map by Geography* since that statute's enactment. With an incidence rate of corruption of 20, Mexico is the worst-rated (American) country, while the highest is China with 49.[6] Put into perspective, these numbers are indeed surprising, given that China's population is ten times that of Mexico.

These parameters reflect the internal and external reality of a country where corruption levels represent up to 10% of gross domestic product[7] and the reality of Mexican citizens who face corruption on a daily basis. Mexicans must invest substantial time and effort if they want to do things the right way, instead of bribing their way through – or alongside – the system.

Modern Mexican politicians tend to blame the previous ruling party for the escalation of corruption; this is not a new or recent phenomenon, however, since historical records show that this has been a long-standing problem.

In its modern phase, Mexico has gone through some efforts to design public policies that aim at tackling corruption to the extent required to make the country desirable and to satisfy economic and political needs, but it has not yet reached the point at which the powerful and corrupt, both in the public and private sectors, have been made to feel uncomfortable and, most of all, responsible for their actions. Efforts of this kind have left out of account the social purpose of fighting corruption and so have failed to make significant changes.

Over the last few decades, the Mexican system of government has drifted toward toleration of corrupt acts, almost reaching their acceptance as an inevitable part of the Mexican character and culture.[8] Society disagrees with this approach but feels disempowered to act against it. Poorly designed control mechanisms, the lack of coordination across the tiers of government and an entrenched culture of impunity have led to wide disenchantment and even wider inaction.

Mexican society is still greatly dissatisfied with its representatives. Internal surveys show that less than one-third of the population (26%) approve of the current administration and that, in late 2017, corruption became the third most reported problem in the country, reaching its highest score since 2001, outstripping poverty and unemployment, which hitherto had typically been higher.[9]

---

5 National Institute of Statistics and Geography (INEGI), 2015 *National Survey of Quality and Governmental Impact*. Results available at http://internet.contenidos.inegi.org.mx/contenidos/productos//prod_serv/contenidos/espanol/bvinegi/productos/nueva_estruc/promo/encig15_principales_resultados.pdf.

6 Stanford Law School, Foreign Corrupt Practices Act Clearinghouse, *FCPA Heat Map by Geography*, available at http://fcpa.stanford.edu/geography.html.

7 As stated by Juan Pablo Castañón, President of the Business Coordinating Council (CCE), based on the 2015 ENCIG results (note 5 above). Available at www.forbes.com.mx/la-corrupcion-cuesta-10-del-pib-mexico-cce.

8 For example, President Enrique Peña Nieto gave a bold assurance that corruption is indeed a cultural problem: see www.animalpolitico.com/2014/09/la-corrupcion-es-un-asunto-cultural-pena-nieto/.

9 *Presidential Assessment Poll* (EPN: Eventos Trimestre 20 de Gobierno), compiled by Consulta Mitofsky. Results available at http://consulta.mx/index.php/estudios-e-investigaciones/evaluacion-de-gobierno/item/990-evaluacion-20-trimestres-de-gobierno-de-enrique-pena-nieto.

Conversely, courageous actors (mainly from the private sector) who are aware that transparency and accountability are essential assets in Mexico, have been fighting ceaselessly to enforce them and are gradually gaining support.

In 2015, after a long struggle, a crucial turning point was reached in the national approach to corruption, when a constitutional amendment that involved the creation of a National Anticorruption System (SNA) was adopted as the first step of a long-distance race against corruption. The three words, 'National Anticorruption System', have come to mean a lot on their own. The 'national' aspect denotes that, at last, the isolated efforts of a few were recognised as inherently unsuccessful and doomed to fail; instead, countrywide coordination was for the first time acknowledged as essential.

Throughout the preceding years, the government had avoided addressing corruption, which is why the creation of an anti-corruption system implies that Mexico as a country is on its way to understanding that problems as complex as corruption are not suitable for single-tracked strategies for their solution.

Emphasis also needs to be addressed to preventive measures, rather than believing that corruption needs to be fought only with harsher penalties. For these reasons, the national perspective is more coherent now, at least on paper.

One of the most sought-after results from the new anti-corruption landscape is to narrow the gap between public officials and citizens – a characteristic issue in representative democracies – to allow accountability and social scrutiny to serve as the main instruments against corruption.

Overall, the new SNA sets out principles and rules, relying on both government and civil society to enforce them, in the hope that individuals will acquire civic responsibility and feel compelled to comply with national norms as much as they demand that public officials should do so. The latter will only be accomplished when Mexicans can firmly believe that the social benefit obtained through complying with norms and preserving the rule of law is greater than the individual convenience of not doing so.

2. 'Corruption' and its definition in Mexico

As with every complex phenomenon, corruption is hard to pinpoint and define. No general definition of the term 'corruption' is provided by the Mexican legal framework. The concept of corruption is, however, spread throughout a number of different and applicable administrative and criminal statutes.

The Federal Criminal Code 1931 (as amended to 2014) extensively describes and penalises corrupt acts in its Tenth Title, 'Corruption Offences'. These include such forbidden conducts as:

- *unlawful exercise of public functions* (article 214): this includes exercising public functions without having been duly appointed, submitting false or incomplete reports and using or hiding privileged information;
- *abuse of power* (article 215): this includes using public powers for particular or personal interests, unduly delaying or denying the provision of services to citizens, unjustifiably denying the administration of justice, unduly depriving a person of his or her liberty (or failing to report this), and requesting fees, handouts or payments;

- *unlawful use of powers and facilities* (article 217): this includes unlawfully granting concessions, permits and licences, signing contracts for debt;
- *extortion* (article 218): this provision applies to demands by public officials for money, anything of value, services, or any other undue benefits, or demands for these things in larger quantities than those authorised or required by law;
- *bribery* (article 222): this provision applies where public officials demand or receive, directly or indirectly, money or any other benefit or accept a promise to do or refrain from doing an act inherent to their functions. It also applies to anyone who gives, promises, or grants any benefit to a public official in exchange for an action or omission inherent to his or her functions;
- *bribery of foreign public officials* (article 222 *bis*): this provision applies to acts of offering, promising or giving money or any other gift to a foreign public official, for the benefit of the offeror or of third parties, to influence that official to do something in the exercise of his or her duties or to do something outside the exercise of those duties;
- *embezzlement* (article 223): this provision applies to the diversion of money, anything of value or any other public good to a private person, or using public funds to promote or damage the public image of another person;
- *unlawful enrichment* (article 224): this refers to the inability of a public official to justify increases in his or her net worth or the origin of his or her assets.

Under the General Law of Administrative Responsibility 2016, the following 'Major Administrative Offences by Public Officials' are equated with corrupt actions:

- *bribery* (article 52): this provision applies to public officials who demand, accept, obtain or attempt to obtain, directly or indirectly, any benefit beyond their official remuneration. The benefit may take the form of money, any other thing of value, movable or immovable assets (including those that have been acquired for a noticeably lower price than that payable in the open market), donations, services, employment opportunities and other undue benefits. Further, the benefit may be for themselves, or their spouses, or relatives by blood or by affinity (eg, in-laws), or third parties with whom they have work or business relationships;
- *peculation* (article 53): this provision applies to a public official who unlawfully and dishonestly authorises, requests or performs acts for his or her personal benefit, or who appropriates public goods, whether material, human or financial, for himself or for any of the other parties to which the offence of bribery applies under article 52;
- *embezzlement* (article 54): this provision applies to a public officer who unlawfully authorises, requests or performs acts aimed at assigning or diverting public goods, whether material, human or financial;
- *unauthorised use of information* (article 55): this provision applies to a public official who acquires (whether for himself or herself, or for any other parties to whom the offence of bribery applies under article 52) movable or immovable assets and things of value that could increase the value or improve the condition of those assets or obtains any advantage or private benefit as a result of having privileged information;

- *abuse of office* (article 57): this provision applies to a public official who exercises powers not inherent to his or her position, or uses those powers to perform or induce arbitrary acts or omissions (whether for personal benefit or the benefit of parties to whom the offence of bribery applies under article 52), or to cause damage to any other person or the public service;
- *conflict of interest* (article 58): this provision applies to a public official who intervenes in dealing with, processing or resolving matters from which he or she is legally ineligible or in relation to which he or she has a conflict of interest;
- *undue hiring* (article 59): this provisions applies to the authorisation of any kind of hiring, selection, appointment or designation of someone who is legally ineligible or barred from occupying a public position or commission or from contracting with public entities;
- *illicit enrichment or concealment of conflict of interest* (article 60): this provision applies to a public official who fails to submit truthful asset and interest declarations with the intention of concealing any increase in wealth, unjustifiable use of goods and services or a conflict of interest;
- *influence peddling* (article 61): this provision applies to a public official who uses his or her position to induce another public official to perform, delay or refrain from performing an act inherent to his or her position, in order to obtain any benefit or advantage for himself or herself or for any other parties to whom the offence of bribery applies under article 52;
- *concealment* (article 62): this provision applies to a public official who, in the exercise of his or her duties, acquires knowledge of acts or omissions that could represent administrative offences and deliberately acts to conceal such acts or omissions;
- *contempt* (article 63): this provision applies to a public official who, upon being required to provide information by a supervisory, judicial, electoral, or human rights authority, provides false information, or fails to provide the required information, or deliberately and unjustifiably delays the delivery or information even after being made subject to enforcement measures;
- *obstruction of justice* (article 64): this provision applies to public officials who are responsible for the investigation, substantiation and resolution of administrative offences that constitute minor offences arising during the investigation of major offences and who fail to report conducts that may constitute major offences or who reveal the identity of an anonymous and protected whistleblower.

Both the Federal Criminal Code and the General Law of Administrative Responsibility define conducts that are considered to be corruption where committed by private sector participants and which involve or encourage illegal conduct by officers in the public sector. The conducts that may lead to the sanctioning of private sector participants in corrupt activities under the General Law of Administrative Responsibility are described at 5 below.

To assume, however, that the only corrupt actions are those typified by the criminal and administrative codes is equivalent to thinking that there are no corrupt practices and no corrupt actors outside of those codes, which is an erroneous approach. Despite the fact that on some occasions it is difficult to tell if an act is corrupt or not, then, if an act is to be labelled as one or the other, corrupt acts are, roughly speaking, those that prevent accountability and transparency from arising and which cause undue advantages to be acquired in public, private or social affairs.

In this regard, academics have devised a very complete definition of 'corruption' that is worth quoting:[10]

Corruption is the violation of a positional duty, contained in the regulatory system, to obtain an extrapositional [sic] benefit, not inherent to the [the official's] position or function. The norms of the system can be rules or principles. Violation of a rule is typical, violation of a principle is atypical. A rule is a given norm that has antecedent, consequence, or sanction. A principle is a legal rule that states a legal value recognized by the system expressly or implicitly.

This definition, unlike those in a number of international instruments, such as the Inter-American Convention against Corruption, does not condition corrupt acts to their statutory typologies.

To sum up, nowadays Mexican legislation better addresses the concept of corruption, while the Criminal Code, which once used the term 'corruption' to refer to the corruption of minors, now includes important elements such as (among other concepts) benefits for third parties, and active and passive bribery. Likewise, the General Law of Administrative Responsibility provides a wider and more accurate description of major offences committed both by public and private actors. Indeed, including every element in a single definition would entail a great deal of effort that would not necessarily be effective and, conversely, may jeopardise its effective application. Thus, referring to the elements and modalities of corruption without creating a definition appears to be most effective approach at the moment.

3. The outcome of public corruption cases in Mexico

3.1 Introduction

There is a Mexican saying that describes the somewhat popular belief of a causal link between cheating and success: *El que no tranza no avanza* ("He who does not cheat, does not succeed"). Sadly, this phrase portrays the philosophy and strategies of many politicians when they reach a privileged position.

Alarming levels of corruption and organised crime have earned Mexico the title of the most corrupt developed country in the world, according to the *2016 World Economic Forum Global Competitiveness Report.* During President Enrique Peña Nieto's administration, an unprecedented number of public officials were the subject of criminal proceedings. These cases included but were not limited to those discussed below.

10 Jaime Cardenas Gracia & Maria de la Luz Mijangos, *Estado de Derecho y Corrupción* (2005, Porrua), at p62.

3.2 The former Governor of Tabasco

The former governor (2007–2012) of Tabasco, one of Mexico's 10 poorest states, was arrested in June 2013 on charges of operations involving illegally-sourced funds and fiscal fraud and accused of the deviation of 2,600 million pesos in 2012, the final year of his administration. In a taped conversation leaked to the media, the former Governor boasted about owning 300 suits, 1,000 shirts and 400 pairs of shoes bought from luxury stores in the United States. Through an investigation carried out under his successor, it was discovered that 190 million pesos were missing from the state treasury. In March 2018, he was sentenced to 10 years, 10 months and 15 days' imprisonment and to pay 195 million pesos as compensation for damage.

3.3 The former Governor of Aguascalientes

In April 2017, the former Governor of Aguascalientes (2004–2010) was initially convicted for selling houses located in a territorial reserve below their real value. He was sentenced to two years and 10 months' imprisonment and to pay 18.9 million pesos as compensation for damage, in addition to being disqualified from exercising any public position for one year and seven months. Following a review of the conviction, a federal judge exonerated the former Governor in October 2017 on the ground that the commission of the offences had not been proved.

Following a further trial against him, this time on charges of embezzlement for the simulated purchase of a tomograph worth 13.8 million pesos (which was never found in the state's hospitals), the former Governor was convicted and sentenced to six years and nine months' imprisonment and to pay 13.8 million pesos as compensation for damage. A review of the conviction by the federal courts is still pending.

3.4 The former Governor of Sonora

The former governor of the northern state of Sonora (2009–2015) was charged with organised crime, fiscal fraud and the laundering of $8.5 million. He surrendered to custody in November 2016, claiming his innocence. Soon after, in an *amparo* action (ie, a federal legal action in order to review the constitutionality of trials), a federal court ordered that his sentence of imprisonment be reviewed in order to consider his defence and evidence in an attempt to prove his innocence. On 8 February 2018, a federal judge found him not guilty of money laundering and fiscal fraud on the ground that the accusation as framed did not fulfil procedural requirements and failed to comply with legal formalities.

3.5 The former Governor of Quintana-Roo

The former governor of Quintana-Roo (1993–1999) was charged with drug trafficking and accused of conspiracy to transport drugs from Colombia to the United States through Quintana-Roo. He was arrested in Cancún in 2001 by agents of the US Drug Enforcement Agency (DEA) and Mexico's *Procuraduría General de la República* (PGR). He was extradited in 2010 to the US, where he pleaded guilty to laundering $19 million and was sentenced to almost 11 years' imprisonment, subject to a deduction of nine years for time previously served in Mexico.

He returned to Mexico in 2017 to serve a sentence of 22 years' imprisonment for having committed crimes against health and money laundering in the form of conspiracy to enable the commission of an illicit act.

3.6 The former Governor of Tamaulipas (1)

The former governor of Tamaulipas (1999–2004) was arrested in Florence in April 2017 after having been a fugitive for five years. He is subject to pending cases in both Mexico and the US, but prosecutors in both countries have agreed that he should be tried first in the US, where he is charged with having laundered drug-trafficking-related money during his tenure and taking bribes from major drug trafficking gangs in Tamaulipas in exchange for allowing them to operate freely in the state.

The Florence Court of Appeal approved his extradition in September 2017. On further appeal in February 2018, however, the court's decision was partially annulled and is being re-examined with a view to a final decision.

3.7 The former Governor of Tamaulipas (2)

Another former governor of Tamaulipas (2005–2010) was indicted by the US Department of Justice in May 2015 on charges of having laundered $30 million dollars. A decision on his extradition to the US is pending.

3.8 The former Governor of Veracruz

The former governor of the eastern Mexican state of Veracruz (2010–2016) is under investigation for organised crime and money laundering. He is accused of diverting 233 million pesos from public funds through ghost companies. Indeed, according to the Federal Superior Audit Office (ASF), criminal diversions have reached 'historical' heights and could exceed 60,000 million pesos.[11]

In early October 2016, the former Governor announced that he would stand down two months ahead of the end of his term and escaped in a state helicopter. He was expelled from his political party, apprehended in Guatemala in April 2017 and finally extradited to Mexico in July 2017. Several luxury apartments and houses in Arizona, Texas, Miami, New York City, Spain and Mexico are among this defendant's properties under investigation. In early 2017, boxes containing 23 million pesos and objects of social assistance, such as wheelchairs and pantries, together with sumptuous objects that included works of art, golf clubs, dinnerware and collectibles, were found in Mexico City and Veracruz. The former Governor has since been imprisoned.

3.9 The former interim Governor of Veracruz

The former interim governor of Veracruz (2016), was appointed to replace the since imprisoned former governor and currently now faces a criminal trial for influence peddling, abuse of power and concealment and is accused of aiding in the former Governor's escape in October 2016. He was released on five million pesos bail and his trial is pending.

---

11 Animal Político, *Los desvíos de Javier Duarte imponen récord histórico para la Auditoría Superior*, available at: www.animalpolitico.com/2016/11/desvios-duarte-veracruz-historicos/.

3.10 The effect of international corruption scandals in Mexico

In addition to local cases of corruption, international scandals are also uncovering significant irregularities in Mexican state-owned companies. In 2017, after Odebrecht had pleaded guilty to bribery in different countries and the US Department of Justice noted that the company had paid nearly $10.5 million to Mexican public officials between 2010 and 2014, three former Odebrecht executives stated that such 'incentives' had been paid to a former CEO of Pemex (the state-owned oil company). Possible further developments are pending.

3.11 Summary

As seen above, multiple corruption investigations in Mexico develop into unsolved and/or undefined cases that leave a sense of doubt and outrage among the population.

An enormous list of corruption cases continues to grow, but some of the examples recounted above reveal that impunity and questionable answers are still the usual outcome. Mexican authorities fail to prove guilt and when convictions and sentences are handed down, justice is delayed until procedural irregularities or defective investigations cause them to be revoked.

It is no surprise that, according to Mexicans against Corruption and Impunity's statistical data, the impunity rate in Mexico is as high as 92.8%.[12] However, more investigations are being conducted and, even if only a few result in convictions, their aftermath would set an example and send a clear message that corruption will no longer be tolerated.

4. The legal framework (1): the international scene

Mexico has signed and ratified three important international instruments on anti-corruption. Under Mexican law, these instruments are considered 'supreme law', provided that they align with constitutional provisions.

4.1 The Inter-American Convention Against Corruption 1996 (IACAC)

This regional convention of the Organization of American States (OAS) was adopted on 29 March 1996 and took effect on 6 March 1997. It was the first to address the problem of corruption internationally. It aims at facilitating cooperation between member states to fight corruption with both punitive and preventive measures, as part of constant and systematic efforts and not only through specific actions.

The IACAC was signed by Mexico on 29 March 1996 and ratified on 27 May 1997. An additional instrument, the Buenos Aires Report on the Establishment of the Mechanism for Follow-up on Implementation of the Inter-American Convention Against Corruption (the Monitoring Mechanism), was adopted by the OAS on 5 June 2001.

One fundamental aspect of the IACAC is the importance it places on the cooperation of civil society, which has recently been emphasised in the Mexican system.

---

12 Maria Amparo Casar, *México: Anatomía de la Corrupción* (2nd Edn, 2016). Available at https://contralacorrupcion.mx/anatomiadigital/content/Anatomia_de_la_corrupcion.pdf.

The implementation of the Monitoring Mechanism is carried out by a specific committee, which has issued several recommendations in its final reports for 2005, 2007, 2010, 2012 and 2016.[13] In general terms, Mexico is reportedly addressing the committee's recommendations, mostly through creating and implementing the SNA.

The fulfilment of a number of the recommendations made in the Second Round of the Monitoring Mechanism is still pending. Most of them are aimed at adopting comprehensive regulations on the protection of public officials and private individuals who report acts of corruption in good faith (ie, whistleblowers). This includes the protection of their identity in accordance with the fundamental principles of the Mexican legal system.[14]

The committee has also made recommendations relating to self-assessment and strategic solutions. For example, it encourages the Federal public administration to analyse why it is not able to attract more qualified candidates in its recruitment rounds and to design campaigns to promote employment opportunities aimed at attracting more candidates and encouraging them to apply for positions.[15]

The Committee's reports also address the design and regulation of public procurement procedures. For example, they suggest that direct-award procedures be more precisely regulated to avoid undue awards and to evaluate whether social witnesses[16] should continue to be paid for their services or if this duty should be *pro bono*.[17]

Altogether, the OAS's recommendations exert pressure on the Mexican government to pursue continuous improvement of anti-corruption legislation, institutional policies and mechanisms that allow and encourage social involvement.

4.2 The Organisation for Economic Co-operation and Development (OECD) Convention on Combating Bribery of Foreign Public Officials in International Business Transactions 1998 (the OECD Convention)

Mexico signed this important convention on 17 December 1997 and ratified it on 17 May 1999. It applies several instruments to implement its provisions. Notably, the Good Practice Guidance on Internal Controls, Ethics and Compliance,[18] and the Recommendation for Further Combating Bribery of Foreign Public Officials[19] are considered by the Mexican government to be tools for shaping national mechanisms against bribery of foreign public officials.

---

13 Available at www.oas.org/juridico/spanish/mex.htm.

14 *Mexico: Final Report on the Implementation of the Provisions of the Convention Selected for Review within the Framework of the Second Round (June 2007).* Available at www.oas.org/juridico/spanish/mesicic_II_inf_mex.pdf.

15 *Mexico: Final Report on the Implementation of the Provisions of the Convention Selected for Review within the Framework of the Fifth Round,* recommendation 37. Available at www.oas.org/juridico/PDFs/mesicic5_inf_mex_sp.pdf.

16 Social witnesses are independent legal entities or individuals that hold a registration from the Ministry of Public Function and are appointed to participate in every stage of a public procurement procedure expressing their opinion and issuing a final public report with their remarks and recommendations.

17 *Ibid.* See recommendations 215–219.

18 *Good Practice Guidance on Internal Controls, Ethics, and Compliance,* adopted 18 February 2010. Available at www.oecd.org/daf/anti-bribery/44884389.pdf.

19 *Recommendation of the Council for Further Combating Bribery of Foreign Public Officials in International Business Transactions.* Released on 9 December 2009 and with amendments adopted by the Council on 18 February 2010. Available at www.oecd.org/daf/anti-bribery/44176910.pdf.

Several phases of evaluation have been conducted under the OECD Convention. Multiple recommendations were made to Mexico as a result of the phase 1, 2 and 3 evaluations conducted in 2000, 2003 and 2011 respectively.[20] These included the following:

- the introduction of additional sanctions for corporations, given that sanctions designed only for individuals may be inadequate or lack practical application to corporations;[21]
- the implementation of specific sanctions regarding participation in public procurement processes, such as temporary or permanent debarment from participating in public procurement and public works, and a general exclusion from entitlement to public benefits or aid;[22]
- the inclusion of an autonomous definition of 'foreign public official' and the inclusion of a reference to a third party as a beneficiary of corrupt acts;[23]
- complementation of the existing legislation on confiscation of goods that proceed from bribery;[24]
- continued improvement in the level of attention devoted to requests for legal assistance in bribery-related cases;[25]
- the enactment of legislation to protect whistleblowers in both the public and private sectors;[26] and
- the introduction of obligations for external auditors to denounce crimes detected during the audits they conduct, granting them protection against possible reprisals.[27]

Although there is still a long way to go in improving the anti-corruption system, a number of these recommendations have been addressed over the years. The SNA laws have wholly or partially addressed a number of the remarks of and recommendations by the OECD Working Group on Bribery.[28]

The evaluations that result from in situ visits certainly have a positive impact on the actions taken by Mexican authorities. Government officials respond better to the recognition of the country as a compliant and hard-working member state than they would to corrective measures (such as sending a high-level mission to the country, a

---

20 Available at www.oecd.org/daf/anti-bribery/mexico-oecdanti-briberyconvention.htm.

21 *Mexico: Phase 2 Report on the application of the Convention on Combating Bribery of Foreign Public Officials in International Business Transactions and the 1997 Recommendation on Combating Bribery in International Business Transactions.* Adopted on 2 September 2004. See items 57–68 in 'Introduction and General Context' and Recommendation 185 d). Available at www.oecd.org/daf/anti-bribery/anti-briberyconvention/33746033.pdf.

22 *Ibid.* See Recommendation 185 d). See also *Mexico: Phase 2 follow-up Report on the Implementation of the Phase 2 Recommendations,* adopted on 4 April 2007. See Recommendation 5 d). Available at www.oecd.org/daf/anti-bribery/anti-briberyconvention/38376307.pdf.

23 *Mexico: Phase 2 Report and the 1997 Recommendation* (*op cit,* note 19 above)). See recommendation 185 b). See also finding 9 in the Summary of findings of this Report.

24 *Phase 3 Report on Implementing the OECD Anti-Bribery Convention in Mexico,* adopted on 14 October 2011. See items 34–38 under heading 'Confiscation of the Bribe and the Proceeds of Bribery' and Recommendation 5. Available at www.oecd.org/daf/anti-bribery/Mexicophase3reportEN.pdf.

25 *Ibid.* See Executive Summary and Recommendation 7.

26 *Ibid.* See Recommendation 15.

27 *Ibid.* See Recommendation 13 b).

28 As concluded by the Working Group in *Mexico: Phase 2 Follow-up Report* (*op cit,* note 20 above) and in *Mexico: Follow-up to the Phase 3 Report & Recommendations,* adopted on 16 June 2014. Available at www.oecd.org/daf/anti-bribery/MexicoPhase3WrittenFollowUpEN.pdf.

critical letter to its relevant ministers or the issuance of a formal public statement), which lack enforceability, but are highly undesirable.

Furthermore, the main purpose of the OECD Convention of raising global awareness of foreign bribery is enshrined in the Federal Criminal Code, as typified in the section 'Bribery of Foreign Public Officials'.

4.3 The United Nations Convention against Corruption 2004 (UNCAC) (also known as the Merida Convention)

Mexico signed this legally binding, universal anti-corruption instrument of uttermost importance on 9 December 2003 and ratified it on 20 July 2004. In doing so, the country adopted an international commitment to guarantee the existence of a specialised, independent and effective body to fight against corruption, by virtue of article 6 of the convention. Moreover, this commitment entails that the country's anti-corruption rules are also applicable to the private sector and that society needs to be involved in the design and implementation of strategies in this regard.

The UNCAC also provides guidelines for the treatment of funds derived from acts of corruption which have been diverted from public treasuries to third countries. The recovery of state-owned assets is promoted because the states parties are obliged to cooperate to prevent and detect these activities.

Two Review Cycles have been performed on Mexico, for Chapters III and IV and for Chapters II and V, respectively. The recommendations made by the Convention's review mechanism as a result of the first Review Cycle include the following:

- criminalising passive transnational bribery;[29]
- criminalising bribery in the private sector;[30]
- entering into agreements with other states for the relocation of witnesses;[31] and
- combating interference in the giving of testimony or the production of evidence through the bribery of a witness or expert.[32]

These recommendations guide the construction of an action-oriented pathway against corruption. The fulfilment of the commitments assumed under the UNCAC review mechanism promotes and encourages effective actions by the Mexican government.

The UNCAC represents a vital input for the implementation of the SNA now that international evaluation and continuous monitoring are determining factors for rebuilding public trust in the government.

5. The legal framework (2): the National Anticorruption System (SNA)

Historic constitutional amendments concerning anti-corruption were published in

---

29 Executive Summary to *Examination by Azerbaijan and Peru on Mexico's Implementation of Articles 15–42 of Chapter III. 'Criminalization and application of the law', and Articles 44–50 of Chapter IV, 'International Cooperation', of the United Nations Convention against Corruption for the 2010–2015 Review Cycle.* See 2.1 in Chapter III. Executive Summary available at www.unodc.org/documents/treaties/UNCAC/WorkingGroups/ImplementationReviewGroup/ExecutiveSummaries/V1505960e.pdf.

30 *Ibid.* See recommendations in 2.3 under 'Criminalization and law enforcement'.

31 *Ibid.* See recommendations in 2.3 under 'Law enforcement'.

32 See observations regarding 'Obstruction of Justice' at 2.1 in Chapter III.

the *Official Gazette* (DOF) on 27 May 2015 as the foundation for secondary legislation enacted on 18 July 2016.

The SNA is a system of coordination between federal and local authorities that are responsible for:

- preventing, detecting and penalising criminal acts of corruption and breaches of administrative responsibilities; and
- controlling public resources.

5.1 The legal framework of the SNA

- The *Constitution of the United Mexican States 1917, as amended.*[33] The SNA is provided for in article 113 of the Constitution, which sets out its description, object, members and minimum conditions for operation.
- *The General Law of the National Anticorruption System (General Law of the SNA) 2016.*[34] The main purpose of this law is to establish coordination and collaboration mechanisms between the institutions that conform with the SNA, which are:
  - the Citizen Participation Committee;
  - the Federal Judicature Council;
  - the National Institute of Transparency, Access to Information and Personal Data Protection;
  - the Federal Superior Audit Office;
  - the Specialized Anticorruption Prosecutor's Office;
  - the Ministry of Public Function Federal Court of Administrative Justice.

  The General Law of the SNA also governs the establishment of the SNA, the implementation of a National Digital Platform and the roles of the Coordination Committee (see 5.2 below), the Citizen Participation Committee (*ibid*) and the Steering Committee of the National Audit System, among other things.
- *The General Law of Administrative Responsibility 2016.*[35] The main purposes of this law are, firstly, to establish the principles for the conduct of public service; secondly, to lay down the responsibilities of public officials (both major and minor) and private individuals; and thirdly, to require public officials to submit statements of their assets and tax declarations and to disclose possible conflicts of interest.

  This law also defines the acts of private corporations and individuals that are related to the category of 'Major Administrative Offences of Public Officials'. These include:
  - *bribery* (article 66): this refers to promising, offering or giving any undue benefit to one or more public officials, directly or through third parties, to induce those officials to perform or refrain from performing an act inherent to their functions or those of another public official, or to abuse

33 Available at www.ordenjuridico.gob.mx/Constitucion/cn16.pdf.
34 Available at www.ordenjuridico.gob.mx/Documentos/Federal/pdf/wo118520.pdf.
35 Available at www.ordenjuridico.gob.mx/Documentos/Federal/pdf/wo114654.pdf.

real or alleged influence in order to obtain or maintain for the offeror or for a third party, a benefit or advantage, regardless of whether the promise, offer or benefit is accepted or received;

- *illicit participation in administrative procedures* (article 67): this refers to performing acts or refraining from participating in administrative procedures, whether federal, local or municipal, when legally ineligible or disbarred from doing so. Further, this provision also applies where a person intervenes in his or her own name but in the interest of an ineligible or disbarred party, with a view to that party obtaining total or partial benefits from participating in the administrative procedure. In such a case, both actors would be penalised;
- *influence peddling* (article 68): this refers to a person using influence, economic or political power, whether real or alleged, over any public official to obtain for that person or for third parties a benefit or advantage, or to cause detriment to another person or the public service, regardless of a public official has been influenced or the intended result obtained;
- *use of false information* (article 69): this refers to providing false information, altered documents or simulating compliance with rules or requirements established in administrative procedures to obtain authorisations, benefits or advantages or to put someone else at a disadvantage. Likewise, it refers to individuals or corporations that, in response to a requirement by a supervisory, judicial, electoral or human rights authority, provides false information, fails to provide the required information, or deliberately and unjustifiably delays providing such information after being made subject to enforcement measures, so as to obstruct investigation activities;
- *collusion* (article 70): this refers to participating, with one or more individuals in federal, local or municipal public procurement procedures, actions aimed at obtaining undue benefits or advantages. It also refers to entering into contracts, agreements, arrangements or combinations between competitors with the object of obtaining an undue advantage or causing damage to the public treasury or the property of public entities;
- *embezzlement* (article 71): this refers to performing acts aimed at appropriating, unduly using or deviating from the object of public resources, whether material, human or financial, when obtaining access to those resources, as well as failing to account for the destination of such resources;
- *undue hiring of former public servants* (article 72): this refers to employing someone who has held public office during the previous year and who, because of that position, has directly obtained privileged information that benefits the private entity or gives it an advantage over its competitors. Both the former public official and the person who hired him or her would be penalised.

Financial penalties for individuals can be of up to twice the value of the benefits obtained or, where the benefits are impossible to measure, an amount of up to approximately 11 million pesos.

Individuals can also be debarred from participating in public procurement procedures for between three months and eight years and can be ordered to pay an indemnity for damage caused to the public finances.

Financial penalties for corporations can be imposed of up to twice the value of the benefits obtained, or, where the value of the benefits obtained is unknown, up to approximately 110 million pesos.

Corporations may be debarred from participating in public procurement processes for between three months and 10 years, and they will also be liable to compensate damage caused to the public finances. Suspension of activities for up to three years and dissolution of a corporation are the severest possible penalties.

An aggravating factor in imposing penalties on corporations arises where it is shown that a corporation was aware of corrupt acts committed by its members but failed to report them.

Conversely, a corporation having an internal integrity policy may act as an extenuating circumstance in imposing penalties, provided that the policy includes (by virtue of article 25):

- organisation and procedure manuals that define and detail the functions and responsibilities of every section;
- a code of conduct, publicly available and known by personnel;
- adequate internal and external reporting systems, as well as disciplinary measures and concrete consequences for non-compliers;
- adequate training and preparation systems;
- mechanisms that ensure transparency and publication of the company's interests;
- adequate and effective control, monitoring and audit systems regarding compliance with integrity standards; and
- human resources policies that prevent the employment of people who represent a high risk to the corporation's integrity.[36]

These aggravating and attenuating criteria perfectly illustrate the duality of the SNA's approach. Corporate stakeholders will not be convinced to comply solely out of fear of punishment, whereas cooperation can be accomplished if incentives are offered to encourage the development of an anti-corruption culture pursuant to one simple idea: that it is more profitable and convenient to comply with anti-corruption norms than it is to break the rules, as the latter could mean the end of a corporation.

Moreover, the General Law on Administrative Responsibility provides for procedures for information exchange on administrative processes and the

36 A UNODC-Ministry of Public Function Project called *Grupo de Trabajo Empresarial* (Entrepeneurial Working Group) has been installed in order to have a standard, affordable and easy to implement Code of Conduct and other related tasks. See www.unodc.org/mexicoandcentralamerica/es/webstories/2017/grupo_de_trabajo_empresaria.htm.

creation of the National System of Sanctioned Public Servants, in order to compile information on all public officials who have been sanctioned for serious corruption offences. These measures seek to meet the objectives stated in article 3 of the IACAC and it is expected that they will allow the generation of information in an orderly and up to date manner to contribute to the effectiveness of the SNA.

The General Directorate of Accountability and Asset Status of the Secretariat of Public Function (SFP), contribute to the content of the Digital Platform of the SNA, through the System of Assets Evolution and Interest Statement, under which every public official is obliged to submit his or her Patrimonial Declaration (declaration of assets) and Declaration of Interests, which must be made public (except with regard to private or confidential information).

- *The Organic Law of the Federal Court of Administrative Justice 2016.* (Federal Administrative Court)[37] One of the main improvements to the anti-corruption system is the creation of the Federal Administrative Court as a jurisdictional body with autonomy and authority to issue binding decisions. The third section of the Federal Administrative Court has competence to:
    - sanction and rule on the administrative responsibility of public officials and private persons and can impose financial penalties to compensate for damage caused to the Federal Public Treasury or public assets;
    - disqualify individuals who engage in acts related to major administrative offences from participating in public procurement procedures; and
    - punish corporations where acts related to administrative offences are performed by individuals acting on their behalf or for their benefit.

  This measure represents a paradigm shift, since questions of administrative responsibility will, for the first time, be resolved by an independent court rather than by the federal public service.
- *The Organic Law of the Federal Public Administration 2016, as amended.*[38] Amendments to this law strengthen the capacity of the Ministry of Public Function (SFP) to prevent and fight corruption. The SFP may exercise its powers to review the income, management, custody and use of federal public resources.

  The SFP carries out audits and evaluations on its own initiative or upon request of the Ministry of Finance and Public Credit (SHCP), in order to supervise and promote efficiency and legality in the management and commissioning of the state's agencies and ministries. It also receives and files patrimonial (asset, property) and interest statements, as well as verifying their content through relevant investigations.
- *The Organic Law of the Attorney General's Office (PGR) 2009.*[39] Amendments to this law have created a Specialized Anticorruption Prosecutor's Office as an autonomous body empowered to investigate and prosecute acts of corruption.

---

37 Available at www.ordenjuridico.gob.mx/Documentos/Federal/pdf/wo118521.pdf.
38 Available at www.ordenjuridico.gob.mx/Documentos/Federal/pdf/wo13235.pdf.
39 Available at www.ordenjuridico.gob.mx/Documentos/Federal/pdf/wo83194.pdf.

This special office has the support of the administrative units of the PGR in matters of expert services required for the drafting of expert opinions.

The head of the Specialized Anticorruption Prosecutor's Office will be nominated and appointed by a two-thirds vote of Senate and may be removed from office by the Attorney General. The head and all of his or her staff are subject to the General Law of Administrative Responsibility and are obliged to submit an annual report of their activities and results.

- *The Federal Criminal Code 1931, as amended.*[40] Broadly speaking, recent reforms impose more severe penalties on those who commit corrupt acts, both public servants and individuals. New offences of bribery, influence peddling, collusion in public procurement, misuse of resources and undue hiring of former public officials have been introduced.

  Article 212 of the amended Criminal Code provides a complete and more comprehensive definition of 'public servant':

  Any person who performs a job, position or commission of any nature in the Federal Public Administration, decentralized agencies, majority state participation companies, organizations and similar companies, public trusts, state productive enterprises, constitutional autonomous organs, the Congress of the Union, the Federal Judicial Power, or anyone who manages federal economic resources.

  The amendments impose penalties on those who are responsible for committing acts of corruption. They include dismissal and disqualification from public office and from participating in acquisitions, leases, services or public works, as well as concessions, for a period of one to 20 years.

- *The Federal Audit and Accountability Law 2016.*[41] Amendments to this law strengthen the Federal Superior Audit Office (ASF) in the fight against corruption. The ASF can carry out reviews in the states and of the federal public accounts. Audits that were once performed annually can now be performed at any time.

  The ASF is also authorised to supervise, in coordination with local entities, all the resources of federal participants that are transferred to governing bodies, and to monitor federal resources that are transferred to trusts, funds and contracts, both public and private.

5.2 Organisational structure of the SNA

The Coordination Committee: The cornerstone of the SNA, the Coordination Committee is a permanent instrument of communication between government entities, with the purpose of establishing effective coordination mechanisms. It is chaired by a citizen in order to reconcile public and social perspectives. Its sessions are held quarterly, with the option of convening extraordinary sessions. Decisions are made by a simple majority, unless a particular situation requires a qualified majority. In the case of a tie, the citizen President (see below) has the casting vote.

40 Available at www.ordenjuridico.gob.mx/Documentos/Federal/pdf/wo83048.pdf.
41 Available at: www.ordenjuridico.gob.mx/Documentos/Federal/pdf/wo114650.pdf.

The members of the Coordination Committee are as follows:

- one representative of the Citizen Participation Committee (see below), who acts as President;
- the head of the Federal Superior Audit Office;
- the head of the Specialized Anticorruption Prosecutor's Office;
- the head of the Ministry of Public Function;
- the President of the Federal Court of Administrative Justice;
- the President of the National Institute of Transparency, Access to Information and Personal Data Protection; and
- One representative of the Federal Judicature Council.

The Committee is supported by an Executive Secretariat, which is headed by a Technical Secretary who is elected every five years. The Executive Secretariat is responsible for submitting specific proposals to the Coordinating Committee.

The Coordination Committee's main functions are:

- to evaluate public policies that target corruption;
- to devise and implement mechanisms, bases and principles for coordination with the audit authorities;
- to produce an annual performance report; and
- to establish the National Digital Platform for the deterrence of administrative faults and acts of corruption.

Acting in its capacity as a reviewing body, the Coordination Committee will issue non-binding public recommendations to the respective authorities and instruct them to adopt measures aimed at institutional strengthening in order to prevent administrative misconduct and acts of corruption as well improving their performance and internal controls and monitoring their implementation.

The establishment of the National Digital Platform is a key element for the successful implementation of the SNA, since it will consolidate all the relevant information relating to:

- public officials' patrimonial (asset/property), tax and conflict of interest declarations;
- public officials who participate in public procurement procedures;
- sanctioned public officials;
- criminal corrupt acts;
- audits; and
- public procurement.

The Citizen Participation Committee: As discussed previously, the creation of the SNA is, to a large extent, a result of social pressure and crisis. The purpose of the Citizen Participation Committee is therefore to contribute to the fulfilment of the objectives of the Coordination Committee, as well as to be the link between social and academic organisations involved in anti-corruption matters.

This committee is the prime example of the connection between the government and civil society. Its component members are five citizens of probity and prestige who stand out for their contribution to transparency, accountability and the fight against corruption. Their appointments are made by a special Selection Committee.

These citizens may not occupy, during the time of their management, a job, position or commission of any nature, in the federal, local or municipal governments, or in any other employment that prevents them from exercising their duties properly. Their membership of the Citizen Participation Committee lasts for five years, with no possibility of re-election. Members are elected in a staggered manner (ie, not all at the same time) and may only be removed for major administrative offences.

To fulfil its functions, the Citizen Participation Committee cooperates with the Coordination Committee by:

- generating coordination mechanisms between civil society, academic and citizens' groups;
- establishing rules for the lodging of citizen complaints against acts of corruption; and
- promoting research on public policies in anti-corruption matters.

In the exercise of its functions, the Executive Committee must propose:

- mechanisms to generate and exchange information concerning the inspection and control of public resources, through the National Digital Platform;
- policies on the prevention of administrative offences; and
- principles for coordination between supervisory authorities.

The Citizen Participation Committee incorporates the concept of governance, as vast majorities approve its members, meaning that appointments of its members are not subject to any political forces, and that they are only removable for major offences. Such characteristics promote fair and impartial performance and are consistent with an entity of an apolitical nature.

The Steering Committee of the National Audit System: The General Law of the National Anticorruption System has established a series of special coordination mechanisms. The National Audit System is one mechanism through which the Federal Superior Audit Office, the Ministry of Public Function, local superior audit entities and local secretariats in charge of internal control will work in coordination.

The Steering Committee comprises representatives of the Federal Superior Audit Office, the Secretary of the Ministry of Public Function and seven rotating members from the local auditing authorities and is chaired in a dual manner by the two federal members.

The Steering Committee's responsibilities are:

- the design, approval and promotion of integrated auditing policies;
- the implementation of coordination mechanisms between all members of the National Audit System; and
- the integration and implementation of mechanisms for the provision, exchange, systematisation and updating of information on the audit and

control of public resources generated by the competent institutions in these matters.

Local systems: Every federal entity is required to develop local anti-corruption systems, which must have an integration mechanism and responsibilities equivalent to those of the National Audit System. This process should have been completed within 180 calendar days from the entry into force of the General Law of Administrative Responsibility. Regrettably, only a few states have been able to complete this important task, as demonstrated in a commentary by the Mexican Institute for Competitiveness entitled the *Anticorruption red light: Monitoring Local Anticorruption Systems*.[42]

5.3 The current standing of the SNA

Nearly two years have passed since the enactment of the SNA legislation. While there are some positive remarks to be made, the picture is still incomplete, owing to political resistance. At the time of writing, the state of play is as described below.

The Selection Committee appointed the five members of the Citizen Participation Committee, who have assumed an active role making statements concerning industrial and commercial espionage to journalists and have brought judicial actions to promote the establishment of local anti-corruption systems and to investigate responsibility for deaths arising out of the collapse of buildings following the earthquakes of September 2017. The Citizen Participation Committee has been extremely proactive in the development of the SNA.

The Senate has failed to appoint both the head of the Anticorruption Prosecutor's Office and the new head of the Federal Superior Audit Office (a position that became vacant as of 1 January 2018).

President Enrique Peña Nieto proposed the appointment of 18 magistrates of the special corruption section of the Federal Court of Administrative Justice. The candidates were subjected to a strenuous process of questioning in the Senate, which has not ratified their appointments, thus creating a void in the implementation of the SNA.

The significant delay in the appointment of the executive arms of the SNA illustrates the political reluctance toward the fight against corruption, despite the grandiloquent speeches of politicians, demonstrating that opposing corruption and impunity are not a priority on their agendas.

Irrespective of the missing pieces of the jigsaw, the seeds have been sown. Citizens increasingly believe that a National Anticorruption System that has taken enormous effort to become a reality must grow into an effective countermeasure. Admittedly, the appointment of the executive heads and specialised magistrates is only the first lap in the race against corruption, and many flaws and shortcomings will undoubtedly come to light as the SNA moves forward. The SNA will naturally require adjustments and improvements, but as of today, its mere existence is a battle won.

---

42 https://imco.org.mx/politica_buen_gobierno/semaforo-anticorrupcion-monitoreo-de-los-sistemas-locales-anticorrupcion.

6. Final thoughts

Until recently, the role of citizens in the fight against corruption was scarce, to say the least. Today, the crisis of Mexican institutions is both a consequence of a long-standing state of apathy and the cause of social awakening.

The scheme introduced by the SNA stands for active citizenship, mainly through the Citizen Participation Committee, but the involvement of individual players and civil society organisations is also key to reshaping the foundations of the Mexican governance and anti-corruption systems. To date, several social actors[43] have exerted pressure to achieve the results that today represent Mexico's opportunity for a change. However, eager individuals need to be coordinated in order to be greater and stronger than the cluster of reluctant actors.

Academics, intellectuals and the media must show themselves to be responsible examples and prove that national progress relies on a more informed and concerned society that exerts pressure on government officials and individuals who look the other way.

Simultaneously, the corporate sector will gradually face the severe consequences of being the counterpart of corrupt institutions and agencies. Corporations will need to focus on developing codes of conduct and reporting mechanisms, and on investing in anti-corruption training up to the highest level.

In the near future, corruption will be a key element in the presidential election. Taking an optimistic view, regardless of the party that will govern in the forthcoming term, the fight against corruption will no longer be a façade behind which the only interests that thrive are those of corrupt actors. Society will hopefully commit to and make this desired change go from paper to rock and, at last, cause discomfort to the corrupt.

43 Such as the Mexican Institute of Competitiveness (IMCO), Transparency Mexico, the Mexican Employers' Confederation (COPARMEX), the International Chamber of Commerce Mexico, Mexicans Against Corruption, *Rumpere Impunitas* and the National Chamber of Consulting Companies (CNEC).

New Zealand

Gary Hughes
Akarana Chambers

1. Country overview regarding corruption matters

New Zealand has a welcome and well-earned reputation for being a relative beacon of low corruption. For many years, the country has sat comfortably high in international estimations, usually listed among the very best-performing nations in the annual Transparency International *Corruption Perceptions Index*[1] and similar global surveys.

This is due to generally high prevailing standards of governance, strong public institutions and courts, rigid application of the rule of law, good freedom of the press and official information disclosure regimes, as well as historically low cultural tolerance of corrupt practices.

However, no country is immune from bribery issues, particularly in the modern globalised era. Increased foreign travel, trade, inward investment and immigration demographics are changing New Zealand, and especially its largest city, Auckland. These remote islands are now a highly multicultural and diverse Asia-Pacific nation.

Possibly as a result of the historical absence of entrenched corruption that can be sadly commonplace in other nations, many New Zealanders have developed a sense of complacency. There remains a perception that because bribery is rare, it is close to non-existent, even where growing evidence suggests otherwise. This collective complacency can manifest itself in a lack of urgency to reform key legislative and regulatory measures, which therefore risk becoming outdated. It also leads to less pressure being exerted upon corporations to adopt and enforce stringent compliance measures. In this area, other developed nations, such as the United Kingdom and the United States, have moved current best practice forward through more detailed compliance and enforcement measures, such as the UK Bribery Act 2010.

New Zealand's enforcement agencies and media are not necessarily complacent. They continue to investigate, strongly call out and prosecute corruption matters. Public sentiment and the courts will condemn those rare instances of outright bribery. However, more could be done in key legal and corporate compliance aspects to ensure vigilance against standards gradually slipping, or against softer forms of corruption gaining a foothold in society.

---

1 Ranked number one in the 2017 edition (released January 2018), marginally ahead of Denmark. Survey available at www.transparency.org.nz/corruption-perceptions-index/.

2. Applicable international anti-corruption treaties and their effect in the fight against corruption

New Zealand is a signatory country to three main international conventions in this area:

- the Organisation for Economic Co-operation and Development (OECD) Convention on Combating Bribery of Foreign Public Officials in International Business Transactions (OECD Convention) (1998, ratified by New Zealand in 2001);
- the United Nations (UN) Convention against Transnational Organized Crime (2000, ratified in 2002);
- the United Nations Convention Against Corruption (UNCAC) (2003, ratified following inexplicable delay in 2015).

New Zealand also participates in regional-level initiatives, such as the Asia-Pacific Economic Cooperation (APEC) Santiago Commitment to Fight Corruption and Ensure Transparency (2004), and via its role in the Asia/Pacific Group on Money Laundering, a financial crime and anti-money laundering intergovernmental forum. The Trans-Pacific Partnership free trade area agreement, currently under re-negotiation following the withdrawal of the US, also has a chapter dealing with transparency matters.

Perhaps the most influential of these international arrangements has been the OECD Convention. Like other signatories, New Zealand is subject to periodic peer review by the OECD; it received a timely international rebuke with the publication of the OECD's Phase 3 Report (2013)[2] on New Zealand's patchy levels of compliance with the convention. This helped spur belated local legislative efforts in response to strengthen a number of elements of New Zealand's domestic anti-corruption frameworks by enacting the Organised Crime and Anti-Corruption legislation reforms in 2015.

Those 2015 reforms comprised a relatively modest package of legislative changes aimed at redressing issues identified by the OECD report. It included measures making technical and definitional amendments to criminal laws, finally ratifying the UNCAC into domestic law and updating provisions to deal with related criminal scourges, such as human trafficking, passport fraud and cross-border identity-related offences.

3. The concept of 'corruption' in New Zealand

An understanding of what amounts to 'corruption' can vary widely among people and firms in New Zealand, reflecting a spectrum of conduct from the ethically ambiguous (eg, conflicts of interest) to more overt levels of dishonesty (eg, kickbacks or secret commissions).

New Zealand has no single agreed or legally binding definition of 'corruption', but the main enforcement agency, the Serious Fraud Office (SFO), is content in practice to apply a broad definition. As such, the SFO may turn to wide notions, such

2 See www.oecd.org/newzealand/new-zealand-not-immune-from-foreign-bribery.htm.

as Transparency International's view that corruption entails "the abuse of entrusted power for private gain",[3] or that of the Asian Development Bank, which refers to:

behaviour on the part of officials in the public or private sector in which they improperly and unlawfully enrich themselves or those close to them, or induce others to do so, by misusing the position in which they are placed.[4]

Bribery is a particularly pernicious subset of corrupt practices, being taken to mean the giving or receiving, whether directly or indirectly, of something of value to influence a transaction. New Zealand's core statute in this area, the Crimes Act 1961,[5] ascribes a fairly mechanical definition of 'bribe' as meaning "any money, valuable consideration, office, or employment, or any benefit, whether direct or indirect".[6] However, in the context of the relevant series of offences laid out in that statute, this neutral definition works in tandem with an additional element of 'corrupt' conduct.

The New Zealand courts have recently had opportunity to examine the statutory meaning and extent of the term 'bribery'. This was in the important case of *Borlase and Noone v R*,[7] which explored where the line should be drawn between lavish but legitimate corporate hospitality and those gifts that would amount to corrupt consideration in return for the award of contracts. As the Court of Appeal explained:[8]

It is the word "corruptly" which introduces the specific element of impropriety. Corruption is established by evidence of the payment of a financial benefit knowing that its receipt is fundamentally inconsistent with the public official's duties. It does not require proof of dishonesty but of a conscious recognition by both the payer and recipient that the benefits are being provided in connection with the official's duties.

This has been New Zealand's highest profile corruption case in recent times. The Crown prosecuted both the recipient of a series of extended and lavish gifts, cash payments, and hospitality who was a senior manager at an Auckland Council-owned public transport infrastructure provider, and the bribe-payer, who ran a roading engineering and construction company, Projenz.

The trial, which was conducted over seven weeks with almost 40 witnesses, exposed a contest over conduct that was argued by the defendants to be acceptable commercial conduct in order to develop business relationships, whereas the Crown alleged that it amounted to long-term and detailed corruption of a person integral to a department that was awarding significant public roading contracts.

The two men each faced charges under section 105 of the Crimes Act for bribery and corruption of a public official. This spanned a seven-year period from 2006 to 2013, during which Projenz routinely paid monthly 'consulting services' invoices issued by the public servant, Mr Noone. The High Court (New Zealand's first instance trial court) concluded that these were a sham and that in substance no consulting services had been provided.

---

3 See www.transparency.org.nz/anti-corruption/.

4 See www.sfo.govt.nz/what-fraud-is-and-what-we-do.

5 Available at www.legislation.govt.nz/act/public/1961/0043/latest/DLM327382.html?src=qs.

6 See Part 6 of the Crimes Act 1961, definition of "crimes affecting the administration of law and justice" in section 99.

7 *R v SJ Borlase and MJ Noone* [2016] NZHC 2970 at first instance (High Court), and [2017] NZCA 514 (Court of Appeal).

8 *Borlase and Noone v R* [2017] NZCA 514 (14 November 2017) at [19].

Earlier case authority confirmed that since the wide scope of section 105 carried a risk of criminalising activity involving unexceptional token gifts or other benefits, there should be allowed a *de minimis* exception for truly minor gifts or what the Crown referred to as "the usual courtesies of life". However, the extravagant benefits provided by Projenz went well beyond the scope of that exception. The Court closely analysed detailed particulars and circumstances of the gifts and payments, and for the most part rejected, various receipts and invoices for lunches, dinners, gifts of wine and whisky, international travel and conferences, iPads, iPhones and holidays for Mr Noone's family members, and payment of personal telephone bills, hotel rooms and taxi travel. These, the court held, went beyond "standard industry business expenses".

The bribery and corruption charges related to the provision of benefits totalling around NZ$1.2 million over seven years by way of:

- payment by Projenz of Mr Noone's monthly invoices said to be for consulting services provided. These were found to be a 'sham' and the payments corrupt;
- the provision of benefits to Mr Noone, such as travel, accommodation, tablets, phones and meals at fancy restaurants. The Crown said these went beyond the "usual courtesies of life" and were corrupt. The defendants countered that these were either normal incidences of marketing and relationship-building with Mr Noone (and within a "culture of collaboration"[9] that was being encouraged at the Council and Auckland Transport), or otherwise provided in connection with the consultancy services. Some of these elements, such as lunches and travel to attend industry conferences, were found to be acceptable; most, however, were not.

The court noted that "happily for New Zealand's international reputation, there is a relative dearth of case law under these provisions". Despite the ordinary meaning usually given to the words 'bribery' and 'corruption', the Crimes Act gives different and less pejorative meanings, with the legislative offence framed in broad terms. In particular, the Court confirmed that this offence does not require:

- any dishonesty on the part of the official receiving the benefit or the person providing it;
- any improper action to be carried out on the part of the official concerned; or
- proof that the person providing the benefit intended to influence the official to carry out an improper act.

Even if there were no evidence of actual involvement by Mr Noone in favourably awarding council contracts to Projenz, the extensive nature of the benefits provided meant it could be inferred that they were only provided to grow and maintain influence with the public official in his role inside the department. Ultimately, both defendants were convicted and given long custodial sentences (as discussed further at 4 below).

9 High Court [2016] NZHC 2970, at [50].

4. Applicable regulations (administrative and criminal) and the authorities in charge of regulating, enforcing against and punishing corruption

4.1 Introduction

There are two main statutory elements to New Zealand's anti-bribery law:

- the series of provisions in the Crimes Act (as mentioned at 3 above), which focus purely on public sector corruption; and
- the Secret Commissions Act 1910,[10] which is now a very elderly piece of legislation but can apply across both the public and private sectors.

There is no general or overarching offence of bribery, but rather a set of specifically defined offences. Further, no detailed compliance programmes or anti-bribery measures are required by statute of business enterprises, these matters typically being left as a matter of commercial and governance choice.

In addition, there are further government regulatory or 'soft law' measures short of statutory powers, which influence the overall make-up of the anti-corruption regime.

While these bribery and corruption offences have a form of extraterritorial application in place, it is more limited than the extensive long-arm reach of the US and UK regimes under, respectively, the Foreign Corrupt Practices Act 1976 and the Bribery Act 2010. New Zealand law can apply to individuals and companies, regardless of whether the factual events and conduct took place locally/domestically or wholly abroad, but the enforcement agencies can only prosecute New Zealand citizens, residents and companies incorporated in New Zealand. Jurisdictional matters have very rarely been tested, but would appear not necessarily to apply to foreign citizens or corporations who merely have assets in or pass transactions through New Zealand.

4.2 Private sector corruption: the Secret Commissions Act 1910

The Secret Commissions Act 1910 (the 1910 Act) contains several bribery and corruption-style offences, couched in the language of principal and agent relationships and undisclosed benefits. Although it is the main private sector anti-corruption law, the 1910 Act is written in archaic and complex drafting style reflective of the time, and has not been the preferred vehicle for prosecutions in the past.

For many years, the prescribed financial penalties applied under the 1910 Act were almost comically low, as the statute had not been updated. Reforms under the 2015 package of changes (see 2 above) corrected this situation by finally increasing maximum penalties for all offences under the 1910 Act to seven years' imprisonment or a potentially unlimited fine both for individuals and for corporations (particularly as the latter cannot be jailed). Nevertheless, the substantive law provisions of the 1910 Act remain in need of major redrafting or replacement by a brand new modern statute.

The key corruption offence under the 1910 Act criminalises the bribing of an

---

10 Available at www.legislation.govt.nz/act/public/1910/0040/latest/DLM177643.html?src=qs.

agent (broadly speaking, someone who works on behalf of a principal). A number of differently defined offences exist under the 1910 Act but, generally speaking, they include actions of corruptly giving, agreeing, offering or accepting/receiving in an agency role any gift or other consideration that is designed to induce or reward an agent's actions relating to the commercial affairs or business of his or her principal.[11]

If a gift or other consideration has been disclosed or has the consent of the principal or relevant party, it is generally not secret and so is often outside the definitions of the offence discussed above. Other offences include:[12]

- failure by an agent to disclose to his or her principal a pecuniary or financial interest in a contract;
- giving a false receipt or invoice to an agent with intent to deceive the principal, or for the agent to do so to his or her principal;
- receipt of a secret reward, inducement, gift or consideration for giving advice to enter a contract with a third party.

4.3 Public sector corruption: the Crimes Act 1961

As foreshadowed in the discussion of the Crimes Act 1961 (the 1961 Act) at 3 above, bribery occurs when a person corruptly gives, receives, accepts or obtains a bribe (which may be done directly or indirectly) for himself or herself or for any other person, with intent to influence the relevant official or person so that he or she acts or refrains from acting in a particular way in his or her official capacity. The main two elements of intent or evaluative nature of the conduct are highlighted by the expressions 'corruptly' and 'with intent to influence'.

A bribe may involve money, valuable consideration, office, employment, a gift, favour, voucher, discount or practically any other tangible benefit in cash or in kind.

The list of office-bearers or public roles to which the offence under the Crimes Act applies is found in sections 100–105 of the 1961 Act and covers New Zealand judges, government ministers, Members of Parliament, police or law enforcement officers and other public officials.

It is also an offence (under sections 105A and 105B of the 1961 Act) to use official information corruptly or to trade in influence or to disclose personal information about an identifiable individual corruptly.

A range of penalties exists for individuals convicted of bribery and corruption of domestic public office-holders, ranging from a maximum of 7–14 years' imprisonment or an unlimited fine.

Most of the provisions of the 1961 Act cannot be subject to a prosecution without leave of the Attorney-General, which serves to curtail significantly any scope for private prosecution and leaves the decision whether to apply for leave in the hands of public enforcement agencies. The same restraint is also to be found under the 1910 Act with regard to private sector cases.

Another set of 1961 Act provisions, sections 105C–105E, criminalise the bribery of foreign public officials in the course of an international business transaction or

11 Sections 3 and 4 of the 1910 Act.

12 See generally *ibid*, sections 5–10.

international aid or trade. These parts of the law were those to which the Phase 3 Review of the OECD Working Group (see 2 above) was directed and to which some criticisms were made. Giving, offering, or agreeing to give a bribe with intent to influence a foreign public official is the cornerstone of these offences, which apply whether or not the bribe is for an act or omission within the scope of the official's authority, and extend to bribes made through third parties or intermediaries.

Acknowledging the seriousness of foreign bribery, the organised crime reform package of 2015 amended the maximum penalties to a term of imprisonment not exceeding seven years and/or a fine not exceeding the greater of:

- NZ$5 million; or,
- if it can be readily ascertained and if the court is satisfied that the offence occurred in the course of producing a commercial gain, three times the value of any commercial gain resulting from the contravention.

The introduction of a commercial gain formula is a positive change, as it better ties the penalty with the gain or profit from the offence, utilising a legal formulation common in other regulatory areas, such as antitrust/competition law penalty cases. The new penalties also mean that individuals convicted of foreign bribery may now incur a fine in addition to a term of imprisonment (not simply as an alternative). These were an important part of New Zealand's response to the Phase 3 Review by the OECD Working Group, to ensure strong monetary penalties would operate as a firm deterrent to any complacency about corporate bribery.

Other key amendments made in 2015 included a number of matters of clarification or updating:

- the offence of foreign bribery no longer contains a dual criminality requirement. This ensures that New Zealand can effectively prosecute foreign bribery under the 1961 Act, regardless of whether it was an offence in the country in which the conduct actually took place;
- the definitions of 'business', 'employee' and 'routine government action' were also updated to ensure that the offence of foreign bribery applies to activities in the provision of international aid and other corporate activities, and to constrain trading businesses abroad in the scope for allowing the pre-existing 'facilitation payments' exception;
- new offences were created to address gaps in the pre-existing anti-corruption framework, for example, so that it is now a specific offence to accept a bribe in return for 'trading in influence' over an official;
- accounting obligations of companies who might be drawn into foreign bribery were clarified, in particular by changing rules under the Companies Act 1993 to ensure record-keeping of any small facilitation payments in a consistent manner. Additionally, the Income Tax Act 2007 now ensures that no bribes can be made tax deductible; and
- additional measures were enacted allowing New Zealand to provide seamless cross-border assistance in corruption investigations and prosecutions by approved overseas agencies, using existing processes under the Mutual Assistance in Criminal Matters Act 1992.

4.4 Facilitation or routine payments in foreign trade

One particularly contentious issue that New Zealand policymakers had to grapple with in 2015 concerned facilitation payments, ie, payments intended to be routine minor payments to speed up an action or process to which the payer is already entitled, such as a standard import process. The historic facilitation payments exception acted as a defence to charges under the 1961 Act but was open to misinterpretation and possibly abuse. The scope of the exception has now been significantly cut back and its definitions firmly clarified, though many commentators (including the writer) feel that it would have been preferable to abolish this confusing and questionable defence altogether. As was colourfully put by a Member of Parliament who criticised the continued existence of such a defence, it serves merely:

> *... to legalise facilitation or 'grease' payments made to foreign public officials to facilitate such activities as the granting of permits or licenses, the provision of utility services, and the loading or unloading of cargo. These 'grease' payments are bribes, no matter their size, and help maintain a culture in some overseas jurisdictions where low-level corruption is permitted and accepted as normal practice when working in some overseas jurisdictions. Internationally, New Zealand is seen as a leader in public sector ethics and transparency. The outlawing of the controversial and unethical practice of facilitation payments will help uphold this international perception.*[13]

However, legitimate competing concerns were raised about potentially putting New Zealand export business at a disadvantage when many other competing trading nations continue to permit some form of routine payments. A facilitation payments exception therefore remains available at law, albeit in very restricted terms.

4.5 Prosecuting bodies and related agencies

Bribery and corruption offences may be investigated and prosecuted by either the New Zealand Police or New Zealand's SFO, a specialist white collar crime unit created to enforce against offences involving matters of high value, complex or otherwise prioritised fraud and corruption cases.[14] By a memorandum of understanding between the two agencies, the SFO will take the lead in investigating any case of corruption or bribery, unless the scale of the matter is very modest.

The SFO has shown itself sufficiently motivated and resourced to make corruption issues a priority, with a team of forensic accountants and a panel of independent external prosecutors, leaving it able to take on challenging cases publicly and aggressively, if necessary.

The SFO frequently also uses additional related charges under the 1961 Act where they may equally fit the circumstances of a corruption or deception matter. For example:

- under section 240, concerning obtaining a benefit or causing a loss by deception (which can expressly apply to sports match-fixing issues);

---

13 Supplementary Order Paper to Parliament, Green Party, during the passage of the Organised Crime and Anti-Corruption Amendment Bill 2015.

14 https://sfo.govt.nz.

- under section 243, concerning money laundering offences;
- under section 249, concerning the accessing of a computer system for a dishonest purpose; and
- under sections 257–260, concerning the forging of documents and false accounting offences.

Other public agencies, such as the Office of the Auditor-General (which audits and investigates the financial affairs of government departments and entities), the State Services Commission and the Office of the Ombudsman, also have a role to play in handling complaints or probing into matters of public sector corruption, misfeasance or conflicts of interest.

5. Relevant public cases and how have they been handled and resolved

5.1 The imprisonment of Taito Phillip Field, Member of Parliament

New Zealand's highest profile corruption case involved a former Member of Parliament (MP) and Associate Minister of the Crown, Taito Philip Field. Mr Field was found guilty of 11 counts of bribery as an MP and 15 counts of attempting to pervert the course of justice. The case concluded with the High Court imposing a six-year prison sentence, four years of which reflected the bribery charges.[15] The decision was appealed unsuccessfully to the Court of Appeal and then finally to the Supreme Court where it was also dismissed.[16]

The case was the first prosecution under section 103(1) of the 1961 Act for corruption and bribery of an MP. Section 103(1) provides that every MP is liable to imprisonment (for a term not exceeding seven years) who corruptly accepts or obtains, or agrees or offers to accept or attempts to obtain, any bribe for himself or herself or any other person in respect of any act done or omitted, or to be done or omitted, by him or her in his or her capacity as an MP. Leave of a High Court judge is required in order to commence a prosecution under this section.

It was in his role as a local electorate MP that Mr Field got into trouble, after he had met a number of Thai immigrants in New Zealand who were facing immigration problems. These Thai nationals were involved in the building industry as tilers, plasterers and painters. Mr Field was very familiar with the immigration system and advised them on how best to achieve their desired outcomes. He did so in his capacity as an MP. The advice included help with immigration issues, such as overstaying, deportation, removal orders and obtaining permanent residence. The advice and assistance they received from Mr Field was effective and the trial judge found it had been more helpful than the paid help they had received from immigration consultants and lawyers.

In return, Mr Field allowed or requested building work to be done by Thai nationals he had assisted on houses owned by him. One of his Thai connections introduced him to another Thai plasterer and a painter, both of whom sought Mr

15 *R v Field*, High Court, Auckland, CRI-2007-092-18132, 6 October 2009.
16 *Taito Phillip Hans Field v R* [2011] NZSC 129.

Field's assistance with their immigration problems around the time that they began working on his property. The work on this property was substantial, all the labour was free and Mr Field soon sold this renovated property for a profit. This type of offending continued over two years; it involved eight Thai individuals who had received advice from Mr Field and five properties that he owned.

Ample evidence was provided to the court to conclude that Mr Field knew the work was done because of and in recognition of the immigration assistance he had provided. This free labour for painting, tiling and plastering undoubtedly helped him sell his properties for a healthy profit.

Although the total value of the unpaid work on Mr Field's properties was only NZ$58,280, the court held that, by any standards, a substantial benefit was conferred. Mr Field knew that his assistance was the basis on which the work was done, and should have known it was wrong. To make matters worse for himself, when interviewed following the instigation of an inquiry, Mr Field provided false statements and urged others to do the same. This included encouraging the Thai nationals to produce false quotations, invoices and statements, for which he was also convicted of perverting the course of justice.

Although Mr Field was not the decision-maker on immigration issues, he had spoken with the ministerial level decision-maker. He had a special relationship with that minister and a special obligation to be honest. The minister was unaware that Mr Field was receiving benefits for vouching for the Thai nationals.

The conviction of Mr Field was later appealed on multiple grounds, including the wrong legal test having been applied. These were in some ways untested waters for the appellate courts, but they firmly dismissed the appeals and made important rulings on legal interpretation, such as confirming:

- that a bribe is corruptly accepted if, in accepting the bribe, the particular member is knowingly outside the recognised bounds of his or her duties;
- that "corruptly", in the language of the offence under the 1961 Act, must be given a wide interpretation, and that in this situation it was simply wrong for an MP or official to accept money, favours or like benefits, including gratuities of a non-financial kind, "in return for what has been done in an official capacity";
- that actions such as those in Mr Field's case tend to promote corruption in future and require a strong response from the court, not least since there is a fundamental inconsistency between "the performance of official functions and the acceptance of private rewards for doing so"; and
- that the law recognised a form of *de minimis* defence where a person was dealing with very small or otherwise token gifts – things that might be considered "of token value which are just part of the usual courtesies of life". An example given by the court was that of a MP, when attending to cut a ribbon at a sports club or open a new sporting facility, who might be given a gift and accepts a sports jersey by the club at or after the ceremony. This would be considered *de minimis* and not amount to bribery, even if the MP was aware in advance of the opening ceremony that there would be a gift.

5.2 The *Borlase and Noone* case – excessive corporate hospitality and sham consulting services

Discussed at 3 above, this case merits further discussion as the most recent and high profile New Zealand court prosecution. It raises two old chestnuts seen in corruption cases worldwide: tendering for and procurement of public infrastructure works, and vague or undocumented fees for 'consulting services'.

The public official, Mr Noone, was said to have provided ongoing and substantial 'business development' consulting services to Projenz during the seven-year period in question. Many of the alleged bribes were paid pursuant to regular monthly invoices issued by him, suggesting that he spent 90–110 hours every month working on 'consulting' for Projenz, in addition to his full-time job with the Auckland Council. The court concluded that Mr Noone did not provide such consulting services and that the defendants' explanation was implausible and defied common sense.

Other key findings by the court on the invoicing scam are worth noting:

- there was no documentary evidence of any of the output or 'work product' of Mr Noone's purported consultancy services over the whole seven years of the payments. Mr Borlase said that all of the consulting advice was verbal: the Court found this to be implausible, given the scale and longevity of the payments made for it;
- highly relevant was the lack of knowledge by other workers and managers in the Council, or in contact with Projenz, about Mr Noone's consulting services arrangement. A number of witnesses who ought to have known about it gave evidence that they did not; and
- related to this, Mr Noone and Projenz had both at important times failed to disclose the arrangements between them, including on occasions where disclosure was plainly required. For example, probity requirements during two specific contract tendering processes would have necessitated disclosure, and Mr Noone in particular had repeatedly failed to disclose to his Council employer these arrangements with Projenz, despite numerous opportunities to do so. He knew his employer had gifting and conflict of interest policies, so this lack of disclosure strongly implied that he knew that the arrangements were wrong.

Overall, this case has shone a deep spotlight into the details of unacceptable and consistently over-the-top corporate hospitality. It also emphasises two of the familiar themes in industries and tendering situations at most risk of corruption: sham 'consulting' work being used as a vehicle to make backdoor payments, and local government officials who are at risk when in a position to influence significant contractual tender rounds if they become cosy with those parties bidding for the work.

Mr Borlase and Mr Noone appealed against their sentences, which gave the Court of Appeal an opportunity to comment on the principles relevant to sentencing for bribery matters. Section 105(2) of the 1961 Act states:

Everyone is liable to imprisonment for a term not exceeding 7 years who corruptly gives or offers or agrees to give a bribe to any person with intent to influence any official in respect of any act or omission by him or her in his or her official capacity.

There were four agreed elements of the charges against Mr Borlase, in that he:

- corruptly
- gave a bribe
- to Mr Noone
- with an intent to influence him in respect of any act or omission by him in his official capacity.

Mr Borlase's appeal against his conviction related to the fourth element. He argued that the Crown had failed to establish that the payments or benefits given to Mr Noone were made with the intention that Mr Noone would act improperly to Mr Borlase's advantage in the tendering of work. The Court of Appeal rejected this submission as contrary to the plain words of section 105(2). It described the purpose of the section as proscribing conduct that is intended to influence the acts or omissions of public officials performed in their official capacity. The offence does not require proof of an additional element of an intention to influence the official to act in a certain way, whether proper or improper. There is no need to enquire into the motives or consequential events resulting from the bribe.

The court applied the earlier case of *Field v R* (see 5.1 above). In doing so, it said that:

corruption is established by evidence of the payment of a financial benefit knowing that its receipt is fundamentally inconsistent with the public official's duties. It does not require proof of dishonesty but of a conscious recognition by both the payer and recipient that the benefits are being provided in connection with the official duties.

Since both payer and recipient were aware that the remuneration package provided by the public authority Council was intended to make up the sole source of financial recompense for Mr Noone in performing his duties, any additional payments disguised as bogus contractual payments would be fundamentally inconsistent with Mr Noone's public duties. The court held that both parties had acted corruptly.

The court then discussed the criminal law concepts of *actus reus* and *mens rea* for this offence. The *actus reus* was the corrupt payment and receipt of the bribe/benefit, and the *mens rea* was the intent to influence Mr Noone in performing his official duties. It may be possible to infer strongly the mental element of intent: "as with many criminal offences, proof of the first requirement will provide a sound if not decisive evidential foundation for proof of the second." The court rhetorically asked: if not as a bribe, what were the payments for Mr Borlase, as a rational businessman, would not pay a public official to act properly and carry out his duties where there was no suggestion that he was acting otherwise, nor would he make such large payments unless he thought he would receive an appropriate return.

Mr Borlase was sentenced to five years and six months' imprisonment, and Mr Noone to five years. The High Court judge set out certain aggravating factors in handing down the sentences:

- the significant harm to the Council as well as the broader community in tarnishing New Zealand's reputation as a country of very low public corruption;

- the seven-year duration of the offending;
- the nature and scale of the amounts paid;
- the breach of trust inherent in the parties taking advantage of a close and lengthy relationship between Mr Borlase's company and the local authorities; and
- the element of deception.

The Court of Appeal decisively upheld those long sentences, noting that multiple offences had been committed over a prolonged period. While each individual offence may not have been of the most serious type, cumulatively they revealed a pattern of criminality on a serious scale. Procurement practices such as this promote a culture in which officials start to expect similar benefits in the future and members of the public who do not provide such benefits receive no assistance.

5.3 Prominent academic convicted for payments in role as trustee

A retired professor *emeritus* and Maori cultural leader was prosecuted for his role in a fraud related to a significant commercial property development in Wellington. Sir Ralph Ngatata Love was jailed for two and a half years in October 2016, having been found guilty of a single charge of obtaining property by deception.[17]

A second alternative charge, of obtaining a secret benefit under the 1910 Act, was laid but, having been found guilty on the first charge, the judge determined that in the event he did not need to go on to consider this charge as it was only an alternative. The maximum penalty either way for the charge would be up to seven years' imprisonment.[18]

The land in question was owned by the Wellington Tenths Trust, of which Sir Ngatata Love was the Chair and a trustee. It administers Maori tribal reserve land largely in the urban Wellington area, for the benefit of all members of the tribe. In commercial negotiations, it emerged that property developers were willing to pay a premium for leasehold rights on the land. Sir Ngatata Love therefore arranged for a total of NZ$1,687,500 to be paid into accounts of his partner, Ms Skiffington, for the pair's benefit. The payments were not disclosed to the remaining trustees and were used to pay down the mortgage on a large home the pair had bought months earlier.

The offending was uncovered only after the Inland Revenue began investigating Ms Skiffington's accountants. She was a lawyer who had held senior advisory roles within central government, but her charges were permanently stayed in August 2015 due to ill-health. Sir Ngatata Love's son also pleaded guilty to a charge under the 1910 Act and was sentenced to six months' home detention. The case attracted heavy media comment due to the public figures involved, and the relatively blatant nature of the secret benefits, which other trustees of the land would not have ratified had they known of them.

---

17 *R v Love* [2016] NZHC 2394, *Sentencing Notes*, 7 October 2016.
18 *R v Love*, Verdict on charges [2016] NZHC 2046, 1 September 2016.

6. The future of New Zealand anti-corruption law: what needs to be modified, strengthened or addressed?

While for many years New Zealand has enjoyed high international estimations as a corruption-free jurisdiction, the country is not exactly immune from corruption. Whether foreign or domestic, the biggest threat to its fortunate position is from complacency. The willingness to enforce corruption cases is there, and the courts do not hesitate to impose strong sentences. However, moving forward with weak and outdated legal measures for corporations and relying on voluntary compliance obligations means that many in the commercial community and citizenry have little awareness of corruption practices. They may not recognise red flags if they were to see corruption, and often have no documented policies or code of conduct about it.

Often, a New Zealand business may only be prompted to institute a specific anti-bribery policy and staff training on the issues because it is required to do so as a precondition of bidding for work in another leading jurisdiction in Europe or North America, where such compliance tools are routine and demanded of those making bids.

Even in a low corruption state, vigilance is important because, over time, minor issues or failings can build up and raise the potential for problems ahead. Typically at risk areas include public procurement and tendering situations in industries such as construction, transport, infrastructure, healthcare, insurance and IT projects. There is at least a degree of concern over conflicts of interest in those sectors, even if evidence of outright corruption is thin. In particular, gifts, travel junkets, corporate hospitality conferences and lavish client entertainment can be the subject of very few rules and norms in New Zealand. Everybody seems to have a different view of what is acceptable, with wide variation by industry, and few firms have actual policies to guide their staff. The *Borlase* and *Noone* case has at least provided some welcome guidance from the courts on where the line should be drawn for ordinary and routine low level hospitality, as opposed to systemic corrupt relationships maintained over time.

Another compliance problem is that formal whistleblowing protocols and policies are rare in the private sector. While there is legislation protecting public sector whistleblowers,[19] not many corporations have implemented confidential hotlines or published guidance to staff on matters such as conflicts of interest and probity in commercial negotiations.

As explained at 4 above, a facilitation payments exception remains available under New Zealand's bribery law, albeit with additional restrictions since 2015 on when it can apply. Most anti-corruption experts would favour doing away with the exception, and even the Ministry of Justice's previous compliance advice to the business community was that they should avoid the use of facilitation payments altogether. The legislative decision to retain a defence to them could be seen as a missed opportunity for New Zealand to remain a leader in cracking down on such areas of low-level institutionalised corruption.

---

19 The Protected Disclosures Act 2000, available at www.legislation.govt.nz/act/public/2000/0007/latest/DLM53466.html?src=qs.

Ironically enough, this sports-mad country has shown that its politicians can move rapidly when motivated to do so, as became clear when news broke that three international cricket players were under investigation for match-fixing in the Indian sub-continent, and Chris Cairns, a leading test match captain, went on trial in England for perjury.[20] With New Zealand due to host the ICC Cricket World Cup in 2015, urgent remedial legislation dealing with match-fixing and corruption in sport was rushed into law after it was realised that no specific offence actually existed for those matters. It would be good to think that addressing matters of commercial corruption and stronger compliance rules will soon be accorded similar political urgency.

20 See, for example, www.theguardian.com/sport/2015/nov/30/chris-cairns-cricket-perjury-trial-how-case-unfolded.

Nigeria

Ayodele Adeyemo
Chukwuma Ezediaro
Babajide O Ogundipe
Sofunde Osakwe Ogundipe & Belgore

---

1. Overview of Nigeria *vis à vis* corruption matters

Nigeria is a federal republic comprising 36 states and a federal capital territory in which the capital, Abuja, is located. With an estimated 185 million people, Nigeria is the most populous country in Africa and the seventh most populous in the world. It is a multi-national state, in that it is populated by more than 500 distinct and separate ethnic groups. Of these 500, the Yoruba, Hausa and Igbo (or Ibo) are the three largest groups, making up about 68% of the population.

The area of what is now Nigeria became a British colony in 1914, following the amalgamation of British protectorates of Northern and Southern Nigeria with the Nigeria Colony (which comprised the Oil Rivers Protectorate and the Lagos Colony). Up until 1939, the administration of the amalgamated territory was conducted separately: on the one hand, the Northern and Southern Nigeria protectorates and, on the other, the Nigeria Colony. In 1939, Southern Nigeria was divided into two provinces, the Eastern and Western. These two provinces, along with Northern Nigeria, became regions in 1946, each having bicameral regional assemblies with limited powers. A central legislative council was established at the same time. In 1957, the Eastern and Western regions became self-governing, with the Northern Region attaining that status in 1959.

Nigeria became independent of Britain on 1 October 1960, with a bicameral Westminster-type federal legislature. A Prime Minister was the head of the government and Queen Elizabeth II remained as the head of state, represented in Nigeria by a Governor-General. In 1963, the constitution was amended to make Nigeria a federal republic, with the Governor-General becoming titular head of state as President. At the same time, the Western Region was reduced in size with the creation of a Mid-Western Region. This system of government remained in place until January 1966, when the army overthrew the civilian government and replaced the regional governments with military governors in what was essentially a unitary government.

It has always been commonly accepted in Nigeria that corruption is a destructive practice. In the first military intervention into governance in Nigeria, the January 1966 coup plotters' spokesperson, Major Kaduna Nzeogwu, referred to corruption as one of the ills that prompted the military's decision to seek the overthrow of the federal and regional governments in the country. This refrain was continued by the perpetrators of each successive military coup until that led by Nigeria's current President, Muhammadu Buhari, when the elected government of Shehu Shagari was overthrown in January 1984. With the return of civilian government in 1999, corruption continued to be viewed as a serious problem, which had clearly not been solved by military interventions in governance. A special anti-corruption agency, the Independent Corrupt Practices Commission, was created in 2000, followed by a special economic and financial crimes agency, the Economic and Financial Crimes Commission, in 2002. Both of these agencies were created by the government led by Olusegun Obasanjo, whose election platform contained a commitment to combat corruption.

Every single federal government in place since 1999 has included a promise to combat corruption in its election platform. In spite of this frequently proclaimed commitment, and some of the best anti-corruption laws, it is generally accepted that Nigeria continues to experience an extremely high level of corruption. It has been estimated that close to $400 billion was stolen from Nigeria's public accounts between 1960 and 1999,[1] and that between 2005 and 2014 some $182 billion was lost through illicit financial flows from the country.[2] Virtually no day passes without an opinion piece in some publication lamenting the scourges of corruption to society in Nigeria, with stories purporting to expose governmental corruption a regular feature in the Nigerian media. In spite of all this, it appears that the authorities remain unable to address the problem meaningfully.

Most Nigerians experience some form of corruption on a daily basis, and this has led to an acceptance that corruption is part of the society and that the governments, in spite of declarations to the contrary, will not take action to stem it. A Chatham House report published in May 2017[3] described the position as tending to foster more corruption, and perpetuating and entrenching injustice in daily life. In turn, such an environment weakens societal values of fairness, honesty, integrity and common citizenship, as the impunity of dishonest practices and abuses of power or position steadily erode citizens' sense of moral responsibility to follow the rules in the interests of wider society.[4]

Nigeria's anti-corruption legislation is, to a large extent, on a par with such legislation around the world. The clear and obvious difference between outcomes in Nigeria and those in other countries where corruption is less of a problem lies in the approach of the authorities, both law enforcement and the courts, to implementation of the laws. Nigeria's problem in this regard is complicated by the fact that not only are the law enforcement agencies not very efficient, even when investigations are conducted and alleged offenders are apprehended, there is also a real likelihood that the agencies themselves may be corrupted by the alleged

---

1 UN Office on Drugs and Crime (2007), Anti-Corruption Climate Change: it started in Nigeria, speech by Antonio Maria Costa at the 6th National Seminar on Economic Crime, Abuja (13 November 2007).

2 This figure represents some 15% of $1.21 trillion, the total value of Nigeria's trade over the period 2005–2014. In 2014 alone, illicit financial flows from Nigeria were estimated at $12.5 billion, representing 9% of the total value of trade of $139.6 billion in that year. See Global Financial Integrity (2017), Illicit Financial Flows to and from Developing Countries: 2005–2014 (April 2017), available at www.gfintegrity.org/wpcontent/uploads/2017/05/GFI-IFF-Report-2017_final.pdf, pp30–34.

3 LK Hoffmann & RN Patel, *Collective Action on Corruption in Nigeria: A Social Norms Approach to Connecting Society and Institutions*, available at www.chathamhouse.org/sites/files/chathamhouse/publications/research/2017-05-17-corruption-nigeria-hoffmann-patel-final.pdf.

4 *Ibid*, p.iv.

offenders. Worse still, Nigeria has, in recent times, been presented with compelling evidence of judicial corruption. This has resulted in persons charged with corruption offences being discharged. Where judicial officers themselves have been charged with corruption offences, the outcomes in recent times have consistently favoured the officers accused.

2. Regulations and authorities in charge of regulating, enforcing against and punishing corruption

2.1 Legislation and other regulations

As noted at 1 above, Nigeria is not lacking in anti-corruption laws and regulations and there are a number of agencies charged with the enforcement of such instruments. The relevant laws and regulations include the following.

(a) The Code of Conduct for Public Officers under the 1999 Constitution (Part 1 of the Fifth Schedule to the Constitution)

The 1999 Constitution (the Constitution) contains a Code of Conduct for Public Officers (the Code). This code stipulates that a public officer must not put himself or herself in a position whereby his or her personal interests might conflict with his or her duties and responsibilities. He or she must not ask for or receive property or benefits of any kind for himself/herself or any other person on account of anything done or omitted to be done by him or her in the discharge of his or her duties. It also requires a public officer to declare his or her assets three months after the Code came into force or immediately after taking office (as the case may be). Thereafter, such declaration is required to be made every four years, or after the expiration of the officer's term of office. The Code further prohibits the offering of a bribe to a public officer or the operation of foreign bank accounts by any public officer.

Responsibility for enforcing the Code is assigned to a special Code of Conduct Tribunal (the Tribunal) under the Code of Conduct Bureau and Tribunal Act (Cap C15, Laws of the Federation of Nigeria 1991). This tribunal has, however, not been terribly successful in enforcing the provisions of the Code. According to data provided by the Tribunal (which at present only goes up to the end of November 2012), a total of 296 cases had been heard by the Tribunal since 1999, when the Constitution came into effect. In 165 of these cases, the defendants had been acquitted and only four convictions had been secured.

(b) The Criminal Code (Cap 77, Laws of the Federation of Nigeria 1990)

As Nigeria is a federal republic, each state is empowered under the Constitution to enact laws creating criminal offences. As a matter of history, states in what was Southern Nigeria (the Eastern and Western regions) enacted a Criminal Code, while those in what was Northern Nigeria have a Penal Code. This is a colonial inheritance that had its roots in the existence of the two British protectorates in the area now known as Nigeria (see 1 above). Although these protectorates were amalgamated in 1914, their criminal laws were, essentially, similar and were based on the Criminal Code of Queensland in Australia until 1960. At independence, Northern Nigeria introduced its Penal Code, which drew on the Sudanese Penal Code, which was in turn based on the Indian Penal Code. In substance, there is no significant difference between the criminal and penal codes. They operate in states that were formerly in the Western and Eastern regions of Nigeria, in the case of the Criminal Code, while the Penal Code operates in areas that were formerly in the Northern Region of Nigeria. A number of offences, the ingredients of which are essentially the same, have different appellations in the two codes and provide for different penalties. The Criminal Code is currently the basis of criminal laws in the 16 states created from the former Eastern, Western and Mid-Western regions, while the Penal Code applies in the 20 states created from what was the former Northern Region and in the federal capital territory, which is located in an area that was formerly within the Northern Region.

Under the Criminal Code, 14 offences relating to corruption and abuse of office in the public service can be found in sections 98–116. Section 98(1) punishes abuse of official duty generally, while section 98(2) penalises corruption by any person employed in the public service. In either case, the accused person is liable, if found guilty, to be sentenced to a maximum term of seven years' imprisonment.

(c) ***The Penal Code (Cap 89, Laws of Northern Nigeria 1963)***

Offences relating to public servants under the Penal Code are contained in sections 115–131. These provisions deal, in the main, with the receipt and giving of bribes (gratification) and other acts of dishonesty by public servants. The punishments provided under these sections range from fines to imprisonment for up to 14 years.

(d) ***The Corrupt Practices and Other Related Offences Act 2000 (Cap C31, Laws of the Federation of Nigeria 2004)***

The Corrupt Practices and Other Related Offences Act established the Independent Corrupt Practices Commission (ICPC), and creates offences similar in nature to those under the Criminal Code (see 2.1(b) above).

(e) ***The Money Laundering (Prohibition) Act 2011 (Act No 11 of 2011) as amended***

The Money Laundering (Prohibition) Act 2011 (the 2011 Act), as amended by the Money Laundering (Prohibition) (Amendment) Act 2012 (Act No 1 of 2012) is relevant in considering anti-corruption provisions because the offences created under the 2011 Act tend to be the ones most used by prosecutors in corruption cases. Given that grand corruption rarely occurs in the open and is frequently difficult to prove, charging defendants with money laundering offences enables prosecutions to be pursued more easily and, in theory, increases the prospects of securing convictions. The predecessor legislation was first aimed at the laundering of proceeds of the trade in prohibited drugs, but was amended after 2000 to enable prosecutions to be more broadly based.

2.2 Enforcement agencies

At present, the primary agencies charged with regulating, enforcing against and punishing corruption are:

- the Nigerian Police Force;

- the Independent Corrupt Practices Commission (ICPC);
- the Economic and Financial Crimes Commission (EFCC);
- the Code of Conduct Bureau (CCB); and
- the courts and tribunals empowered to try offences created under the legislation discussed at 2.1 above.

3. International anti-corruption treaties applicable in the country and their concrete effects in the fight against corruption

The international anti-corruption treaties applicable in Nigeria are the United Nations Convention against Corruption 2004 (UNCAC) and the African Union (AU) Convention on Preventing and Combating Corruption 2003 (AUCPCC). Nigeria signed the UNCAC on 9 December 2003 and the AUCPCC on 12 December 2003, ratifying them on 14 December 2004 and 26 September 2006 respectively.

Neither convention has yet made any significant impact on anti-corruption efforts within Nigeria. In terms of the five main areas on which the UNCAC requires Nigeria to focus – prevention, law enforcement, international cooperation, asset recovery, and technical assistance and information exchange – it is fair to say that there has been very little real progress in any of these areas. No legislation in Nigeria makes any specific reference to the UNCAC, and there do not appear to have been any international cooperation, asset recovery or technical assistance efforts in Nigeria that reference the UNCAC.

One particularly interesting development that has occurred in Nigeria that does not reference the UNCAC, but appears to be related and is likely to be of significance in combating corruption, relates to the amount of information that is being collected by (one assumes, as it is unclear in certain instances) the federal government concerning individuals and corporations. The Federal Inland Revenue Service (FIRS) is deploying the use of Tax Identification Numbers (TINs) to track financial transactions. It is understood that TINs will be shared with authorities in other countries and will be used to trace cross-border flows of money. During 2017, the government also introduced regulations related to National Identity Numbers (NIN) that must be obtained by every Nigerian citizen upon registration under the National Identity Card scheme. These NINs are required by the regulations to be used for all manner of transactions, including the opening and maintenance of bank accounts (which are already subject to Bank Verification Numbers (BVNs), the mandatory use of which was introduced in 2015) and all land transactions.

The objectives of the AUCPCC are to:

- promote and strengthen the development in Africa by each state party of mechanisms required to prevent, detect, punish and eradicate corruption and related offences in the public and private sectors;
- promote, facilitate and regulate cooperation among the state parties to ensure the effectiveness of measures and actions to prevent, detect, punish and eradicate corruption and related offences in Africa;
- coordinate and harmonise the policies and legislation between state parties for the purposes of prevention, detection, punishment and eradication of corruption on the African continent;

- promote socio-economic development by removing obstacles to the enjoyment of economic, social and cultural rights as well as civil and political rights; and
- establish the necessary conditions to foster transparency and accountability in the management of public affairs.

While the extent to which there is any coordination or harmonisation between Nigeria and other AU state parties is unclear, the steps listed above would appear to fit into efforts within Nigeria to improve the detection of corruption offences, which should aid the prosecution and punishment of offenders. These steps do not, however address the challenges posed by limited law enforcement capacity, poor judicial processes and a poor judiciary (see 1 above).

It must be acknowledged that, between 1999 and 2007, during the two terms of President Obasanjo, Nigeria made progress in reducing corruption. Following the election of President Umaru Yar'adua in 2007, however, such progress as had been made began to be reversed almost immediately. Yar'adua suffered ill health almost from the very beginning of his term and, a little over two years after he was sworn in, he became seriously incapacitated and unable to function as President. He travelled to Saudi Arabia for medical treatment in November 2009 and although he returned to Nigeria in February 2010, he never again appeared in public. He died on 5 May 2010 and the Vice President, Goodluck Jonathan, was sworn in as President. Jonathan was elected President in his own right in 2011 but lost his bid for re-election to Muhammadu Buhari in 2015. The general consensus is that such progress as had been made in the anti-corruption field between 1999 and 2007 was completely reversed by 2015 and President Buhari has had to endeavour, with limited success, to restart the fight against corruption.

Consequently, in terms of the prevention of corruption, any progress has been hard to assess. In terms of enforcement, the focus of President Buhari's administration has been, primarily, on the prosecution of allegedly corrupt politicians and their associates. This effort has brought mixed results. While there have been numerous arrests and several prosecutions (as to which, see 4 below), a combination of limited law enforcement capacity, poor judicial processes and a poor judiciary has meant that convictions have been few and far between. In addition to the focus on prosecutions, law enforcement has also made – mainly unstructured – attempts to recover assets acquired as a result of corruption. This focus has resulted in some successes. However, while the federal government trumpets that it has recovered the equivalent of almost US$3 billion since it took office in May 2015, few details of how this sum has been computed have been made available.

In the area of technical assistance and information exchange, the government appears to be laying down strong foundations. One of the first concrete steps taken towards combating corruption and money laundering by President Buhari's government upon taking office was to enter into a number of agreements with a number of countries, one of which was the United Arab Emirates. Among the agreements signed by the governments of the two countries on 19 January 2016 were agreements on extradition, the transfer of sentenced persons and mutual legal assistance in criminal, civil and commercial matters. These agreements are being used by the Nigerian government in efforts to seek the seizure and return to Nigeria of assets alleged to have been unlawfully obtained by former politicians and government officials. In addition, the government has instituted proceedings in the United Kingdom seeking the return of monies alleged to be the proceeds of corruption involving Nigerian government officials and politicians; there has been one significant success related to the proceeds of the sale of an oil mining lease that is alleged to have involved the bribery of government officials.

All these efforts, do not, however, specifically reference either the UNCAC or the AUCPCC. While these treaties may have had some relevance to them, the nature of their influence is difficult to measure.

4. Relevant corruption cases and how they have been handled and resolved

Since the Buhari government took office in 2015, there have been a number of prosecutions of politicians associated with the previous government of Goodluck Jonathan. These have included the prosecution of President Jonathan's National Security Adviser (NSA) for the alleged misuse of monies appropriated for national security purposes, such as the fight against Boko Haram insurgents in the north-eastern area of the country. It is alleged that these monies were diverted by both the NSA and senior military personnel charged with utilising the funds. The NSA is accused of having diverted some of the monies to support both President Jonathan's re-election campaign and the campaigns of his party's gubernatorial candidates. The bulk of these prosecutions were commenced in 2016 and 2017. However, the poor judicial system and poor judiciary previously referred to at 1 above have meant that none of the trials have made any significant progress and are mostly bogged down by objections raised in the trial courts as well as in the Court of Appeal. This is notwithstanding the fact that, under the Criminal Procedure Act (Cap 80, Laws of the Federation of Nigeria 1990) (the 1990 Act), technical objections are to be determined at the end of the trial, along with the issue of the guilt or innocence of the defendant. Although the Supreme Court has recently re-affirmed the provisions of the 1990 Act, it is expected that appeals against the refusal of judges to entertain objections in isolation will continue to be pursued and proceedings will continue to be stayed pending such appeals, in spite of express provisions of the act prohibiting such stays.

In addition to cases involving the former NSA, gubernatorial candidates and former armed forces service chiefs, a number of corruption cases against judges are ongoing. In one of the trials, an accused judge was acquitted without being called upon to enter a defence, the court ruling that the prosecution had not presented any evidence to support the charge against him. It is an overwhelmingly held view within the legal profession that there was more than sufficient evidence to warrant the judge being required to answer the charges against him, and the view is that the decision was improperly favourable to him.

The prosecution has appealed against that decision, but its prospects of success in that appeal appear to have been dented by a decision of the Court of Appeal in a case involving another judge, who was accused of having received money from lawyers to deliver decisions in favour of their clients. In what has been widely considered to be an extremely bizarre decision, the Court of Appeal held that serving judges could not be prosecuted for corruption unless the National Judicial Council, the body responsible for the appointment and discipline of judges, had first dealt with the allegations against a judge. The Court of Appeal consequently dismissed the charges against the judge in this case. The decision of the Court of Appeal has been appealed to the Supreme Court. However, there is concern that members of the judiciary appear too willing to deliver decisions of doubtful merit in favour of their judicial colleagues, and that this attitude might be prevalent in the Supreme Court, where a panel of at least five judges sit as a court of final appeal.

5. What needs to be modified, strengthened or addressed?

5.1 Introduction

As stated previously, Nigeria's anti-corruption legislation is, by and large, satisfactory. There may be areas where improvements can be made, but that is not where the problem with corruption in Nigeria lies at the present time.

In terms of the prevention and detection of corruption, there is a great deal already in place that enables corrupt activities to be detected.

5.2 Facilitating the detection of corruption

Firstly, the anti-money laundering legislation contains provisions that can facilitate the detection of corruption. There are restrictions on the use of cash for commercial transactions. Cash transactions above a specific and fairly low sum are prohibited, thereby requiring high value transactions to be conducted through banks. Banks are required to have biometric details of their customers – photographs and fingerprints – as well as addresses and dates of birth, and are obliged by the legislation to report suspicious transactions and transactions above a certain sum. The introduction of the NIN regulations requiring the mandatory use of NINs for a variety of transactions increases the ability of the authorities to detect illicit flows of money. However, given the nature of the allegations in charges preferred against politicians as to how monies were moved and the absence of charges against banks or bank officials, there is clearly scope for better enforcement of the reporting obligations of banks under money laundering legislation. If the allegations made against politicians are correct, then banks that were involved in the transactions that resulted in the charges preferred ought also to have been prosecuted for money laundering offences. The absence of such charges seems to be a significant lapse.

5.3 Enhancing the capacity of enforcement agencies to make proper use of available provisions

Secondly, in order to use the available provisions properly, the capacity of the enforcement agencies needs to be greatly enhanced. At present, they struggle with poor and inadequate personnel and facilities, and corruption within their ranks is rife. This needs to be addressed. Given the progress that was seen between 2000 and

2007, it is clear that this is something that can be achieved if what is frequently described as 'political will' is present. This 'political will' requires more than just the provision of adequate training for personnel and of the tools with which the agencies can better discharge their functions. It requires more of a commitment from the whole of Nigerian society to reject corruption at all levels. The discussion here is focused primarily on high level corruption rather on the day to day corruption that ordinary people encounter in their lives, such as traffic enforcement officials extorting money from vehicle operators, low level government functionaries extorting money from people wishing to do things like obtaining driving licences and even registering for NINs. As a consequence of this, there appears to be a significant level of apathy within society. The absence of any significant convictions and the imposition of any meaningful sanctions does not help. Clearly, a huge, top-down effort across society is required to address this issue.

The enforcement agencies all need to be strengthened and funded adequately to enable them to carry out their various functions. In terms of funding, since the National Assembly is charged with the duty of approving budgets for these agencies, legislators are effectively able to hamper the agencies' capacity by denying them the funds that they require. This is fairly easy to achieve, since governments never have sufficient funds. It has been contended that one of the reasons the ICPC has been unable to perform its statutory functions properly is due to underfunding. This may, in part, be responsible for the widely held perception that the performance of this agency is lacklustre at best.

The personnel (investigators and prosecutors) of the NPF, EFCC and ICPC require constant training and retraining to keep abreast of modern trends in anti-corruption investigation and changes in technology if they are to stay one step ahead in the fight against corruption. The current mode of investigation utilised by these bodies frequently amounts to little more than hauling in suspects upon the receipt of complaints, and attempting to coerce incriminatory statements from them. Little is done by way of investigating whether there is merit in the complaints in the first instance. In addition, investigations are rarely completed before the preferment of charges in court. This is usually due to the fact that the agencies are under pressure to file charges once they have taken the suspects into custody as the agencies cannot hold them without charge beyond the period stipulated by the Constitution. The resultant effect is that, more often than not, the prosecution is unable to muster the evidence required to secure convictions. This in turn leads to persons being acquitted in circumstances where a conviction could have been secured. This reinforces the general perception that there is no real desire to fight corruption and leads to the weakening of societal values of fairness, honesty, integrity and common citizenship and the erosion of citizens' sense of moral responsibility to follow the rules in the interests of the wider society.

5.4 The need to address the state of the judiciary and the judicial process

Thirdly, the judiciary and the judicial process need to be addressed. A situation in which senior members of the legal profession are accused of giving money to judges, but face no disciplinary sanctions whatsoever from the profession, should not be considered to be an acceptable situation. The recourse to notions of 'culture' to justify the giving of money to judicial officers and the couching of such things as 'traditional gifts' should not be considered to be acceptable. Judges should not, under any circumstances, accept 'gifts' of money or other things of value from legal practitioners. It does not matter that the judge is burying a parent or is celebrating the wedding of a daughter. He or she should not receive gifts from legal practitioners or litigants. If it were to be accepted that legal practitioners may give 'traditional gifts', provisions should be enacted to regulate such a practice by, for example, requiring that the 'gifts' be declared and that they may not exceed a specified amount.

5.5 Declaration of 'gifts' by politicians

Fourthly politicians must similarly declare all 'gifts' received by them. Every legislature should have a register of members' interests and rules as to what is permissible and not permissible. Given the Nigerian legislation as it currently stands, the receipt of money or anything of value by a public officer is deemed to be for an improper purpose unless the recipient proves otherwise. The receipt of 'gifts' should therefore not be proper and, even if a concession were to be made to 'culture', limits to the value of such 'gifts' need to be imposed and enforced.

5.6 Publicising asset declarations by public office holders

Finally, asset declarations that public office holders are required to make should be made public. At present, there is no such requirement. While the current President and Vice President voluntarily made their asset declarations public when they assumed office, their examples have not encouraged others to do the same; their voluntary disclosures do not appear to have been emulated by any other public officers. Secret declarations of assets made only to the CCB are of limited value, especially given the lack of capacity in the Bureau to investigate the initial accuracy of the declarations properly and to police their continued accuracy. If there were free access to information about public officers' asset declarations and to government records, then civic-minded members of the public would be able to draw the attention of the authorities to instances in which public officers have made incorrect declarations. The present freedom of information provisions (that is, the Freedom of Information Act, which was signed into law by former President Goodluck Jonathan on 28 May 2011) are inadequate and cumbersome to operate, with the result that they do not offer the access that is necessary to enable members of the public and the press to access information about public officials.

6. Conclusion

As stated previously, the laws in place to address corruption and related matters are quite robust and, if properly applied, should enable corrupt practices to be detected and perpetrators to be punished. This should, in turn, deter offenders and lead to a reduction in the level of corruption. The problem currently is that the laws are not being applied properly. The procedural laws are designed to reduce delays and enhance the expeditious resolution of cases. Unfortunately, for reasons such as weaknesses in the judiciary and the failure to sanction defence counsel who fail to adhere to the provisions of the legislation, corruption cases, like most criminal trials, take an eternity to reach a verdict. Indeed, the existence of such delays in bringing criminal cases to a conclusion supports the view that an adjournment is close to an acquittal. It is not unusual for criminal cases to take several years to pass through the courts, resulting in the loss of evidence and witnesses as a result of such delays.

Panama

Darío Sandoval Shaik
Fabrega Molino

---

1. Overview

The Republic of Panama is an isthmus located in the centre of the American continent, covering a territorial area of just under 30,000 square miles. It forms the narrow stretch of land joining North and South America.

Even before its discovery in 1501 by Christopher Columbus on his second voyage to the New World, the inhabitants of Panama based their economy mostly on the service sector; transportation and trade being the main sources of revenue.

Panama became a Spanish colony and remained so until 1821, when it attained independence from Spain. Thereafter, the isthmus became a province of Grand Colombia. In 1903, it became the present Republic of Panama.

Panama is a crossroads territory, with a ceaseless commercial bustle that has seen an intense level of arrivals and departures of locals and foreigners for many centuries. This internationally minded and open country embraces trade as part of its identity.

Today, Panama's economy continues to be based on the service sector: The main sources of the nation's gross domestic product (GDP) are the Panama Canal (which has been attracting record revenues since its recent expansion); the Colon Free Trade Zone (the second largest free trade zone in the world after Hong Kong); the financial services industry (with a dollarised monetary system but without a central bank); a banking centre integrated into the international system; commercial openness; a taxation system based on low taxes, and a range of fiscal incentives for investment.

With an estimated population of four million people, the country is a unitary presidential constitutional republic with a President and a Vice President elected by universal suffrage for a five-year term. In addition to the President and Vice President, the executive branch comprises a Cabinet appointed by the President. Presidents may not be re-elected for immediately successive terms.

The legislative branch (the National Assembly) comprises 71 congressmen who are elected by party nomination or free nomination, by direct popular vote, in circuits that guarantee representation. Its management board comprises the President and the two Vice Presidents.

The judicial branch comprises the Supreme Court of Justice as the highest judicial authority. It consists of nine justices, each appointed by the Cabinet Council for a ten-year term and taking office following confirmation by the National Assembly. There are 15 higher courts, which are distributed among four Judicial Districts, which are in turn divided into Judicial Circuits comprising Judicial Municipalities.

The legal system is based on Roman civil law and most statutes are collected in codes. Due to the close commercial relationship between Panama and the United States, there is a certain degree of influence by American law in commercial statutes, such as those concerning bills of exchange, admiralty and corporations; the last of these is regulated by Law No 32 of 26 February 1927, otherwise known as the General Corporation Law of Panama (*Ley de Sociedades Anónimas*). This is a hybrid adaptation of the corporation law of the US State of Delaware to the requirements of a civil law system such as that of Panama. Since its enactment, this statute has been subject to very few amendments; one of these is a recent custody regime applicable to the bearer shares, established with the purpose of allowing the identification of the beneficial owner of a corporation at the request of competent Panamanian authorities, either in the case of investigations under national legislation for money laundering or any illicit activity, or to comply with international agreements signed by Panama.

2. The concept of 'corruption' in Panama

Despite its outstanding business climate and sustained GDP growth, disturbing tendencies have been observed in Panama in recent years, including a perception of the weakening of governance structures. Although Transparency International placed Panama in 87th position (out of 176 countries surveyed) in its *Corruption Perceptions Index 2016*, making the country one of the best ranked in the region, corruption remains an issue of concern, particularly in the aftermath of the Odebrecht scandal.[1]

A recent report by Transparency International on corruption in Latin America[2] has found that perceptions of corruption are rising in Panama and that confidence in government and public officials is deteriorating. This worsening in corruption perceptions comes despite ongoing campaigns to crack down on wrongdoing following popular clamour over a series of high-level scandals. With these campaigns as yet appearing to have limited impact on public sentiment, the fight against corruption will be a key issue heading into the busy 2019 election year.

In *People and Corruption: Latin America and the Caribbean*, which collates the latest regional results of Transparency International's *Global Corruption Barometer* survey, many people expressed worry about the level of corruption in the country and the survey results revealed a not so positive outlook: 52% of people questioned believed that corruption had risen in Panama in the preceding 12 months.

Citizens were very critical of government efforts to fight corruption: 57% said that the government was doing a bad job at this.

With regard to their experiences of corruption, bribery was a common experience for 38% of people questioned, who said they had to pay a bribe, give a gift or provide a favour in the 12 months prior to the survey in order to obtain access to basic public services.[3] The six key basic services included in the survey, and the percentages of corruption reported in relation to them, were:

---

1 Which is currently pending final judgment in Panama.

2 Transparency International: *People and Corruption: Latin America and the Caribbean (Global Corruption Barometer*, October, 2017).

3 Q: "How often, if ever, did you have to pay a bribe, give a gift or provide a favour for: a teacher or school official; a health worker or clinic or hospital staff; a government official in order to get a document, a government official in order to receive utilities services; a police officer, or a judge or court official?"

- public health care services (including urgent lifesaving treatments): 21–30%;
- public education: 21–30%;
- delivery of identity documents: 11–20%;
- policing (to avoid arrest or a fine): 11–20%;
- utilities: 11–20%; and
- courts: 11–20%.

In Panama, 64% of citizens agreed that it was socially acceptable to report corruption. In other words, there is no social stigma in the country against people coming forward to report corruption. However, while reporting corruption was in theory seen as socially acceptable, in practice few people actually reported corruption when they experienced it.

The survey then posed a final and key question. Panamanians were asked whether they thought ordinary people could make a difference in the fight against corruption. A large majority of citizens said that they were hopeful about the positive role citizens could play in tackling graft: 68% agreed that ordinary people could make a difference.

Panama is due to hold presidential elections in May 2019, and corruption issues will play a major role in the election campaign, contributing to increased uncertainty over the outcome. In this environment, the electoral picture currently remains unclear, just a year and a half ahead of the polls.

There is no unique legal concept of 'corruption' in Panama with regard to the use of powers by government officials for illegitimate private gain. Instead, there are several forms of corruption, which are classified under the laws summarised below.

- Law No 33 of 25 April 2013, which creates the National Authority of Transparency and Access to Information. Numeral 10, article 6 of this law provides:

  actions that may be considered acts of corruption, such as…public servants without specific functions assigned, overpricing in purchases and provision of goods or services, duplicity of functions, excess of bureaucratic processes and other behaviors, not restricted to the aforementioned, that affect the good progress of the public service and cause unnecessary expenditures to the treasury…
- By contrast, Executive Order No 246 of 15 December 2004, which provides for a Uniform Code of Ethics of Public Servants who work in the entities of the Central Government, lays down general principles according to which public servants must act, strictly to avoid involvement in corruption, such as probity, prudence, justice, temperance, suitability, responsibility, transparency, equality, respect and leadership. At the same time, it defines particular principles such as aptitude, training, legality, evaluation, truthfulness, obedience, discretion, obligation to report, and the obligation to submit an affidavit for the cases specified in article 304 of the Constitution of Panama (among others).
- The Criminal Code classifies several forms of conduct perpetrated by officeholders as types of corruption, such as bribery, extortion, unjustified

enrichment, influence peddling, graft, embezzlement, and facilitating a criminal enterprise (such as drug trafficking, money laundering and human trafficking, among others).

3. Multilateral anti-corruption treaties ratified by Panama

3.1 List of agreements

The following list reflects the legally binding international anti-corruption agreements ratified by Panama.

- The United Nations (UN) Convention against Corruption (UNCAC). Adopted by the UN General Assembly on 31 October 2003. Signed by Panama in Mérida, Yucatán, Mexico on 9 December 2003. Ratified in Panama by Law No 15 of 10 May 2005.
- The Inter-American Convention against Corruption (IACAC). Adopted by the member countries of the Organization of American States on 29 March 1996. Signed by Panama 29 March 1996. Ratified by Law No 42 of 1 July 1998.

3.2 The concrete effect of these agreements in the fight against corruption

Little evidence exists on whether these international agreements have had a direct impact on levels of corruption or whether they have contributed towards stemming it. This may be explained in part by the fact that these phenomena are, in and of themselves, difficult to measure. While it may not be possible to attribute direct impact as a result of these treaties, they have resulted in a number of positive related developments.

These multilateral initiatives have become transmission mechanisms that have entrenched international norms, including anti-corruption norms, in Panamanian domestic jurisdiction as well as in developed countries. Multilateral agreements have a substantial impact on the development and codification of anti-corruption norms at the national level.

These agreements also serve as a basis for development partners to engage with partner countries to promote global standards on combating corruption, as well as to provide technical support to this end. However, the impact of these agreements on compliance with anti-corruption measures and policies in developing countries such as Panama generally appears to be limited.

4. Laws and regulations and the authorities responsible for regulating, enforcing against and punishing corruption

4.1 Laws and regulations

- the Constitution of the Republic of Panama (1972, as amended);
- Unified Text of the Criminal Code (made under Law No 14 of 18 May 2007, as amended);
- the Code of Criminal Procedure (made under Law No 63 of 28 August 2008, as amended);
- Law No 19 of 19 July 2001, which modifies and adds provisions to the

Criminal Code and the Code of Criminal Procedure and lays down rules for the prevention of corruption;

- Law No 6 of 22 January 2002, which (among other things) lays down norms for transparency in public management and establishes the action of *habeas data*;[4]
- Law No 33 of 25 April 2013, which creates the National Authority of Transparency and Access to Information;
- Executive Order No 13 of 24 January 1991, which lays down Ethical Principles of Public Servants;
- Executive Order No 246 of 15 December 2004, which lays down a Uniform Code of Ethics of Public Servants who work in the entities of the Central Government;
- Law No 23 of 27 April 2015, otherwise generally known as the anti-money laundering law;
- Executive Order No 363 of 13 August 2015, otherwise generally known as the anti-money laundering regulation;
- Law No 15 of 10 May 2005, which ratified the UNCAC;
- Law No 42 of 1 July 1998, which ratified the IACAC;
- Law No 32 of 8 November 1984, otherwise generally known as the General Comptroller of the Republic law;
- Law No 38 of 31 July 2000 on General Administrative Procedure.

4.2 Authorities responsible for anti-corruption rules

- the National Assembly (lawmaking);
- the President of the Republic with the participation of relevant ministers (regulation-making).

4.3 Authorities responsible for enforcing against and punishing corruption

- the National Authority of Transparency and Access to Information;[5]
- special anti-corruption prosecutors;
- Circuit courts;[6]

---

4 Every person is entitled to bring an action for *habeas data* in order to guarantee the right of access to the information provided for by Law No 6 of 22 January 2002. The right of action arises where a public official who is responsible for registration, a file or databank in which the information or personal information claimed is found, has not supplied the requested information of has provided it insufficiently or inaccurately.

5 The National Authority of Transparency and Access to Information has, among others, powers to: (1) require institutions to respond to requests for access to information in a timely manner; (2) require public entities to design corruption combating and control programmes and to verify compliance with the objectives of those programmes; (3) advise the Executive branch on the establishment of public policies to fight corruption that guarantee efficient, effective and transparent public management; (4) address complaints and situations that affect the right to petition, the right of access to public information, transparency, ethics and the fight against corruption; and (5) bring before the relevant institution(s) instances where people have been prevented from fully exercising their rights, with a view to correcting such instances and imposing fines on the perpetrators, in accordance with Law No 33 of 25 April 2013.

6 Now called Courts of Judgment, pursuant to amendments to the Code of Criminal Procedure. These courts are collegiate and exercise jurisdiction over alleged offences that attract imprisonment for periods exceeding one year.

- the National Assembly (in the exercise of jurisdiction and powers over crimes committed by the President of the Republic (though not the Vice President) or Supreme Court justices);
- The Supreme Court of Justice (with regard to crimes committed by ministers of the Cabinet, the Attorney General, the Attorney General for Administration, congressmen, police commanders and the General Comptroller of the Republic, among other officers).

5. Relevant public cases

The *Moncada* affair: In October 2014, a criminal complaint made by the National Bar Association and backed by several civil society organisations was filed before the National Assembly against the then justice of the Supreme Court Alejandro Moncada for alleged corruption felonies. The complaint sought to persuade the assembly to investigate Moncada for the alleged commission of the crimes of graft, unjustified enrichment, money laundering and falsification of public documents.

After the criminal complaint was delivered to the General Secretariat of the National Assembly, it was sent to the assembly's Credentials Committee. A sub-committee of three congresswomen (Ana Matilde Gómez, Zulay Rodríguez and Katleen Levy) was appointed to handle the case as a judicial panel, and a single congressman (Pedro Miguel González) was appointed as prosecutor in the case.

Two weeks later, and following a preliminary hearing, the prosecution continued and resulted in the judicial panel making the following orders:

- removal of Justice Moncada from office;
- a ban on the defendant leaving the country;
- home confinement of the defendant; and
- seizure of bank accounts and two apartments located in an exclusive neighbourhood, all of which were related to the investigation.

Justice Moncada subsequently reached a plea agreement with the prosecutor and disclosed it. The defendant pleaded guilty to unjustified enrichment and falsification of public documents, while the prosecutor recommended a five-year prison sentence and moved to dismiss the other charges. In March 2015 the judicial panel accepted the plea agreement and imposed the recommended sentence. Mr Moncada served most of his sentence at the *El Renacer* Penitentiary. In the writer's opinion, the former justice deserved a more severe punishment.

6. Next steps

The following issues need to be addressed in order to reduce political corruption.

- Government should streamline bureaucratic procedures to avoid lengthy and discretionary decision-making processes.
- Government should invest in e-government platforms (and improve the current ones) to enable applications for services to be made without face-to-face interactions with public officials.

- Government should involve civil society as part of the effort to fight corruption. This would increase the credibility of these efforts.
- Government should invest in measures to strengthen access to justice and the rule of law by ensuring an objective and transparent process for appointing Supreme Court justices and judges and implementing protections for judicial salaries and working conditions.
- Government should strengthen the institutions involved in the detection, investigation and prosecution of corruption-related crimes.

Despite the challenges discussed in this chapter, many citizens stand ready and willing to join the fight against corruption. Engaging them in the anti-corruption movement and sustaining their enthusiasm must be the priority for governments and civil society organisations working to wipe out the scourge of corruption.

A strong, clean and transparent judicial system will be vital for sustaining this public engagement, as people wish to see public officials receive due punishment for any crimes committed. Without this, citizens will become further disillusioned with the governance system in Panama and this positive energy for change will be lost for an entire generation.

Peru

César Guzmán-Barrón
Lawyer in management of social conflicts, compliance and arbitration

---

The world is a dangerous place to live; not because of the people who are evil, but because of the people who don't do anything about it.
(Albert Einstein)

1. Overview of the country *vis-à-vis* corruption matters

1.1 Corruption in the history of Peru

The Peruvian historian Alfonso Quiroz in his work, *History of corruption in Peru*, whose analysis ranges from the establishment of the colony in 1750 to 2012, states that corruption has not been sporadic but rather has been systematic, rooted in the structures of the society. This analysis shows that there is a connection between frustrated economic development and levels of corruption. Likewise, the economic and institutional costs generated by corruption affect an impoverished population, having a strong impact on the governability, politics and development of the country.[1]

When analysing the main periods and cycles of corruption, Quiroz highlights the colonial period as:

> *the colonial roots of the systematic administrative corruption of the patrimonial vice royal courts, backed by a retinue of patronage that is benefited with monopolies, privileges and official positions purchased. The corrupt colonial practices favored the abuse and exploitation of indigenous people, the neglect of the administration of the mines and the widespread contraband ...*[2]

Such conduct of corruption continued following the independence of Peru from Spain. This featured:

> *the domination of the caudillos through networks of patronage that allowed the dispossession and expropriation of private property and the so-called patriotic 'looting', a venal diplomacy and an entrenched contraband, aspects that undermined the New Republic.*[3]

This situation continued, but more so, in the 'guano era', during which corrupt ties between the then rulers and a number of foreign interests contributed to extensive corrosion. This was one of the causes of the disastrous War of the Pacific (1879–1883).

---

1. Alfonso W Quiroz, *History of corruption in Peru* (2013, Lima: *Instituto de Estudios Peruanos*), pp25–29.
2. *Op cit*, p40. Author's free translation throughout all references.
3. *Op cit*, p25.

In the 20th century came governments like that of President Augusto B Leguía, which used controls or means that facilitated corruption. In later years there also emerged electoral pacts that were contrary to the public interest. As pointed out by Quiroz, the governments of the period 1963 to 1989 were involved in cases of corruption. There then followed the complex corruption of the regime of President Alberto Fujimori that would end with the former president being imprisoned following judicial process. Later governments, far from avoiding corruption, regrettably engaged in it, to the point that two of the most recent presidents are currently subjected to judicial proceedings deriving from acts of corruption, particularly with regard to public works contracts.

Over the years, this situation has led (as will be discussed in 2 below) to a perception that corruption has existed and exists as part of everyday life in Peru, resulting in both moral damage to the population in general and high economic costs affecting poverty in a country that has so many natural resources. Regarding the high cost of corruption, according to calculations made by Quiroz, between 1820 and 2000, successive waves of corruption:

> *could have involved the diversion or misallocations of funds equivalent to an average [of] between 30 and 40 percent of the government expenditures, and between 3 and 4 percent of the gross domestic product. These losses would represent between 40 and 50 percent of the country's development possibilities in the long term (considering that for this to take place, a sustained growth of between 5 and 8 percent of GDP must be achieved).*[4]

2. Public perceptions of corruption

2.1 Public opinion on the incidence of corruption

Given this framework of systematic corruption in Peru, there is an increasing perception by the population that it is the biggest of the major problems that the country faces.

Commissioned by Proética (the Peruvian chapter of Transparency International) since 2002, Ipsos Peru has been surveying public opinion about perceptions of corruption in the country. Men and women aged 18 years and over, from all socio-economic levels and resident in the main cities, were surveyed. The main results of the *Tenth National Survey on Perceptions of Corruption* (September 2017) (the Proetica study) show that, over the last year, the perception of corruption as a national problem has increased, along with increased crime. These problems are the two main concerns of citizens, with corruption being placed first, even among those surveyed in the interior of the country.

The results also revealed that the main problem facing the state is the corruption of officials and authorities, which impacts upon the confidence of citizens toward the state and reduces employment opportunities.

According to the Proetica study, the majority of the population are well informed about corruption issues that happen in the country, so the general perception is that

4 *Op cit*, pp425–426.

this problem has not improved in recent years and that there will not be many improvements over the next five years. There is a great distrust of the judiciary, leading to pressure for penalties and sanctions for corruption to be increased and the Peruvian judicial system reformed.

Likewise, so-called 'micro-corruption' is seen as a problem, such as paying bribes to avoid a fine, speeding up procedures or hacking public services. However, two out of three respondents to the Protetica study do not consider these actions as negative, which is one of the negative consequences of perceiving a high index of corruption on the part of the rulers. Among those who claim to have paid some kind of bribe to an authority or to receive a service, one of the main reasons for the perception of micro-corruption is that, if one does not pay, things do not work. Likewise, a high proportion of people consider that making these types of payment is an acceptable habit.

On the other hand, according to the Proetica survey, one-third of respondents consider that the government of President Alan García is one of the most corrupt, followed by Alberto Fujimori and Ollanta Humala. Conversely, 75% of respondents describe the efforts of President Pedro Pablo Kuczynski's government in the fight against corruption as ineffective. The judiciary is considered the most corrupt institution in the country, followed by Congress and the Peruvian National Police Force. However, the study also highlights that the perception of corruption in the police has been reduced since 2015.

People view the bureaucracy as one of the factors that encourages entrepreneurs to offer bribes; however, the majority also identify entrepreneurs as accomplices in the corruption of officials who engage in such transactions. For almost all survey respondents, informality in dealings is seen as negative for the country. Among those who do not consider it negative, 23% believe that less corruption is generated.

For 68% of survey respondents, organised crime has deeply infiltrated politics. This occurs mainly through the financing of political campaigns with illicit money. Conversely, responses show that the rejection of corruption in politics has increased by comparison with 2013; however, the public would still tolerate not sanctioning public officials who are seen as working for the benefit of the population.

The results of the 2017 Proetica survey are set out in figures 1 and 2 on the next page.

Furthermore, the high incidence of corruption has impacted upon the economy and reduced confidence in the state. This is demonstrated by figure 3 on the next page.

Respondents observe that, without corruption, the economy of the country would improve and there would be greater confidence in the state. Thus, facing corruption is fundamental, as figure 4 shows.

Figure 1. Perception of corruption

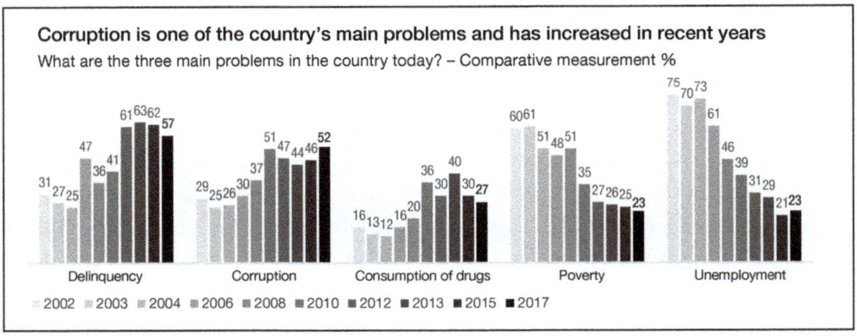

Source: www.proetica.org.pe/contenido/encuesta-nacional-sobre-percepciones-de-la-corrupcion-en-el-peru/.

Figure 2. Perception of corruption

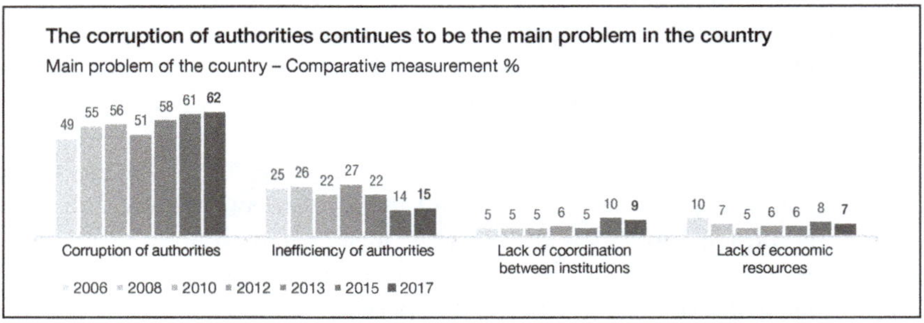

Source: www.proetica.org.pe/contenido/encuesta-nacional-sobre-percepciones-de-la-corrupcion-en-el-peru/.

Figure 3. Perception of corruption

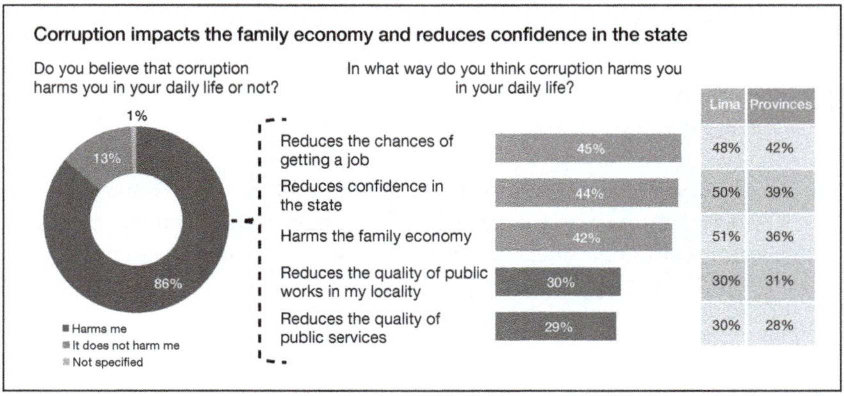

Source: www.proetica.org.pe/contenido/encuesta-nacional-sobre-percepciones-de-la-corrupcion-en-el-peru/.

Figure 4. Corruption in politics

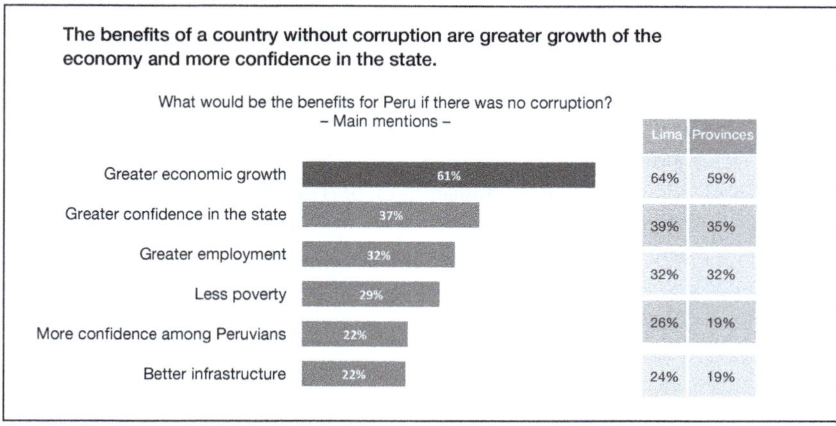

Source: www.proetica.org.pe/contenido/encuesta-nacional-sobre-percepciones-de-la-corrupcion-en-el-peru/.

2.2 Causes and effects of corruption in Peru

According to the following chart prepared by Transparency International, Peru is ranked 101 out of 137 countries surveyed worldwide for levels of corruption.

Figure 5. Ranking of the most corrupt countries in the world

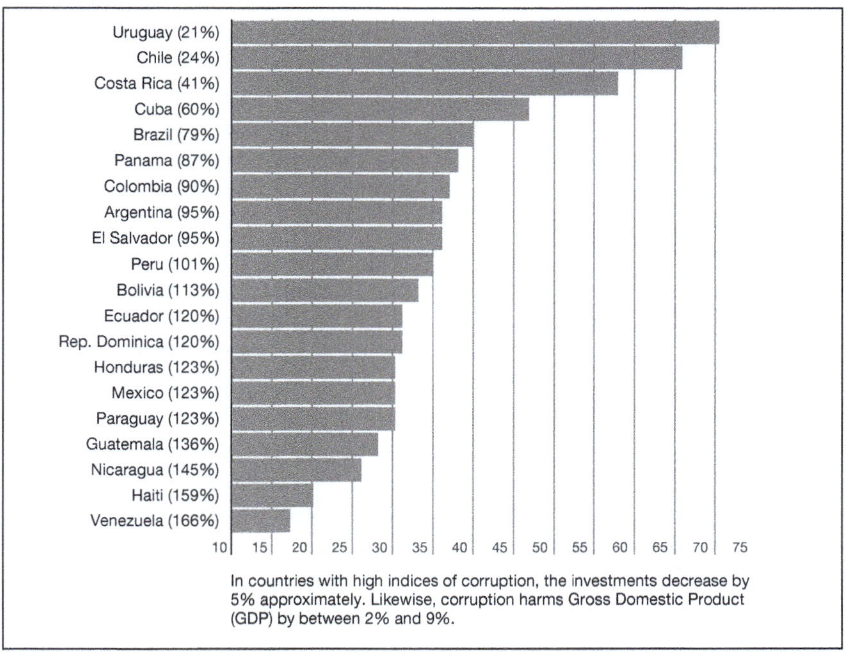

Source: Transparency International, www.transparencyinternational.org.

Further, the main causes of corruption in Peru are set out in the National Anti-Corruption Policy, a document approved by Supreme Decree DS 092-PCM-2017 of 14 September 2017. This document contains the results of an analysis of corruption and makes the following findings.

- *Too little coordination between entities responsible for preventing, controlling and investigating corruption.* It is recognised that although some important landmarks have been established, such as the creation of the High Level Anticorruption Commission, it is necessary to strengthen this area and achieve deeper interrelationships with regard to more specific and concrete activities.

  The findings affirm that corruption networks are complex and present at all levels of government and that, in order to face them, the state must propose strategic improvements.
- *Information gaps and uneven and non-standardised information on corruption.* The existence of asymmetries in mechanisms to design, implement, monitor and evaluate policies, plans, programmes and projects to prevent, control and sanction corruption hinders the articulation of functional responsibility between public entities.
- *Limited scope of anti-corruption actions at the regional or local level.* This causes difficulties when establishing mechanisms that attack medium- and small-sized corruption in regional and local areas, thus limiting preventive action and punishment.
- *Insufficient capacity of the mechanisms for early detection (prevention).* The role of prevention is to prevent corrupt agreements from materialising, thus avoiding the economic, political and social consequences that these entail.

  The persistence of acts of corruption, despite initiatives in terms of control mechanisms, transparency, access to information and the strengthening of ethics reveal the limited capacity of the state in this matter.
- *Scarce mechanisms to improve the state's capacity to sanction corruption.* Improving the state's capacity to punish corruption does not have as its central axis the norms necessary to increase sanctions or penalties in the face of acts of corruption. On the contrary, the probability of obtaining a sanctioning resolution or a condemnatory sentence from actors whose powers are to investigate and punish corruption is low.
- *Lack of leadership oriented to the fulfilment of responsibilities.* It often happens that public officials responsible for decision-making in public entities prioritise regulatory compliance over the proper fulfilment of their responsibilities, thus failing to make decisions aimed at managing problems.
- *Little recognition of ethical principles and moral values.* This is reflected in the levels of tolerance shown by the population towards acts of corruption. In its Ninth Survey (2015), Proética observed that only 22% of respondents showed a definitive rejection of acts of corruption, while 70% of them fell within the group called 'medium tolerance', that is, those who are indifferent to acts of corruption.

The same document summarises the effects of corruption in Peru as follows.

- *Effect on human rights.* Since 2013, the UN, through its Office of the High Commissioner for Human Rights, has recognised the negative relationship that corruption produces with the enjoyment of human rights. This relationship occurs at an individual level, at a collective level and within society in general. In the first case, it is linked to discriminatory access to public services, to the detriment of the principle of non-discrimination by generating undue advantages and preferential access. In the second case, corruption affects specific groups of people, especially vulnerable or at-risk populations. In the third case, it and affects society by violating democratic principles and the rule of law, cracking the confidence of the population in the government.
- *Diversion of crucial resources for development.* This reduces the availability of financial resources to meet citizens' demands for the irregular benefit of a few. The calculations made by the Comptroller General of the Republic of Peru estimate losses linked to acts of corruption to be equivalent to 10% of GDP, or $3 billion per year.

  Given, however, that corruption is characterised as a surreptitious activity, it is important to bear in mind that these figures are only approximations to the real amounts.
- *Distrust in institutions, loss of confidence in the system of rules and institutions of a democracy.* Such distrust and loss of confidence close the vicious circle of corruption, thus promoting and encouraging the emergence of opportunistic behaviours that preclude compliance with the formal rules established for good co-existence. In this scenario of tension and confrontation between different groups, it becomes of little importance to reform the institutions, thus generating a vicious cycle making the formulation, implementation and evaluation of public policies difficult.

3. The concept of 'corruption' in Peru

There are many definitions of 'corruption' that are arise in the public, academic and legal spheres.

The *Defensoría del Pueblo* (Office of the Public Defender) defines 'corruption' as the misuse of public power, which is understood as a breach of both the principles of good governance and the ethical precepts present in society. Acts of corruption have the purpose of obtaining undue advantages or benefits for the person acting in a corrupt capacity or for third parties, to the detriment of the general welfare.

According to Transparency International, 'corruption' is defined as the abuse of public power for private benefit.

The broadest definition is, however, that given in Peru's National Anticorruption Plan (see 2.1 above), which defines 'corruption' as:

The misuse of public or private power to obtain an undue benefit; economic, non-economic or advantage; direct or indirect; by public, private or citizen agents; violating ethical principles and duties, norms and fundamental rights.

In turn, Quiroz understands 'corruption' to mean the misuse of bureaucratic political power by cliques of officials, in collusion with petty private interests, in order to obtain economic or political advantages contrary to the goals of social development through the misappropriation or diversion of public resources, together with the distortion of policies and institutions. Corruption is, in fact, a broad and varied phenomenon that includes public and private activities. It encompasses undue favouring, the receipt of bribes, the misappropriation and misallocation of funds and public expenditure, electoral fraud (such as the illegal financing of political parties in return for securing undue favours) that awaken a reactive perception in the public.[5]

4. International anti-corruption treaties applicable to Peru and their concrete effects in the fight against corruption.

4.1 The United Nations Convention against Corruption (2003) (UNCAC)

The UNCAC, approved in 2003 and in force in Peru since 2005, is the most comprehensive global instrument in the fight against corruption. Currently, it has been signed by 140 states, of which more than half have ratified it. Peru was a promoter of this convention and has participated in the Pilot Program to Review the Implementation of UNCAC.

The norms established by, for example, article 29, which prescribes the crimes to which the UNCAC applies, have been taken into account in provisions recently issued for this purpose (and which are discussed below). This is particularly important given that the convention requires limitation periods to be adequate to allow the effective sanctioning of acts of corruption, and so to avoid a hitherto frequent occurrence in Peru, viz, the impunity from these criminal offences due to expiration of a time prescription.

Another aspect considered in recent legislation is that a person sanctioned and convicted of acts of corruption may return to the public service, which is consistent with that established in article 7 of the UNCAC.

Undoubtedly, the UNCAC is very useful to the Congress of the Republic, even in respect of modifications that would broaden the concept of 'public official' and additional measures that can be adopted in a code of conduct adopted in accordance with article 8 of the convention.

4.2 The Inter-American Convention against Corruption (1996) (Organization of American States)

Since 1997, Peru has been a party to the OAS Inter-American Convention against Corruption, which has also been useful by virtue of its regulations and reports regarding the specific case of 'imprescriptibility' of crimes against public property and the disqualification of public officials generally referred to as 'civil death'.

---

5 *Op cit*, p30.

5. Laws and regulations applicable to anti-corruption and the authorities that are responsible for regulating, enforcing against and punishing corruption

5.1 Laws and regulations

The adaptation of legislation in criminal matters to international standards has been carried out, in particular with regard to the international treaties to which Peru is a party (see 4 above). The main adjustments made to Peruvian anti-corruption law as a consequence include the following.

- The amendment of article 2 of the Penal Code by virtue of Law No 30076 of 19 August 2013, which introduced the penalty of 'confiscation of value', thus allowing a value equivalent to that of the proceeds of crime to be confiscated.
- The penalty of a fine was established for civil servants who commit crimes of corruption, by virtue of Law No 30111 of 26 November 2013.
- By virtue of Law No 30424 of 20 April 2016, the administrative liability of legal persons was established for the crime of transnational active bribery. Subsequently, on 7 January 2017, Legislative Decree 1352 extended the administrative responsibility of legal entities to crimes of generic active bribery, specific active bribery, money laundering, illegal mining and organised crime.

Additionally, through Supreme Decree No 092-2017-PCM of 13 September 2017 (see 2.1 above), the National Policy on Integrity and the Fight against Corruption was approved. This is of mandatory application to all entities of the state, autonomous constitutional bodies and the different levels of government, all of which must adapt their normative frameworks to this norm.

The National Policy on Integrity and the Fight against Corruption is also of mandatory application to the private sector and to civil society in a number of respects; where it is not so applicable, it serves as a guide or a guidance instrument.

In addition to the extraordinary powers granted by the legislature, the executive branch has issued a number of Legislative Decrees.

- Legislative Decree 1243 of 22 November 2016, which amends the Criminal Code and the Code of Criminal Enforcement in order to establish and extend the term of the penalty of principal disqualification, to impose a penalty of perpetual disqualification for crimes committed against the public administration, and to create a Unified Registry of Disqualified Persons.
- Legislative Decree 1265 of 16 December 2016, which creates the National Registry of Lawyers sanctioned for professional malpractice.
- Legislative Decree 1279 of 28 December 2016, which establishes a duty to register kinship and other links derived from the inscriptions carried out by the National Registry of Identification and Civil Status aimed at contributing to the effectiveness of the fight against the corruption.
- Legislative Decree 1291 of 29 December 2016, which approves tools for the fight against corruption in the interior sector.
- Legislative Decree 1295 of 30 December 2016, which modifies article 242 of

Law 27444 of 20 March 2017 (the General Administrative Procedure Law), which lays down provisions to guarantee integrity in public administration.
- Legislative Decree 1307 of 30 December 2016, which modifies the Criminal Procedure Code to provide effective measures to prosecute and punish the offences of corruption of officials and organised crime.
- Legislative Decree 1326 of 5 January 2017, which restructures the administrative system for legal defence of the state and creates the State Attorney General's Office.
- Legislative Decree 1327 of 6 January 2017, which establishes protection measures for whistleblowers and penalises whistleblower complaints made in bad faith.
- Legislative Decree 1353 of 7 January 2017, which creates the National Transparency Authority and a right of access to public information, strengthens the personal data protection regime and strengthens the regulation of interest management.

5.2 Competent authorities

A large number of public bodies are involved in different ways in investigating, enforcing against and punishing acts of corruption.

- The High Anticorruption Commission is responsible for monitoring and evaluating the National Policy on Integrity and the Fight against Corruption and the National Plan for Integrity and the Fight against Corruption.
- The Regional Anti-Corruption Commissions, which, within their jurisdictions, collaborate with and support the General Coordination of the High Anticorruption Commission in monitoring and evaluating the National Policy on Integrity and the Fight against Corruption.
- The Office of the Ombudsman (or Public Defender) is responsible for defending the constitutional and fundamental rights of the person and the community, supervising the fulfilment of the duties of the state administration and the efficient provision of public services to citizens. It investigates, on its own initiative or at the request of interested persons, facts or situations arising in the public administration that could be irregular; prepares reports on issues of the competence of officials (the so-called 'defensorial' reports); supervises compliance with the duties of the state administration; intervenes in constitutional processes in order to defend human rights and the principle of constitutional supremacy; and promotes the signing, ratification, adhesion to and dissemination of information on international human rights treaties.
- Ministries, which are responsible for coordinating the execution and supervision of policies and plans at the national level; efficient management; the promotion and protection of rights; the prevention of corruption; the promotion of public integrity in their sectors, and the cooption of citizens in watching over the good use of the resources allocated to the provision of services that correspond to them.

  Ministries are likewise responsible for coordinating administrative investigations into alleged acts of corruption, developing good practices in the prevention and punishment of corruption within their respective entities, and pursuing allegations of corruption against civil servants.

- The Congress of the Republic is responsible for legislating on corruption, overseeing the actions of the main public authorities and exercising political control. In this regard, it carries out investigations into the acts of the administration and the state authorities and exercises control over the use and disposition of public goods and resources.

  The Congress is also in charge of overseeing the functional performance of the Comptroller General of the Republic, the Office of the Ombudsman and members of the executive branch.
- The Constitutional Court, which is responsible for hearing, in a single instance, actions for unconstitutionality, and hearing, in the final instance, appeals against decisions denying *habeas corpus* and decisions involving injunctions, *habeas data* and compliance that may result from proceedings brought in the judiciary about corruption.
- The Specialised Attorney in Anticorruption Crimes, who is responsible for intervening in preliminary investigations, preparatory investigations and judicial proceedings concerning the commission of the criminal acts covered by sections II, III and IV of Chapter II of Title XVIII of the Second Book of the Criminal Code, as a consequence of a complaint by a party, a news item or intervention by a public ministry.
- Legal defence of the state in proceedings for corruption offences, which has responsibility for assisting in the clarification of the acts constituting corruption offences as well as evaluating and requiring payment of civil compensation from those responsible for such offences.
- The Supervisory Body for Contracting of the State (OSCE), which is responsible for promoting compliance with the contracting regulations of the state, promoting best practices in both the procurement processes for goods and services and the execution of works, carrying out actions of *ex officio* supervision in a random and/or selective manner with regard to the contracting methods contemplated by the law and carrying out supervisory actions at the request of a party.
- The National Council of the Judiciary, which appoints judges and prosecutors at all levels on their merits and personal evaluation through public competition, and ratifies the reappointments of judges and prosecutors at all levels every seven years. It may also apply the sanction of dismissal to members of the Supreme Court and to Supreme Prosecutors and, at the request of the Supreme Court or the Board of Supreme Prosecutors, as the case may be, to judges and prosecutors at all instances.
- The Financial Intelligence Unit, which is responsible for requesting, receiving and analysing information about suspicious transactions submitted by obligated persons; analysing the transaction registers; requesting obligated persons to provide information relevant to the prevention and analysis of money laundering or of assets; informing the public prosecutor about those

transactions that, after investigation and analysis, are presumed to be linked to money or asset laundering activities; analysing reports of suspicious operations of money laundering linked to alleged acts of corruption; promoting the implementation of systems to prevent and detect suspicious operations of money laundering related to alleged acts of corruption; participating in joint investigations; and providing technical assistance to detect and expose the commission of corruption offences, such as money laundering.

5.3 Organisations and civil society authorities

Civil society actors from the following fields are members of the High Anticorruption Commission:

- the Association of Universities of Peru;
- the National Council for Public Ethics (Proetica);
- the National Confederation of Private Business Institutions (CONFIEP);
- the National Society of Industries (SIN); and
- the Chamber of Commerce of Lima (CCL).

Furthermore, it should be noted that CONFIEP has constituted a Private Anticorruption Council.

6. Relevant public cases and how they have been handled and resolved.

6.1 The *Fujimori* and *Montesinos* cases

During the government of President Alberto Fujimori (1990–2000), a secret police and military group was formed to:

> *capture and manipulate the State, as well as perpetrate abuses of human rights. At the center of the covert mechanisms of political control, repression, manipulation and corruption was the National Intelligence Service (SIN) headed by [Vladimiro] Montesinos. The hoarding of secret funds for bribes in the SIN derived from bribes in military acquisitions; the embezzlement of military pension funds; the quotas for drug trafficking; and the assistance given to foreign and local private pressure groups, among many other mechanisms of corruption, was used to finance influence peddling and bribery in practically all areas of the State.*[6]

As mentioned by Quiroz:

> *From the immense amount of evidence contained in approximately 2300 videos, analyzed and transcribed by parliamentary committees formed during the Government of Valentín Paniagua, by July 2003 approximately 1250 people had been processed and more than 225 million dollars in Secret bank accounts had been confiscated. In September 2002 Montesinos was put on trial for more than fifty charges. He has been found guilty of more than thirty charges, having received jail sentences for up to 25 years. While the trial against Fujimori for the charges of human rights violations, corruption and criminal conspiracy began in December 2007, after a prolonged extradition process*

6 *Op cit*, p399.

in Japan and Chile ... finally the Peruvian judicial system was able to condemn Fujimori in a series of trials imposing prison sentences for up to twenty-five years.[7]

6.2 The *Odebrecht* case

Figure 6 shows a range of payments for bribes made by the Brazilian Odebrecht company in several Latin American countries and the amount in millions of dollars they represent, including Peru with a total of $29 million.

Figure 6. Payment of bribes by Odebrecht

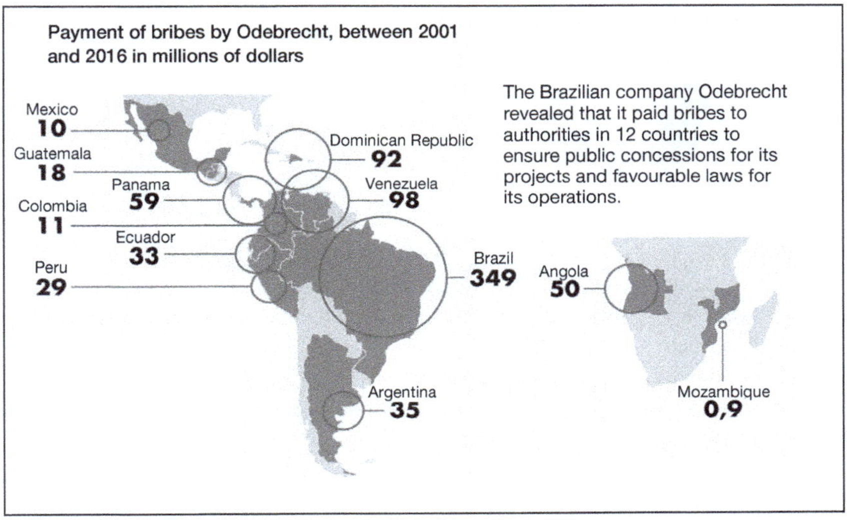

Source: www.proetica.org.pe/contenido/encuesta-nacional-sobre-percepciones-de-la-corrupcion-en-el-peru/.

In Peru, Odebrecht has been engaged in judicial proceedings that have involved or continue to involve ex-presidents, regional governors, ex-ministers and officials of the last three governments for having received bribes in exchange for public concessions.

According to the US Department of Justice, between 2005 and 2014, Odebrecht paid approximately $29 million dollars to Peruvian government officials to secure public works contracts.

The IIRSA case has indicated an approximate amount of $4,600 million in cost overruns for the contracted works. In these works there were 42 arbitrations, of which Odebrecht won 35, while the state won seven. Odebrecht won more than $250 million from these proceedings.

In a very complex case called the *Lava Jato* case, particularly in relation to several processes during the investigation stage, it will be essential to follow up and then determine how they were handled and resolved. It is worth noting the impact that

7 *Op cit*, pp418–419.

this case has generated among the Peruvian population. The following table is from the 2017 Proética population perception survey.

Figure 7. The current context

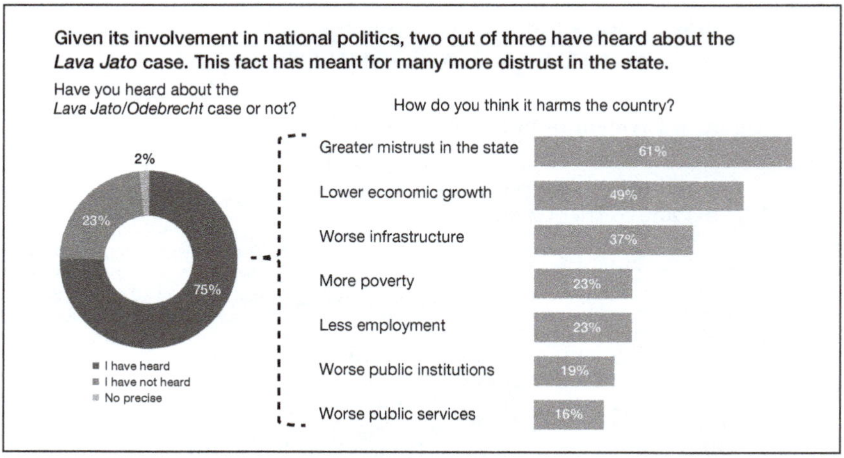

Source: www.proetica.org.pe/contenido/encuesta-nacional-sobre-percepciones-de-la-corrupcion-en-el-peru/.

7. Next steps: comments on what needs to be modified, strengthened or addressed

7.1 What the government proposes

First of all, it is important to highlight the recognition of the current government pursuant to the National Anticorruption Plan of the causes and effects of corruption that are highlighted in section 2.2. The plan suggests a series of measures that should be adopted.

- Generate mechanisms that allow the submission of sworn statements for the prevention of conflicts of interest.
- Continue with the processes of legislative adaptation to the parameters set by international instruments on integrity and the fight against corruption.
- Carry out further studies on the impact and effectiveness of existing state penalties.
- Deepen and optimise the protection mechanisms that facilitate reporting by citizens and by civil servants themselves.
- Provide for uniform criteria and frameworks of action of the bodies responsible for the fight against corruption and the promotion of integrity in each of the public entities.
- Implement mechanisms to measure the effectiveness of training programmes linked to sensitive areas in the fight against corruption, including with regard to public hiring, disciplinary regimes, and prohibitions and incompatibilities in the public service.

- Guarantee transparency and access to public information in state entities.
- Strengthen mechanisms for the management of complaints of alleged acts of corruption.
- Guarantee integrity in the contracting of works, goods and services.
- Strengthen risk management within each public entity.

Given the current situation in Peru, however, there is little confidence among citizens about prospects for improvement. The following results from the 2017 Proética survey are informative.

Figure 8. Democracy and politics

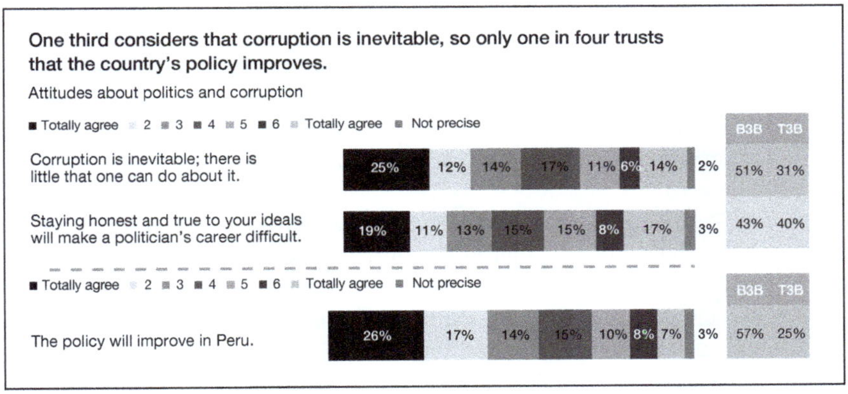

Source: www.proetica.org.pe/contenido/encuesta-nacional-sobre-percepciones-de-la-corrupcion-en-el-peru/.

Figure 9. Fight against corruption

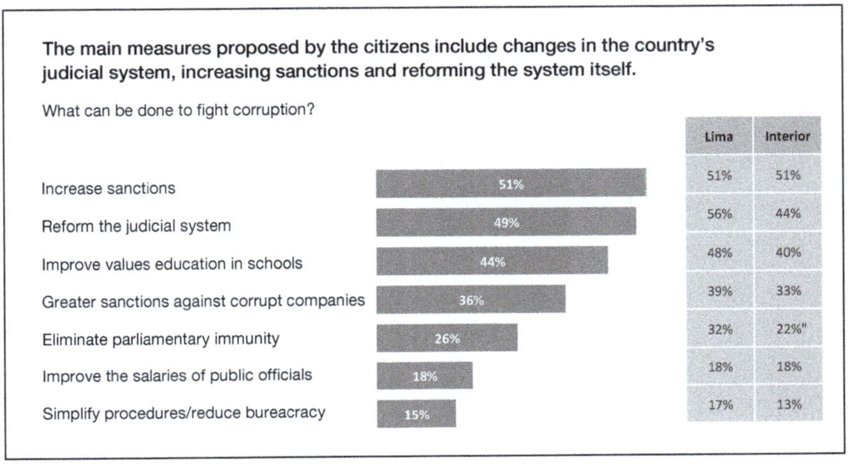

Source: www.proetica.org.pe/contenido/encuesta-nacional-sobre-percepciones-de-la-corrupcion-en-el-peru/.

7.2 Challenges and opportunities

In the writer's opinion, the current situation poses challenges and opportunities that should basically introduce the following improvements.

- Measures to ensure the personal integrity of professionals and business people.
- The institutionalisation of public authorities with a view to empowerment.
- Promoting public awareness about the irreparable damage caused by corruption and the socio-economic benefits of a professional and business ethic.
- Essential measures to clean up the public sector, reorganise and establish parameters for the election of public officials, and promote and implement effective controls.

In terms of measures, mechanisms such as (among others) so-called 'compliance' must be applied to all public entities, as well as implementing the ISO 37001 international standard rating to anti-bribery systems, implementing the 'civil death' of corrupt officials and incorporating mandatory anti-corruption clauses in public contracts.

With regard to the private sector, civic, professional and social responsibilities should be promoted, sources of corruption identified, trade union collaboration promoted for self-regulation of economic agents, and measures adopted such as excluding corrupt companies from the unions. The use of international standards such as ISO 37001 should also be promoted.

It is also up to civil society to become aware of corruption so as not to be part of it, to establish mechanisms for citizen oversight of public management and to promote a system of rewards and protection for citizens who denounce corruption.

In the same way, it is essential in the public sector that there should be political will, proven and trained officials, and an effective and comprehensive anti-corruption system and plan in place. In the private sector, anti-corruption policies should be adopted and anti-corruption tools applied, while civil society should be actively co-opted for surveillance and denunciation of corruption. Citizens should not offer or give bribes, however small.

Finally, it is proposed that an ethical pact between the public sector, the private sector and civil society should be concluded in order to promote a climate of unity for the effective confrontation of corruption.

Russia

Anastasia Kayukova
Roman Vedernikov
German Zakharov
ALRUD Law Firm

1. Overview of the country *vis-à-vis* corruption matters

Russian anti-corruption legislation was formerly quite outdated and required a complex process of revision. Passing the necessary measures has been undertaken by the Russian authorities over the past few years. This reform process was necessitated, in particular, by the existence of the former Soviet Union, which was generally characterised by the absence of a modern regulatory framework for corruption.

The attitude of Russian society to corruption is also a one of the crucial factors to have triggered developments in this area. For example, Transparency International's *Transparency Perceptions Index 2016* scored Russia at 29 on a scale from 0 (highly corrupt) to 100 (very clean), giving a ranking of 129 out of 176 countries surveyed.[1] Due to the existence of problems in anti-corruption regulation, Russia has significantly strengthened and developed its anti-corruption legislation over the last few years.

The modern phase in the development of anti-corruption regulation in Russia actively started in 2008, with the adoption of the Presidential Decree No 815 of 19 May 2008: On measures to combat corruption. This decree provided for the creation of the Presidential Anti-Corruption Council headed by the President. Moreover, Federal Law No 273-FZ of 25 December 2008: On Combating Corruption (the Anti-Corruption Law) formed the basis for regulation.

The next step in legislative developments occurred in 2013–2014. In particular, changes were made to the Anti-Corruption Law requiring companies to develop measures to prevent corruption, such as (among other things) designating officers responsible for the prevention of corruption offences, adopting corporate compliance and ethical codes and preventing informal reporting. This process was accompanied by amendments to the Russian Criminal Code, No 63-FZ of 13 June 1996 (the Criminal Code) and the Code of Administrative Offences, No 195-FZ of 30 December 2001. On the one hand, these amendments imposed greater liability for corruption offences while, on the other, they were aimed at liberalising criminal legislation for economic crimes.

In addition, national anti-corruption plans are adopted regularly. For example, the National Anti-Corruption Plan for 2016–2017[2] sets out the strategic goals in combating corruption in the Russian regions, with a view to minimisation of

1 www.transparency.org/news/feature/corruption_perceptions_index_2016.
2 http://en.kremlin.ru/events/president/news/51626.

corruption risks with regard to different sectors and the procurement of goods. The current state of anti-corruption policy is also characterised by active and ongoing investigations against high public officials, which generally meet requirements of time.

2. International anti-corruption treaties that are applicable to the country and their concrete effect in the fight against corruption

With regard to international cooperation, Russia is a signatory to a number of international treaties dedicated to the fight against corruption. The following instruments are among the main ones.

On 1 February 2012, Russia ratified the Organisation for Economic Co-operation and Development Convention on Combating Bribery of Public Officials in International Business Transactions 1998 (the OECD Convention) and commenced introducing amendments to Russian legislation to bring it up to the standards of the OECD Convention.

Russia is also a signatory to the United Nations Convention against Corruption 2003 and the Council of Europe Criminal Law Convention on Corruption 1999. It takes part in the activities of the Council of Europe's Group of States against Corruption (GRECO) and the Financial Action Task Force on Money Laundering (FATF).

Implementation of these international conventions as part of the Russian legal order has resulted in significant changes in Russian legislation and its adaptation to modern international standards.

3. The concept of corruption in the country

3.1 The definition of 'corruption' in Russia as a general concept

The Anti-Corruption Law defines 'corruption' as:

- abuse of an official position, giving and taking a bribe, receiving a bribe, abuse of powers, commercial bribery, or other illegal use of an official position by an individual, contrary to the lawful interests of society and the state, for the purpose of acquiring a benefit in the form of money, valuables, other property or material services, other property rights (whether for oneself or for third parties), or the illegal provision of such benefit to a person by other individuals; and
- the commission of the acts specified above on behalf of, or in the interests of, a legal entity.

Russian criminal legislation distinguishes two main types of bribe:

- bribes given to public officials ('public' bribery); and
- commercial bribes ('private' bribery).

The main difference between them is whether a bribe is given to a public official or an official of a commercial organisation.

3.2 'Public' bribery

Article 285 of the Russian Criminal Code defines the term 'public officials'. According to this definition, 'public officials' are persons who perform the functions of a representative of government on a permanent or temporary basis, or by special authority, or who perform organisational and regulatory, administrative and economic functions in state bodies, municipal bodies, governmental and municipal institutions, state corporations, state companies, state and municipal unitary enterprises, companies in which the Russian Federation (constituent entities of Russia or municipal bodies) has a controlling stake, and also in the armed forces of the Russian Federation, and in other troops and military formations of the Russian Federation.

Modern Russian criminal legislation provides for the following types of public corruption-related crime:

- *taking a bribe*: this offence is committed by an official, foreign official or an official of a public international organisation, in person or through an intermediary, in the form of money, securities or other property or in the form of unlawful rendering of services of a proprietary nature, or the granting of other property rights (including where a bribe, at the direction of an official, is transferred to another person or entity), for actions taken or refrained from in favour of a bribe-giver or persons he or she represents, if such actions or inaction form part of the official's powers or, if the latter, by virtue of his or her official position, may facilitate these actions, and also as a matter of patronage or connivance in the civil service;
- *giving a bribe:* this offence is committed by a person who gives a bribe to an official, foreign official or an official of a public international organisation, in person or through an intermediary (including where a bribe, at the direction of an official, is transferred to another person or entity);
- *intermediation in bribery:* this is the direct transfer of a bribe under the instructions of a bribe-giver or bribe-taker or other kind of assistance to the bribe-giver and/or bribe-taker in achieving or implementing an agreement between them on taking or giving a bribe;
- *a promise or proposal to intermediate in bribery:* see 'intermediation', above; and
- *minor bribery:* this is the offence of taking or giving a bribe, in person or through an intermediary, in an amount not exceeding Rb 10,000 (approximately €150).

3.3 'Private' bribery

'Private' bribery (referred to in the Criminal Code as 'Commercial Bribery') is regulated in the same manner as 'public' bribery. In this sense, there are only two conceptual differences with regard to commercial bribery:

- the subject, ie, a person performing management functions in a commercial or other corporate entity; and
- the amount of fines that may be imposed (though these do not differ significantly).

3.4 Facilitation payments and bribery 'threshold'

Russian anti-corruption legislation provides neither for exemptions nor for facilitation payments. Formally, any sum of money given for certain acts to be done within the authority of a recipient (or omitted to be done) may qualify as a bribe.

It should be noted in particular that Russian civil legislation allows gifts to be made to state servants where the value of such gifts does not exceed Rb 3000 (approximately €43). In this regard, it is very important to understand what constitutes a gift and a bribe under Russian law. A gift may be made only gratuitously, while bribes, according to the definitions discussed above, are given in exchange for certain acts to be done (or not done) in favour of a bribe-giver – ie, there must be corrupt intent.

Thus, the Rb 3000 threshold cannot of itself be considered to be a barrier distinguishing a bribe and a gift. As stated previously, a gift may only be made gratuitously. This means that courts will always pay attention to intention and the particular circumstances of the situation when a gift was made, ie, whether the bribe-giver derived a certain benefit.

3.5 Public officials' reporting obligations

Russian legislation provides for one of the most extraordinary anti-corruption measures: declaration of income by state officials. Declaration has become one of the most important anti-corruption financial control measures. Currently, state officials are obliged to reveal the value of their income and property (including the property and income of their spouses and infant children). The information must be published on the official website of the relevant state authority. Thus, for example, all Federal Antimonopoly Service (FAS) officials up to the Head of the FAS must report their income annually, and the relevant information is available on the internet.

Moreover, certain categories of state official are prohibited from holding overseas bank accounts and are obliged to report not only their income but also their expenses.

Another measure for combating corruption is the restriction on state officials from being engaged in any commercial activity apart from scholastic, science and arts activities.

4. Regulations and authorities that are responsible for regulating, enforcing against and punishing corruption

4.1 National anti-corruption regulation in Russia

Anti-corruption matters in Russia are regulated by the Anti-Corruption Law as amended. This is the basic law on bribery in Russia and contains the main provisions on fighting corruption.

Penalties for giving or taking bribes are laid down by the Criminal Code Code of Administrative Offences (see 1 above).

Moreover, from time to time the Russian Supreme Court issues clarifications on various types of corruption. In this sense, the most important source is Resolution of

Plenum of the Supreme Court No 24, "On court practice in bribery cases and other corruption offences", dated 9 July 2013.[3]

Laws and other rules regulating state and municipal service also contain provisions aimed at combating corruption, for example, Federal Law No 79-FZ of 27 July 2004: On State Civil Service in the Russian Federation, or the Regulation of the Government No 10 of 9 January 2014, which regulates the procedure for reporting by state and municipal officials of the receipt of gifts during protocol events, official trips and other formal occasions.

4.2 Anti-corruption enforcement

The main public authorities responsible for enforcement of anti-corruption regulation in Russia are the following:

- the Investigation Committee of the Russian Federation and its territorial divisions, as well as investigatory bodies of the Ministry of Internal Affairs, both of which are responsible for (among other things) the investigation of crimes of bribery (investigations are mainly conducted by the Investigation Committee; the Ministry of Internal Affairs has quite limited jurisdiction in this area);
- the Prosecutor's Office of the Russian Federation, which is responsible for (among other things) compliance with the Anti-Corruption Law by those to whom it applies. Prosecutors in Russia also perform the role of state prosecution during court proceedings;
- the courts of the Russian Federation, which have jurisdiction to adjudicate all cases, including those related to anti-corruption matters under Russian legislation.

4.3 Liability for breach of anti-corruption legislation

Corruption-related offences may result in liability under the relevant legislation. The main categories of liability are criminal, administrative, disciplinary and civil.

- *Criminal liability:* An individual may face a criminal fine, disqualification from holding specific offices or imprisonment for a term up to 15 years for bribery-related crimes, depending on the particular circumstances and the gravity of the offence. Such offences include commercial bribery, bribe-giving, bribe-taking, intermediation in bribery, a promise or proposal to act as an intermediary in bribery and minor bribery (see 3.2 above).

  It is very important to note that criminal liability in Russia may be imposed only on individuals. Legal entities are not subject to criminal liability.
- *Administrative liability:* This category applies to unlawful remuneration on the part of a legal entity and may entail the imposition of an administrative fine upon that entity in the amount of up to 100 times the amount of the bribe received.

---

3 Resolution of the Plenum of the Supreme Court of the Russian Federation "On court practice in bribery cases and other corruption offences", No 24, dated 9 July 2013 (amended as of 3 December 2013).

In this regard, the liability of a legal entity does not exclude the imposition of criminal liability on an individual who has committed a related crime of corruption.

- *Disciplinary liability:* Russian labour legislation imposes disciplinary responsibility, which applies to all breaches of labour discipline. Sanctions for breach include a warning, a reprimand and a discharge on appropriate grounds. A number of federal laws also impose special disciplinary responsibility on public servants.
- *Civil liability:* Russian civil legislation also imposes liability on a bribe-giver and/or bribe-taker to reimburse losses caused by bribery, in whole or in part.

5. Relevant public cases and how they have been handled and resolved

5.1 Statistics and trends in high-profile cases

According to official statistics prepared by the Supreme Court in 2016, about 1,300 people were convicted of receiving bribes in Russia and about 3,800 people for giving them, including intermediaries in bribery. Most of the bribes related to small sums (around Rb 10,000 – approx €160) and involved police officers, teachers and doctors; in other words, small bribes constituted approximately 70% of all cases.

At the same time, recent trends show that a number of investigations have been initiated against high-profile public officers. These include Alexei Ulyukayev (an ex-Minister of Economic Development of the Russian Federation), Aleksandr Khoroshavin (an ex-Governor of Sakhalin region: see 5.2(b) below), several high officials of the Investigation Committee of the Russian Federation, and several other cases. Recent practice also shows that rather strict penalties are often imposed on high officials following the completion of investigation and court proceedings.

These investigations may reveal a high level of motivation on the part of the Russian government in fighting corruption. For example, although Mr Ulyukayev was trusted by the President, this did not help him to avoid investigation and a criminal penalty.

5.2 Examples of high-profile anti-corruption cases

Several high-profile cases have resulted from major investigations.

(a) *The* Oboronservice *case*

This case concerned one of the most high-profile recent corruption scandals in Russia. Officials of the company were suspected of fraud amounting to over several hundred million roubles in connection with the sale of non-core military assets. During the investigation, Anatoly Serdyukov, the Defence Minister of the Russian Federation, was dismissed and several individuals were imprisoned.

(b) The ex-Governor of Sakhalin region *case*

One of the most significant cases was initiated in 2015 following the arrest of Aleksandr Khoroshavin, an ex-Governor of Sakhalin region, for taking a bribe of an amount exceeding RUB 500 million. In February 2018, the court completed proceedings and Mr Khoroshavin was sentenced to 13 years' imprisonment and a criminal fine of Rb 500 million. Strict penalties were also imposed on several other officials of the Sakhalin region.

(c) The European Bank for Reconstruction and Development (EBRD) *case*

This corruption scandal involved Elena Kotova, an ex-director of the EBRD, and Igor Lebedev, the senior vice-president of VTB Bank. They were involved in an illegal scheme by which they demanded more than $1.4 million from a Canadian oil and gas company for the issuance of credit. Kotova and Lebedev were given suspended prison sentences of, respectively, five and four years. However, both were later released under an amnesty.

6. Next steps

Russian anti-corruption legislation has developed significantly over recent years. Generally speaking, it currently meets the best international standards. Over the past decade, Russian anti-corruption legislation has been strengthened to a certain extent. However, it is still subject to further development and adaptation to practical needs. The most serious area for development, in the authors' opinion, is real and ongoing enforcement of existing anti-corruption rules. The effective fight against corruption is also impossible without concentrating primarily on cases of public sector bribery, in which the level of corruption may be quite high. This cannot be done without further positive and systematic changes in the Russian judicial and law enforcement systems.

President Vladimir Putin, who has been highly concerned about the problem of corruption, has implemented the National Anti-Corruption Plan for 2016–2017 (the Plan).[4] The objectives of the Plan, which was implemented effectively during 2016, according to law enforcement statistics, include:

- strengthening control over the expenses of civil servants and expropriation of assets of which they fail to prove a lawful origin;
- intensification of international cooperation for the discovery, seizure and recovery from other jurisdictions of assets that prove to be proceeds of crime; and
- a further propaganda campaign in the mass media to make society more intolerant of corruption.

On the other hand, there may also be a certain liberalisation of the Criminal Code, including with regard to economic-related crimes. For example, judicial fines may be imposed for first time low and medium gravity offences (including bribes of insignificant sums). The judicial fine concept was introduced into Russian criminal legislation in summer 2016 and is now actively applied in practice. As a further step, discussions are currently under way on the introduction of a new term into criminal legislation – 'misdemeanour', that is, a criminal offence of low gravity that would not be punishable by imprisonment. In the authors' opinion, this concept would

4 Presidential Decree No 147 of 1 Apri 2016. See note 2 above.

potentially allow increased enforcement of anti-corruption rules without increasing the workload of the prison system.

Finally, commercial corruption should not be forgotten. Companies should continue developing and implementing appropriate anti-corruption programmes, including compliance and codes of practice. Although the Anti-Corruption Law currently obliges companies to do so, failure to take appropriate organisational measures does not result in any serious consequences.

Singapore

Hamidul Haq
Istyana Ibrahim
Rajah & Tann

1. Overview of the country *vis-à-vis* corruption matters

Corruption is viewed and treated as a serious offence in Singapore. The first anti-corruption legislation was introduced in 1937 with the enactment of the Prevention of Corruption Ordinance (the 1937 Ordinance or the Ordinance).[1] However, the Ordinance and the Anti-Corruption Branch (ACB) under the Criminal Investigation Department (CID) were relatively ineffective, as the Ordinance specified only three instances of corrupt behaviour. Further, corruption was a non-seizable offence (ie, an arrest could not ordinarily be made without a warrant), and the Ordinance afforded limited powers of investigation.[2]

The 1937 Ordinance was revised in 1946, making corrupt offences seizable and giving police officers much wider powers of arrest, search and investigation.[3] However, the ACB remained largely ineffective, largely due to its limited manpower and competition with other branches of the CID for resources.[4] The ACB was eventually abolished and replaced in 1952 with the Corrupt Practices Investigation Bureau (CPIB), which came under the purview of the Attorney-General.[5]

When Singapore attained internal self-government in 1959, the CPIB was transferred to the Ministry of Home Affairs.[6] The Prevention of Corruption Act, introduced by the then Minister for Home Affairs Ong Pang Boon, was enacted in 1960 (the PCA).[7] The PCA contained significant provisions aimed at eliminating the deficiencies of the 1937 Ordinance and empowering the CPIB to conduct its investigations and exercise its enforcement duties.[8] In 1963, the CPIB came under the purview of the Prime Minister's Office (PMO), but was later transferred to the Attorney-General's Chambers in 1965.[9] In 1969, responsibility for the CPIB was returned to the PMO, where it has since remained.

To date, Singapore ranks joint sixth worldwide (based on Transparency International's *Corruption Perceptions Index*) and first in Asia for the least corrupt economy. In 2016, Singapore was ranked eighth, and in 2015, it was ranked eighth

1 www.cpib.gov.sg/about-cpib/our-heritage.
2 *Ibid.*
3 *Ibid.*
4 *Ibid.*
5 *Ibid.*
6 *Ibid.*
7 *Ibid.*
8 *Ibid.*
9 *Ibid.*

in Transparency International's index; prior to 2014, the country had finished in fifth position for three years, before slipping to seventh place.

Corruption cases have taken the spotlight in recent years, with a spate of high-profile investigations involving the heads of the Singapore Civil Defence Force and the Central Narcotics Bureau, a law professor from the National University of Singapore and high-ranking executives of government-linked company ST Marine. These investigations have emphasised Singapore's zero tolerance approach toward corruption and that no person, even one in a senior position, is above the law.

In January 2015, Prime Minister Lee Hsien Loong announced that the PCA would undergo review and that the CPIB's manpower and capabilities would be increased. Indeed, corruption offences are viewed so seriously that the Home Affairs Minister has issued preventive detention orders under the Criminal Law (Temporary Provisions) Act (Cap 67) (the 1955 Act, as amended) against a group of people for their alleged role in a global football match-fixing syndicate.[10] The 1955 Act, which allows for detention without trial, was historically used to target secret societies, drug traffickers and unlicensed moneylenders, and has only recently been used against alleged match-fixers, who may be considered 'financial crime-type' offenders.

Corruption offences therefore appear to have a special place in the enforcement process in Singapore, with the CPIB having direct responsibility under the PMO and the exemption of prosecutions under the PCA from the criminal case disclosure process implemented by the 2010 revision of the Criminal Procedure Code (Cap 68) (CPC)[11] (although the common law duty of disclosure pursuant to *Muhammd bin Kadar v Public Prosecutor*[12] also applies to corruption prosecutions).

2. International anti-corruption treaties applicable to Singapore and their concrete effects in the fight against corruption

Singapore became a signatory to the United Nations Convention against Corruption 2004 (UNCAC) on 11 November 2005 and ratified this convention on 6 November 2009. The convention only has concrete effect in the local fight against corruption to the extent that it has been incorporated in national legislation. To review state parties' implementation of their UNCAC obligations, a country review process was established in 2009 whereby each state party would be reviewed by two other states parties. Singapore has been a reviewing state party for Argentina in 2010 and El Salvador in 2012.[13] Singapore underwent its own review of its implementation of UNCAC chapters III (Criminalisation and Law Enforcement) and IV (International Cooperation) in the fourth year (2013/2014) of the current review cycle (2010/2015), with Lebanon and Swaziland as its reviewers.[14] The next cycle of the review, concerning states parties' implementation of UNCAC chapters II (Preventive

10 See also *Tan Seet Eng v Attorney-General and another* [2015] SGCA 59.

11 See section 159(1) of the CPC, read together with the Second Schedule.

12 [2011] 3 SLR 1205.

13 www.cpib.gov.sg/about-cpib/international-engagement.

14 *Ibid.* For further reading, see the UNCAC Country Review Report for Singapore (2016) www.unodc.org/documents/treaties/UNCAC/CountryVisitFinalReports/2016_07_06_Singapore_Final_Country_Report.pdf

15 www.cpib.gov.sg/about-cpib/international-engagement.

Measures) and V (Asset Recovery), commenced in 2015 and is likely to end in 2020.[15]

While Singapore is not a member of the Organisation for Economic Co-operation and Development (OECD) Convention on Combating Bribery of Foreign Public Officials in International Business Transactions 1998, the CPIB represents Singapore at a variety of fora, such as the Asian Development Bank (ADB)-OECD Anti-Corruption Initiative for Asia and the Pacific, the Asia-Pacific Economic Cooperation (APEC) Anti-Corruption and Transparency Experts' Working Group (ACTWG), the Economic Crime Agencies Network (ECAN), the G20 Anti-Corruption Working Group (ACWG), the International Association of Anti-Corruption Authorities (IAACA) and the South East Asia-Parties Against Corruption (SEA-PAC) meetings between parties to a regional Memorandum of Understanding (MOU).[16]

Further, on 12 April 2017, Spring Singapore and CPIB launched the new Singapore Standard ISO 37001 (SS ISO 37001), an anti-bribery standard developed by the International Organization for Standardization (ISO) in October 2016. SS ISO 37001 on anti-bribery management systems is a voluntary standard designed to help companies establish, implement, maintain and improve their anti-bribery good practice.

3. The concept of 'corruption' in Singapore

The main statute governing offences of corruption in Singapore is the Prevention of Corruption Act (Cap 241, 1993 Rev Ed) (the 'PCA'), which applies to both public and private sector bribery. The Penal Code (Cap 224, 2008 Rev Ed) also creates specific offences related to corrupt conduct involving Singaporean public officials.

Corrupt transactions are generally covered by sections 5 (general corruption) and 6 (corruption involving agent) of the PCA. The ambit of the offences under these provisions is broad and includes the soliciting, receiving, giving, promising or offering of a bribe. Singapore does not provide any exception for facilitation payments.

In addition to sections 5 and 6 of the PCA, there are several specific provisions. These are sections 10, 11 and 12, which prohibit bribery in the public sector. Section 10 creates the offence of corruptly procuring the withdrawal of tenders for contracts from the government or any public body. Section 11 prohibits both active and passive bribery in respect of Members of Parliament, while section 12 prohibits the bribery of members of a public body. Furthermore, sections 161–165 deal specifically with corruption by or relating to public servants.

Generally, in order to establish an offence of corruption, the prosecution must show that there was a corrupt element in a transaction according to the ordinary and objective standard, accompanied by guilty knowledge on the part of the accused that what he or she was doing was, by that standard, corrupt.[17] Both of these limbs of the offence must be satisfied beyond a reasonable doubt and the question of what is 'corrupt' would be determined on the facts of the individual case.

---

16 *Ibid.*

17 *Chan Wing Seng v Public Prosecutor* [1997] 1 SLR(R) 721 at [25]; *Hassan bin Ahmad v Public Prosecutor* [2000] 2 SLR(R) 567 at [15]; *Foo Ser Joo William v Public Prosecutor* [2000] 3 SLR(R) 12 at [27]; *Pandiyan Thanaraju Rogers v Public Prosecutor* [2001] 2 SLR(R) 217 at [34].

However, "the factual permutations of corruption can be endless."[18] In *Hassan bin Ahmad v Public Prosecutor*,[19] the High Court (per the then Chief Justice Yong Pung How) described the act of corruption as follows:

> *It was ... not necessary for the Prosecution to prove a nexus between each receipt and a particular act; it only sufficed to demonstrate that the payments were not made innocently, but to purchase the recipient's servitude. This is the essence of being 'bought over' – that the recipient of the gratification be at the beck and call of the payor, prodded into action by his recollection of the payor's generosity even when no specific act was demanded at the time of payment.*

The corrupt element (the first limb) is made out by ascertaining the accused's intention in receiving the alleged gratification, and then determining, on an objective standard, whether that intention, given the facts, taints the transaction with a corrupt element.[20] The second limb is made out by determining the accused's state of mind as a question of fact.[21]

The determination of a corrupt element is ultimately an objective assessment based on the intention of the giver or the recipient.[22] In coming to its decision, the court will look at the particular circumstances of the case. Some of the factors that the court will generally consider are:

- the purpose behind the giving of gratification;
- any prior communication or solicitation before payment of gratification (however, it should be noted that it is not necessary in law for an express request for a bribe or an express reference to a favour to be shown in order to establish a charge of corruption);
- the proximity of time between the act of the receiver and the giving of gratification;
- any furtiveness or surreptitious element in the transactions;
- the nature and frequency of the gratification;
- the quantum of gratification (ie, whether it is excessive, extravagant or non-justifiable);
- the relationship between the parties; and
- whether the recipient has in fact shown or has the power to show favour to the giver.

The question of whether the accused possesses the relevant guilty knowledge is a subjective one.[23] However, there is still an objective element, in that the guilty knowledge is that of knowing or realising that what the accused did was corrupt by the ordinary and objective standard.[24]

---

18 *Chan Wing Seng v Public Prosecutor* [1997] 1 SLR(R) 721 at [26].

19 [2000] 2 SLR(R) 567 at [20].

20 *Hassan bin Ahmad v Public Prosecutor* [2000] 2 SLR(R) 567 at [15].

21 *Ibid.*

22 *Chan Wing Seng v Public Prosecutor* [1997] 1 SLR(R) 721 at [20]; *Fong SerJjoo William v Public Prosecutor* [2000] 3 SLR(R) 12 at [27].

23 *Chan Wing Seng v Public Prosecutor* [1997] 1 SLR(R) 721 at [23]; *Fong Ser Joo William v Public Prosecutor* [2000] 3 SLR(R) 12 at [31].

24 *Fong Ser Joo William v Public Prosecutor* [2000] 3 SLR(R) 12 at [33].

The court in *Chan Wing Seng v Public Prosecutor*[25] observed that if rules or laws were breached knowingly, then it would be easier for the court to infer that the accused knew what he did was corrupt according to the ordinary and objective standard. The court also observed that there could be instances where the accused's actions were so obviously corrupt by the ordinary and objective standard that he must have known that his conduct was corrupt.

Under section 2 of the PCA, the term 'gratification' includes money or any gift, loan, fee, reward, commission, valuable security or other property or interest in property; any office, employment or contract, any part or full payment, release from or discharge of any obligation or other liability, and any other service, favour or advantage of any description whatsoever.

Under section 8 of the PCA, a presumption of corruption operates against the offender if it is proved in any legal proceedings that gratification has been paid to or received by a person in the employment of the government or any department thereof or of a public body by or from a person or agent of a person who has or seeks to have any dealing with the Government or any department thereof or any public body.

Under section 9(1) of the PCA, for the purposes of corrupt transactions with agents, an agent shall be guilty of an offence notwithstanding that he did not have the power, right or opportunity to do so, show or forbear or that he accepted the gratification without intending to do so, show or forbear or that he did not in fact do so, show or forbear or that the act, favour or disfavour was not in relation to his principal's affairs or business.

Offenders under sections 5 or 6 of the PCA shall be liable on conviction to a maximum fine of S$100,000 and/or a maximum term of five years' imprisonment. In certain cases, prison terms may be extended by up to seven years (ie, if the offence relates to a Member of Parliament, a member of a public body or a contract or sub-contract with the government or any public body). Any person convicted of an offence committed by the acceptance of any gratification under the PCA shall also be ordered to pay a penalty sum equivalent to either the amount or the value of that gratification, which will be recoverable as a fine (or in default, punishable by a term of imprisonment).

Offences under the PCA apply both to the public and the private sectors. There is a strong focus on private sector corruption, which forms the majority of cases registered for investigation by CPIB. The main industries of concern are the construction industry, wholesale and retail businesses as well as warehousing, transport and logistics services. Additionally, both individuals and companies can be held liable for bribery, pursuant to the PCA or the Penal Code.

Singapore's anti-corruption laws also have extra-territorial application in relation to Singapore citizens: see, in this regard:

- generally, section 37(1) of the PCA;
- as to public servants, section 4 of the Penal Code; and
- as to offences of the abetment in Singapore of offences committed outside

25 [1997] 1 SLR(R) 721, at [66] and [67].

Singapore, abetment outside Singapore or an offence committed in Singapore, section 29 of the PCA, read together with sections 108A and 108B of the Penal Code.

4. Regulations (administrative and criminal) and the competent authorities that are responsible for regulating, enforcing against and punishing corruption

The relevant anti-corruption legislation in Singapore comprises the following:

- the PCA;
- the Penal Code;
- the Corruption, Drug Trafficking and Other Serious Crimes (Confiscation of Benefits) Act (Cap 65A);
- the Criminal Procedure Code (Cap 68);
- the Prisons Act (Cap 247);
- the Evidence Act (Cap 97);
- the Extradition Act (Cap 103); and
- the Mutual Assistance in Criminal Matters Act (Cap 190A).

The relevant authorities in the fight against corruption are:

- the Corrupt Practices Investigation Bureau (CPIB);
- the Attorney-General's Chambers (AGC);
- the Commercial Affairs Department (CAD) of the Singapore Police Force; and
- the Ministry of Home Affairs.

5. Relevant public cases and how have they been handled and resolved

5.1 Introduction

The main sentencing considerations in corruption cases are deterrence and punishment. The Singapore courts generally do not regard public sector bribery as any less culpable than bribery in the private sector. There is no presumption in favour of a non-custodial sentence for private sector cases.

5.2 The *Romel* case

In *Public Prosecutor v Syed Mostofa Romel*[26] (*Romel*), the High Court (per Chief Justice Sundaresh Menon) observed that where private sector agents are concerned, offences that register a lower level of culpability can be dealt with by the imposition of fines; these are generally cases where the amount of gratification is below S$30,000 and where there is no real detriment to the interests of the principal. However, Menon CJ affirmed the position that there is no presumption in favour of non-custodial sentences wherever private sector corruption is involved. The specific nature of the corruption is of first importance and where private sector corruption involves:

- a significant amount of gratification;

26 [2015] 3 SLR 1166.

- gratification that has been received over a lengthy period of time; or
- the compromise of the accused's duty or a serious betrayal of trust,

the starting point is likely to be a custodial sentence.[27]

The High Court in the *Romel* case identified three broad and non-exhaustive categories in which private sector corruption could manifest itself:

- where the receiving party was paid to confer on the paying party a benefit that was within the receiving party's power to confer without regard to whether the paying party ought properly to have received that benefit;
- where the receiving party was paid to forbear from performing what he was duty bound to do, thereby conferring a benefit on the paying party;
- where a receiving party was paid so that he or she would forbear from inflicting harm on the paying party, even though there was no lawful basis for such harm to be inflicted.

While these three categories were only analytical tools and could shade into one another, the third category was characterised by the heightened culpability of the recipient through

- seeking out of payment from the paying party; and
- the threat to inflict harm on the paying party without any lawful basis.

Offenders falling within the second and third categories could generally expect a custodial sentence.[28]

In the *Romel* case, the accused, a marine surveyor, faced three charges under section 6(a) of the PCA. The first and second charges were proceeded with, while the third was taken into consideration for sentencing. On the first charge, the accused had highlighted several alleged 'high-risk defects' to the captain of a vessel which the latter thought were minor ones that were easily rectified. In return for a bribe payment solicited by the accused, the vessel was allowed to enter the oil terminal. The second charge involved a 'sting' operation by the CPIB whereby the ship was prepared with high-risk defects beforehand and the accused was assigned to carry out an inspection of the vessel. The accused solicited a bribe in return for not including these defects in his report. The third charge involved the accused soliciting a bribe from the captain in return for issuing a favourable inspection report, such that the vessel was allowed to enter the oil terminal.

The facts of the first charge fell within the third category of private sector corruption identified by the High Court and discussed above. The vessel's captain wanted access to the oil terminal for his vessel and was entitled to it so long as his vessel was sufficiently safe, yet he faced the prospect of having to pay a bribe in order to secure access. The facts of the second charge could be associated with the second and third categories, as the accused had forborne to do an act he was duty bound to

27 At [17], [20] and [23] respectively.
28 *Ibid*, at [26]-[31].

do. The association with the third category arose from the payment having been solicited by the accused as the receiving party, with a view of his breaching his duty in return for such payment. In that light, the sentence of two months' imprisonment imposed by the District Court on the first and second charges respectively was inadequate. As the legitimate business rights of the captain and ship's master had been interfered with, and the offending acts were premeditated and deliberate, carried out over three months, and involved a total of US$7,200 which compromised the safety of premises and workers in a strategic industry, the High Court increased the sentence to six months' imprisonment for each of the two charges, with the sentences running concurrently.[29]

The High Court held that the public service rationale was not the only consideration that might cause the custodial threshold to be crossed. Other considerations were:

- where the policy considerations and gravity of the offence as measured by the mischief or likely consequence of the corruption warranted it;
- the size of the bribes;
- the number of people involved in the web of corruption; and
- the prevalence of the conduct.

The court further observed that the public service rationale did not determine whether a custodial sentence was warranted in a case of private sector corruption.[30] The public service rationale did not apply in *Romel*, as no regulatory or oversight considerations were involved and the arrangement was purely commercial.

However, the potentially damaging economic and physical harm that could have resulted was a separate aggravating consideration.[31] In relation to the second charge, there were clearly high-risk defects which were overlooked because of the bribes paid).[32]

5.3 The *Song Men Choon* case

In *Song Meng Choon Andrew v Public Prosecutor*,[33] the appellant had pleaded guilty to two charges under section 5(b)(i) of the PCA for corruptly giving a gratification to one P as a reward for P arranging a 'U-turn' into Singapore for Filipina hostesses in order to have the validity period of their stay in Singapore extended. Both P and one M, an Immigration and Checkpoints Authority (ICA) officer, then hatched a scheme to facilitate the 'U-turn' of these foreigners in return for a standard fee payable to M. The District Court had sentenced the appellant to four months' imprisonment per charge and ordered that they run consecutively. On appeal, one of the grounds raised was that the District Judge had failed to apply the relevant sentencing precedents decided under sections 5(a)(i) and 5(b)(i) of the PCA which established that a fine

29 *Ibid*, at [32]–[34].
30 *Ibid*, at [39].
31 *Ibid*, at [24], [25] and [36].
32 *Ibid*, at [44] and [45].
33 [2015] 4 SLR 1090.
34 *Ibid*, at [19(a)].

should be imposed for small sums of gratification, notwithstanding that the impugned transaction affects a public service.[34]

The sentence was reduced to six weeks' imprisonment per charge, which resulted in a global term of 12 weeks' imprisonment (both sentences to run consecutively). The High Court (per Justice Chan Seng Onn) held that a court should not be overly concerned with whether a charge was brought under section 5 or section 6 of the PCA but should focus on the specific nature of the corruption in the particular case.[35] The High Court observed that a charge brought under sections 6(a) and 6(b) of the PCA could, in most cases if not all, be reframed as a charge under section 5 simply because of the sheer breadth of that provision.[36] However, it was not the case that an offence framed under section 6 of the PCA was necessarily a more serious or aggravated offence than one under section 5: the range of punishments was the same in both provisions. Given this and the considerable overlap between sections 5 and 6, in the sense that section 5 might well be broad enough to encompass all cases under section 6, it was not Parliament's intention that an offence under section 6 should necessarily be regarded as more serious or aggravated by comparison with one under section 5, or vice versa. Much depended on the nature and factual circumstances of the offence.[37]

Having regard to the specific nature of the corruption in the *Song Meng Choon* case, the High Court noted that the appellant was charged for corruptly giving a gratification to a private individual and not to the ICA officer directly. A custodial sentence was warranted because the appellant would have known that a public officer had to be bribed somewhere along the line, though not by him, and therefore knowingly partook in a criminal scheme that would lead to an erosion of public confidence in the essential institutions of government. The public service rationale was therefore engaged.[38] However, the appropriate sentence in this case was six weeks per charge (making a global term of 12 weeks' imprisonment), which reflected the need for deterrence in cases where public confidence in government institutions was compromised, the degree of culpability of the appellant in the scheme, the fact that multiple offences were committed, that there was premeditation, the relatively small amount of the bribe, the appellant's cooperation with authorities and his remorse.[39] Had the appellant been charged for directly bribing the ICA officer, the custodial sentence handed down by the District Judge would have been justifiable, since the very acts which undermine public confidence would have been done by the appellant and so the public service rationale would have applied more strongly (at [46]).[40]

5.4 The *ST Marine* cases

The ST Marine line of prosecutions involved former senior executives of a

35 *Ibid*, at [36].
36 *Ibid*, at [29] and [30].
37 *Ibid*, at [31].
38 *Ibid*, at [42].
39 *Ibid*, at [44]–[46], [79] and [80].
40 *Ibid*, at [46].

government-linked company who conspired to make thousands of false entries in ST Marine petty cash vouchers relating to more than S$6.5 million in entertainment expenses that were allegedly bribes. Two members of this group were sentenced to fines of S$210,000 and S$300,000 respectively for charges under section 477A of the Penal Code, whereas others were sentenced to jail terms ranging from four to 10 months, depending on their level of culpability and seniority for charges under section 477A of the Penal Code or section 6(b) of the PCA (or both).

5.5 The *Keppel* case

This case was the first case in which a Singapore company had reached a global resolution announced on 23 December 2017 with the criminal authorities in the United States, Brazil and Singapore, bringing closure to investigations into corrupt payments made by a former agent of KOM in Brazil. KOM would pay fines totalling US$422 million to the three jurisdictions.

As part of the global resolution, KOM accepted a conditional warning from the Corrupt Practices Investigation Bureau (CPIB) in Singapore, and entered into a Deferred Prosecution Agreement (DPA) with the US Department of Justice (DOJ), while Keppel FELS Brasil, a wholly-owned subsidiary of KOM, reached a Leniency Agreement with the Public Prosecutor's Office in Brazil, the *Ministério Público Federal* (MPF).

5.6 The *Teo Chu Ha* and *Leng Kah Poh* cases

(a) *Introduction*

Two criminal references of 2014 under section 397 of the Criminal Procedure Code concerned complex scenarios of corruption and showed an inclination on the part of the courts to recognise corruption even in complicated forms.

(b) Teo Chu Ha

A transaction may still amount to corruption even if the accused has paid consideration in relation to the transaction. The prosecution does not need to prove that the payment was a sham or that the consideration was inadequate. In *Public Prosecutor v Teo Chu Ha,*[41] the accused's employer (Company A) carried out a tender exercise to award contracts in 2004 ('the tender exercise'). The accused agreed with a third party to influence the tender exercise in favour of Company B, which was a private company formed solely for the receipt of financial benefits from Company A as a result of being successful in the aforementioned tender exercise. In exchange, it was agreed that the accused could buy 20,000 shares in Company B for S$6,000. Company B eventually won the tender exercise.

Company B also won tender exercises conducted by Company A in 2005 and 2007. The accused received a total of 11 dividend payments from his Company B shares. He faced 12 charges. The first charge was for corruptly accepting 20,000 shares in Company B, contrary to section 6(a) of the PCA. The remaining charges related to the 11 payments which the prosecution asserted were also corruptly received. The

41 [2014] 4 SLR 600.

District Judge found the accused guilty of all charges. The High Court judge ('the judge') reversed the conviction. In relation to the first charge, the judge held that there was no evidence that S$6,000 was insufficient consideration for the shares and was, on that basis, not satisfied that the share transfer was objectively corrupt. As for the remaining charges, the judge found that there was no correspondence in time between the tender exercises and the 11 payments. In those circumstances, the judge held that the payments could not be said to be objectively corrupt.

One of the two questions for determination by the Court of Appeal by way of a criminal reference was whether, in determining if a transaction was objectively corrupt for the purposes of section 6 of the PCA where consideration was paid for the gratification, the prosecution must prove that the consideration was inadequate or that the transaction was a sham.

The Court of Appeal answered this question in the negative. While the consideration paid by an accused was a factor which the court could take into account, it was not necessary for the prosecution to prove that the consideration was inadequate or that the transaction was a sham before an offence under section 6 of the Act was made out.[42] If so, this would go against the "broader spirit and policy" of the PCA, which is to "prevent corruption in all its various forms and all the more so with regard to deliberate and involved as well as sophisticated schemes".[43] There is a need to examine "the substance of the entire scheme and its context" rather than the "actual (and more specific) transaction involving payment for the shares themselves".[44] The proposition of law which was the subject of this question was premised on the notion that the gratification in the first charge consisted only of the shares *per se* and nothing else, which was an unduly narrow and technical approach.

In the appropriate case, it was the opportunity to purchase the shares and/or the assistance rendered in purchasing them which, together with the shares, constituted the gratification. The Court of Appeal recognised that Teo (the accused) would not have been able to purchase the shares in the open market, given that the company was a private one. The gratification lay not merely in the shares *per se* but in what they represented, for instance, the necessary 'key' that 'unlocked' the many 'doors of opportunity' for the subsequent material gratification in the form of dividend payments. If an accused allowed himself to be 'bought over' by a third party who gave him an opportunity to acquire the shares, and the shares 'unlocked the door' to subsequent material gratification, then whether he paid the full consideration for the shares could not by itself be decisive: it was entirely possible in such a situation for the agent to have paid an amount in excess of the market value for the shares and still be corrupt.[45]

The Court of Appeal therefore ordered that Teo's original conviction and sentence in the District Court should stand.

---

42 *Ibid*, at [73].
43 *Ibid*, at [71]
44 *Ibid*, at [55].
45 *Ibid*, at [56], [58] and [64]–[67].

(c) Leng Kah Poh

In *Public Prosecutor v Leng Kah Poh,*[46] the respondent was a manager in charge of food and beverage of IKANO Pte Ltd, a Singapore company operating IKEA furniture stores in Singapore. He was charged with 80 counts of corruptly accepting gratification under section 6(a) of the PCA for obtaining gratification from a person as a reward for showing favour in relation to the company's affairs by being partial in placing orders for food products with two third parties. At all times, the money constituted one-third of the profits made by the two third parties. The accused was found guilty by the District Court but the conviction was reversed on appeal.

The High Court found that, for a conviction under section 6(a), it was insufficient to find dishonesty and that there had to be inducement on the part of the third party to the respondent for the latter to act in a certain way. The High Court held that the respondent had not been induced as he was the mastermind or co-conspirator in the transactions. Additionally, the profits made by the two third parties were not rewards as a form of gratification but, rather, secret benefits, and there was a reasonable chance that the respondent was paying himself in a profit-sharing scheme, which indicated some element of equal ownership over the scheme.

The prosecution referred the following two questions to the Court of Appeal by way of a criminal reference:

- *Question 1:* For the purposes of section 6 of the PCA, where an agent initiated, masterminded or co-conspired in the payment of a gratification to himself, does this *ipso facto* mean that he was not induced or rewarded in respect of his principal's affairs?
- *Question 2:* For the purposes of section 6 of the PCA, where an agent used his position *vis-à-vis* his principal to create an arrangement for the payment of a gratification that conflicts with the interests of his principal, does this *ipso facto* mean that the agent was not, by such arrangement, induced or rewarded for showing favours in respect of his principal's affairs?

Question 1 pertained to whether an agent could be "induced or rewarded" in respect of his principal's affairs where the idea of receiving a gratification from the third party did not come from the third party but from the agent himself. The focus of this question was on the roles of the agent and the third party in the conception of the transactions and whether they mattered in establishing a "gratification" for the purposes of s 6(a).

Question 2 pertained to whether, in a situation where the agent has some beneficial or legal interest in the third party, the agent's drawing of his share of the profits obtained by that third party from the benefits conferred could be considered a "gratification" for the purposes of s 6(a).

Both questions were answered in the negative.

Regarding Question 1, the Court of Appeal held that inducement as an act of persuasion and "inducement" as a description of a "gratification" within s 6(a) of the PCA should not be conflated. According to the provision, what acted as the

46 [2014] 4 SLR 1264.

inducement or a reward was the gratification and it was not an enquiry about the presence of an act of inducement by the third party.

As a matter of principle, whether an objective corrupt element existed, and was related to a finding of a "gratification", could not be dependent on who initiated the promise of a gift.[47]

Establishing the gratification as an inducement or reward was only part of the factual enquiry. It had to be linked as the cause or consequence of the conferment of the benefit upon the third party as an analysis under the rubric of an objective corrupt element (the third element). Thus, the correct question to consider was: was there a gratification by inducement or reward to the agent that led to a dishonest or improper gain or advantage being conferred by the agent on the third party?[48]

Regarding Question 2, the paradigm of corruption under section 6(a) of the PCA involved three parties: the principal, the agent and the person who gave the gift, ie, the third party. Section 6(a) was intended to criminalise the influence the gift from the third party had on the agent as this influence was concerned with weakening the agent/principal relationship given this influence.[49]

The separate legal entity doctrine applied in the context of s 6(a). Some form of ownership in a legal entity did not preclude it from being considered a third party for the purposes of that provision and so an agent's ownership in the entity did not alter the fact that it was a separate legal entity and was a third party distinct from the agent and his principal.[50]

Where the three parties were established and section 6(a) was engaged, whether the secret profits received by the agent would be considered a "gratification" would be dependent on the same factual inquiry of an objective corrupt element.

In considering whether a corrupt element exists, the court would balance the fact that the agent had an entitlement to the profits made by the beneficially owned legal entities with the other facts which might otherwise show that an objective corrupt element was still present. The beneficial ownership and the agent's share of the profits obtained were only part of the picture, and a proper enquiry had to be made into the "true nature of the arrangements between the agent and the third party".[51]

The Court of Appeal held that relevant, but non-exhaustive, factors would include:

- the workings of the scheme;
- how the secret profits were derived;
- the setting up of the third party;
- the duration and purpose of the third party;
- fair competition against other entities for contracts with the principal;
- fair competition against the principal for contracts by other parties; and
- the agent's actions *vis-à-vis* the principal and the third party in making the profit.

47 *Ibid*, at [42] and [43].
48 *Ibid*, at [43].
49 *Ibid*, at [23], [24] and [37].
50 *Ibid*, at [55] and [56].
51 *Ibid*, at [43] and [57]–[59].

Depending on the facts of the case, the scheme may be considered as having an objectively corrupt element despite the agent's beneficial interest in the moneys received by the third party.[52]

There could be situations in which, due to the fact that the agent owned the third party, the lines between the agent and the third party might be blurred (eg, where the third party is a 'sole proprietorship with the agent being the proprietor' or an 'incorporated company with the agent being the sole shareholder'). In such circumstances, arguably the agent and the third party could be considered (looking at the substance) to be the same or identical.[53]

6. Deferred Prosecution Agreements (DPAs)

Following the *Keppel* case, the Minister for Law suggested in January 2018 that Deferred Prosecution Agreements (DPA) could be introduced in Singapore, whereby corporates could be taken to task and could pay a much higher sum by comparison with what the criminal law provides.

Under the Criminal Justice Reform and the Evidence (Amendment) Bills, which were passed in Parliament on 19 March 2018, one key amendment is the introduction of DPAs.

Under a DPA, the prosecution agrees not to prosecute a corporation if the latter complies with stipulated conditions, eg, to implement compliance programmes, and/or to cooperate in investigations into wrongdoing by individual officers.

The key features of the DPA framework are as follows:

- it applies only to:
  - corporate offenders with counsel, and
  - scheduled offences;
- High Court approval will be required. The High Court can only approve a DPA if:
  - it is in the interests of justice; and
  - its terms are fair, reasonable and proportionate.

Generally, all DPAs must be published after receiving High Court approval, and are not available to individuals.

7. Next steps: authors' comments on what needs to be modified, strengthened or addressed

The authors make the following suggestions in relation to anti-corruption laws in Singapore:

- corruption offences should be covered by the criminal case disclosure regime;
- a full defence should be accorded to a commercial organisation in terms similar to the UK Bribery Act 2010 if it can shown that, despite a particular incident of bribery having occurred it nevertheless had adequate procedures in place to prevent persons associated with it from committing bribery;

---

52 *Ibid*, at [58].
53 *Ibid*, at [56].

- a right against self-incrimination should be accorded to accused persons under the PCA, resulting in the repeal of section 27 of same;
- a definition of 'corruptly' should be provided in the PCA (eg, by adopting the concept of being "bought over" in *Hassan bin Ahmad v Public Prosecutor*).[54]

54 [2000] 2 SLR(R) 567.

United Kingdom

Chris Hardjasa
Morgan J Miller
Paul Hastings LLP

1. Overview

1.1 A brief history of bribery and corruption in the UK

In recent decades, corruption was generally not considered endemic in the modern United Kingdom of Great Britain and Northern Ireland (the UK).[1] As a highly developed, politically and legally complex nation with the fifth highest GDP in the world, the UK ranks number 10 on the Transparency International *Corruption Perceptions Index* (TI CPI) with a score of 81, placing the UK in the top 10 list of countries with the least corruption in both 2015 and 2016.[2]

However, the UK was not always viewed, either internally or externally, as such a 'clean' nation. Much of the country's history was rife with corruption, particularly widespread in the Great Britain of the 18th and 19th centuries.[3] While the UK is now considered to have one of the most far-reaching anti-bribery laws in the world, it is important to understand how the law evolved in context.[4] Public attitudes and legislation regarding bribery and corruption have evolved considerably over the past centuries.

In many ways, the UK has been a leader in establishing concepts of corruption and bribery now taken for granted in the modern world. British history, tarnished with numerous scandals, is dotted with efforts to introduce reforms – at times hastily and reactively – to eradicate corruption.[5]

Bribery originated as a common law crime, rarely prosecuted until the 19th century.[6] Before then, Great Britain as a state was generally more focused on

---

1 The United Kingdom of Great Britain and Northern Ireland has been the formal full title of the state since 1927. The United Kingdom as a unified, sovereign state was originally known as the United Kingdom of Great Britain, starting in 1707 with the unification of the kingdoms of England and Scotland. In 1800, the union added the kingdom of Ireland, creating the United Kingdom of Great Britain and Ireland. Prior to 1945, the UK was more generally known as 'Britain' or 'Great Britain'. When discussing pre-1900s history, therefore, this chapter will refer to the state as Great Britain.

2 Transparency International, *Corruption Perceptions Index 2016*, available at www.transparency.org/news/feature/corruption_perceptions_index_2016; Transparency International, *Corruption Perceptions Index 2015*, available at www.transparency.org/cpi2015.

3 Transparency International UK, *Corruption in the UK: Overview and Policy Recommendations*, at p5, available at www.transparency.org.uk/wp-content/plugins/download-attachments/includes/download.php?id=857 (March 2012), hereinafter TI-UK (2012).

4 *Ibid.*

5 Professor Mark Knights, *Old Corruption: What British History Can Tell Us About Corruption Today*, available at www.transparency.org.uk/wp-content/plugins/download-attachments/includes/download.php?id=5977 (November 2016), (Knights (2016)).

6 *Ibid.*

extortion, abuse of power and embezzlement.[7] The general public, by contrast, was incensed by excessive taxation by self-serving state officials and the corruption of the electoral system, as well as what they perceived to be the corrupting influence of the monarchy on Parliament.[8]

The complexities of British history and the evolution of corruption as a concept are beyond the scope of this chapter, though suffice to say that it was not until the 18th and 19th centuries that secular concepts of corruption became increasingly important – as did the idea of anti-corruption.[9] In earlier times, public office was considered personal property that could be sold[10] Over time, after certain scandals related to the sale of public offices and resulting prosecutions, the notion of power as being wielded in 'public trust' emerged.[11]

A fundamental shift occurred in Britain wherein holders of office became accountable and responsible to the people, rather than the Crown.[12] The concept of a public trust, which appears in Roman writings, was exported anew throughout the English-speaking world, bringing with it the fundamental principles that underpin anti-corruption efforts today. As this concept of trust developed, it fostered the evolving idea of accountability in the public sphere.[13]

1.2 Bribery and corruption in the UK today

Concepts of public trust and accountability, traceable back to the evolving Great Britain of the 17th to 19th centuries, have shaped public perceptions as well as international discourse regarding corruption. The UK's reforms have historically driven anti-corruption efforts forward. These ideas travelled with Great Britain to its colonies and overseas territories, including the future United States (US) – and arguably set the foundation for anti-corruption legislation and international conventions around the world. The UK of today has built upon these fundamental principles by enacting the UK Bribery Act 2010 (the 2010 Act), the country's modern anti-bribery legislation.[14] The 2010 Act applies to the entirety of the UK – England & Wales, Scotland and Northern Ireland.

The then Secretary of State for Justice, Kenneth Clarke, stated in the Ministry of Justice (MoJ) publication, *The Bribery Act 2010: Guidance* (MoJ Guidance)[15] that the UK wants to play a "leading role in stamping out corruption and supporting trade-led international development." He further stated that "addressing bribery is good for business ... everyone agrees bribery is wrong and that rules need reform. In implementing [the 2010 Act], [the UK is] striking a blow for the rule of law and growth of trade."

The UK has transformed significantly beyond the monarchical state of the last

---

7 *Ibid.*
8 *Ibid.* The public believed this influence undermined the independence of Members of Parliament by improperly rewarding MPs with offices, patronage and money.
9 *Ibid*; TI-UK (2012), at p5.
10 Knights (2016).
11 *Ibid.*
12 *Ibid.*
13 *Ibid.*
14 Available at www.legislation.gov.uk/ukpga/2010/23/contents (2010).
15 Available at www.justice.gov.uk/downloads/legislation/bribery-act-2010-guidance.pdf (March 2011).

few centuries, in which seats in Parliament could be bought and sold.[16] Despite commendable statements by the UK Government and high-level public commitments to defeat corruption, however, a lack of transparency combined with a number of high-profile scandals affected public perception of domestic corruption.[17] Transparency International-UK (TI-UK), the UK chapter of the global anti-corruption civil society group, conducted an extensive study on corruption in the UK in 2011 – the year in which the 2010 Act came into effect. TI-UK's conclusion was that corruption is a greater problem in the UK than is recognised by government policy.[18]

TI-UK found corruption in some areas of UK society and institutions to be a much greater problem than recognised and the UK government's response inadequate to meet this growing threat. Significantly, TI-UK found that corruption was often met with complacency and that key institutions were refusing to confront the problem. TI-UK specifically emphasised problems in prisons, with political parties, in Parliament and in the world of sport.[19]

More recently, some members of the UK press have reported more sceptically regarding the UK's top-10 ranking on the TI CPI. Public perception of the UK has faced numerous challenges. Reported overseas bribery by UK companies resulted in the first settlements under the 2010 Act (described in more detail later in this chapter). Extensive money laundering through London's financial institutions, purportedly lax regulation, the naming of numerous British political figures in the so-called Panama Papers, lack of transparency in British-controlled tax havens and various political and corruption scandals in the UK itself have more recently cast the country in a negative light.[20] Toward the end of 2017, the revelations of the Paradise

16 TI-UK (2012).

17 One of the most significant corruption scandals arising in recent years (prior to the numerous scandals that plagued 2017) was the Members of Parliament (MPs) expenses scandal that emerged in 2009, in which it was revealed that numerous MPs had submitted significant improper personal expenses for public reimbursement (including cleaning their second homes, moat-cleaning, chandeliers, a duck island), though few MPs were prosecuted. It resulted in many resignations, de-selections, public apologies and the repayment of expenses, with the Speaker of the House of Commons forced out of office for the first time in 300 years. Despite the scandal, MP expenses today continue to be a point of contention that draw public ire. See, for example, Andrew Grice, the Independent, *Review of the year 2009: Expenses scandal*, available at: www.independent.co.uk/voices/commentators/andrew-grice/review-of-the-year-2009-expenses-scandal-1847865.html; Press Association, the Independent, *MPs' expenses scandal: the timeline*, available at www.independent.co.uk/news/uk/politics/mps-expenses-scandal-the-timeline-1888349.html (3 February 2010).

18 TI-UK (2012).

19 *Ibid*, at p25.

20 Rachael Davies, The Independent: *Does Britain deserve its top 10 ranking in the Corruption Perceptions Index?*, available at www.independent.co.uk/voices/does-britain-deserve-its-top-10-ranking-in-the-corruption-perceptions-index-a6841636.html (29 January 2016); Joe Churcher, The Independent: *Corruption Experts Brand Cameron's Government 'Extraordinarily Inept'*, available at www.independent.co.uk/news/uk/politics/corruption-experts-brand-david-camerons-government-extraordinarily-inept-a6836101.html; Rachel Davies, *Don't Look, Don't Find: Corrupt Money in the UK*, available at www.transparency.org.uk/dont-look-dont-find-corrupt-money-in-the-uk/#.WgN85mTTPIU (23 November 2015); Robert Barrington, *How Corrupt is Britain?*, Huff Post UK, available at www.huffingtonpost.co.uk/robert-barrington/corruption-britain_b_6911052.html (22 May 2015). With specific regard to money laundering, according to the National Crime Agency (NCA), billions of pounds of corrupt funds are routed through the UK every year. The UK government's own risk assessment, as of 2015, indicated that only a small proportion of those funds are being identified and investigated. See also Transparency International UK, *Corrupt Money in the UK*, available at www.transparency.org.uk/our-work/corrupt-money-in-the-uk/#.WgN5cGTTPIU (2017).

Papers regarding offshore tax havens and financial secrecy with regard to senior members of the UK government and the Royal Family itself, combined with ongoing scandals related to sexual harassment in the UK government and Parliament, have stoked significant public anger and frustration.[21]

In TI-UK's *Global Corruption Barometer* report for 2015–2016, for which approximately 1,000 UK citizens were interviewed, those citizens responded negatively (60% or more respondents said 'very badly' or 'fairly badly') to the question of whether the government was doing a good job of fighting corruption. Their response was moderately negative to the questions asking how corrupt Members of Parliament (MPs) were (20–40% of respondents stated 'most' or 'all' MPs are corrupt), and whether corruption was one of the biggest problems facing the country (15%–35% of respondents agreed it was one of the biggest problems facing the country).[22] If the survey were to have been repeated in 2017, it is likely that the results would have been even more negative.

The current focus on exiting the European Union has brought about further confusion regarding the UK government's priorities. Significant divisions within the country have given rise to a growing sense of uneasiness on the international stage. The UK government has asserted its commitment to anti-corruption enforcement, though the current Prime Minister has refused to confirm whether she will follow through on her predecessor's promise to create a public register of beneficial owners of offshore companies and trusts.[23]

2. International anti-corruption treaties

2.1 The OECD Anti-Bribery Convention 1997

On 21 November 1997, the member states of the Organisation for Economic Co-operation and Development (OECD) adopted the Convention on Combating Bribery of Foreign Public Officials in International Business Transactions (the OECD Convention). This convention came into force in February 1999.

---

21 The Guardian, *The Paradise Papers*, available at www.theguardian.com/news/series/paradise-papers (8 November 2017); Transparency International UK, *Paradise Papers give snapshot of gaping loopholes in the global financial system UK services, territories and systems complicit*, available at www.transparency.org.uk/press-releases/paradise-papers/#.WgN4vGTTPIU (5 November 2017).

22 Transparency International UK, *Global Corruption Barometer 2015–2016*, available at www.transparency.org/research/gcb/gcb_2015_16 (2016). In 2013, TI's *Global Corruption Barometer* noted that corruption in the UK was increasing. Survey participants identified the media as the most corrupt sector, closely followed by political parties. The report indicated that 65% of people in the UK believed that corruption had increased between 2011 and 2013. This represents a stark contrast to Transparency International's 2010 survey, which indicated that less than 40% believed the sector had a corruption problem. By 2013, the figure had risen to 69%, placing it as the sector people believed to be most affected by corruption. That survey indicated that 67% of respondents viewed political parties as being affected by corruption, and 55% believed that the British Parliament had a corruption problem. A shocking 90% of survey participants believed that the UK government was run by a few big entities acting in their own interests, and 62% believed that the government's actions were ineffective in tackling corruption. *See* Transparency International, *Global Corruption Barometer 2010–11*, available at: www.transparency.org/gcb201011 (2010–2011); Transparency International, *Global Corruption Barometer 2013*, available at www.transparency.org/gcb2013 (2013).

23 Jessica Elgot, The Guardian, *Paradise Papers: Theresa May refuses to promise register of offshore trusts*, available at www.theguardian.com/politics/2017/nov/06/paradise-papers-theresa-may-refuses-to-promise-register-of-offshore-trusts (6 November 2017).

The OECD Convention requires each signatory state to enact national legislation to implement the functional equivalence of the convention and create legally binding standards that criminalise bribery of foreign public officials.[24] The UK ratified the OECD Convention on 14 January 1998 and implemented legislation that came into effect on 15 February 1999.

The OECD also requires each signatory state to cooperate in its monitoring and peer review processes. Its most recent peer review report on the UK, the Phase 4 Report published in 2017, discusses the status of the UK's implementation of the convention and the extent to which it is abiding by the convention's requirements.[25]

2.2 The United Nations Convention Against Corruption 2003

The United Nations Convention against Corruption (UNCAC) was approved by the UN General Assembly on 31 October 2003 and has been signed by over 140 countries, including the UK, which signed the convention on 9 December 2003 and ratified it on 9 February 2006.[26]

The UNCAC, which addresses many different forms of corruption, covers five main subject areas:

- preventive measures;
- criminalisation and law enforcement;
- international cooperation;
- asset recovery; and
- technical assistance and information exchange.[27]

The asset recovery provisions of the UNCAC stipulate that, where public funds have been embezzled, confiscated property should be returned to its rightful owners – including countries from which it had been taken illicitly.[28] In similar fashion to the OECD Convention, the UNCAC offers a peer review and monitoring process.[29]

2.3 The Council of Europe's Group of States Against Corruption (GRECO), the Criminal Law Convention on Corruption and the Civil Law Convention on Corruption

The Group of States against Corruption (GRECO) was established in 1999 by the Council of Europe.[30] GRECO's primary objective is to improve the capacity of its member states to battle corruption by monitoring their compliance with the Council

24 United Kingdom – OECD Anti-Bribery Convention, www.oecd.org/daf/anti-bribery/ unitedkingdom-oecdanti-briberyconvention.htm.

25 OECD Working Group, *Implementing the OECD Anti-Bribery Convention, Phase 4 Report: United Kingdom*, available at www.oecd.org/corruption/anti-bribery/UK-Phase-4-Report-ENG.pdf (2017) ("OECD Phase 4 Report").

26 United Nations Office on Drugs and Crime, *United Kingdom of Great Britain and Northern Ireland Country Profile Page*, available at www.unodc.org/unodc/treaties/CAC/country-profile/CountryProfile.html?code=GBR.

27 *Ibid.*

28 United Nations Convention against Corruption (UNCAC), available at www.unodc.org/unodc/en/corruption/uncac.html (31 October 2003).

29 *Ibid.*

30 Council of Europe, Group of States Against Corruption, *About GRECO*, available at www.coe.int/en/web/greco/about-greco (2017).

of Europe's anti-corruption standards through its mutual evaluation and peer review process.[31] Currently, GRECO comprises 49 member states (48 European states, including the UK, plus the US).[32]

The Council of Europe adopted the Criminal Law Convention on Corruption in 1999, and subsequently adopted the Civil Law Convention on Corruption in the same year.

- The Criminal Law Convention, which entered into force in 2002, requires states parties to criminalise a wide variety of acts of corruption, including the promise, offer, gift, solicitation and receipt of bribes by domestic and foreign officials, as well as commercial bribery, and for states parties to provide for effective deterrent sanctions and measures.[33] The UK ratified the convention on 9 December 2003.[34]
- The purpose of the Civil Law Convention is to establish common international rules regarding civil law and corruption, and to prohibit the receipt of bribes in both the public and private sectors.[35] The convention requires states to provide legal remedies to those who have suffered damage due to corruption, and to enable them to defend their rights and interests, including potentially obtaining compensation for damage suffered.[36] The UK signed the Civil Law Convention in 2000.

2.4 The Global Declaration Against Corruption

The Global Declaration Against Corruption[37] (the Declaration) is not an international treaty but a voluntary declaration made by the UK government as part of its Anti-Corruption Summit in 2016 and signed by multiple other governments. Under the Declaration, signatories agree to expose, punish and drive out corruption, including by ending the misuse of anonymous companies to hide the proceeds of corruption. The signatories also pledge to increase the transparency of government budgets, tax information and procurement, deter tax evasion and expose the theft or misuse of taxpayers' money. They further promise to make it easier for people to report corruption.[38]

In May 2017, TI-UK updated its *Anti-Corruption Pledge Tracker*, which tracks the

---

31 GRECO also aims to to help identify deficiencies in national anti-corruption policies, thus prompting necessary legislative and practical reforms. GRECO also provides a platform to share best practices in the prevention and detection of corruption: *ibId.*

32 *Ibid.* Note that membership of GRECO is not limited to Council of Europe member states. Any state which becomes a state party to the criminal or civil law conventions on corruption automatically accedes to GRECO and its evaluation procedures.

33 Council of Europe, Criminal Law Convention on Corruption, 27 January 1999, available at www.coe.int/en/web/conventions/full-list/-/conventions/treaty/173.

34 *Ibid.*

35 Civil Law Convention on Corruption, 4 November 1999, available at www.coe.int/en/web/conventions/full-list/-/conventions/treaty/174.

36 *Ibid.*

37 Cabinet Office, Prime Minister's Office, 10 Downing Street, Global Declaration against Corruption, available at www.gov.uk/government/publications/global-declaration-against-corruption/global-declaration-against-corruption (2016).

38 *Ibid.*

39 Transparency International UK, *Anti-Corruption Pledge Tracker*, available at ukanticorruption pledgetracker.org (May 2017).

status of the pledges made by the declarants in the Declaration. As of the last update, 40% of the UK's pledges are complete, 20% are under way, 20% are pending and 20% are overdue.[39]

3. The concept of corruption in the UK

The 2010 Act, the UK's primary legislation defining and criminalising bribery and corruption, defines 'bribery' as giving or receiving a financial or other advantage in connection with the 'improper performance' of a position of trust, or a function that is expected to be performed impartially or in good faith.

Another source providing insight into the current concept of corruption in the UK is the UK Anti-Corruption Plan (the 2015 Plan) produced by the UK government in 2015. In the Plan, the UK government noted that there is no universally accepted definition of 'corruption' and cites various well-accepted definitions for corruption, including TI's definition of 'corruption' as "the abuse of entrusted power for private gain", and the World Bank's definition of a 'corrupt practice' as the "offering, giving, receiving or soliciting, directly or indirectly, of anything of value to influence improperly the actions of another party."[40]

The 2015 Plan provides the UK government's view and efforts to combat "what the UK public may commonly view as corruption."[41] Activities discussed in it include domestic and foreign bribery, the use of corruption by criminals to enable their crimes, the abuse of position by individuals for personal gain, and the systems and processes which those engaging in corruption exploit to achieve gain for themselves or others.[42]

Based on the results of the TI *Global Corruption Barometer* in recent years, it appears that the British public generally perceives corruption in line with the evolution of concepts of corruption originating from the UK, regarding the abuse of public positions and entrusted power for private gain. TI-UK labels corruption in the UK as encompassing activities which include:

- bribery;
- collusion;
- conflict of interest;
- nepotism;
- fraud;
- money laundering;
- taking advantage of figurative revolving doors between public office and private companies; and
- lobbying.[43]

---

40 HM Government, UK Anti-Corruption Plan, available at www.gov.uk/government/uploads/system/uploads/attachment_data/file/388894/UKantiCorruptionPlan.pdf (December 2014).

41 *Ibid.*

42 *Ibid.*

43 Transparency International UK, *Corruption – Dirty Business: Just How Clean is Britain?*, available at www.pinterest.co.uk/pin/507499451731011487/.

4. Laws regulations and enforcement authorities

4.1 The Bribery Act 2010

(a) Overview

The 2010 Act is the UK's main anti-corruption law. The act, which came into force in 2011, codified the common law offences related to bribery and replaced and consolidated the country's earlier corruption laws, viz, the Public Bodies Corrupt Practices Act 1889 and the Prevention of Corruption Acts 1906 and 1916. The old law continues to apply to conduct that pre-dates the 2010 Act.

As written, the 2010 Act is one of the most stringent anti-bribery laws in the world. It addresses both domestic and foreign bribery, has broad extraterritorial jurisdictional reach, and does not distinguish between commercial and public bribery. It also creates a strict liability offence for corporations engaging in bribery.

(b) Offences

The 2010 Act, which prohibits both commercial/private bribery and public bribery, creates four key offences under the following provisions:

- section 1 – active corruption;
- section 2 – passive corruption;
- section 6 – active bribery of a foreign official; and
- section 7 – corporate failure to prevent bribery by associated persons.

Section 1: Under section 1 of the 2010 Act, it is an offence for a person to offer, promise or give a financial or other advantage to another person:

- with the intent:
  - that the advantage induces a person to perform improperly a relevant function or activity; or
  - to reward a person for the improper performance of such a function or activity

OR

- with the knowledge or belief that the acceptance of the advantage itself constitutes the improper performance of a relevant function or activity.

It does not matter if the advantage is offered, promised or given by the person to the recipient directly or through a third party, or that the recipient or intended recipient is the same person who is to perform or has performed the relevant function or activity.

The terms "relevant function" and "relevant activity" are very broadly defined in section 3 of the 2010 Act as functions or activities subject to an expectation that they will be performed in good faith and/or impartially, or performed in accordance with a position of trust, and include:

- any function of a public nature;
- any activity connected with a business (including any trade or profession);
- any activity performed in the course of a person's employment; and

- any activity performed by or on behalf of a body of persons (whether corporate or unincorporated).

The expression "improper performance" means performance of a function or activity that breaches the expectation that a person will act in good faith, impartially or in accordance with a position of trust in carrying out that performance. Expectation is determined by what a reasonable person in the UK would expect with respect to the performance of the function or activity.

Section 2: Section 2 of the 2010 Act criminalises the receipt and solicitation of bribes. It prohibits a person from requesting, agreeing to receive or accepting a financial or other advantage with the intention that, as a consequence, a relevant function or activity will be performed improperly. It does not matter if the bribe is received directly or from a third party and it is similarly irrelevant whether the recipient, or the intermediary for the bribe, knows or believes the performance of the function or activity is improper.

The definitions applicable to section 1 are also applicable to section 2. As with section 1, the prosecution must provide evidence of improper performance or the intention to induce such performance.

Section 6: Section 6 creates an offence of bribery of a foreign public official. It requires the prosecution to show that the person who bribes an official has the intention of influencing the foreign official in his or her capacity as a foreign official, as well as the intention to obtain or retain business or an advantage in the conduct of business. Section 6 has a lower evidential requirement than the section 1 and 2 offences, as there is no need to prove that 'improper performance' occurred or that there was an intention to induce it. The bribe may be committed through a third party.

Unlike the section 1 and 2 offences, section 6 covers only the offering, promising and giving of bribes, not the acceptance or solicitation of bribes by foreign public officials. The term 'foreign public official' includes both government officials as well as individuals working for public international organisations.

Section 7: Section 7 contains the key new measure of the 2010 Act, which is the failure of a relevant commercial organisation to prevent bribery. The corporate entity will be guilty of a section 7 offence if it fails to prevent a person associated with the company from bribing another person with the intention of obtaining or retaining business or an advantage in the conduct of business for the corporate entity. The company will only have a defence to a section 7 charge if it can show that it had in place 'adequate procedures' designed to prevent persons associated with the company from engaging in such conduct.

The section 7 offence pertains particularly to offering, promising or giving a bribe by an associated person; it does not criminalise the failure to prevent the taking of bribes. It is immaterial for the purposes of this offence where the relevant conduct took place.

The MoJ *Guidance* notes that to be liable under section 7, the commercial organisation must have failed to prevent conduct that would amount to a contravention of section 1 or section 6, though it is irrelevant whether a person has been convicted of such an offence.

Moreover, the MoJ *Guidance* notes that the section 7 offence is additional to, and does not displace, liability arising out of either section 1 or section 6 of the 2010 Act where the company itself commits an offence by virtue of the common law 'identification' principle, which provides that corporate liability arises where the offence is committed by a natural person who is the "directing mind or will of the organisation."[44]

(c) ***Senior officers***

Under section 14 of the 2010 Act, senior officers of companies who "consent or connive" to commit bribery commit the same offence: there are no separate offences for 'consent' and 'connivance'. In order to bring a case against a senior officer, it must first be shown that the corporate entity has been guilty of an offence under sections 1, 2 or 6. If such an offence has been committed, section 14 provides that the senior officer is guilty of the same offence if he or she has consented to or connived in the commission of the offence, and he or she has a close connection to the UK.

(d) ***Jurisdiction***

The 2010 Act is perceived as one of the most sweeping anti-corruption laws enacted, due to its extremely broad jurisdictional reach as written. By its terms, the act applies regardless of where the acts on which it is predicated occurred, so long as the target entity:

- is a UK resident;
- is incorporated in the UK; or
- carries on any part of its business in the UK, even if that business has nothing to do with the improper payment or predicate act itself.

This means that violations with no actual territorial nexus to the UK may be prosecuted under the law.

Broadly, an offence under sections 1, 2 and 6 of the 2010 Act may be prosecuted if:

- any act or omission forming part of the offence takes place in the UK; or
- it is performed outside of the UK, but is committed by a person having a 'close connection' with the UK by virtue of being a British national, ordinarily resident in the UK or a corporate body incorporated in the UK.

The section 7 offence has even greater breadth, as it does not require any 'close connection with the UK' and a commercial organisation can be liable for conduct constituting a section 1 or section 6 offence on the part of a person who is neither a

44 MoJ *Guidance*, at p9.

UK national nor resident in the UK, nor a body incorporated or formed in the UK. It is irrelevant whether the acts or omissions that form part of the section 7 offence take place in the UK or elsewhere, as that provision encompasses any corporate entity, wherever incorporated, which carries on a business or part of a business in any part of the UK. This provision is as yet untested in the UK courts, but would seem to encompass foreign businesses that do business in the UK.

The MoJ *Guidance* suggests that the mere listing of securities in the UK would be sufficient on its own to indicate that a company carries on business there.[45] The SFO has made statements in the past indicating that it intends to use the extraterritorial jurisdiction provided by the 2010 Act.[46] It is not yet clear the extent to which the SFO will use this jurisdictional reach.

(e) Defences

Local law: It is a defence to charges under sections 1, 2 and 6 if the relevant transaction or act were permissible under an applicable written law.

Adequate procedures: It is potentially a full defence to a section 7 charge for a corporate body to show that it had 'adequate procedures' in place at the time the relevant offence was committed. Neither the 2010 Act nor the MoJ *Guidance* defines the expression 'adequate procedures.' The MoJ *Guidance* indicates that there is no single 'one size fits all' solution and states that whether or not a company has adequate procedures in place is a matter of the facts and circumstances of each case.

The MoJ has indicated that companies should be informed by its six key principles, which are:

- proportionate procedures;
- top-level commitment;
- risk assessment;
- due diligence;
- communication and training; and
- monitoring and review.

(f) Penalties

An individual who is guilty on indictment of one of the offences under sections 1, 2 and 6 risks an unlimited fine and/or up to 10 years' imprisonment. Corporate bodies are subject to an unlimited fine.

For companies, direct penalties are in addition to potential indirect sanctions, such as loss of public financing or exclusion from public procurement processes.

---

45 *Ibid*, at p15.

46 For example, Richard Alderman, the former head of the SFO, stated that "I shall have jurisdiction in respect of corruption committed by those corporates anywhere in the world even if the corruption is not taking place through the business presence of the corporate in this jurisdiction... Assume that quite separately that foreign corporate is involved in corruption in a third country. We have jurisdiction over that corruption," FCPA Blog, *SFO to Foreign Companies: Watch Out*, available at www.fcpablog.com/blog/2011/1/26/sfo-to-foreign-companies-watch-out.html (26 January 2011).

Under the UK Proceeds of Crime Act 2002,[47] companies may face asset confiscation. Other potential collateral consequences include director disqualifications, debarment from the World Bank and partner development banks, and other similar issues.

(g) ***Associated persons***

The 2010 Act's concept of an 'associated person' broadly encompasses any person, whether an entity or an individual performing a service for, or on behalf of, the relevant corporate body, including employees, subsidiaries or agents. The MoJ *Guidance* indicates, however, that corporate liability resulting from acts of such associated persons would not necessarily be triggered by a mere shareholding or a simple investment, as in the case of a joint venture or a subsidiary.[48] The *Guidance* notes that relevant elements for consideration in determining the level of association are the degree of control by the corporate body over the subsidiary or a joint venture.

(h) ***Facilitating payments***

Unlike the United States' Foreign Corrupt Practices Act 1977 (FCPA), the 2010 Act does not contain any exception for so-called 'facilitating (or facilitation) payments'. This is consistent with more recent anti-corruption laws enacted globally as well as the OECD's 2009 Recommendation, which recognised the "corrosive effect" of facilitating payments and asked member states to discourage companies from making such payments.[49]

4.2 Other laws

The UK has a host of other laws that may also be wielded against individuals or companies engaging in bribery or other corruption. These include the Companies Act 2006, the Financial Services and Markets Act 2000 and the Criminal Finances Act 2017.[50]

---

47 The UK Proceeds of Crime Act 2002 provides for criminal confiscation, civil recovery, cash seizure and taxation powers with respect to criminal assets or proceeds of crime. It constitutes the UK's principal money laundering legislation. The act also provides for a number of investigative powers, including search and seizure powers and freezing of assets. See the Proceeds of Crime Act 2002, available at www.legislation.gov.uk/ukpga/2002/29/contents (2002).

48 MoJ *Guidance*, at p40.

49 OECD, Recommendation of the Council for Further Combating Bribery of Foreign Public Officials in International Business Transactions, available at www.oecd.org/daf/anti-bribery/44176910.pdf (26 November 2009).

50 The Companies Act 2006 includes a wide range of offences relating to non-compliance, with requirements on auditing, company formation and listing, reporting, etc. Even administrative non-compliance may be considered an 'economic crime' if there is an impact on investors. *See* Timothy Edmonds, House of Commons Library, Briefing Paper: *Corporate Economic Crime: Bribery & Corruption*, available at http://researchbriefings.files.parliament.uk/documents/CBP-7359/CBP-7359.pdf (22 March 2017). The Financial Services and Markets Act 2000 applies to financial services firms regulated by the Financial Conduct Authority (see 4.3 below), which has stringent regulations for financial reporting and disclosure, and expects all entities it regulates not only to abide by the 2010 Act but also to adopt measures to prevent and detect corruption. See the Financial Services and Markets Act 2000, available at www.legislation.gov.uk/ukpga/2000/8/contents (2000). The UK's recently enacted Criminal Finances Act 2017 creates corporate offences regarding the failure to prevent tax evasion, regardless of whether a corporate entity has any relationship with or presence within the UK. See the Criminal Finances Act 2017, available at www.legislation.gov.uk/ukpga/2017/22/contents/enacted (2017). The Criminal Finances Act, in similar fashion to the 2010 Act, provides a defence of 'reasonable procedures'.

4.3 Enforcement authorities

Several UK agencies have the authority and power to take enforcement action against those who engage in financial crimes, such as bribery and corruption. The Serious Fraud Office (SFO) is the main enforcement agency responsible for investigating and prosecuting violations of the 2010 Act specifically. In Scotland, the Scottish Crown Office maintains its own self-reporting regime for 2010 Act violations.[51]

In addition, the Financial Conduct Authority (FCA) regulates, investigates and enforces breaches of financial regulations against entities within the financial sector, and the relatively new National Crime Agency (NCA) has an International Corruption Unit ICU) that works in partnership with the UK government's Department of International Development to investigate international corruption cases and related money laundering.[52]

(a) The SFO

The SFO's stated aims are to reduce fraud and corruption and the cost of such behaviour, deliver justice and the rule of law, and maintain confidence in the UK's business and financial institutions.[53] The SFO works closely with police in England & Wales, but retains its independence.

The SFO has an operating budget of £35.7 million for 2017–2018, holding steady from its 2016 core budget, which saw a modest increase from £33.8 million in 2015–2016.[54] The SFO reported during the OECD Phase 3 Evaluation, however, that it did not have enough funds to investigate every allegation and therefore had to take a balanced approach.[55]

The OECD Working Group on Bribery has called on the UK to provide the SFO with sufficient resources to ensure that enforcement of the 2010 Act is strengthened.[56] The SFO's conviction rates, while rising, are still relatively low and the Working Group remains concerned that the SFO is not able to investigate fully the allegations it receives or of which it learns.[57] The OECD Working Group, TI-UK and law firms have all advocated for the SFO to receive more funding in order to meet the government's commitment to enforcing the 2010 Act.[58]

---

51 Laura Clare & Rob Elvin, *Bribery in Scotland – Civil Settlement Under Bribery Act and the Scottish Crown Office*, The Anticorruption Blog, available at www.anticorruptionblog.com/united-kingdom/bribery-in-scotland-civil-settlement-under-bribery-act-and-the-scottish-crown-office/ (19 April 2016). Civil settlements in Scotland are handled by the Scottish Crown Office's Serious and Organised Crime Division in cooperation with the Scottish Civil Recovery Unit.

52 National Crime Agency, International *Corruption Unit*, available at www.nationalcrimeagency.gov.uk/about-us/what-we-do/economic-crime/international-corruption-unit-icu.

53 UK Serious Fraud Office, *What We Do and Who Do We Work With*, available at www.sfo.gov.uk/about-us/what-we-do-and-who-we-work-with.aspx.

54 SFO, *Annual Report 2016–2017*, available at www.sfo.gov.uk/download/annual-report-2016-2017/?wpdmdl=16932 (19 July 2017).

55 TaylorWessing, *The UK's implementation of the OECD Anti-Bribery Convention*, available at https://united-kingdom.taylorwessing.com/en/insights/corporate-crime-matters/the-uks-implementation-of-the-oecd-anti-bribery-convention (12 April 2017). In addition, funding is set to decrease for the SFO in 2018–2019 to £34.3 million and further in 2019–2020 to £33.5 million. *See* SFO, (note 54 above) at p36.

56 OECD Phase 4 Report

57 *Ibid.*

(b) ***The NCA***

The NCA is a relatively newly created agency with national and international reach, granted the authority to work in partnership with other law enforcement entities in order to address serious and organised crime.[59] The NCA's investigations include business crime, including bribery and corruption. The NCA's International corruption Unit (ICU) is now the central investigator of international corruption in the UK.[60]

5. Relevant public cases

5.1 Introduction

Enforcement of the 2010 Act has been rising following two significant cases for the SFO in 2015. These involved:

- the first use by the SFO of a deferred prosecution agreement (DPA) to settle an investigation under the act – similar to those used by the US enforcement authorities in settling charges under the FCPA 1977; and
- the first section 7 corporate conviction secured by the SFO.

In 2016, the SFO imposed two significant fines for bribery offences, in the UK's second-ever DPA for a 2010 Act settlement, and announced several new corporate investigations. In 2017, the SFO announced a 2010 Act settlement with Rolls-Royce plc. In 2018, two individuals were sentenced following the first contested prosecution under section 7 of the UKBA, in which the relevant company, Skansen Interiors Limited ('SIL'), was also found guilty by a jury.

5.2 Standard Bank (2015)

In November 2015, the SFO entered into the UK's first-ever DPA with Standard Bank (now ICBC Standard Bank plc) for £26.6 million.[61] Standard Bank was also the first example of a company brought before the UK courts for a section 7 offence (the corporate offence of failure to prevent bribery discussed at 4.1 above).[62]

Standard Bank also settled with the US Securities and Exchange Commission

---

58 Transparency International UK, *SFO Resource Deficit Endangers Anti-Bribery Effort*, available at www.transparency.org.uk/press-releases/sfo-resource-deficit-endangers-anti-bribery-effort/#.WgOWy2TTPIU (6 September 2012); TaylorWessing, *op cit* (note 55 above); Pinsent Masons, Out-Law.Com, *SFO budget cuts restricting its ability to seize assets from convicted UK white collar criminals, says expert*, available at www.out-law.com/en/articles/2014/march/sfo-budget-cuts-restricting-its-ability-to-seize-assets-from-convicted-uk-white-collar-criminals-says-expert/ (11 March 2014); Eversheds Sutherland, *Eversheds comment: UK SFO's budget needs upping*, available at https://press.eversheds-sutherland.com/news/22821/eversheds-comment-uk-sfos-budget-needs-upping (8 January 2016).

59 National Crime Agency, *International Corruption Unit*, available at www.nationalcrimeagency.gov.uk/about-us/what-we-do/economic-crime/international-corruption-unit-icu. The ICU replaces the Metropolitan Police Service Proceeds of Corruption Unit and the City of London Police Overseas Anti-Corruption Unit.

60 National Crime Agency, *National Strategic Assessment of Serious and Organised Crime*, available at www.nationalcrimeagency.gov.uk/publications/560-national-strategic-assessment-of-serious-and-organised-crime-2015/file.

61 SFO, *SFO Agrees First DPA with Standard Bank*, available at www.sfo.gov.uk/2015/11/30/sfo-agrees-first-uk-dpa-with-standard-bank/ (30 November 2015).

62 *Ibid.*

63 SFO, Deferred *Prosecution Agreement - SFO v ICBC SB PLC*, available at www.sfo.gov.uk/download/deferred-prosecution-agreement-sfo-v-icbc-sb-plc/?wpdmdl=7600 (18 May 2016).

('SEC') for $4.2 million. The SFO DPA required Standard Bank to pay the government of Tanzania a further $7 million in compensation, plus £330,000 for the SFO's investigation costs.[63] The SFO DPA also required Standard Bank to cooperate with the SFO and have an independent review of its existing anti-corruption compliance programme.[64]

The SFO alleged that Stanbic Bank Tanzania, an affiliate of Standard Bank, paid $6 million in March 2013 to a local partner.[65] The partner was allegedly intended to use the funds to influence Tanzanian government officials to favour Stanbic Tanzania in a $600 million private placement to be carried out on behalf of the government.[66] This placement reportedly generated transaction fees of $8.4 million for Stanbic Tanzania and Standard Bank.

Standard Bank self-disclosed the matter to the SFO in April 2014 and commissioned external counsel to conduct an investigation. The SFO stated publicly that the judgment (in which the court approved the DPA, a requirement for DPAs in the UK) provided helpful guidance to those advising corporate bodies, and applauded Standard Bank for its "frankness with the SFO and their [sic] prompt and early engagement" with the SFO.[67]

5.3 Sweett Group (2016)

In February 2016, the SFO completed the first prosecution under section 7 of the 2010 Act, against the Sweett Group PLC (Sweett Group). The Sweett Group pleaded guilty to a charge of failing to prevent an act of bribery intended to secure and retain a contract in December 2015.[68] The company was sentenced in February 2016, and ordered to pay £2.25 million as a result of its conviction.[69]

Cyril Sweett International Ltd (Cyril Sweett), a foreign subsidiary of the Sweett Group, had allegedly made improper payments to a board member of an insurance company in order to obtain a contract to provide the insurance company with project management and cost-consulting services for the construction of a hotel in Abu Dhabi.[70] In sentencing the Sweett Group, the judge stated that the "whole point of Section 7 is to impose a duty on those running such companies throughout the world properly to supervise them. Rogue elements can only operate in this way – and operate for so long – because of a failure properly to supervise what they are doing and the way they are doing it."[71]

---

64 *Ibid.*

65 SFO, *Deferred Prosecution Agreement - Statement of Facts - SFO v ICBC SB PLC*, available at www.sfo.gov.uk/download/deferred-prosecution-agreement-statement-facts-sfo-v-icbc-sb-plc/?wpdmdl=7603 (18 May 2016).

66 *Ibid.*

67 SFO, *SFO Agrees First DPA with Standard Bank*, available at www.sfo.gov.uk/2015/11/30/sfo-agrees-first-uk-dpa-with-standard-bank/ (30 November 2015).

68 SFO, *Sweett Group PLC sentenced and ordered to pay £2.25 million after Bribery Act conviction*, available at www.sfo.gov.uk/2016/02/19/sweett-group-plc-sentenced-and-ordered-to-pay-2-3-million-after-bribery-act-conviction/ (19 February 2016).

69 SFO, *Sweett Group*, available at www.sfo.gov.uk/cases/sweett-group/ (12 May 2016).

70 SFO, *Sweett Group PLC sentenced and ordered to pay £2.25 million after Bribery Act conviction*, available at www.sfo.gov.uk/2016/02/19/sweett-group-plc-sentenced-and-ordered-to-pay-2-3-million-after-bribery-act-conviction/ (19 February 2016).

71 *Ibid.*

Notably, the Sweett Group was not offered a DPA. This was the first case in which a company was convicted and sentenced in the UK for the section 7 offence of failing to prevent bribery by an associated person.

On 21 December 2016, a former Sweett Group executive was convicted of two destruction of evidence offences, pursuant to the UK Criminal Justice Act 1987.[72] The executive, Richard Kingston, was a managing director of the Sweett Group's Middle East and India operations and was found guilty of concealing, destroying or otherwise disposing of two mobile phones, knowing or suspecting that the data stored on them was relevant to the SFO's investigation into alleged bribery by the Sweett Group.[73] Kingston was sentenced to 12 months' imprisonment on each count, to run concurrently.

5.4 Smith & Ouzman Ltd (2016)

Smith & Ouzman Ltd was convicted in January 2016 of pre-2010 Act offences.[74] This was the first SFO trial to have resulted in a corporate conviction for foreign bribery, and concluded an investigation that had begun in 2010.[75] Under the pre-2010 Act legislation, it was necessary to demonstrate that the "directing mind and will" of the body corporate was involved in the relevant conduct, or that the conduct could be imputed to such directing mind and will (though this is no longer necessary to prosecute a section 7 offence under the 2010 Act).[76]

In the Smith & Ouzman case, the SFO provided sufficient evidence to demonstrate to the jury that two senior individuals were the directing mind and will of the body corporate and had been involved in the improper conduct, and so secured a conviction.[77]

5.5 XYZ Limited (2016)

The SFO's second DPA involved a company that was anonymised as XYZ Limited.[78] The DPA received court approval in July 2016 and XYZ Limited faced an indictment

---

72 SFO, *Richard Kingston convicted and sentenced for destroying bribery and corruption evidence*, available at www.sfo.gov.uk/2016/12/21/richard-kingston-convicted-sentenced-destroying-bribery-corruption-evidence/ (21 December 2016).

73 *Ibid.*

74 SFO, *Convicted printing company sentenced and ordered to pay £2.2 million*, available at www.sfo.gov.uk/2016/01/08/convicted-printing-company-sentenced-and-ordered-to-pay-2-2-million/ (8 January 2016).

75 SFO, *Smith and Ouzman Ltd*, available at www.sfo.gov.uk/cases/smith-ouzman-ltd/ (4 April 2017)

76 Under the English common law 'identification principle', to prosecute a company, the Crown had to show that the commission of an offence could be imputed to the 'directing mind and will' of a body corporate. In practice, the 'directing mind and will' of a body corporate was generally a member (or members) of the board of directors, the company's managing director or other very senior executives who could bind the company. Section 7 of the 2010 Act created a corporate offence for bribery that eliminated this requirement, which historically had been a difficult standard to meet for prosecutors. See, for example, Ole Mückenberger, Jonathan Pickworth, Jonah Anderson & Moritz Mussman, *Approaching the fifth anniversary of the UK Bribery Act*, available at www.businesslaw-magazine.com/wp-content/uploads/sites/4/2016/03/5_BusinessLawMagazine_1-2016.pdf (3 March 2016)*;* Henry Garfield, Joanna Ludlam, Charles Thomson & Ben Ko (Baker & McKenzie United Kingdom), *Corporate Liability in the United Kingdom*, available at https://globalcompliancenews.com/areas-of-law/white-collar-crime-2/corporate-liability-handbook/corporate-liability-in-the-united-kingdom/ (2016); Kumar Subramani, *BRIBERY ACT IN UK: First corporate convicted for bribe paid overseas*, available at www.linkedin.com/pulse/bribery-act-uk-first-corporate-convicted-bribe-paid-kumar-subramani/ (12 January 2016).

77 *Ibid.*

78 SFO, *SFO secures second DPA*, available at www.sfo.gov.uk/2016/07/08/sfo-secures-second-dpa/ (8 July 2016).

79 *Ibid.*

alleging conspiracy to corrupt and to bribe under the pre-2010 Act laws as well as under section 7 of that act of failure to prevent bribery in relation to certain overseas supply contracts.[79]

XYZ Limited agreed to pay £6.6 million, comprising a £6.2 million disgorgement and a £352,000 financial penalty. The judge and the SFO both remarked on the company's exemplary cooperation with the SFO.[80]

According to the judgment, a significant percentage of the company's employees and agents had engaged in systematic bribery for nearly 10 years to obtain contracts to supply XYZ's products.[81] XYZ apparently learned of these activities shortly after its parent company implemented a global compliance programme in 2012. XYZ acted quickly in retaining external counsel to conduct an investigation, and initially reported to the SFO on an anonymous and oral basis in 2012.[82] Subsequently, in January 2013, XYZ formally self-reported its findings to the SFO, following which the SFO then conducted its own investigation based on that report.[83]

5.6 Rolls Royce plc (2017)

On 17 January 2017, US, UK and Brazilian authorities announced that they had entered into settlements with UK-based Rolls-Royce plc (Rolls-Royce). Rolls-Royce, a company operating in the global civil and defence, aerospace, marine and energy industries, entered into a DPA with the SFO, pursuant to which it agreed to pay £500 million for conspiracy to corrupt, false accounting and failure to prevent bribery, in addition to a nearly $170 million US$ penalty in the US under a DPA with the US Department of Justice (DOJ).[84] Rolls-Royce was also required to reimburse the SFO's investigations costs of £13 million. The conduct addressed in the SFO DPA is distinct from the activities addressed in the US DPA, and the UK resolution focuses on conduct between 1989 and 2013 across seven jurisdictions – Indonesia, Russia, Nigeria, China, Malaysia, Thailand and India.[85]

While Rolls Royce did not self-report to the SFO, the judge who approved the settlement, Lord Justice Leveson, approved the DPA and referenced what the SFO described as "extraordinary cooperation" from Rolls Royce.[86]

Notably, Rolls-Royce had appointed an external compliance adviser, Lord Gold, in 2013. The US resolution did not require Rolls-Royce to enter into a monitorship under an independent compliance monitor, instead requiring that Rolls-Royce engage in a self-monitorship. The SFO DPA, however, formalised Lord Gold's appointment, requiring

80 *Ibid.*

81 SFO, *XYZ Final Redacted Judgment*, available at: www.sfo.gov.uk/download/xyz-final-redacted/?wpdmdl=13285 (11 July 2016).

82 *Ibid.*

83 *Ibid.*

84 SFO, *SFO Completes £497.25m Deferred Prosecution Agreement with Rolls-Royce PLC*, available at www.sfo.gov.uk/2017/01/17/sfo-completes-497-25m-deferred-prosecution-agreement-rolls-royce-plc/ (17 January 2017).

85 SFO, *Deferred Prosecution Agreement – SFO v Rolls Royce PLC*, available at www.sfo.gov.uk/download/deferred-prosecution-agreement-sfo-v-rolls-royce-plc/?wpdmdl=14777 (17 January 2017).

86 Judgment of Sir Brian Leveson, President of the Queen's Bench Division, at [19], available at www.judiciary.gov.uk/wp-content/uploads/2017/01/sfo-v-rolls-royce.pdf (17 January 2017).

87 SFO, *Deferred Prosecution Agreement – SFO v Rolls Royce PLC*, available at www.sfo.gov.uk/download/deferred-prosecution-agreement-sfo-v-rolls-royce-plc/?wpdmdl=14777 (17 January 2017).

him to draft a third compliance report by 31 March 2017 and stating that if he resigned, or was unable to fulfil his obligations, Rolls-Royce would be required to notify the SFO immediately.[87] A replacement would then have to be approved by the SFO.

This was the third DPA ever used by the SFO, demonstrating that the UK continues to increase enforcement using US-type methodologies and strategies.

5.7 Skansen Interiors Limited

SIL was a small dormant company in the fit-out construction sector, and was convicted by a jury under section 7 of the UKBA in March 2018. The individuals who were identified as responsible for paying and receiving the improper payments both pleaded guilty to bribery offences under sections 1 and 2 of the UKBA, while SIL defended itself in court but was found guilty.

The two individuals were sentenced to 12 and 20 months' imprisonment respectively and were both disqualified from acting as directors. In sentencing the two individuals, the judge referenced the Sentencing Guidelines on Fraud, Bribery and Money Laundering, considering the individuals' culpability as well as the harm they caused.

These prosecutions indicate that CPS is demonstrably willing to pursue cases that do not involve large sums of money against individuals and that small, even dormant companies will not escape prosecution if they are identified as having engaged in improper conduct.

6. Next steps

6.1 Background

The UK government is facing an increasingly tumultuous political landscape, with Brexit looming on the horizon. The EU, and the world beyond, has expressed deep uncertainty as to what the future holds for the country, including with respect to anti-corruption and anti-bribery efforts.

6.2 Commitment to enforcement, transparency and addressing domestic corruption

The UK should ensure that it keeps its promises with respect to anti-corruption enforcement and makes efforts to ease the EU and other states' concerns regarding the effect of Brexit on its anti-corruption efforts. The UK should also clarify whether it will remain a signatory and state party to the Council of Europe's anti-corruption conventions.

The UK government must also heed the concerns raised by civil society groups such as Transparency International UK and address the domestic issues, including corruption and impropriety in Parliament and in the government, facilitation of tax evasion and money laundering through the City of London and City property and other related issues. The UK government should firmly commit to creating the public register of beneficial ownership as well as limiting the use of offshore tax havens to facilitate tax evasion. In order truly to champion robust anti-corruption enforcement, the UK government must take concrete action to address the underlying issues that undermine its anti-corruption efforts.

The UK has a noble and unarguably important history, having played a significant role in developing the concepts of public trust and accountability and the framework for anti-corruption in the world. Without greater efforts being placed on transparency and fairness in enforcement, as well as in its own governance, the country risks tarnishing that proud history. Its focus should not merely be on the blockbuster cases the US has become well-known for on the world anti-corruption stage, but on identifying and remedying the more endemic and less obvious forms of corruption that pervade British society.

United States

Hillary Levun
Perkins Coie LLP

1. Introduction

Corruption:

> *[A]n impairment of integrity, virtue, or moral principle [including] the impairment of a public official's duties by bribery [or] [a] fiduciary's or official's use of a station or office to procure some benefit either personally or for someone else, contrary to the rights of others; an act carried out with the intent of giving some advantage inconsistent with official duty and the rights of others.*[1]

The United States consistently ranks high in global anti-corruption surveys and is generally perceived to have low levels of corruption compared to many other countries around the world.[2] This is not, of course, to say, that corruption does not exist in the US. On the contrary, these perceptions are likely due to the high levels of anti-corruption enforcement by US law enforcement forces and prosecutors.[3]

The prevention of corruption is built into the fabric of American jurisprudence, dating back to the drafting of the US Constitution. Indeed, the Constitution contains a number of provisions intended to discourage corruption in government affairs and limit opportunities for corrupt self-enrichment. For instance, the Constitution permits impeachment of any officer of the United States, including the President, for bribery,[4] and prohibits anyone holding "any Office of Profit or Trust . . . without the consent of the Congress, [from accepting] any present, Emolument, Office, or Title, of any kind whatever, from any King, Prince, or foreign State."[5]

In the more than 230 years since the Constitution was drafted, American anti-corruption law has continued to develop and become more accessible. Some of the largest companies in the world have been prosecuted for bribery in the US, providing deterrent examples for others in the global marketplace as well as billions of dollars in funding (through the imposition of penalties) for further anti-corruption enforcement efforts.[6] Naturally, the glamour and prestige of these cases has attracted significant attention to and for the US Foreign Corrupt Practices Act 1976 (FCPA),[7]

1 *Black's Law Dictionary* (10th Edition, 2014).
2 See *Transparency International Corruption Perceptions Index* (2016), available at www.transparency.org/news/feature/corruption_perceptions_index_2016.
3 The enforcement of US anti-corruption laws is uniquely decentralised. In addition to the prosecutors in the US Department of Justice, there are more than 70 independent inspectors general embedded in various federal agencies who are specifically charged with investigating and enforcing ethics and anti-corruption laws.
4 US Constitution, article II, § 4.
5 *Ibid*, article I, § 9, clause 8.

the law under which these cases were all brought, making that act the first, and sometimes only, statute that people think of when American anti-corruption law is mentioned.

Yet, the United States has a robust set of purely domestic anti-corruption and anti-bribery statutes that are invoked far more frequently than is the FCPA, and that do just as much to promote integrity in US government and business relations.[8] Indeed, in 2016 alone, 982 federal, state and local government officials and employees and bribe payers were prosecuted under federal domestic anti-corruption and anti-bribery statutes.[9] Of those, 886 individuals (90%) were ultimately convicted.[10] By contrast, 2016 saw 30 individual and corporate prosecutions (or guilty pleas) under the FCPA.[11] Similarly, between 2013 and 2015, there were 16 corporate resolutions and 34 cases in which individuals were charged or pleaded guilty under the FCPA.[12] During that same period, 3,152 individuals were charged, of whom 2,930 (93%) were convicted, under the domestic anti-bribery and anti-corruption statutes.[13]

Section 2 of this chapter discusses in detail the main federal anti-bribery law in the United States, which is applicable only to federal government officials, employees and agents, and examines some recent limitations on the reach of the statute. Section 3 introduces a handful of other federal statutes that may be invoked to extend federal jurisdiction to state and local actors. Section 4 moves outside the public sector and details the various ways in which federal law enforcement can regulate private sector, or commercial, bribery. Finally, section 5 contains some brief concluding impressions.

---

6 See, for example, the following US Department of Justice press releases: (1) *Rolls-Royce plc Agrees to Pay $170 Million Criminal Penalty to Resolve Foreign Corrupt Practices Act Case* (17 January 2017); (2) *Teva Pharmaceutical Industries Ltd Agrees to Pay More Than $283 Million to Resolve Foreign Corrupt Practices Act Charges* (22 December 2016); (3) *Odebrecht and Braskem Plead Guilty and Agree to Pay at Least $3.5 Billion in Global Penalties to Resolve Largest Foreign Bribery Case in History* (21 December 2016); (4) *Avon China Pleads Guilty to Violating the FCPA by Concealing More Than $8 Million in Gifts to Chinese Officials* (17 December 2014); and (5) *Ralph Lauren Corporation Resolves Foreign Corrupt Practices Act Investigation and Agrees to Pay $882,000 Monetary Penalty* (22 April 2013).

7 15 USC §§ 78dd-1, 78dd-2, 78dd-3, 78m, 78ff.

8 As discussed further below, those who accept bribes may be prosecuted to the same extent under domestic anti-bribery laws as those who pay bribes. The FCPA criminalises the payment of bribes but has no similar provision to prosecute the receipt of bribes.

9 Public Integrity Section, Criminal Division, US Department of Justice, *Report to Congress on the Activities and Operations of the Public Integrity Section 20* (2016), available at www.justice.gov/criminal/file/1015521/download. The Public Integrity Section focuses on public corruption, ie, crimes involving abuses of public trust by government officials.

10 *Ibid.*

11 Fraud Section, Criminal Division, US Department of Justice, *Fraud Section Year in Review 2016*, available at www.justice.gov/criminal-fraud/page/file/929741/download (Foreign Corrupt Practices Act Unit enforcement statistics). There were also five FCPA pilot programme declinations, which are beyond the scope of this chapter.

12 Fraud Section, Criminal Division, US Department of Justice, *Fraud Section Year in Review 2015*, available at www.justice.gov/criminal-fraud/file/833301/download (Foreign Corrupt Practices Act Unit enforcement statistics).

13 Public Integrity Section, Criminal Division, US Department of Justice, *Report to Congress on the Activities and Operations of the Public Integrity Section 22* (2016), available at www.justice.gov/criminal/file/1015521/download.

2. The federal anti-bribery statute

In the domestic context, bribery of federal public officials falls within the ambit of 18 USC Section 201.[14] This general anti-bribery statute[15] prohibits, directly or indirectly, corruptly giving, offering or promising anything of value to any federal public official, or any person selected to be a federal public official, with intent either to:

- influence that person's official act;
- commit, collude in or allow a fraud upon the United States; or
- do or omit to do any act in violation of his or her lawful duty.[16]

The statute also criminalises any federal public official or a person selected to be a federal public official who:

- corruptly demands, seeks, receives, accepts, or agrees to receive or accept anything of value personally, or for any other person or entity, in return for being influenced in the performance of an official act;
- commits, colludes in or allows a fraud upon the United States; or
- does or omits to do any act in violation of his or her lawful duty.[17]

Violations of these provisions are punishable by a fine and imprisonment for a term of up to 15 years. Violators may also be disqualified from holding further government office.[18]

Section 201 also prohibits the direct or indirect solicitation or payment of "gratuities."[19] The elements of a gratuities violation overlap significantly with those of a bribery violation, though gratuities need not be paid with the intent of actually influencing an official to act or not act in a certain way.[20] Rather, a payment to a federal official may constitute an illegal gratuity if it is given "for or because of any official act performed or to be performed" by the official.[21] Because there is no requirement that the gift actually produce any specific result, a gift given to an official after an act that is favourable to the giver has been taken could still trigger Section 201(c).[22] Illegal gratuities violations may be punished by a fine and up to two years' imprisonment.[23]

---

14 18 USC Section 201 applies only to federal officials, not to state or local officials. However, as explained further below, certain other federal statutes can be used to prosecute state and local actors for corrupt conduct that otherwise violates Section 201. Bribery involving state and local public officials is also prohibited by the laws of each state, which are individually beyond the scope of this chapter.

15 There are a number of other federal statutes that criminalise giving or receiving payments in the context of specific industries and business sectors. See, for example, 41 USC § 51 (2009) (prohibiting payments to contractors to secure sub-contracts); 18 USC § 215 (1990) (prohibiting payments to bank officers to influence the consideration of loans); 29 USC § 186 (1984) (prohibiting payments to labour union officials); 47 USC § 509(a)(2) (1960) (prohibiting bribery of television game show contestants).

16 18 USC § 201(b)(1).

17 18 USC § 201(b)(2).

18 18 USC § 201(b).

19 18 USC § 201(c).

20 Compare 18 USC § 201(b) with 18 USC § 201(c).

21 18 USC § 201(c).

22 See *United States v Verrusio*, 762 F 3d 1 at 17 (DC Cir 2014) (finding that, because the defendant accepted a number of gifts and benefits knowing they were given "for the particular act of influencing the language of [a] bill," it was completely irrelevant that the briber's preferred language was not ultimately included in the final bill).

23 18 USC § 201(c).

Section 201 liability may attach when a bribe or gratuity is paid directly to a federal official, reaches a federal official indirectly through a third party or intermediary, or is simply promised or offered (although never actually paid) to a federal official.[24] Moreover, anything of value can constitute a bribe.[25] A prosecutor need not establish a minimum value in order to secure a bribery conviction.[26] Rather, it is enough that the item, service or other thing of value offered, provided, or requested has some subjective value to the recipient.[27]

Section 201 defines the term "public official" expansively to include members of Congress; any person "selected to be a public official" (ie, any person nominated or appointed, such as a federal judge); officers, employees, and delegates of all branches and agencies of the federal government; and federal jurors.[28] In fact, an individual need not even be a formal employee of the federal government to qualify as a public official; a public official need only be "a person acting for or on behalf of the United States."[29]

The term 'official act' is defined by the statute as "any decision or action on any question, matter, cause, suit, proceeding or controversy, which may at any time be pending, or which may by law be brought before any public official, in such official's official capacity, or in such official's place of trust or profit."[30] An official act may be established by custom rather than by statute or a written rule or regulation, need not be a formal part of an official's decision-making process, and may include an official's attempt to influence the official act or decision of another public official (through, for example, advice or pressure).[31]

Like the definition of 'public official', the definition of 'official act' appears expansive. However, in 2016, the Supreme Court weighed in, limiting the reach of the term. In *McDonnell v United States*, prosecutors alleged that former Virginia Governor Robert McDonnell and his wife accepted approximately $175,000 in loans, gifts, and other things of value from a Virginia businessman in exchange for performing official acts intended "to legitimize, promote, and obtain research studies" for the businessman's products.[32] The alleged official acts included arranging

---

24 18 USC § 201.

25 18 USC § 201(b).

26 *Ibid.*

27 *United States v Renzi*, 769 F 3d 731 at 744 (9th Cir 2014) (explaining that broad interpretation of "anything of value" serves the congressional purpose of punishing abuses of public office). See also *United States v White Eagle*, 721 F 3d 1108 at 1122 (9th Cir 2013) (ruling that the value of a benefit may include subjective components and is not limited to just "the face amount of the transaction"). This does not mean, however, that the definition of the term is without limit. Noting the *quid pro quo* nature of bribery offences, one court recently observed that a "proposal to trade one public act for another, a form of logrolling, is fundamentally unlike the swap of an official act for a private payment", and therefore vacated a former governor's conviction resulting from his proposal to appoint an individual to the US Senate in exchange for his appointment to the President-Elect's cabinet: *United States v Blagojevich*, 794 F 3d 729 at 734 (7th Cir 2015) (but affirming bribery-related charges based on requests for donations and 'campaign contributions' in exchange for the Senate appointment and supporting certain legislation).

28 18 USC § 201(a)(1–2).

29 *Ibid.*

30 18 USC § 201(a)(3).

31 *McDonnell v United States*, 579 US ___, 136 S Ct 2355 at 2371 (2016) (citing, among others, *United States v Birdsall*, 233 US 223, at 230–231 (1914)).

32 *McDonnell v United States*, 136 S Ct 2355 at 2361, 2365.

meetings and facilitating relationships between the businessman and other Virginia public officials to discuss the products, hosting events at the Governor's mansion at which the businessman was allowed to promote the products to doctors, and contacting other officials concerning research studies on the products.[33] McDonnell (together with his wife) was charged with (and convicted of) a number of crimes, all predicated on the acceptance of bribes as prohibited by 18 USC Section 201.[34]

On appeal, the Supreme Court was asked to determine whether arranging meetings, hosting events and contacting other officials were 'official' enough to bring them within the type of activity that the federal anti-bribery statute was meant to proscribe.[35] The government argued that an official act could be nearly any activity undertaken by a public official, concerning any subject, touching upon any broad policy issue (ie, economic development) relevant to the official's position.[36] McDonnell, on the other hand, argued that routine acts not directed towards the resolution of "specific governmental decision[s]" were not official acts, especially because setting up meetings with other officials was something he did "literally thousands of times" as Governor.[37]

Although the Supreme Court flatly rejected the conclusion that McDonnell's conduct "typif[ied] normal political interaction between public officials and their constituents", the Court also agreed with McDonnell that not every decision or action customarily performed by a public official could count as an official act.[38] The Court held that setting up a meeting, talking to another official, or organising an event did not — without more — rise to the level of an official act under 18 USC Section 201, "even if the event, meeting, or speech [wa]s related to a ... question or matter" generally relevant to the official's function.[39] Instead, the Court held, an official act requires a public official to take an action proactively or make a decision on a question or issue that involves a formal exercise of governmental power.[40]

Because the government's definition of 'official act' in *McDonnell* was over-inclusive, the Court vacated McDonnell's conviction.[41] Soon thereafter, the government announced that it would not seek to retry the McDonnells on federal

---

33 *Ibid* at 2361.

34 *Ibid* at 2365–2366. McDonnell (a state official) and his wife were technically charged with honest services wire fraud and Hobbs Act extortion, both of which may be characterised by bribery as defined by 18 USC Section 201. See *Skilling v United States*, 561 US 358 at 404 (2010) (construing honest services fraud (see 3.2 below) to forbid "fraudulent schemes to deprive another of honest services through bribes or kickbacks" *Evans v United States*, 504 US 255 at 260, 269 (1992) (construing Hobbs Act extortion to include "taking a bribe"). Accordingly, their conduct was examined by reference to 18 USC Section 201, even though they were not charged with Section 201 violations.

35 See *McDonnell v United States*, 136 S Ct 2355 at 2361.

36 *Ibid.*

37 *Ibid* at 2366, 2367.

38 *Ibid* at 2372.

39 *Ibid* at 2370 (citing *United States v Birdsall*, 233 US 223 at 234 (1914)).

40 *Ibid* at 2371–2372, 2374. The Court voiced concern that, if it were to interpret 'official act' any more broadly, 'conscientious public officials' who appropriately address constituents' concerns by, for instance, arranging meetings, contacting other officials on their behalf and including them in events, would be dissuaded from doing so, fundamentally undermining the US tradition of representative government: *ibid* at 2372.

41 *Ibid* at 2375.

42 US Department of Justice Press Release 16-1025, *Justice Department Moves to Dismiss McDonnell Charges* (8 September 2016), www.justice.gov/opa/pr/justice-department-moves-dismiss-mcdonnell-charges.

bribery charges.[42] Accordingly, conduct like Governor McDonnell's, about which even the Supreme Court voiced disapproval, must be regulated under other statutes.[43]

3. Application of federal law to state and local officials

3.1 Introduction

As noted above, 18 USC Section 201 applies only to federal officials, not to state or local public servants. However, at least two other federal statutory schemes can be invoked to prosecute state and local officials for acts of corruption, including the federal mail and wire fraud statutes and the Hobbs Act.[44]

3.2 Public sector mail, wire and honest services fraud

Although the federal mail and wire fraud statutes do not specifically mention corruption, bribery, graft, or kickbacks, they are often invoked to prosecute corruption in the public sector. The elements of mail and wire fraud are:

- a scheme or artifice to defraud or obtain money or property by false or fraudulent pretences; and
- use of the mails or means of interstate wire communications in furtherance of that scheme or artifice.[45]

Each instance of mail or wire fraud is punishable by up to 20 years' imprisonment.[46]

For the purposes of the statute, the term 'wire communications' is defined broadly to include radio transmissions, telephone calls and e-mails.[47] Further, for decades after the mail and wire fraud statutes were enacted, appellate courts interpreted the term 'scheme or artifice to defraud' to include deprivations not only of money or property but also of intangible rights.[48] It was not until after the Supreme Court "stopped the development of the intangible-rights doctrine in its tracks," strictly construing the reference to "money or property" in the statute,[49] that Congress enacted a sister section to the mail and wire fraud statutes providing that the term "scheme or artifice to defraud" as used in those statutes "includes a scheme

---

43 Each branch of the federal government (executive, legislative, and judicial) is also governed by internal ethics regulations that limit or prohibit the acceptance of gifts or other items of value from certain individuals (eg, lobbyists, foreign officials or those doing business with or regulated by a recipient's agency) or under certain circumstances (eg, in connection with events organised by lobbyists or in one-on-one interactions not 'widely attended' by others).

44 The Racketeer Influenced and Corrupt Organizations (RICO) Act may also be used to prosecute acts of public corruption at the state and local levels. Among other things, RICO makes it unlawful for any person, including a public official, "employed by or associated with any enterprise engaged in . . . interstate or foreign commerce, to conduct or participate, directly or indirectly, in the conduct of such enterprise's affairs through a pattern of racketeering activity": 18 USC § 1962(c). A "pattern of racketeering activity" requires at least two "predicate acts", which may include mail and wire fraud or Hobbs Act violations: see 18 USC § 1961(1), (5).

45 See 18 USC § 1341 (mail fraud); 18 USC § 1343 (wire fraud).

46 18 USC § 1341; 18 USC § 1343.

47 See USAM 9-43.100.

48 *Skilling v United States*, 561 US 358 at 400 (2010) (citing, among others, *Shushan v United States*, 117 F 2d 110 (5th Cir 1941)).

49 *Ibid* at 401 (citing *McNally v United States*, 483 US 350 (1987)).

or artifice to deprive another of the intangible right of honest services."[50] It is this language that makes the mail and wire fraud statutes particularly useful in the prosecution of corrupt public officials.

Unlike the typical mail or wire fraud case, in which a violator wrongfully obtains the money or property of a victim (a symmetrical change of hands), the typical public official honest services mail or wire fraud case is characterised by the acceptance of bribes, kickbacks or something else of value in exchange for actions, such as awarding government contracts to, or directing business through, the bribe payers to the benefit of both the official and the bribers.[51] No identifiable victim or tangible loss is required.[52] The following illustration is helpful:

> [I]*f a city mayor (the offender) accept[s] a bribe from a third party in exchange for awarding that party a city contract, yet the contract terms [a]re the same as any that could have been negotiated at arm's length, the city (the betrayed party) w[ill] suffer no tangible loss. Even if the scheme occasion[s] a money or property gain for the betrayed party, courts reason ... [that] actionable harm [rests] in the denial of that party's right to the offender's "honest services".*[53]

Indeed, there was no identifiable victim or tangible loss in *United States v Renzi*, and yet the court affirmed the honest services fraud conviction in that case.[54] There, former Arizona Congressman Richard Renzi persuaded a third party (the Aries Group) to purchase land owned by his friend and business associate James Sandlin in exchange for a commitment to use his authority to obtain passage of a bill benefiting Aries in the disposition of the land.[55] Although the sale was made at fair market value, Renzi failed to disclose to Aries that Sandlin owed Renzi roughly $700,000, which he began to repay with the proceeds from the sale of the land.[56] Renzi argued that, because Sandlin owed him money independently of the land sale to Aries, and because Aries was not victimised by the "equal value sale", the government could not prove that he obtained anything of value to which he was not otherwise entitled.[57] The court disagreed, noting that Renzi had used his office to secure the "early repayment of a large private debt" and that "[t]his money clouded his judgment in performing his official duties and deprived his constituents of the honest services of their elected representative."[58]

3.3 The Hobbs Act

The Hobbs Act criminalises obstructing, delaying, or affecting interstate or foreign commerce by robbery or extortion.[59] For the purposes of the act, the term 'extortion' means "the obtaining of property from another, with his consent, induced by

---

50 18 USC § 1346.
51 See *Skilling v United States*, 561 US 358 at 400, 410 (2010).
52 *Ibid* at 400.
53 *Ibid* (citation omitted) (emphasis in original).
54 *United States v Renzi*, 769 F 3d 731 at 744 (2014). As noted below, the court also affirmed a number of Renzi's other convictions, including one under the Hobbs Act (see 3.3 below): *ibid* at 743.
55 *Ibid* at 741.
56 *Ibid* at 740.
57 *Ibid* at 742–743.
58 *Ibid* at 744.
59 18 USC § 1951(a).

wrongful use of actual or threatened force, violence, or fear, or under color of official right."[60] Moreover, consistent with the federal bribery statute and the mail and wire fraud statutes, the Hobbs Act defines the term 'property' broadly to include anything of value that can be exercised, transferred, or sold, and does not require the extortionist to receive directly the fruits of the extortion himself or herself.[61] Hobbs Act violations are punishable by up to 20 years' imprisonment.[62]

The Hobbs Act is made applicable to public corruption through the "under color of official right" language, which derives from the common law meaning of 'extortion'. "At common law, extortion was an offense committed by a public official who took 'by colour of his office' money that was not due to him for the performance of his official duties."[63] This, according to the Supreme Court in its watershed Hobbs Act case, is "the rough equivalent of what we would now describe as 'taking a bribe'."[64]

In *Evans*, a member of the DeKalb County, Georgia Board of Commissioners was convicted of a Hobbs Act violation for accepting campaign contributions from a real estate developer who, on numerous prior occasions, had solicited assistance in rezoning a tract of land for residential use.[65] Evans sought reversal of the conviction, arguing that his "passive acceptance" of a campaign contribution did not amount to extortionary coercion.[66] The Court flatly rejected the notion that a public official was required to take any specific action to 'induce' the payment of a bribe, and noted that the required coercive element arose from the existence of the public office (and thus the appearance of power) itself.[67] The Court concluded that, so long as an official knows that a payment is made in exchange for (or in expectation of) an official act, the passive acceptance of that payment will run afoul of the Hobbs Act.[68]

4. Private sector/commercial bribery

4.1 Introduction

Private sector, or commercial, bribery is the direct or indirect giving or offering to give anything of value to any private agent, employee or fiduciary, without the knowledge and consent of the principal or employer, with intent to influence such

60 18 USC § 1951(b)(2).

61 *United States v Renzi*, 769 F 3d 731 at 742–743 (2014) (citing *Scheidler v National Organization for Women Inc*, 537 US 393 at 405 (2003)) (affirming a Hobbs Act conviction for payment made to Renzi's business associate, who, as a result of the payment, was able to repay his own previous prior debts to Renzi). Contrast *United States v Blagojevich*, 794 F 3d 729 at 736 (7th Cir 2015) (citing *Sekhar v United States*, 570 US 729 (2013)) (noting that the "Hobbs Act must not be extended just to penalize shady dealings," and thus, "property" must be limited to what one owner can transfer to another and does not include government positions).

62 18 USC § 1951(a).

63 *Evans v United States*, 504 US 255 at 260 (1992).

64 *Ibid*. The Court later rejected Evans' argument that the evidence against him was more conducive to a bribery conviction than a Hobbs Act extortion conviction, noting that the two crimes were not mutually exclusive, especially where public officials acting "under colour of official right" were involved: *ibid* at 267 n 18.

65 *Ibid* at 257. As it turned out, the 'developer' was actually an undercover FBI agent.

66 *Ibid* at 267–268.

67 *Ibid* at 265.

68 *Ibid* at 258, 268.

agent's, employee's or fiduciary's action in relation to his or her employment duties. Although honest services mail and wire fraud often involves bribery of public officials, courts recognise private-sector honest services fraud as well.[69] In addition, prosecutors may look to the Interstate and Foreign Travel or Transportation in Aid of Racketeering Enterprises statute, more commonly known as the 'Travel Act' (see 4.3 below), to keep bribery and corruption in the private sector at bay.[70]

4.2 Private sector mail, wire, and honest services fraud

In the earliest application of honest services mail/wire fraud to commercial bribery, one court observed that:

> [w]*hen one tampers with [the employer-employee] relationship for the purpose of causing the employee to breach his duty [to his employer], he in effect is defrauding the employer of a lawful right. The actual deception that is practi[s]ed is in the continued representation of the employee to the employer that he is honest and loyal to the employer's interests.*[71]

In that vein, court after court has recognised that any employee, public or private, can be prosecuted under the mail and wire fraud statutes for breaching his or her allegiance to an employer by accepting bribes or kickbacks in the course of carrying out an employment duty.[72]

Thus, while the application of the mail and wire fraud statutes to both the public and private sectors can no longer be questioned, whether the law extends to the deprivation of honest services by any means other than bribes or kickbacks was, until just recently, open to question. In 2010, however, the question was squarely presented to the Supreme Court in *Skilling v United States*, resulting in the significant limitation of the reach of 18 USC Section 1346.

In *Skilling*, prosecutors charged Enron Corporation's former Chief Executive Officer and others with conspiracy to commit 'honest services' securities and wire fraud (among other charges), alleging that Skilling and his co-conspirators "deceive[d] [investors] about the true performance of Enron's businesses by: (a) manipulating Enron's publicly reported financial results; and (b) making public statements and representations about Enron's financial performance and results that were false and misleading."[73] In the process, prosecutors alleged, Skilling and his co-conspirators "enriched themselves . . . through salary, bonuses, grants of stock and stock options, other profits, and prestige."[74] No bribes or kickbacks were alleged.

Ultimately, the Supreme Court declined to characterise "the taking of official

---

69 See *Skilling v United States*, 561 US 358 at 401 (2010).

70 The line between public and private sector bribery is less pronounced in the context of 18 USC Section 666, which prohibits, in part, offering, soliciting, or accepting bribes or gratuities in connection with any business transaction of $5,000 or more with any organisation that receives at least $10,000 in federal funding in any year. See 18 USC §§ 666(a)(1)(B), (a)(2), (b). The statute is specifically designed to facilitate prosecution of those who steal or divert money or property from state and local governments or private organisations – for example, universities, foundations and corporations – that are entrusted with federal resources.

71 *Skilling v United States*, 561 US 358 at 401 (2010) (citing *United States v Procter & Gamble Co*, 47 F Supp 676 at 678 (D Mass 1942)).

72 *Ibid.*

73 *Ibid* at 369.

74 *Ibid.*

action by [one] that furthers his own undisclosed financial interests while purporting to act in the interests of those to whom he owes a fiduciary duty" as honest services fraud.[75] Instead, the Court limited the statute to deprivations of honest services achieved only through bribes and kickbacks, reasoning that Congress must have meant to cover at least that conduct, but that any broader reading of the statute would result in unconstitutional vagueness.[76] The Court justified the limitation by noting that the honest services doctrine had its genesis in bribery prosecutions[77] and that Section 1346 had been enacted in response to the Court's earlier refusal to apply the honest services doctrine in a kickback case,[78] before which application of the doctrine to any other conduct had been amorphous and inconsistent.[79] Because Skilling was not alleged to have engaged in bribes or kickbacks, the Court concluded that his conduct could not fall within 18 USC Section 1346 and reversed his honest services fraud conviction.[80]

4.3 The Travel Act

Although *Skilling*, like *McDonnell*, effectively limited the federal anti-corruption arsenal, some might say that the Travel Act simply picks up where honest services fraud leaves off. Among other things, the Travel Act prohibits travel in interstate or foreign commerce or using the mails or any facility in interstate or foreign commerce with intent to

- distribute the proceeds of any unlawful activity;[81] or
- promote, manage, establish, carry on or facilitate the promotion, management, establishment or carrying on, of any unlawful activity.[82]

Punishment for each individual Travel Act violation may include up to five years' imprisonment and a $250,000 fine.[83]

Arguably, the Travel Act may be considered the broadest of all of the federal anti-bribery statutes. Indeed, because the term 'facility in interstate or foreign commerce' has been defined broadly to encompass all means of transportation and communication both within and outside the United States, commercial bribery (no matter where in the world it occurs) falls squarely within the ambit of the Travel Act.[84] Moreover, because the term 'unlawful activity' is defined to include not only violations of federal anti-bribery laws (eg, 18 USC Section 201 and the FCPA)[85] but also violations of their state counterparts,[86] the Travel Act effectively 'federalises' state

---

75 *Ibid* at 409. It should be noted that the Court did not countenance the alleged behaviour, but simply held that such conduct did not fall within the purview of Section 1346: *ibid* at 412.

76 *Ibid* at 408.

77 See *Shushan v United States*, 117 F 2d 110.

78 See *McNally v United States*, 483 US 350.

79 *Skilling v United States*, 561 US 358 at 410 (2010). Justice Scalia dissented, arguing that, even if bribery and kickbacks could be said to form the "core" of the honest services fraud doctrine, the Court was not justified in reading a *limitation* to bribery and kickbacks into the statute: *ibid* at 421.

80 *Ibid* at 368.

81 18 USC § 1952(a)(1).

82 18 USC § 1952(a)(3).

83 18 USC § 1952(a).

84 Andrew S Boutros, T Markus Funk & James T O'Reilly, *The ABA Compliance Officer's Deskbook* (2016) p35.

85 18 USC § 1952(b)(i)(2).

86 18 USC § 1952(b). See also Brian P Loughman & Richard A Sibery, *Bribery and Corruption: Navigating the Global Risks* (2012), p24.

private commercial bribery laws. Finally, the Travel Act has been held to apply to bribery between private entities only and need not involve any element of public corruption.[87] Thus, the Travel Act may provide jurisdiction where other statutes may have left federal oversight lacking.

Such was the case in *Perrin*, wherein the Supreme Court affirmed a Travel Act conviction based on the defendant's participation in a scheme to exploit confidential geological exploration data stolen from a private company.[88] The data at issue was stolen by a company employee who had been promised a percentage of the profits of the scheme, and the defendant was brought into the scheme as a consultant to analyse and interpret the data that the employee stole.[89] The co-conspirators engaged in a number of telephone calls across state lines in furtherance of the scheme.[90]

In his defence, Perrin argued that he had not been appropriately charged under the Travel Act because there was no federal statute applicable to commercial (as opposed to public sector) bribery and neither he nor any of the other participants in the scheme were public officials.[91] The Court flatly rejected Perrin's contention, noting first that the Travel Act was intended to stem the growing tide of interstate organised crime, and there could be "little doubt that . . . bribery of private persons was widely used in highly organized criminal efforts to infiltrate and gain control of legitimate businesses."[92] Moreover, the Court found that the statute's explicit definition of the Travel Act offences by reference to existing state and federal law demonstrated Congress's clear intent to supplement state authority by allowing federal enforcement of state commercial bribery statutes.[93]

5. Conclusion

As discussed above, there are a number of federal laws that prohibit and punish corrupt conduct in the United States. The existence of these statutes, and their relatively frequent invocation to prosecute domestic wrongdoers, no doubt contributes to the relatively low perception of corruption in the country. That said, however, there is clearly more work to be done to incentivise legitimacy and honesty in American government and business relations so that it can become less and less necessary to invoke those statutes.

87 *See Perrin v United States*, 444 US 37 (1979).
88 *Ibid* at 40, 50.
89 *Ibid* at 40.
90 *Ibid*.
91 *Ibid* at 41.
92 *Ibid* at 48.
93 *Ibid* at 42 (noting that the Travel Act criminalised "extortion [or] bribery ... in violation of the laws of the State in which committed or of the United States"), 50.

The United States Foreign Corrupt Practices Act

Josh Christensen
Timothy L Dickinson
Derek Turnbull
Paul Hastings LLP

1. Introduction

It is no longer sufficient to simply sigh and say that is the way business is done. It is time to treat the issue for what it is: a serious foreign policy problem.[1]

These were the words of United States Senator Frank Church in his opening remarks at the Senate's 'Church Committee' hearings in 1975. Senator Church was referring to the then-recently discovered practices of major American companies making secret payments of questionable legality to foreign government officials and political parties, and purposely misrecording these payments in the companies' books to hide them from disapproving investors and regulators. The Senator from Idaho had convened the committee amid a sense of 'post-Watergate morality,' following the coincidental uncovering of these questionable transactions during the domestic political scandal's burgeoning investigations.[2]

At the height of the Cold War, US companies were being singled out for criticism across the world based on allegations of corruption in developing nations and among US allies such as South Korea and Italy, where political parties had received major donations in secret from US oil corporations. The US government saw these practices as a crisis in moral leadership that threatened to undermine America's self-perceived role as a reliable alternative to communist oppression. Lockheed Martin, a major American defence contractor, was found to have been funnelling money to rightist political parties in Japan via a major figure in that country's organised crime networks. In several nations in which political party contributions had been made, the communists were gaining support at the expense of pro-American political forces, the latter now seen as "the handmaidens of foreign and domestic financial interests", as Senator Church characterised the perception.[3]

The response by the US government, following a series of hearings and input from the State Department, the Defense Department and commercial interests, among others, was to adopt the Foreign Corrupt Practices Act of 1977 (the FCPA). The FCPA, it was thought, would put an end to illicit payments to government

1 *Multinational Corporations and United States Foreign Policy: Hearings Before the Subcommittee on Multinational Corporations of the Senate Committee on Foreign Relations*, 94th Congress 2 (1975) (statement of Senator Frank Church, Chairman of the Subcommittee on Multinational Corporations. (Senator Church's Statement.)

2 Milton S Gwirtzman, *Is Bribery Defensible?*, *New York Times Magazine*, 5 October 1975, at 19.

3 Senator Church's Statement (note 1 above).

officials abroad by US companies and restore a degree of openness to the bookkeeping practices of US issuers, thereby repairing the image of US economic interests.

2. What is the FCPA?

The FCPA consists of two primary components. Firstly, the 'anti-bribery provisions' (15 USC § 78dd-1–3) make it illegal for a company or individual to make payments or give anything of value to a foreign official for the purposes of obtaining or retaining business or to gain a business advantage. Secondly, the 'accounting provisions' (15 USC § 78m) require "issuers" to keep accurate books and records, as well as to maintain internal accounting controls reasonably devised to prevent corruption or the subversion of the company's accurate accounting practices.

2.1 To whom does the FCPA apply?

The FCPA's bribery provisions apply to "issuers," "domestic concerns," and foreign persons or foreign non-issuers who act in furtherance of a corrupt payment inside the territory of the United States.[4]

- The term "issuers", as defined in the FCPA, includes all companies that issue securities on a US national securities exchange or that have a class of securities in the over-the-counter US market and are required to file reports with the Securities and Exchange Commission (SEC).
- The term "domestic concerns" means US citizens, nationals or residents, as well as all companies organised under the laws of the United States or based in the United States.

A 1998 amendment added to these classes of persons and companies those who take – or cause to be taken – any act whatsoever inside the United States in furtherance of a corrupt payment to a foreign official.

The FCPA's accounting provisions, meanwhile, apply only to issuers and any individuals connected to those issuers.[5]

2.2 The anti-bribery provisions: a closer look

The US Department of Justice (DOJ) expands upon the simple definition found above as follows:

> *[T]he anti-bribery provisions of the FCPA prohibit the willful use of the mails or any means of instrumentality of interstate commerce corruptly in furtherance of any offer, payment, promise to pay, or authorization of the payment of money or anything of value to any person, while knowing that all or a portion of such money or thing of value will be offered, given or promised, directly or indirectly, to a foreign official to influence the foreign official in his or her official capacity, induce the foreign official to do or omit to do an act in violation of his or her lawful duty, or to secure any improper advantage in order to assist in obtaining or retaining business for or with, or directing business to, any person.*[6]

---

4 15 USC § 78dd-1 – 78dd-3.
5 15 USC § 78m.

However, even this more fulsome explanation may not do justice to how far-reaching the law truly is. Below are set out the key elements of the law.

The first element is that the law only applies – as described above – to "issuers" or "domestic concerns", as well as their employees, agents and other individuals acting on their behalf. It also applies to foreign persons or foreign non-issuers who act in furtherance of a corrupt payment inside the territory of the United States.

The second element is that the individual or entity involved must have wilfully used the mail or another tool of interstate commerce in connection with the alleged crime. This could mean that a letter was sent, a telephone call was made, or an email or text message was exchanged. In the modern, digitally interconnected world, nearly every bribe payment above the level of slipping a dollar bill across a handshake will satisfy this element (assuming jurisdiction applies in the first place).

The third element consists of a payment or an offer, promise, or authorisation of payment. This means that the party charged with the violation need not have made the payment himself or herself, nor does an actual payment even need to have occurred, because the offer is enough.

The fourth element of a violation – that the 'payment' consists of 'anything of value' – encompasses not only payments of money but also the provision of myriad other benefits to a foreign official. Punishments have been handed out for everything from job offers to vacations, and even charitable donations to an official's preferred organisation.

The fifth element – that the payment be destined for a foreign official – also encompasses far more than it would appear to at first glance. Under the FCPA, a "foreign official" does not only mean a minister of finance or an elected official. Foreign officials can include nearly anyone employed in almost any capacity by a foreign government (federal, provincial, municipal, etc), in addition to candidates and representatives of political parties, and officials of public international organisations (such as development banks). In countries like China or Venezuela, where entire industries may be nationalised, foreign officials may include all those employed at state-owned enterprises, such as the local utility company, the provincial university, oil companies, shipping conglomerates, tobacco purveyors and sometimes even airlines.[7] It is also illegal to make payments to such individuals through third parties or intermediaries.

Finally, the sixth element – that the payment be directed to obtaining or retaining business – is one of the more straightforward elements. The payment must be provided with intent to induce the official to misuse his or her official position in order to gain some business advantage. Paying cash to a minister of defence to purchase his or her car at fair market value, without other facts, would likely not

---

6 US Department of Justice, *Foreign Corrupt Practices Act: An Overview*, (updated 3 February 2017), available at www.justice.gov/criminal-fraud/foreign-corrupt-practices-act.

7 Not every employee of every organ connected to a government necessarily qualifies as a foreign official. Courts employ a complex factor-based test (called the '*Esquenazi* test', after the 11th Circuit case which formulated it) to determine whether a foreign government controls the relevant entity, and whether that entity performs a government function – which could mean different things in different countries. Suffice to say, though, that legal scholars almost universally agree that the *Esquenazi* test confirms a very broad definition of foreign officialdom.

constitute a crime under the FCPA. Handing the minister a suitcase of cash in return for his or her assignation of a contract for fighter jets, on the other hand, clearly would qualify. The intent to obtain government contracts or business, however, is not needed to fulfil this element, as it can also be satisfied when the payment was made to gain any business advantage. This could include paying lower tax than legally mandated or having one's goods clear customs without proper inspections.

2.3 The accounting provisions: books and records and internal controls

The FCPA's accounting provisions include requirements that companies accurately record payments and transactions and maintain strong internal controls. The "books and records" provision requires issuers to "make and keep books, records, and accounts, which, in reasonable detail, accurately and fairly reflect the transactions and dispositions of the assets of the issuer."[8] Under this part of the law, enforcement authorities need not prove every element of violation of the anti-bribery provision to secure a conviction, but merely the telltale signs of a cover-up (eg, payments listed to a third party but lacking "reasonable detail" as to the purposes of the payments).[9] In other words, FCPA liability can arise not only where there is fire but also where there is merely the right kind of smoke.

The "internal controls" provision requires issuers to devise and maintain a system of internal accounting controls sufficient to provide reasonable assurances that, among other things, transactions are executed in accordance with management authorisation, and that they are recorded, as necessary, for the preparation of financial statements in conformity with generally accepted accounting principles.[10] An example of poor internal controls that would constitute a violation would be if a company were to maintain a discretionary slush fund for its CEO without any sort of approval process or documentation required for spending it. FCPA enforcers target these kinds of arrangement as a recipe for improper payments.[11]

While most people think of anti-corruption laws as consisting of the more glamorous anti-bribery provisions, the accounting provisions actually afford the government deceptively wide latitude in pursuing suspected wrongdoers. The accounting provisions serve the important purpose of attempting to head off bribery violations before they occur, but have the added benefit of sweeping up conduct that might indicate past illicit payments where direct evidence is lacking. This may be thought of as being a little like the infamous Al Capone prosecution strategy: the authorities knew Capone had committed serious crimes (extortion and murder, among others) but they just could not prove it, so prosecutors took a careful look at Capone's books and convicted him of tax evasion. For FCPA enforcement, this scenario applies to those occasions when the government may suspect a company of having made improper payments but lacks the smoking gun of a *quid pro quo* transaction, such as an email chain about bribes, invoices showing kickbacks, or

8 15 USC § 78m(b)(2)(A).

9 *Ibid.*

10 15 USC § 78m (b)(2)(B).

11 'Improper payments' is an industry term of art, often used by defence lawyers. Prosecutors might prefer the more common term, 'bribes'.

eyewitnesses willing to testify. In cases like these, the government can step in and subpoena the company's books, then go line by line and verify every item of expenditure in the relevant business unit. If indeed improper payments were made, then at some point investigators will invariably find outlays marked as having:

- gone to non-existent corporations;
- been paid to third parties with no evidence of substantive services rendered in return; or
- gone out while otherwise lacking the proper supporting documentation.

That said, the SEC will vigorously enforce the accounting provisions independent of any suspicion of actual bribery having taken place. Going back to the original purposes of the FCPA, enforcement authorities care deeply about preserving transparency and integrity in US issuers' record-keeping, and this is an area where the SEC has particular expertise and a mandate for enforcement, which is expounded upon below.

2.4 The exception and defences

So far as defences are concerned, the FCPA's bribery provisions provide one exception and two affirmative defences.

The exception applies to what are known as 'facilitation payments', ie, payments that facilitate or expedite "routine governmental action[s,]" or, in other words, acts that "ordinarily and commonly are performed by a foreign official ...."[12] Facilitation payments are permissible, for example, when the payment is meant to speed the issuing of a permit which the foreign official is already duty-bound to issue. It is interesting to note that, although the FCPA allows facilitation payments, not every country sees them the same way; the United Kingdom's Bribery Act 2010, for example, does not permit them and such payments are almost always illegal under the laws of the country in which they are made.

The FCPA's two affirmative defences consist of:

- a *bona fide* promotional defence; and
- a local law defence.

The promotional defence refers to the allowance of *bona fide* expenditures "directly related to the promotion, demonstration, or explanation of products or services, or the execution or performance of a contract with a foreign government or agency thereof."[13] That is, a company can legally reimburse travel expenses, for example, while legitimately attempting to market a product or service to a foreign government.

The local law defence applies to payments that are permitted under the local law of the jurisdiction where they are made. The SEC has issued guidance stressing the fact that local 'law' means what it says: the law must be written, so that customs and so-called 'everybody does it' excuses do not suffice.[14]

---

12 SEC Office of Investor Education and Advocacy, Investor Bulletin: The Foreign Corrupt Practices Act – Prohibition of the Payment of Bribes to Foreign Officials (October 2011), p2, available at www.sec.gov/investor/alerts/fcpa.pdf.

13 *Ibid.*

14 *Ibid.*

3. How is the FCPA enforced?

FCPA enforcement can come from two different directions: criminal and civil. The DOJ enforces criminal sanctions under the law, and the SEC is responsible for civil enforcement actions. While private plaintiffs have tried before to use the FCPA as a ground for recovery, US courts have stated that the legislation provides no private right of action, and so private plaintiffs may not bring claims for such a recovery.[15]

Violators of the FCPA may face criminal and civil fines, disgorgement of profits plus interest, and jail time. The text of the law itself states that corporations may face criminal fines of up to $2 million per violation of the bribery provisions, while individuals face criminal fines of up to $100,000 in addition to up to five years' imprisonment.[16] The accounting provisions, meanwhile, allow for corporate fines of up to $25 million, while individuals may be fined up to $5 million and imprisoned for up to 20 years.[17]

Courts and enforcement authorities alike, however, have almost universally adopted the approach of imposing the far harsher penalties allowed under the Alternative Fines Act, 18 USC § 3571(d), which authorises a punishment to be levied equal to up to twice the benefit obtained by virtue of the improper payment, leading to some of the more eye-popping settlements reached by enforcement authorities in recent years.[18]

Civil fines for the anti-bribery provisions can be statutorily up to $16,000 per violation for both individuals and companies, and for the accounting provisions, can range up to $150,000 for individuals and $725,000 for companies.[19] However, the SEC may obtain civil penalties for accounting provision violations up to the greater of either of these limits or "the gross amount of the pecuniary gain … as a result of the violations …."[20] In addition, criminal convictions can lead to suspensions and debarments, which can include being blocked from doing business with the US government or receiving financing from major international development banks – a potential death sentence for companies relying on government contracts or development projects for their revenues.

The DOJ pursues both individuals and companies in its criminal enforcement efforts. In general, companies tend to come to settlements with the government, while individuals have a greater incentive to insist on having their day in court. Extensive scholarship exists elsewhere on this phenomenon, but the consensus seems to be that companies wish to avoid the financial and reputational costs associated with drawn-out legal fights, choosing instead to – when given the opportunity – face the one-time reputational hit of a DOJ press release publicising their alleged wrongdoing, pay a negotiated amount in penalties or disgorgement,

---

15 See *Lamb v Phillip Morris, Inc*, 915 F. 2d 1024 (6th Cir. 1990).

16 15 USC §§ 78dd-2(g)(2)(A), 78dd-3(e)(2)(A), 78ff(c)(2)(A).

17 15 USC § 78ff(a).

18 Note also that this law caps individual fines at $250,000, making this the true cap on individual fines per violation.

19 15 USC §§ 78dd-2(g), 78dd-3(e), 78ff(c) & 15 USC § 78u(d)(3).

20 US Department of Justice & US Securities and Exchange Commission, *FCPA: A Resource Guide to the US Foreign Corrupt Practices Act* (12 November 2012), p69, available at www.sec.gov/spotlight/fcpa/fcpa-resource-guide.pdf.

and, in some cases, implement certain mandated changes to the way they do business. Businesses also value predictability, so there is a bonus for the company that pleads out and pays a sum that was negotiated over a matter of months, as compared with the company that heads into a potentially years-long legal battle with no certainty over how the judge or jury will find at the end of the road. Individuals, on the other hand, can face life-ruining convictions and long jail sentences even when offered plea deals, so they are more apt to take their charges to court in the hope of having their names cleared entirely.

Adding to the tendency for companies to seek out-of-court solutions after FCPA violations is the credit the DOJ will extend to them in return for self-reporting and cooperation. In 2016, the DOJ debuted what it calls its 'FCPA pilot program': a one-year programme (since extended indefinitely) under which companies – if they demonstrate sufficient alacrity and commitment in investigating, disclosing and remediating their FCPA-related missteps – could receive significant reductions in their penalties, or even declination letters (statements from the DOJ that it does not plan to prosecute, so long as certain conditions are met).[21] The principles of this programme existed previously – that the DOJ would look to hand out lighter punishments for companies that exhibited greater signs of engagement and cooperation – but the 'pilot program' has formalised and publicised these principles, while also enhancing the benefits offered to companies that are willing to cooperate.

The SEC upholds the civil side of the law. The SEC typically pursues the twin remedies of disgorgement and civil penalties, though it generally gives credit for any criminal penalties or other payments levied on the defendant by the DOJ. The SEC has no equivalent to the DOJ's 'pilot program', but will take into account a company's efforts at self-reporting and remediation when coming to a settlement. Like the DOJ, the SEC can pursue individuals who violate either the bribery or the books and records provisions of the FCPA on behalf of the issuers falling under the SEC's jurisdiction.

4. Enforcement trends

Within a year of the FCPA's passage, the law saw its first two cases in *Securities and Exchange Commission v Page Airways Inc et al* and *Securities and Exchange Commission v Katy Industries Inc et al*. Neither case resulted in any monetary penalties, though Page Airways was required to engage an independent compliance monitor, a tool not seen again in settlements until 2002, but used much more commonly since.[22] Even with this quick start to prosecution of the law, though, 1978 began a period of rather slow enforcement that lasted for more than two decades. Including these two cases and through the year 2000, there were only a total of 52 FCPA enforcement actions:

---

21 See US Department of Justice, *Criminal Division Launches New FCPA Pilot Program* (5 April 2016), available at www.justice.gov/archives/opa/blog/criminal-division-launches-new-fcpa-pilot-program.

22 Compliance monitors are independent third parties engaged to review a company's policies and procedures, and to keep an eye on the company's business for a specified period of time, usually one to three years. The monitor reports back to the government at regular intervals, certifying that the company remains in compliance with the terms of the settlement – or refusing to grant that certification, potentially leading to further penalties.

41 initiated by the DOJ and 11 by the SEC.[23] Following a slight uptick in the early 2000s, the number of enforcement actions per year drastically increased in 2007, with double-digit numbers of actions coming out of both agencies during most years since.[24]

Then, in 2008, the DOJ and SEC settled FCPA charges with a German company, Siemens AG, in what would remain the largest FCPA settlement in history (by amount paid to US authorities) until September 2017, when it was supplanted by an action against a Swedish telecommunications company. The German conglomerate had allegedly paid bribes and kickbacks stretching back into the mid-1990s in efforts to obtain government contracts around the world, including in the now-infamously corrupt United Nations Oil-for-Food Programme in Saddam Hussein's Iraq. Siemens – a US issuer – disgorged $350 million to the SEC and paid a $450 million fine to the DOJ for criminal violations.[25]

Before this $800 million settlement, no company had ever paid even a tenth of that amount for FCPA violations. While there had been a marked increase in FCPA cases over the previous two years, the *Siemens* case shocked the international legal community because the FCPA had been on the books for over 30 years and many observers still did not know much about it; certainly, a settlement this large was as yet practically uncontemplated. A *New York Times* article announcing the settlement named the law just once, and omitted any use of the now-common initialism 'FCPA', noting merely that "the case was part of a noticeable spike in the [DOJ]'s foreign corrupt practices investigations, with 42 cases brought in the last four years compared with 17 in the four years before that."[26]

The *Siemens* settlement was at the midpoint of the era from 2001 to 2016, which saw 435 enforcement actions: 250 initiated by the DOJ and 185 by the SEC.[27] In other words, there have been more than eight times as many enforcement actions in the 16 years of FCPA enforcement after the year 2000 as there were in the first 23 years of the law's existence. While the precise reasons for increased FCPA enforcement are up for debate, the upward trend in enforcement has been clear for some time. Further, from 2008 on, settlements with multinational corporations became much larger than they had usually been previously, reaching into the double and even triple-digit millions of US dollars in disgorgement and penalties on a regular basis.

This trend can best be seen in a recent enforcement action, described by the DOJ as the "largest foreign bribery case in history', in which construction conglomerate Odebrecht and petrochemical company Braskem, both Brazil-based, agreed to pay penalties of $3.5 billion to settle charges with US, Brazilian, and Swiss authorities. The combined FCPA enforcement action concluded in December 2016 following a years-long investigation by those authorities. The two companies were alleged to

---

23 Stanford Law School, Foreign Corrupt Practices Act Clearinghouse, *DOJ and SEC Enforcement Actions*, available at http://fcpa.stanford.edu/statistics-analytics.html (Stanford).

24 *Ibid.*

25 See Securities and Exchange Commission press release, *SEC Charges Siemens AG for Engaging in Worldwide Bribery* (15 December 2008), available at www.sec.gov/news/press/2008/2008-294.htm.

26 Eric Lichtblau & Carter Dougherty, *Siemens to Pay $1.34 Billion in Fines, The New York Times* (15 December 2008), available at www.nytimes.com/2008/12/16/business/worldbusiness/16siemens.html.

27 Stanford (note 23 above).

have created an entire business unit within Odebrecht, devoted to channelling bribes to officials located in countries around the world. From 2001 onwards, the business unit allegedly paid $788 million in bribes, with the knowledge and direction of company executives, in order to steer contracts and rig bids. The bribe-paying unit – though it reported to the highest levels within the company – operated off-the-books and used coded messages to conceal its payments and purpose. From 2006 to 2014, Braskem joined in on the bribe-paying system, contributing around $250 million to Odebrecht's accounts in order to take advantage of its corrupt capabilities.

In a sign of the global trend in anti-corruption enforcement, US authorities cooperated with Brazilian and Swiss investigators in uncovering the operation and amassing evidence to bring prosecutions. Furthermore, even as Odebrecht and Braskem agreed to pay massive penalties and institute sweeping changes in their internal controls, they also agreed to continue cooperating with investigations in the three countries aiming to bring to justice various individuals connected with the scheme.[28]

Other recent trends have included hybrid enforcement actions and the increased use of deferred prosecution agreements (DPAs).

Hybrid actions are concerned with the urge by enforcement authorities to pursue repugnant conduct where the intricacies of jurisdiction mean that the FCPA may not cover all of the conduct, for example where bribes were paid both to government officials and to purely commercial actors. In these kinds of case, prosecutors have shown a willingness to bring in other laws, such as the Travel Act, 18 USC § 1952, which in relevant part federalises certain violations of state laws, such as commercial bribery. Pursuing the bribe-payer on both FCPA and Travel Act theories means that punishments can be levied for the improper payments to government officials and also for those made to non-governmental actors.

Meanwhile, DPAs have seen an increase in usage as companies have become more aware of the incentives for cooperation. Under a DPA, charges may be articulated but never officially brought, so companies can escape the black mark of having a conviction so long as they tightly adhere to the terms of the agreement, which will often include disgorgement and significant remedial actions.

5. The future of the FCPA

This country is absolutely crazy – they prosecute people for going over to China and Mexico and other countries and getting business and creating jobs in this country.... Wh[y] are we prosecuting people to keep China honest? ... It's a horrible law, and it should be changed.[29]

That was Donald Trump, Chairman and President of the Trump Organization, speaking about the FCPA in May 2012. Four and a half years later, having just

28 US Department of Justice press release, *Odebrecht and Braskem Plead Guilty and Agree to Pay at Least $3.5 Billion in Global Penalties to Resolve Largest Foreign Bribery Case in History*, (21 December 2016), available at www.justice.gov/opa/pr/odebrecht-and-braskem-plead-guilty-and-agree-pay-least-35-billion-global-penalties-resolve.

29 *Trump: Dimon's Woes & Zuckerberg's Prenuptial*, CNBC, 15 May 2012, www.cnbc.com/video/2012/05/15/trump-dimons-woes-zuckerbergs-prenuptial.html?play=1 at minutes 14:59-15:30.

assumed his position as the 45th President of the United States, he evidently still held the same view, telling his new Secretary of State Rex Tillerson, as recently as February 2017, that American businesses being punished for overseas bribery were "being unfairly penalized."[30] To the lawyers and enforcement officials working in the area of FCPA enforcement, and perhaps also to enforcement authorities around the globe, these were worrying words from the leader of the free world.

Mr Trump's sentiments are not his alone. A certain school of thought has found robust support from some quarters – as far back as the debate over the FCPA's passage in the 1970s – for the idea that punishing American companies or individuals for corrupt practices in other countries puts them at a needless competitive disadvantage. Prosecuting Americans for paying bribes, the thinking goes, prevents US businesses from competing on a level playing field in countries where anti-corruption enforcement is not as robust as citizens of many developed nations have come to expect. How, ask these critics, can an American company hope to compete in China against Chinese firms, if only the local firms are willing to pay the prices demanded by the local officials?

Those who disagree with this criticism, however, argue that the understanding of the FCPA which underpins this criticism by the law's opponents has several fundamental flaws. First of all, the criticism underestimates the degree to which the FCPA has been deployed against non-US companies and nationals. As of October 2017, seven of the top ten largest FCPA enforcement actions in history were against non-US-based companies.[31] Perhaps US companies have become accustomed to the FCPA, or they have better access to legal advice than foreign firms struggling to implement effective compliance programs; or perhaps US enforcement agencies simply do not see an incentive in throwing the book at American violators when foreign competitors with US nexuses exist aplenty. Whatever the reason, the reality is clearly that the FCPA's consequences bear on domestic and non-US companies and individuals alike, and may even disproportionately lean on non-US entities.

Moreover, criticisms of the FCPA based on arguments about competitiveness ignore the rapidly expanding enforcement efforts readily apparent in nations like China and Brazil. China's Communist Party has undertaken a massive anti-corruption effort in the last several years, as the country's anti-bribery drive has become General Secretary Xi Jinping's signature initiative. Dubbed by some the 'Tiger and Flies campaign' because of comments Xi made in 2013, shortly before ascending to China's presidency, referring to the high-level officials ('tigers') and low-level bureaucrats ('flies') whom he intended to pursue, China's effort to rid itself of corruption has brought down thousands of officials, including former members of some of the Party's top governing organs. As part of this campaign, Chinese enforcers have not shied away from pursuing foreign violators – such as the UK pharmaceutical giant GlaxoSmithKlein and some of its executives, who were prosecuted and

30 Dexter Filkins, *Rex Tillerson at the Breaking Point*, *The New Yorker* (16 October 2017), available at www.newyorker.com/magazine/2017/10/16/rex-tillerson-at-the-breaking-point.

31 The FPCA Blog, *Telia Tops Our New Top Ten List (After We Do Some Math)*, (22 September 2017), available at www.fcpablog.com/blog/2017/9/22/telia-tops-our-new-top-ten-list-after-we-do-some-math.html. This calculation of the top ten largest enforcement actions looks at dollar amounts agreed to be paid to US enforcement authorities for FCPA violations.

punished for bribery in 2014 – and in fact the Communist Party, like many governing authorities, could easily see an advantage in focusing on foreign players' roles in corruption scandals.

In Brazil, a sprawling investigation dubbed 'Operation Car Wash' – a reference to the money-laundering and corruption allegations which sparked it – has engulfed dozens of federal government legislators and executives at several large companies, including Petrobras, Brazil's state-owned oil company. That investigation crossed into the US and other countries, with enforcement authorities in Brazil, the United States and Switzerland ultimately cooperating in their investigations (as mentioned earlier, with the Odebrecht/Braskem settlement).

Meanwhile, the UK Bribery Act 2010 has been applied with increasing frequency and effectiveness as the UK's Serious Fraud Office (SFO) has looked to expand its footprint; even before the SFO secured its first ever conviction under the relatively new 2010 Act in 2016, companies around the globe were taking that law into account in formulating their compliance programmes and educating their employees.

An argument exists that the FCPA in fact makes US companies more competitive, for example by inoculating them against demands for bribes; that is, even in countries where bribes are expected, bribe-takers now know that US companies cannot pay them, and so they do not even ask. Companies from other countries without the long arm of an FCPA-like law might still encounter costly or time-consuming hiccups when greedy officials demand lavish attention, or hold up projects expecting their cut. Furthermore, US companies theoretically have historically had easier access to expert advice on FCPA compliance, which is an area reserved for US-educated – and therefore largely US-based – attorneys, though in an increasingly interconnected global community this factor may have less weight today than it has in the past.

While some commentators point to the FCPA as an example and an inspiration for other countries looking to build up the rule of law, the FCPA's role in sparking foreign enforcement is somewhat beside the point. Whether the US government continues to pursue enforcement of the law aggressively or not, most US companies operating abroad have to make their behaviour conform with the increasingly strict laws of other countries in which they have touchpoints, including those looking to exercise extra-territorial jurisdiction – such as the UK – and those cracking down on abuses within their borders, such as China. In early 2017, Jay Clayton, President Trump's nominee at the time for the chairmanship of the Securities and Exchange Commission, said at his confirmation hearing:

> *...[H]ow do you advise a client who is subject to the Foreign Corrupt Practices Act, who may be entering into business in a country that is well known for corruption[?] I think you have to tell that client to think long and hard about whether you want to have the potential exposure to ... not just the Foreign Corrupt Practices Act, but thankfully now – which was not the case five, seven years ago – similar oversight and enforcement from other OECD countries. And, in fact, there are some jurisdictions where in the vast majority of the cases, it may make sense just not to participate.*[32]

32 Jay Clayton, SEC Nominee Confirmation Hearing, 23 March 2017, available at www.c-span.org/video/?425840-1/sec-nominee-jay-clayton-defends-prior-work-lawyer-goldman-sachs&start=7412 at 2:03:35–2:04:22.

Chairman Clayton was confirmed a little over a month after making that statement, and thus far no evidence has contradicted his view of the situation: companies must remain cognisant of an increasingly large body of foreign bribery laws enacted by countries other than the United States. So long as this is the case, the United States stands to gain little from relaxing its pursuit of violators, as the FCPA definitionally only applies to conduct with some extraterritorial nexus, and US companies with such nexuses must already be taking steps to prevent their employees from making improper payments or engaging in other corrupt misconduct.

Moreover, the FCPA has proved to be a lucrative focus for US enforcement agencies, netting billions in fines and disgorgement as a result of comparatively low-cost settlements and the occasional prosecution. Some scholars argue that enforcement agencies, run by individuals, will sometimes gravitate to the enforcement actions that will bring them the greatest public recognition with the least effort expended; furthermore, the large, headline-grabbing settlements characteristic of FCPA investigations, where companies nevertheless have a strong incentive to settle, are exactly the kinds of enforcement action where the payoff-to-effort ratio is greatest.[33] With these incentives and the inertia of government investigation units already practised in bringing these kinds of enforcement action, the DOJ and SEC bodies in charge of these investigations would seem to have little upside in shifting their focuses.

A year into the Trump administration, no overt moves have yet been taken that would suggest a drop-off in FCPA enforcement; in fact, one of the largest FCPA enforcement actions of all time was concluded in September 2017, when Telia Company AB, a Swedish telecommunications company, agreed to pay $965 million in combined criminal and civil penalties to US and Dutch authorities.[34] While this enforcement action began under the Obama administration, it was aggressively pursued through to its end eight months after Mr Trump took office. It also post-dates comments by Acting Assistant Attorney General Kenneth Blanco, made in March 2017, that "[t]he Criminal Division remains committed to doing its part by vigorously investigating and prosecuting international crime when it violates US laws, and by remaining committed to international collaboration in our nations' shared struggle to safeguard our citizens, our markets and financial systems, and our networks."[35]

If anything, FCPA enforcement actions may increase in number in the near future, as enforcement authorities shift their focus to prosecuting individuals. Since

---

33 See, for example, Vikramaditya Khanna, *Corporate Crime Legislation*, 82 Wash U L Rev 95 at 126–130 (2004) (arguing that prosecutors have an incentive to bring cases that will satisfy the public while reducing their own workload).

34 US Department of Justice press release, *Telia Company AB and Its Uzbek Subsidiary Enter Into a Global Foreign Bribery Resolution of More Than $965 Million for Corrupt Payments in Uzbekistan* (21 September 2017), available at www.justice.gov/opa/pr/telia-company-ab-and-its-uzbek-subsidiary-enter-global-foreign-bribery-resolution-more-965.

35 US Department of Justice press release, *Acting Assistant Attorney General Kenneth A Blanco Speaks at the American Bar Association National Institute on White Collar Crime* (10 March 2017), available at www.justice.gov/opa/speech/acting-assistant-attorney-general-kenneth-blanco-speaks-american-bar-association-national.

September 2015, when Deputy Attorney General Sally Yates issued the 'Yates Memorandum' indicating the DOJ's intention to pursue individual violators more aggressively than it had previously, the DOJ has determined to focus on gathering evidence for individual prosecutions even as it undertakes corporate investigations. One of the prime ways in which corporations can gain remedial credit is now by offering evidence on internal bad actors whose actions have led to the corporations' own liability, which in turn encourages follow-up enforcement actions to grow out of corporate investigations.

6. Conclusion

It appears likely that the FCPA will remain an important component of US enforcement and corporate compliance moving forward, given both the global climate and an informed understanding of the institutional forces at play in the US and abroad.

In fact, FCPA enforcement has shown a trend toward increased multi-jurisdictional cooperation, and one can expect to see more such cooperative investigations – such as the *Odebrecht/Braskem* case – in the future. If anything, this means that FCPA compliance efforts are likely to become more complex, as companies and individuals now have to take into account more than just the FCPA and have to contend with more than just US authorities. Today, when considering potential FCPA violations, such violations could include violations of another country's domestic laws and the results of any US investigation could end up being shared with another country's investigators.

The FCPA has become entrenched in how companies and individuals view their engagement in the world economy, and in how enforcement authorities around the world view that engagement, and these facts appear unlikely to change anytime soon.

About the authors

Ayodele Adeyemo
Associate, Sofunde, Osakwe, Ogundipe & Belgore
aaadeyemo@sooblaw.com

Ayodele Adeyemo is an associate in the dispute resolution group of Sofunde, Osakwe, Ogundipe & Belgore. He holds a law degree and has been engaged in active legal practice in Nigeria for over seven years. He has represented leading financial institutions in a number of contentious commercial litigation cases. He has also been part of legal teams representing clients in high profile corruption cases in Nigeria.

Roberto P Bauzá
Partner, Rattagan Macchiavello Arocena
rpb@rmlex.com

Roberto P Bauzá is a partner of Rattagan Macchiavello Arocena in Buenos Aires, Argentina. His areas of expertise include general corporate counselling, anti-corruption and compliance, mergers and acquisitions, international contracts and foreign investment, finance and capital markets. He was previously a partner in Allende & Brea in Buenos Aires. He also worked as a foreign associate for Gibson, Dunn & Crutcher in New York, with a focus on Latin America.

Mr Bauzá is currently a co-chair of the Anticorruption Committee of the American Bar Association (Section of International Law) and a member of the Public Bar of the City of Buenos Aires. He has published articles in international journals and speaks frequently in Argentina and abroad about matters within his expertise.

Mr Bauzá holds a law degree from the *Universidad Nacional de Cuyo* (Mendoza, Argentina) and an LLM from Columbia University School of Law (New York City).

Lorena de la Barrera
Integrity specialist, UNODC LPO Mexico
lorena.delabarrera@un.org

Ms de la Barrera holds a BA in International Relations and an MA in Public Policy from the School of Government and Public Transformation of the Monterrey Institute of Technological and Superior Studies. She has participated in international academic exchanges with the Institute of Political Science in Paris, the School of Government of Harvard University and the University of Carleton in Ottawa, Canada. She has been involved in the international public service since the beginning of her career. From 2005 to 2008 she was with the OECD Multilateral Tax Centre in Mexico.

At the same time, Ms de la Barrera was appointed as National Consultant for Mexico in Anticorruption for the United Nations Office on Drugs and Crime (UNODC), coordinating and collaborating in several projects related to democratic governance and the right to water with indigenous communities in Honduras, Nicaragua and south-western Mexico. It is from this experience that her specialisation in the anti-corruption mandate of UNODC in Mexico stems.

Wendy Berman
Senior partner, Cassels Brock & Blackwell LLP
wberman@casselsbrock.com

Wendy Berman, a senior partner in the Toronto office of Cassels Brock & Blackwell LLP, is recognised as one of Canada's leading securities litigators by *Chambers Global*, the *Canadian Legal Lexpert Directory* and *Best Lawyers in Canada*. She practises commercial litigation with an emphasis on securities-related regulatory investigations and proceedings and has extensive experience dealing with Canadian regulatory and law enforcement agencies. She regularly provides strategic advice and representation to companies and their directors and officers in all aspects of matters relating to allegations of corporate misconduct, including internal investigations and Canadian and cross-border parallel civil, regulatory and criminal investigations and proceedings.

Ms Berman has represented public companies and directors and officers in some of Canada's largest investigations and proceedings involving disclosure violations, insider trading and other fraud-related allegations, corruption and anti-bribery, shareholders' remedies, litigation aspects of takeover bids and other acquisitions, corporate governance (including directors' and officers' liability) and securities class actions.

Ashleigh Buckett
Lawyer
ashleigh.buckett@gmail.com

Ashleigh Buckett is a former legal adviser with the IBA's Legal Policy & Research Unit (LPRU), during which time she led projects on whistleblowers, sextortion, sanctions and the Women Business Lawyers Initiative. An Australian lawyer, she holds a BA in Political Science/Spanish, an LLB, a Graduate Diploma of Legal Practice and an LLM in International Law. Ms Buckett now practises as part of a team of lawyers undertaking strategic litigation addressing human rights abuses in Australia, particularly in relation to indigenous Australians and refugees.

Ada SW Chan
Associate, Haldanes
ada.chan@haldanes.com

Ada Chan is an Associate in the Criminal Litigation Department of Haldanes in Hong Kong. She holds degrees in law and commerce, and has been admitted as a solicitor in Hong Kong and in New South Wales, Australia. In particular, she has been heavily involved in numerous headline cases, including corruption, money laundering and commercial fraud. She specialises in criminal defence, with a focus on regulatory and commercial offences, and is experienced in immigration matters.

Ms Chan is currently leading the Haldanes team on a number of internationally renowned cases to be heard at the High Court of Hong Kong, including an 80-day riot trial, a murder trial, and cross-border forfeiture order and restraint order hearings.

Kamen Chanov
Junior associate, Kinstellar
kamen.chanov@kinstellar.com

Kamen Chanov is a junior associate in Kinstellar's Sofia office. He focuses on compliance, competition and technology law. Kamen has valuable experience in working on compliance matters (including internal investigations, integrity due diligence of business partners, examining possible conflict of interests and more generally research with regard to politically exposed persons), but also on antitrust and merger proceedings before the Bulgarian competition authority and before the Supreme Administrative Court. He also advises clients on compliance with the GDPR, including conducts data protection audits (gap assessments) and localisation of policies and procedures.

Kamen has working experience with the Council of the European Union in Brussels and at the Embassy of the Republic of Bulgaria in The Hague. He speaks Bulgarian, English and French.

Josh Christensen
Associate, Paul Hastings LLP
joshchristensen@paulhastings.com

Josh Christensen is an associate in the Litigation practice of Paul Hastings and is based in the firm's Washington DC office. His practice focuses on matters relating to the US Foreign Corrupt Practices Act and international anti-corruption law. He counsels clients regarding anti-corruption compliance programmes, risk assessments, conducting due diligence on third parties and in connection with acquisitions and corruption-related internal investigations. He has worked as part of independent corporate monitoring teams as well as preparing clients for corporate monitors.

Mr Christensen received his law degree from the University of Wisconsin Law School, where he served as a vice president of the Moot Court Board and articles editor of the *Wisconsin Law Review*. He is admitted to practise law in the District of Columbia, Maryland and Wisconsin.

Marco Dalla Vedova
Attorney, Dalla Vedova Associazione Professionale
mdv@dallavedova.com

Marco Dalla Vedova achieved a law degree at the School of Law of La Sapienza University in Rome in 1985. He received a Japan JT Scholarship in 1986. In 1993, he worked at EUTELSAT, based in Paris, as a visiting attorney. He was admitted to the Italian Bar in 1986 and qualified to practise before the Supreme Court in 2002.

As managing partner at Dalla Vedova Associazione Professionale and head of the telecommunication, technology, media and payments practice, he advises companies and governments on key corporate and regulatory issues and handles complex litigation cases.

Listed in *Chambers* and *Legal 500* Italy, he is a regular speaker at major international conferences worldwide and at restricted audience national and international government and federal consultancy focus groups and meetings. He has also authored several publications concerning telecommunications, technology, media and payments.

Kristýna Del Maschio
Junior associate, Kinstellar
Kristyna.DelMaschio@kinstellar.com

Kristýna Del Maschio is a junior associate in Kinstellar's Prague office. She is a member of the Compliance, Risk & Sensitive Investigations team and her specialisations include white-collar crime defence, corporate criminal liability and corporate investigations. During her studies, she spent a year at university in Germany and was involved in projects restructuring companies in Rwanda and Zambia. She also completed an internship at the District Court for Prague 1. She has advised a number of clients in matters relating to internal investigations (including a global pharmaceutical company) and white collar crime matters (including an international automotive company and a major Czech chemical company).

Stéphane de Navacelle
Partner, Navacelle
sdenavacelle@navacellelaw.com

Stéphane de Navacelle has worked in the field of white collar crime/corporate crime in New York, London and Paris (at Engel & McCarney and Debevoise & Plimpton LLP).

With extensive experience in French and US white collar crime, he has participated in landmark cases involving FCPA and embargo restrictions (OFAC), market abuse/insider trading, fraud (Forex), benchmark manipulation (LIBOR/Euribor), investigations by development banks and criminal and internal investigations in Europe, the Americas and Africa. He advises companies with setting up and auditing compliance programmes; he was appointed Independent Compliance Monitor – pursuant to a World Bank Negotiated Resolution Agreement – by an infrastructure group with global operations.

Mr de Navacelle has been identified as a leading practitioner by *Chambers & Partners, Legal 500 France, Legal 500 EMEA, Who's Who Legal, Leaders' League/Décideurs, GIR* (40 under 40 – world's leading young investigation specialists) and the *Expert Guide for White-Collar Crime/Business Crime, Investigations and Stock Market Litigation.*

Mr de Navacelle is a regular participant at seminars and is consulted on issues relating to regulatory and criminal investigations in Europe and the United States.

Timothy L Dickinson
Partner, Paul Hastings LLP
timothydickinson@paulhastings.com

Timothy L Dickinson is a partner in the Litigation practice of Paul Hastings' Washington DC office. With over 30 years' experience in the field of international anti-corruption law, he works closely with a wide range of industries on FCPA matters, including the establishment and implementation of compliance programmes, due diligence for third parties and acquisitions, and special investigations and defence before regulators in the US and abroad. He has been recognised by *Chambers USA* every year since 2009 as one of very few attorneys ranked as top-tier FCPA experts.

Mr Dickinson is currently a Professor from Practice at the University of Michigan Law School, where he co-founded the International Transactions Clinic. He has been selected many times to serve as an independent compliance monitor in conjunction with settlements with US enforcement authorities, and was chosen by the World Bank to assist with the development of its Voluntary Disclosure Program.

Sandrine dos Santos
Counsel, Navacelle
sdossantos@navacellelaw.com

Before joining Navacelle, Sandrine dos Santos worked in a top-tier litigation French boutique and at the Paris Prosecutor Office from 2007 to 2010. She dealt with cases related to economic and financial crime or organised crime and damages to persons or property, and acquired a strong expertise in white-collar crime.

Ms dos Santos has worked on complex international corruption matters involving high-profile political stakeholders and large-scale companies in Africa and South America. She also handled sensitive FCPA & LIBOR-related matters.

Ms dos Santos has assisted clients in setting up global compliance training and she is a regular participant at conferences organised by the French Institute for Higher National Defence Studies (*Institut des Hautes Etudes de Défense Nationale*, IHEDN).

Vanya Evtimova
Associate, Kinstellar
vanya.evtimova@kinstellar.com

Vanya Evtimova is an associate in Kinstellar's Sofia office. She focuses on corporate, compliance (including commercial and employment aspects) and litigation law. She has over six years of experience advising both local and international clients on a vast range of corporate and M&A matters, employment and compliance matters. In the area of compliance, Vanya has worked on several internal investigations, on integrity due diligences of business partners and on employment and corporate aspects of internal investigations, as well as on devising compliance programmes for clients. She also has a background in advising major beneficiaries of European funding programmes in Bulgaria. She speaks Bulgarian and English.

Chukwuma Ezediaro
Senior associate, Sofunde, Osakwe, Ogundipe & Belgore
ccezediaro@sooblaw.com

Chukwuma Ezediaro is a senior associate in the dispute resolution group of Sofunde, Osakwe, Ogundipe & Belgore. He holds a combined degree in Political Science and History and a degree in Law. He has specialised mainly in anti-corruption and anti-money laundering advisory work along with commercial and civil litigation for over 14 years while based in Lagos, Nigeria. In particular, he has been a regular co-contributor to the Nigerian chapters of *Getting The Deal Through* publications on anti-corruption regulation and anti-money laundering. He has also delivered papers at conferences on anti-corruption matters.

Dessislava Fessenko
Of counsel, Kinstellar
dessislava.fessenko@kinstellar.com

Dessislava Fessenko is an of counsel and head of the Sofia Compliance, Risk and Sensitive Investigations practice, with over fifteen years of experience advising on compliance, data protection, antitrust/competition and technology matters.

Dessislava has advised clients in a number of compliance audits and internal investigations in the pharmaceutical, financial services, retail, oil and gas sectors. She regularly advises on anti-corruption compliance, corporate investigations, avoiding conflicts of interest, dealings with politically exposed persons, integrity due diligences and anti-money laundering in the retail, pharmaceutical, banking and insurance, energy and mining, electronic payments and online gaming sectors. Dessislava also supports clients in policy advocacy initiatives related to compliance and anti-money laundering. She has delivered compliance training to pharmaceuticals and industrial manufacturers in Bulgaria on a number of occasions. Dessislava also provides advice on the legal aspects of technology, data protection, intellectual property and technology agreements (including software licences). Dessislava speaks Bulgarian, English and German.

Juan Eduardo Figueroa
Partner, FIHS Abogados
jef@fihs.cl

Juan Eduardo Figueroa has 30 years' experience as counsel to diverse construction companies and property developers and is a specialist in urban planning and construction law. He was a judge of the Supreme Court of Chile. He is also an arbitrator for the Arbitration and Mediation Center of the Santiago Chamber of Commerce, for the International Centre for Dispute Resolution (ICDR) of the American Arbitration Association (AAA), for the Arbitration Center of the Chamber of Commerce Brazil–Canada (CAM CCBC) and for the Chamber of Arbitration of the Engineering Institute of Sao Paulo, Brazil. He has been recognised by *Chambers Latin America* and by *Ranking Leading Lawyers* as a leading real estate lawyer.

Jocasta Giles
Senior associate, King & Wood Mallesons
jocasta.giles@au.kwm.com

Jocasta Giles is a senior associate specialising in dispute resolution. She advises companies and individuals across a broad range of industries in the private sector on commercial and contractual disputes, as well as investigations and prosecutions brought by regulatory bodies in Australia (including the Australian Federal Police and the Australian Securities and Investments Commission).

At the time of co-writing her chapter, Ms Giles was part of the dispute resolution team at Johnson Winter & Slattery (having joined the firm in 2011). Ms Giles spent time in 2016/2017 working with the conflicts team at Clifford Chance LLP in London before returning to Johnson Winter & Slattery in Sydney in 2017. Ms Giles subsequently joined King & Wood Mallesons in March 2018.

César Guzmán-Barrón
Lawyer in management of social conflicts, compliance and arbitration
cguzman@pucp.pe

César Guzmán-Barrón holds a master's degree in Humanities and is a lawyer, specialising in compliance, arbitration and other alternative means of dispute resolution. He is currently director of the firm Consensere, specialising in advice and on the prevention and management of corruption cases, both in the application of compliance programmes and other anti-bribery systems, such as ISO 37001.

Mr Guzmán-Barrón has more than 40 years' experience in the fields of negotiation, evaluation and conflict management, having acted as mediator, conciliator, facilitator and arbitrator. He has been director of the Conflict Resolution and Analysis Center of the Pontifical Catholic University of Peru. He has a deep and solid academic vocation that is expressed not only in his professional experience and practice but also in university teaching in a number of institutions, both in undergraduate and postgraduate courses in Socio-Environmental Conflict, International Trade and Negotiation, Dispute Boards and Arbitration.

Hamidul Haq
Partner, Rajah & Tann Singapore LLP
hamidul.haq@rajahtann.com

Hamidul Haq is a partner in the Commercial Litigation department of Rajah & Tann Singapore LLP. He has an LLB from the National University of Singapore and an LLM from University College London. He is a former senior prosecutor with the Attorney's General Chambers and Commercial Affairs Department in Singapore and has dealt with many high profile cases, both for the defence and the prosecution, over the last three decades.

Mr Haq has received recommendations from a number of legal directories, including the *Expert's Guide 2014, Who's Who Legal 2014, Asia Law Profiles 2007, Who's Who Legal, Singapore 2008* and *Asia Pacific Legal 500* (2006–2007). He also authored the book *Financial Crimes in Singapore* in 2014.

Chris Hardjasa
Senior associate, Paul Hastings LLP
christinahardjasa@paulhastings.com

Chris Hardjasa is a senior associate in the Investigations and White Collar Defence practice at Paul Hastings LLP and is based at the firm's London office. She previously practised at the firm's Washington DC office, and is admitted to practise law in Virginia, Washington DC and as a solicitor in England and Wales. She counsels clients on matters relating to the US Foreign Corrupt Practices Act, the UK Bribery Act of 2010 and other international anti-corruption laws.

Ms Hardjasa has extensive experience advising numerous multinational companies and individuals on developing, assessing and enhancing anti-corruption compliance programmes, compliance with reporting requirements to the US Department of Justice and the US Securities and Exchange Commission, and conducting complex, cross-border internal investigations, global risk assessments, due diligence on third parties and other similar matters. She has worked as part of an independent corporate monitoring team and has also counselled clients subject to such monitorships.

Carlos Hernández
Anti-corruption Unit Coordinator, UNODC LPO Mexico
carlos.hernandez@un.org

Mr Hernández studied law at the National Autonomous University of Mexico, and since October 2006 has provided advice and coordination skills pursuant to the mandate of the United Nations Office on Drugs and Crime (UNODC) at the Mexico Office. Projects he has led include Integrity Initiatives with both the public and private sectors from 2011–2014. In the Central America region, he assisted the project for the establishment of a regional network for reintegration and treatment for drug rehabilitation, where the first research on HIV and its relationship with drug consumption was established.

Mr Hernández has negotiated projects throughout Mexico and the Central America region in the fight against corruption and in prison reform, crime prevention and drug treatment. He has also worked for a private firm providing legal advice on criminal justice for private clients. Within the federal government, he worked as an intern for the National Migration Institute.

Roberto Hernández-García
Managing partner, COMAD, SC
rhernandez@comad.com.mx

Roberto Hernández-García is an international attorney specialising in construction law (transactional and disputes), public procurement law (transactional and disputes) and compliance and investigations in those areas of practice. He obtained a master's degree in Mexican Administrative Law from the *Universidad Panamericana*, Mexico City with an investigation on corruption and public procurement. He has served in diverse positions in a number of national and international anti-corruption groups, such as chair of the Anticorruption Commission of ICC México (2006–2018); vice president of Ethics and Anticorruption at the National Chamber of the Consulting Industry (CNEC) and representative for Latin America and co-vice chair of the Anticorruption Committee of the International Bar Association (IBA).

Mr Hernández-García has acted as an adviser for specific projects for anti-corruption organisations, such as the United Nations Office on Drugs and Crime (UNODC), *Transparencia Mexicana* and the Mexican-German Chamber. He has been invited as international speaker in anti-corruption topics for such organisations as the OECD in Colombia, the Guatemala Chamber of Industry and the American Bar Association Construction Forum in the US.

Mr Hernández-García advises national and international companies in compliance matters in diverse sectors such as oil and gas, construction and engineering and information technology, provides training and attends administrative investigations and legal proceedings. He is the coordinator of the ICC-Universidad Panamericana Anticorruption Program for Law Students and of the Anticorruption Diploma for Lawyers and Executives.

Gary Hughes
Barrister, Akarana Chambers
gary@garyhughes.nz

Gary Hughes is a senior lawyer specialising in all types of regulatory investigations and cases. Key areas include anti-trust (competition/consumer law), anti-money laundering, fraud and anti-bribery and corruption. He provides advocacy for clients under investigation, promotes resolution with regulators, representation in court proceedings, and strategic risk management advice. His expertise, developed over 22 years, includes a significant insurance law and financial markets conduct (securities) practice, and related issues such as D&O insurance, privacy, technology and board governance cases.

In 2016, Mr Hughes established an independent barrister's practice after a career in leading law firms, including firms in the large national (Chapman Tripp), leading boutique (Wilson Harle), and global (Clyde & Co, London) categories. He is a director of ACAMS Australasia (the global AML professional body), and is the International Bar Association's Anti-Corruption division New Zealand Officer. His work has been ranked by leading lawyer guides, including *Chambers Asia-Pacific, Legal 500, AsiaLaw Profiles* and *Who's Who Legal.*

Sergio Huidobro Martínez
Partner, FIHS Abogados
sah@fihs.cl

Sergio Huidobro Martínez has 22 years' experience in economic criminal litigation. He has been a partner with Figueroa, Illanes, Huidobro & Salamanca since 1996. He has been a Professor of Criminal Law since 2008 at the University del Desarrollo and Professor of Company Laws and Criminal Liability since 2010 at the same institution.

Mr Huidobro holds a postgraduate degree in Economics and Finance for Lawyers from the Faculty of Economic and Administrative Sciences of the University of Chile (2001) and diplomas in Corporate Governance from the University del Desarrollo (2012) and Economic Sanctions Law: Administrative and Penal from the University de los Andes (2015). He is a member of the Bar Association of Chile AG, of the Institute of Criminal Sciences and of Construlegal (Working Alliance of Construction Law Firms for the Americas).

Istyana Ibrahim
Partner, Rajah & Tann Singapore LLP
istyana.ibrahim@rajahtann.com

Istyana Ibrahim is a partner in the Commercial Litigation department of Rajah & Tann Singapore LLP. She graduated with an LLB from the National University of Singapore in 2010 and was called to the Singapore Bar in 2011.

Ms Ibrahim has been with Rajah & Tann Singapore LLP since 2011, having been involved in both high-profile criminal and civil proceedings in almost all levels of the Supreme Court of Singapore. She frequently advises on anti-bribery compliance matters and has assisted in a variety of significant reported cases involving white-collar crime and/or regulatory offences, including the first extradition case in Singapore which resulted in the release of the defendant, as well as a landmark case involving detention without trial under the Criminal Law (Temporary Provisions) Act, which also resulted in the release of the detainee.

Naoki Iguchi
Partner, Nagashima Ohno & Tsunematsu
naoki_iguchi@noandt.com

Naoki Iguchi is a leading partner with the international infrastructure/construction projects and arbitration practice team of Nagashima Ohno & Tsunematsu, Tokyo. He has advised construction, investment and infrastructure management companies in nuclear/gas/coal/renewable power plant, chemical plant, water, railway, highway, crude oil pipeline, shopping centre, hospital and other infrastructure projects in Asia, Africa, the UK and the US, as well as in Japan. He has also advised clients on public procurement regulation and procedures, including under WTO agreements, and on anti-corruption regulations in Japan and other Asian jurisdictions, and represented clients in international arbitration.

Mr Iguchi studied at University of Tokyo (LLB, LLM), Stanford (LLM) and Beijing (Mandarin Training) and has worked in law firms in Japan, China, Taiwan and the United States. He is a member of the Japan ICC Arbitration Committee. He is fluent in English and Chinese (Mandarin) as well as Japanese and also understands Spanish.

Lara Jackson
Partner, Cassels Brock & Blackwell LLP
ljackson@casselsbrock.com

Lara Jackson is a partner in the Toronto office of Cassels Brock & Blackwell LLP. She has an active and varied commercial litigation practice with particular expertise in securities litigation, including Canadian and cross-border civil and regulatory proceedings. She has also represented clients in a broad range of commercial cases involving proxy contests, takeover bids, shareholder disputes, oppression remedies and insolvency disputes, and has defended class actions in a number of areas, including securities misrepresentation, competition law, employment and oppression. She is recognised as a leading lawyer by the *Canadian Legal Lexpert Directory, The Best Lawyers in Canada* and *Benchmark Litigation.*

Anastasia Kayukova
Attorney, ALRUD Law Firm
AKayukova@alrud.com

Anastasia Kayukova is an attorney at ALRUD Law Firm, Moscow. She graduated from the Law Faculty of Lomonosov Moscow State University (LLB, LLM). She has advised clients on antitrust and anti-corruption legislation as well as other regulatory matters. As a member of the white-collar crime, compliance and internal investigations practice, she is involved in such projects as antitrust/anti-corruption due diligence, assisting with investigations and compliance with anti-corruption regulation requirements. She also represented clients following dawn raids carried out by FAS Russia as part of a series of cartel investigations.

Sophia SY Lam
Trainee solicitor, Haldanes
sophia.lam@haldanes.com

Sophia Lam is a trainee solicitor with Haldanes in Hong Kong. She graduated with an LLB from the City University of Hong Kong. Prior to her traineeship, she worked as a legal executive in the Enforcement Division of the Hong Kong Securities and Futures Commission (SFC). She was part of the team that assisted in the SFC's defence against an application by HSBC Private Bank (Suisse) SA to review the SFC's disciplinary decision.

During her training in the Criminal Litigation Department of Haldanes, Ms Lam assisted in a number of criminal and regulatory investigations instituted by the Independent Commission Against Corruption, the Hong Kong Monetary Authority, the SFC, the Hong Kong Police Force and the Customs & Excise Department. In particular, she has experience in assisting private sector clients facing charges under section 9 of the Prevention of Bribery Ordinance.

Hillary Levun
Counsel, Perkins Coie LLP
HLevun@perkinscoie.com

Hillary Levun is a counsel in the Commercial Litigation Practice at Perkins Coie's Chicago, Illinois office and is a member of its White Collar & Investigations group. Her practice focuses on the representation of both individual and corporate clients facing allegations of securities fraud, insider trading, tax fraud and Foreign Corrupt Practices Act (FCPA) violations before the US Department of Justice and the Securities Exchange Commission. She has participated in numerous international internal investigations aimed at identifying regulatory violations and has drafted advisory reports on potential exposure to civil and criminal penalties. She also assists clients in evaluating their compliance and anti-corruption programmes and provides recommendations to strengthen internal controls, combat regulatory violations and reduce future liability.

Jitka Logesová
Analyst, General Prosecutor's Office (Czech Republic)
logesova@gmail.com

Jitka Logesová is an analyst at the General Prosecutor's Office (Czech Republic) working on the Corporate Compliance Defence rules for the state prosecutors. She was a partner of an international law firm and spent several years as head of its Compliance, Risk & Sensitive Investigations practice. She has been appointed senior vice-chair of the IBA's Anti-corruption Committee and acts as its country coordinator. She is also the Czech exclusive member of ICC–FraudNet (a worldwide network of specialists in asset recovery).

Ms Logesová has led several corporate investigations – including cross-border matters – in a number of sectors, notably pharmaceuticals, construction, infrastructure, financial services, chemicals, retail and IT. She has also advised a number of companies on US FCPA-triggered investigations. She has broad experience in advising clients on crisis communications strategy in connection with governmental and corporate investigations. She has also represented clients in a number of litigation and arbitration proceedings. Ms Logesová is a guest lecturer in the Business Ethics class at the Anglo-American University in Prague. She has published a number of articles about corporate investigations, compliance and corruption in Central and Eastern Europe (CEE), specifically the Czech Republic.

Morgan J Miller
Partner, Paul Hastings LLP
morganmiller@paulhastings.com

Morgan Miller is a partner in the Investigations and White Collar Defense practice at Paul Hastings LLP and is based in the firm's London and Washington DC offices. His practice focuses on representing companies and individuals in white collar defence, anti-corruption, securities enforcement and related investigations before the US Securities and Exchange Commission, the US Department of Justice, the UK Serious Fraud Office and other international regulators. Mr Miller's particular areas of expertise include cross-border investigations involving complex financial and accounting issues and anti-corruption matters, including under the US Foreign Corrupt Practices Act and the UK Bribery Act, as well as internal and special committee representations, regulatory compliance and corporate governance.

Felix KH Ng
Partner, Haldanes
felix.ng@haldanes.com

Felix Ng is a partner at Haldanes and specialises in complex white-collar crime, securities regulations and competition law. He is admitted in Hong Kong, England & Wales and Dubai International Financial Centre and holds practice certificates in all three jurisdictions.

Mr Ng frequently advises listed companies, multinational corporations and individuals in cross-border investigations concerning bribery and corruption, commercial fraud, market misconduct, cartels, money laundering, tax crime and antitrust issues, and frequently represents clients at various levels of the criminal courts. Apart from defending clients in internationally renowned corruption trials and appeals in Hong Kong, he also has substantial experience in handling US Foreign Corrupt Practices Act (FCPA)-related investigations.

Mr Ng is recommended in *Who's Who Legal Thought Leaders – Business Crime Defence 2017* and *Chambers & Partners Asia-Pacific 2017*, and is author of a number of international criminal law publications.

David Ofosu-Dorte
Senior partner, AB & David
david@abdavid.com

David Ofosu-Dorte is the senior partner of AB & David, which has offices in Ghana, Zambia, Botswana and Zimbabwe and affiliate firms in many other African countries.

His experience cuts across project finance, the power sector, policy reform and public-private partnerships (PPPs). He led the government of Ghana's legal advisory team for Ghana's Millennium Challenge Compact One negotiations with the US government and the preparation of the Public-Private Partnership draft Bill for Ghana. He has also been the lead adviser in numerous infrastructure transactions. He has been recognised by *IFLR1000* and *Chambers Global*.

Mr Ofosu-Dorte also holds master's degrees in Public Administration and in Applied Business Research from the Swiss Business School and Fellowship of the Chartered Institute of Logistics

& Transport (UK). He is currently pursuing a doctorate in Business Administration.

Babajide Ogundipe
Partner, Sofunde, Osakwe, Ogundipe & Belgore
boogundipe@sooblaw.com

Babajide Ogundipe is a founding partner of Sofunde, Osakwe, Ogundipe & Belgore and has more than 35 years' experience as a commercial litigator in Nigeria. He specialises in acting for the victims of fraud and other financial malfeasance in seeking the recovery of losses resulting from such activity, and advises on compliance issues and the conduct of due diligence on behalf of non-Nigerians seeking to invest in Nigeria.

Mr Ogundipe is one of Nigeria's most senior arbitrators. He held leadership positions in the Nigeria branch of the Chartered Institute of Arbitrators between 1997 and 2009, including as branch chairman from 2006 to 2009. He is a former president of the Lagos Court of Arbitration and a current member of the board of directors. He has served as a member of a number of International Bar Association's committees, including the Anti-Corruption Committee. He is ICC FraudNet's Nigeria representative.

Cynthia Irene Osio Sanchez
Associate, COMAD, SC
cosio@comad.com.mx

Cynthia Osio obtained her law degree from the *Universidad Iberoamericana Puebla*. She served in the judicial branch, gaining experience in civil and business litigation. She is currently an associate at COMAD, SC, where her professional practice is mainly focused on construction law, public procurement, compliance and dispute resolution processes. She advises national and international companies in such industries as construction, transportation, information technology and pharmaceuticals. She is a member of the American Bar Association's Forum on Construction Law and co-author of *Getting the Deal Through: Construction 2018*, *Getting the Deal Through: Public Procurement 2018*, and *Doing Business 2018* published by the World Bank Group.

Leopoldo Pagotto
Partner, Freitas Leite Advogados
pagotto@fladv.com.br

Leopoldo Pagotto is in charge of the anti-corruption and compliance practices at Freitas Leite Advogados. Besides being an anti-corruption & compliance private practitioner approved by the Latin American Corporate Counsel Association (LACCA), he has been recognised by Chambers and Partners as a foreign expert in competition law and M&A for Japanese clients. Mr Pagotto is currently vice-chair of the Anti-Corruption Committee of the International Bar Association (IBA). He was a reporter for the Chamber No 20 and Chamber No 1 of the Ethics Tribunal of the Brazilian Bar Association, São Paulo Chapter. He holds a PhD in Financial-Economic Law (*Universidade de São Paulo*), an LLM in Financial-Economic Law (*Universidade de São Paulo*), an MSc in Regulation (London School of Economics and Political Science) and an LLB (*Universidade de São Paulo*).

Rocío Paniagua
Senior legal manager, Legal Policy & Research Unit, International Bar Association
Rocio.Paniagua@int-bar.org

Rocío Paniagua is currently acting as senior legal manager with the Legal Policy & Research Unit. She has extensive experience and academic credentials in international law and project management, with a focus on anti-corruption and business and human rights. Rocío completed her law degree at the Autonomous University of Madrid and undertook additional law studies at the Roma Tre University in Italy and the Complutense University of Madrid, where she earned a master's in International Cooperation for Development. A member of the Madrid Bar

Association, she has previously worked as a legal officer in the International Department of the Spanish National Bar Association and for two major reinsurers in London and Dublin.

Rocío is currently leading IBA legal projects in the areas of corporate and judicial integrity, including anti-corruption and business and human rights.

Estefania Paz
Associate, Ferrere
espaz@ferrere.com

Estefanía Paz is an associate in Ferrere's Bolivia offices and a member of the Disputes team and the regional Risk Management & Compliance team.

Ms Paz's practice focuses on risk management and anti-corruption compliance and commercial disputes. She regularly counsels clients regarding corruption risks in Latin America. She frequently contributes to research for Ferrere's regional compliance publications, identifying trends in anti-corruption and anti-money laundering compliance in Bolivia, Ecuador, Paraguay and Uruguay.

Ms Paz additionally has significant experience in alternative dispute resolution and commercial and corporate law matters.

Ms Paz obtained her law degree, with honours, from *Universidad Privada Boliviana* in Cochabamba, Bolivia and obtained an LLM from the University of Pepperdine in Malibu, California. She was awarded a Fulbright Scholarship to pursue an LLM at Pepperdine. Her native language is Spanish and she is fluent in English.

Luca Pietrantuono
Trainee attorney, Dalla Vedova Associazione Professionale
lp@dallavedova.com

Luca Pietrantuono obtained a degree at the School of Law of Roma Tre University with a dissertation on *The role of the CONSOB in the criminal protection of the financial markets*. After graduating, he was admitted as a scholarship recipient into a Second-Level Professional Master's Programme in Business Criminal Law at LUISS Guido Carli, based in Rome, and obtained a diploma with a dissertation on *The obstacles to the exercise of the functions of public supervisory bodies*.

Having gained his initial professional experience with a local law firm, Mr Pietrantuono joined Dalla Vedova Associazione Professionale in February 2017. He currently provides legal assistance pursuant to a multidisciplinary approach, embracing international public and private law to criminal and company law, with a focus on advising primary operators of electronic communications with regard to commercial contracts and the relevant regulatory framework.

Santiago Oliva Pinto
Senior associate, Rattagan Macchiavello Arocena
sop@rmlex.com

Santiago Oliva Pinto is a senior associate of Rattagan Macchiavello Arocena in Buenos Aires, Argentina. His areas of expertise include general corporate counselling, anti-corruption and compliance, mergers and acquisitions, international contracts and foreign investment. He also works in aviation law transactions, representing clients in the leasing and financing of aircraft. Between 2004 and 2012, he was a corporate counsel for Arcor, Argentina's largest grocery manufacturing and processing conglomerate.

Santiago earned his law degree from the *Universidad Blas Pascal*. He has specialisations in tax law (from the *Universidad Austral*) and labour law (from the *Universidad Católica*). He attended the international private law course of The Hague Academy of International Law (Netherlands) and the course on American and international law of the Academy for American and International Law (CAIL, USA). He has published articles on commercial, tax and labour law.

Santiago is a native Spanish speaker, is fluent in English, and has basic command of Portuguese and French.

Volker D Popp
Compliance and AML Officer
volkerdpopp@gmail.com

Volker D Popp is a Compliance and Anti-Money Laundering Officer based in Mexico City. He holds an MBA degree from Kellogg School of Management/Northwestern University and has participated in the executive education program of Columbia University in New York City. He is also a Certified Internal Auditor and Certified Fraud Examiner with over 15 years' experience in the automotive sector.

Mr Popp has considerable experience in conducting international investigations and white collar crime prevention. In his current role, he acts as consultant to top management and independent distributors with a view to preventing reputational and legal risks. Much of his work focuses on applicable anti-corruption and anti-money laundering legislation, training and communication.

Mr Popp is president of the Compliance Managers Committee of the International Chamber of Commerce Mexico. He is frequently invited to speak on anti-corruption practices at national and international conferences.

Mariana Duprat Ruggeri
Compliance analyst, Camargo Corrêa Infra
duprat_@hotmail.com

Mariana Duprat acts in the areas of corporate compliance, anti-corruption and fraud investigation in the infrastructure, pharmaceutical, food and automotive industries. She has experience in matters involving: review and development of internal policies and codes of conduct; development, structuring and review of compliance programmes and related training materials; and due diligence, risk assessments and background checks. Ms Duprat has also acted in a number of large internal investigation cases (including multi-jurisdictional).

Darío Sandoval Shaik
Senior associate, Fabrega Molino
dsandoval@fmm.com.pa

Darío Sandoval is a senior associate in the Banking, Securities and Insurance department of Fabrega Molino in Panama City, Panama. He holds a PhD in Law from Complutense University of Madrid, and has specialised for over 15 years in securities public offerings, the setting up and obtaining of licences from the Superintendency of the Securities Market, the Superintendency of Banks and the Superintendency of Insurance and Reinsurance, and in setting up investment vehicles (mutual funds).

Dr Sandoval acts for local and international banks, trust companies, insurance and reinsurance companies, broker-dealer houses, investment advisers, investment administrators, registered issuers, investment companies and market value providers. His paper, *Arbitration in Insurance and Reinsurance Disputes*, received an award in Panama for '2016 Best Article in the Field of Economics and Finance'.

Viviane Schiavi
Senior manager, Anti-corruption and corporate responsibility, International Chamber of Commerce
viviane.schiavi@iccwbo.org

Viviane Schiavi is senior manager for Anti-corruption and Corporate Responsibility with the International Chamber of Commerce (ICC), overseeing ICC's work to promote anti-corruption, responsible business conduct and corporate responsibility worldwide. These objectives are pursued through a combination of policy advocacy with regard to the UN, the G20 and other fora, and of concrete, practical tools for business.

Ms Schiavi is a member of the New York Bar, with over 20 years' experience in international policy and commercial practice. Of dual American and French nationality, she is a graduate of Bard College and the City University of New York Law

School. She practised international commercial law in New York City and with Arthur Andersen International in Paris, before joining the ICC. Her areas of legal practice included litigation, international contracts, and mergers and acquisitions.

Denis Simonneau
Senior vice president, Group Institutional Affairs, L'Oréal
Denis.Simonneau@loreal.com

A graduate of Sciences Po and the *École Nationale d'Administration* in Paris, Denis Simonneau holds a master's degree in Economics.

As a French diplomat, Mr Simonneau served in India (1988–1989), South Africa (1993–1996), was adviser to the then Minister of European Affairs, Michel Barnier (1996–1997), counsellor at the French Permanent Representation to the EU in Brussels (1997–2001) and consul general and head of the French Trade Economic Mission in Houston, Texas (2001–2005). Deputy spokesperson for the Department of Foreign Affairs (2005–2007), he was chief of staff to the French secretary of state in charge of European Affairs, Jean-Pierre Jouyet, (July 2007–December 2008). In 2009, Mr Simonneau joined GDF SUEZ (now ENGIE) and was appointed diplomatic adviser to the group's chairman and CEO, Gérard Mestrallet, the then senior vice president for international relations. In May 2011, he became member of the executive committee in charge of European and international relations. Since 2018, he has been senior vice president for Group Institutional Affairs at l'Oréal.

Mr Simonneau has chaired ICC's Commission on Anti-corruption and Corporate Responsibility since October 2015 and is also president of EUROPANOVA, a French NGO.

Filip Široký
Legal intern, Kinstellar
Filip.Siroky@kinstellar.com

Filip Široký is a Legal intern in Kinstellar's Prague office and a member of the Compliance, Risk & Sensitive Investigations team. He is currently in the fourth year of his studies at the Faculty of Law of the Charles University. He previously worked as a compliance manager assistant with Mercedes-Benz and then as a paralegal with CMS Cameron McKenna Nabarro Olswang. He also successfully completed an internship at the District Public Prosecutor's Office for Prague 7. He took part in two summer law schools that helped him in terms of international experience: one was oriented on financial crime and held in Thessaloniki, Greece, while the other one focused on IP rights and was held in Tbilisi, Georgia.

Lindsay Sykes
Partner, Ferrere
lsykes@ferrere.com

Lindsay Sykes is a partner in Ferrere, one of Latin America's largest law firms, with offices in Bolivia, Ecuador, Paraguay and Uruguay. She leads Ferrere's regional Compliance group, assisting clients in the firm's four jurisdictions with compliance with international anti-corruption regulations, including the US Foreign Corrupt Practices Act (FCPA), and the assessment and management of risks related to potential mergers, acquisitions and other transactions. She also advises corporate clients on the design and execution of internal investigations into possible corporate misconduct, as well as on risk assessments of the practices of business partners and potential partners. Prior to joining Ferrere, Ms Sykes was an attorney with Cleary Gottlieb Steen & Hamilton LLP in Washington DC, where she represented clients in a wide range of cross-border matters, including in investigations by US regulators into allegations of illegal corporate practices, as well as complex commercial litigation.

Derek Turnbull
Associate, Paul Hastings LLP
derekturnbull@paulhastings.com

Derek Turnbull is an associate in the Litigation practice of Paul Hastings LLP and is based in the firm's Washington DC office. His practice focuses on white collar defence, primarily the Foreign Corrupt Practices Act and US sanctions regulations. He has worked on corruption- and sanctions-related internal investigations for large multinational corporations, investigated financial fraud in a mid-sized domestic firm and contributed advice to clients on the rapidly evolving sanctions frameworks against Russia and Iran.

Mr Turnbull received his law degree in 2016 from the University of Michigan Law School, where he was an associate editor of the *Michigan Journal of International Law*. He has previously lived and worked in China and Israel. He is admitted to practise law in the District of Columbia and New York.

Ramesh K Vaidyanathan
Managing partner, Advaya Legal
ramesh@advayalegal.com

Ramesh K Vaidyanathan is a general corporate lawyer with extensive experience in M&A, projects and infrastructure, construction and aviation. Before founding Advaya Legal, he was in private practice as resident partner of the Mumbai office of a large Indian law firm and as the general counsel to a large Indian infrastructure company. During his initial stint in private practice, he specialised in all aspects of corporate law. He helped set up several international companies in India, which involved advice on such matters as company formation, joint venture documentation, regulatory approvals and employee agreements. His in-house role primarily involved the development and modernisation of Mumbai International Airport. His key practice areas in Advaya are general corporate, projects and infrastructure and aviation.

Mr Vaidyanathan is an officer of the Asia Pacific Forum of the International Bar Association (IBA) and a member of the International Young Lawyers Association (AIJA) and the Inter Pacific Bar Association (IPBA). He teaches some modules for the Indian law course at the Michigan State University in the US.

Roman Vedernikov
Senior attorney, ALRUD Law Firm
rvedernikov@alrud.com

Roman Vedernikov is a senior attorney at ALRUD Law Firm, Moscow. He advises clients on compliance with Russian antitrust and anti-corruption legislation, participates in the conduct of antitrust/anti-corruption due diligence and cartel investigations, and represents clients following dawn raids by FAS Russia. As a member of the white-collar crime, compliance and internal investigations practice, he also actively participates in projects related to internal investigations and developing internal anti-corruption policy for both Russian and foreign companies doing business in Russia.

Mr Vedernikov graduated from MGIMO-University, International Trade Law Department. He completed a master's programme at the National Research University – Higher School of Economics, Law Department.

François Vincke
Attorney, Member of the Brussels Bar
francoisvincke@gmail.com

François Vincke is a member of the Brussels Bar with extensive legal experience, including with Wilkie, Farr & Gallagher until 2006. He served until July 2000 as secretary general of Petrofina, the multinational energy and chemicals corporation. Since 1994, he has been head of anti-corruption at ICC, first as chairman of the Commission on Anti-corruption and later as vice chair of the Commission on Corporate Responsibility and Anti-corruption. He has also led a number of Commission publications.

Mr Vincke is a renowned international expert on anti-corruption and self-regulation. He has also co-authored a number of books and articles on corporate governance and corporate practice, including: *Anti-corruption in Belgium – corporate good practices; Companies and globalization – opportunities and risks, legal strategies; Legal tracks I, Essays on contemporary corporate and finance law; Legal tracks II, Essays on international and domestic contracts and torts;* and *ICC Ethics and Compliance Training Handbook.*

Stephanie Voudouris
Associate, Cassels Brock & Blackwell LLP
svoudouris@casselsbrock.com

Stephanie Voudouris is an associate at Cassels Brock & Blackwell LLP. She has an active commercial litigation practice with a focus on securities litigation. She has acted for companies, directors and officers, and shareholders in transactional litigation arising from shareholder disputes, oppression claims, proxy fights and class actions, including primary and secondary market liability claims. She has also acted in a wide range of commercial litigation matters involving contract disputes and insolvency proceedings. She has appeared before a number of courts and has experience with private arbitration and mediation proceedings.

Ms Voudouris received her JD in 2013 from Osgoode Hall Law School, where she graduated in the top ten per cent of her class. She is an active member of the Hellenic Canadian Lawyers' Association and sits on the Board of Directors of Young Women in Law.

Robert Wyld
Partner, Johnson, Winter & Slattery
robert.wyld@jws.com.au

Robert Wyld specialises in dispute resolution and has advised many national and international clients, including individuals, public and private companies and statutory authorities in the banking and securities, telecommunications, health and pharmaceutical, aviation, construction, and power and energy industries. His work has a particular focus on commercial crime and fraud, anti-corruption and bribery investigations (arising from employment and business conduct) and prosecutions, sanctions, money-laundering, extradition and domestic and international taxation-related disputes.

Mr Wyld was the co-chair of the International Bar Association's Anti-Corruption Committee for 2015–2016. He appears regularly across the Australian media as a specialist and expert on bribery and corruption issues. He has published foreign bribery texts in Australia, the United Kingdom, Germany and France (with the OECD) and has been recognised as a leading anti-corruption lawyer by *Chambers Asia Pacific* (2016–2017), *Best Lawyers in Australia* (Litigation), the *Global Awards Corporate LiveWire 2017* (Anti-Corruption Law services), *Who's Who Legal for Business Crime and Investigations* and the 2018 *Who's Who Legal: Thought leaders – Investigations* in Australia.

Zhaopeng Yang (Neo Yang)
Associate, Zhong Lun Law Firm
yangzhaopeng@zhonglun.com

Neo Yang is an associate with Dr Haixiao Helen Zhang's team at Zhong Lun Law Firm in Shanghai. He graduated from Fudan University in 2017. Prior to joining Zhong Lun Law Firm, He worked as an intern with CMS Hasche Sigle Shanghai, Gowling WLG and other leading local firms, and has participated in various projects in the foreign direct investment, M&A and corporate compliance fields.

German Zakharov
Partner, ALRUD Law Firm
gzakharov@alrud.com

German Zakharov is a recognised expert in the antitrust regulation field and supports clients on a wide range of antitrust issues, including coordination of merger control transactions with FAS Russia, cartel investigations, advising on distributorship agreements, and analysing compliance of commercial agreements with antitrust requirements. He represents companies during 'dawn raids' carried out by FAS Russia and its territorial sub-divisions, and also represents clients before the courts. As a member of the firm's white-collar crime, compliance and internal investigations practice, he renders legal support to companies with regard to compliance with applicable criminal and antitrust legislation, and assists in drafting and implementing internal policies and compliance procedures.

Mr Zakharov graduated with honours from the Law Faculty of Lomonosov Moscow State University and completed 'Economics in Competition Law' and 'EU Competition Law' programmes at King's College London.

Haixiao Helen Zhang
Partner, Zhong Lun Law Firm
haixiaozhang@zhonglun.com

Dr Haixiao Helen Zhang is a partner with Zhong Lun Law Firm in Shanghai. She graduated from the University of Pennsylvania in 2002 and graduated with an LLB and a doctoral degree from Fudan University in 1995 and 2013 respectively. She was admitted to practise law in the PRC in 1995.

Dr Zhang is one of the leading PRC legal counsel for multinational companies doing business in China and advises on regulatory compliance and IP. She has also been retained as main legal counsel by the Shanghai Pudong government since 2013 and by Shanghai MOFCOM since 2016. She is a member of the Administrative Review Committee of the Shanghai Pudong government and has been selected to deal with cases in the Shanghai Free Trade Zone since 2015.

Prior to joining Zhong Lun Law Firm eight years ago, Dr Zhang worked as a senior lawyer and partner with Weil Gotshal & Manges LLP and other leading international and local firms for a total of 20 years.

Julie Zorrilla
Associate, Navacelle
jzorrilla@navacellelaw.com

Prior to joining Navacelle in 2012, Julie Zorrilla previously worked in the Direction of Legal Affairs at the French Ministry of Economic Affairs and Finance in 2012 and was a law clerk to the Paris Court of Appeal in 2011.

Over the past few years, Ms Zorrilla has worked on cases with complex cross-border financial and criminal implications (including embargos, index manipulation and SSA) and involving top executives and major foreign and French financial institutions. Ms Zorrilla has also handled large-scale corruption cases advising on both legal and communication strategies.

Ms Zorrilla has assisted clients in setting up internal investigations in relation to litigation and pre-litigation matters.

New journal – Modern Legal Practice

Globe Law and Business

Modern Legal Practice

Business • Strategy • Leadership

Editorial
Katherine Cowdrey

Opinion **The effect of Brexit on London as a centre for dispute resolution**
Deborah Finkler
Robert Brittain

Strategy **The new normal lawyer – legal practice in the 21st century**
Tony King

Remuneration **Table manners: rewarding performance without 'eat what you kill'**
Norman Clark

Technology and innovation in the in-house context
Bjarne Tellmann

Procurement **Why you need to know about legal procurement**
Dr Silvia Hodges Silverstein

Diversity **Retaining women lawyers: the need for new perspectives**
Ida Abbott

Finance and strategy **Finance issues facing firms**
Brian Dunlop

Interpersonal skills **Finding a new way through difficult conversations**
Alison Nolan

GC Perspectives Who should be the culture and ethics guardian?
Jeremy Barton

Meet the board
Tony King

Book review
Brighter thinking for law firms by Peter Noyce
Reviewed by Professor Stephen Mayson

July 2017 • www.globelawandbusiness.com

Globe Law and Business

Founder Subscriber Offer

Subscribe today as a founder subscriber, and receive:

- Your first issue free of charge
- Over 20% discount on your first year's subscription

Publication dates:
Quarterly
Hard copy ISSN:
2398 - 5410
Hardcopy only:
£295 per annum
Discounted price:
£236 per annum

Go to **http://modernlegalpracticeoffer.globelawandbusiness.com** for full details and subscription offer.

About Globe Law and Business

Globe Law and Business was established in 2005 as an imprint of Globe Business Media Group. We set out to create law books which are sufficiently high level to be of real use to the experienced professional, yet still accessible and easy to navigate. Most of our authors are drawn from Magic Circle and other top commercial firms, both in the UK and internationally.

In Autumn 2015, we had an exciting turn in our history when Globe Law and Business was bought by a management team which includes my colleague Jim Smith and me, Sian O'Neill.

We love books, and our hardback titles are carefully produced, with the utmost attention paid to the editorial, design and production processes. We hope this results in high-quality titles which are easy to read, and a pleasure to own.

Our customers and authors are of paramount importance – we are committed to devoting time and attention to each book as well as everyone involved in the publishing process.

We'd very much like to hear from you with your thoughts on our titles or ideas for improving what we offer. Please do feel free to email me on sian@globelawandbusiness.com with your views.

Sian O'Neill
Managing director
Globe Law and Business

www.globelawandbusiness.com

New Special Reports from Globe Law and Business

Globe Law and Business

We are pleased to announce the launch of our new special reports series. A4 and softback in format, the special reports will offer cutting edge analysis into specific areas of legal practice and law firm management, along with handy tools and best practice guidelines.

The first report, by Professor Heidi Gardner and Anusia Gillespie, is on *Smart Collaboration for Lateral Hiring* launching in September.

For full details, go to **www.globelawandbusiness.com/subjects/special-reports**